Direito em Debate

Direito em Debate

VOLUME 2

2020

Maria Helena Diniz
Coordenadora

ALMEDINA

DIREITO EM DEBATE
VOLUME 2

COORDENADORA: Maria Helena Diniz

DIRETOR ALMEDINA BRASIL: Rodrigo Mentz
EDITORA JURÍDICA: Manuella Santos de Castro
EDITOR DE DESENVOLVIMENTO: Aurélio Cesar Nogueira
ASSISTENTES EDITORIAIS: Isabela Leite e Larissa Nogueira

DIAGRAMAÇÃO: Almedina
DESIGN DE CAPA: Almedina

ISBN: 978-85-8493-642-7
Dezembro, 2020

Dados Internacionais de Catalogação na Publicação (CIP)
(Câmara Brasileira do Livro, SP, Brasil)

Direito em Debate: volume 2 /
Maria Helena Diniz, coordenadora.
– São Paulo: Almedina Brasil .

Bibliografia.
978-85-8493-642-7

1. Direito 2. Direito - Brasil I. Diniz, Maria
Helena.

20-47557 CDU-34

Índices para catálogo sistemático:

1. Direito 34
Cibele Maria Dias - Bibliotecária - CRB-8/9427

Este livro segue as regras do novo Acordo Ortográfico da Língua Portuguesa (1990).

EDITORA: Almedina Brasil
Rua José Maria Lisboa, 860, Conj.131 e 132, Jardim Paulista | 01423-001 São Paulo | Brasil
editora@almedina.com.br
www.almedina.com.br

SOBRE A COORDENADORA

Detentora de inúmeros prêmios desde os tempos de seu bacharelado na PUC-SP, **Maria Helena Diniz** ostenta brilhante carreira acadêmica, com cursos de especialização em Filosofia do Direito, Teoria Geral do Direito, Direito Administrativo, Tributário e Municipal. Fez o Mestrado na Faculdade de Direito da USP e o Doutorado na PUC-SP, tendo nesta última obtido os graus de Mestre, Doutora, Livre-Docente e Titular, por concurso de provas e títulos.

A autora é Professora Titular de Direito Civil na PUC-SP, onde leciona essa matéria nos cursos de graduação e pós-graduação. É também coordenadora do Núcleo de Pesquisa em Direito da PUC-SP. Leciona ainda Direito Civil Comparado, Filosofia do Direito e Teoria Geral do Direito nos cursos de pós-graduação (mestrado e doutorado) em Direito da PUC-SP.

Parecerista e autora de mais de trinta títulos que se tornaram referência na área jurídica, a autora também traduziu consagradas obras do direito italiano, e escreveu mais de cem artigos em importantes revistas jurídicas nacionais e internacionais.

É membro da Academia Paulista de Direito (Cadeira 62 – patrono Oswaldo Aranha Bandeira de Mello), da Academia Notarial Brasileira (Cadeira 16 – patrono Francisco Cavalcanti Pontes de Miranda) e do Instituto de Direito Comparado Luso-brasileiro. Presidente do Instituto Internacional de Direito – IID, com sede em São Paulo.

É incontestável a importância do trabalho desta autora, sem dúvida uma das maiores civilistas de todos os tempos.

A editora

SOBRE OS AUTORES

Alessandro Pelizzon

Doutor pela Universidade de Wollongong – Austrália. LLM pela Universidade de Turim – Itália. Palestrante Sênior da Escola de Direito e Justiça da Southern Cross University – Austrália.

Álvaro Villaça Azevedo

Professor Titular da Faculdade de Direito da USP. Livre-docente e Doutor em Direito pela USP. Bacharel em Direito pela Universidade Presbiteriana Mackenzie.

Ana Cristina de Barros Monteiro França Pinto

Procuradora do Município de São Paulo. Advogada.

Armando Rafael Aquino Britos

Professor Adjunto de Direito Político e Direito Constitucional da Faculdade de Direito da Universidade Nacional do Nordeste – Argentina. Advogado.

Christiano Cassettari

Pós doutorando em Direito Civil pela USP. Doutor e Mestre em Direito Civil pela USP. Registrador Civil em Salvador-BA.

Claudia Cristina dos Santos Abrosio

Mestranda em Direito pela PUC-SP. Especialista em Direito Tributário pelo IBET – Instituto Brasileiro de Estudos Tributários. Advogada.

Claudio De Cicco

Livre-docente e Doutor em Direito pela USP. Professor da Faculdade de Direito da PUC-SP.

Daniella Gonçalves Stefanelli

Mestranda e Bacharel em Direito pela Universidade Federal do Espírito Santo. Membro do Grupo de Pesquisa "O direito civil na pós-modernidade jurídica". Advogada.

Dinorá Adelaide Musetti Grotti

Doutora e Mestre em Direito pela PUC-SP. Professora da Faculdade de Direito da PUC-SP.

Giovanni Chiarini

Doutorando em Direito pela Universidad de Insubria – Itália. Advogado.

Giselda Maria Fernandes Novaes Hironaka

Professora Titular da Faculdade de Direito da USP. Livre-docente, Doutora e Mestre em Direito pela USP. Coordenadora e Professora Titular do Programa de Mestrado e Doutorado da FADISP. Coordenadora Titular da área de Direito Civil da Escola Paulista de Direito. Ex-Procuradora Federal. Fundadora e Diretora Nacional do IBDFAM (região sudeste). Diretora Nacional do IBDCivil (região sudeste).

Jonathan Barros Vita

Doutor e Mestre em Direito pela PUC-SP. Coordenador e professor do Mestrado e Doutorado em Direito da UNIMAR. Conselheiro do Conselho Municipal de Tributos de São Paulo. Ex-Conselheiro do CARF, Conselho Administrativo de Recursos Fiscais. Ex-Juiz do Tribunal de Impostos e Taxas do Estado de São Paulo. Ex-Secretário da Comissão Especial de Direito Tributário do Conselho Federal da OAB. Contador e Advogado.

José Luiz Ragazzi

Doutor em Direito Processual Civil pela PUC-SP. Mestre em Direito pela Faculdade de Direito de Bauru. Professor do mestrado e doutorado da Instituição Toledo de Ensino- ITE. Advogado.

Julcira Maria de Mello Vianna Lisboa

Doutora em Direito pela PUC-SP. Professora de Direito Tributário nos Cursos de Graduação e Pós-Graduação da PUC-SP. Vice Coordenadora do Curso de Direito da PUC-SP. Coordenadora da Cadeira de Direito Tributário da Faculdade de Direito da PUC-SP. Advogada.

Lucas Abreu Barroso

Doutor em Direito pela PUC-SP. Professor na Faculdade de Direito da Universidade Federal do Espírito Santo. Líder do Grupo de Pesquisa "O direito civil na pós-modernidade jurídica". Advogado.

Luiz Alfredo Angelico Soares Cabral

Mestre em Direito pela PUC-SP. Advogado.

Mariana Ribeiro Santiago

Pós-doutora em Direito pela *Justus-Liebig-Universität Giessen*. Doutora e Mestre em Direito pela PUC-SP. Bacharel em Direito pela Universidade Federal da Bahia. Professora do Programa de Mestrado e Doutorado em Direito da Universidade de Marília. Editora-chefe da Revista *Argumentum*. Advogada.

Milton Flávio de A. C. Lautenschläger

Doutor, Mestre e Bacharel em Direito pela PUC-SP. Diretor Administrativo do Instituto dos Advogados de São Paulo – IASP (2016-2018). Advogado.

Mônica Aguiar

Doutora em Direito pela PUC-SP. Professora da Universidade Católica do Salvador e da Universidade Federal da Bahia.Coordenadora do Mestrado em Direito da Universidade Católica do Salvador.

Odete Novais Carneiro Queiroz

Doutora e Mestre em Direito pela PUC/SP. Professora da Faculdade de Direito da PUC-SP. Advogada.

Olivia Raposo da Silva Telles

Doutora pela Universidade de Paris 1 (Panthéon-Sorbonne). Bacharel em Direito pela USP. Colaboradora em matéria de direito eleitoral do Movimento de Combate à Corrupção Eleitoral. Advogada.

Paulo de Barros Carvalho

Livre Docente, Doutor, Mestre e Bacharel em Direito pela PUC-SP. Professor Titular da Faculdade de Direito da PUC-SP. Professor Titular da Faculdade de Direito da USP. Presidente do IBET – Instituto Brasileiro de Estudos Tributários. Advogado.

Rafael Chagas Mancebo

Doutor, Mestre e Bacharel em Direito pela PUC-SP.

Romualdo Baptista dos Santos

Doutor e Mestre em Direito Civil pela USP. Especialista em Direito Contratual e Direito de Danos (Contratos y Daños) pela Universidade de Salamanca. Professor convidado em cursos de pós-graduação. Membro do Instituto Brasileiro de Estudos da Responsabilidade Civil – IBERC. Advogado.

Sara Bomfim Santa Rosa

Mestranda em Direito pela Universidade Católica do Salvador. Advogada.

Sergio Iglesias Nunes de Souza

Doutor e Mestre em Direito pela PUC-SP. Professor Concursado Titular de Direito Civil na Faculdade de Direito de São Bernardo do Campo. Advogado.

APRESENTAÇÃO

Há vinte anos abracei uma carreira duplamente jurídica e editorial, e nessa jornada como profissional do livro aprendi preciosas lições. Uma das mais relevantes, sem dúvida, foi que ser convidado para escrever a apresentação de uma obra é uma das maiores honras que alguém pode receber.

Pois bem. Entre pesquisas para o doutorado e a elaboração de pareceres editoriais, fui surpreendida com um convite da consagrada jurista Maria Helena Diniz para escrever a apresentação de uma nova série, coordenada por ela. Na hora pensei "como vou introduzir um livro de uma autora tão profícua, que publicou mais títulos do que, tristemente, muitas pessoas já leram?". Mas, como sempre gostei de desafios, eis aqui o resultado.

Sempre tive pra mim que transferir pensamentos para o mundo concreto é uma arte, e isso pode se dar por diversas formas, inclusive por meio das palavras faladas e das palavras escritas. Penso que escrever é a maneira mais generosa, significativa e corajosa de perpetuar ideias, e, claro, de se expor a críticas. É atitude reservada aos que não temem o bom combate. E esse é justamente o caso da coordenadora desta inovadora coleção.

Nesta era em que "mudança" tornou-se palavra de ordem, o Direito tem sido chamado para apresentar soluções rápidas e, por vezes, milagrosas. Em congruência com esse cenário, a série *Direito em Debate* convida o leitor a refletir sobre temas atuais por meio de estudos consistentes, plurais e dinâmicos, que percorrem temas relevantes e interdisciplinares, lançando mão de explanações lúcidas e consistentes. Como resultado, os artigos aqui apresentados conduzem o estudioso à construção do arcabouço da doutrina exposta, bem como o incentiva a navegar pela estrada, por vezes tortuosa, de alternativas práticas.

Em seu compromisso com a difusão do conhecimento, a editora Almedina, conhecida e respeitada casa portuguesa de publicações jurídicas, que agora também expande suas fronteiras além-mar, nos brinda com essa primorosa coleção, que se destina para estudiosos e docentes da área jurídica, além de advogados especializados e pesquisadores de áreas fronteiriças com o Direito, interessados no desenvolvimento do pensamento jurídico reflexivo.

Para fechar essa breve nota gostaria de deixar registrado meu orgulho e minha satisfação pessoal por contar com a amizade da querida autora. Esta série reflete mais um resultado decorrente de suas qualidades como estudiosa do Direito, e o convite para escrever esta apresentação é uma demonstração da generosidade infindável com que abraça seus alunos.

São Paulo, inverno de 2020.
Pandemia da Covid-19.

Manuella Santos de Castro
Editora Jurídica e Advogada.
Doutoranda em Direito Civil pela USP.
Mestre em Direito Civil Comparado pela PUC-SP.
Bacharel em Direito pela PUC-SP.
Cursa Faculdade de História na USP.
Professora convidada de cursos de pós-graduação *lato sensu* em Direito.

SUMÁRIO

THE "HARMONY WITH NATURE": PARADIGM IN BRAZIL

Alessandro Pelizzon*
Mariana Ribeiro Santiago**

INTRODUCTION

In 2015, the Municipality of São Paulo proposed the Amendment to the Organic Law[1] of the Municipality nº 04-00005/2015, in which it suggested to include a new provision (180A), 'considering that the members of nature have intrinsic rights to life and maintenance of their ecosystem processes, in interdependence with the dignified life of the citizens, with the aim of achieving sustainability in the city' (SÃO PAULO, 2015). Shortly thereafter, in 2017, the Municipality of Bonito, in the State of Pernambuco, amended its Organic Law to recognize the rights of Nature (PERNAMBUCO, 2020), and was soon followed, in 2018, by the Municipality of Paudalho, also in the State of Pernambuco, which, equally recognized Nature as a subject of rights (PERNAMBUCO, 2018).

* Doutor pela Universidade de Wollongong – Austrália. LLM pela Universidade de Turim – Itália. Palestrante Sênior da Escola de Direito e Justiça da Southern Cross University – Austrália.

** Pós-doutora em Direito pela *Justus-Liebig-Universität Giessen*. Doutora e Mestre em Direito pela PUC-SP. Bacharel em Direito pela Universidade Federal da Bahia. Professora do Programa de Mestrado e Doutorado em Direito da Universidade de Marília. Editora-chefe da Revista *Argumentum*. Advogada.

[1] In Brazil, in addition to the Federal Constitution, States and Municipalities have a type of law similar to a "local constitution". Municipalities call this law the Organic Law.

From this brief overview, it seems that rights of Nature arguments are increasingly becoming commonplace in Brazil. In a parallel, but ultimately similar development, the Superior Court of Justice decided, in March 21, 2019, that non-human animals can be conceived of as subjects of law, making them the object of custody, not possession, by their human companions (Appeal nº 1.797.175-SP). Ingo Wolfgang Sarlet and Tiago Fensterseifer suggest that, through an ecological reading of the principle of the dignity of the human person (prompted by what is, in fact, an emergency in the face of an ecological crisis), this judgment challenges and ultimately dismantle a fundamentally Kantian anthropocentric paradigm (SARLET; FENSTERSEIFER, 2017, p. 62).

The ontological, epistemological, and ultimately normative, transformative potential of the emergence of a rights of Nature paradigm is profound and cannot be overstated. As mentioned above, such a proposal does more than rearranging the existing categories of legal subjectivity, or even rewriting its fundamental constituents, and rather challenges century-old assumptions about the role of humanity in the cosmos and the normative and legal protocols such assumptions have produced. Cast against the most recent and widely reported global environmental disasters, this challenge highlights the insufficiency of the mainstream discourse for the effective protection of the environment, as well as the quality of life of both current society and future generations.

This article is thus prompted by the (increasingly more widely shared) perception of the seriousness of environmental issues that affect global society today (both internationally and, more specifically, in Brazil), with its consequential quest for alternative solutions focused on a novel conceptualization of legal subjectivity that aims to include Nature within its fold. Many new proposals designed to offer an increased preservation of the environment through rights of Nature initiatives have already been embraced by several countries, while an overall ecocentric shift has been advocated by the United Nations through its Harmony with Nature programme. In contextualizing the Brazilian experience among those examples, this article aims to appraise and evaluate the evolution of rights of Nature considerations within Brazilian legislation, to analyze recent biocentric and ecocentric trends within Brazilian jurisprudence, and, finally, to reflect upon the adequacy of such an approach within the Brazilian legal system.

1. ECOLOGICAL JURISPRUDENCE RISING

While the right to development was internationally recognized as an inalienable human right through the Declaration on the Right to Development (UNITED NATIONS, 1986), the articulation of a *sustainable* development has been steadily increasing over the past few decades, through Brundtland Report (UNITED NATIONS, 1987), Rio 92 (UNITED NATIONS, 1992), Johannesburg Declaration on Sustainable Development (UNITED NATIONS, 2002), Rio + 20 (UNITED NATIONS, 2012) and Sustainable Development Summit (UNITED NATIONS, 2015). *Sustainability*, albeit often misused as a concept, reveals an underlying dissatisfaction with the ultimately anthropocentric and tautological cosmology embodied by the very idea of 'development', an idea that emerged relatively recently in human history. Heron José de Santana Gordilho suggests that the Modern Age, by instrumentalizing the meaning of things, placed man at the axiological centre of the moral universe, and thus, as a result, solidified the triumph of an anthropocentric ontological worldview accompanied by materialism and laicization, with a rejection of any spiritual value to be found in the cosmos itself and a consequent devaluation of different worldviews (GORDILHO, 2008, p. 23-25).

In contrast, in 1972, Professor Christopher Stone concluded a property law lecture at the University of Southern California with a rather provocative question: should *trees* have standing, he asked? While 'greeted ... with [laughter and] uproar' (STONE, 2010, xiii), the question had been prompted by the proposed development, in the Southern Sierra Mountains, of a resort that would have destroyed an extensive portion of the original old growth forest inhabiting the mountains. The attempt to block the development by the Sierra Club was, however, frustrated, in *Sierra Club v. Morton*, by the argument that, by not being directly damaged by the proposed development, the Sierra Club lacked standing. That notwithstanding, Stone argued, something – the old growth forest itself – *was* being damaged, and thus in need of immediate protection; such an argument convinced Justice Douglas who, in his dissenting opinion, suggested that, 'if standing were the barrier, why not designate ... the wilderness area as the plaintiff "adversely affected"' (STONE, 2010, xiii).

It is impossible not to wonder as to what, within contemporary legal imagination, made the Sierra Mountains old growth forest legally *invisible* (or at least legally *irrelevant*). While it is inherently difficult to accurately identify the origin of an idea, it is undoubtable that the underpinning worldview of modern legal theoreticians and practitioners alike is directly linked to the very idea of "nature" as evolved within Mediterranean and European civilizations over the past two or three millennia. It is likely that a radical change occurred in the worldview of the first villagers and farmers, whose environment morphed from a holistic cosmological fabric within which the entirety of the cosmos was both enshrined and rigorously mapped to a wilderness to be replaced by agriculturally productive lands. However, it is in the earliest philosophical document that the roots of the modern conception of "nature" is clearly articulated.

In the writing of pre-Socratic philosophers, the quest for the definition of "nature" became synonymous with the quest for the understanding of "matter". Concerned with the question as to whether matter is a single substance capable of multiple expressions, or rather a collection of separate and ultimately independent components, Democritus's answer arguably is, to the present day, the most notable one, conceiving of "matter" (and thus, by extension of 'nature') as an interplay of distinct and ultimately separate units called "atoms". Democritus's view, of nature as a collection of ontologically independent material components, became the basis of modern science, leading to a worldview that Brian Swimme and Mary Evelyn Tucker define as "[d]eterministic materialism ... a worldview that [has] three tenets: that all things in the universe [are] composed of tiny particles of matter; that these particles [are] purely material, without any degree of subjectivity, and that these particles [move] according to fixed, mathematical laws." (SWIMME; TUCKER, 2011, p. 103-104)

Such a view was further solidified, at the onset of the Modern Age, in the writings of Rene Descartes, who, informed by Judeo-Christian medieval metaphysics, argued that only humans possess a "mind", with all other 'things' being nothing more than "things", material collections of particles moving in a somewhat mechanical manner. Cartesian deterministic materialism, therefore, enshrined not only within natural but also within political philosophy the idea that only human could be conceived of as *subjects*, with everything else only being capable of being an ontological, political, and ultimately legal *object*: "for centuries scientists have attempted to explain the universe by means of physical laws expressed in mathematical equations. The universe was thought to consist of mechanisms within mechanisms." (SWIMME; TUCKER, 2011, p. 49)

Nature thus conceived became, in its inherent material "alienness", a mere collection of objects to be harnessed for the benefit of thinking humans, capable of reaching its full potential only when properly "developed", leading to the (hopefully unintended) consequences we observe today. "Dynamized by their technology and their dreams of material progress", Swimme and Tucker write, "modern humans transformed the planet into a bundle of resources. They produced food in quantities never seen in history, and consequently populations exploded." As a result, "feeding and housing these many humans ... led to the depletion of the oceans, the degradation of the forests, and the loss of topsoil ... The paradox of unintended consequences is now becoming evident. The oceans, the rivers, the atmosphere, and the soil have all been severely degraded by our actions". As Yuval Noah Harari suggests, the collective power of humans to shape the environment is now, due to its sheer contemporary magnitude, akin to a geological force (HARARI, 2014).

Such a transformative power, however, was harnessed from its ontological promise by specific legal structures. It is the normative and legal structures deployed by European colonial societies first, and then by the rest of the globalized world, that allowed natural landscapes to be reshaped in the manner we collectively observe today, according to conquering (and often colonial) ideas as discussed above. Nicole Graham suggested the term "lawscape" to describe the legal reshaping of the world, arguing that, due to contemporary human ubiquity, every landscape we collectively observe (and inhabit) today is the direct result of the interplay between law, property regimes and environmental ontologies (GRAHAM, 2011). In this sense, nature can only be conceived of as a collection of objects, in particular a collection of objects of other subjects' property rights.

If nature is just an *object* of rights, and if the *subjects* of such rights have absolute power over that which is the object of such rights, then, naturally, the environmental damage suffered by the Sierra Mountains old growth forest and decried by Stone in 1972 was indeed legally invisible. Stone's question was thus particularly provocative, as it recognised the profound interplay between normative structures and ecological alterations, and thus, in proposing to remove 'nature' from the category of legal *things*, or *objects*, and rather casting it as a legal *subject* in order to increase its legal protection, it allowed the modern legal world to imagine the natural world as an active participant within human legal proceedings.

Stone's proposed shift from an *anthropocentric* legal ontology to a *biocentric* or even *ecocentric* one, suggesting a much more cautious approach to our interaction (as a collective species) with the rest of nature, answered Rachel Carson's call who, in 1962, had written that "the earth's vegetation is part of a web of life in which there are intimate and essential relations between plants and the earth, between plants and other plants, between plants and animals. Sometimes we have no choice but to disturb these relationships, but we should do so thoughtfully, with full awareness that what we do may have consequences remote in time and place" (CARSON, 1962, p. 64). Gordilho further suggests a growing dissatisfaction, within the scientific community over the last few centuries, with the anthropocentric view articulated above:

First, when Copernicus demonstrated that the earth was not the center of the universe, but only a small fragment of a vast cosmic system. Second, ... Charles Darwin proved that the human species did not emerge ready, as the Bible says, and there is a common ancestor with the great primates. And finally, when Freud demonstrated human irrationality and that the ego is not lord within its own home, since most of our actions are unconscious (GORDILHO, 2008, p. 33)

Carson and Stone's proposals were further expressed, two decades later, by eco-theologian and self-described 'earth scholar' Father Thomas Berry first, and South African environmental lawyer Cormac Cullinan shortly after. Underpinned by deep ecological perspectives (Arne Naess and the Deep Ecology movement had argued for decades the inherent value of nature, regardless of any human utility), Berry's invitation to articulate in political and legal terms an *ecocentric* worldview was fully articulated by Cullinan in his book *Wild Law*, where he defined this novel *Earth Jurisprudence* as

a philosophy of law and human governance that is based on the idea that humans are only one part of a wider community of beings and that the welfare of each member of the community is dependent on the welfare of the Earth as a whole. From this perspective, human societies will only be viable and flourish if they regulate themselves as part of this wider Earth community and do so in a way that is consistent with the fundamental principles that govern how the Universe functions (the 'Great Jurisprudence') (in BURDON, 2011, p. 13)

While a full analysis of Cullinan's usage of the term 'Great Law' or 'Great Jurisprudence' is beyond the scope of this paper, it is without a doubt that

Cullinan's writing established the theoretical terrain from which a number of Constitutional, judicial and legislative initiatives granting nature both rights and legal subjectivity emerged as part of a larger theoretical trend challenging the inherently reductionist and anthropocentric dominant view of both ontology and normativity, a trend defined by the authors of the present article as an *Ecological Jurisprudence.* (PELIZZON, 2014)

Furthermore, the emergence of an Ecological Jurisprudence has been profoundly influenced, from its inception, by many Indigenous ontologies. Rogério Roque Amaro, for example, explains that the idea of 'Buen Vivir' (or 'Good Life'), central to the Ecuadorian and Bolivian experiences discussed below, was based upon the Spanish translation of four distinct Andean concepts and expressions: 'Sumak Kawsay' (common among the Quechua people of Ecuador, Bolivia, Peru, Argentina, Chile and Colombia), which conveys the sense of communion with Mother Earth, or 'Pacha Mama'; 'Suma Qamaña' (common among the Aymará people of Bolivia, Argentina, Chile and Peru), which equally conveys the meaning of 'full life', 'good life', and 'living together'; 'Teko Porã' (common among the Guarani people of Bolivia, Argentina, Brazil, Paraguay and Uruguay), with its meaning of 'good living'; and lastly, 'Teko Kavi' (also from the Guarani people) meaning 'the good life' or the 'good way of being and living'. (AMARO, 2018)

It is equally important to remember that similar concepts also originated in what Amaro calls 'Southern Epistemologies'. A prominent example is the concept of 'Gross National Happiness' adopted in Bhutan, which is based upon a combination of Buddhist-inspired ideas such as psychological well-being, health, balanced use of time, community vitality, education, diversity and cultural resilience, ecological resilience, good governance and healthy standard of living. Equally, the concept of 'Ubuntu' (originated from the Xhosa people from South Africa and now widespread in the Southern part of the continent), highlights the importance of the interconnection of human beings with one another, with the welfare of one being inextricably linked to the welfare of the other. The term 'noflay' (from the Wolof language, spoken in Senegal) is the Senegalese equivalent of the Andean concept of 'buen vivir', emphasizing the cultural, philosophical and moral perspectives of all human beings.

The attempt to transcend a dominant anthropocentric worldview entailed by the emergence of an Ecological Jurisprudence thus necessarily implies the profound recognition and valuing of many traditional societies of the global South, including their ancestral knowledge, with a particular emphasis on their community relations and their respect and reverence for Nature. The effort to search for a new collective worldview, in which man and nature share the role of protagonist as interconnected and equally integral parts of the same planet, is thus, clearly, truly global.

2. JUDICIAL AND LEGISLATIVE PRECEDENTS

If Cullinan's book *Wild Law* represents a symbolic threshold between a previously more theoretical discussion on the emerging legal subjectivity of nature and the actual implementation of rights of Nature initiatives around the world, the Ecuadorian Constitution of 2008 (often called the "Montecristi Constitution") is the symbolic marker by which this emerging theory became globally recognised as firmly enshrined in practice. The Ecuadorian example, however, followed a 2006 precedent, when, for the first time in recorded legal history, the Community Environmental Legal Defense Fund (CELDF) in the United States included the local ecosystem as a subject of rights in a local ordnance drafted by the small community of Tamaquah Borough, in Schuylkill County, Pennsylvania. Since then, in the USA, more than a hundred local ordnances have been drafted by local communities with CELDF's assistance, the most recent of them being the *Lake Erie Bill of Rights*, adopted by the residents of Toledo, Ohio, in the attempt to prevent the lake's water from being further polluted. While the practical success of these ordnances in legal courts has been questioned, they nonetheless represent a profound desire for an alternative governance model (based on an *ecological jurisprudence*) from (at least a section of) the population.

As mentioned above, notwithstanding the local relevance of these first U.S. examples, it is Ecuador's recognition, in 2008, of Nature's intrinsic rights, guaranteed by four Constitutional provision, that undoubtedly represents the most momentous event in the emergence of Nature's legal subjectivity in practical terms. The Constitutional assembly was deeply influenced by local Indigenous worldviews via the Indigenist movement and political party *Pachakutik Plurinational Unity Movement* (see Mijeski and beck, 2011), and thus, at the same time, inscribed within a foundational legal document both rights of Nature (capitalized in the Constitutional text) and a previously excluded (or at least marginalized) worldview – the idea of *Pachamama*, often translated from the original quechua as 'Mother Earth', found within a pan-Andean cosmology. Following the enactment of the 2008 Constitution, the Ecuadorian courts soon began to test the implications of Nature's subjectivity. In 2011, the first successful rights of Nature case (in the world) was litigated in the Provincial Court of Justice of Loja, where the decision by the Municipality of Loja to build a road that would have altered the natural flow of the Vilcabamba river was challenged by two private citizens acting *on behalf of the river*. In a relatively short (and inevitably protean) decision, the Court found in favour of the river, issuing an injunction for the Municipality to repair the damage caused by its actions. Over the decade since the *Vilcabamba case*, more than 35 rights of Nature cases have been litigated in Ecuador, most of them proving successful (KAUFFMAN; MARTIN, 2016).

Then President of neighbouring Bolivia Evo Morales, an Aymara man himself, convened, in 2010, a *World People's Conference on Climate Change and the Rights of Mother Earth* in Tiquipaya, just outside the city of Cochabamba, as a direct and explicit response to the perceived failure of C.O.P. negotiations in Copenhagen at the end of 2009. More than 30000 delegates participated in the conference, including Cormac Cullinan, CELDF and a number of Ecuadorian representatives, and together they drafted a *Universal Declaration of the Rights of Mother Earth*, since then a central document for the entire rights of Nature movement. Inspired by the results, Bolivia passed, in 2010, the *Ley De Derechos De La Madre Tierra* (Mother Earth Rights Law), and, in 2012, the *Ley Marco De La Madre Tierra y Desarrollo Integral Para Vivir Bien* (Law of Mother Earth and Integral Development for Living Well). Bolivian rights of Nature legislation has been, since its inception, less concerned with individualized rights than with collective responsibilities, not only by explicitly articulating a language of *Mother Earth* rights directly cast against rights of *Nature*, but also by developing a comprehensive program for the "integral management of life systems" called a "socio-communitarian productive education model" (ZAMBRANA, 2019).

These Latin-American pioneering examples were soon to be followed by a host of initiatives worldwide. In 2009, following a proposal by the Bolivian government titled 'Harmony with Nature', the United Nations General Assembly proclaimed 22 April as International Mother Earth Day, and, in so doing, launched the Harmony with Nature programme. As a result, U.N. Members States have begun to recognize that the Earth and its ecosystems are our collective common home and that we collectively need to promote Harmony with Nature in order to strike a fair balance between present and future economic, social and environmental needs. Not long thereafter, the *European Citizen's Initiative for the Rights of Nature* was launched in 2013 in the United Kingdom, while the Green Party of England and Wales endorsed a rights of Nature policy platform in 2016. Pope Francis authored, in 2015, the encyclical *Laudato Sí*, subtitled *On care for Our Common Home*. New Zealand, as a result of extensive negotiations with traditional Maori Iwis, granted legal personhood to the Te Urewera forest in 2014 and the Whanganui River in 2017, and is currently negotiating the same recognition for a third geographical feature of the North island, Mt. Taranaki. The Whanganui River legislation is of particular significance as the first instance whereby Nature (or, more specifically, an identifiable natural feature) has been explicitly articulated as a legal *person*. Moreover, it directly and explicitly influenced the 2017 decisions (currently stayed) by the High Court of Uttarakhand, in India, which granted legal personhood to the Ganges and Yamuna rivers and their tributaries, as well as their glaciers, lakes, air, meadows, dales, jungles, forests, wetlands, grasslands, springs and waterfalls. Still in 2017, Mexico City adopted legislation to "recognize and regulate the broader protection of the rights of nature formed by all its ecosystems and species as a collective entity subject to rights", the Australian State of Victoria passed the *Yarra River Protection (Wilip-gin Birrarung murron) Act 2017* (Vic.), which declared the Yarra River (or *Birrarung* in the traditional Woi-wurrung language of the local Aboriginal people) "one living and integrated natural entity", and the NGO *Deep Green Resistance* commenced litigation (since then unsuccessful) in the U.S. in the name of the *Colorado River Ecosystem* in the U.S. District Court in Denver, Colorado, seeking to have the entire ecosystem declared a juridical person. In 2019, Uganda passed the *National Environmental Act* of 2019 recognizing nature as having 'the right to exist, persist, maintain and regenerate its vital cycles, structure, functions and its processes in evolution', while the High Court of Bangladesh explicitly acknowledged the rights of rivers. Following the decisions, first in 2017, by the Constitutional Court of Colombia on the Atrato river, which recognized the Atrato river as a legal subject, and then in 2018 by the Supreme Court of Colombia, which also recognized the entire Amazon basin as a legal subject, a veritable flood of similar decisions occurred, beginning in

2019, such as the Coello, Combeima and Cocora Rivers case (decided in the Regional Court of Tolima), the Cauca River case (decided in the Superior Court of Medellín), the Plata River case, and the Páramo in Pisba (a high Andean ecosystem) case (decided in the Administrative Court of Boyacá) (Herrera-Santoyo, 2020).

Although certainly present from the onset of the movement, Indigenous voices became even more prominent over the last five years. In the USA, the Ho-Chunk Nation voted for a rights of Nature tribal Constitutional amendment in 2016, the Ponca Nation of Oklahoma adopted a customary law recognizing the same in 2018, the White Earth band of the Chippewa Nation recognized the rights of manoomin (wild rice) in 2019, and, in the same year, the Yurok tribe recognized the legal rights of the Klamath River. It appears that Indigenous peoples in the United States are now strategically adopting – by aptly using the unique features of U.S. Tribal Constitutional Law, which protects Indigenous sovereign tribes from State interference – rights of Nature as a legal tool that is, at the same time, understandable by the colonial legal system and capable of conveying some of the (otherwise excluded) metaphysical complexities of traditional worldviews.

What all the initiatives discussed above have in common, however, it the recognition that an *ecocentric* perspective, one where "the earth does not belong to humans, but rather it is humans who belong to the earth" (*Atrato case*, 5.9), is not only preferable but effectively indispensable to prevent an environmental catastrophe capable to threaten human survival. Moreover, what all these approaches show is that "the environmental patrimony is not exclusive to a geographically, jurisdictionally and temporally bounded human community, but rather belongs to humanity in general, including all future generations" (Clark et al, 2019).

3. THE BRAZILIAN CONTEXT

The Brazilian Constitution refers to the concept of development both in its Preamble[2] and in its Article 3, II[3], in this case as a fundamental objective of the Federal Republic of Brazil. Additional reference to technological and

[2] "We, representatives of the Brazilian people, gathered in the Constituent National Assembly to establish a Democratic State, designed to ensure the exercise of social and individual rights, freedom, security, welfare, development, equality and justice as supreme values of a fraternal, pluralistic and unprejudiced society founded on social harmony and committed,

economic development, specifically linked to industrial inventions, can also be found in Article 5, XXIX.[4] Despite the lack of an express definition of development, the right to development is commonly understood as a fundamental right. Firstly, because the material concept of fundamental law goes beyond the express constitutional provision, and secondly, because the right to development is provided for as a human right in a number of international treaties ratified by Brazil.

However, the principles of human dignity and social solidarity – found, respectively, in Articles 1, III,[5] and 3, I[6] of the Brazilian Constitution – allow for an interpretation of the concept of development that implies the concept of sustainability. Equally, Article 170, in disciplining the general principles of economic activity, indirectly point to the concept of sustainability. In terms of environmental sustainability, the Article establishes the "defense of the environment, including through differentiated treatment according to the environmental impact of products and services and their processes of elaboration and rendering" (Item VI); in terms of social sustainability, the Article calls for a "reduction of regional and social inequalities" (Item VII); and finally, in terms of economic sustainability, it refers to "the pursuit of full employment" (Item VIII) and to "favored treatment to small companies incorporated under Brazilian law and that have their headquarters and administration in the country" (Item IX).

Moreover, and more specifically in relation to the environment, Article 225 of the Brazilian Constitution affirms, in its caput, that "[e]veryone has the right to an ecologically balanced environment, a common good of the people and essential to a healthy quality of life, imposing itself to the

in domestic and international order, to the peaceful settlement of disputes, we promulgate, under the protection of God, the following Constitution of the Federative Republic of Brazil."

3 Art. 3: "The fundamental objectives of the Federative Republic of Brazil are: (...) II – to guarantee national development."

4 Art 5, XXIX: "The law will grant authors of industrial inventions temporary privilege for their use, as well as protection of industrial creations, trademark ownership, company names and other distinctive signs, in view of the social interest and the technological and economic development of the country."

5 Art. 1: "The Federative Republic of Brazil, formed by the indissoluble union of States and Municipalities and the Federal District, constitutes a Democratic State of Law and is founded on: (...) III – the dignity of the human person."

6 Art. 3: "The fundamental objectives of the Federative Republic of Brazil are:
I – build a free, just and solidary society."

Government and to the community the duty to defend it and preserve it for present and future generations." In order to ensure the effectiveness of this right, it is incumbent upon the State to

> I – preserve and restore essential ecological processes and provide for the ecological management of species and ecosystems;
> II – preserve the diversity and integrity of the country's genetic heritage and supervise entities dedicated to research and manipulation of genetic material;
> III – define, in all units of the Federation, territorial spaces and their components to be specially protected, being the alteration and suppression allowed only by law, forbidden any use that compromises the integrity of the attributes that justify their protection;
> IV – require, in accordance with the law, for installation of work or activity potentially causing significant degradation of the environment, prior environmental impact study, which will be publicized;
> V – control the production, marketing and use of techniques, methods and substances that pose a risk to life, quality of life and the environment;
> VI – promote environmental education at all levels of education and public awareness for the preservation of the environment; and
> VII – to protect the fauna and flora, forbidden, according to the law, the practices that endanger their ecological function, cause the extinction of species or subject the animals to cruelty. (Article 225, paragraph 1)

Additionally, in terms of civil liability for environmental damage, the Brazilian Constitution, under Article 225, paragraphs 2 and 3, provides that anyone who exploits mineral resources is obliged to restore any degraded environment, and that conduct and activities considered harmful to the environment will result in criminal and administrative sanctions. Finally, paragraph 4 states that the Brazilian Amazon Forest, the Atlantic Forest, the Serra do Mar, the Mato-Grossense Pantanal and the Coastal Zone are considered national heritage, and their use will be permitted under conditions that ensure the preservation of the environment, including the use of natural resources.

This brief analysis of the Brazilian Constitution, and in particular of Article 225, suggests that rights related to environmental concerns are both foundational and superior to other rights. The rights to a balanced environment and to a healthy quality of life are inherently diffused, belonging to each and every one at the same time, without the possibility of identifying a singular holder. Gordilho argues that such perspective, however, is still inherently anthropocentric, based as it is upon human dignity. Alternative expressions, such as "common interest of the people" or "diffuse interest", would instead facilitate the characterization of nature as a hybrid good, at the same time both public and private, with public, community and cultural relevance (Gordilho, 2008, p. 137-138).

At a legislative level, the Brazilian legal system presents a multifaceted landscape. The Brazilian Forest Code (Law nº 12.651/2012) establishes the preservation of forests and other forms of native vegetation, as well as biodiversity, soil, water resources and the integrity of the climate system, its declared objective being the wellbeing of present and future generations, while the idea of sustainability permeates the whole text. On the other hand, the Brazilian Civil Code perpetrates a clearly anthropocentric ontology, by treating all things – including natural features – as 'goods' to be used by the entity to which they belong (Article 103). A number of Acts exist in relation to animal rights and welfare, such as Law nº 9.605/1998, which criminalizes acts of animal cruelty (such as the abuse, mistreatment, injury or mutilation of native or exotic wild animals, domestic or domesticated), Law nº 7.173/1983, which governs the functioning of zoos, Law nº 7.643/1987, on protection of marine cetaceans; Law nº 11.794/2008, regulating scientific activities involving animals, and Law nº 10.519/2002, on the hygiene and care of animals involved in rodeos and similar fields. According to Gordilho, "the juridical status of animals is already halfway between property and legal personality, since the Constitution expressly detaches them from the ecological perspective to consider them under an ethical approach, prohibiting practices subjecting them to cruelty." (Gordilho, 2008, p. 122) The Constitutional and legislative context presented here is thus the necessary background against which, as we will discuss shortly, biocentric arguments are currently emerging in Brazil.

4. THE 'RIGHTS OF NATURE' PARADIGM IN BRAZIL

While the terrain for the introduction of a rights of Nature paradigm in Brazil appears to be either Constitutional or legislative, as discussed above, it is the Judgment of Appeal 1.797.175-SP by the Superior Court of Justice, reported by Minister Og Fernandes in March 21, 2019, that represents the first explicit introduction of rights of Nature in Brazil. The case involved the custody of a wild animal (specifically, a parrot), seized by the Brazilian Institute of Environment and Renewable Natural Resources, which is responsible for the protection of the Brazilian fauna. The lower Court of the Municipality of Ubatuba, in the State of São Paulo, had been requested the annulment of the infraction notices issued by the Brazilian Institute of the Environment and Renewable Natural Resources for the improper possession of the wild animal, as well as the restoration of what the claimant called “the original guardianship” of the wild animal apprehended by the institute. The claim was initially deemed groundless. However, the Appeal Court of the State of São Paulo decided, with regard to the “guardianship” of the animal, that it should continue, on a provisional basis, with the claimant, based on Resolution nº 457/2013[7], due to the lack of basic animal care while the animal was under the custody of the Brazilian Institute for the Environment and Renewable Natural Resources. This provisional guardianship, however, would cease as soon as the Brazilian Institute of the Environment and Renewable Natural Resources could prove the viability of the animal’s destination and that proper care could be provided, at which point the animal would be immediately sent to an appropriate place capable of providing daily care.

The decision, however, was not deemed satisfactory by the claimant. According to her, 23 years of close cohabitation between the bird in question and his human companions had created a unique affective bond, which, in turn, had caused the bird to acquire habits incompatible with life in the wild. This argument authorized a special appeal to the Superior Court,[8] in which it was argued that, in removing the wild animal from a long life spent with the plaintiff, the decision of the appellate court contradicted Article 5 of the Law of Introduction to the Rules of Brazilian Law.[9]

[7] In Brazil, an administrative resolution is an order that pronounces the person in charge of a public service. It is a standard whose scope is limited to the context of the service in question and whose compliance is mandatory. The Resolution nº 457/2013 was edited by the National Council of Environment. It deals with temporary deposit and custody of wild animals seized or rescued by the organs members of the National System of the Environment.

[8] In Brazil there exist two Supreme Courts, the first one (Supremo Tribunal Federal) with jurisdiction over extraordinary appeals based on violation of the Federal Constitution, and the second one (Superior Tribunal de Justiça) with jurisdiction over what is called ‘special appeal’, based on violation of Federal law in general.

[9] Article 5: ‘In the application of the law, the judge will attend to the social ends to which it is directed and to the requirements of the common good.’

Considering that the coexistence between the claimant and the animal had continued for more than 23 years, it was argued, a provisional guardianship would have induced high levels of uncertainty and anxiety, destabilizing the emotional and physical wellbeing of the claimant. Moreover, and more importantly for the purpose of this paper, the claimant also argued that the removal of the wild animal after a long period of domestication also implied a violation of the animal's own rights.

The Superior Court argued that, while recognizing that the overall protection of wild fauna is inscribed within a Constitutional framework[10] (which makes the action of the Brazilian Institute for the Environment and Renewable Natural Resources to curb wildlife trafficking commendable), contextual conditions suggest that "the bird's reintegration into its natural habitat, while possible, may cause more damage than benefits, considering that the parrot in question has had pet bird habits for about 23 years." (Supremo Tribunal Federal, 2019) Furthermore, "the constant lack of definition of the animal's final destination clearly violates the dignity of the claimant as a human person, because, despite allowing a temporary relationship, it imposes the end of the affective bond and the certainty of a separation that is not known when it may occur." (Supremo Tribunal Federal, 2019)[11]

As mentioned in the introduction, Sarlet and Fensterseifer contend that this judgment ultimately addresses the principle of the dignity of the human person from an ecological perspective, with the consequence of unsettling a Kantian anthropocentric paradigm (SARLET; FENSTERSEIFER, 2017, p. 62). Vanessa Hasson de Oliveira suggests that the court could have instead selected the expression "planetary dignity", which proposes the guarantee of the dignity of human life within its larger ecological community, thus including the perception and appreciation of the existence and maintenance of the diversity of life on the planet, which is indispensable to the existence and maintenance of the dignity of the life of the

[10] Article 225, caput and paragraph 1, VII.

[11] The granting of custody in the case in question, however, was conditional on some measures: a) a semiannual visit by a veterinarian specialized in wild animals, to conduct educational training with the person responsible for the bird; b) an annual inspection of the conditions of the enclosure and the animal by the Brazilian Institute for the Environment and Renewable Natural Resources, whose observations must be implemented under the penalty of loss of custody.

human person (Oliveira, 2016, p. 71). It is indeed without doubt that the decision by the Superior Court of Justice casts wild animals as object of human *custody*, not *possession*, thus departing from the understanding traditionally applied to them by civil law, whereby animals are considered mere goods, object of possession and property.

In implicitly recognizing non-human animals as subjects (rather than objects) of law, the decision makes express mention of Article 20 of the German Constitution as a step beyond anthropocentrism (which provides that "[w]ithin the framework of the constitutional order, the State protects the natural bases of life and animals, also taking into account its responsibility to future generations, through legislative power, and according to the law and through executive and judicial powers"), as well as the Constitutions of Ecuador and Bolivia, with a particular emphasis on the influence of their Andean culture. Moreover, the decision also refers to previous animal rights cases, a prime example being the Habeas Corpus nº 833085-3/2005-TJBA159, with judgment on September 28, 2005, which intended to grant freedom to a chimpanzee on the grounds that she was trapped alone in a zoo cage, which had caused clear suffering and loneliness (before a decision could be issued, however, the chimpanzee was found dead in her cage).[12]

While the decision goes beyond the traditional protection afforded to animals by Brazil's Federal legislation, as well as adopting an ultimately biocentric perspective, the decision is not binding and applies only to the specific case. Indeed, it is important to remember that Brazil is a Civil Law country belonging to the Roman-Germanic tradition, with a rigid Constitution and centrality of legislation, not of judicial decisions. John Gilissen points out the radical differences of the common law tradition and its emphasis on jurisprudence (Gilissen, 1995, p. 20), which account for the judicial evolution of rights of Nature arguments in common law countries. In the Brazilian case, therefore, influenced as it is by the Roman-Germanic tradition, judicial decisions are not, *per se*, sufficient to award dignity to the environment in a structurally solid legal manner, considering that,

[12] Another emblematic case was the Habeas Corpus 002637-70.2010.8.19.0000-TJ-RJ, also aiming to free a caged chimpanzee in a zoo, kept in a small and poorly structured cage. This second claim was extinguished without resolution of the merits, with the argument that, even though the court sympathized with the plea, the measure of habeas corpus belongs exclusively to the human being.

as a rule, they are not binding, their effects being restricted to specific claims and claimants. On the other hand, paradigmatic decisions, such as the one briefly analyzed above, *do* exercise political force, in a type of judicial activism that can generate social mobilization and legislative action. Judicial decisions, therefore, *do* play a fundamental role in influencing new court decisions, and thus, ultimately, in introducing rights of Nature within the Federal legal system. Gordilho asserts that "judicial litigation should not be seen in a different way from politics. Litigation is political activity, connected to political practices and aspirations, although it does not always represent a solid path to social change" (GORDILHO, 2009, p. 101).

Since the Brazilian Constitution establishes the hierarchy between the different types of law, in its article 59, municipal legislation also runs the risk of being declared unconstitutional. Nonetheless, as discussed at the opening of this paper, in 2015, the Municipality of São Paulo proposed an Amendment to the Organic Law of the Municipality[13] nº 04-00005/2015, in which it suggested to include a new provision (180A), "considering that the members of nature have intrinsic rights to life and maintenance of their ecosystem processes, in interdependence with the dignified life of the citizens, with the aim of achieving sustainability in the city" (SÃO PAULO, 2015). Shortly thereafter, in 2017, the Municipality of Bonito, in the State of Pernambuco, amended its Organic Law to recognize the rights of Nature (PERNAMBUCO, 2020), and was soon followed, in 2018, by the Municipality of Paudalho, also in the State of Pernambuco, which, equally recognized Nature as a subject of rights (PERNAMBUCO, 2018).

In all these cases, where proposed legislative amendments undertook the municipal route, the issue is articulated rather briefly, without clarifying many relevant substantive and procedural issues, such as the legitimacy for proposing a legal action and the representation of nature as a subject of law. Given the Brazilian Code of Civil Procedure does not mention Nature as a subject of legal action, such issues require further, extensive and more profound scrutiny. The relative superficiality of the municipal approach, therefore, may run the risk of municipal legislation about rights on Nature being declared unconstitutional. Consequently, the desire to grant sub-

[13] In Brazil, in addition to the Federal Constitution, States and Municipalities have a type of law similar to a "local constitution". Municipalities call this law the Organic Law.

jectivity to Nature within the Brazilian legal system necessarily requires radical amendments to the Brazilian Constitution itself.

However, while Constitutional amendments are the necessary precursor to engender any form of stability for the novel rights of Nature perspective currently being proposed, Article 225 of the Brazilian Federal Constitution does not permit any obscurity to arise in regard to its interpretation. The issue raised by the Judgment of Appeal 1.797.175-SP and by the municipal rights of Nature proposals, therefore, has broader implications in regard to legal certainty, since, as Celso Antonio Bandeira de Mello points out, an individual must be able to foresee the consequences of one's actions and plan one's future (MELLO, 2002, p. 113). While Recaséns Siches poetically equates the feeling of security with the feeling of stepping on firm ground (while the impression of insecurity is equivalent to the fear of falling: SICHES, 1973, p. 301), and Antonio-Enrique Pérez Luño admits that security is an ingrained desire in the life of humanity, who feels terror at the insecurity of one's existence the face of the unpredictability and uncertainty to which one is subjected (PÉREZ LUÑO, 1991, p. 17), José Afonso da Silva links the theme to the stability of subjective rights. According to da Silva, an important condition of legal certainty is in the relative certainty that individuals have that relations established under a norm must last even when that norm is replaced (SILVA, 1996, p. 412).

The combined analyses of a biocentric jurisprudential perspective and of proposed municipal rights of Nature amendments in Brazil, therefore, indicate unequivocally the need for a significant change inscribed within the Brazilian Federal Constitution, if a rights of Nature discourse had to achieve any form of lasting certainty within Brazil. On the other hand, these Brazilian examples also add to the international discourse introduced in this paper, indicating the global desire for a universal declaration on the rights of Nature under international law capable of bypassing the limitations of domestic law. Karl Larenz wrote, in 1985, that peace and justice, the two main components of the idea of law, are always in a dialectical relationship, constantly shaping each other. If the legal system is unjust, peace cannot be safeguarded. On the other hand, where legal peace is lacking, justice often disappears (LARENZ, 1985, p. 51). Thus, while the unbridled quest for legal security always runs the risk of immobility and stratification, once society evolves and changes, the law cannot turn a blind eye to social transformations, lest it becomes unjust. Recognizing the limitations of Brazilian legislation in embracing a rights of Nature discourse is thus the first step towards any effective and credible effort towards an ecocentric paradigm that is consistent with the current demands of the global environment.

REFERENCES

LEGISLATION

BOLIVIA. *Constitución del Estado Plurinacional de Bolivia* 2008 [Constitution of the Plurinational State of Bolivia 2008].

BOLIVIA. *Ley De Derechos De La Madre Tierra* [Mother Earth Rights Law], Ley N 71, 21 December 2010.

BOLIVIA. *Ley Marco De La Madre Tierra y Desarrollo Integral Para Vivir Bien* (Law of Mother Earth and Integral Development for Living Well], Ley N 300, 15 October 2012.

BRASIL. *Código Civil* (January 10, 2012a). Available in: http://www.planalto.gov.br/ccivil_03/leis/2002/l10406.htm. Access in: October 28, 2019.

BRASIL. *Constituição Federal* (October 5, 1988). Available in: http://www.planalto.gov.br/ccivil_03/constituicao/constituição.htm. Access in: October 15, 2019.

BRASIL. *Lei nº 12.651* (May 25, 2012b). Available in: http://www.planalto.gov.br/ccivil_03/_Ato2011-2014/2012/Lei/L12651.htm. Access in: October 28, 2019.

NEW ZEALAND. *Te Urewera Act 2014*.

NEW ZEALAND. *Te Awa Tupua (Whanganui Claims Settlement) Act 2017*.

PERNAMBUCO. Lei Orgânica do Município de Bonito (December 26, 2016). Available in: https://camarapaudalho.pe.gov.br/2018/12/lei-municipal-no-8782018-declara-como-patrimonio-natural-ambiental-cultural-a-fonte-de-agua-mineral-em-sao-severino-do-ramos-e-da-outras-providencias/. Access in: March 22, 2020.

PERNAMBUCO. Lei Municipal de Paudalho 878/2018. Available in: http://camarapaudalho.pe.gov.br/wp-content/uploads/2018/04/LEI-ORG%C3%82NICA-MUNICIPAL-OFICIAL.pdf. Access in: March 22, 2020.

SÃO PAULO. *Project of Amendment to the Organic Law of the Municipality number 04-00005/2015*. Available in: http://splegisconsulta.camara.sp.gov.br/Pesquisa/IndexProjeto. Access in: March 23, 2020.

UNITED NATIONS. *Agenda 21* (1992). Available in: https://sustainabledevelopment.un.org/content/documents/Agenda21.pdf. Access in: October 22, 2019.

UNITED NATIONS. *Declaration on the Right to Development* (December, 4 1986). Available in: http://legal.un.org/avl/ha/drd/drd.html. Access in: October 22, 2019.

UNITED NATIONS. *Future We Want* – Outcome document (2012). Available in: https://sustainabledevelopment.un.org/futurewewant.html. Access in: October 23, 2019.

UNITED NATIONS. *Harmony with Nature*. Available in: http://www.harmonywithnatureun.org/. Access in: October 23, 2019.

UNITED NATIONS. *Johannesburg Declaration on Sustainable Development* (2002). Available in: https://www.un.org/esa/sustdev/documents/WSSD_POI_PD/English/POI_PD.htm. Access in: October 23, 2019.

UNITED NATIONS. *Report of the World Commission on Environment and Development: Our Common Future* (1987). Available in:: https://sustainabledevelopment.un.org/content/documents/5987our-common-future.pdf. Access in: October 23, 2019.

UNITED NATIONS. Sustainable Development Summit (2015). Available in: ment.un.org/sdgsummit. Access in: October 23, 2019.

UNITED NATIONS. *United Nations General Assembly*, GA RES 63/278, 63rd session, Agenda Item 49(d), UN Doc A/RES/63/278 (22 Apr 2009).

Yarra River Protection (Wilip-gin Birrarung murron) Act 2017 (Vic), 1(a)

JURISPRUDENCE

BRASIL. Superior Tribunal de Justiça. Recurso Especial nº 1.797.175-SP. Relator: Ministro Og Fernandes. Julgado em: 21 de marco de 2019.

COLOMBIA. Corte Constitucional [Constitutional Court], Decision T-622 10/11/2016 (*Atrato case*).

ECUADOR. *Wheeler et al. v. Director de la Procuraduria General del Estado*, Judgment 11121-2011-0010 (31 March 2011) (Corte Provincial de Justicia de Loja [Provincial Court of Justice of Loja]) (*Vilcabamba case*).

INDIA. *Lalit Miglani v State of Uttarakhand & others* (March 30 2017) MCC 139/2017 (March 30 2017) (*Glaciers case*).

INDIA. *Mohd. Salim v. State of Uttarakhand & Others*, Uttarakhand H.C. 126 (India) (March 20 2017) (High Court of Uttarakhand, India) (*Ganges and Yamuna case*).

U.S. *Sierra Club v. Morton*, 405 U.S. 727 (1972).

SECONDARY MATERIALS

AMARO, Rogério Roque. Desenvolvimento ou Pós-Desenvolvimento? Des-Envolvimento e... Noflay! *Cadernos de Estudos Africanos [Online]*, 34 | 2017, posto online no dia 11 abril 2018. Disponível em: http://journals.openedition.org/cea/2335 ; DOI : 10.4000/cea.2335. Acesso em: 25.10.2019.

BERRY, Thomas. *The Dream of the Earth*, San Francisco: Sierra Club Books, 1988.

BERRY, Thomas. *The Great Work*. New York: Random House, 1999.

BERRY, Thomas Berry. *The Sacred Universe*. New York: Columbia University Press, 2009.

BURDON, Peter. *Earth Jurisprudence: Private Property and the Environment*. London: Routledge, 2015.

CARSON, Rachel. *Silent Spring*. Boston: Houghton Mifflin, 1962.

CLARK, C; EMMANOUIL, N; PAGE, J; PELIZZON, A. Can you hear the rivers sing? Legal personhood, ontology, and the nitty-gritty, *Ecology Law Quarterly*, vol. 45, no. 4., 2019, pp. 787-844.

COMMUNITY ENVIRONMENTAL LEGAL DEFENSE FUND (Web Page, 30 January 2020) <https://celdf.org/advancing-community-rights/rights-of-nature/rights--nature-timeline/>.

CULLIMAN, Cormac. *Wild Law. 2 ed.* Chelsea Green, 2011.

CULLIMAN, Cormac. A History of Wild Law. Peter Burdon (ed.) In *Exploring Wild Law*. South Austrália: Wakefield, 2011, pp. 12-24.

DINIZ, Maria Helena. *Compêndio de introdução à ciência do direito*. 13 ed. São Paulo: Saraiva, 2001.

DINIZ, Maria Helena. *Lei de Introdução ao código civil brasileiro interpretada.* 3 ed. atual. São Paulo: Saraiva, 1997.

FODOR, Amanda Cesario. *A defesa dos direitos dos animais não-humanos como parte integrante do ordenamento jurídico brasileiro.* Monograph presented in the Law Graduation Course. Universidade Federal Fluminense, Rio de Janeiro, 2016.

GILISSEN, John. *Introdução histórica ao direito (Introduction historique au droit).* 2. ed. Translation A. M. Hespanha e L. M. Macaísta Malheiros. Lisboa: Fundação Calouste Gulbenkian, 1995.

GORDILHO, Heron José de Santana. *Abolicionismo animal.* Salvador: Evolução, 2008.

GRAHAM, Nicole. *Lawscape.* London: Routledge, 2011).

HARARI, Yuval Noah. *Sapiens: A Brief History of Humankind.* New York: Harper, 2014.

KAUFFMAN, Craig; MARTIN, Pamela. Testing Ecuador's Rights of Nature: Why Some Lawsuits Succeed and Others Fail. Speech, *International Studies Association Annual Convention,* Atlanta, 18 March 2016.

LARENZ, Karl. *Derecho justo.* Translation Luis Díez-Picazo. Madri: Civitas, 1985.

LUÑO, Antonio-Enrique Pérez. *La seguridad jurídica.* Barcelona: Ariel, 1991.

MELLO, Celso Antônio Bandeira de. *Curso de direito administrativo.* 15 ed. atual. São Paulo: Malheiros, 2002.

MIJESKI, Kenneth; BECK, Scott. *Pachakutik and the Rise and Decline of the Ecuadorian Indigenous Movement.* Athens: University of Ohio Press, 2011.

OLIVEIRA, Vanessa Hasson de. *Direitos da Natureza.* Rio de Janeiro: Lumen Juris, 2016.

PELIZZON, Alessandro. Earth laws, rights of nature and legal pluralism. Michelle Maloney & Peter Burdon (eds.). In *Wild Law – In Practice.* London: Routledge, 2014.

RUSSELL, Bertrand. *A History of Western Philosophy.* New York: Simon and Schuster, 1945.

SANTOYO, Hector Herrera. The Rights of Nature (Rivers) and Constitutional Actions in Colômbia. Available in: <https://gnhre.org/2019/07/08/the-rights-of-nature-rivers--and-constitutional-actions-in-colombia/>. Access in: January 30, 2020.

SARLET, Ingo Wolfgang; FENSTERSEIFER, Tiago. *Direito constitucional ambiental*: Constituição, direitos fundamentais e proteção do ambiente, 5. ed. São Paulo: RT, 2017.

SICHES, Recaséns. *Nueva filosofía de la interpretación del derecho.* 2 ed. ampl.. México: Porruá, 1973.

SILVA, José Afonso da. *Curso de direito constitucional positivo.* 11 ed. São Paulo: Malheiros, 1996.

STONE, Christopher. Should Trees Have Standing? Towards Legal Rights for Natural Objects. *California Law Review,* vol. 45, 1972, pp. 450-501.

STONE, Christopher. *Should Trees Have Standing?.* 3 ed. Oxford: Oxford University Press, 2010.

SWIMME, Brian; TUCKER, Mary Evelyn. *The Journey of the Universe.* Neu Haven: Yale University Press, 2011.

ZAMBRANA-FLORES, Ivan. Mother Earth approach in the implementation of Education and Climate Change. *UN Harmony with Nature program.* Available in: http://files.harmonywithnatureun.org/uploads/upload808.pdf. Retrieved March 20, 2020.

AFETO NA RELAÇÃO FAMILIAR

ÁLVARO VILLAÇA AZEVEDO*

1. PATERNIDADE BIOLÓGICA E PATERNIDADE SOCIOAFETIVA

Apesar dos avanços da tecnologia biomédica, nos últimos anos, a paternidade biológica exerce um papel secundário no Direito de Família, especialmente quando confronta com os princípios da afetividade, da igualdade entre os filhos e da dignidade da pessoa humana, que imperam na convivência familiar. Esses princípios, que fundamentam a paternidade socioafetiva, foram consagrados pelo nosso ordenamento jurídico e, por isso, sobrepõem-se e prevalecem até mesmo ante uma prova biológica, por exemplo, um exame de DNA com resultado positivo, que aponte o verdadeiro genitor, mas que jamais teve uma convivência familiar com os filhos biológicos mencionados no exame.

Em nossa Constituição Federal de 1988, além do artigo 1º, inciso III, que define a dignidade da pessoa humana como um dos princípios fundamentais de nossa ordem jurídica, destacam-se outros dispositivos que cuidam, especificamente, de relações familiares entre pais e filhos. Realmente, o artigo 227, §6º, estabelece que todos os filhos são iguais, independentemente de sua origem, incluindo, especialmente, nesse âmbito da igualdade de direitos, os filhos havidos por adoção. O *caput* desse mesmo

* Professor Titular da Faculdade de Direito da USP. Livre-docente e Doutor em Direito pela USP. Bacharel em Direito pela Universidade Presbiteriana Mackenzie.

dispositivo constitucional assegura à criança e ao adolescente o direito à convivência familiar, sem qualquer negligência, crueldade ou discriminação, não sendo prioridade, portanto, a origem genética. O artigo 226, §4º, atribui à comunidade formada por qualquer dos pais e seus descendentes a mesma dignidade de família constitucionalmente protegida.

No âmbito infraconstitucional, nosso Código Civil de 2002, em seu artigo 1.593[1], reconhece outras espécies de parentesco civil (outras origens), além do decorrente da adoção, acolhendo, assim, essa nova base de vínculo parental, a paternidade socioafetiva fundada na posse de estado do filho. Outros dispositivos do Código Civil de 2002 destacam-se também no sentido de acolherem o paradigma da paternidade socioafetiva. O artigo 1.596 estabelece que todos os filhos, independentemente de sua origem, possuem os mesmos direitos, conforme se verifica de sua redação, *verbis*: "Os filhos, havidos ou não da relação de casamento, ou por adoção, terão os mesmos direitos e qualificações, proibidas quaisquer designações discriminatórias relativas à filiação". O artigo 1.597, inciso V, ao presumir concebido na constância do casamento o filho havido por inseminação artificial heteróloga, com a prévia autorização do marido, acaba admitindo uma origem parcialmente biológica desse filho, pois o marido que autorizar a reprodução humana assistida com utilização de sêmen alheio, será um pai exclusivamente socioafetivo, o que não poderá ser impugnado por investigação de paternidade posterior, uma vez que a lei autoriza o aludido procedimento artificial.

O artigo 1.605, inciso II, prevê que, na falta ou defeito do termo de nascimento, poderá ser provada a filiação por qualquer modo admissível em direito, especialmente, "quando existirem veementes presunções resultantes de fatos já certos", por exemplo, quando existe um tratamento pessoal e afetivo recíproco entre duas pessoas, como pai e filho e *vice versa*; quando uma pessoa provê a educação e o sustento da que é por ele criada, o que também é conduta típica entre pai e filho; quando duas pessoas se apresentam em público, reciprocamente, como pai e filho, sendo essa convivência pessoal e afetiva, específica e típica do relacionamento entre pai e filho, reconhecida pela sociedade e pela família; entre outros exemplos possíveis. Esse dispositivo legal consagra a posse de estado de filiação, que

[1] Art. 1.593: "O parentesco é natural ou civil, conforme resulte de consanguinidade ou outra origem".

abrange as hipóteses do filho de criação e da adoção de fato, esta também denominada "adoção à brasileira".

E o artigo 1.614 admite que o filho rejeite o reconhecimento do estado de filiação, requerido posteriormente pelo pai biológico que não efetuou o registro após seu nascimento. Como se nota, as aludidas normas constitucionais e infraconstitucionais demonstram que a paternidade e a filiação socioafetivas foram acolhidas e consagradas pelo nosso ordenamento jurídico, de maneira a possibilitar o seu reconhecimento, mesmo que não exista vínculo biológico. Tratando do instituto jurídico da adoção, João Baptista Villela já vislumbrava a afetividade como essência do vínculo da paternidade, ressaltando que "As transformações mais recentes por que passou a família, deixando de ser unidade de caráter econômico, social e religioso para se afirmar fundamentalmente como grupo de afetividade e companheirismo, imprimiram considerável reforço ao esvaziamento biológico da paternidade"[2].

Alerta, ainda, que o equívoco, "a propósito da investigação de paternidade, está, pois, em não se distinguir que posso obrigar alguém a responder patrimonialmente pela sua conduta – seja esta o descumprimento de um contrato, a prática de um ilícito ou o exercício de uma atividade potencialmente onerosa, como o ato idôneo à procriação –, mas não posso obrigar, quem quer que seja, a assumir uma paternidade que não deseja. Simplesmente porque é impossível fazê-lo, sem violentar, não tanto a pessoa, mas a própria ideia de paternidade. Tem tanto esta de autodoação, de gratuidade, de engajamento íntimo, que não é susceptível de imposição coativa. Pai e mãe ou se é por decisão pessoal e livre, ou simplesmente não se é. Assim, a lei e a Justiça desrespeitam gravemente uma criança, quando lhe dão por pai quem, em ação de investigação de paternidade, resiste a tal condição. Um ser com todos os vícios e crimes, mas que aceite verdadeiramente a paternidade, é preferível àquele que a recuse, ornado, embora, de todos os méritos e virtudes, se se tomar como critério o bem da criança. Imagine-se cada um tendo como pai ou mãe, quem só o é por imposição da força : ninguém experimentará mais viva repulsa, nem mais forte cons-

[2] *Desbiologização da Paternidade*, conferência realizada em 09/05/1979 e publicada na Revista da Faculdade de Direito da Universidade Federal de Minas Gerais, Belo Horizonte, ano XXVII, nº 21, maio de 1979; texto revisto pelo autor e reproduzido *in* Revista Forense Comemorativa – 100 anos, tomo IV, Direito de Família e Sucessório, Coord. Eduardo de Oliveira Leite e José da Silva Pacheco, Ed. Forense, Rio de Janeiro, 2006, pp. 244, 245 e 246

trangimento. Todo o direito de família tende a se organizar, de resto, sob o princípio basilar da liberdade, tão certo é que as prestações familiais, seja entre cônjuges, seja entre pais e filhos, só proporcionam plena satisfação quando gratuitamente assumidas e realizadas".

Cuidando do tema e referindo-se às bases da filiação socioafetiva, elucida Luiz Edson Fachin[3]: "O reconhecimento do fundamento biológico da filiação, com o desenvolvimento das técnicas da engenharia genética, a atenuação da presunção *pater is est*, a vedação constitucional ao tratamento discriminatório e o consequente acesso dos filhos outrora ilegítimos ao estatuto jurídico da filiação, em patamar de igualdade com os denominados filhos legítimos, foram significativos avanços do Direito no que tange a questão do estabelecimento da paternidade. Todavia, sendo a paternidade um conceito jurídico e, sobretudo, um direito, a *verdade biológica* da filiação não é o único fator a ser levado em consideração pelo aplicador do Direito: o elemento material da filiação não é tão-só o vínculo de sangue, mas a expressão jurídica de uma *verdade socioafetiva*. O elemento socioafetivo da filiação reflete a verdade jurídica que está para além do biologismo, sendo essencial para o estabelecimento da filiação".

E continua: "O *fato* a ser tomado pelo Direito como filiação não constitui apenas um fato biológico, mas, também, um fato social, que se revela tanto na sua manifestação perante o grupo social, como, especialmente, na esfera psicológica e afetiva dos sujeitos (...) Prepondera, pois, o laço afetivo. A verdade sociológica da filiação se constrói, revelando-se não apenas na descendência, mas no comportamento de quem expende cuidados, carinho no tratamento, quer em público, quer na intimidade do lar, com afeto verdadeiramente paternal, construindo vínculo que extrapola o laço biológico, compondo a base da paternidade"[4].

No mesmo sentido, esclarece Maria Berenice Dias[5] que "A necessidade de manter a estabilidade da família, que cumpre a sua função social, faz com que se atribua um papel secundário à verdade biológica. Revela a constância social da relação entre pais e filhos, caracterizando uma paternidade que existe não pelo simples fato biológico ou por força de presunção legal,

[3] Comentários ao Novo Código Civil, vol. XVIII, Artigos 1.591 a 1.638, Ed. Forense, Rio de Janeiro, 2008, p. 24.

[4] Comentários ao Novo Código Civil, cit., pp. 24 e 25.

[5] Manual de Direito das Famílias, Ed. Revista dos Tribunais, São Paulo, 5ª ed., 2009, pp. 338 e 339.

mas em decorrência de uma convivência afetiva. Em matéria de filiação, a verdade real é o fato de o filho gozar da posse de estado, que prova o vínculo parental (...) Constituído o vínculo da parentalidade, mesmo quando desligado da verdade biológica, prestigia-se a situação que preserva o elo da afetividade. Não é outro o fundamento que veda a desconstituição do registro de nascimento feito de forma espontânea por aquele que, mesmo sabendo não ser o pai consanguíneo, tem o filho como seu" (destaques do original).

Outro não é o entendimento de nossos Tribunais, que, igualmente, vêm admitindo a paternidade socioafetiva, como se verifica nas decisões adiante citadas: "Apelação Cível. Reconhecimento de paternidade socioafetiva. Criança que foi acolhida aos três meses de idade, criada como se filho fosse ante a impossibilidade biológica do casal em gerar filhos. Adoção não formalizada. A verdade real se sobrepõe a formal, cumprindo-nos conhecer o vínculo afetivo-familiar criado pelo casal e a criança, hoje adulto, ainda que não tenha havido adoção legal. Paternidade socioafetiva que resulta clara nos autos pelos elementos de prova"[6]. "Apelação Cível. Negatória de paternidade. Paternidade socioafetiva. Ainda que o autor, pai registral, não seja o pai biológico do réu, mantém-se a improcedência da negatória da paternidade, se estabelecida a paternidade socioafetiva entre eles. Em se tratando de relação de filiação, não se pode compreender que seja descartável, ao menos em casos como o presente, onde por vinte anos o réu teve como genitor o autor. Pretensão que afronta o princípio constitucional da dignidade da pessoa humana, porque o réu ficaria sem pai registral, ou seja, sem filiação e sobrenome paterno. Precedentes doutrinários e jurisprudenciais"[7].

"O código atual abandonou a sistemática e passou a chamar de civil o parentesco decorrente da adoção, aquele vindo de inseminação artificial heteróloga consentida (artigo 1597, V) e o vindo da afinidade. É possível aqui incluir, inclusive, a filiação sócio-afetiva, conforme já reconheceu o Superior Tribunal de Justiça (REsp. 83371/RS, julgado em 17.05.2007) e estabelece o enunciado número 256 do Conselho Nacional de Justiça: 'Art. 1593 : A posse do estado de filho (parentalidade socioafetiva) cons-

[6] Tribunal de Justiça do Rio Grande do Sul, 7ª Câmara Cível, Relator Desembargador Ricardo Raupp Ruschel, Apelação Cível nº 70023877798, j. 27/08/2008, *in* DJ 03/09/2008.

[7] Tribunal de Justiça do Rio Grande do Sul, 8ª Câmara Cível, Relator Desembargador José Ataídes Siqueira Trindade, Apelação Cível nº 70022895072, j. 05/06/2008, *in* DJ 12/06/2008.

titui modalidade de parentesco civil'. O parentesco consanguíneo, sem dúvida, garante a inclusão no plano de saúde da requerida. Essa situação não é contestada pela requerida e o comprova o fato de outros filhos do autor serem seus dependentes nele. À filiação civil há de se atribuir o mesmo direito. Isso porque a Constituição Federal equiparou, para todos os efeitos, os filhos, qualquer que fosse a sua categoria (artigo 227, §6º)"[8].

"(...) aqui está absolutamente configurada uma 'adoção à brasileira' em que a pessoa, embora ciente da ausência de vínculo biológico, reconhece o outro como filho. Nesses casos, o que prevalece não é a verdade biológica, mas a socioafetiva, porquanto a pessoa que teve reconhecida a paternidade passa a gozar do estado de filho, que não lhe pode ser retirado simplesmente por ato unilateral do pai registral, como se o ato fosse de mero capricho, o reconhecimento é irrevogável e irretratável, pois caracterizada uma adoção. Em verdade, apenas nas hipóteses de o filho desejar estabelecer a verdade biológica é que a jurisprudência tem admitido a revogação do reconhecimento levado a efeito (...) No mais, desimportante tenha o exame pericial excluído a paternidade, consoante o posicionamento já externado, em ações desse jaez, em que ocorrida típica 'adoção à brasileira', o princípio da verdade socioafetiva sobrepuja ao da biológica. Nesse diapasão, escorreita a condução da dilação probatória pelo Juízo a *quo*, porquanto este cuidou em determinar a realização de estudos social e psicológico exatamente para aferir a existência de vínculo afetivo entre as partes"[9].

Registre-se, nesse passo, a decisão do Tribunal de Justiça do Ceará[10], que "enfatiza manifestação de vontade exercida pelo pai no reconhecimento de filho que sabia não ser biologicamente seu", *verbis*: "o reconhecimento espontâneo da paternidade por quem sabe não ser o pai biológico tipifica verdadeira adoção (adoção à brasileira), a qual é irrevogável, descabendo postular-se anulação do registro de nascimento, salvo se demonstrada de forma convincente a existência de vício de consentimento, o que inocorreu no caso em foco". " 'O estado de filiação não está necessariamente ligado

[8] Tribunal de Justiça de São Paulo, 9ª Câmara de Direito Privado, Relator Desembargador José Luiz Gavião de Almeida, Apelação nº 527.250-4/8-00, j. 29/07/2008.

[9] Tribunal de Justiça de São Paulo, 8ª Câmara de Direito Privado, Relator Desembargador Joaquim Garcia, Apelação com Revisão nº 534.955-4/1-00, j. 08/10/2008.

[10] Apel. Cív. n. 116.24200080601761 – Fortaleza, Rel. Des. Sérgia Maria Mendonça Miranda, 6ª Câm. Cív, registro em 21.07.2010, citado pela mesma Relatora na Apel. Cív. n. 59402-26.2007.8.06.0001/1,j. em 09.09.2011.

à origem biológica e pode, portanto, assumir feições originadas de qualquer outra relação que não exclusivamente genética. Em outras palavras, o estado de filiação é gênero do qual são espécies a filiação biológica e a não biológica (...) Na realidade da vida, o estado de filiação de cada pessoa é único e de natureza socioafetiva, desenvolvido na convivência familiar, ainda que derive biologicamente dos pais, na maioria dos casos' (Mauro Nicolau Júnior *in* 'Paternidade e Coisa Julgada. Limites e Possibilidade à Luz dos Direitos Fundamentais e dos Princípios Constitucionais', Curitiba: Juruá Editora, 2006)"[11].

Por isso, Luiz Edson Fachin[12] destaca esse "reconhecimento pelos tribunais de uma situação que se coloca como base das relações familiares. Se não há dúvida acerca da relevância do reconhecimento dos laços biológicos da filiação, o vínculo que une pais e filhos, e que lhes oferece tais qualificações, é mais amplo que a carga genética de cada um: diz respeito às relações concretas entre eles, o carinho dispensado, o tratamento afetuoso, a vontade paterna em se projetar em outra pessoa, a quem reconhece como filho, não só em virtude do sangue, mas em virtude do afeto, construído nas relações intersubjetivas concretas. Tais relações são, não raro, dotadas de objetiva recognicibilidade, inclusive por inferência de comportamentos concludentes".

Por outro lado, mesmo ressalvando o direito à busca da origem genética na relação familiar socioafetiva, elucida Wania Andréa Luciana Chagas Duarte de Figueiredo Campos[13] que "a investigação de paternidade é capaz de indicar o pai biológico e não de dar um pai ao investigante. Através da ação judicial o indivíduo tem conhecimento da existência ou não do vínculo biológico. Conhecer a origem significa entender seus traços socioculturais, devendo ser compreendido como um direito fundamental do ser humano. O direito à identidade genética deve ser entendido, com base no princípio da dignidade da pessoa humana, somo elemento intrínseco ao direito da personalidade".

[11] Superior Tribunal de Justiça, 4ª Turma, Relator Ministro Hélio Quaglia Barbosa, Recurso Especial nº 234.833-MG, j. 25/09/2007, *in* DJ 22/10/2007, p. 276). No mesmo sentido, a decisão no Recurso Especial nº 450.886-MG, do mesmo Relator, j. 04/12/2007, *in* DJ 17/12/2007, p. 173.

[12] Comentários ao Novo Código Civil, cit., pp. 28 e 29.

[13] *O direito à busca da origem genética na relação familiar socioafetiva*, *in* A Ética da Convivência Familiar e sua Efetividade no Cotidiano dos Tribunais, Coord. Tânia da Silva Pereira e Rodrigo da Cunha Pereira, Ed. Forense, Rio de Janeiro, 2006, p. 356.

E continua: "O reconhecimento do direito à identidade genética não implica, necessariamente, gerar uma relação de parentesco, e, por conseguinte, seus efeitos patrimoniais, mas dar a quem investiga a possibilidade de conhecer mais sobre si, adequando sua realidade à sua verdade, e, assim, manter uma convivência plena com o meio social que o cerca". Por essa razão, conclui que "aos filhos provenientes da adoção, e até mesmo de reprodução assistida heteróloga (considerando a possibilidade nos casos especiais que envolvam a prevenção da própria vida, em razão da saúde), deve ser assegurado o direito ao conhecimento de suas origens, sem que, no entanto, essa identificação importe na desconstituição da paternidade/maternidade da filiação jurídica ou socioafetiva, ou seja, não cause quaisquer efeitos sobre a relação de parentesco, pois não deve haver valoração da identidade biológica sobre os laços afetivos presentes na relação entre pais e filhos"[14] .

Aliás, nesse sentido, decidiu a 7ª Câmara Cível do Tribunal de Justiça do Rio Grande do Sul, sendo Relator o Desembargador Sérgio Fernando de Vasconcellos Chaves[15], que "a possibilidade de investigação não traz necessariamente sequelas obrigacionais e patrimoniais. Reconhecida a filiação socioafetiva, a investigação de paternidade não leva a desconstituição ou anulação do registro de nascimento, mas se limita a atender a possibilidade de se conhecer a paternidade sem gerar sequelas patrimoniais". Concluiu-se, ainda, nesse julgado: "Se identificada a paternidade biológica, julgo procedente, mas sem anulação do registro pelo reconhecimento da filiação socioafetiva, o que atende ao direito constitucional de busca da identidade biológica".

Tive oportunidade de dar Parecer em caso, em que, embora tenha sido constatada, por exame pericial de DNA, a paternidade biológica de determinadas pessoas não se pode simplesmente ignorar e descartar quarenta anos de convívio intenso e diário de seus filhos biológicos com o pai afetivo (registral), à base de carinho, amor, afeto, dedicação, assistência imaterial e comprometimento recíprocos, com efetiva e constante participação do pai na criação e educação de seus filhos registrados. Com fundamento nesse meu Parecer, julgou o Tribunal de Justiça do Ceará[16] que, com esteio na doutrina e na jurisprudência", mostra o mesmo Parecer que "os laços de

[14] *O direito à busca da origem genética*, cit., p. 358.

[15] Apelação Cível nº 70004131520, julgada em 22/05/2002.

[16] TJCE, Apel. Cív., 59402-26.2007.8.06.0001/1, Re. Des. José Mário dos Martins Coelho, 6ª Câm. Cív.,, j. em 09.09.2011..

afeto não podem ser olvidados para se anular a titulada "adoção à brasileira", em prol da gênese biológica".

No mesmo sentido, outros julgados devem ser considerados, reconhecendo que "O reconhecimento da paternidade é ato irrevogável (art. 1º da Lei n. 8.560/92 e art. 1.609 do CC)."[17] Como demonstram os entendimentos doutrinários e jurisprudenciais citados, a posterior constatação pericial da paternidade biológica, no caso estudado nesse Parecer, não tem o condão de simplesmente descartar e apagar um vínculo jurídico de paternidade e filiação socioafetivas, consolidado por convívio familiar de quarenta anos de afetividade, dedicação e comprometimento do pai na criação e educação dos filhos que registrou como seus. Daí a possibilidade até de manutenção da paternidade constante do registro, mesmo em detrimento da prova pericial da paternidade biológica, especialmente quando declarada e admitida como fato incontroverso, em processo judicial, a existência de uma sólida e duradoura relação paterno-filial socioafetiva.

Ressalta-se, finalmente, com Paulo Luiz Netto Lobo[18] que "A paternidade socioafetiva não é espécie acrescida, excepcional ou supletiva da paternidade biológica; é a própria natureza do paradigma atual da paternidade, cujas espécies são a biológica e a não-biológica. Em outros termos, toda a paternidade juridicamente considerada é socioafetiva, pouco importando sua origem. Nas situações frequentes de pais casados ou que vivam em união estável, a paternidade e a maternidade biológicas realizam-se plenamente na dimensão socioafetiva. Sua complexidade radica no fato de não ser um simples dado da natureza, mas uma construção jurídica que leva em conta vários fatores sociais e afetivos reconfigurados como direitos e deveres. Superou-se a equação simplista entre origem genética, de um lado, e deveres alimentares e participação hereditária, de outro. A paternidade é múnus assumido voluntariamente ou imposto por lei no

[17] Apel, Cív. n. 70040230336, 7ª Câm. Cív., TJRS, Rel. Des. André Luiz Planella Villarinho, j. em 25.05.2001, Apel. Cív. n. 70039342936, TJRS, Rel. Des. Rui Portanova, j. em 26.05.2011; Apel. Cív. 20060310218213, Rel. Des. Donizete Aparecido, 5ª T. Cív., j. em 05.08.2009, DJ de 15.10.2009, p. 92; STJ, REsp 1000356-SP, Rel. Min. Nancy Andrighi, 3ª Turma, j. em 25.05.2010, DJe, j. em 07.06.2010; Ação Rescisória n., 70026560961, 4ª G. de Câm.Cív, TJ RS, Rel. Des. Rui Portanova j. em 11.12.2009.

[18] *Paternidade socioafetiva e o retrocesso da Súmula nº 301/STJ, in* Família e Dignidade Humana – Anais do V Congresso Brasileiro de Direito de Família, do Instituto Brasileiro de Direito de Família – IBDFAM, Coord. Rodrigo da Cunha Pereira, Impresso por IOB Thomson, São Paulo, 2006, p. 808.

interesse da formação integral da criança e do adolescente e que se consolida na convivência familiar duradoura".

E complementa: "Nem toda paternidade socioafetiva resulta da consanguinidade, pois o direito assegura igualdade de direitos e deveres ao pai que assumiu voluntariamente o estado de filiação nas hipóteses de adoção, de inseminação artificial heteróloga e de posse de estado. Em todas o estado de filiação assim constituído é inviolável e não pode ser desfeito por decisão judicial, salvo na situação comum de perda do poder familiar (art. 1.638 do Código Civil). A paternidade desaparece em face do genitor biológico em virtude da perda do poder familiar, nas hipóteses de adoção e de declaração judicial de posse de estado de filiação", ressaltando, finalmente, que a "paternidade socioafetiva decorrente da posse de estado de filiação não pode ser contraditada"[19].

2. INDENIZAÇÃO POR ABANDONO AFETIVO

Por outro lado, o abandono afetivo paterno tem sido reconhecido pelos Tribunais como causador de indenização por danos morais. Assim, não basta o pagamento regular de pensão alimentícia, mas é preciso que existam cuidados pessoais com os filhos pensionados, como um dever inafastável decorrente da paternidade ou da maternidade.

Os pais não são obrigados a amar seus filhos, mas a cuidar deles, material e imaterialmente. O princípio da dignidade da pessoa humana, previsto no art. 1º, inciso III, da Constituição Federal de 5 de outubro de 1988, exige esse respeito devido à pessoa. Os direitos e deveres da personalidade devem ser cumpridos, para que se valorize a pessoa com a dignidade necessária no convívio social. Julgado do Tribunal de Alçada de Minas Gerais[20] "reconheceu ao filho o direto a ter reparados os danos morais decorrentes do abandono paterno, fixando indenização correspondente a 200 salários mínimos", com a seguinte ementa: 'Indenização danos morais – Relação paterno-filial – Principio da dignidade da pessoa humana – Princípio da afetividade'". Destaque-se, nesse julgado, que "O papel dos pais não se limita ao dever de sustento, de prover materialmente o filho com os meios necessários à subsistência orgânica. Vai muito além, para abranger a sub-

[19] *Paternidade socioafetiva*, cit., pp. 808 e 809.

[20] AC n. 408.550-5, da 7ª Câm. Cível, Rel. Juiz Unias Silva,de 01.04.2004. Relato de Luiz Felipe Brasil Santos, *in* COAD/ADV, Seleções Jurídicas, fevereiro/2005, p. 25.

sistência emocional, e a função psicopedagógica, de educação e assistência em geral. Na medida em que não é cumprido esse irrenunciável papel, por injustificável ausência paterna, exsurge o dano que há de ser reparado".

Muitas decisões existem nesse sentido[21], como a do juiz Mário Romano Maggioni, da 2ª Vara de Capão da Canoa (RS), de agosto de 2003 (proc. 1.030.012.032-0) que "condenou um pai a pagar 200 salários mínimos à filha que alegou abandono material e psicológico" e a do juiz Luís Fernando Cirillo, da 31ª Vara Cível de São Paulo-SP (proc. 01.36747-0) que "condenou um pai a pagar à filha indenização de R$50 mil por danos morais e para custear tratamento psicológico". Em recente julgamento do Superior Tribunal de Justiça, pronunciou-se a Ministra Nancy Andrighi[22] que "Amar é faculdade; cuidar é dever". Nesse caso, a decisão favoreceu uma mulher de 38 anos, que litigava há 12 anos, sob fundamento de que ela deveria ter sido cuidada em sua infância e juventude por seu pai, que foi, por esse descuidado, condenado a pagar indenização de 200 mil reais de danos morais. Essa filha obteve o reconhecimento da paternidade por via judicial. Declarou a Ministra Relatora em seu voto que "O cuidado é fundamental para a formação do menor e do adolescente"... "Não se discute mais a mensuração do intangível - o amor -, mas sim, a verificação do cumprimento, descumprimento ou parcial cumprimento de uma obrigação legal: cuidar".

E continua: entre pais e filhos, além dos vínculos afetivos, existem os legais". "... entre os deveres inerentes ao poder familiar estão o convívio, o cuidado, a criação, a educação, a transmissão de atenção e o acompanhamento do desenvolvimento sociopsicológico dos filhos. Essas obrigações existem tanto em relação aos filhos biológicos quanto aos adotivos". E acrescento, também, quanto aos filhos na paternidade e na maternidade afetiva, em que o dever paterno e materno nascem do amor e do respeito à pessoa, que não pode ser abandonada e esquecida. Nessa reportagem citada, ressalta-se que o Tribunal de Justiça de São Paulo, nesse caso de abandono afetivo, sendo o pai "abastado e próspero", o havia condenado ao pagamento de danos morais de 415 mil reais, valor que foi reduzido no STJ a 200 mil reais. Nessa reportagem fui consultado e me manifestei favo-

[21] *In* Revista Consultor Jurídico, de 14 de junho de 2004.

[22] *In* JT Cidade, Jornal da Tarde de 03 de maio de 2012, Reportagem de Mariângela Gallucci, p. 9 A. julgamento do STJ, 3ª Turma, no REsp 1159242.

rável a essa decisão, lembrando, na oportunidade, que "Estamos na era do afeto, tudo é afetivo. A Justiça decide agora sobre uma série de problemas que antigamente não se consideravam". E acrescentei quanto ao valor da indenização fixada que o juiz leva em conta o poder econômico do pai, destacando "O STJ deve ter avaliado a vida do pai, se ele é um milionário, se leva uma vida de vantagens e se privou sua filha de certos benefícios".

Ao seu turno, manifesta-se favoravelmente à indenização decorrente de abandono afetivo, nessa relação entre pais e filhos, Giselda Maria Fernandes Novaes Hironaka[23], afirmando que "O dano causado pelo abandono afetivo é, antes de tudo, um dano à personalidade do indivíduo". Giselda analisa, nessa oportunidade, uma decisão[24] do Tribunal de Justiça de Minas Gerais, comentando que, ao assistir a entrevista dada pela vítima, desse processo, na TV, que "Havia a expressão de alguma coisa que poderia ser chamada de dor ou de solidão, mas que era bem mais do que isso". Em 50 anos de advocacia, tenho presenciado casos dolorosos de rejeição de paternidade, de pessoas que colocam o patrimônio à frente do sentimento ou que usam o interesse material para tirar vantagens indevidas, geralmente à época da morte dos responsáveis. Reconhecer-se a paternidade, nem sempre, justifica o reconhecimento de direitos materiais. A dor pelo não reconhecimento do amor é constante nos atos de nossa existência e necessitam de uma indenização, para penalizar a negligência, ao descaso, ao desamor, que deve ser medido de caso para caso, ainda que sua configuração material seja *pro forma*, simbólica.

Ninguém pode ser obrigado a amar, pois esse é também um direito da personalidade de quem exerce esse sentimento. Por tal razão, como menciona a Ministra Nancy Andrighi, a falta de cuidado deve ser apenada, para que não se desrespeite essa verdadeira responsabilidade social. Quem gera um filho não está autorizado, pelo Direito Natural, a desprezá-lo, seja qual for a origem desse nascimento, se querido ou não. O ser humano deve ser respeitado, essencialmente, como obra da Natureza, que precisa ser preservada, além das querelas e das fraquezas do ser humano.

[23] Direito ao pai: dano decorrente de abandono afetivo na relação paterno-filial, entrevista no Boletim IBDFAM, julho/agosto, 2005, p. 3.

[24] TJMG, AC n. 408.550-5, 7ª Câm. Cív, publ. no DJM6 de 24.04.2004, em que foi advogado Rodrigo da Cunha Pereira.

TESTAMENTO PÚBLICO: BREVES CONSIDERAÇÕES

Ana Cristina de Barros Monteiro França Pinto*

O direito das sucessões disciplina a transferência dos bens da pessoa, após sua morte, ao seu herdeiro ou legatário, seja em decorrência da lei, seja em decorrência de testamento. É o que decorre do art. 1.786 do Código Civil, segundo o qual a sucessão se dá por lei ou por disposição de última vontade, prevendo as duas formas de sucessão do direito brasileiro, a legítima, por força da lei, e a testamentária, advinda de testamento. Por essa forma procura o legislador regular a destinação do patrimônio de uma pessoa após sua morte. Na sucessão legítima a lei estabelece a transferência dos bens a pessoas expressamente indicadas, demonstrando o apreço que tem o direito brasileiro pela família, nos termos do art. 1.788: morrendo a pessoa sem testamento, transmite a herança aos herdeiros legítimos. O mesmo ocorrerá quanto aos bens não compreendidos no testamento, subsistindo a sucessão legítima se o testamento caducar, ou for julgado nulo. Idêntica a solução em caso de revogação do testamento.

A lei contempla uma relação fechada de herdeiros legítimos: somente as pessoas ali elencadas serão consideradas sucessoras por força de lei, de acordo com uma ordem previamente estabelecida, e que se denomina ordem de vocação hereditária, prescrita no art. 1829. Assim, são chamados a suceder: I – os descendentes, em concorrência com o cônjuge sobrevivente, salvo se casado no regime da comunhão universal, ou no regime

* Procuradora do Município de São Paulo. Advogada.

da separação obrigatória de bens; ou se, no regime da comunhão parcial, ou de participação final nos aquestos, o falecido não houver deixado bens particulares; II – os ascendentes, em concorrência com o cônjuge; III – o cônjuge sobrevivente; IV – os colaterais até o 4º grau.

Deve-se assinalar que no julgamento do Resp 878.694/MG o Supremo Tribunal Federal proclamou ser inconstitucional a distinção de regimes sucessórios entre cônjuges e companheiros prevista no art. 1.790, devendo ser aplicada em ambos os casos a regra do art. 1.829. Dessarte, onde o legislador impôs a participação do cônjuge na sucessão do marido, deve-se entender que a mesma disposição legal deve ser aplicada ao companheiro nas mesmas circunstâncias, atendidos os requisitos legais previstos para sua situação, notadamente estar vivendo com o falecido ao tempo do óbito. Cabe lembrar que de acordo com a moderna orientação ditada por nossos costumes e julgados, a equiparação ocorre também em uniões homoafetivas.

Por outro lado, ao disciplinar a sucessão testamentária, o legislador estabeleceu quem são os herdeiros necessários, que são herdeiros obrigatórios, aos quais será destinada compulsoriamente metade dos bens do falecido – a legítima – de modo que o testador só terá livre disponibilidade sobre metade de seus bens – a porção disponível. Na ausência desses herdeiros necessários, o testador poderá dispor de seus bens como bem entender, sem qualquer restrição.

São herdeiros necessários (art. 1.845): os descendentes, os ascendentes, o cônjuge sucessível e o companheiro sucessível. Nota-se sempre a preocupação do legislador em prestigiar a família, assegurando a seus integrantes participação na herança do extinto. WASHINGTON DE BARROS MONTEIRO assim conceitua testamento: é negócio jurídico unilateral e gratuito, de natureza solene, essencialmente revogável, pelo qual alguém dispõe de seus bens para depois de sua morte, ou determina a própria vontade sobre a situação dos filhos e outros atos de última vontade, que não poderão, porém, influir na legítima dos herdeiros necessários. (Curso de Direito Civil, vol.VI, ed. Saraiva, 39ª ed., pág. 147, 2016).

Alguns aspectos ressaltam desse conceito: é negócio jurídico unilateral – a declaração de vontade é proveniente de uma só parte, isolada, sendo vedada a participação de dois ou mais declarantes. É ato gratuito, embora eventualmente possa apresentar algum aspecto oneroso, como a estipulação de um encargo. É ato jurídico solene, prevendo o legislador cuidadosamente todas as formalidades de que se deve revestir, sob pena de invalidação. Compreende-se o rigorismo formal, sempre proclamado por doutrinadores e aplicadores da lei: destinado a produzir efeitos quando não mais vive o testador, não admite qualquer esclarecimento, correção ou adequação.

O testamento é ato personalíssimo a ser praticado exclusivamente pelo testador, que declara sua vontade pessoalmente, diretamente, não podendo fazê-lo por intermédio de representante de qualquer natureza. Ao praticar o ato, deve reunir as condições exigidas por lei para legitimidade do ato, que deve ser iniciado e concluído na mesma oportunidade, atendidos todos os requisitos legais. Por isso, em caso de perda ou destruição, não há que se falar em reconstituição do testamento. Daí a grande vantagem que se vislumbra na segurança oferecida pelo testamento público.

O testamento é ainda negócio jurídico "mortis causa", apto a produzir efeitos somente após a morte do testador, podendo ser revogado a qualquer momento em vida do testador – não só revogado, como modificado, total ou parcialmente, sem necessidade de justificativa para esse fim. Podem ser objeto de testamento disposições pertinentes a totalidade ou parte dos bens do testador, além de servir ao reconhecimento de filho, embora a adoção não seja tolerada por esse meio por exigir formalidades específicas. Serve ainda para a nomeação de tutor ao descendente órfão, perdão ao indigno, deserdação de herdeiro, imposição justificada de cláusulas restritivas à legítima, nomeação de administrador dos bens de descendente incapaz.

Washingon de Barros Monteiro assinala outras finalidades possíveis a serem alcançadas por meio de testamento: instituir fundação, substituir beneficiário na estipulação em favor de terceiro, constituir condomínio por unidades autônomas, dispor do próprio corpo após a morte (op. cit. págs. 148/149). Serve ainda para instituir a multipropriedade. O testamento exige agente capaz à época de sua elaboração. Em princípio, todos podem testar, excluídos apenas aqueles que o legislador especifica: os menores de dezesseis anos e aqueles que não tiverem condições, por causa permanente ou transitória, de exprimir sua vontade, ou não tiver pleno discernimento.

A capacidade é aferida no momento da confecção do testamento. É no instante mesmo do ato que o testador deve reunir condições de plena capacidade, não importando se incapaz nesse momento, posteriormente a causa de incapacidade veio a desaparecer. Da mesma forma, a incapacidade superveniente não invalida o testamento feito quando o testador apresentava plena capacidade. Não afetam a capacidade testamentária ativa a idade avançada, nem doença de que o testador seja portador, mas que não comprometa a sua sanidade mental, nem a proximidade da morte.

Os testamentos são classificados em ordinários e especiais. São testamentos ordinários: o público, o cerrado e o particular. Os especiais são o marítimo, o aeronáutico e o militar, admitidos em circunstâncias especiais e por isso mesmo quase nunca empregados. Não se admitem outras formas de testamento, entre as quais não se inclui o codicilo, previsto no art. 1881, que, embora destinado a providências após a morte da pessoa, é admitido para disposições sobre enterro, esmolas de pouca monta e legado de móveis, roupas e joias de pouco valor. Pela segurança que oferece o testamento público é o mais utilizado.

Testamento público é aquele feito pelo testador perante o oficial de cartório de notas, lavrado em livro especial na presença de duas testemunhas. A forma que deve seguir é estabelecida integralmente pelo legislador com o intuito de cercar o ato de toda segurança para o oportuno cumprimento da vontade do testador exposta naquele ato solene. A designação de público pode ser explicada pela circunstância de ser lavrado pelo notário público, a quem a lei atribui fé pública, que o conserva em seus registros e confere a certeza de que foi elaborado de acordo com a lei e de que não será destruído ou subtraído à sua execução. Mas não significa que esteja acessível ao conhecimento do público em geral, de modo a poder ser conhecido por qualquer pessoa – é a natureza do cargo público do tabelião que lhe atribui a denominação, contrapondo-se ao testamento particular, este redigido pelo testador em presença apenas de três testemunhas a confiado à guarda de pessoa escolhida livremente pelo testador.

Ao lavrar testamento público, o notário verifica desde logo a identidade do testador, ao mesmo tempo em que pode certificar-se de que ele se encontra em perfeita saúde mental, plenamente consciente do ato que pretende praticar. O testador pode ditar ou declarar as determinações a serem incluídas no testamento; pode também trazê-las redigidas por advogado e apenas entregá-las ao oficial. Importa, porém, sejam expostas em português, de modo a ser compreendido por todos os participantes do ato, oficial, testador e testemunhas. É necessária, portanto, a presença de duas testemunhas que assistam ao ato em sua integralidade, ditado, redação e leitura pelo oficial ou pelo testador, de modo a se certificarem da efetiva vontade do testador. Assim será evidenciada a correspondência entre o conteúdo escrito e a vontade manifestada pelo testador. Concluído o ato, todos os presentes assinarão. Na impossibilidade de o testador assinar, porque não sabe ou não pode, assinará em seu lugar, a rogo, uma das testemunhas testamentárias, sendo tudo certificado pelo tabelião.

O Código não mais se refere a impedimentos para servir como testemunha de testamento, mas parece evidente que não podem ser admitidas pessoas que de alguma forma possam ter interesse nas disposições contidas no ato de última vontade, tal como havia no direito anterior. Assim, além dos menores de dezesseis anos, incapazes para todos os atos da vida civil, bem como daqueles que não tenham plena capacidade para reger sua pessoa e ou seus bens, não podem ser admitidas como testemunhas testamentárias: o herdeiro instituído ou o legatário, seus ascendentes ou descendentes, irmãos, cônjuge ou companheiro. Mas nada impede sejam testemunhas serventuários do cartório, assim como o testamenteiro, que dará cumprimento às determinações do testador. Embora o testamenteiro seja a pessoa indicada pelo testador para dar cumprimento às disposições constantes no ato de última vontade, não se vislumbra motivo para impedi-lo de servir como testemunha do mesmo.

O testamento público é, sem dúvida, o melhor meio de testar, mais seguro e confiável para que se conheça a vontade do autor da herança. É o meio de que se podem valer o analfabeto, aquele que não puder assinar, o surdo que saiba ler e o cego, caso em que o testamento será lido duas vezes. Os ébrios habituais e os viciados em tóxicos poderão ser admitidos a fazer testamento público em períodos de abstinência, em que possam exprimir sua vontade com plena compreensão do ato. Caberá ao oficial público certificar-se das circunstâncias em que se apresentam para o ato, verificando se gozam de pleno discernimento naquela oportunidade. Será sempre ocasião a exigir toda atenção e cuidado.

Também os pródigos poderão fazer testamento público, uma vez que, dispondo de seus bens para depois da morte, não estarão comprometendo ou dilapidando seus bens. O tema da capacidade civil sofreu profundas modificações em nosso sistema jurídico, que instituiu o processo de tomada de decisão apoiada (Lei nº 13.146/2015), pelo qual o deficiente pode eleger duas pessoas para dar-lhe suporte na tomada de decisão nos atos da vida civil. Assim, em princípio, parece que o testamento estaria entre esses atos. Evidentemente hão de incluir-se entre aqueles que não podem ser contemplados na condição de herdeiros os dois apoiadores, havendo também impedimento para serem testemunhas do ato seus descendentes, ascendentes, irmãos, cônjuge e companheiro.

Enquanto for vivo o testador nenhuma objeção de outra pessoa é cabível contra suas disposições, pois o testamento só produzirá efeitos depois da morte do autor da herança, o qual, no entanto, pode revogá-lo ou modificá-lo a qualquer tempo enquanto viver. Permitir o contrário seria condescender com discussão sobre herança de pessoa viva, o que é inadmissível. As formalidades impostas na confecção do ato de última vontade visam garantir a veracidade e a espontaneidade das declarações ali contidas, de modo que, quando de seu cumprimento, possa ser executado com segurança e seriedade, atendendo a sua finalidade. No Resp. 802.372/MG a 3ª Turma do STJ afirmou que o testamento é a expressão da liberdade no direito civil, cuja força é o testemunho mais solene e mais grave da vontade íntima do ser humano.

Como regra, em caso de impugnação do testamento, procuram nossos tribunais pesquisar a efetiva vontade do testador, que é o valor a ser preservado. Em caso de cláusula duvidosa, que remeta a interpretações distintas, deve prevalecer aquela que melhor se harmonize com a vontade manifestada pelo testador. (Resp 1532544/RJ – STJ). Nesse acórdão, alguns princípios de interpretação podem ser observados na apreciação do testamento: a) na busca da real vontade do testador deve-se atender aquela que confira maior eficácia e utilidade à cláusula escrita; b) para saber-se a real vontade do testador é necessário apreciar o conjunto das disposições testamentárias e não apenas determinada cláusula; c) quando forem possíveis várias interpretações, será escolhida a que observar melhor a vontade do testador; d) a interpretação deve ser buscada no próprio testamento, deve emergir do próprio texto.

De acordo com o art. 610 do Código de Processo Civil, havendo testamento ou interessado incapaz, o inventário há de ser judicial. Na ausência de testamento, sendo todos os interessados capazes, estando todos de acordo, sem objeções entre si, permite o parágrafo 1º desse dispositivo legal optem as partes por inventário e partilha por escritura pública. Recentemente, porém, no Resp 1808767/RJ, o Superior Tribunal de Justiça entendeu que havendo partes harmoniosas e concordes, devidamente representadas por advogado, tendo feito previamente o registro judicial do testamento, devidamente mandado cumprir, poderiam também nesse caso optar por inventário extrajudicial.

FAKE NEWS (NOTICIAS FALSAS): VERDAD, JUSTICIA Y DEMOCRACIA (O QUE EL ÁRBOL NO TAPE EL BOSQUE)

ARMANDO RAFAEL AQUINO BRITOS*

1. VERDAD Y DERECHOS

Vivimos inmersos en la dinámica de un mundo globalizado donde la intercomunicación instantánea de lo que ocurre en lo más recóndito del planeta nos brinda la información propicia para formarnos una opinión como ciudadanos comprometidos de esta aldea global. De lo bueno, poco; de lo lindo, escasas veces, pero de lo malo o pernicioso, mucho; no solo porque ocurre con más frecuencia, sino que es lo que más y mejor se difunde e informa. La sociedad soporta las inclemencias del hombre que en su ambición sin límites conspira contra la convivencia colectiva. Tal situación nos interpela a ser mejores; nos compromete a participar para defender el espacio común, nos obliga a custodiar los mejores valores y nos hace militantes de los más nobles propósitos: la verdad y la justicia en un ámbito de libertad son valores que enaltecen a la información. Mientras la justicia se institucionaliza mediante ordenamientos legales y sistemas judiciales, la verdad se desenvuelve en otra dimensión (moral, social y política) y se transmite mediante información publicada.

La publicación ya no solo es escrita (la menos), oral y televisiva, sino que se desenvuelve (cada vez más) por internet y sortea todo tipo de fronteras. Las redes sociales la difunden, no sin cargar opinión sobre ella. La

* Professor Adjunto de Direito Político e Direito Constitucional da Faculdade de Direito da Universidade Nacional do Nordeste – Argentina. Advogado.

información sobre los hechos debe entonces ser veraz, clara y categórica y estar expresada en valor neutro para que cada ciudadano elabore su juicio sobre ella y se comprometa, pues "los hechos son sagrados, pero las interpretaciones libres", nos enseñó Fayt, cuando al pie de su automóvil, casi como última lección póstuma, explicaba una causa a los periodistas. La dinámica del mundo actual suma al vértigo de estos tiempos los intereses, por allí oscuros, de quienes pretenden un juicio colectivo pronto, aunque infundado, ya que la verdad no se conoce, o se la vierte parcialmente y de manera tendenciosa. Desde el punto de vista del derecho se puede decir que "la verdad de un hecho o suceso jurídico es el desarrollo de un comportamiento (conducta) humano en un momento determinado y la cual como actuación del hombre que ha trasgredido un derecho ajeno particular, o, colectivo debe establecerse mediante un proceso reglado que busca la paz social la solución justa al litigio a través de un tercero (el Juez)"[1]. La interrelación de la verdad – en todas sus formas – es de vital importancia para la defensa de los más elementales derechos humanos y por tal motivo la ONU ha establecido el 24 de marzo[2] como Día Internacional del Derecho a la Verdad en relación con Violaciones Graves de los Derechos Humanos y de la Dignidad de las Víctimas, advirtiendo que los derechos civiles, políticos, económicos, sociales y culturales son universales, indivisibles e interdependientes y estrechamente interrelacionados. Existen varias formas y modos de conspirar contra la verdad. Pero esta siempre muere en manos de la mentira.

Las manifestaciones injuriosas de antaño – desde el rumor a la publicación incierta – hoy tienen otro comportamiento más letal. Actualmente el mecanismo masivo se manifiesta con el fenómeno de las fake news (noticias falsas) que preocupa, en todos los ámbitos, pero más en la labor de la justicia que debe necesariamente apoyarse – siempre – en la verdad. Obliga esto a repensar los valores de una prensa libre y sin restricciones, pero también de un periodismo comprometido con la verdad. Es imperioso que se resguarden la limitación y el respeto a la esfera de intimidad, que son la clave de bóveda, más allá de la libertad sin cortapisas, para emitir una opinión

[1] Ramírez Roa, Luis A., "Debido proceso y derecho a la verdad como defensa de los Derechos Humanos", en AA.VV., Las garantías constitucionales y convencionales, aplicadas al proceso, Ed. Instituto de Estudio e Investigación Jurídica (INEJ), Managua, 2017, p. 232.

[2] Res. 65/196 del 21/12/2010, aprobada por la Asamblea General, en la 71ª Sesión Plenaria de la ONU.

que debe ser siempre libre de todo tipo de censura. El presupuesto de una democracia constitucional exige una prensa libre y comprometida con la verdad, además de partidos políticos que articulen la relación de la sociedad con el Estado. Ellos formarán una opinión comprometida del ciudadano. Una noticia falsa o parcialmente verdadera puede ser nociva para el proceso democrático, y peor para la justicia, donde lo verosímil suplanta a la verdad y los juicios populares condicionan la labor de tribunales permeables a un "juicio" ya elaborado y vertido de antemano en otras esferas que no son precisamente los tribunales.

Preocupa y obliga esta situación. La ley fue la expresión del más débil; igualó a quien contaba con muchos medios y recursos a aquel que solo contaba con la verdad, y así la justicia pudo hacer lo suyo apoyándose en la "verdad procesal" y la "verdad material" como principios rectores del procedimiento y la sentencia, con lo que se ponía fin a las controversias. Mucho se avanzó. El desafío actual es que los avances de la ciencia y de la técnica no terminen con los valores y no afecten la democracia constitucional como sistema de vida colectivo. Es tan letal para la democracia deliberativa la noticia falsa como la proliferación de información irrelevante que orienta al ciudadano a analizar situaciones superfluas o insignificantes cuando se omite poner el foco y la lupa en situaciones que pueden comprometer el futuro de la sociedad, el funcionamiento de las instituciones o cambiar su forma y modo de vida. Es el abarrotamiento de la información secundaria, como técnica de manipulación. Es la desinformación. Se explica bien la situación actual, pues ha emergido una infobesidad o sobrecarga informativa (information overload) que se puede tornar sumamente peligrosa porque en pos de la libertad de expresión facilitada por múltiples medios, fuentes y plataformas que brindan una accesibilidad masiva y una verdadera descentralización informativa, aparecen y subyacen las falsas noticias (fake news) como una expresión de toxicidad informativa que busca producir el efecto contrario: la desinformación.

Los blancos de esta situación son, además, del ciudadano comprometido con el sistema, la justicia como ámbito de resolución de conflictos, y el sistema democrático donde influirá el ciudadano cuando elabore sus opiniones[3]. La verdad engloba el derecho individual y colectivo; es una forma

[3] Vaninetti, Hugo A., "Las noticias falsas (fake news) y la libertad de expresión en internet", LA LEY, 2019-A, 924.

de preservar la identidad colectiva, evitar futuras violaciones de derechos humanos que siempre vienen con procesos como ser el negacionismo, o revisionismo, donde la parcialidad es manifiesta o la verdad total se oculta – y niega –, o se la esboza parcial y tendenciosamente. De allí la necesidad de que la información sea cierta, ya que el ciudadano es quien construye su opinión con base en ella. Es un derecho colectivo que tenemos como sociedad, al mismo tiempo que subjetivo ya que nos puede afectar directamente. Empero, siempre debemos ser conscientes del derecho a la información y que la libertad de prensa es la libertad preferida, como elemento indispensable del sistema democrático y que hace a nuestra forma de vida.

2. EL DERECHO A LA INFORMACIÓN

Basterra magistralmente define el derecho a la información "como la facultad que tienen los ciudadanos de comunicar o recibir libremente información veraz por cualquier medio de difusión"[4] (4). Antes, expresa con acierto que "el derecho a la información es una prerrogativa distinta de la libertad de expresión, con entidad propia, aun cuando tradicionalmente se los ha identificado. En tal sentido, corresponde diferenciar a la libertad de expresión del derecho a la información, a partir de la distinción de aquello que se transmite, ideas u opiniones, o hechos, datos o noticias. "Esta diferenciación puede visualizarse a través de tres elementos que son a) el derecho a comunicar, común a ambas libertades; b) el derecho a investigar, propio de la libertad de información y; c) el derecho a recibir, común a la libertad de expresión y a la libertad de información.

"Se acogen dos derechos distintos por su objeto y sus titulares. Por un lado, el derecho a la libertad de pensamiento o ideología – libertad de expresión o de opinión –; mientras que, por el otro, se construye el derecho de información en una doble dirección, comunicarla y recibirla". Sin dudas que la libertad de prensa (que para nosotros integra el derecho a la información) es una de las que goza, necesariamente, de mayor tutela por nuestro ordenamiento jurídico. Bianchi acertadamente la encuadra dentro de las libertades preferidas, mas entiende que ella no es absoluta, ya que "un gobierno democrático nos brinda numerosísimos medios para expresar nuestras ideas, desde los más simples hasta los más sofisticados, desde

[4] Basterra, Marcela, "Derecho a la información y a la libertad de expresión", LA LEY, 2011-D, 794.

los más corrientes hasta los más impactantes todos ellos protegidos ¿por qué elegir el peor de ellos y por qué protegerlos en aras de la libertad? ¿De quién, del agresor o de los agredidos?"[5].

La protección constitucional al ejercicio de los derechos de la prensa – conforme a los arts. 14 y 32 de la CN, reforzados por los tratados internacionales de aplicación directa en la especie, conforme al art. 75, inc. 22, de nuestro máximo cuerpo legal, tal el art. 13 de la CADH – constituye una condición indispensable y necesaria para la difusión de las ideas, para el control social – u horizontal – a través de este medio por parte de la ciudadanía de la actividad gubernamental e incluso como un medio por el cual el gobierno da a conocer sus actos y los publicita. Es condición necesaria, mas no suficiente, para garantizar el funcionamiento verdaderamente libre del derecho a la información y la libertad de prensa, en el proceso democrático donde el ciudadano común debe ser el centro y objetivo del funcionamiento mismo del sistema. Empero, no se puede desconocer que el destinatario es el hombre común y que este, como parte integrante de la sociedad, debe primero saber y conocer la verdad, formarse luego opinión y hasta verter juicios sobre ello si lo considera necesario. No siempre ocurre esto; por lo contrario, el proceso es difícil y escabroso. Es cierto que ya no se presentan en el mundo civilizado actos como la irrupción de fuerzas policiales o parapoliciales para tomar un medio de prensa y – con o sin orden judicial, con o sin pátina de legalidad en sus procedimientos – clausurar un medio o ejercer una censura directa.

La heroica recepción jurisprudencial del amparo es una muestra clara de aplicación directa de la Constitución; la efectivización garantista de los derechos fundamentales más allá de la libertad, y por supuesto en el caso concreto la protección del ejercicio de los derechos y libertades de una persona, y desde luego la libertad de la prensa. No se conocen en los tiempos modernos formas directas y desembozadas de censura por el accionar directo del Poder Ejecutivo, y el bagaje normativo que podía impedir el ejercicio libre, aunque responsable, de la prensa se fue morigerando paulatinamente desde la consolidación del sistema democrático, desde 1983 a la fecha. Por ello se morigeraron algunas figuras penales y se derogaron otras. Es un proceso plausible. Es que siempre existieron vanos intentos por regular el ejercicio de la prensa; mas está claro que para proteger los

[5] BIANCHI, Alberto B., "Control de constitucionalidad", Ed. Ábaco, Buenos Aires, 1992, p. 484.

derechos que se ejercen a través de ella no existe otra ley que la libertad, lo que no significa que no existan responsabilidades, sanciones o restauración de derechos lesionados, cuando existen excesos, extralimitación ilegal o hasta la dolosa intención de inferir daño por su intermedio; mas la prensa, en toda la comprensión y latitud de su concepción, debe ser protegida.

Este tema debe ser analizado tomando los derechos de una manera bifronte: por un lado, los derechos del editor, del periodista o de la persona que ejerce el derecho por medio de la prensa; por el otro, del ciudadano que debe tener acceso a la información veraz y responsable, ya que con ella formará su juicio, volcará su opinión, y con ella participará en el proceso deliberativo de una democracia social y participativa. Expresó con acierto la Corte IDH que "La libertad de expresión es una piedra angular en la existencia misma de una sociedad democrática. Es indispensable para la formación de la opinión pública. Es también conditio sine qua non para que los partidos políticos, los sindicatos, las sociedades científicas y culturales, y en general, quienes deseen influir sobre la colectividad puedan desarrollarse plenamente. Es, en fin, condición para que la comunidad, a la hora de ejercer sus opciones, esté suficientemente informada. Por ende, es posible afirmar que una sociedad que no está bien informada no es plenamente libre"[6].

El ejercicio pleno de derechos genera también responsabilidades, por ello es que las describimos anteriormente; pero esto no mengua el aporte de la prensa libre al funcionamiento institucional claro y con controles sociales ya que es funcional al principio cardinal de la soberanía popular y de la forma republicana de gobierno. Carpizo[7] señala muy bien que "los medios masivos de comunicación son indispensables a la democracia, pero dentro de un Estado de Derecho que a todos beneficie y a todos obligue".

No se puede lograr la autonomía de la voluntad sin conocimiento cierto de las cosas y con ello aportar la parte alícuota de cada ciudadano al proceso democrático y ser partícipe de un eslabón de la construcción de la expresión soberana de una sociedad; y la articulación de control social que hace al sistema republicano de gobierno. Estos derechos están en cabeza

[6] Corte IDH, "La colegiación obligatoria de periodistas", opinión consultiva OC-5/85 del 13/11/1985, párr. 70.

[7] Carpizo, Jorge, "Los medios masivos de comunicación y el estado de derecho, la democracia, la política y la ética", Asociación Arg. Dcho. Constitucional, 167, año XVI, p. 6.

de toda la sociedad, pero puede en cada caso particular, depende del grado de afectación generar un derecho subjetivo. Ha sido la propia CIDH que señaló la doble dimensión de este derecho al explicar que comprende "dos dimensiones igualmente importantes y que deben ser garantizadas simultáneamente: una individual y otra social. La primera reconoce el derecho de los individuos a no ser arbitrariamente impedidos – total o parcialmente – de expresar su propio pensamiento. La segunda implica el derecho de todos los miembros de la sociedad a conocer información u opiniones que otros puedan difundir"[8]. El termómetro institucional para medir la temperatura o funcionamiento del Estado de Derecho material de una sociedad pasa por el control de la prensa libre e independiente. A menor control, más libertades públicas; o cuanto mayor control, más restricciones sobre los derechos de los ciudadanos. El proceso en la Argentina fue plausible pues se derogó la figura del desacato (art. 244, Cód. Penal) para cumplir con el principio que dice: "Los funcionarios públicos están sujetos a un mayor escrutinio por parte de la sociedad. Las leyes que penalizan la expresión ofensiva dirigida a funcionarios públicos generalmente conocidas como 'leyes de desacato' atentan contra la libertad de expresión y el derecho a la información" (principio 11 – CIDH – Declaración de Principios sobre Libertad de Expresión).

Por la ley 26.551, como consecuencia del caso "Kimel", se modificó la figura penal de calumnias e injurias, donde el marco de libertades se amplió ostensiblemente; no obstante, Basterra señala que la Corte IDH rescata que "la sociedad tiene derecho a no recibir informaciones falsas o sustancialmente cambiadas, de los acontecimientos informados por la prensa"[9]. La CIDH entiende que "la protección al honor, en abstracto, puede considerarse como un fin legítimo. Sin embargo, cuando el aparato represivo del Estado se dirige, por medio de una sanción penal, contra las expresiones sobre asuntos de interés público, la legitimidad de la sanción penal se diluye ya sea porque no existe un interés social imperativo que la justifique, o porque se convierte en una respuesta desproporcionada o, incluso, en una restricción indirecta"[10] y por ello la eliminación de sancio-

[8] "La libertad de expresión en la jurisprudencia de la CIDH", Asociación por los Derechos Civiles, p. 14, www.adc.org.ar, documento elaborado por el equipo de trabajo del Programa sobre el Sistema Interamericano de Protección de los Derechos Humanos.

[9] BASTERRA, Marcela, ob. cit.

[10] CIDH, informe anual 2002, nota 13, cap. V, párr. 23.

nes punitivas es un avance notable, pues impide el mecanismo intimidatorio se dio en llamar "autocensura" ya que se tiene miedo a la prisión o al pago de un supuesto resarcimiento económico por la crítica y ello lleva, naturalmente, a una restricción del derecho.

Aclara bien la Corte IDH que esto "no significa que el honor de los funcionarios públicos no ha de ser protegido jurídicamente, sino que dicha protección debe ser acorde con los principios del pluralismo democrático. La distinción en cuestión no se funda, por lo tanto, en la calidad del sujeto sino en el interés público de sus actividades o actuaciones"[11]. Entiende la CIDH que los llamados delitos contra el honor por parte de los funcionarios eran utilizados de la misma manera que la figura del desacato, para acallar las críticas de la prensa a su actividad. Es que la interpretación del art. 13 de la CADH señala que la lectura y la interpretación de este artículo permiten establecer que la adopción de responsabilidades ulteriores debe fundamentarse en leyes claras y previamente adoptadas, debe perseguir fines legítimos acordes con este artículo y ser necesaria para satisfacer un interés público.

El libre debate democrático y el pluralismo político de una sociedad abierta exigen un margen de tolerancia a la manifestación de ideas, informaciones y opiniones que puedan considerarse ofensivas; particularmente respecto de la función pública y de quienes la ejercen; y, por el contrario, son los funcionarios públicos los que deben excitar el debate, alentar la investigación, promover el control de la cosa pública, ya que con ello se logra mayor transparencia del sistema institucional y merced a tal comportamiento cada funcionario pone a resguardo su honra y honor, caso contrario cuando se lesiona la verdad o el honor queda el recurso de respuesta o replica (art. 14, CADH) para reparar la injusticia que se comete cuando se falsea la verdad o se vierte una opinión subjetiva y equivocada, mas no la prisión o el pago de una indemnización, salvo, claro está que la noticia o la idea publicada o emitida sea dolosa y maliciosamente incierta. El mecanismo punitivo en el doble sentido, penal y económico, debe ser el caso extremo donde se sancione la malicia o la actitud absolutamente desinteresada del informante con la verdad, con la honra o reputación de una persona, o su intimidad; ya que estos tipos de leyes pueden tener un efecto disuasivo en quienes desean participar en el debate público por

[11] Corte IDH, 02/07/2004, "Herrera Ulloa vs. Costa Rica", serie C 107, párr. 129.

temor a acciones judiciales o a las sanciones; particularmente cuando no distinguen entre los hechos y los juicios de valor. La posibilidad de probar la verdad, al transferir la carga de la prueba a quien se manifiesta, no reduce este efecto, especialmente en los casos de los juicios de valor que no admiten prueba.

2.1. NOTICIAS FALSAS

Esta última década, sin resignar las premisas antes mencionadas, la doctrina se abocó a analizar la incidencia de los recursos científico-tecnológicos que se manifestaron por el uso de las computadoras que permitieron la transmisión, el almacenamiento y el manejo de la información. Internet y las redes sociales ampliaron la manera de generar y socializar la información que dio en llamarse la sociedad del conocimiento, producto de la revolución tecnológica, generando derechos al usuario. Se transita de una sociedad de la información, con información disponible, organizada, compartible, confiable y necesaria, como fuerza constitutiva en la sociedad, para constituirse como sociedades del conocimiento, que utilizan ampliamente la información para crear nuevo conocimiento" dice Técuatl Quechol[12]. Por ello siempre debe cuidarse la verdad como "la conformidad de las cosas con el concepto que de ellas forma la mente"; "conformidad de lo que se dice con lo que se piensa"; "propiedad que tiene una cosa de mantenerse siempre la misma sin mutación alguna" o "juicio o proposición que no se puede negar racionalmente"; "cualidad de veraz", dice el Diccionario de la RAE, indispensable para constituir una democracia deliberativa con base en la participación en el proceso democrático por cada ciudadano.

En su contra conspira la posverdad, que tiene como característica la de ser un fenómeno global donde las fronteras entre la verdad y la mentira; entre la honradez y la falta de honradez, la ficción y la no ficción son difusas, se entremezclan a punto tal que una mentira puede ser asumida como verdad. Este fenómeno se nutre y alimenta de una desinformación producida por una noticia falsa, o parcialmente falsa, y tiene por característica dirigirse a grupos indeterminados, apelando a las emociones; por ello carece de precisión y fundamentación argumentativa. Tiene la carac-

[12] TÉCUATL QUECHOL, María Graciela M., "La información: entre la verdad y la posverdad", en MORALES CAMPOS, Estela (coord.), La posverdad y las noticias falsas: el uso ético de la información, (coord.), Ed. Universidad Nacional Autónoma de México, México 2018, p. 37.

terística de inmediatez, urgencia y repetición por varios medios o canales comunicativos; es verosímil (creíble por situaciones o hechos parecidos), por lo que busca generar un estado de ánimo o emocional del cual, por más que se conozca después la verdad, resulta difícil despejar la duda.

La posverdad, como técnica de manipulación, necesita de un ciudadano frágil, desinformado y desinteresado del proyecto colectivo como sociedad o nación y, por supuesto, es funcional para ello que los partidos políticos no cumplan con su misión. La perversidad de la posverdad es utilizada para conspirar, crear malestar, provocar el recelo o la hostilidad de grupos sociales, para lo que se recurre a las fake news o noticias falsas y engloba a "los contenidos intencionalmente engañosos publicados para obtener provecho o por motivos políticos, bajo la forma de información legítima y acorde a los hechos"[13].

2.2. LA FORMA DE PRODUCCIÓN DEL CONTENIDO FALSO

A sabiendas se emiten y difunden: a) noticias fraudulentas para obtener un provecho para beneficiarse por motivos financieros, particularmente para beneficiarse de la publicidad online; b) noticias fraudulentas por motivos políticos, financiados o distribuidos por ciudadanos individualmente o como parte de movimientos u organizaciones, con el fin de apoyar un partido político, un candidato o una ideología; c) desinformación proveniente del gobierno, financiados o distribuidos por el sector estatal o grupos afines; y d) las teorías conspirativas, vale decir, noticias falsas que son consideradas verdaderas por quienes las inventan, pero cuyo grado de verificabilidad es nulo[14]. Como mencionamos antes, algunas conductas distorsivas emitidas por la prensa son pasibles de ser sancionadas, pero otras todavía no tienen la regulación necesaria y demanda un debate profundo a fin de salvaguardar no solo el principio cardinal de la libertad de información, a publicar por la prensa las ideas sin censura previa, etc., sino también a respetar los llamados derechos informáticos que algunos creen conforman una nueva generación de derechos, aunque no estemos de acuerdo con tan singular teoría.

Reiteramos que tales derechos son tutelados por los arts. 14, 32 y 75, inc. 22, de la CN; ya que la CADH lo reconoce en el art. 13; en tanto en el

[13] Ibid.

[14] Melo, Verónica E., "La inmunidad de los proveedores de servicios de internet (isp) ante el fenómeno de las fake news", RCyS 2020-I, 3.

art. 19 de la DUDH se produce similar resguardo, al igual que en el art. 19 del PIDCyP, como así también en el art. 13 de la CDN. Empero la legislación ordinaria local parece insuficiente para repeler las injurias o las difamaciones vertidas por proveedores de fake news, dado que esta operación fraudulenta puede ser concebida y desarrollada fuera de nuestro territorio, o también difícil de encontrar el centro de difusión originario.

Las llamadas redes sociales, como Twitter, que surgió en el año 2006 como una red de comunicación entre amigos para comunicar instantáneamente una noticia o hecho, se extendió de manera inconmensurable, que confía en su autorregulación y el control posterior del contenido. El medio, idóneo para la difusión de ideas, carece de un filtro que detecte lo procaz, lo injuriante, lo calumnioso o lo falso. Google, como buscador capaz de organizar información y hacerla universalmente accesible y útil, se apoya en un algoritmo neutro que determina cada hecho, noticia o imagen que aparece ante la búsqueda del usuario, pero es insuficiente o no tiene capacidad para detectar las noticias falsas; empero, se preocupó por difundir las políticas de su contenido para alertar a sus usuarios y, más allá de la transparencia y los nobles propósitos, no logra impedir que se filtren noticias falsas.

Facebook, como red social que articula más personas que cualquier otra plataforma de red social, permite la circulación de fake news por la comunicación entre usuarios, agravado por su elevado número de asociados pues es un mecanismo apto para compartir información en forma dinámica, actual y fácil. Las empresas titulares de estos servicios han efectuado ingentes y apreciables esfuerzos por quitar el contenido falso; ora de personas, ora de noticias, etc.; y también quitar información que puede ser lesiva, obscena o falsa con un rigor en la política de que condiciona al usuario a las normas comunitarias de los integrantes de la red social como también en los contenidos que, se advierte, serán condicionados, prohibidos o declarados inaceptables, siendo un modo de declarar como "spam" noticias que atenten contra la integridad y autenticidad o expresen representaciones engañosas.

En este ámbito de la comunicación se depende de la formación del usuario, como también de la autorregulación de las empresas que sostienen las redes sociales. Dice Sbdar que regular las fake news resulta "un desafío, pues es necesario identificar los cientos de casos posibles: plataformas digitales construidas ex professo, replicadores acríticos, redes sociales que brindan información a empresas, entre otras construcciones posibles, con una lógica mercantil incluso para los casos de manipulación electoral"[15]. En lo que gravita notoriamente es en las campañas electorales o los procesos políticos, donde se utilizan plataformas de comunicación para difundir noticias falsas y así poder incidir y gravitar sobre el electorado, para ello se recurre también a otros medios de comunicación como el WhatsApp que permiten la difusión sin control de estos a modo de caricatura (memes).

El mecanismo de autorregulación y las sanciones económicas que se imponen en otras latitudes con regulaciones preventivas son demostrativos de la magnitud del problema advertido en julio del 2018 por la Asociación de Entidades Periodísticas Argentinas (ADEPA). Esta situación se suma a una suerte de inconsciente colectivo, más propio de la psicología social: pretendemos creer (y creemos que sabemos) y entonces cuestionamos todo; hasta lo evidente, sumado a que somos presa fácil de las noticias falsas, pues "la verdad es lo que queremos creer que es cierto, lo que nos conviene o lo que les conviene que creamos. Este juego de palabras es un círculo que solo se rompe si reflexionamos y tenemos instituciones que tengan el prestigio suficiente para que podamos discutir críticamente lo que nos presentan los medios"[16].

3. LA BÚSQUEDA DE LA VERDAD

Estamos convencidos de que este proceso se revierte si se fortalece al ciudadano, y si a este le dan las herramientas necesarias para: a) lograr una información verdadera; b) producir una información veraz; y c) colaborar aportando la verdad al proceso democrático y deliberativo, y no mediante regulaciones que restrinjan la libertad de prensa. Ahora bien, las empresas de medios de comunicación, de plataformas digitales, de medios de vinculación social (redes sociales), como el Estado mismo (siempre a través del gobierno de turno), deben entender que la libertad se obtiene con la verdad, permitiendo el intercambio de información y no pretendiendo tener el monopolio de una información, o peor aun difundiendo una noticia falsa.

Este desafío se soluciona, como toda crisis, saliendo para adelante, superando las contingencias: el camino es fortalecer al ciudadano, permitiendo elaborar un juicio crítico. El Estado debe entender que debe garantizar la

[15] Sbdar, Claudia, "¿Fake news?", LA LEY, 2019-B, 1216.

[16] Ibid.

pluralidad, la diversidad e impedir los monopolios que restringen la verdad, reglamentar y democratizar la pauta oficial de publicidad, así como tener una agencia estatal dirigida por técnicos que no ejerzan tendencia política en contenidos o preferencias de medios[17]. Los medios de comunicación deben saber que son titulares de derechos de una libertad preferida pero que no tienen la omnipotencia de difundir lo que quieren sino la verdad, sin lesionar el honor o la moral, y sin injerencias abusivas sobre la privacidad de las personas que afecten la protección que les otorga a estos el principio de reserva (art. 19, CN).

Encontramos la solución en lo que determina el art. 14 de la CADH, el derecho de réplica, como una acción amplia y que contribuya a la formación de la verdad sobre la realidad de los hechos; dicho artículo expresamente dispone: "Derecho de Rectificación o Respuesta: 1. Toda persona afectada por informaciones inexactas o agraviantes emitidas en su perjuicio a través de medios de difusión legalmente reglamentados y que se dirijan al público en general, tiene derecho a efectuar por el mismo órgano de difusión su rectificación o respuesta en las condiciones que establezca la ley. "2. En ningún caso la rectificación o la respuesta eximirán de las otras responsabilidades legales en que se hubiese incurrido. "3. Para la efectiva protección de la honra y la reputación, toda publicación o empresa periodística, cinematográfica, de radio o televisión tendrá una persona responsable que no esté protegida por inmunidades ni disponga de fuero especial". La epopeya del reconocimiento operativo de tal derecho se dio en 1993 (antes de la reforma constitucional de 1994) donde se estableció el estándar que 1) los tratados tienen rango superior a la ley; 2) los derechos son operativos al estar reconocidos 3) la protección amplia a través del amparo de la verdad, repeler la injuria o calumnia y no lesionar el honor, dándole al amparo promovido una naturaleza de "acción popular"[18]. En efecto, en el caso "Ekmekdjian, Miguel Á. c. Sofovich, Gerardo y otros", sentenciado el 07/07/1992, la CS[19], le otorgó una legitimación amplísima a la pretensión articulada por este derecho que se conquistó merced a la tesonera actitud del recordado profesor Miguel Ekmekdjian, luego morigerada en el prece-

[17] Lo desarrollamos ampliamente en AQUINO BRITOS, Armando – BRAILLARD POCARD, Pedro, "El derecho de réplica, rectificación o respuesta", Librería de la Paz, 2013.

[18] QUIROGA LAVIÉ, Humberto, "Ha nacido el amparo colectivo con motivo del derecho de réplica", LA LEY, 1992-D, 879.

[19] Fallos 315:1492.

dente "Petric, Domagoj c. Diario Página/12", del 16/04/1998[20]. En acertada glosa de aquel fallo decía Gelli que "desde luego, si de lo que se trata es de responder sobre hechos, el límite de la respuesta será preciso y el equilibrio entre la dimensión personal y social del derecho se mantendrá. Pero, franquear la línea de los hechos y trasladar las razones justificatorias de la doctrina de la real malicia al derecho de rectificación o respuesta altera la garantía de la prensa libre en una sociedad democrática.

"En efecto, la doctrina de la real malicia tiene una función social: evitar la autocensura y, por esa vía, facilitar el control político. En cambio, exorbitar la rectificación o respuesta puede acarrear el efecto contrario: neutralizar la disidencia desde que, en cambio, de operar como un escudo protector contra el control estatal, impone una carga adicional y transforma a la rectificación o respuesta en réplica ideológica. Ese desborde, estimo, no se compadece con la libertad expresiva garantizada en la Constitución Nacional"[21]. El derecho de réplica, rectificación o respuesta, desde nuestra visión tiene determinadas formas: rectificación es la actividad tendiente a demostrar que un hecho histórico difundido es falso, distorsionado e inexacto, sea que involucre lugares, personas o cosas. El afectado tiene pleno y total derecho a hacer rectificar por el mismo medio y de la misma forma y proporción lo que se difundió falsa o erróneamente en ese medio. "No es otra cosa que buscar que la noticia o información esté reducida y circunscripta a la conveniente exactitud los dichos o hechos que se le atribuyen a una persona"[22].

La respuesta fue un derecho/deber que algunos creen ver en el derecho romano, el ius respondi, como prerrogativa de los jurisconsultos encumbrados, lo que ulteriormente se conoció en la Francia como el droit de réponse, modelo que adoptó Bélgica. En Francia, a comienzos del siglo XIX se instauraron los derechos de rectificación para proteger a los funcionarios de los ataques de la prensa, dándoles a estos la posibilidad de aclarar, desde su punto de vista, los hechos que los involucraban, y en 1822 la Ley de Represión de los Delitos de Prensa, donde se consagraba el derecho de respuesta y daba la posibilidad a los ciudadanos particulares en caso de

[20] Fallos 321: 885 (1998).

[21] GELLI, María Angélica, "El caso 'Petric' ¿valor agregado de la rectificación o respuesta?", LA LEY, 1998-F, 53.

[22] AQUINO BRITOS, Armando – BRAILLARD POCARD, Pedro, ob. cit., p. 167.

que estos argumentaran ser víctimas de difamación o vieran afectados su honor o reputación por la prensa[23].

Es también una obligación impuesta a los representantes como una forma de rendición de cuentas, tal como lo recepta el art. 6º in fine de la Constitución de la provincia de Corrientes[24]. Este concepto comprende una estricta protección legal de la persona contra la publicidad de datos o de actos personales que se ponen en conocimiento del público, sin noticia o permiso de la persona afectada[25]. La réplica tiene su fundamento en la afectación sobre la honra, los aspectos más salientes y fundamentales, que el sujeto afectado las considera particularmente agraviantes para la conformación de su personalidad moral y que integra su reputación personal. Rivarola Paoli considera que el alcance del derecho, en esta modalidad, debe extenderse también a los agravios o "ataques contra opiniones o creencias esenciales de una persona, sus opiniones que perfilen y definan su personalidad y respondan a la escala axiológica normal y que tales ataques se efectúen con medios injustos y razonables"[26]. La réplica siempre es más amplia y lo que no se puede proteger por medios jurídicos, pues no enerva derechos subjetivos reconocidos al peticionante, debe ser responsabilidad de la sociedad democrática por otros medios no punitivos.

4. EL MECANISMO DE PROTECCIÓN

Es la búsqueda de la verdad – como expresión material y concreta del derecho a informar lo que interesa – y para ello el derecho de réplica o de respuesta es indispensable para construir el juicio de la verdad sobre el que

[23] Ver ROSAS MARTÍNEZ, Alejandro, "¿Derecho de rectificación, derecho de respuesta o derecho de réplica?", 03/06/2011, Biblioteca Jurídica virtual del Instituto de Investigaciones Jurídicas de la UNAM.

[24] Constitución de Corrientes. Art. 6º. – La libertad de la palabra hablada y escrita es un derecho. Toda persona puede ilimitada y libremente, en cualquier forma, manifestar sus ideas y opiniones, examinar y censurar la conducta de los poderes y funcionarios públicos, pero será responsable del abuso que haga de esta libertad. No se dictarán leyes ni medida alguna que restrinjan el ejercicio de aquella y en las causas a que diera lugar su abuso, se admitirá la prueba, siempre que fuese el injuriado un funcionario o empleado público. Es obligación de los funcionarios o empleados públicos, acusar toda publicación en que se les imputen faltas o delitos cuya averiguación interese a la sociedad (destacado nos pertenece).

[25] EKMEKDJIAN, Miguel A. – PIZZOLO, Calógero, "Hábeas data: el derecho de la intimidad frente a la revolución informática", Ed Depalma, Buenos Aires, 1995, p. 8.

[26] RIVAROLA PAOLI, Juan Bautista, "Derecho de Información", Intercontinental Editora, Asunción, 1995, p. 131.

se edifica el derecho a la información. Siempre debe primar que el medio de difusión acepte, tolere y brinde la posibilidad de buscar la verdad y producir el intercambio de opiniones, más aún cuando se da la situación de error, inexactitud histórica o agravio a una persona en su honor y otros derechos. Ahora bien, la acción en estos tiempos no debe ser el amparo como se proponía[27] en otros tiempos, sino la medida autosatisfactiva, el recurso sencillo, rápido y directo; porque la verdad a la que se rehúye es la mentira que se instala.

La acción de tutela urgente de la medida autosatisfactiva implica equidad y equilibrio entre los derechos fundamentales en juego (verdad sobre los hechos, tutela del honor o protección de la intimidad) por un lado, y la libertad protegida de la libertad de prensa y difundir por ella las ideas sin censura previa. Este concepto comprende una estricta protección legal de la persona contra la publicidad de datos o de actos personales que se ponen en conocimiento del público, sin noticia o permiso de la persona afectada[28]. El ordenamiento jurídico provee, por este medio, una solución ante la noticia falsa. Para ello hay que dar efectividad al derecho de réplica y regular el mismo más allá de la oposición manifiesta de los grandes medios y del gobierno, siempre proclive a manipular la información mediante mecanismos de control directo o indirecto (órganos y publicidad estatal). Es fortalecer al ciudadano, armarlo en defensa de sus derechos y poner la garantía de los derechos en manos del Poder Judicial que así se legitima como actor democrático, por cuanto realiza y hace realizar los mandatos constitucionales.

La vía idónea es la medida autosatisfactiva, dada la dinámica y frenética actividad de los medios – y su gravitación e incidencia – sobre órganos de gobierno, en particular, el Poder udicial. Es reconocer que tal herramienta judicial es el "recurso sencillo y rápido" que señala el art. 25[29] de la CADH,

[27] Ley 5855 de la provincia de Corrientes, cuyo art. 1º dice: "Toda persona que por cualquier medio de comunicación masivo, sea lesionada públicamente, en su reputación, honra, vida privada, familiar; o bien mencionada por información errónea, tendrá derecho a que en forma gratuita y por el mismo medio en que se haya difundido la información o efectuado la referencia que se juzga lesiva o incierta, a que se publique o difunda su réplica, rectificación y/o defensa a tal información".

[28] Ekmekdjian, Miguel A. – Pizzolo, Calógero, ob. cit., p. 8.

[29] CADH, art. 25, Protección judicial: 1. Toda persona tiene derecho a un recurso sencillo y rápido o a cualquier otro recurso efectivo ante los jueces o tribunales competentes, que la ampare contra actos que violen sus derechos fundamentales reconocidos por la Constitución,

en armonía con el art. 2º del PIDCyP, garantía que goza de la operatividad que dispone el art. 75, inc. 22, de la CN. Las características básicas de las medidas autosatisfactivas siempre son: la urgencia – pudiendo disponerse inaudita parte – y de ejecución inmediata, como su carácter autónomo.

La urgencia es solución rápida a situaciones conflictivas que requieren inmediatamente una decisión jurisdiccional, dada la afectación cierta y notoria de un derecho fundamental gravemente lesionado, más allá de la causa o razón. Debe existir una fuerte probabilidad de que la petición esté fundada en un derecho fundamental afectado por la flagrante ilegalidad del hecho que lo produce; en el caso de quien difundió la noticia inexacta o agraviante, con la clara demostración del perjuicio concreto, que es evidente.

La naturaleza del medio comisivo tanto como la producción del daño tornan innecesaria la acreditación de otro remedio procesal más idóneo que esté fundado en la urgencia, por ello se infiere que decisión judicial que la adopta no puede admitir recurso con efecto suspensivo ni incidente que pueda suspender su ejecución. De allí que "la autonomía de las medidas autosatisfactivas es la segunda gran característica que, a diferencia de la primera, constituye la principal distinción entre ellas y las medidas cautelares que, como es sabido, son siempre instrumentales de un proceso principal. La medida autosatisfactiva se agota en sí misma, resuelve la situación conflictiva urgente de manera definitiva – de ahí el nombre de "autosatisfactiva" – por lo que su eficacia no queda condicionada al resultado de un proceso posterior que no existe", dice con acierto Picó I Junoy[30].

Con ello se protege al ciudadano; se cuida la verdad y se tutela el honor, los que siempre son lesionados por noticias arteras, tendenciosas o falsas. Son los titulares de los poderes salvajes (aquellos que con poder económico actúan al margen de la ley), por un lado, por el otro el gobierno,

la ley o la presente Convención, aun cuando tal violación sea cometida por personas que actúen en ejercicio de sus funciones oficiales. 2. Los Estados Partes se comprometen: a) a garantizar que la autoridad competente prevista por el sistema legal del Estado decidirá sobre los derechos de toda persona que interponga tal recurso; b) a desarrollar las posibilidades de recurso judicial, y c) a garantizar el cumplimiento, por las autoridades competentes, de toda decisión en que se haya estimado procedente el recurso.

[30] Picó I Junoy, Joan, "De las medidas cautelares a las medidas autosatisfactivas, ¿un avance del derecho procesal?", Revista Jurídica Española de Doctrina, Jurisprudencia y Bibliografía, 2001, ps. 1468 y ss.

cualquiera sea su ocupante provisorio, quienes pueden afectar directa o indirectamente el derecho a la información veraz y objetiva cuyo titular es la sociedad en su conjunto o un derecho subjetivo en particular que afecte a un ciudadano. Es grave cuando la puja entre ellos tiene como escenario la sociedad pues el daño colectivo es inconmensurable ya que la fake new (noticia falsa) se torna común y corriente. La sociedad, cual teatro de operaciones, es la víctima, además del afectado directo.

Es la expresión de la llamada crisis de la democracia por "arriba" como dice Ferrajoli, que se genera por el patrimonialismo que es la confusión entre la "esfera pública y esfera privada, o sea, entre poderes políticos y poderes económicos (...) por la estrecha alianza entre poderes políticos públicos y poderes económicos privados y por la sustancial subordinación de los primeros a los segundos. Bajo este aspecto los conflictos de intereses, en las formas de la corrupción o del intercambio político con los lobbies corporativos y, sobre todo, con los medios de comunicación son hoy fenómenos endémicos en todos los ordenamientos democráticos, en los que resulta cada vez más fuerte la relación entre dinero, información y política", todo a expensas de los derechos de la sociedad que se dice representar"[31].

Siempre la solución será mantener inalterable la letra, pero también el espíritu de la Constitución y de la ley, como también fortalecer al ciudadano. Un proverbio africano dice: "cuando los elefantes se pelean, el que pierde es el pasto", válida metáfora para entender que medios de comunicación concentrados y gobierno no quieren fortalecer al ciudadano sino defender sus respectivos intereses. Así no se construye una sociedad democrática en cuanto que una noticia falsa que se instala y difunde siempre será la verdad que no se conocerá nunca, o se conocerá muy tarde y allí la reivindicación será post mortem de los derechos humanos más elementales.

5. EVITAR MALES MAYORES

Se ha dicho, en algunos casos con razón, que los medios de comunicación y las redes sociales actúan sobre el Poder Judicial y a caballo de la posverdad y con alguna verosimilitud en los hechos socavan la decisión de un tribunal, generando un condicionamiento a su decisión que debe ser siempre fundada – máxime en materia penal – sobre la veracidad de los hechos y

[31] FERRAJOLI, Luigi, "Poderes salvajes. La crisis de la democracia constitucional", Ed. Trotta, Madrid, 2011, p. 53.

sobre su irrefutabilidad mediante pruebas incontrovertidas, para emitir un decisorio conforme al ordenamiento jurídico vigente.

El poder de los medios, ayudado por este fenómeno social, necesita de un juez o tribunal permeable a los condicionamientos; no obstante, el resguardo de las garantías funcionales (inamovilidad en el cargo e intangibilidad en sus remuneraciones) y que el justiciable acuda a la inhibición o la recusación como mecanismos para garantizar la imparcialidad de sus decisiones. Estas formas y modos de garantizar la independencia de su actuación ceden ante la presión mediática o del gobierno.

Por ello es imperioso fortalecer las garantías. La ley, el proceso y el juez, revestido, además, de las garantías funcionales de imparcialidad, permiten garantizar los derechos humanos que las impunidades de la mentira lesionan, restringen, alteran o amenazan. Para ello también es imprescindible que existan políticas públicas orientadas en el sentido tuitivo de la verdad apoyado en un sistema de justicia ágil y dinámico. Lejos de buscar fortalecer al ciudadano en el proceso democrático en busca de la verdad de los hechos, sobre todo en la rendición de cuentas de la labor de los funcionarios públicos, se recurre a la desmesura del mismo modo que resultan criticables los mecanismos de las fake news o la manipulación de la información que genera la posverdad.

Se busca incidir gravemente sobre el Poder Judicial, aduciendo la nomenclatura bélica del lawfare por parte de figuras políticas cercanas a un gobierno, cuando no figuras de la oposición que, con base en hechos inciertos o parcialmente exactos, promueven denuncias falsas o carentes de sustento jurídico de relevancia. Es un juego macabro que toma por asalto al Poder Judicial y condiciona la democracia constitucional, pues es el último refugio de los derechos fundamentales. Es este donde se legitima el debido proceso constitucional mediante la satisfacción de las garantías y no debe ser el escenario de disputa de los poderosos.

Se condiciona o censura al Poder Judicial, mientras que so pretexto de la legitimación u otra verdad se levantan tribunales populares con marcada identificación y parcialidad, además de una ilegalidad manifiesta.

Ambos comportamientos son censurables y condenables. Es reprochable que estos "tribunales éticos" de la verdad, como modo de combatir el lawfare, oficien de presión al Poder Judicial como una suerte de moderna inquisición que controla a este por quienes se creen depositarios de la verdad revelada. Son vulgares comisiones especiales que ponen en vilo al

Poder Judicial y se alzan contra el mandato del art. 18 de la CN. Tampoco se sanciona con severidad las denuncias falsas o la proliferación de fake news que son estimuladas por grandes medios, sectores con intereses creados o sectores políticos – opositores u oficialistas –, en cuanto menoscaban o manipulan la verdad.

Se busca la impunidad por medio de sufragio. Algunos funcionarios electos para ejercer cargos públicos adquieren una tutela que los ponen al margen de la investigación de hechos que se deben fundar en la verdad de lo acontecido. Se evade la sanción, por la inmunidad de "proceso" ya que no se investiga si tales hechos violaron o no la ley vigente, sobre cuya obligación de acatar y cumplir no quedan dudas. Merece la enérgica condena también la celeridad de un proceso donde la verdad procesal y la verdad material se soslayen, motivados por un proceso político y social que emite un juicio provisorio, parcialmente fundado en hechos sesgados y tendenciosamente expuestos para gravitar sobre el Poder Judicial.

La verdad no se legitima de otra forma que no sea descubriéndola mediante mecanismos previstos en la ley, con carácter de irrefutabilidad para fundamentar un castigo; de lo contrario volvemos a la Inquisición. El camino es fortalecer al ciudadano, dotándolo de herramientas como la acción mencionada para que pueda demostrar la verdad y con ello formar una opinión libre. Se requiere una información veraz y objetiva. Una democracia constitucional de matriz deliberativa tiene como contraseña de entendimiento el cumplimiento de la Constitución, se nutre con el diálogo y se fortalece con la participación del ciudadano en el proceso democrático; para ello es indispensable la verdad, base de todo consenso mínimo y edificante. De lo contrario el árbol siempre tapará al bosque. El ciudadano es el titular de la parte alícuota de la soberanía popular, cuyo titular colectivo es el pueblo, no un gobierno ni sectores concentrados de poder económico.

A DERROGAÇÃO DO ART. 1.725 DO CÓDIGO CIVIL EM RAZÃO DO RECONHECIMENTO DA INCONSTITUCIONALIDADE DO ART. 1.790 PELO STF

CHRISTIANO CASSETTARI*

No dia 10 de maio de 2017, os Ministros do Supremo Tribunal Federal, por seu Tribunal Pleno, sob a presidência da Ministra Cármen Lúcia, por maioria de votos, apreciando o Tema 498 da repercussão geral, nos termos do voto divergente do Ministro Luís Roberto Barroso, que redigiu o acórdão, deram provimento ao RE 646.721/RS, para reconhecer de forma incidental a inconstitucionalidade do art. 1.790 do Código Civil de 2002 e declarar o direito do recorrente de participar da herança de seu companheiro em conformidade com o regime jurídico estabelecido no art. 1.829 do Código Civil de 2002, vencidos os Ministros Marco Aurélio (Relator) e Ricardo Lewandowski. Em seguida, acordaram, vencido o Ministro Marco Aurélio (Relator), e ausentes, justificadamente, os Ministros Dias Toffoli e Celso de Mello, e, neste julgamento, o Ministro Gilmar Mendes, em fixar a tese nos seguintes termos:

> "É inconstitucional a distinção de regimes sucessórios entre cônjuges e companheiros prevista no art. 1.790 do CC/2002, devendo ser aplicado, tanto nas hipóteses de casamento quanto nas de união estável, o regime do art. 1.829 do CC/2002." A ementa do julgado ficou assim definida: Direito constitucional e civil. Recurso extraordinário. Repercussão geral. Aplicação do artigo

* Pós doutorando em Direito Civil pela USP. Doutor e Mestre em Direito Civil pela USP. Registrador Civil em Salvador-BA.

> 1.790 do Código Civil à sucessão em união estável homoafetiva. Inconstitucionalidade da distinção de regime sucessório entre cônjuges e companheiros. 1. A Constituição brasileira contempla diferentes formas de família legítima, além da que resulta do casamento. Nesse rol incluem-se as famílias formadas mediante união estável, hétero ou homoafetivas. O STF já reconheceu a "*inexistência de hierarquia ou diferença de qualidade jurídica entre as duas formas de constituição de um novo e autonomizado núcleo doméstico*", aplicando-se a união estável entre pessoas do mesmo sexo as mesmas regras e mesas consequências da união estável heteroafetiva (ADI 4277 e ADPF 132, rel. Min. Ayres Britto, j. 05.05.2011). 2. Não é legítimo desequiparar, para fins sucessórios, os cônjuges e os companheiros, isto é, a família formada pelo casamento e a formada por união estável. Tal hierarquização entre entidades familiares é incompatível com a Constituição de 1988. Assim sendo, o art. 1790 do Código Civil, ao revogar as Leis n. 8.971/1994 e n. 9.278/1996 e discriminar a companheira (ou o companheiro), dando-lhe direitos sucessórios bem inferiores aos conferidos à esposa (ou ao marido), entra em contraste com os princípios da igualdade, da dignidade humana, da proporcionalidade como vedação à proteção deficiente e da vedação do retrocesso. 3. Com a finalidade de preservar a segurança jurídica, o entendimento ora firmado é aplicável apenas aos inventários judiciais em que não tenha havido trânsito em julgado da sentença de partilha e às partilhas extrajudiciais em que ainda não haja escritura pública. 4. Provimento do recurso extraordinário. Afirmação, em repercussão geral, da seguinte tese: "*No sistema constitucional vigente, é inconstitucional a distinção de regimes sucessórios entre cônjuges e companheiros, devendo ser aplicado, em ambos os casos, o regime estabelecido no art. 1.829 do CC/2002*" (RE 646.721/RS).

Como vimos, a tese fixada pelo STF tem como base ser inconstitucional a distinção de regimes sucessórios entre cônjuges e companheiros, ou seja, com isso não se pode fazer diferenciação entre ambos, pois de agora em diante tudo o que se aplica ao cônjuge se aplica ao companheiro na sucessão. Dessa forma, todas as regras sucessórias destinadas ao cônjuge se aplicam, também, ao companheiro. Com o citado julgamento, o artigo que tratava da sucessão do companheiro (art. 1.790 do CC) foi declarado inconstitucional, e a regra que passou a viger é a do art. 1829 do CC, onde nele está escrito "cônjuge" na sucessão devemos colocar uma "barra" e incluir o "companheiro" (cônjuge/companheiro). O art. 1.829 do Código Civil estabelece a ordem da vocação hereditária, nos seguintes termos:

> Art. 1.829. A sucessão legítima defere-se na ordem seguinte: (Vide Recurso Extraordinário nº 646.721) (Vide Recurso Extraordinário nº 878.694)
>
> I – aos descendentes, em concorrência com o cônjuge sobrevivente, salvo se casado este com o falecido no regime da comunhão universal, ou no da separação obrigatória de bens (art. 1.640, parágrafo único); ou se, no regime da comunhão parcial, o autor da herança não houver deixado bens particulares;
>
> II – aos ascendentes, em concorrência com o cônjuge;
>
> III – ao cônjuge sobrevivente;
>
> IV – aos colaterais.

Assim sendo, quais são as principais consequências que a declaração de inconstitucionalidade do art. 1.790 do Código Civil produz no Direito das Sucessões?

1) A regra sucessória que será aplicada na sucessão do companheiro é a mesma aplicada ao cônjuge, consoante ao art. 1.829 do Código Civil.
2) Com isso, o companheiro passa a ser terceiro na ordem da vocação hereditária, recebendo toda a herança se só existirem ele e colaterais do falecido, que por esse motivo estariam excluídos da sucessão.
3) Além disso, o companheiro sobrevivente poderá concorrer com descendentes e ascendentes do falecido, nos mesmos moldes que o cônjuge.
4) O companheiro passa a ter direito à reserva legal de1/4 da herança, se, quando concorrer com descendentes, for ascendente de todos os herdeiros com quem concorrer.
5) Os companheiros passam a ser herdeiros necessários, já que o cônjuge assim já é reconhecido pelo art. 1.845 do Código Civil. Dessa forma, ele não poderá ser excluído por testamento, pois terá direito à legítima; venda de ascendente para descendente deve ter autorização do companheiro (art. 496 do CC); doação entre companheiros importa adiantamento de legítima, e por isso deverá ser levada à colação etc.
6) É sepultada de vez a polêmica sobre o direito real de habitação do companheiro, que já era reconhecido pela jurisprudência, mas sem consenso sobre qual seria o fundamento, motivo pelo qual não se sabia quando ele seria extinto. De agora em diante se aplica o art. 1.831 do Código Civil na sucessão do companheiro, que terá direito

real de habitação vitalício, se preenchido os requisitos do dispositivo, também aplicado ao cônjuge.

7) Será aplicado na sucessão do companheiro o art. 1.830 do Código Civil, e com isso o companheiro sobrevivente estará excluído da sucessão se estiver separado de fato do falecido na data do óbito.

Porém, alguns problemas surgirão com essa igualdade sucessória determinada pelo STF, e terão que ser solucionados. O maior deles, em nossa opinião, se refere a regra patrimonial da união estável. A mudança do regime de bens no casamento só pode ocorrer com autorização judicial (art. 1.639 do CC), o que evita fraude na sucessão pela dificuldade imposta, já que ele é importante para saber se haverá ou não concorrência do cônjuge com o descendente do falecido (art. 1.829 do CC). Agora, na união estável não há essa dificuldade, podendo o casal mudar, por simples contrato escrito, por instrumento particular ou escritura pública, o regime de bens, sem intervenção judicial, conforme o art. 1.725 do Código Civil. Assim sendo, há uma porta aberta para a fraude sucessória, pois, fazendo esse contrato antes do falecimento, é possível colocar ou tirar o companheiro da concorrência sucessória com o descendente, dependendo do regime escolhido, já que tal concorrência dele depende.

Mas ocorre que o direito de herança é indisponível, previsto em cláusula pétrea no art. 5º, XXX, da CF, e por isso não pode ser objeto de disposição, senão teríamos um pacta corvina, repudiado pelo art. 426 do Código Civil. Dessa forma, para evitar fraude sucessória, e considerando que foi objeto de desejo geral uma equiparação da união estável a casamento, ela agora deverá ser plena e não apenas na parte boa, ou seja, deve ocorrer em tudo.

Portanto, para evitar uma fraude sucessória, é necessário interpretar o art. 1.725 do Código Civil no sentido de dizer que os conviventes não mais poderão mudar a regra da comunhão parcial de bens por contrato escrito de união estável, devendo uma nova regra patrimonial depender de autorização judicial, como ocorre no casamento (art. 1.639 do CC). O art. 1.725 do Código Civil estabelece que vigora na união estável a regra do regime da comunhão parcial de bens, sendo tais normas aplicadas na hipótese da extinção da união. Porém, o citado dispositivo permite que a regra seja modificada por um contrato escrito celebrado entre as partes, seja por escritura pública ou instrumento particular. Para alteração dessa regra, para qualquer outra prevista ou não no Código Civil, o artigo fala na celebração de um "contrato de convivência", denominação dada por Francisco José Cahali, de cuja obra recomendamos a leitura[1]. Poderia, inclusive, ser criado regime híbrido (assim como ocorre no pacto antenupcial).

No contrato de convivência podem constar a regra patrimonial, a data de início da união estável, constituição de direitos reais (como a habitação ou o usufruto, por exemplo), regras quanto à administração dos bens dos companheiros e de instituição de arbitragem. Questão interessante que sempre é levantada é se podem os conviventes, em contrato de convivência, estabelecer efeitos patrimoniais retroativos para a união estável. Em outras palavras, pode o casal estabelecer que o regime de bens por eles eleito vale desde o início da sua união? Em recente julgado, o Superior Tribunal de Justiça entendeu pela impossibilidade de os conviventes atribuírem efeitos retroativos (*ex tunc*) ao contrato de união estável, a fim de eleger regime de bens aplicável ao período de convivência anterior a sua assinatura, como já tinha sido decidido no REsp 1.383.624/MG, rel. Min. Moura Ribeiro, 3ª Turma, j. em 2-6-2015:

> Escritura pública de reconhecimento de união estável. Regime da separação de bens. Atribuição de eficácia retroativa. Não cabimento. Precedentes da Terceira Turma. 1. Ação de declaração e de dissolução de união estável, cumulada com partilha de bens, tendo o casal convivido por doze anos e gerado dois filhos. 2. No momento do rompimento da relação, em setembro de 2007, as partes celebraram, mediante escritura pública, um pacto de reconhecimento de união estável, elegendo retroativamente o regime da separação total de bens.3. Controvérsia em torno da validade da cláusula referente à eficácia retroativa do regime de bens. 4. Consoante a disposição do art. 1.725 do Código Civil, "na união estável, salvo contrato escrito entre os companheiros, aplica-se às relações patrimoniais, no que couber, o regime da comunhão parcial de bens". 5. Invalidade da cláusula que atribui eficácia retroativa ao regime de bens pactuado em escritura pública de reconhecimento de união estável. 6. Prevalência do regime legal (comunhão parcial) no período anterior à lavratura da escritura. 7. Precedentes da Terceira Turma do STJ. 8.Voto divergente quanto à fundamentação. 9. Recurso especial desprovido (REsp 1.597.675, rel. Paulo de Tarso Sanseverino, 3ª Turma, j. 25-10-2016).

[1] *Contrato de convivência na união estável*. São Paulo: Saraiva, 2002.

Segundo o entendimento fixado, o regime de bens entre os companheiros começa a vigorar na data da assinatura do contrato, assim como o regime de bens entre os cônjuges começa a produzir efeitos na data do casamento (art. 1.639, § 1º, do Código Civil). Em outros dizeres, o contrato de união estável é plenamente válido, mas somente pode gerar efeitos para o futuro, não sendo lícita a produção de efeitos pretéritos. Incabível, pois, cláusula de retroatividade do pacto patrimonial celebrado pelos conviventes. Essa regra se aplica à primeira escritura feita pelos conviventes, bem como a outras, realizadas no decorrer de uma união estável, para modificar escrituras anteriores. Lembrando que, como se aplica a regra da separação obrigatória à união estável, não é possível fazer escritura de união estável, como mudança de regra patrimonial, a partir de quando um dos conviventes completar 70 anos.

O TJSC decidiu, em 18-8-2015, que pode ser pactuado efeito *ex nunc* (não retroativos) no contrato de convivência de união estável, na Apelação Cível n. 2015.026497-8, 3ª Câmara de Direito Privado, relatada pela Desembargadora Maria do Rocio Luz Santa Rita. Cumpre ressaltar que o contrato de namoro, denominado pela imprensa dessa forma, é nulo de pleno direito, pois tem o condão de afastar a aplicação das normas da união estável, afastando lei imperativa do caso concreto. Por tais motivos, acreditamos que o art. 1.725 do Código Civil foi derrogado, pois permite mudar o regime da comunhão parcial, imputado para as uniões estáveis, por meio do contrato escrito, manipulando a regra patrimonial que irá viger no final da união quando ocorrer o falecimento, que pode ser próximo a celebração do contrato ou não, para que inclua ou retire a concorrência sucessória do companheiro com o descendente, ao arrepio da norma que seria aplicada se o regime continuasse sendo o da comunhão parcial.

Isso pode estimular uma burla sucessória, já que o STJ decidiu que o referido contrato produz efeito *ex nunc* na meação, mas na sucessão prevaleceria o último escolhido, incluindo ou excluindo o companheiro da sucessão, caracterizando um verdadeiro *pacta corvina*, vedado pelo art. 426 do Código Civil, que proíbe que seja objeto de contrato a herança de pessoa viva. Por ser uma união informal, a celebração do contrato de convivência é facultativa, podendo ela ocorrer mediante escritura pública ou por instrumento particular, em razão da omissão de normas quanto à forma desse negócio jurídico. Todo contrato só produz efeitos *inter partes*, ou seja, entre as partes, por força do princípio da relatividade dos efeitos do contrato. Para que um contrato produza efeitos *erga omnes*, é necessária a existência de lei que assim determine e que estabeleça em qual local ele deve ser registrado.

O Provimento n. 37 do CNJ, que faculta o registro da escritura e sentença no Livro "E" do Cartório de Registro Civil das Pessoas Naturais, tem o condão de dar efeito perante terceiro do seu conteúdo. Cumpre lembrar, conforme explicamos anteriormente, que existem Estados que possuem normas locais, de suas Corregedorias estaduais, que permitem o registro da escritura pública de união estável no Registro Imobiliário, para que tenha oponibilidade *erga omnes* e efeitos semelhantes do pacto antenupcial registrado no mesmo local, consoante o art. 1.657 do Código Civil, que não parece ser a saída mais adequada, por força do Provimento n. 37 do CNJ.

Por isso é que defendemos que a existência da união estável deve ser averbada no termo de nascimento dos conviventes, para que não se tenha mais de uma união estável, e também para que se tenha notícia da existência do contrato escrito entre as partes, pois qualquer mudança de regra patrimonial só poderia ocorrer com autorização judicial. Essa regra já é aplicada ao casamento, por disposição expressa da Lei 6.015/73.

Outra forma de mudar a regra da união estável sem autorização judicial seria a conversão da união estável em casamento, hipótese em que outro regime poderia ser escolhido. Assim sendo, com o julgamento do RE 646.721/RS em 10 de maio de 2017, quando o Supremo Tribunal Federal apreciando o Tema 498 da repercussão geral, que reconheceu de forma incidental a inconstitucionalidade do art. 1.790 do Código Civil de 2002 e que fixou tese no sentido de que deve ser aplicado o regime jurídico estabelecido no art. 1.829 do Código Civil de 2002, tanto nas hipóteses de casamento quanto de união estável, o artigo art. 1725 do Código Civil foi derrogado, e vigora, atualmente, apenas a parte que cita ser aplicada na união estável a regra do regime da comunhão parcial de bens.[2]

Isso de dá porque a equiparação sucessória entre cônjuges e companheiros terá que ser feita, também, na modificação do regime de bens, aplicando em ambos os tipos de constituição de família a regra do art. 1.639, parágrafo segundo do Código Civil, que exige autorização judicial. Essa autorização judicial se faz necessária para que não se estimule uma fraude sucessória, onde seria permitido os companheiros manipularem a regra

[2] Cassettari, Christiano. *Elementos de Direito Civil*. 8. Ed. São Paulo: Saraiva, 2020.

sucessória, fazendo um contrato escrito, particular ou público, adotando a regra de um regime de bens que retire ou coloque o companheiro na concorrência sucessória, diferentemente do que ocorreria se fosse comunhão parcial, cuja concorrência depende da existência de bens particulares.

O PRINCÍPIO DA CAPACIDADE CONTRIBUTIVA COMO INSTRUMENTO CONCRETIZADOR DA JUSTIÇA SOCIAL E FISCAL

Claudia Cristina dos Santos Abrosio*
Julcira Maria de Mello Vianna Lisboa**

INTRODUÇÃO

Na atualidade, o contexto de desigualdade social é considerado condição *sine qua non* para abertura de debates dos mais diversos temas, em sua maioria de viés político e econômico, com ênfase na exigência por justiça social, na intenção de um coletivo solidário e provedor de maior assistência aos que mais necessitam.

Em uma sociedade que surgiu da colonização, é compreensível historicamente os motivos pelos quais a distribuição de renda seja desigual. Países no caminho de um almejado desenvolvimento ou estagnados neste processo, não têm como prioridade equilibrar direitos e obrigações dos indivíduos, como se fosse o significado de desfrute generalizado, independente da geração de renda produzida.

A desigualdade em seu princípio é econômica e como um rio, deságua na questão social, onde naturalmente é observado que maiores provedores usufruem de melhores condições e os de menor colaboração possuem

* Mestranda em Direito pela PUC-SP. Especialista em Direito Tributário pelo IBET – Instituto Brasileiro de Estudos Tributários. Advogada.

** Doutora em Direito pela PUC-SP. Professora de Direito Tributário nos Cursos de Graduação e Pós-Graduação da PUC-SP. Vice Coordenadora do Curso de Direito da PUC-SP. Coordenadora da Cadeira de Direito Tributário da Faculdade de Direito da PUC-SP. Advogada.

direitos limitados. Assim, evidente a necessidade de equiparar os direitos, através da justiça social que acolhe o conceito de forma funcional.

René Descartes (1596 – 1650), em sua filosofia cartesiana considera essencial a construção do sujeito ético, detentor do conhecimento verdadeiro. Em "Discurso do método", Descartes propõe o uso de sua metodologia para o alcance do conhecimento legítimo, como conclusão de quatro etapas: (i) dar clareza e distinção as evidências apresentadas, evitando precipitar uma conclusão, no uso do pensamento independente de crenças e vivências pessoais, questionáveis em seu teor natural, ou seja, a evidência será aceita como verdadeira, quando indubitável; (ii) fragmentar o problema de acordo com a necessidade de análise do processo, a fim de resolvê-lo de forma mais eficiente; (iii) organizar os pensamentos de forma a resolver os problemas em escala gradual e evolutiva, dos mais simples aos mais complexos, até que sejam resolvidos, e (iv) revisar por completo as etapas anteriores para que se possa alcançar uma conclusão isenta de omissões. A célebre frase *"Penso, logo existo"* idealiza a forma com a qual é construído o pensamento crítico em busca da verdade incontestável. [1]

Para o filósofo, a dúvida edifica o pensamento e este prova a existência, sendo a própria existência a única verdade que não pode ser questionada. A partir do momento que o indivíduo manifesta a dúvida, inicia-se o processo de julgamento, com finalidade de encontrar a verdade que traz a justiça.

Dito isso, embora não exista uma definição unívoca para o vocábulo "justiça", é possível concluir que se trata de um instrumento que institui regras e traz equidade para sociedade, reconhecendo de forma igual o direito de cada indivíduo. Na contemporaneidade, erguem-se reflexões sobre a sociedade em geral, indivíduos e instituições que lidam com um sistema insuficiente e inadequado, disseminando assim um modo de sobrevivência a este, mesmo que tenhamos eventos sociais e econômicos que nos permitam conceber novas maneiras de contribuir, já que moralmente devemos pagar os impostos.

Desde sempre temos a concepção de que o tributo é devido como forma de subsídio para o bem comum no desenvolvimento da coletividade. Neste sentido, cabe trazer à baila, por oportuno, uma narração do discípulo Mateus (22:21): *"Dai, pois, a César o que é de César, e a Deus o que é de*

[1] DESCARTES, René. Discurso do Método; tradução de Jacó Guinsburg e Bento Prado Júnior (Coleção Os Pensadores). 2ª ed. São Paulo: Editora Abril Cultural, 1979, p. 46.

Deus", para compreensão de que é licita a cobrança de impostos ordenada pelo imperador, que possui o domínio sobre o governo, e dele originam-se as riquezas e os benefícios oferecidos a sociedade. Feitas essas considerações e, diante das regras aplicáveis na sociedade, faz-se imprescindível a reivindicação da justiça social e fiscal para o bom direcionamento da coletividade como um todo, fator fundamental do Direito.

É neste contexto que a justiça fiscal vem ganhando destaque nos últimos anos, uma vez que o Sistema Tributário é movido pela exigência de tributos, no entanto, o Estado deve assegurar uma tributação justa e equânime, com fundamento de validade, trazendo verdadeira efetivação ao princípio da capacidade contributiva, de estatura constitucional. Neste artigo pretendemos investigar a ideia de justiça tributária, demonstrando como o princípio da capacidade contributiva se insere no ordenamento jurídico, na medida em que representa um instrumento de extrema relevância para o equilíbrio no modelo de arrecadação e distribuição das riquezas.

1. O CONCEITO DE JUSTIÇA

É evidente que desenvolver um conceito de justiça que seja unânime ao anseio de todos os indivíduos é uma tarefa árdua. Em um mundo em constante transformação, onde há diversas características peculiares e regras que a sociedade impõe aos indivíduos, e que cada qual tem um pensamento do que é justo e injusto, faz-se necessário discutir acerca desse conceito, que envolve um estudo intelectual, humano e jurídico, ocasionando uma visão pluridisciplinar. A este respeito, importante observar que juristas e estudiosos que versam sobre justiça divergem em alguns aspectos, reivindicando para si a certeza do seu conceito, levando em consideração as diferentes opiniões, experiências, marcos históricos e as dimensões sob as quais o conteúdo foi tratado.

2. A TEORIA DE IMMANUEL KANT

Immanuel Kant (1724 – 1804) organizou uma ciência do direito precisamente lógica, através da distinção entre o Direito e a moral, sob o prisma formal e não material.

Importante mencionar que os sistemáticos do direito natural não estavam vinculados a nenhuma fonte positiva do Direito. Nas palavras de Tércio Sampaio Ferraz Jr. "o Direito Natural do Iluminismo em Kant, por exemplo, se de um lado aparece como uma "filosofia social da liberdade", de outro atribui à liberdade um valor moral que se manifesta expressamente numa teoria dos direitos subjetivos." [2]

Kant explanava o direito natural através do uso da razão, logo, o que legitima a atividade do legislador é a sua obediência ao direito natural do indivíduo, distanciando-se do positivismo. Para o filósofo, a função do Direito consiste em assegurar a liberdade, que é o direito básico humano, já que este é essencial para a garantia de todos os outros direitos humanos e sociais.

Nesta linha de raciocínio, adota o posicionamento de que é mediante o arbítrio que o ser humano conscientemente estabelece a distinção entre o justo e injusto, constituindo a fórmula racional para saber o que deve ou não ser realizado juridicamente, o que, em última instância, sugere sopesar que a razão prática é capaz de fundar o direito positivo, de situar a proporção exata de convivência em direção a uma paz perpétua, de modo que a justiça entra em conformidade a estas prescrições racionais. [3]

Na sua visão o direito é estritamente ligado à coação, na medida em que exerce função limitadora dos excessos da liberdade, ou seja, ele limita a liberdade de um para que ela não prejudique a liberdade do outro, proporcionando o pleno gozo da liberdade por todos os indivíduos. Por conseguinte, é possível afirmar que nesta teoria o conceito de justiça está vinculado ao agir de forma a conviver com a liberdade dos demais envolvidos. [4]

3. A TEORIA DE HANS KELSEN

Em sentido oposto, a Teoria Pura do Direito de Hans Kelsen (1881 – 1973) está intimamente ligada ao movimento positivista, consequentemente, restringe-se à análise estrutural da lei positiva, livre de qualquer ideologia social, religiosa ou política. Essa teoria afirma existir apenas o direito

[2] FERRAZ JR., Tércio Sampaio. A Ciência do Direito. 3ª ed. São Paulo: Atlas, 2014, pp. 27-28.

[3] DOS SANTOS, Rafael Padilha. A Moral e a Justiça no Pensamento de Immanuel Kant. Tese: Mestrado em Filosofia. Universidade Federal de Santa Catarina. Florianópolis: 2011, p. 132. Disponível em: <https://repositorio.ufsc.br/bitstream/handle/123456789/95997/293089.pdf?sequence=1&isAllowed=y> Acessado em 04 de ago. de 2020.

[4] SERRETTI, André Pedrolli. O fundamento moral da Teoria do Direito em Kant. São Paulo: Revista Âmbito Jurídico nº 74, 2010. Disponível em: <https://ambitojuridico.com.br/edicoes/revista-74/o-fundamento-moral-da-teoria-do-direito-em-kant/> Acessado em 04 de ago. de 2020.

positivo, provida de pureza metódica e objetivismo científico, afastando do campo de análise tudo que não pertença a seu próprio objeto, tornando o estudo do direito autônomo e desvinculado de qualquer outra área de conhecimento. Esse pensamento busca desprender a ciência jurídica de todos os componentes que lhe são alheios.

Nesse contexto, Kelsen faz uma diferenciação entre o mundo do "*ser*", próprio das ciências naturais que atuam com base nas premissas de verdadeiro/falso, e do "*dever-ser*" que tem por fundamento as premissas de válido/inválido, no qual o Direito estaria centrado. De tal modo, a norma jurídica residiria no mundo do "*dever-ser*" e obedeceria ao princípio da imputação, com base em um respectivo comando ou mandamento. Para Kelsen o sistema de normas – como ordem jurídica – possui um caráter dinâmico, uma vez que a norma jurídica não é revestida de validade tendo em vista o seu conteúdo, mas sim porque é criada de uma forma determinada. E é por esta razão que ela pertence à ordem jurídica, cujas normas são elaboradas de conformidade com a norma fundamental.[5]

Ou seja, o conteúdo da norma é meramente formal, sem qualquer dependência valorativa ou material. Assim, se uma norma preenche todos os requisitos legais para a sua existência, mesmo que injusta, será obrigatória. Para Kelsen não há que se falar nas denominadas leis injustas, por ponderar que a justiça é apenas relativa, idealizando como injustiça a não aplicação da norma jurídica ao caso concreto. Logo, a justiça se perfaz com a aplicação da norma, sendo irrelevante avaliar a norma jurídica como justa ou injusta.

Nesse contexto, cabe mencionar os seguintes ensinamentos da Teoria Pura do Direito: "Dado que o fundamento de validade de uma norma somente pode ser outra norma, este pressuposto tem de ser uma norma: não uma norma posta por uma autoridade jurídica, mas uma norma pressuposta, quer dizer, uma norma que é pressuposta sempre que o sentido subjetivo dos fatos geradores de normas postas de conformidade com a Constituição é interpretado como o seu sentido objetivo."[6] Portanto, como essa norma pressuposta é a norma fundamental de uma ordem jurídica,

5 KELSEN, Hans. Teoria Pura do Direito; tradução de João Baptista Machado. 8ª ed. São Paulo: Editora WMF Martins Fontes, 2020, p. 221.

6 KELSEN, Hans. Teoria Pura do Direito; tradução de João Baptista Machado. 8ª ed. São Paulo: Editora WMF Martins Fontes, 2020, p. 224.

esta estabelece as proposições basilares, representando fundamento de validade comum para as demais normas inferiores. Neste ponto, percebe-se que as normas não podem ser ordenadas no mesmo plano hierárquico, situadas uma ao lado da outra, uma vez que há uma graduação escalonada, com diversas classes e níveis.

Diante dessas breves considerações, inegável que o Direito evoluiu, no entanto, apesar das críticas a que a Teoria Pura do Direito está sujeita, tendo em vista principalmente que nem sempre a justiça estará disposta na norma, constata-se que o ordenamento permanece fundamentado em uma estrutura escalonada, sendo que a norma mais importante da hierarquia, que subordina as demais normas jurídicas inferiores, é a chamada norma hipotética fundamental. Neste particular, menciona-se que no ordenamento jurídico brasileiro, a Constituição Federal de 1988 se coloca no vértice do sistema jurídico, impondo-se como fundamento de validade das demais normas inferiores.

4. JUSTIÇA SOCIAL E FISCAL

O conceito de justiça social abrange questões como igualdade de direitos, garantias ao indivíduo e solidariedade. No entendimento de quanto maior a concentração de riquezas, maior a desigualdade social, em todos os seus desdobramentos. Deve-se compreender a justiça social como fator determinante na promoção de um melhor desenvolvimento do país, reduzindo as desigualdades econômicas e sociais. Neste sentido, vale mencionar que em novembro de 2007, a Assembleia Geral da Organização das Nações Unidades (ONU) decretou o dia 20 de fevereiro como o Dia Mundial da Justiça Social. A relevância que este tema tem alcançado auxilia no fortalecimento da busca ao desenvolvimento social e crescimento econômico, uma vez que o mundo anseia por melhores condições e oportunidades, em prol da convivência pacífica das nações, sendo este o propósito da organização, em todas as áreas nas quais atua.

Oportunidade e conhecimento são privilégios designados parcialmente à sociedade. As condições com as quais o indivíduo se relaciona – em sua maioria de cunho econômico – garantem o acesso à informação, conduzidos inclusive através da educação. A economia está além da questão social, pois desta forma, o Estado atinge um maior controle sobre os bens e indiretamente sobre os indivíduos. Entre nós, leciona Aline Vitalis: “as capacidades relacionam-se diretamente a concepção de igualdade de oportunidades, ou seja, de igualdade no 'ponto de partida', de modo a possibilitar a cada cidadão exercer livremente suas escolhas de vida, viabilizando, assim, a construção de um sistema fundado na justiça social." [7]

O Estado tem por dever cumprir com as obrigações impostas na Constituição Federal, assegurando à sociedade os direitos previstos na norma fundamental, que compreendem, entre outros, a saúde, o saneamento básico, a segurança e a educação, partindo do conceito de equidade e garantindo iguais condições de tratamento para todos, como é de direito de cada cidadão. Através das capacidades contributivas, exerce-se a justiça fiscal a partir da justiça social. É imposta uma tributação de maior escala aos que dispõem de maiores riquezas. Nesse contexto, o tributo, desde épocas remotas, tem acompanhado as organizações políticas como ferramenta para promover a manutenção do sistema público, tendo em vista a necessidade de recursos para assegurar a garantia de determinados valores indispensáveis ao desenvolvimento de uma sociedade.

No período do Estado Patrimonial, o tributo era aplicado como um pacto entre os detentores do poder e a sociedade, constituindo uma exigência obrigatória sobre o patrimônio, sendo que o período do Estado Fiscal foi marcado por grandes evoluções, que envolveram a liberdade humana e às iniciativas individuais e, por conseguinte, o tributo alcançou determinadas limitações. É neste momento que surge o mecanismo da capacidade contributiva de cada indivíduo, adquirindo conotação de princípio fundamental na organização de uma sociedade, onde o tributo passa a ser visto como dever de cidadania. [8] Nesse contexto de busca pela justiça fiscal, oportuno mencionar as lições de Norberto Bobbio "toda norma jurídica pode ser submetida a três valorações distintas, e que estas valorações são independentes uma das outras. De fato, frente a qualquer norma jurídica podemos colocar uma tríplice ordem de problemas: (1) se é justa ou injusta; (2) se é válida ou inválida; (3) se é eficaz ou ineficaz. Trata-se dos três problemas distintos: da *justiça*, da *validade* e da *eficácia* da norma jurídica". [9] (grifos no original)

[7] VITALIS, Aline. Justiça Fiscal, Neutralidade e Compliance. 8ª ed. Rio de Janeiro: Editora Lumen Juris, 2018, p. 70.

[8] BONOMO, Carla. A eficácia da capacidade contributiva e a justiça social. Londrina: Revista do Direito Público, v. 4, n. 2, 2009. Disponível em: <http://www.uel.br/revistas/uel/index.php/direitopub/issue/view/728> Acessado em 04 de ago. de 2020.

[9] BOBBIO, Norberto. Teoria da Norma Jurídica; tradução de Fernando Pavan Baptista e Ariani Bueno Sudatti. 2ª ed. Bauru: Edipro, 2003, pp. 45-46.

Para Regina Helena Costa, a noção de justiça tributária sofreu lenta sedimentação até adquirir a configuração dos dias atuais. Ainda, observa que a Lei Maior, ao evidenciar os objetivos fundamentais da República Federativa do Brasil, estabeleceu o de "construir uma sociedade livre, justa e solidária", nos termos do artigo 3°, inciso I. Neste particular, a justiça em questão deve ser entendida em toda a sua extensão, a qual compreende inclusive a justiça tributária. De tal modo, o indivíduo possui o direito de ser tributado de uma forma justa, direito fundamental amparado por cláusula pétrea, com fundamento constitucional no artigo 60, §4°, inciso IV. [10] Essa justiça fiscal deve ser implantada pelo Estado, de modo a atender esses objetivos fundamentais, expostos pela Carta Magna. Todas as formas e critérios devem ser adotados pelas pessoas políticas, através de lei, que atenda aos princípios constitucionais que informam a tributação.

5. A EVOLUÇÃO HISTÓRICA DA CAPACIDADE CONTRIBUTIVA

No Brasil, após a Constituição Imperial, a capacidade contributiva deixou de constar nas Cartas de 1891, 1934 e 1937, reaparecendo apenas com a democrática Constituição de 1946, da seguinte forma: "Art. 202 – Os tributos terão caráter pessoal, sempre que isso for possível, e serão graduados conforme a *capacidade econômica do contribuinte*." (grifamos) Ocorre que, representando notório declínio no âmbito do Direito, a Emenda Constitucional n° 18 de 1965, ao apresentar a reforma tributária, expurgou o princípio da capacidade contributiva do texto constitucional.

Em momento posterior, e de forma acertada, o postulado foi reprojetado na Constituição Federal de 1988: "Art. 145. A União, os Estados, o Distrito Federal e os Municípios poderão instituir os seguintes tributos: (...) § 1º Sempre que possível, os impostos terão caráter pessoal e serão graduados segundo a *capacidade econômica do contribuinte*, facultado à administração tributária, especialmente para conferir efetividade a esses objetivos, identificar, respeitados os direitos individuais e nos termos da lei, o patrimônio, os rendimentos e as atividades econômicas do contribuinte." (grifamos) Em que pese a história constitucional, de acordo com alguns estudiosos, supõe-se que a noção de capacidade contributiva como teoria surgiu com a ciência das finanças clássica do século XIX, sendo que a introdução do tema como

[10] Costa, Regina Helena. Praticabilidade e Justiça Tributária: Exeqüibilidade de Lei Tributária e Direitos do Contribuinte. São Paulo: Malheiros, 2007, pp. 376-379.

uma preocupação da ciência jurídica teve por fundamento o estudo realizado pelo professor Benvenuto Griziotti, em 1929, e da escola de seus discípulos, denominada por Escola de Pávia, tendo em vista que o assunto até então estava restrito aos estudiosos das finanças. Neste sentido, para Griziotti, a capacidade contributiva era a própria causa da exigência tributária. [11]

Nas palavras do jurista espanhol Carlos Palao Taboada, citadas por Regina Helena Costa, após uma primeira fase na qual o princípio da capacidade contributiva foi compreendido como sendo uma ideia prontamente deduzida do princípio de justiça, foi posteriormente concebido como noção necessária para dotar de conteúdo material o princípio da igualdade, então assimilado no aspecto puramente formal. [12] Isto posto, da leitura e reflexão do dispositivo constitucional (artigo 145, §1°, da CF/88) surge, de modo inequívoco, a relação do princípio da capacidade contributiva com o fator econômico e jurídico. No mais, este princípio também está intimamente ligado com a solidariedade, uma vez que aqueles que podem devem pagar impostos para o bem da coletividade.

É preciso esclarecer que o princípio da capacidade contributiva tem por finalidade conferir condições equivalentes de capacidade econômica, assegurando que todos os sujeitos contribuam na mesma equivalência em razão das suas riquezas, uma vez que estes devem pagar tributos de modo a não comprometer seus direitos fundamentais.

Regina Helena Costa explica que no plano jurídico-positivo o princípio da capacidade contributiva estabelece que um sujeito é titular de direitos e obrigações nos termos da legislação tributária vigente, que é quem vai dispor sobre a capacidade e seu respectivo âmbito. No âmbito ético-econômico, a capacidade contributiva se vincula com a justiça econômica tributária. Dessas lições se extrai o entendimento que o princípio em questão está vinculado a dois elementos: (i) o volume de recursos que o indivíduo possui para satisfazer o ônus tributário e (ii) a necessidade dos recursos envolvidos. [13]

Nas palavras de Roque Carrazza "o princípio da capacidade contributiva hospeda-se nas dobras do princípio da igualdade e ajuda a realizar, no

[11] TABOADA, Carlos Palao. Isonomia e capacidade contributiva. RDTributário 4/127.

[12] COSTA, Regina Helena. Princípio da Capacidade Contributiva. 4ª ed. São Paulo: Malheiros, 2012, p. 20.

[13] COSTA, Regina Helena. Princípio da Capacidade Contributiva. 4ª ed. São Paulo: Malheiros, 2012, pp. 26-27.

campo tributário, os ideais republicanos (...) é justo e jurídico que quem, em termos econômicos, tem muito pague, proporcionalmente, mais imposto do que quem tem pouco." [14] Em vista de todo o exposto, é irrefutável que o princípio da capacidade contributiva age como instrumento concretizador da justiça fiscal no ordenamento jurídico. Para Hugo de Brito Machado é possível compreender que, independentemente da disposição na Constituição Federal de 1988, o princípio em questão deve ser apreciado como um princípio de justiça, levando em consideração que o fim da norma tributária consiste em uma arrecadação fundamentada na capacidade contributiva dos sujeitos eleitos a satisfazer os tributos. [15]

Embora a Constituição Federal de 1988 estipule a capacidade contributiva apenas para os impostos, como ensina Leandro Paulsen, cuida-se de princípio fundamental de tributação aplicável a todas as espécies tributárias, concluindo que "a possibilidade de graduação do tributo conforme a capacidade contributiva pressupõe, evidentemente, que tenha como hipótese de incidência situação efetivamente reveladora de tal capacidade, do que se depreende que o princípio encontra aplicação plena aos tributos com fato gerador não vinculado." [16] Por fim, interessante observar que, tendo em vista que a capacidade contributiva possui vinculação com fatos econômicos, a própria Receita Federal do Brasil (RFB) já dispôs publicamente que, dentre outras ações, a fiscalização é realizada atualmente com foco nos contribuintes de maior capacidade contributiva.

Neste sentido, de acordo com o Plano Anual da Fiscalização da RFB para 2019 e Resultados de 2018, através de um consistente processo de capacitação e do desenvolvimento de ferramentas tecnológicas, os resultados a partir do ano-calendário de 2010 evidenciam um aumento consistente na atuação junto aos grandes contribuintes, que representam 60% da arrecadação total. [17] Vejamos:

[14] CARRAZZA, Roque Antonio. Curso de Direito Constitucional Tributário. 32ª ed. São Paulo: Malheiros, 2017, p. 79.

[15] MACHADO, Hugo de Brito. Os Princípios Jurídicos da Tributação na Constituição Federal de 1988. 6ª ed. São Paulo: Malheiros, 2019, p. 72.

[16] PAULSEN, Leandro. Curso de Direito Tributário Completo. 11ª edição. São Paulo: Saraiva, 2020, p. 77.

[17] Plano Anual da Fiscalização da Receita Federal do Brasil para 2019 e Resultados de 2018, pp.13-14. Disponível em: <https://receita.economia.gov.br/dados/resultados/fiscalizacao/arquivos-e-imagens/2019_05_06-plano-anual-de-fiscalizacao-2019.pdf>. Acessado em: 04 de ago. 2020.

Ano	Grandes Contribuintes – PJ	Variação ano anterior	Valor total das autuações pela Fiscalização da RFB	Variação ano anterior	Participação dos CG nas autuações
2009	R$ 55.940.711.486,00		R$ 85.722.778.908,00		65,26%
2010	R$ 55.737.977.458,00	-0,4%	R$ 84.818.059.397,00	-1,1%	65,71%
2011	R$ 74.560.935.507,00	33,8%	R$ 103.354.779.871,00	21,9%	72,14%
2012	R$ 86.840.125.794,00	16,5%	R$ 108.969.478.480,00	5,4%	79,69%
2013	R$ 152.539.000.000,00	75,7%	R$ 181.616.552.959,00	66,7%	83,99%
2014	R$ 104.238.000.000,00	31,7%	R$ 144.556.799.956,00	-20,4%	72,11%
2015	R$ 94.659.500.058,00	-9,2%	R$ 125.227.321.703,00	-13,4%	75,59%
2016	R$ 80.716.870.856,00	-14,7%	R$ 117.794.178.958,00	-5,9%	68,52%
2017	R$ 158.017.453.718,27	95,8%	R$ 199.127.165.381,01	69,0%	79,36%
2018	R$ 149.032.681.643,49	-5,7%	R$ 181.627.463.778,79	-8,8%	82,05%

Em que pese o dever de pagar tributos por parte dos indivíduos, que faz parte da engrenagem institucional do Estado, ressalta-se que fato despido de significação econômica não autoriza a exigência de tributo, sendo necessário avaliar a legalidade e as características próprias de cada tributo para a efetiva concretização do fato gerador da exação, notando os limites no que diz respeito as relações jurídicas, com base nos fundamentos de validade previstos na Lei Maior, afastando possíveis exigências com viés nitidamente arrecadatório, que resulta em confisco. Ressalta-se a ligação que a própria Constituição aponta entre os princípios da legalidade e da capacidade contributiva, na medida em que os tributos só podem ser exigidos por lei (artigo 150, inciso I, da CF) e a expressão " sempre que possível" expressa no artigo145, § 1º, da CF, reconhece a obrigatoriedade da aplicação do princípio da capacidade contributiva sempre que o fato, apontado pela lei, possibilitar a medida da capacidade econômica do contribuinte.

6. CASOS JURÍDICOS

Em vista das considerações já apresentadas, este é o momento pertinente para adentrar nos casos jurídicos práticos no âmbito do direito tributário, de forma a evidenciar que a capacidade contributiva representa um eficiente instrumento para promover a justiça fiscal, traduzindo-se numa das mais significativas expressões do "Estatuto do Contribuinte".

7. IPI E PIS/COFINS – VALORES MÍNIMOS (SETOR DE BEBIDAS)

Antes de adentrarmos ao caso concreto, cabe observar que o Imposto sobre Produtos Industrializados (IPI) é um tributo de competência federal, instituído pela União, incidente sobre produtos industrializados, que tem seu fato gerador e base de cálculo definidos por lei complementar, nos termos dos artigos 146, inciso III, alínea "a", e 153, inciso IV, da Constituição Federal de 1988.

Cumprindo o seu papel, o Código Tributário Nacional, aprovado pela Lei nº 5.172 de 1966, determina seu fato gerador como sendo a saída do produto industrializado do estabelecimento industrial que o manufaturar, ou seja, *aquele que lhe modifique a natureza ou a finalidade, ou o aperfeiçoe para o consumo*, ou do importador que o importar, com base nos artigos 46 e artigo 51.

No tocante a base de cálculo do IPI, o STF (Supremo Tribunal Federal) julgou, em sede de repercussão geral (RE nº 567.935/SC), que ela corresponde ao preço da saída da mercadoria, tal como definida na alínea "a" do inciso II do artigo 47 do Código Tributário Nacional: "Art. 47. A base de cálculo do imposto é: (...) o valor da operação de que decorrer a saída da mercadoria". Contextualizando o conteúdo apresentado, cumpre destacar que o valor da operação indica a capacidade econômica do contribuinte do IPI, aspecto fundamental relacionado à materialidade do imposto. Além disso, com base no artigo 149 da Constituição Federal de 1988, a União Federal pode instituir Contribuições Sociais, incluindo Contribuições de Seguridade Social, desde que observado as seguintes disposições constitucionais: artigo 146, inciso III, artigo 150, incisos I e III e artigo 195, § 6º.

Especificamente em relação às Contribuições de Seguridade Social, a Carta Magna estabeleceu seus possíveis fatos geradores e bases de incidência, incluindo-se entre estas o faturamento ou receita bruta, como se verifica no seu artigo 195, inciso I, alínea "b". Deste modo, o fato gerador e a base de cálculo da Contribuição para o Programa de Integração Social (PIS) e da Contribuição para o Financiamento da Seguridade Social (COFINS) estão limitados à efetiva incorporação de recursos econômicos ou financeiros ao patrimônio da pessoa jurídica, ligados ao exercício da atividade empresarial em caráter definitivo e passível de mensuração.

No contexto da incidência desses tributos (IPI e PIS/COFINS), a Lei nº 13.097 de 2015[18], com vigência a partir de 1º de maio de 2015, dispõe

[18] Em momento anterior à vigência da Lei nº 13.097 de 2015, a legislação federal estipulava outro regime de tributação para as bebidas frias – Regime Especial de Tributação de Bebidas

sobre o atual regime tributário incidente sobre a venda de bebidas frias (água, refrigerantes, refrescos, cervejas, entre outras), com regulamentação específica no Decreto nº 8.442 de 2015. Em síntese, esse regime tributário estabelece que as empresas importadoras, industriais e atacadistas de bebidas ficam submetidas ao IPI, PIS e COFINS sob alíquotas *ad valorem*, fixando valores mínimos para pagamento desses tributos.

No caso do IPI, a legislação estabeleceu alíquotas de 6% ou 4% sobre os produtos sujeitos ao regime, nos termos do seu artigo 15 da Lei nº 13.097 de 2015. Por outro lado, estabeleceu alíquotas gerais de 2,32% e 10,68% para o PIS e a COFINS, nos termos do artigo 25 da Lei nº 13.097 de 2015.[19] No entanto, apesar da legislação prever a tributação com base em alíquotas *ad valorem* sobre as receitas de comercialização das bebidas frias, o artigo 33 estabeleceu valores mínimos para recolhimento desses tributos, em função da classificação fiscal na Tabela de Incidência do Imposto sobre Produtos Industrializados (TIPI), com base no tipo de produto e na capacidade do recipiente, nos termos do Anexo I da Lei nº 13.097 de 2015. Regulamentando essa exigência, o artigo 30 do Decreto nº 8.442 de 2015 assim determina:

> "Art. 30. *Ficam estabelecidos valores mínimos do IPI, da Contribuição para o PIS/Pasep, da Cofins, da Contribuição para o PIS/Pasep-Importação e da Cofins-Importação em função da classificação fiscal na Tipi*, do tipo de produto e da capacidade do recipiente, conforme Anexo I. (...)
>
> § 2º Excetuado o caso previsto no § 1º, *os valores dos tributos de que trata o caput não podem ser inferiores aos valores mínimos de que trata este artigo*, mesmo após a aplicação de qualquer das reduções de alíquotas previstas neste Decreto." (grifamos)

Frias – REFRI (vigente entre janeiro de 2009 até abril de 2015), que antecipava a arrecadação tributária incidente sobre tais produtos, concentrando a tributação do setor nos fabricantes e importadores de bebidas, nos termos do artigo 58-J da Lei nº 10.833 de 2003, o qual foi revogado pela Lei nº 13.097 de 2015.

19 No caso de vendas realizadas para pessoa jurídica varejista ou consumidor final, as alíquotas ficam reduzidas em:
I – 19,82% (dezenove inteiros e oitenta e dois centésimos por cento), no caso da Contribuição para o PIS/Pasep;
II – 20,03% (vinte inteiros e três centésimos por cento), no caso da Cofins.

Em termos práticos significa dizer que, o contribuinte deve, em cada operação de venda efetuar dois cálculos distintos, realizando um comparativo entre (i) o valor resultante da aplicação das alíquotas *ad valorem* sobre a base de cálculo e (ii) o valor da pauta mínima, efetuando o recolhimento dos tributos com base no maior valor, independente do resultado econômico auferido pela pessoa jurídica, afastando de plano o real alcance da capacidade contributiva da pessoa jurídica.

Deste modo, o legislador determinou que o sujeito passivo deve efetuar o pagamento dos valores mínimos independente (i) do valor da operação de que decorrer a saída da mercadoria (IPI) e (ii) da receita auferida na atividade (PIS/COFINS), ignorando a base de cálculo definida para os tributos em questão. Essa exigência viola os direitos e garantias dos contribuintes do setor de bebidas, que compreende inclusive a igualdade e a vedação ao confisco. Neste particular, vale destacar que para fins de verificação da validade da norma, é imprescindível avaliar a justificativa para aplicação do regime diferenciado em situação com aparentes condições de igualdade, sendo vedado se utilizado injustificadamente (RE 640.905/SP), o que é o caso.

Ademais, no caso ora analisado o fator de discriminação (setor de bebidas) não guarda pertinência com a distinção entre o regime atribuído a esse ramo com as demais empresas industriais. Em vista do exposto, conclui-se que o "valor mínimo" estabelecido na legislação aplicável é inconstitucional, subverte a lógica dos tributos, na medida em que não possui qualquer fundamento de validade na Lei Maior, que ocupa o vértice da pirâmide no sistema jurídico.

8. ICMS – SUBSTITUIÇÃO TRIBUTÁRIA – NÃO EFETIVAÇÃO DO FATO PRESUMIDO

Com fundamento na Constituição Federal de 1988, o Imposto sobre Operações relativas à Circulação de Mercadorias e sobre Prestações de Serviços de Transporte Interestadual e Intermunicipal e de Comunicação (ICMS) é um imposto de competência estadual que incide sobre as operações relativas à circulação de mercadorias e sobre prestações de serviços de transporte interestadual e intermunicipal e de comunicação (artigo 155, inciso II). No que diz respeito a possível tributação sob regime de substituição tributária, cabe apontar que a Carta Constitucional atribuiu competência à lei complementar para regular o regime, nos termos dos artigos 146, inciso III, e 155, § 2º, inciso XII, alínea "b".

Ao tratar das normas gerais de direito tributário, o artigo 128 do Código Tributário Nacional estabelece que a responsabilidade tributária pode ser conferida por lei de forma expressa e desde que o substituto tributário tenha relação com o fato gerador. Neste sentido, a Lei Complementar nº 87 de 1996 (conhecida como Lei Kandir) autoriza os Estados e o Distrito Federal a atribuírem à terceira pessoa a responsabilidade de recolher o tributo, tanto em caso de operações antecedentes (substituição tributária "para trás"), como em caso de operações subsequentes (substituição tributária "para frente"), nos termos do artigo 6º.

Isto posto, ao julgar o RE 593.849/MG, com repercussão geral reconhecida, o STF se manifestou no sentido de ser direito de todos os contribuintes a restituição do ICMS pago no regime de substituição tributária nos casos em que a base de cálculo efetiva for inferior à presumida, fixando a seguinte tese: "É devida a restituição da diferença do Imposto sobre Circulação de Mercadorias e Serviços – ICMS pago a mais no regime de substituição tributária para frente se a base de cálculo efetiva da operação for inferior à presumida". Em suma, a tese autoriza os contribuintes examinarem eventual dissonância entre o ICMS cobrado com base no regime de substituição tributária e o negócio efetivamente incorrido (ICMS-ST pra frente), trazendo maior efetividade às relações jurídicas sujeitas a esta metodologia de tributação.

Esse caso também compreende conceitos jurídicos que têm raiz constitucional, uma vez que o STF foi expresso em consignar que o princípio da praticidade tributária não prevalece na hipótese de violação de direitos e garantias dos contribuintes, especialmente os princípios da capacidade contributiva, igualdade e vedação ao confisco. Diante disso, fica evidenciado que a regra estabelecida pela norma inferior não pode transformar uma ficção jurídica em uma presunção absoluta na esfera tributária, onerando o contribuinte de modo alheio à realidade de determinado acontecimento econômico.

CONCLUSÕES

A desigualdade está enraizada em nossa cultura. Partindo do princípio que a nação é de todos, com seus direitos e deveres, o Estado deve garantir aos cidadãos a dignidade humana e as condições para o mínimo existencial. A busca por igualdade social e econômica caminha com a solidariedade. Esta por diversas vezes é aclamada mediante ação específica e de potencial limitado, através de organizações que carecem de auxílio não governamental, tornando sua aplicabilidade deficiente para um contexto contributivo e coletivo.

O conceito de solidariedade deve ser compreendido por meio da consciência individual em prol do coletivo. É necessário praticar a empatia nos mais diversos níveis com o objetivo de auxiliar na justa distribuição de renda, visando a necessidade do outro e colaborando com o incentivo às oportunidades. O Estado tem por obrigação prover direitos iguais aos cidadãos, que compreende condições de saúde, educação, emprego e rendimento, entre outros. Ações que a longo prazo podem contribuir com a saúde dos cofres públicos.

No atual cenário, políticas públicas são decisivas para a transformação e avanço da sociedade. O equilíbrio do sistema através da equidade, proporciona benefícios a todos que dela fazem parte. Enquanto houver concentração de riquezas, não haverá prosperidade social. Ainda que diante da exposição das relações de domínio do poder público sobre a sociedade, é fato que o cidadão não está habituado a perceber e indagar a forma com a qual os recursos provenientes da receita são empregados. É evidente que a falta de entendimento sobre a carga tributária no Brasil afeta consideravelmente a participação ativa do contribuinte em prol de mudanças na forma de arrecadação.

Nesse contexto, sob a ótica do contribuinte, importante registrar que o princípio da capacidade contributiva consiste em um instrumento que visa tributar as riquezas na proporção dos recursos individuais, na medida em que o sujeito deverá suportar o gravame fiscal apenas na sua equivalência, garantindo uma justiça social e fiscal eficiente. Assim, tal princípio tem por desígnio orientar toda a tributação, gerando eficácia no ordenamento jurídico como um todo, seja do ponto de vista do legislador, seja do ponto de vista do aplicador. Diante do estabelecido, é possível afirmar que a igualdade dos indivíduos diante da lei é compreendida de igual modo pela lei tributária.

Esse tema traz à tona uma série de questionamentos, motivo de debates e reflexões entre os estudiosos e juristas, haja vista algumas arbitrariedades presentes no âmbito do direito tributário, inseridas nas normas inferiores sem fundamento de validade na Constituição Federal de 1988, patamar mais elevado da pirâmide do ordenamento jurídico. Evidente que direitos dessa estatura não podem ter seu exercício tolhido pelo Estado através da exigência de tributos sem significação econômica, sobre bases de cálculo fictícias, sendo que a capacidade contributiva não deve ser pensada apenas como horizonte, mas sim como um instrumento que traz efetivação e justiça fiscal, sob pena da tributação não concretizar sua finalidade de atenuar as desigualdades. De tal modo, conclui-se que quando da inobservância do princípio da capacidade contributiva por parte dos entes federados, às leis injustas devem ser objeto de reivindicação pelos contribuintes e tribunais, afastando um possível confisco. Ora, se a segurança jurídica atua como fator de estabilidade social, coerente que deve prevalecer os fundamentos de validade previstos na Lei Maior, com o fito de afastar quaisquer injustiças estabelecidas pelo Estado nas normas inferiores.

REFERÊNCIAS

BOBBIO, Norberto. Teoria da Norma Jurídica; tradução de Fernando Pavan Baptista e Ariani Bueno Sudatti. 2ª ed. Bauru: Edipro, 2003.

BONOMO, Carla. A eficácia da capacidade contributiva e a justiça social. Londrina: Revista do Direito Público, v. 4, n. 2, 2009. Disponível em: <http://www.uel.br/revistas/uel/index.php/direitopub/issue/view/728> Acessado em 04 de ago. de 2020.

CARRAZZA, Roque Antonio. Curso de Direito Constitucional Tributário. 32ª ed. São Paulo: Malheiros, 2017.

COSTA, Regina Helena. Praticabilidade e Justiça Tributária: Exeqüibilidade de Lei Tributária e Direitos do Contribuinte. São Paulo: Malheiros, 2007.

COSTA, Regina Helena. Princípio da Capacidade Contributiva. 4ª ed. São Paulo: Malheiros, 2012.

DESCARTES, René. Discurso do Método; tradução de Jacó Guinsburg e Bento Prado Júnior (Coleção Os Pensadores). 2ª ed. São Paulo: Editora Abril Cultural, 1979.

DOS SANTOS, Rafael Padilha. A Moral e a Justiça no Pensamento de Immanuel Kant. Tese: Mestrado em Filosofia. Universidade Federal de Santa Catarina. Florianópolis: 2011, p. 132. Disponível em: <https://repositorio.ufsc.br/bitstream/handle/123456789/95997/293089.pdf?sequence=1&isAllowed=y> Acessado em 04 de ago. de 2020.

FERRAZ JR., Tércio Sampaio. A Ciência do Direito. 3ª ed. São Paulo: Atlas, 2014.

KELSEN, Hans. Teoria Pura do Direito; tradução de João Baptista Machado. 8ª ed. São Paulo: Editora WMF Martins Fontes, 2020.

MACHADO, Hugo de Brito. Os Princípios Jurídicos da Tributação na Constituição Federal de 1988. 6ª ed. São Paulo: Malheiros, 2019.

PAULSEN, Leandro. Curso de Direito Tributário Completo. 11ª edição. São Paulo: Saraiva, 2020.

Plano Anual da Fiscalização da Receita Federal do Brasil para 2019 e Resultados de 2018. Disponível em: <https://receita.economia.gov.br/dados/resultados/fiscalizacao/arquivos-e-imagens/2019_05_06-plano-anual-de-fiscalizacao-2019.pdf>. Acessado em: 04 de ago. 2020

SERRETTI, André Pedrolli. O fundamento moral da Teoria do Direito em Kant. São Paulo: Revista Âmbito Jurídico n° 74, 2010. Disponível em: <https://ambitojuridico.com.br/edicoes/revista-74/o-fundamento-moral-da-teoria-do-direito-em-kant/> Acessado em 04 de ago. de 2020.

TABOADA, Carlos Palao. Isonomia e capacidade contributiva. RDTributário 4/127.

VITALIS, Aline. Justiça Fiscal, Neutralidade e Compliance. 8ª ed. Rio de Janeiro: Editora Lumen Juris, 2018.

UMA RELEITURA DA TEORIA TRIDIMENSIONAL DO DIREITO DE MIGUEL REALE: O RELATIVISMO DO PROCESSO HISTÓRICO-CULTURAL EM FACE DAS INVARIANTES AXIOLÓGICAS DA PESSOA HUMANA

Claudio De Cicco*

1. A TEORIA TRIDIMENSIONAL DO DIREITO NA HISTÓRIA DO PENSAMENTO JURÍDICO DO SÉCULO XX

A "teoria tridimensional do direito', elaborada pelo Professor Miguel Reale (1910-2006), dada à luz em 1941, surgiu, em grande parte, como resultado de uma reflexão sobre o fenômeno jurídico que data de seus trabalhos juvenis, buscando sempre integrar a realidade fática com a dimensão axiológica e a normativa do direito. Consideramos que foi uma meta alcançada depois de longo percurso, sempre balizada por sua atuação prática como advogado. Se, num segundo momento, foi tida como uma reação contra o normativismo monista de Hans Kelsen (1881-1973), cremos não fosse esta a inicial intenção de Reale, sabendo dos riscos de se raciocinar "a contrario sensu" de alguém. Reale reconhece, em seus escritos, o propósito de Kelsen, – de construir uma "teoria pura do direito", pondo a ciência jurídica a salvo, tanto dos que lhe negavam caráter científico, por falta de base experimental, como o Círculo de Viena, como dos que queriam transformá-la em capítulo da Sociologia ou da Moral.

Mas, é claro que sua própria reflexão autônoma o levou em vários textos, como por exemplo em uma de suas primeiras obras, ***Fundamentos do Direito***,em março de 1940, a considerar a visão kelseniana por demais

* Livre-docente e Doutor em Direito pela USP. Professor da Faculdade de Direito da PUC-SP.

reducionista, (consulte-se o Capítulo IV desse livro, agora em 4ª edição. O direito não poderia ser reduzido ao sistema normativo, como não poderia ser classificado apenas como um fato social entre outros fatos sociais, como pretendia Émile Durkheim, nem reduzido a valores morais, como defendia Giovanni Gentile.

O direito deveria ser estudado em suas três dimensões: a do fato, a do valor e a da norma. Seriam três os polos que dialeticamente se implicariam, num processo histórico-cultural. Apresentou então Miguel Reale uma nova noção de dialética, a dialética de implicação entre fato, valor e norma, diversa da dialética hegeliana ou dialética de oposição. De modo que Reale não nega a importância do normativo, nem do social, nem do axiológico, desde que vistos de modo integrado e dialético. Uma das maiores preocupações de Miguel Reale, ao expor sua teoria tridimensional do direito, foi a de sublinhar seu aspecto histórico-cultural.

Mostrava que as três dimensões do fenômeno jurídico, o fato, o valor e a norma, em contínua dialética de implicação e polaridade, só poderiam ser compreendidas se inseridas num contexto histórico. "Sempre dei razão a Giambattista Vico (1688-1714) quando nos ensina que não se pode conhecer algo na história dos homens ("storia degli uomini") sem conhecer o modo do nascimento ("la guisa del nascimento". É da nomogênese, em suma, que resulta o conceito de norma, não podendo ser posta entre parêntesis a tensão fático-axiológica da qual e na qual ela emerge." (Miguel Reale. ***Teoria Tridimensional do Direito,*** pag. 96, da 5ª edição, de 1994).

Uma visão estática prejudicaria todo o significado da teoria que, abstraindo do contexto histórico, seria uma explicação demasiado mecânica, longe da realidade. Se não houver um cuidado muito grande em acentuar este aspecto importante da tridimensionalidade, os estudiosos do direito poderão ficar com uma noção estática da tríade "fato, valor e norma", como se fosse uma estrutura imutável. A obra do jurista Miguel Reale pode ser melhor entendida dentro desta premissa: as normas jurídicas mudam no tempo e no espaço, pois mudam os valores, mudam os fatos e os três polos mutuamente se implicam: dialética de implicação e polaridade, num processo histórico-cultural. Por tais afirmações, se vê a utilização do método antropológico, denominado do "relativismo cultural", ainda que não explicitado.

2. O MÉTODO DO RELATIVISMO CULTURAL EM OPOSIÇÃO À DECLARAÇÃO UNIVERSAL DOS DIREITOS HUMANOS?

O método do relativismo cultural foi o método elaborado pelo antropólogo Franz Boas (1858-1942), no início do século passado, para evitar que – numa visão colonialista herdada do século anterior – se estabelecesse a civilização ocidental como ponto de referência para estudar as outras culturas do mundo, prejudicando e deformando a objetividade da análise.Era uma novíssima aplicação do princípio "Tudo é relativo", enunciado em meados do século XIX por Auguste Comte e que significava que nenhum fato pode ser estudado sem levar em conta o conjunto de fatos a que ele pertence e com os quais se relaciona. Havia um preconceito a superar: o dogma evolucionista de ver nossa civilização, tecnicamente mais desenvolvida, como a forma mais evoluída do modo humano de ser. Aliás, nisto que Boas chamava de "etnocentrismo", estava exatamente a legitimação do colonialismo sobre povos "primitivos", "inferiores na escala evolutiva".

Foi preciso esperar e ver ao que nos conduziu nosso orgulho civilizatório: duas terríveis conflagrações mundiais em menos de cinquenta anos do século XX; holocausto de milhões de prisioneiros, nos campos de concentração, duas bombas atômicas. Nunca seres humanos se apresentaram tão anti-humanos.Como continuar chamando de "selvagens" quem nunca imaginou sequer a possibilidade de tais chacinas? Os fatos levaram a metodologia de Boas a ser aceita e utilizada, trazendo uma objetividade aos estudos antropológicos, sociológicos e históricos, nunca antes presenciada, sem os velhos preconceitos etnocêntricos.

O culturalismo e o relativismo, a ele inerente, começaram a ganhar adeptos em quase todos os ramos das ciências humanas. A ciência do direito não poderia ficar imune ao novo clima cultural e um dos seus principais defensores do "relativismo cultural" aplicado ao direito foi Gustav Radbruch (a que se refere Reale em ***Fundamentos do Direito***, no capítulo V). Por outro lado, o final dessa guerra levou os vencedores a instituir tribunais para julgar os perdedores como criminosos. É obvio que os réus tentaram se inocentar, valendo-se do argumento de que "seus atos foram praticados segundo leis vigentes em seus países", e "só agora eram considerados como crimes pelos vencedores". Foram condenados por "crimes contra a humanidade". E logo depois se fez a "Declaração Universal dos Direitos Humanos" para que jamais se repetissem os horrores da Segunda Guerra ou se invocasse uma legislação nacional para encobrir ou justificar massacres hediondos. Os direitos humanos existem porque os seres humanos estão dotados de uma natureza comum, apesar das diversidades culturais. Era a mensagem evidente da Declaração de 1948. Depois desta digressão, voltemos à teoria de Miguel Reale.

3. UMA CONTRADIÇÃO INTERNA NA TEORIA TRIDIMENSIONAL DO DIREITO?

Como conciliar uma metodologia histórico-cultural relativista com a noção de direitos universais? Em outras palavras: como conciliar o relativismo do culturalismo com a antiga ideia de direitos naturais, agora restaurada com o nome de direitos humanos? Parece, à primeira vista, impossível tal conciliação. Acresce que Reale cunhou a expressão lapidar: " a pessoa é o valor-fonte de todos os valores".Daí as " constantes ou invariantes axiológicas", os valores permanentes que defendem a dignidade da pessoa humana, limitando o relativismo cultural, na classificação do que é bom e do que é mau, do que é moral e do que é imoral, do que é justo e do que é injusto, como categorias estáveis, acima das diferenças culturais no espaço e no tempo.

Seria, então, uma afirmação de algo de permanente em uma teoria que pressupunha a mutabilidade histórico cultural dos valores?Haveria uma contradição interna? Seria utilizado um artifício para não admitir um relativismo total? Os adeptos da teoria tridimensional do direito, por outro lado, não se contentariam com tão grande contradição interna na teoria. Exigia-se, para tudo esclarecer, uma explicação que compatibilizasse o permanente e o transitório, no pensamento de Miguel Reale.

4. A SOLUÇÃO DO PROBLEMA NA FILOSOFIA DA HISTÓRIA

A teoria tridimensional do direito deveria supor, pois, uma visão histórica, antropológica,mas também uma filosofia da história. Mas, poder-se-ia objetar, não é normal que um jusfilósofo se refira ao fator histórico? Que pensador sério pode prescindir dele? É possível pensar nos problemas sociais, sem olhar para o processo que lhes deu origem? O simples fato de realçar a importância da historicidade faria de Miguel Reale um filósofo da História. Primeiramente, perguntemos: o que é um filósofo da História? Confunde-se ele com um historiador? Evidente que todo historiador, ao selecionar os fatos que para ele são relevantes para reproduzir determinada época, tem sua filosofia da história, implícita no próprio processo seletivo dos fatos considerados históricos.

O historiador marxista destacará os interesses econômicos conflitantes. O historiador católico ressaltará os problemas morais da época estudada e a maior ou menor penetração das máximas evangélicas numa sociedade. A filosofia da história é, por isso mesmo, considerada por Jacques Maritain (1882-1973) como "uma filosofia moral, adequadamente explicitada", considerada de certo modo, cronologicamente. Mas é filosofia moral, não é filosofia da arte nem da economia. Ou seja, não há como esconder o papel educativo da narrativa histórica, a qual, como sentenciava Cícero, é mestra da vida (*storia magister vitae*) e leva a aceitar esta ou aquela visão de mundo.

Neste sentido, nenhum historiador é filosoficamente neutro. No livro de sua juventude, ***Atualidades de um Mundo Antigo***, (1936) nos dizia Reale: "O positivismo construiu uma história simétrica, unilinear e precisa. (...) Essa história sacrificou o homem. Desde que o determinismo penetra na história e expulsa o finalismo, dela sai o homem, porque se lhe rouba a liberdade, a autonomia, o poder de querer e de agir. (...) Com efeito, a contradição só existe onde há liberdade. Se a história fosse obra imediata e exclusiva de Deus, ou se resultasse do determinismo cego da matéria, não haveria contradição. Nas contradições históricas está manifestada a liberdade do homem. Elas se verificam nos claros que Deus deixou à liberdade humana...". Por aí se vê que Reale não seguia a filosofia materialista de cunho determinista.

Com Benedetto Croce (1866-1952), aprendera a ver na história a manifestação do espírito humano como liberdade. Mas além de Croce estava Giambattista Vico. Assim sendo, entenderemos melhor o corte epistemológico que faz Miguel Reale, quando se refere a "invariantes axiológicas", quando classifica a pessoa humana como "valor fonte de todos os demais valores", no desenvolvimento de uma teoria que aceita a mutabilidade dos valores.

5. FUNDAMENTOS HISTÓRICO-FILOSÓFICOS DA DIGNIDADE DA PESSOA HUMANA

O homem para a Filosofia Antiga era um animal político ou social, como o definia Aristóteles, cujo valor maior era ser cidadão de um Estado. Batista Mondin (1926-2015), chegou a afirmar que "na filosofia antiga falta até mesmo o termo para exprimir a pessoa, pois o único termo que se tinha era –em latim – "persona" (a máscara de um personagem de teatro). É verdade que, com o fim da Cidade-Estado, na época helenística (3ºséc.A.C.), a Escola Estóica começou a reconhecer algo de comum entre o romano, o grego ou o persa, a natureza humana, entendendo o mundo como uma unidade, a Cosmópolis, do qual se dizia cidadão o imperador filósofo, Marco-Aurélio. Séculos depois, esta ideia será retomada pelo jusnaturalismo moderno nos séculos dezessete e dezoito.

A quem sustente que a firmação do sofista pré-socrático Protágoras "o homem é a medida de todas as coisas" é uma afirmação da dignidade do homem. Mas, no contexto de Atenas de Sócrates, estaria ele se referindo à relatividade da verdade, da mutabilidade das opiniões, de acordo com a conveniência de cada um e – no fundo – negando a possibilidade objetiva daimportância mesma de cada ser humano.

De modo claro, a ideia de que cada ser humano tem um valor em si mesmo, surgiu historicamente com o Cristianismo, ao proclamar afiliação divina de todos – como lemos em Paulo :" Não há judeu nem grego; não há escravo nem livre; não há homem e mulher, porque todos sois um só em Cristo Jesus" (Gálatas 3, 27-28). Historicamente, porém, em todo o final de Antiguidade e durante a Idade Média não se desenvolve a ideia de tal dignidade, a não ser de modo implícito como "filho de Deus", na "família humana". O conceito de dignidade da pessoa, tal como o temos explicitado hoje, é uma conquista cultural do pensamento ocidental que se desenvolveu a partir do Humanismo, no século XV.

Não é um dado da natureza, e sim uma construção da cultura ocidental cristã. Mais precisamente, foi o filósofo italiano, Giovanni Pico della Mirandola(1463-1494),que no discurso "De Dignitate Hominis" (Sobre a Dignidade do Homem), de 1480,justifica a importância da busca humana pelo conhecimento, numa perspectiva neoplatônica. Ele afirma que "Deus, tendo criado todas as criaturas, foi tomado pelo desejo de gerar uma outra criatura, um ser consciente que pudesse apreciar a criação, mas não havia nenhum lugar disponível na cadeia dos seres terrestres, desde os vermes até primatas. Então Deus criou o homem, que ao contrário dos outros seres,era capaz de aprender sobre si mesmo e sobre a natureza, além de poder emular qualquer outra criatura existente." Desta forma, segundo Pico, quando o homem filosofa, ele ascende a uma condição angélica e comunga com a Divindade, entretanto, quando ele falha em utilizar o seu intelecto, pode descer à categoria dos seres mais baixos, na escala da Criação."

A ideia de que o homem pode ascender na cadeia dos seres pelo exercício de suas capacidades intelectuais foi a garantia de dignidade da existência humana na vida terrestre. A raiz da dignidade reside na sua afirmação que somente os seres humanos podem mudar a si mesmos pelo seu livre-arbítrio. Ele observou na história humana que filosofias e instituições estão sempre evoluindo, fazendo da capacidade de auto-transformação do homem a única constante. Em conjunto com sua noção de que toda a criação constitui um reflexo simbólico da divindade, a filosofia de Pico della Mirandola teve uma profunda influência no pensamento europeu.

No século XVII se inicia a grande marcha rumo ao reconhecimento dos direitos inerentes à natureza humana,que culmina na Declaração de Direitos de 1688, visivelmente inspirada na concepção política antiabsolutista do filósofo John Locke (1632-1704). A proclamação do valor distinto da pessoa humana terá como consequência lógica a afirmação de direitos específicos de cada homem, o reconhecimento de que, na vida social, ele, homem, não se confunde com a vida do Estado, além de provocar um "deslocamento do direito do plano do Estado para o plano do indivíduo, em busca do necessário equilíbrio entre a liberdade e a autoridade".

Para Immanuel Kant (1724-1804), na sua investigação crítica sobre a teoria do conhecimento, o sujeito torna-se o centro de que parte o conhecimento. Deu-se então que ele mesmo denomina a "revolução copernicana" na Gnosiologia. Ou seja, em vez de o sujeito cognoscente girar em torno dos objetos, são estes que giram em seu redor.Não mais nossa inteligência deve amoldar-se aos objetos, como na visão ontológica clássica – que na verdade nunca deu muita atenção ao sujeito cognoscente -, mas estes devem ajustar-se ao nosso pensamento. Analogamente, na ordem ética, "o ser humano põe-se como personalidade, sujeito a uma ordem que não é a ordem das coisas. Como pessoa passa a representar um valor radical, unidade instituidora de um processo no qual e pelo qual as coisas possuem validade". (***Teoria Tridimensional do Direito,*** pag. 133). Em outras palavras, o ser humano, dotado de uma dignidade especial, nunca pode ser meio para os outros, mas sempre fim em si mesmo. Ou seja, o homem é um fim em si mesmo e, por isso, tem valor absoluto, não podendo, por conseguinte, ser usado como instrumento para algo, e, justamente por isso, tem dignidade, é pessoa. A título de exemplo, citemos nosso texto constitucional que coloca a dignidade da pessoa humana como princípio fundamental da República Federativa do Brasil. Isto significa que o Estado existe, em nosso país, em função das pessoas e não estas em função do Estado.O Estado é instrumento para a realização da dignidade de todos os membros de sua população, para que todos possam ser dignos de respeito.

6. AS DIVERSAS CONCEPÇÕES DA DIGNIDADE DA PESSOA HUMANA: INDIVIDUALISMO, TRANSPERSONALISMO E PERSONALISMO

Utilizando-nos da terminologia empregada por Miguel Reale, na densa obra ***Filosofia do Direito,*** (pag. 277 a 279, da edição de 1990) constatamos, historicamente, a existência de, basicamente, três concepções da dignidade da pessoa humana: individualismo, transpersonalismo e personalismo. "No âmago do pensamento do individualismo existe a tese essencial de que cada homem, cuidando dos seus interesses, protege e realiza, "Ipso facto", o interesse coletivo.Daí que a função do Estado se esgotaria na tutela jurídica das liberdades individuais. "(pag. 277)

Podemos dizer que tal conceito da dignidade do indivíduo corresponde a um modo de se compreender os direitos fundamentais do homem como se este vivesse isolado. "Ao se interpretarem os códigos, cuidar-se-á sempre de preservar o indivíduo contra as interferências do poder público." (pag.278). Ao lado desta posição há os que contestam a possibilidade de uma harmonia entre o bem do indivíduo e o bem do todo. Só adquire autenticidade e plenitude a existência humana quando a serviço do bem social. É o transpersonalismo." (pag.277). Nega-se, portanto, segundo esta doutrina, a pessoa humana como valor supremo. Enfim, a dignidade da pessoa humana realiza-se tão somente no bem comum da nação. Radicalizações desta corrente são as concepções nacionalista ou socialista, das quais a mais representativa é, em nossos dias, a visão marxista.

Sua consequência lógica será uma tendência na interpretação do direito que limita a liberdade das pessoas individuais em favor do Estado, pretenso realizador da igualdade. O que se observou na realidade histórica ou "socialismo real" foi o aparecimento de regimes oligárquicos, de partido único, mantenedores de desigualdades abissais entre a massa da população e a elite dos privilegiados membros do partido, chegando ao requinte, como em Cuba e na Coréia do Norte de se estabelecerem dinastias de governantes de uma mesma família, que se sucedem, como nas velhas monarquias absolutas. A terceira corrente, que ora se denomina personalismo, rejeita quer a concepção individualista, quer a coletivista; busca ela, principalmente, a compatibilização, a inter-relação entre os valores individuais e valores coletivos.

Em consequência, não há que se falar no predomínio do indivíduo ou no predomínio do todo. A solução há de ser buscada num princípio, o princípio de subsidiariedade: o da ação subsidiária do grupo social maior para determinada tarefa que o grupo menor não possa realizar por si mesmo. Não há absorção de todos os grupos e pessoas num magma coletivo impessoal. Também não se retorna a uma concepção do indivíduo como ser isolado, "Robinson Crusoé' solitário em sua ilha. Pelo contrário, o ser humano vive e se realiza como pessoa em grupos sociais diversos: nasce em uma família, estuda em uma escola, trabalha em uma empresa, ora em uma igreja, diverte-se em um clube, trata-se em um hospital, mora em um bairro, em um município, em uma região, em uma nação. Cabe ao Estado contribuir eficazmente para que em todos esses grupos ele atinja o fim almejado, com paz e segurança, interferindo diretamente sempre que tais fins sejam frustrados, quer para auxiliar, quer para reprimir os comportamentos indesejados, na forma da lei. Neste sentido, defende-se que a pessoa humana, enquanto tal, é um absoluto.

7. A DIGNIDADE DA PESSOA HUMANA, UMA PREOCUPAÇÃO SEMPRE PRESENTE NO PENSAMENTO DE MIGUEL REALE

A importância desse valor fundamental da pessoa humana sempre esteve presente na longa trajetória intelectual de Miguel Reale. Lemos, por exemplo, em sua obra escrita com apenas 24 anos de idade, em 1934, ***"O Estado Moderno"***, republicado na coleção em 3 volumes de sua "Obra Política-1ª Fase"- com comentários do autor, pela Editora da Universidade de Brasília, em 1983: "O Estado aristotélico é uma unidade, mas não abstrata e vazia; é um organismo no qual os homens realizam valores particulares e coletivos. (...) Uma das características da unidade orgânica é precisamente esta de integrar discriminado. O todo não deve absorver as partes – como no totalitarismo, mas integrar os valores comuns respeitando os valores específicos e exclusivos (integralismo)".(cfr. pag.129,132 da edição da UNB, vol.II)

Mais incisivo ainda foi seu artigo "Nacionalismo e Democracia",publicado às vésperas do golpe doEstado Novo, na revista, que ele mesmo dirigia, ***"Panorama"*** n ° 14, de outubro de 1937: "A Democracia sempre foi nosso ideal e foi por amor á Democracia que repudiamos o Liberalismo e o Socialismo que dela tem se servido como mero instrumento, ora para a prepotência das minorias plutocráticas, ora para a exploração demagógica dos sofrimentos populares."(pag.1e segs.) E ainda : "Nacionalismo quer dizer

Democracia Integral, baseada na consideração do homem político, moral e econômico". (...) "quer realizar uma Democracia de fins e não de meios. Quer salvar a dignidade do homem do torvo materialismo dos capitalistas e dos comunistas."Ainda que Miguel Realenão fosse tomista, sua retidão intelectual faz suas ideias serem análogas ao que ensinava a Doutrina Social da Igreja, pelo papa Pio XI (1857-1939) na encíclica "***Quadragesimo Anno***" , de 1931,comemorativa da célebre "***Rerum Novarum***"de Leão XIII, que incentivara a criação de associações operárias, em 1891: "Recentemente iniciou-se, como todos sabem, uma nova organização sindical e corporativa, à qual, vista a matéria desta Nossa carta encíclica não podemos deixar de Nos referir, com alguma consideração oportuna. O Estado reconheceu juridicamente o sindicato. (...) As corporações são constituídas pelos representantes dos sindicatos dos operários e dos patrões pertencentes à mesma arte e profissão, e, como verdadeiros e próprios órgãos e instituições do Estado, dirigem e coordenam os sindicatos nas coisas de interesse comum. (...) Basta refletir um pouco, para ver as vantagens desta organização, embora apenas sumariamente indicada: a pacífica colaboração das classes, a repressão das organizações e violências socialistas, a ação moderadora de uma magistratura especial. " (cfr. ***Documentos da Igreja***, Pio XI, Editora Paulus, 2004, pag.310,311.). Porém, o século XX, que segundo Michail Manoilesco (1891-1950), deveria ser o "século do corporativismo" teria seu rumo distorcido pelo nazismo, pelo comunismo e pelo americanismo,que lutavam pela expansão de seusimpérios e isto levaria aos pactos, às traições e às simplificações que comprometeram e enodoaram para sempre as ideias de nação e corporação, tudo encaminhando para o odioso racismo, que só poderia levar ao medonhoconfronto da Segunda Guerra, em que a pessoa humana foi aviltada como nunca anteriormenteo fora.

Mas, já em 1940, Reale dava à luz sua ***"Teoria do Direito e do Estado",*** onde lecionava: "A concepção do Estado por nós exposta concilia as exigências da autoridadee da liberdade, tanto no plano interno, como no plano internacional.Internamente, o Estado, como pessoa jurídica destinada a realizar o bem comum, ou seja, a realizar o conjunto das condições sociais de uma vida plenamentehumana, não pode deixar de ver em cada indivíduo uma pessoadotada de liberdade, pois personalidade e liberdade constituem a condição essencial sem a qual nenhum bem pode ser alcançado em sua plenitude.O Estado que fere a liberdade da pessoa atinge a sua própria essência. No plano do Direito não se concebe soberania com exclusão da liberdade.Quando se nega a personalidade jurídica dos sujeitos, temos uma situação que, no grau atual de evolução cultural, não pode deixar de ser consideradasimples situação de fato." (pag.326).

8. A FILOSOFIA DA HISTÓRIA DE GIAMBATTISTA VICO, INTERPRETADA E ATUALIZADA POR MIGUEL REALE

Então temos que ir à compreensão neoplatônica da história adotada pelo filósofo napolitano do século XVIII, Gianbattista Vico (1668-1744), ao apresentar a história como ciência nova, que estuda os ciclos de "corsi e ricorsi" em diferentes fases (mítica, heroica e racional) da variável civilização humana "in concreto", como representação de uma imutável história ideal eterna, na mente divina. É possível encontrar mais de um laço entre Miguel Reale e o neoplatonismo de Vico: as constantes axiológicas seriam próprias à dignidade da pessoa humana, tal como a quer Deus. O mutável no acontecer histórico-dialético dos fatos e valores, levando a diferentes construções jurídicas, se deveria à liberdade humana.

Isto aproxima o cogitar realeanoda reflexão de um autor infelizmente pouco conhecido entre nós: Gioele Solari (1872-1952). Solari foi aluno do grande Giuseppe Carle *1845-1917), o promotor do retorno a Vico no final do século XIX, com sua densa obra ***"La Vita del Diritto"***(1890). Carle e depois Solari manifestavam pouca ou nenhuma simpatia por um jusnaturalismo abstrato à maneira dos séculos XVII-XVIII e sincera atração por tudo o que falasse de concreção e historicidade. É o denominador comum entre a obra citada do mestre Carle e as obras clássicas de Gioele Solari, publicadas entre 1930 e 1949: ***"Individualismo e Diritto Privato", "Storicismo e Diritto Privato", "Studi Storici di Filosofia Del Diritto".***

Em Gioele Solari o ideal do justo como algo arquetípico se realiza no campo social através da história, tal como o jurídico na solução do caso concreto. A isso ele denominava "idealismo social e jurídico". Seria um tridimensionalismo com uma dialética de implicação e ***verticalidade***, apontando para o valor do justo como ideal sempre perseguido pelos juristas. Miguel Reale também, partindo de Giuseppe Carle, entre outras leituras de sua vasta erudição, em que é notável a marca do pensamento italiano, chega até o tridimensionalismo, teoria jurídica que lhe granjeou merecida fama. Esta importância da base histórica da reflexão jurídica que depois na história mesma se concretiza, parece-nos uma constante no seu pensamento.

Trabalhando de forma independente, e a partir também da ideias de Giorgio Del Vecchio (1878-1970) – que distingue o conceito puro de direito da sua concreção no direito positivo -nos parece que Reale, ao admitir as constantes axiológicas da pessoa humana, dentro do processo histórico--cultural, escapa de um relativismo total e retoma o conceito vichianode uma história ideal eterna que se realiza nas mutações e relatividades dos "corsi e ricorsi"da história humana. Atenua então a polaridade igualitária entre fato, valor e norma para, no conceito de "constantes axiológicas", verticalizar nos valores fundantes da dignidade humana. Miguel Reale não faz alarde dessa filosofia da história. Ela passa desapercebida na dinâmica da implicação dialética de fato-valor-norma.

Refere-se a ela, no entanto em mais de um momento de sua clássica ***Filosofia do Direito.*** Partindo da definição de jurisprudência do célebre jurisconsulto Ulpiano (A jurisprudência é o conhecimento das coisas divinas e humanas, a ciência do justo e do injusto – ***Digesto***, I,1,10), nosso Autor sentencia:"a jurisprudência é o conhecimento das coisas humanas com base no conhecimento das coisas divinas. A definição de Ulpiano resulta desdobrada em dois planos: na primeira parte não seria uma definição da ciência do direito, mas sim de seus pressupostos mais altos; na segunda parte, delimitaria, como consequência a aplicação dos critérios transcendentes do justo ao campo variável e concreto do lícito."(pag.632-633). É esta a filosofia da história que nos faz passar de Clio a Themis, da história para o direito. Explica-nos Reale, no prefácio de 1956 ao livro, aliás de título muito sugestivo ***Horizontes do Direito e da História***: "É mister que o ideal de justiça seja devolvido à consciência atuante do homem. (...) é possível que a meditação da história nos torne mais conscientes das razões concretas da atividade jurídica, de maneira que as necessárias estruturas e processos formais não se convertam em rígidos entraves à atualização espontânea dos fins que compõem a constante ética do Direito".

E se reuniu vários artigos de cunho histórico, unindo apreciações sobre a filosofia grega e romana, sobre o Cristianismo e o Renascimento, sobre a descoberta do mundo da cultura por Vico, a ensaios sobre as teorias de Rousseau, Kant e Hegel,nessa obra ***Horizontes do Direito e da História***, isto se deu porque se manteve fiel à mesma filosofia da história: "As nações são formações históricas. Sem compreensão da história não pode haver verdadeiro estudioso da política. Em verdade, a política é uma ciência experimental que encontra na história o seu laboratório de experiência. Somente a história assegura ao político a capacidade de ***distinguir o que é universal do que é particular, específico e transitório nas instituições e nas leis***; somente a história nos previne contra o engano das palavras que permanecem as mesmas enquanto que os seus significados se sucedem, às vezes da maneira mais contraditória e paradoxal; somente a história nos ensina a não julgar os fatos pela moldura das formas de governo, mas pelo que nelas se contenha de real e de vivo. (...)".

Para nos certificarmos de que não laboramos em erro quando tanto aproximamos Reale de Vico bastaria ler o ensaio acima citado na obra ***Horizontes*** com o título "Giambattista Vico, a Jurisprudência e a descoberta do mundo da cultura"(pags.113 a 127, da edição de 2002). Com efeito, ali podemos ler: "A preferência de Vico pelo platonismo é mais um elo que o prende aos grandes pensadores italianos do Renascimento." (Pag.120, nota 12) E, mais adiante: "Pode-se dizer que é na filosofia de Vico que o conceito de Humanidade (humanitas) atinge sua plena concreção como uma força una e diretora da história, como força a que tão somente a Providência transcende. Destarte, o progresso do direito se insere na história ideal do gênero humano." (pag. 124).

"Essa ideia de que no direito se casam um elemento universal e eterno e elementos variáveis e contingentes encontrará na ***"Scienza Nuova" (Ciência Nova , a História***) outros fundamentos gnosiológicos decorrentes da extensão de seu novo critério de verdade ao mundo dos fatos históricos. É, em suma, através de estudos jurídicos que Vico se orienta no sentido da especificidade do mundo da cultura. Ao se propor a estudar uma nova ciência, Vico desde logo observa que tal ciência se adquire com base na ideia de "direito das gentes' que tiveram os jurisconsultos romanos. (***Scienza Nuova***, livro I, cap. IV). Se, por conseguinte, Vico se contrapõe ao direito natural abstrato de Grócio e Pufendorf, aproxima-se cada vez mais às estruturas que os romanos haviam construído, todo feito de experiência". (pag.118-120). "Condenando o abstracionismo jusnaturalista da sua época, Vico refugiava-se na experiência histórica do direito romano, na qual via se desenvolver gradativamente um "direito natural concreto" que não se esgotava nos fatos e que, sob a insondável direção da Providência Divina, conduzia a espécie humana rumo à realização de uma república ideal e justa, posta como valor a traduzir-se no tempo, valor ideal só apreensível nos quadros da filosofia platônica." (pag. 120)

Fica, para nós, bastante clara a fonte última de que brotou a noção realeana das invariantes ou constantes axiológicas. Por outro lado, em Vico encontramos também a constatação da mutabilidade dos valores e das normas em função de fatos, que se alteram continuamente, na ideia de que "o mundo histórico é indubiamente cognoscível pelo homem , porque é por ele mesmo gerado. " (pag. 122). "Torna-se assim possível o conceito de um "direito universal", feitura da mente humana, traduzindo-se em experiências jurídicas particulares, cujo estudo servirá para compreender as demais experiências que compõem o todo do mundo da cultura." (pag.122).

9. *"CORSI E RICORSI"*

Sabemos que para o filósofo napolitano as nações cumprem um percurso passando de uma fase **mítica**, em que tudo se explica pela ação divina imediata sobre o mundo humano, para uma fase **heroica**, em que surgem os grandes vultos da humanidade, fundando impérios e codificando ordenamentos jurídicos por sua própria inteligência e vontade, para finalmente chegar a uma fase propriamente **humana**, em que todos participam enquanto humanos da elaboração das leis. São as fases mítica ou teocrática; heroica ou aristocrática e por fim a fase simplesmente humana ou democrática.

Se tal democracia degenerar em anarquia, os governos em demagogia, a Providência, para salvar aquela nação, fa-la-á voltar à fase primitiva mítica, o que Vico chamava de "barbárie ritrovata". (barbárie reencontrada). De modo que não se pode desprezar uma cultura que tem menos tecnologia do que nós, pois ela pode já ter sido muito avançada há séculos, do que restam sinais perceptíveis para o bom arqueólogo.

Assim um naturalista alemão, Carlos Frederico Von Martius (1794-1868), no Brasildo primeiro reinado, além de ter estudado nossa fauna e nossa riquíssima flora, conviveu com os indígenas e tirou uma conclusão curiosa: "Ainda não há muito tempo era opinião geralmente adotada que os indígenas da América foram homens diretamente emanados da mão do Criador. (...) Enfeitados com as cores de uma filantropia e filosofia enganadora, consideravam este estado como primitivo do homem: procuravam explicá-lo, e dele derivavam os mais singulares princípios para o Direito Público, a Religião e a História. Investigações mais aprofundadas, porém, provaram ao homem desprevenido que aqui não se trata do estado primitivo do homem, e que pelo contrário o triste e desagradávelaspecto que nos oferece o atual indígena brasileiro, não é senão o resíduo de uma muito antiga, posto que perdida civilização."(Cfr. ***O Estado de Direito entre os autóctones do Brasil.*** Publicado pela EDUSP e Itatiaia, em 1982).

10. CONVIVÊNCIA DE DIFERENTES CULTURAS, EM DIFERENTES FASES

De modo que podem conviver em uma mesma época e em um mesmo país, culturas e comunidades humans em diferentes fases históricas – mítica, heróica, humana, para conservar a terminologia de Vico – com valoresrespectivos de uma mentalidade religiosa, aristocrática, democrática, devendo todas mutuamente se respeitar e encorajar para alcançar a plenitude da humanidade, alcançada, para Vico como para Platão na "República ideal" eterna, da tríplice função: dos orantes, dos beligerantes, dos operantes, com suas respectivas virtudes da sabedoria, da coragem e da temperança.

A justiça seria a conjugação das vitudes na felicidade comum dos cidadãos, cada qual se consagrando com satisfação à sua parte na construção do bem comum, para o qual todos as tarefas são importantes e insubstituíveis. É um modo de conceber o "relativismo cultural" de Franz Boas a partir de uma matriz –no fundo hesiódica – da história como cíclos=corsi e ricorsi- em que a uma fase decadente se seguiria uma nova idade de ouro-tal como ficou imortalizada no clássico poema "***Os Trabalhos e os Dias***" de Hesíodo (pag.91 a 95 da edição francesa de 1995).

Também é verdade que, infelizmente,em nome do relativismo cultural de Franz Boas, não poucos antropólogoschegam a manifestar verdadeira execração pela cultura ocidental, em que só sabem ver mazelas, com uma romântica glorificação de outras culturas – tidas comoúnicas "boas e humanas", caindo num etnocentrismo de sentido contrário, como a do "bom selvagem" de Rousseau (1712-1778). Já a concepção não linear da história, tal como a de Vico, tem o mérito de reconhecer a diversidade cultural, sem correr o risco de quebrar a unidade do gênero humano, quebra que representa pavoroso retrocesso, depois da Declaração Universal dos Direitos Humanos de 1948.Aliás, o título de uma obra de Reale por nós citada, tem uma certa consonância com tal filosofia vichiana: ***Atualidades de um mundo antigo.***

Vemos então a possível conciliação do mundo ideal, arquetípico, com o mundo real da história humana, bem ao modo de Vico: mundos pensados como distintos, mas nunca opostos, pois em contínua interação, como a dizer: ***conhecemos o ideal quando se projeta no real e o real quando se eleva ao ideal.*** Em consequência, conhecemos o direito justo quando elaboramos a norma que o faz se tornar realidade concreta na vida social. ***Sabemos que uma norma positivada é justa quando percebemos que ela nos conduz a um princípio superior de equidade.*** É claro que a vasta obra de Miguel Reale não se resume ao tema que aqui abordamos. Mas consideramos que se fazia necessária uma releitura de certos pontos da "teoria tridimensional do direito" e da afirmação das "invariantes axiológicas da pessoa humana ", para esclarecer e harmonizar conceitos apenas aparentemente conflitantes. Se o conseguimos ou não, caberá, ao amável leitor deste artigo, tirar a sua conclusão.

REFERÊNCIAS

BIDNEY, David. *Theoretical Anthropology*. Nova York, Schocken Books, 1970, 2ª edição.

BOAS,Franz. *Antropologia Cultural*. Trad.Celso Castro. Rio de Janeiro, Ed. Zahar, 2010,6ª edição.

CARLE, Giuseppe. *La Vita del Diritto*. Turim, Editora Fratelli Bocca, 1890.

CHAIX-RUY, Jules. *La Formation de la Pensée Philosophique de G.B.Vico*. Nova York. Arno Press, 1979.

CROCE, Benedetto. *La Filosofia di Giambattista Vico*. Roma. Ed. Laterza, 1980.

HESÍODO.*Les Travaux et les Jours*. Tradução de Claude Terreaux. Paris, Editora Arléa,1995.

PLATÃO. *Timée*. Tradução de Luc Brisson. Paris, Editora Flammarion, 1992.

REALE, Miguel. *Fundamentos do Direito*. Ribeirão Preto, Editora Migalhas, 2014,4ª edição.

____. *Horizontes do Direito e da História*.São Paulo, Editora Saraiva,1999,3ª ed. 2002, 2ª tiragem.

____. *Personalismo e Historicismo Axiológico* in *Teoria Tridimensional do Direito* (suplemento II).São Paulo, Ed.Saraiva,1994, 5ªed.

____. *Filosofia do Direito*. São Paulo, Editora Saraiva, 2002, 20ª edição.

____. *Atualidades de um Mundo Antigo*. São Paulo, Editora José Olympio, 1936.

____. *O Estado Moderno*. São Paulo, Editora José Olympio, 1935, 3ª edição.

SOLARI, Gioele. *Studi Storici di Filosofia del Diritto*. Turim, Editora Giappichelli,1949.

VICO, Giambattista . *A Ciência Nova*.Tradução de Marco Lucchesi. Rio de Janeiro, Editora Record, 1999.

____. *Princípios de uma Ciência Nova*.Tradução de Antonio Lázaro de Almeida Prado. São Paulo, Editora Abril. Col. "Os Pensadores", vol XX, 1974.

VON MARTIUS, Carlos Frederico. *O Direito entre os Autóctones do Brasil*. São Paulo,EDUSP e Ed. Itatiaia, 1982.

FUNÇÃO SOCIAL DA PROPRIEDADE PRIVADA

DINORÁ ADELAIDE MUSETTI GROTTI*

1. CONSIDERAÇÕES GERAIS

1.1. EVOLUÇÃO

O tema do direito de propriedade e as questões que o permeiam são antigos, polêmicos e objeto de acirradas disputas. Seu conceito e extensão variaram de tamanho, de forma ou de padrão no decorrer da história, mas sempre apresentando relevância em todos os sistemas políticos das sociedades organizadas.[1] A propriedade evoluiu do sentido individual para o

* Doutora e Mestre em Direito pela PUC-SP. Professora da Faculdade de Direito da PUC-SP.

[1] O Código de Hamurabi, como lembra Adilson Abreu Dallari, previa, por exemplo, que o proprietário perderia o direito sobre a sua propriedade caso ela não fosse cultivada dentro de determinado limite de tempo. Verifica-se, portanto, que o interesse social, representado pela manutenção de condições de subsistência do povo, se sobrepunha ao interesse particular na manutenção da terra (*Desapropriação para fins urbanísticos*. São Paulo: Forense, 1981, p. 28). No Império Romano o direito de propriedade era, em princípio, individual e absoluto, mormente porque as propriedades eram locais de prática de culto religioso dos familiares e, portanto, pertencente, única e exclusivamente, àquela família. Com a queda do Império Romano do Oriente e o advento da Idade Média, o direito de propriedade passou a ser regulado, em cada propriedade, pelo respectivo senhor feudal, representando, por isto mesmo, um poder ilimitado e soberano ao seu proprietário. Com o advento da Revolução Francesa e seu ideário de igualdade, garantidor da liberdade individual em face dos arbítrios da nobreza e do clero, o tratamento jurídico dado à propriedade foi exacerbadamente individualista. Neste momento histórico o direito de propriedade apresentava como principais características o caráter absoluto, exclusivo e perpétuo. O individualismo pregado e perpetrado pelos ideais iluministas encontrou, na República de Weimar (1.919), o primeiro grande movimento de reação no continente europeu sendo o marco inicial do novo perfil do direito de propriedade,

social,[2] deixando de ser o mais amplo direito real, o qual engloba o direito de usar, gozar e dispor da coisa, de forma absoluta, exclusiva e perpétua, bem como o de reivindicá-la de quem quer que injustamente a detenha. A concepção individualista de propriedade, dominante no período feudal e revivida após a Revolução francesa, passou a sofrer, a partir de meados do século XIX, progressivas injunções públicas, as quais afastaram seu caráter absoluto e acabaram por lhe atribuir funcionalização social, percebida, especialmente, nas áreas do direito urbanístico e agrário. [3]

1.2. DISTINÇÃO ENTRE PROPRIEDADE PÚBLICA E PRIVADA

Embora apresentem pontos comuns, a propriedade pública e a privada são distintas.[4]

qual seja, sua finalidade (ou função) social. Verifiquem-se, a propósito, os artigos 153 e 155 da Carta Magna daquela República, que previam, respectivamente, *"A propriedade obriga. Seu exercício deve ser ao mesmo tempo um serviço prestado ao bem comum"* e, no que se refere à propriedade rural, *"o possuidor da terra está obrigado, frente à comunidade, a trabalhar e explorar o solo"*. Assim, as Constituições subseqüentes passaram a reconhecer os direitos sociais delimitadores do âmbito de abrangência dos direitos individuais. A propriedade acaba por perder seu caráter absoluto, assumindo uma nova estrutura, por força da função social que lhe é atribuída.

[2] A origem mais próxima do princípio da função social da propriedade é a doutrina social da Igreja Católica Apostólica Romana, tal como tratada nas Encíclicas *Mater et Magistra* do Papa João XXIII, de 1961, e *Centesimus Cennus, de 1991,* de João Paulo II, nas quais se vincula a propriedade à concretização do bem comum , ou seja, "à função de servir de instrumento para a criação de bens necessários à subsistência de toda a humanidade"(Di Pietro, Maria Sylvia Zanella. *Direito administrativo,* 33. ed. Rio de Janeiro: Forense, 2020, p.169).

[3] Medauar, Odete. *Direito administrativo moderno.*21. ed. rev., atual. e ampl. Belo Horizonte: Fórum,2018. p. 343.

[4] A distinção entre propriedade pública e propriedade privada está calcada na diferença dos regimes jurídicos que disciplinam uma ou outra propriedade e não no ramo do direito a que pertençam, pois, quanto ao ramo, a doutrina diverge a respeito do ramo a que pertence o direito de propriedade. A maioria o encarta no Direito Privado, enquanto uma minoria de autores, entre eles, Oswaldo Aranha Bandeira de Mello e Celso Antônio Bandeira de Mello, o encartam no Direito Público. De acordo com Celso Antônio Banmdeira de Mello, "o direito de propriedade – ou seja, o reconhecimento que a organização jurídica da Sociedade (Estado) dispensa aos poderes de alguém sobre coisas – encarta-se, ao nosso ver, no Direito Público e não no Direito Privado. É evidente que tal Direito comporta relações tanto de Direito Público quanto de Direito Privado. Entretanto, o direito de propriedade, como aliás sempre sustentou o prof. Oswaldo Aranha Bandeira de Mello é, essencialmente, um direito configurado no Direito Público e – desde logo – no Direito Constitucional". [...]

"Com efeito, basta ver que, dependendo do tratamento que for dispensado ao direito de propriedade, um Estado será socialista ou capitalista, com todas as implicações jurídicas

Sílvio Luís Ferreira da Rocha aponta, como primeiro traço distintivo, o conteúdo excludente da propriedade privada em contraposição ao conteúdo includente da propriedade pública. Ou seja, a característica da primeira é a possibilidade de o titular do direito de propriedade excluir qualquer outra pessoa da posição de desfrutar do bem, salvo se autorizada por ele. Daí destacar-se ter o direito de propriedade eficácia *erga omnes*, obstando terceiros de desfrutar do bem ou de promover sua exploração econômica, salvo se autorizado pelo seu titular.[5]

De acordo com a doutrina tradicional, o direito de propriedade consubstancia três caracteres: é absoluto, exclusivo e perpétuo. "É direito absoluto porque assegura ao proprietário a liberdade de dispor das coisas, legitimamente adquiridas, do modo que lhe aprouver. É direito exclusivo porque respeita ao proprietário e a ninguém mais; quer dizer: é imputado ao proprietário; só a ele, em princípio, cabe. É direito perpétuo porque não desaparece com o fim da vida do proprietário, porquanto passa a um sucessor, significando, pois, que tem duração ilimitada (CC, art.1.231), nem se perde pelo não uso".[6]

Estas características do direito de propriedade privado, em certo sentido também acolhidas nos arts. 1.228, 1.229 e 1.231 do Código Civil,[7] opõem-se ao conteúdo inclusivo da propriedade pública, tornando o bem compartilhado ou compartilhável. O segundo traço de distinção diz respeito à alienação dos bens públicos e privados. O bem, objeto do direito de propriedade privado, não só está sujeito à imposição de ônus, mas também pode ser livremente alienado, a título oneroso ou gratuito, por seu titular.

daí decorrentes. Trata-se, portanto, de um direito nodular à caracterização político-social do Estado e, por isso, de todo o quadro jurídico da sociedade; logo um Direito Público, por excelência". (Novos aspectos da função social da propriedade no direito público. *Revista de Direito Público*, São Paulo, v. 20, n. 84, p. 39-45, out./dez. 1987. p. 39).
"De resto, ao falar-se em função social da propriedade está-se, *ipso facto*, fazendo referência à caracterização que o Direito Público lhe irroga. É o Direito Constitucional quem outorga esta fisionomia à propriedade". (ROCHA, Sílvio Luís Ferreira da. *Função social da propriedade pública*. São Paulo: Malheiros, 2005. p. 67-68).

[5] ROCHA, Sílvio Luís Ferreira da. *Função social da propriedade pública*. São Paulo: Malheiros, 2005. p. 68.

[6] SILVA, José Afonso da. *Direito urbanístico brasileiro*, 5.ed., rev. e atual. São Paulo: Malheiros, 2008. p. 399.

[7] SILVA, José Afonso da. *Direito urbanístico brasileiro*, 5.ed., rev. e atual. São Paulo: Malheiros, 2008p. 399.

O bem público, por sua vez, tem sua disponibilidade vinculada a uma finalidade pública, à existência de interesse público, devidamente justificado, tal como exige o art. 17 da Lei nº 8.666/93. As duas espécies de propriedade, embora distintas, devem cumprir a função social.[8]

2. FUNÇÃO SOCIAL DA PROPRIEDADE

A noção de propriedade só assume contornos jurídicos com o delineamento dos poderes atinentes ao proprietário e correlatas limitações, isto é, o direito de propriedade é o resultado do perfil definido pelo ordenamento jurídico de determinado país em determinado momento histórico. Assim, o direito de propriedade, quando configurado pelo sistema normativo, é integrado pelas limitações administrativas. Por isso, rigorosamente falando, não há limitações administrativas ao direito de propriedade; as limitações restringem tão só a propriedade [9]. E, por serem, as limitações administrativas à propriedade, simples conformação do direito, não geram qualquer direito à indenização, salvo se ocorrer abuso.[10] Diferem os atos que condicionam dos que sacrificam os direitos, pois os primeiros têm a finalidade de delimitação do próprio direito e das condições de seu exercício regular, e, os segundos são a supressão, total ou parcial, de algo que fora atribuído pela ordem jurídica ao administrado.[11]

Vale observar que estas formulações teóricas nem sempre são de fácil assimilação diante do caso concreto. De acordo com Carlos Ari Sundfeld,

[8] ROCHA, Sílvio Luís Ferreira da. *Função social da propriedade pública*. São Paulo: Malheiros, 2005. p. 69-70.

[9] BANDEIRA DE MELLO, Celso Antônio, *Curso de direito administrativo*. 34. ed. rev e atual. São Paulo: Malheiros, 2019, p. 869.Conforme diz Zanobini, a ideia de limitação deriva do próprio conceito de direito subjetivo, pois "tudo o que é juridicamente garantido é também juridicamente limitado" (*Corso di Diritto Amministrativo*, 5. ed., Milano, Giuffrè, 1958, v. IV, p. 191). No mesmo sentido, Ruy Cirne Lima aproxima as ideias de garantia e limitação (*Princípios de Direito Administrativo*. 5. ed. São Paulo: RT, 1982, p. 105).

[10] Como bem esclarece Celso Antônio Bandeira de Mello, "as limitações ao exercício da liberdade e da propriedade corrrespondem à configuração de sua área de manifestação legítima, isto é, da esfera jurídica da liberdade e da propriedade tuteladas pelo sistema. É precisamente esta a razão pela qual as chamadas limitações administrativas à propriedade não são indenizáveis. Posto que através de tais medidas de polícia não há interferência onerosa a um direito, mas tão-só definição que giza suas fronteiras, inexiste o gravame que abriria oportunidade a uma obrigação pública de reparar"(*Curso de direito administrativo*. 34. ed. São Paulo: Malheiros, 2019. p. 871-872).

[11] SUNDFELD Carlos Ari. *Direito administrativo ordenador*. São Paulo: Malheiros, 2003. p. 56.

o que deve orientar o intérprete e aplicador do direito é que as limitações administrativas (conformações de direitos) devem respeitar um "conteúdo mínimo de direito".[12] Ou, em doutrina de Celso Antônio Bandeira de Mello, é a ideia de "funcionalidade" que deve conduzir à solução do caso concreto: "o direito estaria sacrificado quando não se pudesse dar ao bem utilização funcional, entendendo-se por 'funcionalidade' a aptidão natural do bem em conjugação com a destinação social que cumpre, segundo o contexto em que esteja inserido".[13]

2.1. A PROPRIEDADE É DIREITO SUBJETIVO?

O direito à propriedade privada vem sendo considerado, desde a Antigüidade e, inclusive, no Estado moderno, mais em razão do sujeito que o titulariza do que da função que o legitima. Daí ser ele estudado, enfaticamente, e enunciado, juridicamente, como direito subjetivo. No âmbito jurídico, Léon Duguit, no início do século XX, criticou a ideia de considerar a propriedade um direito subjetivo anterior à própria constituição do Estado e sustentou a ideia de função social da propriedade, segundo a qual a propriedade deixaria de ser um direito do indivíduo para converter-se em uma função social do detentor da riqueza e que por ele deve ser cumprida.

Mostra-se equivocada a premissa do raciocínio desenvolvido por Léon Duguit de não ser, a propriedade, um direito, mas uma riqueza passível de proteção pelo direito objetivo violado por terceiros, quando, na verdade, não se duvida de que a propriedade constitua um direito subjetivo.[14] A função social da propriedade pode ser concebida como um dever-poder do proprietário de exercer o seu direito de propriedade sobre o bem de acordo com o fim ou interesse da coletividade que integra, observadas as políticas públicas estabelecidas e voltadas para a melhoria da qualidade de vida, o bem-estar geral e o desenvolvimento das gerações presentes e futuras.[15] É, portanto, comportamento obrigatório em benefício de terceiro.[16].

[12] SUNDFELD Carlos Ari. *Direito administrativo ordenador.* São Paulo: Malheiros, 2003. p. 56.

[13] BANDEIRA DE MELLO Celso Antônio. Natureza jurídica do zoneamento- Efeitos. *Revista de Direito Público,* São Paulo, n. 61, p. 34-47, 1982.p. 39.

[14] ROCHA, Sílvio Luís Ferreira da. *Função social da propriedade pública.* São Paulo: Malheiros, 2005. p. 71.

[15] ROCHA, Sílvio Luís Ferreira da. *Função social da propriedade pública.* São Paulo: Malheiros, 2005. p. 71.

[16] Ensina Antonio H. V. Benjamin que, "dentro das relações jurídicas, a função significa toda atuação em razão de um fim jurídico, em sua dupla esfera: privada e pública. A expressão vem

Não se pode, portanto, conceber a função social como algo exterior à propriedade, mas como elemento integrante de sua própria estrutura. Não são incompatíveis o dever do proprietário, de atender ao bem-estar comum, e o direito de usar, fruir e dispor dos bens, pois a função social apenas condiciona o exercício dos direitos inerentes à relação jurídica de propriedade.[17] Não se confundem, também, a função social da propriedade e limites ou restrições[18] a ela impostos, pois a função social, fator que determina a atuação do proprietário, serve como fonte de estímulos e sanções, ou como meio de impor, a aquele, deveres positivos – pelo fato de ser titular da propriedade – em relação a outros sujeitos determinados, ou perante a coletividade.

Como registra Carlos Ari Sundfeld, enquanto as limitações administrativas à propriedade são a "condição para o exercício de direito", a função social da propriedade consiste no "dever de exercitar" este mesmo direito.[19] Em suma, enquanto as limitações administrativas à propriedade são os contornos do próprio direito, a conformação jurídica que possibilita o exercício concreto de um direito, a função social representa um dever, imposto ao proprietário, de orientar o uso e fruição de sua propriedade de modo a amparar, em alguma medida, o interesse da coletividade.

No trabalho "Novos aspectos da função social da propriedade", elaborado ainda à luz da Constituição Federal de 1969, Celso Antônio Bandeira de Mello afasta a ideia de que a propriedade seja uma função social, ou seja, bem protegido apenas na medida em que realiza aquela função, pois

do latim para a forma portuguesa: "*functione(m)*", que se prende à raiz do verbo depoente "*fungor, eris, functus sum, fungi*", cujo sentido é executar, cumprir, desempenhar"(Benjamin, Antonio H. V. Função Ambiental. In: Benjamin, Antonio H. V (coord.). *Dano ambiental:* prevenção, reparação e repressão. São Paulo: Revista dos Tribunais, 1993, p. 9-82. p. 26), ou, ainda, desempenhar uma função política, cumprir um dever, uma missão (Gaffiot, Félix. *Dictionnaire illustré latin français*. Paris: Hachette, 1934; Torrinha, Francisco. *Dicionário latino português*. Porto: Marânus, 1945). O vocábulo função tem, na língua portuguesa, entre outras acepções, as de exercício de uma atividade, de um cargo, de uma missão (Bueno, Francisco da Silveira. *Grande dicionário etimológico-prosódico da língua portuguesa*. São Paulo: Saraiva, 1968).

17 Loureiro, Francisco Eduardo. *A propriedade como relação jurídica complexa*. 2001. Dissertação (Mestrado em Direito) – Faculdade de Direito, Pontifícia Universidade Católica de São Paulo, São Paulo, 2001. p. 95.

18 O direito de propriedade sofre restrições. Estas restrições decorrem da Constituição, das leis, dos princípios gerais de direito e da vontade da parte.

19 Sundfeld, Carlos Ari. *Direito administrativo ordenador*. São Paulo: Malheiros, 2003. p.11.

isso levaria à conclusão de que propriedades não cumpridoras de função social estariam desprotegidas à luz do ordenamento jurídico, o que não corresponde à realidade, tendo em conta que, como regra, a proteção existe também para a propriedade que desatenda a função social.[20] A expressão função social da propriedade pode ser tomada, de acordo com Celso Antônio Bandeira de Mello, em duas acepções.

A primeira, "no sentido de que a propriedade deve cumprir um destino economicamente útil, produtivo, de modo a satisfazer as necessidades sociais preenchíveis pela espécie tipológica do bem", exigindo "que o bem seja posto em aptidão para produzir sua utilidade específica, ou, ao menos, que o seu uso não ocorra em desacordo com a utilidade social".[21] Frise-se que, mesmo esta perspectiva, ligada exclusivamente ao destino produtivo do bem, já permitiria a adoção de várias providências adequadas à conformação da propriedade ao proveito coletivo, como a instituição de "pesada e progressiva tributação sobre imóveis rurais e urbanos ociosos ou insatisfatoriamente utilizados, a proteção legal a posses produtivas sobre prédios rústicos inaproveitados por seus titulares ou sobre terrenos urbanos estocados para valorização e não edificados".[22]

A segunda acepção cogitada pelo citado autor procura atribuir à expressão "função social da propriedade" conteúdo atrelado a objetivos de Justiça Social, ou seja, comprometido com a realização de uma sociedade mais

[20] Diz o referido autor: "Estamos em crer, que ao lume do direito positivo constitucional, a propriedade ainda está claramente configurada como um direito que deve cumprir uma função social e não como sendo pura e simplesmente uma função social, isto é, bem protegido tão só na medida em que a realiza. Deveras, a entender-se que o protegido é a propriedade função-social, ter-se-ia, conseqüentemente, que concluir ausente a proteção jurídica a ou às propriedades que não estivessem cumprindo função social. Estas, pois, deveriam ser suscetíveis de serem perdidas, sem qualquer indenização, toda e cada vez que fosse demonstrável seu desajuste à função social que deveriam preencher.[...] *Ergo*, existe proteção também para a propriedade que contrarie a função social, conquanto tal proteção seja menos completa, pois neste caso, a indenização devida não se apura segundo um "justo" perquirível ao lume do valor efetivo do imóvel, mas segundo os critérios que a lei estabelecer e far-se-á "em títulos especiais da dívida pública, resgatáveis no prazo de vinte anos, em parcelas anuais e sucessivas ..." tudo como dispõe o referido art. 161. (Novos aspectos da função social da propriedade no direito público. *Revista de Direito Público*, São Paulo, v. 20, n. 84, p. 39-45, out./dez. 1987. p.41).

[21] Novos aspectos da função social da propriedade no direito público. *Revista de Direito Público*, São Paulo, v. 20, n. 84, p. 39-45, out./dez. 1987. p.43.

[22] Novos aspectos da função social da propriedade no direito público. *Revista de Direito Público*, São Paulo, v. 20, n. 84, p. 39-45, out./dez. 1987. p. 44.

justa e igualitária, havendo possibilidade de adoção de medidas normativas que tomem como rumo estes objetivos.[23] Em nosso país, a função social da propriedade ganha reconhecimento em âmbito constitucional a partir da Constituição Federal de 1.934, que, no art. 113, 17, garantia o direito de propriedade, mas impedia o respectivo exercício contra o interesse social ou coletivo, segundo o que a lei determinasse. Embora silente a respeito do tema, a Constituição de 1937 assegurou, no art. 122, o direito de propriedade, ressalvada a desapropriação por necessidade ou utilidade pública, mediante indenização prévia.

A seu turno, na Carta de 1946, o uso da propriedade foi condicionado ao bem-estar social (art. 147).[24] Coube, no entanto, à Constituição Federal de 1967, consagrar expressamente a função social da propriedade, embora como princípio da ordem econômica (art. 157, III), o que foi mantido na Emenda nº 1 de 1.969 (art. 160, III). Na Constituição de 1988, o art. 5º, inciso XXII, garante o direito de propriedade, mas, o inciso XXIII determina que a propriedade (em geral) atenderá à sua função social. Bastava essa disposição para que toda forma de propriedade fosse intrinsecamente permeada daquele princípio constitucional, mas a Constituição não se limitou a isso. Reafirmou a instituição da propriedade privada e a sua função social como princípios da ordem econômica (art. 170, II e III), que têm por fim "assegurar a todos existência digna, conforme os ditames da justiça social" (art. 170, "caput"). Além disso, inscreveu o princípio da função social da propriedade, com conteúdo definido em relação às propriedades urbana e rural, com sanções para o caso de não ser observado (arts. 182, 184 e 186).

[23] Novos aspectos da função social da propriedade no direito publico. *Revista de Direito Público*, São Paulo, v. 20, n. 84, p. 39-45, out./dez. 1987. p. 44. No Brasil, assevera Luís de Lima Stefanini, já havia preocupação com o cumprimento da função social da propriedade na época da concessão das sesmarias, posto que entre as obrigações impostas aos sesmeiros encontrava-se a de cultivar a terra (*A propriedade no direito agrário*. São Paulo: Revista dos Tribunais, 1978. p. 57).

[24] Para Celso Antônio Bandeira de Mello "sem dúvida alguma, este preceptivo é um marco jurídico. Com efeito, não apenas se prevê a desapropriação por interesse social, mas se aponta, no aludido art. 147, para um rumo social da propriedade, ao ser prefigurada legislação que lhe assegure justa distribuição, buscando mais que a tradicional igualdade perante a lei, igualdade perante a oportunidade de acesso à propriedade". (Novos aspectos da função social da propriedade no direito público. *Revista de Direito Público*, São Paulo, v. 20, n. 84, p. 39-45, out./dez. 1987. p.40).

Deflui, portanto, da configuração do ordenamento jurídico em vigor, que a propriedade deve ser concebida como um direito subjetivo, mas também acrescida do dever de atender a uma função social. Ao agregar a intelecção de função social à propriedade, a Constituição Federal prescreveu uma dimensão pública a um direito que historicamente se consagrava com aspectos exclusivamente privados. Dessa forma, a propriedade não é uma função social – como inicialmente defendia Léon Duguit –, mas há uma função social que orienta, e por isto condiciona o exercício dos poderes inerentes ao domínio, o que conduz ao reconhecimento de um direito individual com feição coletiva.

A função social não se contrapõe à propriedade, mas se projeta, em razão da necessidade de adequar o direito individual e o interesse público, de modo a imprimir um dever jurídico, ao proprietário ou possuidor, que contenha como propósito a integração do direito individual com um fim público.[25]

2.2. FUNÇÃO SOCIAL DA PROPRIEDADE NO CÓDIGO CIVIL DE 2002

Na esteira e tendo como fundamento a Constituição de 1988, o Código Civil brasileiro de 2002 (Lei nº 10.406, de 10 de janeiro de 2002), ao cuidar deste tema (arts. 1.228 e segs.), enfatizou e estendeu o princípio da função social da propriedade. É princípio de ordem pública, que não pode ser revogado por vontade das partes. O parágrafo único do art. 2.035 é expresso neste sentido, ao preceituar que "nenhuma convenção prevalecerá se contrariar preceitos de ordem pública, tais como os estabelecidos por este Código para assegurar a função social da propriedade e dos contratos" Quanto aos contratos, estatui o Código:

> Art. 421. A liberdade contratual será exercida nos limites da função social do contrato. (Redação dada pela Lei nº 13.874, de 2019)

[25] De acordo com Marina Mariani de Macedo Rabahie, o princípio da função social qualifica o direito subjetivo de propriedade, nele inserindo um dever-poder sem, contudo, aniquilá-lo. Na verdade, com base na lição de Eros Roberto Grau, a citada autora julga que "não é o bem apropriável que tem uma função (pois a função só tem sentido e valor na medida em que for exercitada) e sim o proprietário a quem incumbe, por imperativo constitucional, exercitar os poderes inerentes ao seu direito, de modo condicionado ao interesse comum." (RABAHIE, Marina Mariani de Macedo. A função social da propriedade. In: DALLARI, Adilson Abreu; FIGUEIREDO, Lúcia Valle (coords.) *Temas de Direito Urbanístico 2*. São Paulo: Revista dos Tribunais, 1991, p. 213-258. p. 229).

Relativamente à propriedade, o Código Civil estabeleceu:

> Art. 1.228. O proprietário tem a faculdade de usar, gozar e dispor da coisa, e o direito de reavê-la do poder de quem quer que injustamente a possua ou detenha.
>
> § 1º O direito de propriedade deve ser exercido em consonância com as suas finalidades econômicas e sociais e de modo que sejam preservados, de conformidade com o estabelecido em lei especial, a flora, a fauna, as belezas naturais, o equilíbrio ecológico e o patrimônio histórico e artístico, bem como evitada a poluição do ar e das águas. [...]

Na hipótese normativa havida no § 1º, do art. 1.228, do Código Civil, segundo Cármen Lúcia Antunes Rocha, há que ser observada a interpretação conforme à Constituição, que "faz sobrelevar o fator social ao econômico, impedindo que o eficientismo econômico sobrepuje ou anule a socialidade a que se volta a função a ser cumprida pelo proprietário"[26]. Por sua vez, Maria Helena Diniz, ao comentar referido dispositivo, afirma que há limitação ao direito de propriedade com o propósito de inibir uso abusivo, que acabe causando prejuízos ao bem-estar social.[27]

Reconhece Sílvio Luis Ferreira da Rocha que o legislador, no art. 1.228, não conseguiu "livrar-se do ranço de definir a propriedade a partir das faculdades reconhecidas ao proprietário, entre elas, a de usar, gozar e dispor da coisa (CC, art. 1.228), quando, na verdade, o que importa é o fato de o exercício da propriedade ter que se revelar útil e proveitoso não apenas para quem é o titular do direito, mas também para a coletividade".[28] Admite, porém, a implementação de avanços consideráveis, destacando especialmente a dignidade conferida ao instituto da posse, que, pela função social, atingiu posição de relevo, seja na usucapião *pro labore* (CC, art. 1.240), seja na desapropriação *pro labore* (CC, art. 1.228,§ 4º).

[26] Rocha, Cármen Lúcia Antunes. O princípio constitucional da função social da propriedade. In: Bacellar Filho, Romeu Felipe (coord.geral); MOTA, Paulo Roberto Ferreira; Castro, Rodrigo Pironti Aguirre de (coord.). *Direito Administrativo Contemporâneo*: estudos em memória ao professor Manoel de Oliveira Franco Sobrinho. Belo Horizonte: Fórum, 2004, p. 55-104. p. 101.

[27] Diniz, Maria Helena. *Código civil anotado*. 9 ed. rev. e atual. São Paulo: Saraiva, 2003. p.785.

[28] Rocha, Sílvio Luís Ferreira da. *Função social da propriedade pública*. São Paulo: Malheiros, 2005. p. 79.

Esta figura expropriatória, prevista no artigo 1.228, § 4º, do Código Civil, configura-se na hipótese de o imóvel reivindicado consistir em extensa área, na posse ininterrupta e de boa-fé, por mais de cinco anos, de considerável número de pessoas, e estas nela houverem realizado, em conjunto ou separadamente, obras e serviços considerados pelo juiz de interesse social e econômico relevante. Preenchidos os requisitos legais, o proprietário, autor de ação reivindicatória, poderá ser privado da propriedade da coisa, em benefício dos réus, mediante justa indenização, fixada pelo juiz (art. 1.228, § 5º).[29] [30]

A norma cria a desapropriação judicial, considerada uma inovação "do mais alto alcance, inspirada no sentido social do direito de propriedade, implicando não só novo conceito desta, mas também novo conceito de posse, que se poderia qualificar como sendo de posse-trabalho".[31]; Trata-se, sem dúvida, de uma das mais significativas alterações efetuadas pelo Código Civil no âmbito do direito da propriedade, que não encontra paradigma na legislação pátria anterior. Cuida-se de modalidade aquisitiva absolutamente *sui generis*, pela qual certo número de pessoas (possuidores), preenchendo os requisitos da lei, passa a ter "direito de adquirir" imóvel alheio mediante pagamento de justa indenização, sempre sob a necessária e imprescindível intervenção judicial. Em novembro de 2011 foi aprovado o Enunciado nº 496, da V Jornada de Direito Civil promovida pelo Conselho da Justiça Federal e pelo Centro de Estudos Judiciários, com o seguinte teor: "O conteúdo do art. 1.228, §§ 4º e 5º, pode ser objeto de ação autônoma, não se restringindo à defesa em pretensões reivindicatórias".

[29] ROCHA, Sílvio Luís Ferreira da. *Função social da propriedade pública*. São Paulo: Malheiros, 2005. p.79-80.

[30] "Art. 1.228 [...]

§ 4º O proprietário também pode ser privado da coisa se o imóvel reivindicado consistir em extensa área, na posse ininterrupta e de boa-fé, por mais de cinco anos, de considerável número de pessoas, e estas nela houverem realizado, em conjunto ou separadamente, obras e serviços considerados pelo juiz de interesse social e econômico relevante.

§ 5º No caso do parágrafo antecedente, o juiz fixará a justa indenização devida ao proprietário; pago o preço, valerá a sentença como título para o registro do imóvel em nome dos possuidores".

[31] REALE, Miguel. Exposição de motivos ao Ministro da Justiça. Diário do Congresso Nacional, Seção I, Suplemento B ao n. 061,13.6.1975n, 27c, p.121.

2.2.1. CONSTITUCIONALIDADE DA CHAMADA DESAPROPRIAÇÃO JUDICIAL

Dúvidas foram levantadas a propósito da eventual inconstitucionalidade desta forma de aquisição da propriedade imóvel e de seus dispositivos reguladores. A defesa do entendimento, que considera inconstitucional[32] a desapropriação judicial, fundamenta-se em interpretação conjugada do art. 5º, *caput* e inciso XXII e do art. 170, II, da Constituição Federal, para afirmar que a Carta Magna, ao garantir o direito de propriedade, resguarda a propriedade privada. Assim, somente a desapropriação estatal por necessidade ou utilidade pública, ou por interesse social, mediante justa e prévia indenização em dinheiro (art. 5º, XXIV, da CF-88) e a desapropriação-sanção, efetivada em virtude do não atendimento da função social pelo proprietário (art. 182, §§ 2º, 3º e 4º, III e arts. 184 e 186 da CF-88), expressamente previstas no texto constitucional, poderiam incidir sobre a propriedade privada. Nenhuma outra modalidade expropriatória seria admitida.

A seu turno, a tese contrária busca demonstrar a constitucionalidade da desapropriação judicial a partir do fundamento do dispositivo do Código Civil. Não se trataria de expropriação-sanção, mas de forma de intervenção que leva em consideração valores sociais aferidos pelo juiz. O próprio texto do dispositivo explicita que a posse, obras e serviços realizados pelos possuidores devem ser "considerados pelo juiz de interesse social e econômico relevante". Deste modo, a lei civil encontra referência expressa na Constituição Federal, que permite a desapropriação por interesse social, mediante pagamento de justa e prévia indenização (art. 5º, XXIV).

Este entendimento é respaldado por vários doutrinadores, que não admitem restrições às expressões *necessidade, utilidade pública* e *interesse social* como inerentes apenas à viabilidade de serviços públicos, advertindo dever-se estabelecer "também a possibilidade de uma desapropriação que não seja por necessidade do Estado em si [...] para qualquer serviço do Estado. Mas devemos possibilitar a desapropriação *sempre que necessária à ordem social, à vida social*".[33] A desapropriação por interesse social referida terá o

[32] Nessa linha: MALUF, Carlos Alberto Dabus. *Novo Código Civil Comentado*. FIÚZA, Ricardo (Coord.) 4. ed. São Paulo: Saraiva, 2005. p. 1133.

[33] CRETELLA JÚNIOR, J. *Comentários à Constituição brasileira de 1988*. 3. ed. Rio de Janeiro: Forense Universitária, 1992. p. 188-189. No mesmo sentido e destacando a amplitude da função social da propriedade, são as lições de FERREIRA FILHO, Manoel Gonçalves. *Curso de direito constitucional*. 32. ed. São Paulo: Saraiva, 2006. p. 307-308; PINTO FERREIRA. *Comentários à*

seu procedimento estabelecido por lei, tal como determina o art. 5º, XXIV, da Constituição Federal, independentemente de vinculação ou exclusividade de competência com o ente expropriante. Conclui-se, então, que a desapropriação judicial, também denominada "expropriação privada", não é feita por particulares, aos quais, para tanto, nenhuma competência é delegada, mas, sim pelo juiz, órgão integrante do Judiciário e, portanto, por um dos poderes do Estado.

A exposição de motivos do Código Civil ressalta ter, este Código, aberto uma "via nova de desapropriação que se não deve considerar prerrogativa exclusiva dos Poderes Executivo ou Legislativo. Não há razão plausível para recusar ao Poder Judiciário o exercício do poder expropriatório em casos concretos, como o que se contém na espécie analisada".[34] Diante dessas considerações, o Enunciado 82, aprovado pela I Jornada de Direito Civil

Constituição brasileira. São Paulo: Saraiva, 1989. p. 104-105; SILVA, José Afonso da. *Curso de direito constitucional positivo*. 36. ed. São Paulo: Malheiros, 2013. p. 283-286; MORAIS, Alexandre de. *Direitos humanos fundamentais*. São Paulo: Atlas, 2000. p. 174-175.

[34] Há controvérsia sobre a natureza jurídica do instituto previsto nos §§ 4º e 5º do art. 1.228 do Código Civil de 2002. Alguns defendem que se trata de nova modalidade de usucapião (entre eles, Carlos Alberto Dabus Maluf, Eduardo Cambi. Controvérsias constitucionais acerca do usucapião coletivo. *Revista Magister de Direito Civil e Processual Civil*, ano II, n. 12, maio/jun. 2006. p. 38; Patricia Waldmann Padin. *Aspectos fundamentais do usucapião coletivo*. 2010. 127 f. Dissertação (Mestrado em Direito) – Faculdade de Direito, Universidade de São Paulo, São Paulo, 2010. p. 89). Outros sustentam que se trata de desapropriação judicial,chamada também por alguns doutrinadores de desapropriação por posse-trabalho ou de desapropriação judicial indireta (entre eles Marco Aurélio Viana – *Comentários ao Novo Código Civil*, dos Direitos Reais. V. XVI. Rio de Janeiro: Forense, 2003. p. 49; Nelson Kojranski. Direitos reais. In: MARTINS FILHO, Ives Gandra da Silva; MENDES, Gilmar Ferreira; FRANCUILLI NETO, Domingos (coord.). *O novo Código Civil*: estudos em homenagem ao Prof. Miguel Reale. São Paulo: LTr, 2003. p. 1002. Por sua vez, Pablo Rentería classifica tal instituto como aquisição de propriedade imobiliária pela acessão invertida social. Preconiza o autor que, a aquisição de propriedade prevista no referido dispositivo guarda estreita relação com a acessão invertida disposta no parágrafo único do art. 1255 do Código Civil, cujo texto legal estabelece que *"aquele que, de boa-fé semeou, plantou ou edificou em terreno alheio, se a construção ou a plantação exceder consideravelmente o valor do terreno, adquirirá a propriedade do solo, mediante pagamento da indenização fixada judicialmente, se não houver acordo"*. Tratar-se-ia de uma acessão invertida de feição marcadamente social, que se prolongaria no tempo, no transcurso do prazo legal (protraindo-se no tempo, de maneira análoga à hipótese do art. 1251 CC), efetivando-se mediante o pagamento de indenização, fixada judicialmente, ao proprietário prejudicado. (A aquisição da propriedade imobiliária pela acessão invertida social: análise sistemática dos parágrafos 4º e 5º do artigo 1228 do Código Civil. In: *Revista Trimestral de Direito Civil,* Rio de Janeiro, v. 9, n. 34, abr./jun. 2008, p. 71-91).

do Centro de Estudos Judiciários do Conselho da Justiça Federal, afirmou a constitucionalidade dos §§ 4º e 5º do art. 1.228 do Código Civil, por sua integral compatibilidade vertical, sob o prisma formal e substancial, com os arts.3º, 5º, XXII, XXIII e XXIV, 170, II e III da Constituição Federal de 1988,[35] da seguinte forma: "É constitucional a modalidade aquisitiva de propriedade imóvel prevista nos §§ 4º e 5º do art. 1.228 do novo Código Civil".

Acresça-se, também, o entendimento de Teori Albino Zavascki, no sentido de que "a norma é constitucional porque resolve a aparente antinomia entre o direito de o proprietário reivindicar a coisa de quem injustamente a possua e a função social da propriedade, com a manutenção do bem com aquele que lhe deu função social com a posse-trabalho".[36] Sílvio Luís Ferreira da Rocha lembra que a desapropriação judicial pode funcionar como instrumento de pacificação de conflitos sociais em torno da disputa da propriedade, principalmente nas áreas rurais, já que o Código Civil não distingue se o imóvel está localizado em área urbana ou rural, ao permitir aos posseiros que adquiram a propriedade do imóvel em litígio, mesmo contra a vontade do proprietário, mediante, no entanto, o pagamento de justa indenização por parte dos réus.[37]

2.2.2. RESPONSABILIDADE PELO PAGAMENTO DA INDENIZAÇÃO

A quem deve ser imputado o pagamento da indenização fixada pelo juiz e devida ao proprietário? Ficará a cargo dos possuidores a prestação indenizatória em todos os casos *sub judice*? Divergências existem acerca dos responsáveis pelo pagamento da indenização. A doutrina se divide basi-

[35] Justificativa apresentada, pelo Desembargador do Tribunal de Justiça do Espirito Santo, Dr. Álvaro Manoel Rosindo Bourguignon, ao Enunciado 82. *I Jornada de Direito Civil do Centro de Estudos Judiciários do Conselho da Justiça Federal, realizada em 12 e 13 de setembro de 2002*. Disponível em: <www.jf.jus.br>. Acesso em: 15 ago. 2008.

[36] Zawascki. Teori Albino. A tutela da posse na Constituição e no Projeto do Novo Código Civil. In: Martins-Costa. *Reconstrução*, p. 854, apud Nery Junior, Nelson; Nery, Rosa Maria de Andrade. *Código Civil Comentado*. 6. ed. rev. amp. e atual. São Paulo: Revista dos Tribunais, 2008. p. 880. No mesmo sentido, Luiz Edson Facchin entende que a garantia do direito de propriedade não pode estar acima do princípio constitucional da função social. (Facchin, Luiz Edson. *O Projeto de Código Civil no Senado Federal*. Brasília: Senado Federal, 1998, v. II, p. 311 e 317, apud Nery Junior, Nelson; Nery, Rosa Maria de Andrade.*Código Civil Comentado*. 6. ed. rev. amp. e atual. São Paulo: Revista dos Tribunais, 2008. p.880).

[37] Rocha, Sílvio Luís Ferreira da. *Função social da propriedade pública*. São Paulo: Malheiros, 2005. p. 80.

camente em dois posicionamentos: um sustenta caber aos possuidores o pagamento da indenização[38] e, outro, ser o Estado responsável pelo seu pagamento.[39] Os partidários da primeira corrente entendem caber o pagamento aos possuidores beneficiados pela desapropriação judicial, uma vez que a propriedade será incorporada ao seu patrimônio.

Os que afirmam ser o Estado o responsável pelo pagamento da indenização, argumentam que o magistrado, ao concluir pela desapropriação judicial, está agindo como parte do Estado, ou seja, como parte da Administração Pública. Isto porque tal instituto teria uma proximidade muito grande com a desapropriação administrativa, que é poder-dever reservado exclusivamente ao Estado, permitindo a transferência compulsória da propriedade, *"com o fim de propiciar justiça social, supondo a utilização inadequada do direito de propriedade "*.[40]As duas correntes têm desvantagens. Em relação ao entendimento de que o dever de indenizar caberia aos possuidores, surge o problema de a coletividade não possuir condições sócio-econômicas suficientes para arcar com a indenização, inviabilizando o instituto, além de favorecer o proprietário que não dá função social à sua propriedade.

Surge, então, como alternativa, o entendimento de que este dever de indenizar caberia ao Estado, tendo em conta o intento do legislador ordinário na referida desapropriação. Como o instituto da desapropriação judicial tem caráter eminentemente social, buscando uma utilização adequada da propriedade, e, não sendo possível a transferência desta, do proprietário

[38] FREITAS, Cleuton César Ripol de. A desapropriação judiciária e os conflitos coletivos pela posse. In: SEMINÁRIO NACIONAL DE DIREITO AGRÁRIO. I, 1975. Anais... Brasília, Associação Brasileira de Direito Agrário, 9 a 13.12.2002 (CD-ROM); VENOSA, Silvio de Salvo. *Direito civil*: direitos reais. 5. ed. São Paulo: Atlas, 2005. v. 5; MALUF, Carlos Alberto Dabus. Direitos reais. In: Seminário Novo Código Civil Brasileiro: o que muda na vida do cidadão, 2003, Brasília. Anais. Brasília: Câmara dos Deputados, Centro de Documentação e Informação, Coordenação de Publicações, 2002, p. 230-241; Gagliano, Pablo Stolze. Controvérsias constitucionais acerca do usucapião coletivo.*Revista Magister de Direito Civil e Processual Civil,* ano II, n. 12, maio/jun. 2006. p.40.

[39] BARROSO, Lucas de Abreu. Hermenêutica e operabilidade dos parágrafos 4º e 5º do art. 1.228 do Código Civil. *Revista de Direito Privado,* São Paulo, n. 21, p. 130-138, 2005; CASTRO, Mônica. *A desapropriação judicial no novo Código Civil.* Disponível em: http://www.mundojuridico.adv.br/sis_artigos/artigos.asp?codigo=486. Acesso em: 03 abr. 2008; NOBRE JÚNIOR, Edílson Pereira. A posse e a propriedade no novo Código Civil. *Revista de Direito Privado,* Disponível em: www.jfrn.gov.br/docs/doutrina180.doc . Acesso em: 16 jan. 2009.

[40] CASTRO, Mônica. *A desapropriação judicial no novo Código Civil.* Disponível em: http://www.mundojuridico.adv.br/sis_artigos/artigos.asp?codigo=486. Acesso em: 03 abr. 2008 .

aos possuidores, sem o pagamento da indenização, tal indenização ficaria a cargo do ente federado competente para realizar a desapropriação administrativa do bem em questão.

No entanto, deste posicionamento originam-se também alguns problemas. O primeiro se dá na esfera processual: com a decisão judicial, uma vez feita coisa julgada, estar-se-ia prejudicando terceiros, que não fizeram parte da relação processual, em desacordo com o art. 472 do Código de Processo Civil. Isto porque a desapropriação judicial só se dará após a resolução de um procedimento processual privado – entre proprietário e possuidores – no qual o Estado não será parte. O Estado não tem porque participar deste processo, uma vez que não é parte interessada. Desta feita, seria injusto atribuir a um terceiro, no caso, o Estado, o dever de pagar indenização ao proprietário que perdeu a sua propriedade, quando não foi o causador desta perda.

Ademais, se se considerasse o Poder Público responsável pelo pagamento da indenização, não haveria desapropriação judicial e, sim, uma desapropriação administrativa indireta. Assim, seriam inúteis tal instituto e o dispositivo que o implementa, visto já existir previsão de um instituto que possibilita a desapropriação de imóveis pelo Estado, sendo este, no caso, o responsável pela indenização. Há, ainda, quem entenda que possuidores e Estado são devedores solidários em relação ao pagamento de indenização ao proprietário do imóvel. Afirma Glauco Gumerato Ramos:

> Partindo-se do princípio de que o Estado é devedor solidário da indenização junto com os possuidores – estes, devedores pelo benefício direto com a aquisição da propriedade; aquele, devedor pelo fato de ter realizado a *desapropriação judicial* -, a denunciação da lide será mecanismo eficaz para garantir ao proprietário que efetivamente seja indenizado pela intervenção expropriatória que redundou no perdimento da propriedade imobiliária.[41]

Este entendimento não deve prosperar, uma vez que, por força do art. 265 do Código Civil, a solidariedade não se presume, o que significa que, para existir, a solidariedade deve estar prevista em lei ou ser pactuada pelas

[41] Ramos, Glauco Gumerato. Contributo à dinâmica da chamada desapropriação judicial: diálogo entre Constituição, direito e processo. *Jus Navigandi,* Teresina, ano 10, n. 931, 20 jan. 2006. Disponível em: http://jus2.uol.com.br/doutrina/texto.asp?id=7857. Acesso em: 09 out. 2008.

partes. Este não é o caso. Não existe previsão legal de solidariedade para a indenização no caso de desapropriação judicial. Se houvesse esta previsão, fácil seria imputar a responsabilidade pelo pagamento da indenização, não havendo celeuma a este respeito. Muito menos há possibilidade de ajuste entre possuidores e Poder Público.

O Centro de Estudos Judiciários do Conselho da Justiça Federal, inicialmente, através de seu Enunciado 84, aprovado na I Jornada de Direito Civil, realizada em setembro de 2002, posicionou-se no sentido de que: "A defesa fundada no direito de aquisição com base no interesse social (art. 1.228, §§ 4° e 5°, do novo Código Civil) deve ser arguida pelos réus da ação reivindicatória, eles próprios responsáveis pelo pagamento da indenização".

A justificativa daquele Enunciado traz, de início, a afirmação de que o próprio Código, já tendo feito menção, "no § 3º do art. 1.228, à desapropriação por interesse social e à requisição como formas de exclusão do domínio; parece estar tratando, nos §§ 4º e 5º, de situação nova, de natureza processual, tanto que o proprietário é qualificado como reivindicante". Posteriormente, no Enunciado 308 (IV Jornada) houve uma evolução dessa posição do Conselho da Justiça Federal, no sentido de que:

> A justa indenização devida ao proprietário em caso de desapropriação judicial (art. 1.228, § 5º) somente deverá ser suportada pela Administração Pública no contexto das políticas públicas de reforma urbana ou agrária, em se tratando de possuidores de baixa renda e desde que tenha havido intervenção daquela nos termos da lei processual. Não sendo os possuidores de baixa renda, aplica-se a orientação do Enunciado 84 da I Jornada de Direito Civil.[42]

Tal mudança foi feita sob a justificativa de que, estando o imóvel reivindicado, urbano ou rural, ocupado por possuidores de baixa renda, uma vez declarada a desapropriação judicial e apurada a verba indenizatória, o pagamento desta deverá ficar a cargo do ente federado que teria competência para desapropriá-lo na esfera administrativa. Para tanto, basta incorporar tal diretriz às políticas públicas em execução com a finalidade de cuidar das questões de reforma urbana ou agrária, ou que se imponha esse ônus à Administração Pública no próprio instrumento decisório.

[42] Jornadas de Direito Civil I, III e IV. Enunciados Aprovados. In: *Jornada de Direito Civil*, organização Ministro Ruy Rosado de Aguiar Jr. Brasília: CJF, 2007, p.67. Disponível em: http://www.jf.jus.br. Acesso em: 15 ago. 2008.

A interpretação proposta para o dispositivo em análise evita duas hipóteses indesejadas: a) que os possuidores de baixa renda, não podendo pagar a justa indenização, sejam obrigados a desocupar o imóvel onde realizaram benfeitorias de relevante interesse social e econômico, cumprindo, assim, a função social da propriedade; b) que a posse do imóvel seja restituída ao proprietário desidioso, que, ademais, praticou abuso de direito ao não observar os ditames constitucionais e infraconstitucionais atinentes ao direito subjetivo da propriedade privada. A aplicação do instituto assim pensada, no que se refere ao pagamento da indenização, levará a efeito mais facilmente a operabilidade a que está constrito, diminuindo os conflitos sociais e representando fator de distribuição horizontal da riqueza, imprescindível para o exercício da cidadania e para a afirmação da dignidade da pessoa humana.[43]

Saliente-se que o pagamento da indenização, calculada em montante suficiente para cobrir o valor do bem, da perda sofrida pelo expropriado, não pode deixar de ser feito. Isto porque sua finalidade é a de preservar o justo equilíbrio entre o direito de propriedade e as exigências do interesse geral.

2.2.3. JUSTA INDENIZAÇÃO

O Código Civil, no § 5º do art. 1.228, preceitua que o juiz fixará a justa indenização devida ao proprietário, numa clara alusão à circunstância de que se trata de um preço que leva em conta, necessariamente, o aspecto social daquela posse. Na III Jornada de Direito Civil do Centro de Estudos Judiciários do Conselho da Justiça Federal foi aprovado o Enunciado 240: "A justa indenização a que alude o § 5º do art. 1.228 não tem como critério valorativo, necessariamente, a avaliação técnica lastreada no mercado imobiliário, sendo indevidos os juros compensatórios".

A justificativa deste Enunciado apresenta pontos que devem ser salientados, a saber: 1) não cuidando, a hipótese em análise, da desapropriação em sua acepção tradicional (§ 3º do art. 1.228 do Código Civil), não é possível cogitar da exigência de laudo elaborado por perícia técnica, como sucede por força do art. 14 do Decreto-lei n.3.365/41, quando o juiz, ao despachar a inicial expropriatória, designa um perito de sua livre escolha

[43] Justificativa apresentada pelo Prof. Lucas Abreu Barroso ao Enunciado 308 da IV Jornada de Direito Civil do Centro de Estudos Judiciários do Conselho da Justiça Federal , v. II, p. 634-635. Disponível em: http://www.jf.jus.br. Acesso em: 15 ago. 2008.

para proceder à avaliação dos bens; 2) tratando-se de aquisição da propriedade com base na denominada posse *pro labore* e, não, de usucapião, a existência de obras e serviços considerados pelo juiz de interesse social e econômico relevante, aliada ao pagamento de justa indenização, permitem a sua concretização; 3) não são devidos os juros de natureza compensatória admitidos nas ações de desapropriação convencionais e que são objeto das Súmulas 69 e 113 do STJ.

Os juros compensatórios destinam-se a ressarcir o expropriado pelo que deixou de ganhar, impedido do uso e gozo econômico do imóvel, em razão do ato restritivo do Poder Público e incidem a partir da antecipada imissão na posse, na desapropriação direta e, da efetiva ocupação do imóvel, na desapropriação indireta. A situação na desapropriação judicial é diversa, posto que, não ocorrendo, no caso, interrupção das atividades lucrativas do proprietário, não se há de falar em restrição de seus rendimentos, até porque a nova modalidade de expropriação requer a caracterização de um presumido abandono do bem pelo titular. [44]

2.2.4. PAGAMENTO DE INDENIZAÇÃO E TRANSFERÊNCIA DE PROPRIEDADE

A propriedade não pode ser transferida aos possuidores enquanto a indenização não for paga ao proprietário do imóvel, pois, nos termos do § 5° do art. 1228, o pagamento é condição para que a sentença de desapropriação judicial valha como título para o registro do imóvel em nome dos possuidores. Até o efetivo pagamento da indenização, a propriedade permanece na titularidade do reivindicante, por força das disposições do *caput* do art. 1.245 do Código Civil, que estabelece regra geral das transmissões imobiliárias em nosso sistema: "Transfere-se entre vivos a propriedade mediante o registro do título translativo no Registro de Imóveis". O Enunciado 241, aprovado, na III Jornada de Direito Civil do Centro de Estudos Judiciários do Conselho da Justiça Federal, assim trata da matéria: "O registro da sentença em ação reivindicatória, que opera a transferência da propriedade para o nome dos possuidores, com fundamento no interesse social (art.

[44] Justificativa apresentada pelo Desembargador Federal do Tribunal Regional Federal da 3ª Região, Luís Paulo Cotrim Guimarães, ao Enunciado 240 da III Jornada de Direito Civil do Centro de Estudos Judiciários do Conselho da Justiça Federal. In: *III Jornada de Direito Civil*, organização Ministro Ruy Rosado de Aguiar Jr., Brasília: CJF, 2005, p. 317-318. Disponível em: http://www.jf.jus.br/. Acesso em: 15 ago. 2008.

1.228, § 5º), é condicionado ao pagamento da respectiva indenização, cujo prazo será fixado pelo juiz".

Ou seja, a sentença referida será ineficaz, embora exista juridicamente e tenha validade,[45] enquanto não se implementar a condição suspensiva: o pagamento do preço justo ao proprietário-reivindicante. Pendente o registro da sentença, a titularidade do domínio permanece em mãos do autor da ação de reivindicação. Regra similar é a contida no § 1º do art. 1.245 do Código Civil: "enquanto não se registrar o título translativo, o alienante continua a ser havido como dono do imóvel." Além de obstar o registro da sentença, o não pagamento do preço justo, no prazo fixado pela decisão judicial, acarretará a imissão do autor da demanda na posse do bem.[46] De outro lado, o Enunciado 311, aprovado na IV Jornada de Direito Civil do Centro de Estudos Judiciários do Conselho da Justiça Federal, afirma: "Caso não seja pago o preço fixado para a desapropriação judicial, e ultrapassado o prazo prescricional para se exigir o crédito correspondente, estará autorizada a expedição de mandado para registro da propriedade em favor dos possuidores".

2.2.5. POSSIBILIDADE DE A DESAPROPRIAÇÃO JUDICIAL SER INVOCADA CONTRA O PODER PÚBLICO

A possibilidade de a desapropriação *pro labore* recair sobre bens públicos e ser invocada contra o Poder Público, pelos réus em ação reivindicatória promovida por este, é controvertida. Tal possibilidade foi inicialmente rejeitada pelo Enunciado 83 do Centro de Estudos Judiciários do Conselho da Justiça Federal: "Nas ações reivindicatórias propostas pelo Poder Público, não são aplicáveis as disposições constantes dos §§ 4º e 5º do art. 1.228 do novo Código Civil".

Todavia, houve uma mudança de entendimento no Enunciado 304 (IV Jornada de Direito Civil): "São aplicáveis as disposições dos §§ 4º e 5º do art. 1.228 do Código Civil às ações reivindicatórias relativas a bens públicos dominicais, mantido, parcialmente, o Enunciado 83 da I Jornada de Direito Civil, no que concerne às demais classificações dos bens públicos".

[45] DINAMARCO, Cândido Rangel. *Instituições de direito processual civil.* 4. ed. São Paulo: Malheiros, 2004, v. 3. p. 685-686.

[46] Justificativa apresentada pelo Desembargador Federal Luis Paulo Cotrim Guimarães ao Enunciado 241 da III Jornada de Direito Civil do Centro de Estudos Judiciários do Conselho da Justiça Federal. In: *III Jornada de Direito Civil*, organização Ministro Ruy Rosado de Aguiar Jr., Brasília: CJF, 2005, p. 319. Disponível em: http://www.jf.jus.br/. Acesso em: 15 ago. 2008.

2.2.6. ELEMENTOS

Compõem o direito de desapropriação judicial: a) com relação ao imóvel: propriedade de outrem, área extensa; b) quanto à posse: ser de boa-fé, isto é, que não seja clandestina, violenta, nem precária, e que a posse seja mansa, pacífica, ininterrupta por mais de cinco anos; ser exercida por número considerável de pessoas; ser caracterizada como posse-trabalho, isto é, exercida por pessoas que realizaram no imóvel, em conjunto ou separadamente, obras e serviços de relevante interesse social e econômico.

A exigência de posse de boa-fé desperta, de imediato, alguns questionamentos, especialmente em vista das disposições do art. 1.201, do Código Civil, cujo *caput* estabelece: "É de boa-fé a posse, se o possuidor ignora o vício, ou o obstáculo que impede a aquisição da coisa". A boa-fé, exigida pelo § 4º do artigo 1.228, do mesmo Código, ajustar-se-ia a este conceito? O Enunciado 309, aprovado na IV Jornada de Direito Civil do Centro de Estudos Judiciários do Conselho da Justiça Federal, cuida da questão: "O conceito de posse de boa-fé de que trata o art. 1.201 do Código Civil não se aplica ao instituto previsto no § 4º do art. 1.228."

A justificativa do Enunciado 309 sustenta ter sido cometido um deslize, nesse parágrafo, capaz de inviabilizar a norma em foco, tendo em conta que será raríssima (ou mesmo inexistente) a hipótese em que considerável número de pessoas tenha se apossado de imóvel com extensa área desconhecendo não ter havido qualquer vício para a aquisição da coisa.[...] Ao que parece, houve um atropelo legislativo, confundindo os conceitos de posse de boa-fé com o de posse justa, já que é possível configurar-se posse de má-fé que não seja injusta.[...] Para que não ocorra a total ineficácia do dispositivo, deverá ser dada interpretação restritiva ao § 4º do art. 1.228 do Código Civil, de modo a excluir a posse de boa-fé do rol dos requisitos para a concessão da figura jurídica ali desenhada. [...] Prestigiar o grave equívoco legislativo, mantendo-se o descompasso do art. 1.201 frente ao § 4º do art. 1.228, com a confusão instaurada entre os conceitos de posse de boa-fé e de posse justa, implicará o esvaziamento, quase completo, do inédito instituto jurídico constante em nosso Código Civil, inutilizando-o como ferramental útil para concretização da função social da propriedade. [47]

[47] Justificativa apresentada pelo Prof. Rodrigo Reis Mazzei ao Enunciado 309 da IV Jornada de Direito Civil do Centro de Estudos Judiciários do Conselho da Justiça Federal). In: *IV Jornada de Direito Civil*, organização Ministro Ruy Rosado de Aguiar Jr., Brasília: Conselho da Justiça Federal, 2007, v. II, p. 632-634. Disponível em: http://www.jf.jus.br/. Acesso em: 15 ago. 2008.

Nas áreas urbanas, a utilidade da desapropriação judicial será de menor importância em razão da introdução, pelo Estatuto da Cidade, da modalidade de usucapião urbana coletiva, não prevista no Código Civil, que apresenta parcial coincidência com o instituto da desapropriação judicial *pro labore*, tornando-a um instituto menos atraente, por depender do pagamento de indenização, enquanto a usucapião urbana coletiva dispensa o pagamento de qualquer indenização para a aquisição da propriedade.

2.2.7. USUCAPIÃO E DIREITO DE SUPERFÍCIE

A disciplina da posse, no Código Civil de 2002, evidencia a influência preponderante dos princípios constitucionais norteadores da criação, interpretação, compreensão e concretização do direito privado. O princípio da função social da propriedade ganha relevo no tocante à aquisição da propriedade por meio da posse qualificada pelo *animus domini*, prevista nas hipóteses da usucapião especial urbana e rural (arts. 183 e 191, da Constituição Federal).

Na hipótese de má utilização da propriedade, a posse sobrepõe-se ao direito de propriedade.[48] Lembra, porém, Sílvio Luís Ferreira da Rocha que a priorização da posse, apontada como um dos principais efeitos da função social da propriedade, não foi totalmente esgotada pelo legislador, uma vez que o Código Civil sujeitou a posse, "enquanto poder de fato exercido sobre um bem no sentido de extrair deste suas utilidades econômicas", prevalecente sobre a propriedade, ao prazo mínimo de duração de cinco anos.[49] Assim, a par da diminuição dos prazos para usucapião, seja na hipótese da usucapião extraordinária (art. 1.238 C.Civil), seja na da usucapião ordinária (art. 1.242 C. Civil), as figuras constitucionais da usucapião urbana e rural foram acolhidas nos arts. 1239 e 1240 do Código Civil. Ressalte-se, ainda, que o Código Civil vai além da Lei nº 10.257/01 porque estende o instituto aos imóveis rurais, não abrangidos pelo Estatuto da Cidade.

O Código Civil, em face do amadurecimento do conceito de função social da propriedade, cuidou, também, em consonância com as disposições

[48] Ramos, Glauco Gumerato. Contributo à dinâmica da chamada desapropriação judicial: diálogo entre Constituição, direito e processo, item 2. Posse, propriedade e Constituição. *Jus navigandi* . Teresina, ano 6, n. 54, fev. 2002. Disponível em http://jus2.uol.com.br/doutrina/texto.asp?. Acesso em 28 set. 2008.

[49] Rocha, Sílvio Luiz Ferreira. *Função social da propriedade pública*. São Paulo: Malheiros, 2005. p. 81.

da Constituição Federal, nos arts. 1.369 a 1.377, do direito de superfície, restaurando e modernizando este instituto, previsto já nas Ordenações Filipinas. Assim, o titular do direito de propriedade pode conceder a outrem, onerosa ou gratuitamente, o direito de construir ou plantar em seu terreno, por tempo determinado, estabelecido em escritura pública, devidamente registrada no Cartório de Registro de Imóveis.

Trata-se de direito autônomo, distinto do direito de propriedade e pode ser instituído em imóvel urbano ou rural, conferindo, ao superficiário, propriedade (propriedade superficiária), de natureza resolúvel. A concessão poderá resolver-se, antes do termo final, se o superficiário der ao terreno destinação diversa daquela para que foi concedida (art. 1.374 C.C.). O direito de superfície já havia sido previsto e instituído pelo Estatuto da Cidade, em seus arts. 21 a 24.

2.3. FUNÇÃO SOCIAL DA PROPRIEDADE URBANA

De acordo com o art. 182, § 2º, da Lei Magna, "a propriedade urbana cumpre sua função social quando atende às exigências fundamentais de ordenação da cidade expressas no plano diretor". A norma se completa com a do § 4º do artigo citado, que faculta ao Poder Público municipal, mediante lei específica para área incluída no plano diretor, exigir, nos termos da lei federal, do proprietário do solo urbano não edificado, subutilizado ou não utilizado, que promova seu adequado aproveitamento, sob pena, sucessivamente, de:

> I – parcelamento ou edificação compulsórios;
>
> II – imposto sobre a propriedade predial e territorial urbana progressivo no tempo;
>
> III – desapropriação com pagamento mediante títulos da dívida pública de emissão previamente aprovada pelo Senado Federal, com prazo de resgate de até dez anos, em parcelas anuais, iguais e sucessivas, assegurados o valor real da indenização e os juros legais.

Portanto, o que ora se faculta ao Poder Público é uma seriação de medidas de cunho inequivocamente coercitivo, as quais desembocam na possibilidade de uma desapropriação com pagamento mediante títulos da dívida pública. A seu turno, os mecanismos de exigibilidade do aproveitamento adequado do solo urbano estão descritos no próprio texto constitucional. A matéria está disciplinada pela Lei 10.257, de 10 de julho de 2001 (Estatuto da Cidade), que regulamenta os artigos 182 e 183 da Constituição Federal e estabelece diretrizes gerais da política urbana, cujos objetivos foram minuciosamente explicitados em seu art. 2º, incisos I a XVII.

As diretrizes gerais de política urbana traçadas pelos incisos I a XIX do art. 2º, do Estatuto da Cidade, são as seguintes: 1 – garantia do direito a cidades sustentáveis; 2 – gestão democrática, por meio da participação da população e de associações representativas dos vários segmentos da comunidade na formulação, execução e acompanhamento de planos, programas e projetos de desenvolvimento urbano; 3 – cooperação entre os governos, a iniciativa privada e os demais setores da sociedade no processo de urbanização, em atendimento ao interesse social; 4 – planejamento do desenvolvimento das cidades, da distribuição espacial da população e das atividades econômicas do Município e do território sob sua influência, de modo a evitar e corrigir as distorções do crescimento urbano e seus efeitos negativos sobre o meio ambiente; 5 – oferta de equipamentos urbanos e comunitários, transporte e serviços públicos adequados aos interesses e necessidades da população e às características locais; 6 – ordenação e controle do uso do solo, de forma a evitar: a) a utilização inadequada dos imóveis urbanos; b) a proximidade de usos incompatíveis ou inconvenientes; c) o parcelamento do solo, a edificação ou o uso excessivo ou inadequado em relação à infra-estrutura urbana; d) a instalação de empreendimentos ou atividades que possam funcionar como pólos geradores de tráfego, sem a previsão da infra-estrutura correspondente; e) a retenção especulativa de imóvel urbano, que resulte na sua subutilização ou não utilização; f) a deterioração das áreaas urbanizadas; g) a poluição e a degradação ambiental; h) a exposição da população a riscos de desastres (Incluído dada pela Lei nº 12.608, de 2012); 7 – integração e complementaridade entre as atividades urbanas e rurais, tendo em vista o desenvolvimento socioeconomico do Município e do território sob sua área de influência; 8 – adoção de padrões de produção e consumo de bens e serviços de expansão urbana compatíveis com os limites da sustentabilidade ambiental social e econômica do Município e do território sob sua área de influência; 9 – justa distribuição dos benefícios e ônus decorrentes do processo de urbanização; 10 – adequação dos instrumentos de política econômica, tributária e financeira e dos gastos públicos aos objetivos do desenvolvimento urbano, de modo a privilegiar os investimentos geradores de bem-estar geral e a fruição dos bens pelos diferentes segmentos sociais; 11 – recuperação dos investimentos do Poder Público de que tenha resultado a valorização de imóveis urbanos; 12 – proteção, preservação e recuperação do meio ambiente natural e construído, do patrimônio cultural, histórico, artístico, paisagístico e arqueológico; 13 – audiência do Poder Público municipal e da população interessada nos processos de implantação de empreendimentos ou atividades com efeitos potencialmente negativos sobre o meio ambiente natural ou construído, o conforto ou a segurança da população; 14 – regularização fundiária e urbanização de áreas ocupadas por população de baixa renda mediante o estabelecimento de normas especiais de urbanização, uso e ocupação do solo e edificação, consideradas a situação socioeconômica da população e as normas ambientais; 15 – simplificação da legislação de parcelamento, uso e ocupação do solo e das normas edilícias, com vistas a permitir a redução dos custos e o aumento da oferta dos lotes e unidades habitacionais; 16 – isonomia de condições para os agentes públicos e privados na promoção de empreendimentos e atividades relativos ao processo de urbanização, atendido o interesse social; 17 – estímulo à utilização, nos parcelamentos do solo e nas edificações urbanas, de sistemas operacionais, padrões construtivos e aportes tecnológicos que objetivem a redução de impactos ambientais e a economia de recursos naturais (Incluído pela Lei nº 12.836, de 2013); 18 – tratamento prioritário às obras e edificações de infraestrutura de energia, telecomunicações, abastecimento de água e saneamento (Incluído pela Lei nº 13.116, de 2015; 19 – garantia de condições condignas de acessibilidade, utilização e conforto nas dependências internas das edificações urbanas, inclusive nas destinadas à moradia e ao serviço dos trabalhadores domésticos, observados requisitos mínimos de dimensionamento, ventilação, iluminação, ergonomia, privacidade e qualidade dos materiais empregados (Incluído pela Lei nº 13.699, de 2018).

Estas diretrizes gerais de política urbana colocaram em discussão temas relevantes, tais como o direito a cidades sustentáveis,[50] a gestão democrática da cidade, a ser exercida por órgãos colegiados de política urbana,[51]

[50] A propósito, Odete Medauar conceitua cidades sustentáveis como "aquelas em que o desenvolvimento urbano ocorre com ordenação, sem caos e destruição, sem degradação, possibilitanto uma vida urbana digna para todos". (Medauar, Odete. Diretrizes Gerais. In: Medauar, Odete; Almeida, Fernando Dias Menezes de (coords.). *Estatuto da Cidade:* Lei 10.257, de 10.07.2001: comentários. 2. ed. rev. atual. e amp. São Paulo: Revista dos Tribunais, 2004, p. 15-40. p.17).

[51] Maria Paula Dallari Bucci propugna pelo deslocamento da formulação da política urbana para o Conselho de Desenvolvimento Urbano, onde houver, desde que conte com recursos técnicos e orçamentários a permitir o desenvolvimentos de suas funções e cuja composição

debates, audiências e consultas públicas, iniciativa popular de projetos de lei, de planos, programas e projetos de desenvolvimento urbano, bem como o plano diretor, de instituição obrigatória em municípios com mais de vinte mil habitantes ou que pretendam utilizar os instrumentos previstos no § 4º do art. 182 da Constituição federal.

Para Hely Lopes Meirelles o plano diretor ou plano diretor de desenvolvimento integrado, como modernamente se diz, é "o complexo de normas legais e diretrizes técnicas para o desenvolvimento global e constante do Município, sob os aspectos físico, social, econômico e administrativo, desejado pela comunidade local".[52]

O plano diretor, meio adequado para dar contorno mais apurado ao conceito de função social da propriedade urbana, mereceu tratamento especial por parte do legislador federal, conforme expresso no Capítulo III, arts. 39 a 42 do Estatuto da Cidade. Esta lei estabeleceu o conteúdo mínimo do plano diretor, as cidades que obrigatoriamente devem elaborá-lo, o prazo para sua revisão, a amplitude do seu alcance, a previsão da integração de suas diretrizes e prioridades na legislação orçamentária e a obrigatoriedade da participação popular na sua elaboração.

Vários instrumentos jurídicos foram especificados pelo Estatuto da Cidade, dentre os quais se destacam a desapropriação, as limitações administrativas, o tombamento de imóveis ou de mobiliário urbano, a instituição de unidades de conservação, a instituição de zonas especiais de interesse social, a concessão de direito real de uso, a concessão de uso especial para fins de moradia, o parcelamento, edificação ou utilização compulsórios, a usucapião especial de imóvel urbano, o direito de superfície, todos com o intento de auxiliar a implementação das diretrizes estabelecidas em seu art. 2º.

2.3.1. DO PARCELAMENTO, EDIFICAÇÃO OU UTILIZAÇÃO COMPULSÓRIOS, IPTU PROGRESSIVO, DESAPROPRIAÇÃO-SANÇÃO

Pela interpretação conjunta do dispositivo constitucional e dos artigos 5º e 8º do Estatuto da Cidade, podem ser apontadas as seguintes exigências

assegure o equilíbrio entre os representantes do Poder Público e os da sociedade civil. A competência consultiva ou deliberativa destes conselhos estaria restrita às matérias não dependentes da edição de lei específica. (Bucci, Maria Paula Dallari. Gestão democrática da cidade (arts. 43 a 45). In: Dallari, Adilson Abreu; Ferraz, Sérgio (coords.). *Estatuto da Cidade*: comentários à Lei Federal 10.257/2001. São Paulo: Malheiros, 2002, p. 322-341. p. 331).

[52] *Direito municipal brasileiro*. 17 ed. São Paulo: Malheiros, 2014, p. 561-562.

para a desapropriação efetuável em nome da política urbana, de competência exclusiva dos Municípios:

a) existência de um plano diretor que defina as exigências fundamentais de ordenação da cidade (art. 182, §§ 1º e 2º, da Constituição); em consonância com o § 1º, o plano diretor, aprovado pela Câmara Municipal, somente é obrigatório para cidades com mais de vinte mil habitantes, constituindo-se em instrumento básico da política de desenvolvimento e de expansão urbana. Contudo, o Estatuto da Cidade, com o objetivo de dar efetividade à função social da propriedade urbana, ampliou, no artigo 41, a exigência constitucional, ao tornar obrigatório o plano diretor para as cidades: I – com mais de vinte mil habitantes; II – integrantes de regiões metropolitanas e aglomerações urbanas; III – onde o Poder Público municipal pretenda utilizar os instrumentos previstos no § 4º do art. 182 da Constituição Federal; IV – integrantes de áreas de especial interesse turístico; V – inseridas na área de influência de empreendimentos ou atividades com significativo impacto ambiental de âmbito regional ou nacional; VI – incluídas no cadastro nacional de Municípios com áreas suscetíveis à ocorrência de deslizamentos de grande impacto, inundações bruscas ou processos geológicos ou hidrológicos correlatos; em consonância com o artigo 42 do mesmo Estatuto, o plano diretor deverá conter, entre outras medidas, a delimitação das áreas urbanas onde poderá ser aplicado o parcelamento, edificação ou utilização compulsórios, considerando, para esses fins, a existência de infra-estrutura e de demanda para utilização;
b) existência de lei municipal específica para área incluída no plano diretor, determinando o parcelamento, a edificação ou a utilização compulsórios do solo urbano não-edificado, subutilizado ou não utilizado, devendo fixar as condições e os prazos para implementação da referida obrigação (art. 5º, *caput*, do Estatuto da Cidade);
c) subutilização do imóvel, ou seja, aproveitamento inferior ao mínimo definido no plano diretor ou em legislação dele decorrente (art. 5º, § 1º);[53]

[53] "O inciso II do § 1º. do art. 5º. do Estatuto da Cidade tinha outra hipótese de subutilização consistente na utilização do imóvel em desacordo com a legislação urbanística ou ambiental, que foi vetado pelo Excelentíssimo Presidente da República com a justificativa de que haveria

Há divergência doutrinária acerca da possibilidade de o plano diretor estabelecer hipóteses diversas de subutilização do imóvel, qualificadas como violadoras do princípio da função social da propriedade ou se, apenas ao Estatuto da Cidade, como veículo normativo previsto na Constituição (art. 182, § 4º), competiria definir subutilização;[54]

d) notificação do proprietário para o cumprimento da obrigação, devendo a notificação ser averbada no cartório de registro de imóveis (art. 5º, § 2º do Estatuto da Cidade).
Embora a lei não preveja expressamente, Sílvio Luis Ferreira da Rocha entende que "a notificação deve ser precedida de verificação que constate a não utilização ou a subutilização do imóvel, pois a subutilização do imóvel constitui o motivo do ato que impõe a obrigação de aproveitar adequadamente o imóvel, devendo, portanto, estar comprovado antes da expedição do referido ato".[55] Em sentido contrário posiciona-se Vera Scarpinella Bueno sob o argumento de não previsão legal e de inexistência de prejuízo para o proprietário, o qual poderia defender-se, atacando a subutilização invocada, antes de sofrer qualquer prejuízo;[56]

uma equiparação inconstitucional, porquanto a Constituição penaliza somente o proprietário que subutiliza o seu imóvel de forma a não atender ao interesse social, não abrangendo aquele que a seu imóvel deu uso ilegal, o qual pode, ou não estar sendo subutilizado". (ROCHA, Sílvio Luís Ferreira da. *Função social da propriedade pública*. São Paulo: Malheiros, 2005. p. 90).

[54] Vera Scarpinella Bueno expressa a opinião de que "a própria Constituição Federal diz que lei municipal pode exigir do proprietário do solo urbano não edificado, subutilizado ou não utilizado o seu adequado aproveitamento *nos termos da lei federal* (art. 182, § 4º). É a lei federal – o Estatuto da Cidade – que trouxe os contornos para a exigência dessa obrigação. Se o Estatuto poderia ter trazido um rol maior de hipóteses de subutilização, esta é outra discussão. O fato é que não o fez. Restringiu o conceito de imóvel urbano subutilizado àquele 'cujo aproveitamento seja inferior ao mínimo definido no plano diretor ou em legislação decorrente'. O Município não tem competência para tratar do assunto, nem para dar uma interpretação que 'encubra'o veto presidencial". (BUENO, Vera Scarpinella. Parcelamento, edificação ou utilização compulsórios da propriedade urbana. In: DALLARI, Adilson Abreu; FERRAZ, Sérgio (coords.). *Estatuto da Cidade*: comentários à Lei Federal 10.257/2001. São Paulo: Malheiros, 2002, p. 87-100. p. 99).

[55] ROCHA, Sílvio Luís Ferreira da. *Função social da propriedade pública*. São Paulo: Malheiros, 2005. p. 91.

[56] BUENO, Vera Scarpinella. Parcelamento, edificação ou utilização compulsórios da propriedade urbana. In: DALLARI, Adilson Abreu; FERRAZ, Sérgio (coords.). *Estatuto da Cidade*: comentários à Lei Federal 10.257/2001. São Paulo: Malheiros, 2002, p. 87-100. p. 96-97.

e) existência de prazo mínimo de um ano, contado a partir do recebimento da notificação, para o proprietário protocolar o projeto no órgão municipal competente e, de dois anos, a partir da aprovação do projeto, para iniciar as obras do empreendimento (§ 4º); excepcionalmente, em empreendimentos de grande porte, a lei municipal específica poderá prever a conclusão em etapas, assegurando-se que o projeto aprovado compreenda o empreendimento como um todo (§ 5º);
f) desatendidos a notificação e os prazos estabelecidos, o Município aplicará o IPTU progressivo no tempo, mediante a majoração da alíquota pelo prazo de cinco anos consecutivos (art. 7º) ou até que se cumpra a obrigação (§ 2º do art 7º); o valor da alíquota a ser aplicada a cada ano será fixado em lei e não excederá a duas vezes o valor referente ao ano anterior, respeitada a alíquota máxima de 15%. Enquanto alguns consideram o percentual de quinze por cento (15%) confiscatório, diante da substancial absorção da propriedade que representará (Regina Helena Costa),[57] outros defendem a constitucionalidade da cobrança, por se tratar de sanção, possuindo, portanto, nítido caráter extrafiscal (Fernando Dias Menezes de Almeida[58] e Diógenes Gasparini[59]).
Nos termos do art. 7º, § 2º do Estatuto da Cidade, dado o caráter sancionador da medida, a cobrança da alíquota máxima obtida pode ser mantida por tempo indeterminado, enquanto o proprietário desatender à obrigação de parcelar, edificar ou utilizar adequada-

A referida autora afirma: "A seguinte questão pode surgir: é necessário que o Poder Público Municipal, antes de notificar o proprietário para dar cumprimento ao disposto nas leis municipais, proceda à vistoria da propriedade, com participação do proprietário do imóvel? Parece-nos que não. Não só porque a lei não previu expressamente este procedimento, mas também porque não traz prejuízo algum ao proprietário o fato de eventual contestação ser posterior à notificação, e não prévia. Não há violação ao princípio do contraditório (CF, art 5º., LIX) pois o proprietário terá oportunidade para apresentar defesa antes que venha a sofrer qualquer gravame".

[57] Costa, Regina Helena. Instrumentos tributários para a política urbana. In: Dallari, Adilson Abreu; Ferraz, Sérgio (Coords.). *Estatuto da Cidade*: comentários à Lei Federal 10.257/2001. São Paulo: Malheiros, 2002, p. 101-136. p.110.

[58] Dos instrumentos da política urbana. In: Medauar, Odete; Almeida, Fernando Dias Menezes de (coord). Medauar, Odete; Almeida, Fernando Dias Menezes de (coords.). *Estatuto da Cidade:* Lei 10.257, de 10.07.2001: comentários. 2. ed. rev. atual. e amp. São Paulo: Revista dos Tribunais, 2004, p. 15-40. p.64.

[59] *O estatuto da cidade.* São Paulo: NDJ, 2002. p. 49.

mente o bem imóvel, havendo, porém, autores, como Regina Helena Costa, que entendem incabível a manutenção da exigência fiscal pela alíquota máxima além do prazo de cinco (5) anos, cabendo, ao Município, recorrer ao instituto da desapropriação, previsto no art. 8º do Estatuto da Cidade;[60]

g) só após decorridos cinco anos de aplicação de IPTU progressivo, sem que o proprietário tenha cumprido a obrigação de parcelamento, edificação ou utilização, é que o Município poderá desapropriar, com pagamento em títulos da divida pública (§ 8º), aprovados pelo Senado e resgatáveis em até dez anos (art. 182, § 4º, III, da Constituição).O valor real da indenização está definido no § 2º do art. 8º do Estatuto da Cidade, devendo "refletir o valor da base de cálculo do IPTU, no caso o valor venal, descontada eventual valorização decorrente de obras realizadas pelo Poder Público na área de localização do imóvel, após a notificação para que o proprietário parcele, edifique ou utilize adequadamente o imóvel. A lei também exclui o pagamento dos lucros cessantes e os juros compensatórios".[61]
Ora, é sabido que nem sempre o valor venal corresponde ao valor real do bem. Ademais, a exclusão de lucros cessantes e juros compensatórios do valor da indenização, determinada pelo Estatuto da Cidade, contrapõe o conceito de real indenização ao de justa indenização, presente na Constituição Federal.
Para alguns, a introdução daquelas restrições, ao valor da justa indenização, seria inconstitucional. Ademais, limitando-se a distinção, no tocante à indenização, entre a desapropriação por interesse público e a desapropriação-sanção prevista no art. 182 da Constituição Federal, ao fato de, nesta última, a indenização não precisar ser prévia e nem em dinheiro, deve prevalecer o entendimento de que o valor real da indenização deve significar o mesmo que justa indenização.[62; 63]

[60] Instrumentos tributários para a política urbana. In: DALLARI, Adilson Abreu; FERRAZ, Sérgio (Coords.). *Estatuto da Cidade*: comentários à lei Federal 10.257/2001. São Paulo: Malheiros, 2002, p. 101-136. p.111-112.

[61] ROCHA, Sílvio Luís Ferreira da. *Função social da propriedade pública*. São Paulo: Malheiros, 2005. p. 97.

[62] BEZNOS, Clóvis. Desapropriação em nome da política urbana. In: DALLARI, Adilson Abreu; FERRAZ, Sérgio (Coords.). *Estatuto da Cidade*: comentários à lei Federal 10.257/2001. São Paulo: Malheiros, 2002, p. 101-136. p. 133.

Para outros, o constituinte desejou um valor indenizatório diverso daquele tradicionalmente pago ao expropriado e o consignou no texto constitucional.[64]

Celso Antônio Bandeira de Mello indaga se a natureza de sanção da desapropriação do imóvel urbano, que não cumpre sua função social, não implicaria o pagamento de indenização diferente da compreendida na expressão "justa indenização" e que, "portanto, não seria apurada segundo um "justo" indagável à luz do valor efetivo do imóvel, mas segundo os critérios estabelecidos no artigo 8º, § 2º, do Estatuto da Cidade, o que significaria a atribuição de menor proteção à propriedade urbana que não cumpre sua função social".[65]

h) uma vez desapropriado o imóvel, deve o Município proceder ao seu aproveitamento adequado, que foi exigido do expropriado; e isso se há de fazer no prazo máximo de cinco anos, contado a par-

[63] Ressalta Maria Sylvia Zanella Di Pietro: o dispositivo é inconstitucional e tem grande possibilidade de ser assim declarado pelo Supremo Tribunal Federal, da mesma forma que o foi, anteriormente, o artigo 11 do Decreto-lei nº 554, de 25-4-69, que dispunha sobre desapropriação para reforma agrária. O dispositivo determinava como teto para a indenização o valor declarado pelo proprietário, para efeito de pagamento o imposto territorial rural, independentemente de considerar se esse teto seria ou não suficiente para recompor integralmente o patrimônio do expropriado. Por essa razão foi declarado inconstitucional (RDA 155/238), tendo sua execução suspensa pelo Senado, por meio da Resolução nº 126, de 8-11-65. A limitação da indenização conflita com a exigência de **indenização justa** contida na Constituição, seja no artigo 5º, inciso XXIV, seja no artigo 182, § 3º. O caráter sancionatório apenas impõe o pagamento em títulos da dívida pública, mas não afeta a exigência de indenização justa, sob pena de a desapropriação adquirir, nesse caso, feição confiscatória. A indenização só é justa quando recompõe inteiramente o patrimônio do desapropriado, abrangendo todos os eventuais prejuízos que decorram da perda da propriedade. (*Direito administrativo.* 33. ed. Rio de Janeiro: Forense, 2020. p.213-214).

[64] GASPARINI, Diógenes. *O estatuto da cidade.* São Paulo: NDJ, 2002. p.62-63.

[65] ROCHA, Silvio Luis Ferreria da. *Função social da propriedade pública.* São Paulo: Malheiros, 2005. p. 99; Celso Antônio Bandeira de Mello, sob a égide da constituição anterior a 1988 sustentou este ponto de vista: "Ergo, existe proteção também para a propriedade que contrarie a função social, conquanto tal proteção seja menos completa, pois, neste caso, a indenização devida não se apura segundo um "justo" perquirível ao lume do valor efetivo do imóvel, mas segundo critérios que a lei estabelecer e far-se-á 'em títulos especiais da dívida pública, resgatáveis no prazo de vinte anos, em parcelas anuais e sucessivas'[...] tudo como dispõe o referido art. 161". (BANDEIRA DE MELLO, Celso Antônio. Novos aspectos da função social da propriedade no direito público. *Revista de Direito Público,* São Paulo, v. 20, n. 84, p. 39-45, out./dez. 1987. p. 41).

> tir da sua incorporação ao patrimônio público, nos termos do § 4º do art. 8º da Lei n. 10.257/01. Por força do "§ 5º do artigo citado, "o aproveitamento do imóvel poderá ser efetivado diretamente pelo Poder Público ou por meio de alienação ou concessão a terceiros, observando-se, nesses casos, o devido procedimento licitatório". O adquirente do imóvel sujeita-se às mesmas obrigações de parcelamento, edificação ou utilização a que se sujeitava o expropriado (§ 6º do art. 8º). Afirma Maria Sylvia Zanella Di Pietro que, embora silente a lei, "é evidente que, se não houver atendimento das exigências quanto ao aproveitamento, o novo proprietário ficará sujeito às mesmas sanções previstas no artigo 182, § 4º, da Constituição, inclusive à desapropriação sancionatória".[66]

Em face da necessidade de atendimento dos requisitos pertinentes a esta modalidade de desapropriação, acima apontados, e sem considerar os prazos para a aprovação do plano diretor e da lei específica, mencionados nas letras *a* e *b*, os demais prazos previstos no Estatuto da Cidade indicam que o decreto de desapropriação não poderá ser expedido antes do transcurso de aproximadamente oito anos. Isto significa que o atendimento de todas as exigências constitucionais e legais passará por três mandatos de prefeito, no mínimo, tornando o instituto difícil de ser aplicado, ainda que juridicamente possível.[67] A Lei nº 10.257/01 não contém normas específicas para o processo de desapropriação, aplicando-se, por esta razão, o mesmo procedimento previsto no Decreto-lei n. 3.365/41 e alterações posteriores[68].

2.3.2. DA USUCAPIÃO ESPECIAL DE BEM IMÓVEL URBANO

O art. 183 da Constituição Federal prevê a possibilidade de usucapião em favor daquele que possuir como sua área urbana de até duzentos e cinquenta metros quadrados, por cinco anos, ininterruptamente e sem oposição, utilizando-a para sua moradia ou de sua família, desde que não seja proprietário de outro imóvel urbano ou rural. É a chamada usucapião

[66] Di Pietro, Maria Sylvia Zanella. *Direito administrativo*, 33. ed. Rio de Janeiro: Forense, 2020. p. 220.

[67] Di Pietro, Maria Sylvia Zanella. *Direito administrativo*, 33. ed. Rio de Janeiro: Forense, 2020. p.198.

[68] Di Pietro, Maria Sylvia Zanella. *Direito administrativo*, 33. ed. Rio de Janeiro: Forense, 2020. p.198

urbana individual. Tal dispositivo foi repetido no artigo 1.240 do Código Civil de 2002.[69]

Por sua vez, o Estatuto da Cidade, no art. 9º, ampliou a abrangência da usucapião urbana individual, possibilitando a sua incidência para área ou edificação urbana de até duzentos e cinquenta metros quadrados. A redação deste dispositivo, se comparada com a redação da Constituição Federal, permitiria a aquisição de edificação, independentemente do terreno ao qual acede.[70]

De outro lado, a ampliação da abrangência da usucapião urbana reabriu discussão a respeito da limitação de duzentos e cinquenta metros quadrados, estabelecida para o bem usucapiendo, que já se pacificara no sentido de que a limitação respeitava apenas o solo, sendo indiferente o tamanho da área construída. A indagação que se propõe é no sentido de saber se o limite de área se refere ao solo, à construção ou a ambos.

A nosso ver, o limite deve atingir tanto a área do terreno, quanto a da edificação, a fim de que seja mantida, sempre, a finalidade, constitucionalmente prevista, deste modo de aquisição da propriedade imóvel. Francisco Eduardo Loureiro acompanha a corrente minoritária, aplicando o limite tanto à área de terreno quanto à construção, sujeitas, ambas, ao teto legal.[71] O direito a esta espécie de usucapião transmite-se aos herdeiros do possuidor, mas, nos termos do § 3º do art. 9º do Estatuto da Cidade, o herdeiro legítimo só continua de pleno direito a posse de seu antecessor se já residir no imóvel no momento da abertura da sucessão. Ou seja, a posse do antecessor falecido continua a ser exercida pelo herdeiro legítimo, que resida no imóvel por ocasião do falecimento do possuidor.

Quando houver pluralidade de herdeiros, e apenas um residir no imóvel no momento da morte, surgem três soluções possíveis: a) todos aguardam o prazo para outras modalidades de usucapião; b) o herdeiro que reside no imóvel nega a composse dos co-herdeiros, afirma ser possuidor

[69] Os requisitos da posse mansa e pacífica por cinco anos de área urbana de até duzentos e cinquenta metros quadrados utilizada como moradia pessoal ou familiar, sem ser proprietário de outro imóvel urbano ou rural configuram atualmente não apenas requisitos da usucapião urbana, como, também, da concessão do direito especial de moradia.

[70] Nesse sentido Loureiro Francisco Eduardo. Usucapião coletivo e habitação popular. *Revista de direito imobiliário*, São Paulo, v. 24, n. 51, p. 133-149, jul./dez. 2001. p. 154.

[71] Loureiro Francisco Eduardo. Usucapião coletivo e habitação popular. *Revista de direito imobiliário*, São Paulo, v. 24, n. 51, p. 133-149, jul./dez. 2001. p. 155.

exclusivo e inaugura novo prazo prescricional e c) a situação jurídica de um herdeiro a todos beneficia.[72] O terceiro posicionamento, adotado por Eduardo Francisco Loureiro,[73] harmoniza-se com a proibição, pelo legislador, na usucapião individual, da *accessio possessionis*, isto é, da soma das posses do antigo e do novo possuidor, adotando entendimento doutrinário e jurisprudencial, que negava aquela possibilidade na usucapião constitucional, exigindo, portanto, posse pessoal do usucapiente.[74]

Todavia, este critério contrasta com o adotado na usucapião coletiva e na concessão de uso especial para fins de moradia, figuras em que a soma das posses é admitida (art. 10, § 1º do Estatuto da Cidade e art. 2º, § 1º, da Medida Provisória nº 2.220, de 4.9.2001). Esclareça-se, ainda, que a concessão da usucapião individual não se vincula ao preenchimento antecipado dos requisitos urbanos e do Plano Diretor da Cidade.[75]

2.3.3. USUCAPIÃO COLETIVA

Determina o art. 10 do Estatuto da Cidade, com a redação dada pela Lei nº 13.465, de 2017, que "Os núcleos urbanos informais existentes sem oposição há mais de cinco anos e cuja área total dividida pelo número de possuidores seja inferior a duzentos e cinquenta metros quadrados por possuidor são suscetíveis de serem usucapidos coletivamente, desde que os possuidores não sejam proprietários de outro imóvel urbano ou rural. Nesta modalidade de usucapião, denominada coletiva, são requisitos a posse qualificada – ininterrupta e sem oposição – por cinco anos ou mais e a impossiblidade de delimitar as áreas ocupadas pelos possuidores, tipificados como população de baixa renda, para sua moradia e desde que não sejam proprietários de outro imóvel urbano ou rural.

O objetivo da usucapião coletiva é tutelar o interesse social de morar, possibilitando a regularização da ocupação de imóveis sem precisa delimitação, nos quais se confundem as moradias existentes, a ponto de não

[72] LOUREIRO Francisco Eduardo. Usucapião coletivo e habitação popular. *Revista de direito imobiliário*, São Paulo, v. 24, n. 51, p. 133-149, jul./dez. 2001. p.156.

[73] Assim no curso da prescrição, caso um dos herdeiros resida no imóvel no momento da morte e eles mantenham composse, poderão todos requerer em litisconsórcio ativo necessário, o usucapião especial.

[74] LOUREIRO Francisco Eduardo. Usucapião coletivo e habitação popular. *Revista de direito imobiliário*, São Paulo, v. 24, n. 51, p. 133-149, jul./dez. 2001. p.155.

[75] LOUREIRO Francisco Eduardo. Usucapião coletivo e habitação popular. *Revista de direito imobiliário*, São Paulo, v. 24, n. 51, p. 133-149, jul./dez. 2001. p.158.

ser possível estabelecer os contornos das áreas ocupadas pelos moradores. Sendo indefinidos os contornos das áreas ocupadas, pode ocorrer até a usucapião coletiva de vielas de acesso, praças e espaços comuns existentes nas áreas ocupadas.[76]

Assevera Eduardo Francisco Loureiro que os imóveis com destinação mista (residencial e comercial) podem ser usucapidos coletivamente, se presente a finalidade residencial. Isto porque os núcleos habitacionais ou favelas formam um todo orgânico, "tratado como unidade pelo legislador, de tal modo que excluir poucos imóveis comerciais – abrindo retalhos dominiais da gleba – pode significar, em casos concretos, a inviabilidade da urbanização futura. Parece que, ocorrendo tal hipótese, qual seja, a de que o recorte de imóveis não residenciais no interior da gleba desfigurem o todo, a aplicação do princípio da razoabilidade e a vocação eminentemente residencial da área, vista como unidade, é que constituem fatores determinantes para o usucapião coletivo."[77]

As disposições do art. 10 do Estatuto da Cidade deram ensejo a questionamentos da doutrina, a respeito da figura por ele criada. Trata-se de saber se a usucapião coletiva constitui nova figura de usucapião. Eduardo Francisco Loureiro e Paulo Eduardo Fucci entendem não ter havido a criação de nova modalidade de usucapião. O primeiro considera a usucapião coletiva "uma espécie de usucapião constitucional urbano, apenas ostentando algumas facetas peculiares para solucionar situações fáticas que encontravam obstáculos de natureza formal para consumação da prescrição aquisitiva",[78] ao passo que o segundo aponta, como inovação, apenas "a instituição de uma modalidade original e temporária do condomínio até que se consume a reurbanização da área ocupada pelo conjunto de moradias, destinada a propiciar a melhoria das condições habitacionais e de saneamento básico, podendo esse condomínio ser extinto a partir de então."[79] Sílvio Luís Ferreira da Rocha, por sua vez, interpretando as disposições do art. 183 da Constituição Federal e as do art. 10 do Estatuto

[76] ROCHA, Sílvio Luís Ferreira da. *Função social da propriedade pública*. São Paulo: Malheiros, 2005. p. 103.

[77] Usucapião coletivo e habitação popular. *Revista de direito imobiliário*, São Paulo, v. 24, n. 51, p. 133-149, jul./dez. 2001. p. 164.

[78] Usucapião coletivo e habitação popular. *Revista de direito imobiliário*, São Paulo, v. 24, n. 51, p. 133-149, jul./dez. 2001. p.159.

[79] FUCCI, Paulo Eduardo. Estatuto da cidade e condomínio especial. *Revista de Direito Imobiliário*, São Paulo, v. 52, jan./jun. 2002. p.140.

da Cidade, no tocante à metragem das áreas usucapiendas, afirma que "a soma das posses individuais pode ultrapassar o limite de duzentos e cinquenta metros quadrados, mas, a área a ser usucapida não pode ultrapassar o múltiplo de autores vezes duzentos e cinquenta metros quadrados.[80]".

O art. 10 do Estatuto da Cidade permite a soma das posses do possuidor atual e de seu antecessor, desde que ininterruptas, para perfazimento do período de cinco anos exigido para a declaração de usucapião. A sentença declaratória de usucapião constitui título a ser registrado no Cartório de Registro de Imóveis. Além disto, a decisão judicial institui condomínio indivisível entre os possuidores, cabendo, a cada um deles, fração idêntica da área do terreno usucapido. Este condomínio não é passível de extinção, exceção feita à hipótese de execução de urbanização posterior à constituição do condomínio, desde que pelo menos dois terços dos condôminos deliberem favoravelmente a ela.

A execução de urbanização posterior à constituição do condomínio, como requisito para a sua extinção, possibilita a realização da reurbanização indispensável para que os residentes possam desfrutar da moradia em condições mais dignas. Se ocorresse a extinção do condomínio antes da execução do projeto de reurbanização, haveria embaraços para eventual remanejamento da localização de habitações e "seria muito mais difícil a obtenção de acordo entre os moradores da área para melhorar as moradias, as condições de saneamento, iluminação e tráfego de pessoas e cargas.[81]

Não há, também, neste condomínio, direito de preferência entre os condôminos, sendo livre a alienação da fração idêntica que cada um deles usucapiu. Ao juiz cabe estabelecer o conceito de "baixa renda", requisito para a concessão da usucapião coletiva. As partes legítimas para propor a ação de usucapião coletiva são as enumeradas no art. 12 do Estatuto da Cidade, a saber: o possuidor, isoladamente ou em litisconsórcio originário ou superveniente; os possuidores, em estado de composse ou, como substituto processual, a associação de moradores da comunidade, regularmente constituída, com personalidade jurídica, desde que explicitamente autorizada pelos representados.

[80] ROCHA Sílvio Luís Ferreira. *Função social da propriedade pública*. São Paulo: Malheiros, 2005. p. 102.

[81] FUCCI, Paulo Eduardo. Estatuto da cidade e condomínio especial. *Revista de Direito Imobiliário*, São Paulo, v. 52, jan./jun. 2002. p.134.

2.3.4. CONCESSÃO DE DIREITO REAL DE USO

Esta figura foi instituída no ordenamento brasileiro pelos arts. 7º e 8º do Decreto-lei 271/67, que dispõe sobre o loteamento urbano, responsabilidade do loteador, concessão de uso do espaço aéreo e dá outras providências. Mais recentemente, a concessão de direito real de uso passou a ser invocada no âmbito do tema da moradia da população de baixa renda.[82] [83] O legislador ampliou o campo de incidência do instituto para atender a outras situações indicativas de interesse social. De acordo com o art. 7º[84] do referido Decreto-lei, com a redação que lhe foi dada pela Lei 11.481,

[82] MEDAUAR, Odete. *Direito administrativo moderno.* 21. ed. rev. e atual. Belo Horizonte: Fórum, 2018. p. 253. A Lei 11.481, de 31-05-2007, em seu art. 7º, alterou o "caput" deste artigo tornando explícito que o instituto em apreço poderia ser utilizado para regularização fundiária e outras modalidades de interesse social.

[83] A Lei 11.481/2007 introduziu na Lei 9.636/98 o art 6º-A que reza: "No caso de cadastramento de ocupações para fins de moradia cujo ocupante seja considerado carente ou de baixa renda, na forma do § 2º do art. 1º do Decreto-Lei nº 1.876, de 15 de julho de 1981, a União poderá proceder à regularização fundiária da área, utilizando, entre outros, os instrumentos previstos no art. 18, no inciso VI do art. 19 e nos arts. 22-A e 31 desta Lei".

[84] Art. 7º É instituída a concessão de uso de terrenos públicos ou particulares remunerada ou gratuita, por tempo certo ou indeterminado, como direito real resolúvel, para fins específicos de regularização fundiária de interesse social, urbanização, industrialização, edificação, cultivo da terra, aproveitamento sustentável das várzeas, preservação das comunidades tradicionais e seus meios de subsistência ou outras modalidades de interesse social em áreas urbanas. (Redação dada pela Lei nº 11.481, de 2007)

§ 1º A concessão de uso poderá ser contratada, por instrumento público ou particular, ou por simples têrmo administrativo, e será inscrita e cancelada em livro especial.

§ 2º Desde a inscrição da concessão de uso, o concessionário fruirá plenamente do terreno para os fins estabelecidos no contrato e responderá por todos os encargos civis, administrativos e tributários que venham a incidir sôbre o imóvel e suas rendas.

§ 3º Resolve-se a concessão antes de seu têrmo, desde que o concessionário dê ao imóvel destinação diversa da estabelecida no contrato ou têrmo, ou descumpra cláusula resolutória do ajuste, perdendo, neste caso, as benfeitorias de qualquer natureza.

§ 4º A concessão de uso, salvo disposição contratual em contrário, transfere-se por ato inter vivos , ou por sucessão legítima ou testamentária, como os demais direitos reais sôbre coisas alheias, registrando-se a transferência.

§ 5º Para efeito de aplicação do disposto no caput deste artigo, deverá ser observada a anuência prévia: (Incluído pela Lei nº 11.481, de 2007)

I – do Ministério da Defesa e dos Comandos da Marinha, do Exército ou da Aeronáutica, quando se tratar de imóveis que estejam sob sua administração; e (Incluído pela Lei nº 11.481, de 2007)

II – do Gabinete de Segurança Institucional da Presidência de República, observados os termos do inciso III do § 1º do art. 91 da Constituição Federal. (Incluído pela Lei nº 11.481, de 2007)

de 2007, a concessão de uso, remunerada ou gratuita, por tempo certo ou indeterminado, incide sobre terrenos públicos ou particulares, "como direito real resolúvel, para fins específicos de regularização fundiária de interesse social, urbanização, industrialização, edificação, cultivo da terra, aproveitamento sustentável das várzeas, preservação das comunidades tradicionais e seus meios de subsistência ou outras modalidades de interesse social em áreas urbanas".

Com a alteração do citado art. 7º, a concessão de direito real de uso passou a ter, entre os seus objetivos, a regularização fundiária, o aproveitamento sustentável das várzeas e a preservação das comunidades tradicionais e seus meios de subsistência. São finalidades de caráter eminentemente social, justificando-se sua menção expressa. Embora se assemelhe à concessão de uso, a concessão de direito real de uso dela difere em dois pontos fundamentais. Na concessão de uso surge relação jurídica de caráter pessoal, tendo as partes relação meramente obrigacional; no presente tipo de concessão de uso é outorgado, ao concessionário, direito real.[85] De outro lado, na concessão de direito real de uso, os fins, nem sempre presentes na concessão de uso, são previamente fixados na lei requladora – urbanização, edificação, industrialização, cultivo ou qualquer outro que traduza interesse social.

A concessão de uso em análise não constava originalmente da relação dos direitos reais contida no Código Civil. Ali foi incluída (art. 1.225, inciso XII), com a alteração introduzida pela Lei nº 13.465, de 2017. Referida lei incluiu, também, a concessão de direito real de uso no rol dos direitos sujeitos à incidência de hipoteca (art. 1.473, IX C.C.). Este direito real pode, ainda, ser objeto de alienação fiduciária, desde que seja passível de alienação. Nas duas hipóteses, se a concessão tiver ocorrido por prazo determinado, a garantia também ficará restrita a esse prazo.[86;87;88] O instituto não é, portanto, específico do direito público, podendo ser utilizado também por particulares (arts. 7º e 8º do Dec-Lei nº 271/67). Pode ter por objeto, além do uso da terra, o uso do espaço aéreo sobre a superfície de

[85] Bandeira de Melo, Celso Antônio, *Curso de direito adminsitrativo*, 34. ed. p. 982.

[86] Art. 1.473, § 2º Código Civil, com a redação da Lei 11.481/2007

[87] Art. 22, § 1º, III e § 2º, da Lei 9.514, de 20-11-97, que disciplina a alienação fiduciária), com a alteração da Lei 11.481/2007.

[88] Carvalho Filho, José dos Santos. *Manual de direito administrativo*. 33. ed. rev. amp. e atual. São Paulo: Atlas, 2019. p. 1267-1269.

terrenos públicos ou particulares, nos mesmos termos e para os mesmos fins impostos para a concessão de uso de terras (art. 8º).

No tocante à sua concessão, a regra é a exigência de licitação; o art. 17, I, "f", "h" e "i" da Lei 8.666/93 a dispensa no caso de imóveis destinados a programas habitacionais ou de regularização fundiária de interesse social, desenvolvidos por órgãos ou entidades da administração pública._(redação dada pelas Leis nº 11.481, de 2007 e 13.465, de 2017). O art. 17, § 2º, da Lei 8.666/93, com redação dada pela Lei nº 11.196, de 2005, e alterado pela Lei nº 13.465, de 2017, prevê que a

> Administração também poderá conceder título de propriedade ou de direito real de uso de imóveis, dispensada licitação, quando o uso destinar-se:
>
> I – a outro órgão ou entidade da Administração Pública, qualquer que seja a localização do imóvel; (incluído pela Lei nº 11.196, de 2005)
>
> II – a pessoa natural que, nos termos de lei, regulamento ou ato normativo do órgão competente, haja implementado os requisitos mínimos de cultura, ocupação mansa e pacífica e exploração direta sobre área rural, observado o limite de que trata o § 1º do art. 6º da Lei nº 11.952, de 25 de junho de 2009 (Redação dada pela Lei nº 13.465, 2017)

Esclareça-se que a regularização do inciso II do § 2º do artigo 17 limita-se às ocupações de áreas não superiores a 2.500 ha (dois mil e quinhentos hectares). A partir da inscrição da concessão de direito real de uso em livro especial de registro público, o concessionário passa a usufruir plenamente do terreno, de acordo com os termos do contrato, e a responder por todos os encargos civis, administrativos e tributários que recaem sobre o imóvel e suas rendas. A concessão transmite-se por ato *inter vivos* ou por sucessão legitima e testamentária, salvo disposição contratual em contrário. Se for dada ao imóvel destinação diversa da prevista no contrato ou alguma cláusula deste for descumprida, a concessão será rescindida, com perda das benfeitorias de qualquer natureza (§ 3º do art. 7º). A concessão poderá ser contratada por instrumento público ou particular ou por simples termo administrativo e será inscrita e cancelada em livro especial (§ 1º do art. 7º). Sua outorga depende de autorização legislativa, salvo exceção legal.[89] A concessão de direito real de uso mostra-se vantajosa, pois

[89] MEDAUAR, Odete. *Direito administrativo moderno.* 21. ed. rev. e atual. Belo Horizonte: Fórum,, 2018. p. 254.

não só salvaguarda o patrimônio da Administração, mas também evita a alienação de bens públicos. De outro lado, o concessionário fica adstrito a destinar o bem ao fim estabelecido em lei, o que resguarda o interesse público pelo qual se pautou a concessão real de uso.[90]

2.3.5. CONCESSÃO DE USO ESPECIAL PARA FINS DE MORADIA

A concessão de uso especial para fins de moradia foi prevista no art. 4º, V, "h" do Estatuto da Cidade (Lei 10.257, de 2001), mas, tendo sido vetados os dispositivos que dela tratavam (arts. 15 *usque* 20), só veio a ser regulada pela MP 2.220, de 04-09-2001, em atenção ao disposto no § 1º do art. 183 da CF. Aplica-se também a imóvel público remanescente de desapropriação, cuja propriedade tenha sido transferida a empresa pública ou sociedade de economia mista (Lei 11.481, de 2007, art. 25).

A concessão de uso especial de que trata a Medida Provisória nº 2.220, de 4 de setembro de 2001, é destinada àqueles que, até 30-06-2001, alterada pela Lei 13.465/17, para até 22 de dezembro de 2016, tinham a posse, por cinco anos ininterruptos e sem oposição, de imóvel público situado em área urbana, de até 250 metros quadrados, utilizando-o como sua moradia, desde que não sejam proprietários ou concessionários de outro imóvel urbano ou rural.[91]

Se a ocupação acarretar risco à vida ou à saúde dos possuidores, o Poder Público garantirá o exercício do direito em outro local (art. 4º, Medida Provisória nº 2.220, de 2001). Neste caso, a Administração está vinculada à outorga desse direito, não podendo decidir de forma diversa. Já nas hipóteses previstas no art. 5º da Medida Provisória nº 2.220, de 2001 (ocupação de imóvel): a) a de uso comum do povo; b) destinado a projeto de urbanização; c) de interesse da defesa nacional, da preservação ambiental e da proteção dos ecossistemas naturais; d) reservado à construção de represas

[90] CARVALHO FILHO, José dos Santos. *Manual de direito administrativo*. 33. ed. rev. amp. e atual. São Paulo: Atlas, 2019. p. 1269.

[91] Os pressupostos são bem semelhantes aos do usucapião especial urbano:
a) posse por cinco anos até 22/12/2016 (v. Lei 13.465, de 11/7/2017);
b) posse ininterrupta e pacífica (sem oposição);
c) imóvel urbano público de até duzentos e cinquenta metros quadrados;
d) uso do terreno para fins de moradia do possuidor ou de sua família; e
e) não ter o possuidor a propriedade de outro imóvel urbano ou rural (art. 1º) (José dos Santos Carvalho. Manual de Direito Administrativo, . 33. ed. rev. amp. e atual. São Paulo: Atlas p. 1270).

e obras congêneres; e) situado em via de comunicação, o legislador conferiu ao Poder Público a faculdade de assegurar o exercício do direito em outro local, rendendo ensejo, assim, à sua atuação discricionária.[92]

A outorga da concessão para moradia pode ocorrer por termo administrativo, quando o benefício for requerido administrativamente. Se houver negativa da Administração Pública, ou esta for omissa na apreciação do pedido, o interessado poderá recorrer ao Judiciário. Os títulos de outorga da concessão especial de uso para fins de moradia – termo administrativo ou decisão judicial – são suscetíveis de registro no Cartório de Registro de Imóveis.[93] (art. 167, I, n. 37, da Lei 6.015/73, alterado pela Medida Provisória nº 2.220/2001). A concessão de uso especial para fins de moradia, à semelhança do direito real de uso, foi incluída, pela Lei nº 11.481/07, entre os direitos reais enumerados no art. 1.225 do Código Civil, bem como entre os bens que podem ser objeto de hipoteca (art. 1.473, VIII, do mesmo Código).

Além disto, o direito de uso especial para fins de moradia passou a figurar como objeto de alienação fiduciária, podendo, portanto, ser transferido, pelo devedor, de forma resolúvel, ao credor, como garantia contratual.[94] [95] Esta concessão especial de uso aproxima-se da concessão do direito real de uso prevista no DL 271/67, mas dela se distingue porque se restringe à finalidade de moradia do possuidor, o que não ocorre naquela. Além disto, trata-se de um direito do possuidor, sobre coisa alheia, concretizado mediante o preenchimento dos requisitos legais. É direito real, resolúvel[96] e pode ser transferido por ato *inter vivos* ou *causa mortis* (art. 7º, Medida Provisória 2.220, de 2007). A outorga de direito real de uso de imóvel público, para fins de moradia do possuidor ou de sua família, é ato administrativo vinculado.[97]

[92] Carvalho Filho, José dos Santos. *Manual de direito administrativo.* 33. ed. rev. amp. e atual. São Paulo: Atlas, 2019. p. 1273.

[93] Carvalho Filho, José dos Santos. *Manual de direito administrativo.* 33. ed. rev. amp. e atual. São Paulo: Atlas, 2019. p. 1272-1273

[94] Art. 22, § 1º, II, da Lei 9.514, de 20-11-97 (que dispõe sobre a alienação fiduciária), com a redação da Lei nº 11.481/2007.

[95] Carvalho Filho, José dos Santos. *Manual de direito administrativo.* 33. ed. rev. amp. e atual. São Paulo: Atlas, 2019. p. 1271.

[96] Meirelles, Hely Lopes Meirelles. *Direito administrativo brasileiro.* 42. ed. atualizada até a Emenda Constitucional 90, por José Emmanuel Burle Filho e Carla Rosado Burle. São Paulo: Malheiros, 2016. p. 649.

[97] Carvalho Filho, José dos Santos. *Manual de direito administrativo.* 33. ed. rev. amp. e atual. São Paulo: Atlas, 2019. p. 1271.

A concessão de uso especial para fins de moradia e a usucapião especial urbana instituída pelo art.183 da Constituição Federal, regulado pela Lei 10.257, de 2001 (Estatuto da Cidade), distinguem-se, em primeiro lugar, quanto ao objeto. Na última, o objeto é imóvel privado; na primeira, é imóvel público (federal, estadual, distrital ou municipal, desde que regular a ocupação). Outro traço distintivo dos dois institutos é a necessidade, na concessão, de preenchimento dos requisitos legais, pelo possuidor, até 22 de dezembro de 2016, ao passo que, na usucapião, não existe termo final previsto para a aquisição do direito.[98] Ressalte-se, ainda, que não há, na concessão de uso especial para fins de moradia, transferência do domínio, tal como ocorre na usucapião.

Na esfera federal, a concessão de uso especial para fins de moradia aplica-se às áreas de propriedade da União, alcançando, inclusive, os terrenos de marinha e acrescidos, desde que os possuidores ou ocupantes preencham os requisitos legais estabelecidos na Medida Provisória nº 2.220, de 4 de setembro de 2001 (art. 22-A da Lei 9.636 de 1998, incluído pela Lei 11.481, de 2007). Esse direito não se aplica a imóveis funcionais (§ 1º). Por outro lado, não há, para o ocupante, direito subjetivo à concessão em foco, relativa à ocupação de imóveis sob administração do Ministério da Defesa ou dos Comandos da Marinha, do Exército e da Aeronáutica; tais imóveis são considerados de interesse da defesa nacional, o que permite que a Administração transfira a concessão para outra área (art. 5º, inciso III, da Medida Provisória nº 2.220 e art. 22-A, § 2º. Lei n. 9.636/1998).

Para evitar o desvio de finalidade do instituto, o direito à concessão de uso especial para fins de moradia só será reconhecido uma vez ao mesmo possuidor. A concessão será gratuita e poderá ser outorgada ao homem ou à mulher, ou a ambos, sendo irrelevante o estado civil dos interessados. No caso de morte do possuidor, o herdeiro legítimo continua a posse do antecessor, desde que já resida no imóvel ao tempo da abertura da sucessão (art. 1º, § 3º). Sem esta condição, não haverá continuidade e, em conseqüência, inviável será a outorga da concessão.[99]

As formas de extinção da concessão de uso especial são as previstas no art. 8º da Medida Provisória nº 2.220/2001, a saber: 1º) ocorrência de desvio

[98] Carvalho Filho, José dos Santos. *Manual de direito administrativo.* 33. ed. rev. amp. e atual. São Paulo: Atlas, 2019. p. 1270.

[99] Carvalho Filho, José dos Santos. *Manual de direito administrativo.* 33. ed. rev. amp. e atual. São Paulo: Atlas, 2019. p. 1270-1271,1272.

de finalidade, ou seja, destinação do imóvel, pelo concessionário, a outro fim que não o de moradia para si ou para sua família; 2º) aquisição, pelo usuário, da propriedade de outro imóvel urbano ou rural. A extinção da concessão deverá ser averbada no Cartório de Registro de Imóveis, a fim de produzir efeitos *erga omnes*.[100]

De acordo com o art.2º da Medida Provisória nº 2.220/2001, com a redação dada pela Lei nº 13.465, de 2017, se o imóvel, ocupado por população de baixa renda, para sua moradia, tiver área superior a duzentos e cinquenta metros quadrados e não for possível discriminar os terrenos ocupados, a concessão será conferida de forma coletiva (art. 2º), preenchidos os demais pressupostos, à semelhança da usucapião especial coletiva de imóvel urbano particular, disciplinada pela Lei nº 10.257/2001 (Estatuto da Cidade). Neste caso, a cada concessionário será atribuída igual fração ideal do terreno, independentemente da área de terreno que cada possuidor ocupe, salvo hipótese de acordo escrito entre os ocupantes, estabelecendo frações ideais diferenciadas. A fração ideal outorgada a cada possuidor não poderá ser superior a duzentos e cinquenta metros quadrados. A José dos Santos Carvalho Filho parece singular, e até mesmo se afigura esdrúxulo, que a concessão seja outorgada para incidir sobre uma fração ideal do terreno. Entretanto, deve considerar-se que o instituto tem caráter urbanístico e visa a regularizar a situação imobiliária de infinito número de pessoas, integrantes do que a lei denominou de "população de baixa renda". Além disso, procurou o legislador assemelhar esse tipo de concessão ao usucapião especial de imóvel urbano privado, figura em que, pela formação de condomínio, o domínio de fração ideal de terreno não acarreta qualquer estranheza. Por fim, é preciso aceitar que a ordem urbanística está mesmo a reclamar medidas jurídicas novas, ainda mais quando se cuida de garantir o bem-estar, a segurança e a comodidade das populações.[101]

2.3.6. DIREITO DE SUPERFÍCIE

"Direito de superfície é aquele pelo qual o proprietário concede a outrem o direito de utilizar, no mínimo, a superfície de seu imóvel na forma pactuada no respectivo contrato. Embora seja contrato de direito privado, nada

[100] Carvalho Filho, José dos Santos. *Manual de direito administrativo*. 33. ed. rev. amp. e atual. São Paulo: Atlas, 2019. p. 1273.

[101] Carvalho Filho, José dos Santos. *Manual de direito administrativo*. 33. ed. rev. amp. e atual. São Paulo: Atlas, 2019. p. 1273-1274.

impede que ente público, desde que haja lei autorizadora, conceda ao administrado o direito de utilizar a superfície do imóvel público.[102] Registre-se, aliás, que o art. 1.377, do Cód. Civil, admite expressamente que o referido direito seja constituído por pessoa jurídica de direito público interno.[103] Fundamental é que haja minuciosa motivação a fim de aferir-se a legalidade do negócio jurídico. Cabe à Administração – enfatize-se – demonstrar limpidamente as razões de ordem administrativa que a levaram à contratação, bem como o interesse público que resultará do contrato".

Trata-se de instituto que pode revelar-se importante instrumento para o cumprimento da função social da propriedade imobiliária, pois permite a construção ou plantação sem necessidade de aquisição do terreno, portanto com menor ônus para o interessado. Tem por principal efeito suspender, por prazo determinado, o efeito aqusitivo da acessão, isto é, a regra geral de que o acessório segue o principal, ou seja, de que o dono do solo (principal) adquire, pelo só fato da acessão, a propriedade do que no seu imóvel for edificado ou plantado (acessório).

"Sem dúvida o direito de superfície é instituto similar à enfiteuse, sobretudo porque, tanto quanto esta, comporta o desmembramento da propriedade, figurando, como *dominus* da nua-propriedade, o proprietário (que pode ser a pessoa estatal) e, como titular do direito de uso, o *superficiário*. Difere da enfiteuse, contudo, porque o superficiário, em princípio, pode alienar seu direito sem anuência do proprietário, o que não ocorria com aquela. Ademais, na enfiteuse o foro (ou cânon) é da essência do instituto, ao passo que o valor ajustado no direito de superfície (solarium) não o é. Por último, o inadimplemento do foro na enfiteuse provoca a extinção desta, ao passo que na superfície a extinção nessa hipótese é eventual.[104] Há duas disciplinas que regulam o direito de superfície. Uma delas encontra-se nos arts. 21 a 24 do Estatuto da Cidade (Lei nº 10.257, de 10.07.2001) e a outra no Código Civil, entre os arts. 1.369 a 1.377. A primeira se insere

[102] CARVALHO FILHO, José dos Santos. *Comentários ao Estatuto da Cidade.* 2. ed. Rio de Janeiro: Lumen Juris, 2006. p. 148.

[103] Na hipótese – dita o dispositivo – aplica-se o Código Civil, *"no* que *não for diversamente disciplinado* em *lei especial"*. Como a Lei 10.257/2001 é lei especial, será ela aplicada a imóveis em áreas urbanas.

[104] A respeito, consulte-se LIRA, Ricardo Pereira. *Elementos* de *direito urbanístico.* Rio de Janeiro: Renovar, 1997, p. 62; CARVALHO FILHO, José dos Santos. *Comentários ao Estatuto da Cidade.* 2. ed. Rio de Janeiro: Lumen Juris, 2006. p. 199.

em *lei especial,* destinada a regular o referido negócio em *áreas urbanas* e voltada especificamente para a política de desenvolvimento urbano (art. 182, CF). Conseqüentemente, o Código Civil, embora materializado por lei mais nova, caracteriza-se como *lei geral,* e, portanto, será aplicável a imóveis situados fora da área urbana. Incide aqui o art. 2º, § 2º, da Lei de Introdução ao Código Civil, segundo o qual não ocorre revogação quando lei geral sucede a lei especial. Ambos os diplomas, por conseguinte, convivem harmoniozamente dentro do sistema, cada um deles incidindo sobre esfera jurídica específica.

O direito de superfície deve formalizar-se por contrato, como consta da lei, revelando as manifestações volitivas do proprietário e do superficiário. No instrumento contratual é que as partes devem pactuar detalhamente os direitos e obrigações atribuídos a cada uma delas. A natureza jurídica é a de *direito real* sobre a coisa alheia. O Código Civil, inclusive, inseriu expressamente o direito de superfície no elenco dos direitos reais (art. 1.225, II). Constituído o direito, deve ser objeto de averbação no respectivo cartório do registro de imóveis. Como corolário, o direito é transferível a terceiros por ato *inter vivos* ou *causa mortis* (arts. 24, § 2º, do Estatuto da Cidade, e 1.369, do Cód. Civil). Pode, inclusive, ser objeto de garantia real no âmbito do sistema financeiro da habitação, cujos agentes não podem recusá-la (art. 13 da Lei n. 11.481, de 31.5.2007). Quanto ao *objeto* do negócio jurídico, a lei refere-se à concessão da superfície do *terreno,* parecendo indicar apenas o solo puro. Entretanto, a lei disse menos do que queria *(minus quam voluit).* Na verdade, tanto pode o terreno puro ser objeto do contrato, como eventual edificação que a ela tenha acedido pelo princípio da acessão natural *(superficies solo cedit).*[105] O terreno, desse modo, é a *reserva mínima* para figurar como objeto contratual, nada impedindo maior extensão.

No cotejo entre as disciplinas do Estatuto da Cidade e do Código Civil, encontram-se algumas diferenças de tratamento da matéria (o que é um complicador indesejável). Vejamos as distinções básicas: 1ª) no Estatuto da Cidade, o direito de superfície pode ser ajustado por prazo determinado ou indeterminado (art. 21), ao passo que no Código Civil o ajuste deve ser apenas por prazo determinado (art. 1.369) (note-se que o Estado, como proprietário, só pode contratar por prazo determinado); 2ª) o direito

[105] Com o mesmo entendimento, ALMEIDA, Fernando Dias Menezes de. *Estatuto da Cidade.* São Paulo: RT, 2009. p. 114.

de superfície no Estatuto abrange, como regra, o direito de utilização do subsolo (art. 21, § 1º), o que não ocorre no Cód. Civil, a menos que a obra seja inerente ao objeto do contrato (art. 1.369, parág. único); 3ª) o Código Civil alude à constituição do direito por pessoa jurídica de direito público interno (art. 1.377), ao passo que o Estatuto é silente a respeito (embora o próprio Código Civil, como vimos, admita a incidência da lei especial, suprindo, pois, a omissão do Estatuto); 4ª) o Código Civil regula a hipótese de desapropriação, estabelecendo que a indenização caberá ao proprietário e ao superficiário, sendo proporcional ao valor do direito real de cada um (art. 1.376); o Estatuto não regulou tal hipótese. Nesse caso, entendemos aplicável, subsidiariamente, por ser lei geral, o Código Civil quando se tratar de desapropriação de imóvel situado em áreas urbanas.

Por fim, releva destacar que, no caso de alienação da propriedade ou do direito de superfície, terão *direito* de *preferência,* respectivamente, o superficiário e o proprietário, em igualdade de condições à oferta de terceiros. Extinto o negócio, o proprietário recuperará a propriedade plena do imóvel, só tendo a *obrigação* de *indenizar* acessões e benfeitorias feitas pelo superficiário se o contrato for expresso a respeito".[106]

2.4. FUNÇÃO SOCIAL DA PROPRIEDADE RURAL

O conceito de imóvel ou propriedade rural, a par de não ter sido objeto de disposição constitucional, também não foi disciplinado pelo atual Código Civil. Todavia, ao longo dos anos, definições de imóvel rural, contidas em dispositivos infraconstitucionais, apontaram, como traço característico da propriedade rural, ora a sua destinação, ora a respectiva localização. Atualmente, o direito positivo brasileiro acolhe dois conceitos de imóvel rural: um, vinculado à destinação do bem, é encontrado na legislação agrária; outro, caracterizado pelo critério da localização do imóvel, exclusivamente para efeitos de desapropriação para fins de reforma agrária. Além disto, por força do art. 29 do Código Tributário Nacional (Lei nº 5.172, de 25.10.1966), é considerado imóvel rural, para fins tributários, o localizado fora da zona urbana do município.[107]

[106] Carvalho Filho, José dos Santos. *Manual de direito administrativo.* 33. ed. rev. amp. e atual. São Paulo: Atlas, 2019. p. 1278-1279.

[107] De acordo com Bastos, Celso Ribeiro. *Comentários à Constituição do Brasil.* São Paulo: Saraiva, 1990, v. 7. p. 253 "o imóvel rural é o que se encontra topograficamente no campo. Será rural todo aquele que não for urbano conforme definido pelo próprio município, respeitadas

Sem embargo da existência de tais conceitos de propriedade rural, adotados por agraristas (critério da destinação do imóvel) e tributaristas (critério da localização), o imóvel rural deve, também, cumprir sua função social. Afirma Alberto Ballarin Marcial que a função social da propriedade rural "consiste, antes de tudo, na obrigação, a cargo do proprietário inerte, de converter-se em empresário ativo, integrando sua terra em uma organização produtiva que alcance índices ótimos do ponto de vista da produtividade e dos demais aspectos sociais".[108] O cumprimento da função social da propriedade rural consiste no atendimento dos requisitos do art. 186 da Constituição Federal, compreendendo o aproveitamento racional e adequado do imóvel, a utilização adequada dos recursos naturais disponíveis e preservação do meio ambiente, a observância das disposições que regulam as relações de trabalho e a exploração que favoreça o bem-estar dos proprietários e dos trabalhadores.

Portanto, o preenchimento dos requisitos da função social da propriedade rural está vinculado a três aspectos: econômico (exploração eficiente e aproveitamento adequado), social (normas trabalhistas e bem-estar dos empregados) e ecológico (proteção do meio ambiente). Estes requisitos, de resto, já haviam sido estabelecidos pelo art. 2° do Estatuto da Terra (Lei nº 4.504/64). A Constituição Federal prevê sanções aplicáveis na hipótese de não atendimento da função social da propriedade rural. Entre elas, encontram-se: o aumento progressivo do ITR, o confisco da terra utilizada para o cultivo de plantas psicotrópicas, a usucapião agrária e a desapropriação por interesse social para fins de reforma agrária.

Além destas, existem outras sanções, de caráter penal, civil e administrativo, trabalhista e ambiental, contidas em nosso ordenamento jurídico, a serem aplicadas ao proprietário do imóvel rural, que não atende a sua função social. O art. 184 da Constituição Federal prevê a desapropriação

as diretrizes gerais em lei da União. É óbvio que se o município se encontra em área urbana, ainda que com destinação agrária, ele não pode ser sujeito da desapropriação própria dos rurícolas [...] Imóvel rural para os fins desse artigo é o que no campo se encontra. Em outras palavras, as áreas rurais são compostas de imóveis rurais com exclusão das pequenas porções de terra que porventura lhe dêem uma destinação não-agrária. Por isso é muito feliz a expressão de Tupinambá Miguel Castro do Nascimento quando diz que "imóvel rural é o localizado em zona rural e cuja destinação econômica, efetiva ou potencial, tem agrariedade" (*A ordem econômica e financeira e a nova Constituição:* arts 170 a 192. Rio de Janeiro: Aide, 1989. p.102).

[108] MARCIAL, Alberto Ballarin. Nueva función social de la propiedad rústica. *Rivista di Diritto Agrario,* Milano, v. 51, n. 1, p. 62, gen./mar. 1972.

por interesse social para fins de reforma agrária, como sanção ao proprietário rural que não cumprir a função social do seu imóvel, ou seja, se este for considerado de grande extensão e improdutivo. Neste caso, a indenização não será em dinheiro, mas em títulos da dívida agrária, com cláusula de preservação do valor real.

A competência para promover esta modalidade de desapropriação, também chamada de desapropriação-sanção, é exclusiva da União.[109] A desapropriação para fins de reforma agrária não pode, nos termos do art. 185 da Constituição Federal, incidir sobre a pequena e a média propriedade rural, definidas na Lei n° 8.629/93, desde que o seu proprietário não possua outra propriedade, ou sobre a propriedade produtiva.[110]

A pequena e a média propriedade rural estão conceituadas no art. 4º da Lei nº 8.629/93, com as alterações produzidas pela Lei 13.465/2017. O artigo citado deixa claro, ainda, que tais propriedades são insuscetíveis de desapropriação desde que seu proprietário não possua "outra propriedade rural". A propriedade produtiva, a seu turno, é definida, pelo art. 6º da Lei nº 8.629/93, como "aquela que, explorada econômica e racionalmente, atinge, simultaneamente, graus de utilização da terra e de eficiência na exploração, segundo índices fixados pelo órgão federal competente".

O pagamento da indenização, no caso, é feito em títulos da dívida agrária. Tratando-se de processo expropriatório sancionador do descumprimento da função social da propriedade, no requisito produtividade, a indenização ao proprietário omisso não é paga em dinheiro, mas em títulos da dívida agrária, com longo prazo para resgate.[111] Ainda no âmbito da

[109] Maria Sylvia Zanella Di Pietro adverte que a competência é da União somente quando o imóvel rural se destine à reforma agrária, podendo os Estados e Municípios desapropriar imóveis rurais para fins de utilidade pública. (*Direito administrativo*, 33. ed. Rio de Janeiro: Forense, 2020. p. 205).

[110] Na ementa do Mandado de Segurança nº 22.022, o Supremo Tribunal Federal considera que "a propriedade produtiva, independentemente de sua extensão territorial e da circunstância de o seu titular ser, ou não, proprietário de outro imóvel rural, revela-se intangível à ação expropriatória do Poder Público em tema de reforma agrária (CF, art. 185,II), desde que comprovado, de modo inquestionável, pelo impetrante, o grau adequado e suficiente de produtividade fundiária"(STF –MS nº 22.022/ES , Pleno, rel. Min. Celso de Mello, j. 7-10-1994, v.u. DJ 04-11-94). No mesmo sentido MS 31735/MC/DF, decisão monocrática, rel Min. Dias Toffoli, j. 04/12/2012; MS 24152/DF, decisão monocrática, rel. Min. Dias Toffoli, j. 11/09/2012; MS22.478/PR, Pleno, rel. Maurício Correa,j. 30/06/97, DJ 26/09/97, p. 47479

[111] Rezek, Gustavo Elias Kallás. *Imóvel agrário*: agrariedade, ruralidade e rusticidade. Curitiba: Juruá, 2007. p. 136.

questão da função social da propriedade rural, são encontrados outros institutos: legitimação de posse, disciplinada pela Lei nº 6.383, de 07 de dezembro de 1976; regularização da ocupação de terras devolutas com área superior a cem hectares; usucapião especial, prevista na Lei nº 6.969, de 10 de dezembro de 1981 e usucapião constitucional.

A legitimação de posse, originalmente contemplada na Lei nº 601, de 18 de setembro de 1850 (Lei de Terras), foi objeto do art. 99 do Estatuto da Terra (Lei nº 4.504, de 1964). A Constituição de 1967, com a redação da Emenda Constitucional nº 1, de 17 de outubro de 1969, cuidou da legitimação de posse no art. 171: "a lei federal disporá sobre as condições de legitimação de posse e de preferência para aquisição, até cem hectares, de terras públicas por aqueles que as tornarem produtivas com o seu trabalho e o de sua família". Nos termos do art. 29 da Lei nº 6.383, de 07 de dezembro de 1976, é prevista a outorga da legitimação ao ocupante de terras públicas, de área contínua de até 100 hectares, que as tenha tornado produtivas com o seu trabalho e o de sua família e que não seja proprietário de imóvel rural e comprove a morada permanente e a cultura efetiva, pelo prazo mínimo de um ano.

A legitimação consiste, conforme determinam os §§ 1º e 3° do art. 29 da Lei nº 6.383 de 1976, no fornecimento de uma Licença de Ocupação, pelo prazo mínimo de quatro anos, findo o qual o ocupante terá preferência para a aquisição do lote, pelo valor histórico da terra nua, satisfeitos os requisitos de moradia permanente e cultura efetiva e comprovada a sua capacidade para desenvolver a área ocupada (art. 29, § 3º da Lei n. 6.383/76). O art. 2º da Lei nº 6.969, de 1981, por sua vez, trata da usucapião especial. Esta se caracteriza pela posse, por cinco anos ininterruptos, sem oposição, de área rural contínua, não superior a 25 hectares, tornada produtiva por todo aquele que, não sendo proprietário rural ou urbano, nela tiver, também, a sua moradia e abrange, na forma daquela lei, terras particulares e terras devolutas em geral.

A doutrina, em face das disposições do parágrafo único do art. 191 da Constituição Federal de 1988 – "os imóveis públicos não serão adquiridos por usucapião" – passou a entender estar proibida a usucapião de terras devolutas. A este entendimento opõe-se Celso Ribeiro Bastos, afirmando que as terras devolutas, embora titularizadas por pessoas jurídicas de direito público, não se sujeitam a um regime jurídico também de direito público, "a que estão normalmente submetidos os bens públicos na plena acepção da palavra", posto que desvinculadas do atingimento de fim público, permanecendo como um estoque de áreas ainda não repassadas aos particulares ou que, tendo saido das mãos destes, voltaram ao patrimônio do Estado. Considerando, portanto, a destinação a que estão afetas as terras devolutas, bem como entendendo que estas terras são possuídas, pelo Poder Público, "à moda de um particular", Celso Ribeiro Bastos afirma estarem, as terras devolutas, sujeitas à usucapião especial. O autor referido fundamenta, ainda, sua assertiva no texto constitucional, dizendo:

> Assim é que o art. 188 da Lei Maior faz referência no mesmo preceito às terras públicas e às terras devolutas, deixando certo que acolheu a distinção esposada cientificamente. Se as terras devolutas fossem públicas, não haveria necessidade da sua referência. Essa só se explica pelo fato de o Texto Constitucional ter perfilhado a tese segundo a qual só são públicos os imóveis quando sujeitos a um regime de direito público. Portanto, é forçoso reconhecer que, nada obstante um imóvel ser público por compor o domínio de uma pessoa de direito público, ele pode ser dominical do ponto de vista da sua destinação ou utilização. Esses são usucapíveis.[112]

Também Sílvio Luis Pereira da Rocha admite a possibilidade de usucapião de bens não afetados a uma finalidade pública (dominicais) apesar da expressa vedação constitucional. Explica o autor que [...] as regras constitucionais que proíbem a usucapião de bens públicos (arts. 183, § 3.º, e 191, parágrafo único, da Constituição Federal) devem ser interpretadas e compreendidas à luz do princípio da função social da propriedade, que, como visto, informa, também, a propriedade pública [...] no caso dos bens dominicais, semelhantes aos bens privados, o princípio da função social da propriedade comporta o efeito de submetê-los à força aquisitiva da posse contínua e pacífica, não bastando para impedir este efeito uma proposição genérica que subtrai os bens públicos do raio de ação da prescrição aquisitiva [...] portanto, há necessidade de interpretarmos a proibição da usucapião dos bens públicos para adequá-la somente em relação aos bens considerados de uso comum do povo e de uso específico ou especial.[113]

[112] *Comentários à Constituição do Brasil*. São Paulo: Saraiva, 1990. v. 7. p. 239-240.

[113] Sílvio Luís Ferreira da Rocha. *Função social da propriedade pública*. São Paulo: Malheiros, 2005. p. 151-153.

Posição semelhante é defendida por Juarez Freitas que, balizado na redação do art. 188 da CF, e se referindo a terras públicas e terras devolutas, teria criado outra categoria de bens (bens não públicos) e, portanto, usucapíveis. Conclui o autor que [...] a leitura combinada e sistemática dos arts. 20, II, 26, IV, 188, "caput", 183, § 3.º, e 191, parágrafo único, da Constituição Federal, desde que atenta ao "telos" inescapável e cristalino de dar adequado uso à propriedade, conduz à conclusão de que a vontade da Constituição no que tange à insuscetibilidade de usucapião de imóveis públicos pode ser relativizada por outros princípios superiores, dentre os quais avulta o da função social, obedecidos determinados requisitos legais e sem ofensa aos comandos dos arts. 183, § 3.º, e 191, parágrafo único, da Carta Ápice, conquanto, indisputavelmente, melhor, sob a ótica científica, sustentar a mudança constitucional que agasalhe expressamente a interpretação oferecida como mais justa.[114] "Há entendimento no sentido de que é vedado usucapião apenas sobre bens materialmente públicos, assim considerados aqueles em que esteja sendo exercida atividade estatal".[115]

Não parece, contudo, ser essa a correta exegese da norma constitucional. A toda evidência, os dispositivos da Constituição que vedam a usucapião de bens públicos não fazem distinção entre categorias de bens para a submissão a essa proteção. Assim, sendo os bens dominicais integrantes da categoria bens públicos, não há razão para retirar-lhes essa garantia. Ademais, correta a lição de Odete Medauar quando identifica que a finalidade da imprescritibilidade é, sobretudo, "a preservação dos bens públicos, protegendo-os até contra a negligência da própria Administração".[116] Maria Sylvia Zanella Di Pietro lamenta a proibição constitucional de qualquer tipo de usucapião de imóvel público,e salienta que"essa proibição constitui um retrocesso por retirar do particular que cultiva a terra um dos instru-

[114] Freitas, Juarez. *Da necessária reclassificação dos bens públicos:* estudos de direito administrativo. São Paulo: Malheiros, 1995. p. 73.

[115] Fortini, Cristiana. A função social dos bens públicos e o mito da imprescritibilidade. *Revista de Direito Municipal*, Belo Horizonte, ano 5, n. 12, p. 113-122, 2004.

[116] Odete Medauar. *Direito administrativo moderno.* 21. ed. Belo Horizonte: Fórum, 2018. p. 250. No mesmo sentido, afirma Floriano de Azevedo Marques Neto que com a imprescritibilidade o Direito impede que possa haver disposição de bem público por omissão administrativa e, não, por decisão legítima. (Marques Neto, Floriano de Azevedo. *Bens públicos*: função social e exploração econômica. O regime jurídico das utilidades públicas. Belo Horizonte: Fórum, 2009. p. 304).

mentos de acesso à propriedade pública, precisamente no momento em que se prestigia a função social da propriedade".[117]

José dos Santos Carvalho Filho observa que já se decidiu, equivocadamente em nosso entender, "que a imprescritibilidade alcança bens da Caixa Econômica, no caso de ser financiado pelo Sistema Financeiro de Habitação, ainda que se trate de pessoa de direito privado.[118] Trata-se de desvio de perspectiva não autorizado nem pela Constituição nem pela lei civil e do qual dissentimos, com a devida vênia. O argumento da função social nos parece infundado, e isso porque se proprietário e financiador se mostram inertes quanto a propriedade, é porque não há nenhuma função social, nem justificativa para prejudicar o direito do terceiro possuidor.".[119]

Trata-se da outra face do poder de intangibilidade dos bens públicos. Pela impenhorabilidade impede-se a perda pela via judicial; pela imprescritibilidade impede-se a perda pela aquisição direta pelo particular. Esse poder de intangibilidade ampliou sobremaneira o direito de sequela do Estado que pode, a qualquer momento, reivindicar um bem público ainda que este esteja na posse de particular por um longo período. Há formas de legitimação da posse de particulares sobre bens públicos, mas não a aquisição automática da propriedade pelo mero fato da posse. Portanto, apenas a posse prolongada de particular sobre bem público não é capaz de torná-lo proprietário como se daria se o bem fosse de outro particular.

"Apesar de alguns autores equivalerem essa "legitimação de posse" à própria alienação do bem público, entendemos que assim não pode ser entendido em razão de o art.31 da Lei n.6.383/76 dispor: 'A União poderá,

[117] DI PIETRO, Maria Sylvia Zanella. *Direito administrativo*, 33. ed. Rio de Janeiro: Forense, 2020. p. 879.

[118] STJ, REsp. 1.448.026, j. 17.11.2016.

[119] CARVALHO FILHO, José dos Santos. *Manual de direito administrativo*. 33. ed. São Paulo: Atlas, 2019, p.1240-1241. José Carlos de Moraes Salles assevera, com apoio nos ensinamentos de Hely Lopes Meirelles, Celso Antônio Bandeira de Mello, Diógenes Gasparini e Maria Sylvia Zanella Di Pietro, que, a partir da promulgação da Constituição de 1988, não haveria a usucapião especial rural sobre terras devolutas rurais: "Não resta, portanto, a menor dúvida de que as *terras devolutas, bens públicos patrimoniais* na definição de Hely Lopes Meirelles [...], não podem ser objeto de usucapião, até porque, atualmente, não só por entendimento consagrado na Súmula 340 do Pretório Excelso, mas e principalmente em virtude de normas expressas da Constituição de 1988 (§ 3º do art. 183 e parágrafo único do art. 191), "os imóveis públicos não serão adquiridos por usucapião".(*Usucapião de bens imóveis e móveis*. 5. ed. São Paulo: Revista dos Tribunais, 1999. p. 280).

por necessidade ou utilidade pública, em qualquer tempo que necessitar do imóvel, cancelar a Licença de Ocupação e imitir-se na posse do mesmo, promovendo, sumariamente, a sua desocupação no prazo de 180 (cento e oitenta) dias.'"[120] "A Lei n. 11.977, de 7.7.2009, que dispõe sobre 'Programa Minha Casa, Minha Vida', prevê a conversão da legitimação da posse em registro de propriedade, 'tendo em vista sua aquisição por usucapião, na forma do art. 183 da Constituição Federal' (art. 60). Infelizmente, o legislador só fez aumentar a confusão sobre a matéria. Na verdade, nem há usucapião, nem o autoriza o art. 183 da CF. A aquisição da propriedade, ao contrário, decorre da própria autorização contida na lei".[121]

2.4.1. USUCAPIÃO CONSTITUCIONAL

A usucapião constitucional, nos termos do art. 191, da Constituição Federal, possibilita a aquisição da propriedade de área de terra, não superior a cinquenta hectares e localizada em área rural, por aquele que, não sendo proprietário de imóvel rural ou urbano, dela tenha a posse ininterrupta e sem oposição, por cinco anos, tornando-a produtiva, por seu trabalho ou de sua família e nela tendo sua morada.

A condição de não proprietário, exigida do ocupante, deve estar presente durante os cinco anos do período aqusitivo. Neste sentido, é a lição de Celso Ribeiro Bastos.[122] Quanto à permanência do possuidor na área usucapienda, entende-se que a sua posse não é descaracterizada por breves ausências, sendo obstáculo, à aquisição da propriedade, a ausência prolongada, anormal, com entrega da área a terceiros, que afasta a pessoalidade da posse.[123] [124]

A Carta de 1934, que deu início ao processo de adoção de normas de caráter social e sedimentou ideias ruralistas já desenvolvidas, entre elas as fundamentadas no projeto de Código Rural de Joaquim Luís Osório, ela-

[120] ARAGÃO, Alexandre Santos de. *Curso de direito administrativo.* Rio de Janeiro: Forense, 2013. p.511, nota de rodapé n.35.

[121] CARVALHO FILHO, José dos Santos. *Manual de direito administrativo.* 33. ed. São Paulo: Atlas, 2019. p. 1241.

[122] *Comentários à Constituição do Brasil.* São Paulo: Saraiva, 1990, v. 7. p. 342.

[123] SALLES, José Carlos de Moraes. *Usucapião de bens imóveis e móveis.* 5. ed. São Paulo: Revista dos Tribunais, 1999. p.256; BASTOS, Celso Ribeiro. *Comentários à Constituição do Brasil.* São Paulo: Saraiva, 1990, v. 7. p.346.

[124] SALLES, José Carlos de Moraes. *Usucapião de bens imóveis e móveis.* 5. ed. São Paulo: Revista dos Tribunais, 1999. p. 256.

borado em 1912 e restrito ao estado do Rio Grande do Sul, criou a usucapião *pro labore*, tendo por objeto áreas rurais de até dez hectares (art. 125). Apesar do evidente retrocesso nos direitos criados pela Constituiçao de 1934, a Carta de 1937 reproduziu, praticamente, no art. 148, os termos do citado artigo 125. O instituto foi mantido pela Constituição de 1946, com ampliação da área suscetível de usucapião para vinte e cinco hectares (artigo 156, § 3º). Nova ampliação, para cem hectares, surgiu com o advento da Emenda Constitucional nº 10, de 09.11.1964. Finalmente, o art. 191 da Constituição Federal de 1988 reduziu, para cinquenta hectares, a área objeto da usucapião constitucional.[125]

José Carlos de Moraes Salles afirma que a usucapião especial rural não é cabível no caso de a posse recair sobre área rural superior a cinquenta hectares, ainda que a pretensão do possuidor seja a de usucapir área menor ou igual "que a do limite imposto pelo art. 191 da Constituição, fazendo-o com fundamento nesta norma". Isto porque, na opinião do citado autor, se possível fosse a hipótese cogitada, "consagrada estaria a burla ao dispositivo constitucional em exame, porque bastaria ao prescribente instalar-se em área maior que a prevista no referido artigo, esperar o decurso do tempo (cinco anos) e preencher os demais requisitos previstos na aludida norma, para, posteriormente, contornar o preceito constitucional, reduzindo suas pretensões a área igual ou inferior a cinquenta hectares". Conclui José Carlos de Moraes Salles:

> A burla se caracterizaria, especialmente, sob o aspecto de que o proprietário "dormidor", atento à circunstância de que o usucapião só se consubstanciaria em prazo maior [...], poderia ter deixado a adoção de providências tendentes à recuperação de seu imóvel para ocasião mais oportuna, dentro daquele prazo maior, vindo a ser surpreendido, entretanto, pelo *usucapião especial rural* do art. 191 da Lei Maior, cujo reconhecimento seria pleiteado pelo prescribente em prazo menor (cinco anos), sobre área igual ou menor que a estabelecida no dispositivo constitucional, situada dentro da área maior inicialmente ocupada e possuída.[126]

125 SALLES, José Carlos de Moraes. *Usucapião de bens imóveis e móveis*. 5. ed. São Paulo: Revista dos Tribunais, 1999. p. 251.

126 SALLES, José Carlos de Moraes. *Usucapião de bens imóveis e móveis*. 5. ed. São Paulo: Revista dos Tribunais, 1999. p. 252-253.

Contrariamente, posiciona-se Celso Ribeiro Bastos, considerando que impedir a usucapião de área superior a cinquenta hectares equivaleria a punir aquele que, zelosamente, tornou produtiva área superior à suscetível de usucapião especial.[127]

CONCLUSÕES

O princípio da função social da propriedade, princípio-garantia (art. 5º, XXIII) e princípio político estruturante da organização econômico-social do Estado (art. 170, III, 182, §2º e 186), tem incidência reconhecida sobre a propriedade privada, conformando-a. Saliente-se que a aplicação do princípio da função social não acarreta a extinção do direito de propriedade, mas, sim, compatibiliza o seu exercício com as normas da Constituição Federal. Por força da observância daquele princípio, o uso e o gozo da propriedade estão condicionados às disposições da Constituição Federal, ficando, o proprietário, obrigado a dar, ao seu bem, destinação que assegure a todos existência digna, segundo os ditames da justiça social e em benefício dos interesses da coletividade.

O potencial do princípio da função social da propriedade poderá ser ampliado pelas decisões de nossos tribunais, aplicando-se a outras hipóteses de exercício do direito de propriedade contrárias à sua finalidade social, além das já previstas nos institutos jurídicos criados para atribuir-lhe a devida eficácia.

REFERÊNCIAS

ALMEIDA, Fernando Dias Menezes de. Dos instrumentos da política urbana. In: MEDAUAR, Odete; ALMEIDA, Fernando Dias Menezes de (coord). *Estatuto da cidade: Lei 10.257, de 10.07.2001: comentários.* 2. ed. rev. atual. e amp. São Paulo: Revista dos Tribunais, 2004, p. 15-40.

ARAGÃO, Alexandre Santos. *Curso de direito administrativo.* Rio de Janeiro: Forense, 2013.

BANDEIRA DE MELLO Celso Antônio. Natureza jurídica do zoneamento- Efeitos. *Revista de Direito Público,* São Paulo, n. 61, p.34-47, 1982.

BANDEIRA DE MELLO Celso Antônio. *Curso de direito administrativo.* 34. ed. rev e atual. São Paulo: Malheiros, 2018

BANDEIRA DE MELLO Celso Antônio. Novos aspectos da função social da propriedade no direito público. *Revista de Direito Público,* São Paulo, v. 20, n. 84, p. 39-45, out./dez. 1987

[127] BASTOS, Celso Ribeiro. *Comentários à Constituição do Brasil.* São Paulo: Saraiva, 1990, v. 7. p.347.

BARROSO, Lucas de Abreu. Hermenêutica e operabilidade dos parágrafos 4º e 5º do art. 1.228 do Código Civil. *Revista de Direito Privado*, São Paulo, n. 21, p. 130-138, 2005.

BASTOS, Celso Ribeiro. *Comentários à Constituição do Brasil*. São Paulo: Saraiva, 1990, v. 7.

BENJAMIN, Antonio H. V. Função Ambiental. In: BENJAMIN, Antonio H. V (coord.). *Dano ambiental:* prevenção, reparação e repressão. São Paulo: Revista dos Tribunais, 1993, p. 9-82.

BEZNOS, Clóvis. Desapropriação em nome da política urbana. In: DALLARI, Adilson Abreu; FERRAZ, Sérgio (Coords.). *Estatuto da Cidade*: comentários à lei Federal 10.257/2001.

BUCCI, Maria Paula Dallari. Gestão democrática da cidade (arts. 43 a 45). In: DALLARI, Adilson Abreu; FERRAZ, Sérgio (coords.). *Estatuto da Cidade*: comentários à lei Federal 10.257/2001. São Paulo: Malheiros, 2002, p. 322-341.

BUENO, Francisco da Silveira. *Grande dicionário etimológico-prosódico da língua portuguesa*. São Paulo: Saraiva, 1968.

BUENO, Vera Scarpinella. Parcelamento, edificação ou utilização compulsórios da propriedade urbana. In: DALLARI, Adilson Abreu; FERRAZ, Sérgio (coords.). *Estatuto da Cidade*: comentários à lei Federal 10.257/2001. São Paulo: Malheiros, 2002, p. 87-100.

CAMBI, Eduardo. Controvérsias constitucionais acerca do usucapião coletivo. *Revista Magister de Direito Civil e Processual Civil*, ano II, n. 12, maio/jun. 2006.

CARVALHO FILHO, José dos Santos. *Comentários ao Estatuto da Cidade*. 2. ed. Rio de Janeiro: Lumen Juris, 2006.

CARVALHO FILHO, José dos Santos. *Manual de direito administrativo*. 33. ed. rev. amp. e atual. São Paulo: Atlas, 2019.

CASTRO, Mônica. *A desapropriação judicial no novo Código Civil*. Disponível em: <http://www.mundojuridico.adv.br/sis_artigos/artigos.asp?codigo=486>. Acesso em: 03 abr. 2008.

COSTA, Regina Helena. Instrumentos tributários para a política urbana. In: DALLARI, Adilson Abreu; FERRAZ, Sérgio (Coords.). *Estatuto da Cidade*: comentários à lei Federal 10.257/2001. São Paulo: Malheiros, 2002.

CRETELLA JÚNIOR, J. *Comentários à Constituição brasileira de 1988*. 3. ed. Rio de Janeiro: Forense Universitária, 1992.

DALLARI, Adilson Abre. *Desapropriação para fins urbanísticos*. São Paulo: Forense, 1981.

DI PIETRO, Maria Sylvia Zanella. *Direito administrativo*, 33. ed. Rio de Janeiro: Forense, 2020.

DINAMARCO, Cândido Rangel. *Instituições de direito processual civil*. 4. ed. São Paulo: Malheiros, 2004, v. 3.

DINIZ, Maria Helena. *Código civil anotado*. 9· ed. rev. e atual. São Paulo: Saraiva, 2003.

FERREIRA FILHO, Manoel Gonçalves. *Curso de direito constitucional*. 32. ed. São Paulo: Saraiva, 2006.

FREITAS, Cleuton César Ripol de. A desapropriação judiciária e os conflitos coletivos pela posse. In: SEMINÁRIO NACIONAL DE DIREITO AGRÁRIO. I, 1975. Anais...Brasília, Associação Brasileira de Direito Agrário, 9 a 13.12.2002 (CD-ROM);

FUCCI, Paulo Eduardo. Estatuto da cidade e condomínio especial. *Revista de Direito Imobiliário*, São Paulo, v. 52, jan./jun. 2002.

GAFFIOT, Félix. *Dictionnaire illustré latin français*. Paris: Hachette, 1934.

GAGLIANO, Pablo Stolze .Controvérsias constitucionais acerca do usucapião coletivo.. *Revista Magister de Direito Civil e Processual Civil*, ano II, n. 12, maio/jun. 2006. p.37-42

GASPARINI, Diógenes. *O Estatuto da cidade*. São Paulo: NDJ, 2002.

JORNADAS DE DIREITO CIVIL I, III E IV. Enunciados Aprovados. In: *Jornada de Direito Civil*, organização Ministro Ruy Rosado de Aguiar Jr. Brasília : CJF, 2007, p.67. Disponível em: <http://www.jf.jus.br>. Acesso em: 15 ago. 2008.

KOJRANSKI, Nelson. Direitos reais. In: MARTINS FILHO, Ives Gandra da Silva; MENDES, Gilmar Ferreira; FRANCUILLI NETO, Domingos (coord.). *O novo Código Civil*: estudos em homenagem ao Prof. Miguel Reale. São Paulo: LTr, 2003. p. 981-1016.

LIMA, Ruy Cirne. Princípios de Direito Administrativo, 5. ed. São Paulo: RT, 1982.

LIRA, Ricardo Pereira. *Elementos* de *direito urbanístico*. Rio de Janeiro: Renovar, 1997.

LOUREIRO Francisco Eduardo. Usucapião coletivo e habitação popular. *Revista de direito imobiliário*, São Paulo, v. 24, n. 51, p. 133-149, jul./dez. 2001.

LOUREIRO Francisco Eduardo. *A propriedade como relação jurídica complexa* . 2001. Dissertação (Mestrado em Direito) – Faculdade de Direito, Pontifícia Universidade Católica de São Paulo, São Paulo, 2001.

MALUF, Carlos Alberto Dabus. Direitos reais. In: Seminário Novo Código Civil Brasileiro: o que muda na vida do cidadão, 2003, Brasília. Anais. Brasília: Câmara dos Deputados, Centro de Documentação e Informação, Coordenação de Publicações, 2002, p. 230-241

MALUF, Carlos Alberto Dabus. *Novo Código Civil Comentado*. FIÚZA, Ricardo (Coord.) 4. ed. São Paulo: Saraiva, 2005.

MARCIAL, Alberto Ballarin. Nueva función social de la propiedad rústica. *Rivista di Diritto Agrario*, Milano, v. 51, n. 1, p. 62, gen./mar. 1972.

MEDAUAR, Odete. *Direito administrativo moderno*. 21. ed. rev. atual.e ampl. Belo Horizonte: Fórum,, 2018.

MEDAUAR, Odete. Diretrizes Gerais. In: MEDAUAR, Odete; ALMEIDA, Fernando Dias Menezes de Almeida (coords.). *Estatuto da Cidade:* Lei 10.257, de 10.07.2001: comentários. 2. ed. rev. atual. e amp. São Paulo: Revista dos Tribunais, 2004, p. 15-40.

MEIRELLES, Hely Lopes. *Direito administrativo brasileiro. Direito administrativo brasileiro.* 42. ed. atualizada até a Emenda Constitucional 90, por José Emmanuel Burle Filho e Carla Rosado Burle. São Paulo: Malheiros, 2016.

MEIRELLES, Hely Lopes. *Direito municipal brasileiro*. 17 ed. 2. tir. DALLARI, Adilson Abreu (coord.) São Paulo: Malheiros, 2014.

MORAIS, Alexandre de. *Direitos humanos fundamentais*. São Paulo: Atlas, 2000.

NASCIMENTO, Tupinambá Miguel Castro do. *A ordem econômica e financeira e a nova Constituição:*arts 170 a 192. Rio de Janeiro: Aide, 1989.

NERY JUNIOR, Nelson; NERY, Rosa Maria de Andrade. *Código Civil Comentado*. 6. ed. rev. amp. e atual. São Paulo: Revista dos Tribunais, 2008.

NOBRE JÚNIOR, Edílson Pereira. A posse e a propriedade no novo Código Civil. *Revista de Direito Privado*, Disponível em: <www.jfrn.gov.br/docs/doutrina180.doc> . Acesso em: 16 jan. 2009.

PADIN, Patricia Waldmann. *Aspectos fundamentais do usucapião coletivo*. 2010. 127 f. Dissertação (Mestrado em Direito) – Faculdade de Direito, Universidade de São Paulo, São Paulo, 2010.

PINTO FERREIRA. *Comentários à Constituição brasileira*. São Paulo: Saraiva, 1989.

RABAHIE, Marina Mariani de Macedo. A função social da propriedade. In: DALLARI, Adilson Abreu e FIGUEIREDO, Lúcia Valle (coords.) *Temas de Direito Urbanístico 2*. São Paulo: Revista dos Tribunais, 1991, p. 213-258.

RAMOS, Glauco Gumerato. Contributo à dinâmica da chamada desapropriação judicial: diálogo entre Constituição, direito e processo. *Jus Navigandi*, Teresina, ano 10, n. 931, 20 jan. 2006. Disponível em: <http://jus2.uol.com.br/doutrina/texto.asp?id=7857>. Acesso em: 09 out. 2008.

RAMOS, Glauco Gumerato. Contributo à dinâmica da chamada desapropriação judicial: diálogo entre Constituição, direito e processo, item 2. Posse, propriedade e Constituição. *Jus navigandi*. Teresina, ano 6, n. 54, fev. 2002. Disponível em <http://jus2.uol.com.br/doutrina/texto.asp?>. Acesso em 28 set. 2008.

REALE, Miguel. Exposição de motivos ao Ministro da Justiça. Diário do Congresso Nacional, Seção I, Suplemento B ao n. 061,13.6.1975n, 27c, p.121.

RENTERÍA, Pablo. A aquisição da propriedade imobiliária pela acessão invertida social: análise sistemática dos parágrafos 4º e 5º do artigo 1228 do Código Civil. In: *Revista Trimestral de Direito Civil*, Rio de Janeiro, v. 9, n. 34, abr./jun. 2008, p. 71-91.

REZEK, Gustavo Elias Kallás. *Imóvel agrário*: agrariedade, ruralidade e rusticidade. Curitiba: Juruá, 2007.

ROCHA, Cármen Lúcia Antunes. O Princípio Constitucional da Função Social da Propriedade. In: BACELLAR FILHO, Romeu Felipe (coord.geral); MOTA, Paulo Roberto Ferreira; CASTRO, Rodrigo Pironti Aguirre de (coord.). *Direito Administrativo Contemporâneo*: estudos em memória ao professor Manoel de Oliveira Franco Sobrinho. Belo Horizonte: Fórum, 2004.

ROCHA, Sílvio Luís Ferreira da. *Função social da propriedade pública*. São Paulo: Malheiros, 2005.

SALLES, José Carlos de Moraes. *Usucapião de bens imóveis e móveis*. 5. ed. São Paulo: Revista dos Tribunais, 1999.

SILVA, José Afonso da. *Curso de direito constitucional positivo*. 36. ed. São Paulo: Malheiros, 2013.

SILVA, José Afonso da. *Direito urbanístico brasileiro*, 5.ed., rev. e atual. São Paulo: Malheiros, 2008.

STEFANINI, Luís de Lima. *A propriedade no direito agrário*. São Paulo: Revista dos Tribunais, 1978.

Controvérsias constitucionais acerca do usucapião coletivo. *Revista Magister de Direito Civil e Processual Civil*, ano II, n. 12, maio/jun. 2006. p.40.

SUNDFELD Carlos Ari. *Direito administrativo ordenador*. São Paulo: Malheiros, 200.

TORRINHA, Francisco. *Dicionário latino português*. Porto: Marânus, 1945.

VENOSA, Silvio de Salvo. *Direito civil*: direitos reais. 5. ed. São Paulo: Atlas, 2005. v. 5.

VIANA, Marco Aurélio. *Comentário ao Novo Código Civil*, dos Direitos Reais. V. XVI. Rio de Janeiro: Forense, 2003.

ZANOBINI, Guido. Corso di Diritto Amministrativo, 5. ed., Milano, Giuffrè, 1958, v. IV.

GIANDOMENICO ROMAGNOSI (1761-1835): ENTRE LA LEY Y EL PROCESO PENAL Y LA FILOSOFÍA DEL DERECHO PÚBLICO[1]

GIOVANNI CHIARINI[*]

INTRODUCCIÓN: LA UNIVERSIDAD DE LOS ESTUDIOS DE ROMAGNOSI

Con mucho placer y orgullo intentaré exponer brevemente la inmensa figura de Gian Domenico Romagnosi, quien merece ser conocido en profundidad incluso en los países de América Latina, dada su importante tradición legal y sus interacciones con nuestro sistema de orden.

Hacer una presentación a este autor eterno es un deber, debido a sus estudios interdisciplinarios y a sus pasiones, y considerando que hoy en día existe una innumerable cantidad de escritos que no han sido ordenados y recopilados. Escribe por ejemplo un profesor autorizado de derecho comparado como Lanchester, Romagnosi es "prolicromado en el espacio y en el tiempo" [2], y además de ser un estudioso de derecho y juicio penal, también afrontó las cuestiones de derecho constitucional y administrativo, especialmente desde un punto de vista filosófico, así como otros temas, como la filosofía política, la economía e incluso la hidráulica. Un autor

[*] Doutorando em Direito pela Universidad de Insubria – Itália. Advogado.

[1] Artículo publicado para el Revista de Ciencia de la Legislación (Argentina) N° 7 Abril 2020; traducido por la Doctora Pamela Eulissa Ambrosi Miranda, hablante nativo de español, graduada en la Universidad Católica del Sagrado Corazón de Piacenza en Gestión Internacional, Facultad de Economía y Jurisprudencia.

[2] F. LANCHESTER, "Romagnosi costituzionalista", pubblicazione per AIC (Associazione Italiana dei Costituzionalisti), rivista n. 4/2011, pag. 1

como Bruno Brunello en este apunto afirma que la figura de Romagnosi permaneció (y permanece) "casi oculta a la sombra de la conciencia de los italianos, aunque generalmente se sabía quién era. [3]" De hecho, se observa que "Romagnosi es, muy a menudo, objeto de mera curiosidad histórica para los mismos amantes de las disciplinas practicadas por él, pero también objeto de distorsión, porque cada uno tiende a construir un Romagnosi adapto a sus propias posiciones, perdiendo así la visión general. [4]" Un constitucionalista como Antonio D'Aloia, por otro lado, escribe que Romagnosi es "un intérprete moderno de una fase extraordinaria de la historia italiana y europea[5]" y un estudioso como Albertoni sugiere que "en realidad su pensamiento político y social es demasiado temprano en el momento real del desarrollo italiano[6]".

En este breve artículo, me detendré en la contribución que Romagnosi ha brindado a la ciencia criminal en general (incluidos en particular los aspectos procesales, considerando obviamente que en ese momento la procedura penal aún no se consideraba un tema totalmente autónomo), así como su análisis en profundidad publicista (administrativo y constitucional), fundamentalmente filosófico. De hecho, parece imposible rastrear un análisis de todas las disciplinas estudiadas por el Supremo, ya que implicaría el riesgo de hacer una colección puramente teórica, que no le daría honor, porque Romagnosi "es grado de hablarnos, de pesar sobre las preocupaciones y los problemas de la actualidad", quedando todavía "envuelto en la bruma de errores y clichés erróneos"[7], errores que, desafortunada-

[3] B. BRUNELLO, "Il pensiero politico italiano dal Romagnosi al Croce", Bologna, Zuffi Editore, 1949, pag. 7 ss. Va ricordato inoltre che il Romagnosi è studiato in gran parte delle Università europee e anglosassoni. Basti citare, ad esempio, l'opera inglese *"The Cambridge History of Eighteenth-Century Political Thought"* o *"From Kant to Croce: Modern Philosophy in Italy, 1800-1950"* oltre che la prestigiosa collana dell' *"Harvard Economic studies"*

[4] F. LANCHESTER, "Romagnosi costituzionalista", op. cit., pag. 1

[5] A. D'ALOIA, "Percorsi del costituzionalismo italiano: il contributo di Gian Domenico Romagnosi", pag. 2, rielaborazione dell'intervento per la conferenza "Alle origini della Costituzione italiana: il contributo di Gian Domenico Romagnosi", Parma, 14 dicembre 2011

[6] A. D'ALOIA, op. cit. pag. 8. Vedi anche R. GHIRINGHELLI, "Modernità e democrazia nell'altro Risorgimento. Studi Romagnosiani", Milano, 2002, pag. 107 e E. A. ALBERTONI, Introduzione a R. GHIRINGHELLI e F. INVERNICI (a cura di), "Per conoscere Romagnosi", Milano, 1982, pag. 14

[7] F. MERUSI "Romagnosi amministrativista", pag. 165, atti del seminario "Le origini del diritto amministrativo nel pensiero di Romagnosi", 9 novembre 2011, Parma

mente, son cada vez más frecuentes en los tiempos modernos que aún vivimos, ricos en palabras pero de poca sustancia, incluso desde el punto di vista legal. Por lo tanto, su lectura puede ser vista como una breve, pero intensa, "reconstituyente", para "consumir" en este desierto de aridez de pensamiento que domina nuestro presente.

1. LAS CUESTIONES PROCESALES Y SUSTANTIVAS DE LA GÉNESIS DEL DERECHO PENAL

En 1791, en que los logros de las conquistas del periodo del iluminismo se fusionaron con las típicas instancias represivas, el Maestro escribió una de sus obras más importantes, el "Génesis del derecho penal". Ya desde las primeras páginas se percibe el genio de este escrito y su impronta interpretativa basada en el equilibrio de los diferentes intereses que intervienen cada vez que se habla, en general, de la ley y el juicio penal. En la introducción, por ejemplo, escribió literalmente que "si es importante, de hecho, un derecho del pueblo, que la legislación no vaya más allá de los límites inmutables de la moderación justa al decretar sanciones, además de ocuparse de toda la sociedad, esto quiere decir que sus individuos deberán ser persuadidos por su justicia. Cuán deseable para el orden social sea ese acuerdo, en el cual el delincuente, en el acto de ser castigado, se dice así mismo: "Me lo he merecido" y el espectador declara que tiene razón"[8], refiriéndose a la importancia de la proporcionalidad de la pena , que no debe desbordarse en un castigo excesivo o anormal, pero que al mismo tiempo debe garantizar las necesidades de la seguridad social y también debe ser percibida como justa incluso en la opinión pública misma, así como en los condenados.

El Maestro, entonces, en la primera parte del trabajo antes mencionado, lleva a cabo un profundo razonamiento en torno al concepto de defensa personal argumentando: "supongamos ahora el caso de una agresión. Está claro que tengo el derecho a preservar la vida, y que venga respetada; por lo tanto, como un medio necesario, tengo el derecho de escapar o rechazar el delito, hasta la seguridad más completa. Este medio se llama defensa", definiendo la defensa legítima como "la eliminación de sí misma de cualquier actual, inminente o ciertamente futuro delito". Curioso, sobre este punto,

[8] G.D Romagnosi, "Genesi del diritto penale", 1791, V edizione, Tipografia Giusti, Prato, 1833, parte prima, p. I dell'introduzione

que los requisitos de actualidad y la inminencia de la defensa legítima sigan siendo hoy las piedras angulares de la discriminante en cuestión. Del mismo modo, con respecto al requisito de necesidad (que todavía es esencial a nivel normativo), Romagnosi sostiene: "el mal que quiero llevar al delincuente, para defenderme, ¿debe ser necesario para ser justo? Necesario es aquello a lo que es imposible ser diferente de lo que es; por lo tanto, preguntarse si la ofensa que cometemos a quienes nos ofenden debe ser necesaria para que pueda considerarse correcta"[9].

La ofensa es necesaria cuando es inevitable y cuando es lo menos posible. De igual interés es el razonamiento que Romagnosi desarrolla alrededor del delito, que parece recordar las teorías modernas del delito contra el llamado bien jurídico (piense en las teorías de Bricola o Nuvolone); "el delito", dice, no le quita ni disminuye los derechos de los demás considerados en sí mismos, sino que solo ofende a su sujeto, a medida que el delito sea un acto injusto.

Un robo es de hecho válido para privarme de la posesión de una cosa, pero nunca del derecho de propiedad. El ladrón está obligado a devolvérmelo y tengo derecho a recuperarlo. Por lo tanto, el campo del crimen es objeto de derechos[10]. Según Romagnosi, cada derecho humano se funda en el principal "derecho a la felicidad" (ya mencionado por los estadounidenses en 1776). De hecho, escribe que "todas las raíces del árbol descienden del mismo y único tronco, y son una rama de las fibras de él. Por lo tanto, todos los derechos son de felicidad. Todas las diferentes ramas, en las que se dividen las raíces, tienden a un solo fin: la vegetación y la prosperidad de la planta, por lo que todos los derechos tienden al único fin de la conservación y la felicidad del hombre", y termina argumentando que por estas razones "el delito contra cada derecho siempre se refiere el bienestar del hombre"[11].

También se cuestiona profundamente sobre la justificación de la pena (hay que decir que, a diferencia de Beccaria, estaba a favor, en ciertos casos, de la pena de muerte) y su especial capacidad preventiva, y escribe que "si después del primer delito hubo una certeza moral que quién lo ha hecho no lo volverá hacer más, la sociedad no tiene derecho a castigarlo. Dire-

9 G.D Romagnosi, op. cit., parte prima, capo primo, p. 7

10 G.D Romagnosi, op. cit., parte prima, capo undecimo, p. 42

11 G.D Romagnosi, op. cit., parte prima, capo undecimo, p. 43

mos, entonces, que el futuro es, por esta razón, única forma de la ley penal, con el fin de excluir cualquier relación con el pasado[12]. Para Romagnosi, el derecho penal es un complejo de reglas fundamentales para garantizar, esencialmente, la defensa de la sociedad, y escribe expresamente que "el derecho penal es en esencia solo el derecho de defensa", como "en la sociedad, admitió la impunidad de los malvados quienes están disponibles o incluso se determinarían infaliblemente a serlo, ciertamente se llevarían a cabo todo tipo de crímenes, donde un crimen futuro es ciertamente un mal futuro para la Sociedad", y "en consecuencia a la impunidad, que al mismo tiempo es una causa, también es equivalente a un ataque, o una suma de ataques. Entonces, en el derecho penal se pregunta ¿qué es el delincuente? El futuro malvado[13]. Para Romagnosi la sociedad entera tiene el derecho de castigar al delincuente, porque toda la sociedad tiene el derecho de defenderse a si misma y a sus miembros de los daños derivados de los delitos, dado que un crimen sin castigo es casi seguro que una recurrencia futura, lo que resulta en un mayor daño a la sociedad; "el derecho penal es responsabilidad exclusiva de todo el cuerpo social"[14] y "el único propósito de las sanciones es distorsionar los crímenes de la sociedad"[15]

Sin embargo, si la penalización excede la proporcionalidad, debe considerarse injusto: pero ¿cuál es la penalización excesiva?, ¿cuándo se puede considerar correcto? Romagnosi sostiene que el terror que inspiran las penas puede evitar la comisión del delito y que, efectivamente, esta concepción "es un hecho luminoso e incontrovertible". El objetivo preventivo, dice Romagnosi, "es el único en el que trataré de establecer la gran teoría de la verdadera norma, a fin de elegir y proporcionar las penas a los dos crímenes"[16]. El autor también distingue entre el elemento subjuntivo y el elemento objetivo del delito. Él escribe, por ejemplo, "en el crimen, por lo tanto, podemos distinguir dos partes; la primera interna, que podemos llamar la parte moral del crimen, porque es el trabajo de las facultades morales del hombre; y la externa, que podemos llamar la parte física, porque es el trabajo de la facultad física y ejecutor del hombre"[17].

[12] G.D Romagnosi, op. cit., parte seconda, capo decimoquarto, p. 85

[13] G.D Romagnosi, op. cit., parte seconda, capo decimoquarto, p. 89

[14] G.D Romagnosi, op. cit., parte seconda, capo ventesimoprimo, p. 105

[15] G.D Romagnosi, op. cit., parte terza, libro I, capo II, p. 128

[16] G.D Romagnosi, op. cit., parte terza, libro I, capo VI, p. 147

[17] G.D Romagnosi, op. cit., parte terza, libro I, capo VIII, p. 156

Tambien escribe sobre la teorización de castigo de los crímenes de ataque (así como de intento), de considerable interés, y sobre la responsabilidad del director por los excesos cometidos por el agente provocador en la acción penal, así como, por ejemplo, apoya la justificación de un castigo mayor (que hoy es una circunstancia agravante) de cometer el delito "bajo las distorsiones de la máscara", más grave que el delito cometido "bajo las formas ordinarias y cognitivas de vestirse y vivir en sociedad"[18]. Para una importante doctrina, Romagnosi "fue la expresión de ese fértil laboratorio de Padano que a partir de la segunda mitad del siglo XVIII puso en juego hombres e ideas para erigir una nueva pena de origen italiano: el fervor de los Verri y de los Beccaria había dejado herederos dignos, comprometidos, entre 1790 y 1810, para conciliar la gran tradición del pasado con las nuevas demandas del presente"[19].

Particularmente curiosa es también su ingeniosa propuesta para la construcción de la llamada "máquina de la plaga", enviada por el propio Romagnosi al entonces Ministro de Justicia del Reino de Italia, Napoleónico Giuseppe Luosi, junto con su propio "proyecto reemplazado" del código penal del 1806[20]. Esta maquina (hecha de madera y con un sistema de palos, manivelas y cuerdas) se ha definido hoy como una "herramienta de ingeniería maquiavélica y pitagórica"[21] y fue diseñado por él para ir en busca del castigo perfecto en el momento de la ejecución de la "flagelación". Este proyecto estuvo acompañado de cálculos y medidas precisas que, de ser respetados, habrían permitido que esta herramienta actuara como un medio de castigo igual y proporcional para todos (sin tener que depender, de vez en cuando, del poder físico del "verdugo" de turno, así como calibrado en relación con las características de la persona condenada (edad, sexo, constitución física) a la identidad y la gravedad del delito. Por otro lado, siempre es necesario contextualizar; pocos saben, por ejemplo, que incluso Beccaria estaba a favor de la "paliza" reeducativa, y solo hacia las clases sociales más bajas, de hecho, escribió: "debe haber mucho sobre la condición de las personas, porque la paliza que puede corregir a un insolente,

[18] G.D Romagnosi, op. cit., parte quarta, libro I, capo X, p. 287

[19] L. Garlati, *La macchina del flagello. Romagnosi alla ricerca della pena perfetta,* nella rivista "Italian Review of Legal History"

[20] Di particolare interesse P. Veneziani, sulla "colpa" nel progetto sostituito, in "L'indice Penale", Gennaio-Giugno 2009, nuova serie, anno XII n. 1, CEDAM, pagg. 335-353.

[21] L. Garlati, *Il volto umano della giustizia, omicidio e uccisione nella giurisprudenza del Tribunale di Brescia, 1831-1851,* Giuffré, Milano, 2008, p. 341

humilla y aniquila a un noble, un comerciante honesto y cualquier persona civilizada, e involucra a toda su familia en la ignominia más triste"[22].

Romagnosi, entonces, desarrolló la *"teoria della spinta criminosa"* definido por los historiadores del derecho como "una de las más agudas percepciones en la historia del derecho penal"[23], afirmando que por cada impulso se necesita un contraataque por parte del Estado, también afirmando de esta manera la proporcionalidad. Nuestros actores escriben que "si el único impulso criminal es administrar la norma para elegir y proporcionar las sanciones, es necesario conocer su verdadera naturaleza íntimamente y presentar las leyes por las cuales se despierta y se pone en práctica"[24] y que "en el magisterio penal no podemos exceder la medida de una defensa legítima"[25].

Volviendo a los aspectos procesales, Romagnosi también examina el valor probatorio de las pistas. El Maestro escribe que "en general, al examinar la naturaleza de las cosas, está claro que todas las pistas que realmente prueban la existencia de un crimen, tomadas en su realidad, solo pueden ser actos libres y externos, y por lo tanto comprobables, con los que el delito en sí mismo se lleva a cabo; como actos externos, por lo tanto, pueden llegar al conocimiento de los demás "y" es cierto que las indicaciones posteriores al acto también se prueban a sí mismas; pero está claro que no pueden hacerlo, excepto porque lo hacen naturalmente supongamos la ejecución previa de él"[26].

Romagnosi también tuvo en cuenta que la seriedad de la sentencia no siempre significa certeza, si no se actúa sobre las disposiciones legislativas en la ejecución de la sentencia misma; Nuestros escribe que "la severidad de la sentencia no se suma a si nada a su certeza"[27] y que la importancia de la efectividad de la sentencia también es fundamental a nivel de prevención social en que "otorgar impunidad después del delito cometido es un recurso inmoral que la fomenta"[28].

Por el contrario, escribe, "la moderación y el contraste utilizados en el acto de la empresa criminal es un arte de prudencia legislativa recomen-

[22] C. BECCARIA, *Brevi riflessioni intorno al Codice generale sopra i delitti e le pene,* in C. Cantù, *Beccaria e il diritto penale,* Firenze 1862, Appendice, p. 350, in L. GARLATI, op. cit. n. 20

[23] R. GHIRINGHELLI, Introduzione a *"Genesi del diritto penale"*, Giuffré, Milano, p. 49

[24] G.D ROMAGNOSI, op. cit., parte terza, libro I, capo VIII, p. 155

[25] G.D ROMAGNOSI, op. cit., parte sesta, capo V, p. 440

[26] G.D ROMAGNOSI, op. cit., parte quarta, libro II, capo VII, p. 269

[27] G.D ROMAGNOSI, op. cit., parte quarta, libro II, capo X, p. 287

[28] G.D ROMAGNOSI, op. cit., parte quarta, libro II, capo X, p. 288

dada por la justicia y la razón para defender a la sociedad". Sin embargo, él es muy consciente del hecho de que antes de alcanzar un castigo (y por lo tanto determinar la comisión del delito) es necesaria una evaluación procesal rigurosa, ya que es "en la forma de proceder o juzgar a los acusados de los delitos" que "adecuadamente se consume todo el magisterio de la certeza del castigo. Pero ¿dónde se resuelve finalmente este magisterio? Un buen código de procedimiento penal constituye la solución de este problema, su ejecución produce su efecto"[29]. En cuanto a la "fuente" de los crímenes, lo identifica en cuatro clases: por maldad (a su vez dividida en avaricia y malevolencia); por licencia; por exceso de poder; por el impulso de otros, en el que no es necesario detenerse aquí[30]. Para Romagnosi, además, la administración de justicia penal es una de las principales justificaciones para los impuestos y el gasto público.

2. NOTAS SOBRE LOS PRINCIPIOS DEL DERECHO ADMINISTRATIVO

Romagnosi, como se mencionó anteriormente, escribió los conocidos "principios fundamentales del derecho administrativo para tejer sus instituciones" de 1814, donde, entre las muchas razones contenidas en él, procedió a una división de poderes en ocho partes (a diferencia de las más famosas divisiones en tres partes: poder ejecutivo, legislativo, judicial de Montesquieu en su " esprit des lois " de 1 748): postulante, moderador, juez, determinante, operativo, convincente, certificador, predominante. Él, escribe D ' Aloia, "no será un simple exégeta, ni un teórico puro, también porque no tiene un sistema regulador completo detrás de él; es, o intentará ser, un constructor de nuevas arquitecturas normativas e institucionales, un jurista orientado a las reformas, a la planificación. Su horizonte finalista es beneficiar el derecho positivo, modificarlo"[31].

Romagnosi fue por algunos considerado el "padre del derecho administrativo"[32] porque se dio cuenta de que el poder, existente en la naturaleza como las autoridades, debía ser definido por la ley y envuelta

[29] G.D Romagnosi, op. cit., parte quarta, libro II, capo X, p. 289

[30] G.D Romagnosi, op. cit., parte sesta, capo V, p. 446

[31] A. D'Aloia, op. cit. pag. 10

[32] Sul punto si veda R. Lombardi, "Gian Domenico Romagnosi: alle origini della scienza del diritto amministrativo in Italia", in R. Ferrara e S. Sicardi (a cura di), "Itinerari e vicende del diritto pubblico in Italia", 1998, Cedam, Padova, pag. 473 ss.

en normas legales. Obviamente estamos hablando de conceptos que no pueden entenderse como los modernos; el mismo término de "derecho administrativo", al que se refiere Romagnosi en su imponente ya mencionado, están escritos de una manera completamente diferente de la configuración de un manual moderno, cuya configuración de tiempo estaba más cerca de lo que ahora llamaríamos "doctrina del estado", y que, por lo tanto, pertenecen al diseño constitucional del poder administrativo *sic et simpliciter*, en el primer esbozo del principio de proporcionalidad en el equilibrio entre el interés público y el interés privado, hasta la cuestión de las autonomías y los municipios. A él se debe, por ejemplo, que la fórmula está presente en todas las etapas de liberación de la construcción de títulos de habilitación: "respetando el derecho de terceros"[33], que representa una válvula de garantía para los puestos de terceros con respecto a un procedimiento que solo puede desarrollarse y concluir entre la administración y la persona que solicita un permiso de construcción. En cuanto a la afirmación del importante canon de proporcionalidad[34] en cambio, escribió una frase llena de significado: "la regla rectora de la administración en este conflicto es hacer que los asuntos públicos prevalezcan sobre los privados con el menor sacrificio posible de propiedad privada y libertad"[35].

Precisamente con respecto a lo que ahora llamaríamos " derecho administrativo ", por lo tanto, Romagnosi era una luminaria: cuando los austriacos regresaron, estaba listo un código de procedimiento administrativo que ya intentaba traducir la necesidad de un corpus orgánico de reglas de procedimiento[36], tanto que, para otros autores, " Romagnosi inventó el derecho administrativo", como un asunto que sirvió para identificar el tema de la disputa administrativa (del entonces nuevo juez de la administración) y así resolver el conflicto de jurisdicción con el juez ordinario. También está escrito que "la historia del derecho administrativo podría comenzar con Romagnosi ". Otra contribución importante se refiere a la

[33] F. MERUSI, "Gian Domenico Romagnosi fra diritto e processo amministrativo", in "Rivista di diritto processuale amministrativo", 2011, Giuffré, pag. 1240 ss.

[34] Si veda, sul punto, anche U. FANTIGROSSI, "Sviluppi recenti del principio di proporzionalità nel diritto amministrativo italiano", *Liuc Papers n. 220, Serie Impresa e Istituzioni, 26, settembre 2008*

[35] G. ROSSI, "L'attualità di Gian Domenico Romagnosi nell'eclissi dello statalismo", in "Rivista di diritto pubblico", 2012, I, pag. 3 ss.

[36] F. MERUSI, op. cit., Ibidem

publicidad de los documentos, en la que insistió particularmente y que vio como una herramienta fundamental para garantizar una conciencia participativa (aunque mínima) de los ciudadanos en la administración pública. Escribió: "Todo lo que demuestra la necesidad y el derecho de una publicidad absoluta de los actos de la administración, de la libertad total y la publicidad y la circulación de opiniones sobre la legislación y la administración del Estado"[37].

3. LOS ASPECTOS CONSTITUCIONALES FUNDAMENTALES

En la "parte" constitucionalista se pueden resaltar algunas obras importantes: en "la introducción al estudio del derecho público universal" de 1805, Romagnosi expresa su especial importancia como "el problema de la relación político-derecha parece resuelto con una sumisión del segundo al primero"[38].

Y aquí comienza el surgimiento del " constitucionalista Romagnosi ", que prosperará en su " Ciencia de las Constituciones" del 1814, en cuya premisa hace una verdadera declaración de autonomía e independencia intelectual: " Nadie quedará feliz". Los cortesanos me despreciarán y me amenazarán, porque me he atrevido a atar las manos del monarca de una manera nueva: la gente popular se quejará de mí, porque le he dado toda la autoridad al rey, y no tengo más remedio que protegerlo. Ejercer dentro de los límites de la necesidad más rigurosa", para luego dictar los principios que debe cubrir una Constitución: "Para ser buena, una Constitución debe armonizarse en sus partes, disciplinarse en su régimen, sanarse en sus ejecuciones, y esto con el poderes tan distintos y bien contrastantes, que lejos de colisionar, tienden a lo contrario. (...) El contraste debe parecerse al de una máquina bien construida: todo está atado, pero sus vibraciones son libres como las del corazón"[39].

Romagnosi, quien propuso como modelo una monarquía nacional representativa (y no una feudal como la monarquía inglesa), tenía en mente los principios del primer constitucionalismo liberal que apenas se afirmaba; "Por lo tanto, cada gobierno verdaderamente constitucional es un

[37] G. D. Romagnosi , "La scienza delle Costituzioni", 1848 (pubblicata postuma), vol. I, parte I, Teoria generale, cap. IV, pag. 41.

[38] F. Lanchester, op. cit. pag. 6-7.

[39] G. D. Romagnosi, "La scienza delle Costituzioni", Introduzione, pag. II & III, 1848 (pubblicata postuma), Losanna, S. Bonamici e compagnia tipografi editori.

gobierno esencialmente republicano. La verdadera monarquía constitucional es, por lo tanto, esencialmente una república con un gobernador jefe"[40], escribe, reiterando el concepto de un estado fuerte (cerca del absolutismo ilustrado), de modo que, para Romagnosi, de hecho, incluso una monarquía absoluta se puede definir republicano, rompiendo con el concepto clásico de "republicanismo".

Sin embargo, el concepto vinculado a la Nación, y no a la "persona física" del Rey, permanece; sobre el punto, de hecho, escribe: "Pero si los gobernantes están sujetos a una ley, por lo tanto, tienen un soberano al que deben obedecer, este soberano es la nación. " Y de nuevo en la soberanía y el ejercicio del poder público: " Los poderes que dan lugar a que los funcionarios públicos reemplacen sus intereses personales con los intereses del Estado siempre serán incompatibles"[41] Si este pensamiento puede parecer contradictorio, sus eruditos, en este sentido, aclaran por escrito que en el trabajo de Romagnosi el pensamiento constitucionalista de la era de la Ilustración y las corrientes políticas de Resurgimiento de autonomía política e independencia del Nación y Romagnosi se erigió como un "puente", como una figura de transición en la que se encontraron ambas corrientes de pensamiento, de modo que llevó a algunos autores a escribir que "la cultura y la tradición italiana adquieren una dimensión auténticamente nacional precisamente en el esencial enlace entre Romagnosi y el sur de Vico, Genovesi, Filangieri y Pagano"[42], y un gran personaje de Risorgimento como Carlo Pisacane se declarará "un deudor y discípulo de Romagnosi"[43].

Sobre la relación entre el gobierno polico y la ley, Romagnosi enmarca el aspecto constitucional en una sotomisión del primero al segundo, y está estrechamente relacionado con el interés colectivo: "Si el gobierno de la administración se realiza de acuerdo con los requisitos de los asuntos públicos, la administración es buena, en caso contrario, la administración es mala"[44].

Con respecto a la forma de gobierno, surge un ajuste y limitación del poder: "La promulgación de la forma de gobierno es saber lo que hace el

[40] *La scienza delle costituzioni*, op. cit., pag. 158-159.

[41] *La scienza delle costituzioni* op. cit. pag 166

[42] E. Albertoni, op. cit. pag. 26

[43] E. Albertoni, op. cit. pag. 34

[44] G. D. Romagnosi, "La scienza delle Costituzioni", 1848 (pubblicata postuma), vol. I, parte I, cap. II, pag. 15

gobierno; para dar a conocer lo que debe proporcionar el gobierno, aquí están los atributos eminentes e inalienables de toda sociedad civilizada dirigida por la dominación regular. Digo eminente e inalienable porque sin estos atributos no existe una garantía sólida de la integridad de la Constitución o ya no puede existir dentro de una nación."[45] Al volver sobre sus obras también notamos cuán frecuente es la referencia de Romagnosi al término "máquina", para indicar la estructura del orden constitucional y el equilibrio de poderes, y que parece describir lo que ahora se llama como "ingeniería constitucional"[46]. Otra contribución importante dada por el Maestro es sobre el debate en torno a los parámetros que incluso hoy definiríamos como "calidad de la ley"; De hecho, escribe: "la única función justa de la ley es imponer esas restricciones que son puramente necesarias para la equidad, la seguridad y la prosperidad común"[47], y de nuevo: "Las malas leyes surgen de la mala constitución del gobierno, por lo que el freno a la mala voluntad del legislador sigue siendo libre; o surgen de la ignorancia de esas relaciones que era conveniente consultar; y muchas respiraciones de ambas razones reunidas"[48]. En otro trabajo, por ejemplo, escribe sobre el equilibrio entre los derechos y deberes como vida ordenada y civilizada: Una serie compuesta de deberes, derechos y leyes, uno con los otros subordinados, y el otro y el otro conspirando a un solo intento, ¿cuál es la conservación más feliz de la especie humana que se puede obtener en esta tierra? [49]

Sus palabras también son fundamentales con respecto a la libertad de prensa y de expresión, ideas claras y revolucionarias para la época en que fueron escritas: "Sé que la libertad de hablar para escribir e imprimir es desagradable para muchos. Pero solo por medio de esta libertad, publicidad y circulación recíproca de parlamentos y escritos, una nación adquiere esa unidad moral y la verdadera personalidad que corresponde a una sociedad

[45] G. D. Romagnosi, "La scienza delle Costituzioni", 1848 (pubblicata postuma), vol. I, parte I, cap. IV, pag. 32

[46] G. Sartori, "Ingegneria costituzionale comparata", 1995, Il Mulino, Bologna

[47] G. D. Romagnosi, "La scienza delle Costituzioni", 1848 (pubblicata postuma), vol. I, parte I, cap. IV, pag. 32vol. I, parte I, cap. VII, pag. 92

[48] G. D. Romagnosi, "La scienza delle Costituzioni", 1848 (pubblicata postuma), vol. I, parte I, cap. VII, pag. 139

[49] G. D Romagnosi, "Introduzione allo studio del diritto pubblico universale, V edizione, 1836, Milano, vol. II, Biblioteca scelta di opere italiane antiche e moderne, vol. 349, Silvestri Editore, Milano pag. 140

de hombres libres e ilustrados.[50]" Otra novedad importante en comparación con el pensamiento liberal de la época es que "Romagnosi no piensa en las limitaciones del censo del derecho al voto, a partir del electorado pasivo, y no se acerca a la participación de las mujeres"[51] ; no es un asunto trivial considerando que teníamos sufragio universal (masculino) en 1913 y el voto a las mujeres en 1946.

Aún en la participación civil, él considera la educación como un elemento fundamental de la responsabilidad cívica de cada ciudadano: en un ensayo titulado "Educación pública", Romagnosi dirá que "la educación civil primaria debe considerarse como necesaria" y el deber público no puede dejarse a una autoridad parental mal concebida", y en la ciencia de las constituciones la educación pública está configurada como una "institución constitucional subsidiaria " como " subsistencia activa " (una especie de asistencia social en el trabajo más que en la asistencia tout court) porque "ambos cooperando de manera fundamental en la celebración del pacto constitucional son una condición para que la gente ame, sirva y defienda mejor al país"[52], haciendo que una fuerte impronta republicana de la "educación cívica" emerja como el elemento fundador de la *res publica* y, al mismo tiempo, como un "deber" de lealtad a la patria, y no al déspota , precisamente porque todo poder templado regula el poder y hace a los hombres, pueblos y gobernantes buenos, iluminados y fuertes. La bondad, la ciencia y el poder son los frutos de la moderación solamente. La maldad, la ignorancia y la debilidad son fruto de la intemperancia.

Componentes "cívicos" que emergen completamente también en el concepto de ciudadanía, que el Maestro vincula a la "pequeña patria", es decir a los municipios: "Los municipios representan formaciones sociales naturales", escribe el autor en "Instituciones de filosofía civil", hasta el punto de que "la nación tiene el derecho de construir estos municipios, y ya no podría oponerse a la prerrogativa principesca"[53]. Una fuerte asonancia con la formulación actual del art. 5 de nuestra Constitución, que dice precisamente que la República "reconoce", así como "promueve las autonomías locales", como si ya existiera incluso antes de su afirmación legal. En el ensayo "Sobre ciudadanía y fortaleza" de 1814 también ofrece

[50] G. D Romagnosi , "La scienza delle Costituzioni", op. cit., vol. I, parte I, cap. IV, pag. 39

[51] A. D'Aloia, op. cit., pag. 39

[52] A. D'Aloia, op. cit., pag. 35-36

[53] "La scienza delle costituzioni", op. cit. pag. 157-158

una configuración entre las dos ciudadanías: la local, "vinculada al municipio", y la general, "vinculada a la unidad de todo el Reino".

Sobre todo el Reino Romagnosi escribe: "No es más que un conjunto de municipios, ya que los municipios son solo un conjunto de familias; entonces se puede decir que la ciudadanía municipal es la base de la ciudadanía del Reino, que llamaremos nacionalidad, por lo que la nacionalidad no es más que una extensión de la ciudad municipal", un paso muy fundamental que lleva a definir (por los constitucionalistas modernos) a Romagnosi como la democracia en América de Tocqueville[54]. Elementos de la ley natural emergen entonces en sus escritos: en sus "Consideraciones sobre los fundamentos particulares del orden moral propio de la humanidad", escribe que "Si las reglas que constituyen la ciencia del derecho público no se derivan de las relaciones reales y necesarias de la sociedad en orden de la naturaleza, serían frustrantes o perjudiciales"[55] y en el siguiente párrafo sobre la necesidad de particularizar las reglas: ¿Desea limitarse a conocer solo los principios abstractos y generales? Todo lo que hará es violar el orden de las cosas y producir serios inconvenientes en la administración pública de los Estados. Por proporcionalmente que un principio, una noción, cualquier concepto es más general, está más despojado de las circunstancias concretas y reales con las que las cosas realmente existen, tienen lugar y se practican en la naturaleza. (...) La gran generalidad de las nociones es, por lo tanto, una imperfección en sí misma, cuando las consideraciones más cercanas al estado concreto, el único que existe en la naturaleza, no se unen posterior y gradualmente[56].

n este sentido (y para aclarar un tema tan poco homogéneo y complejo), el constitucionalista D' Aloia escribe que la interpretación que puede mantener todas estas elaboraciones juntas "se puede encontrar en la importancia inevitable de los principios de derecho público y natural como base para comprender la jurisprudencia civil."[57] Romagnosi escribe que "cuando la

[54] A. D'ALOIA, op. cit., pag. 37

[55] G. D ROMAGNOSI, "Introduzione allo studio del diritto pubblico universale", V edizione, 1836, Milano, vol. II, Biblioteca scelta di opere italiane antiche e moderne, vol. 349, Silvestri Editore, Milano, pag. 6

[56] G. D ROMAGNOSI, "Introduzione allo studio del diritto pubblico universale", V edizione, 1836, Milano, vol. II, Biblioteca scelta di opere italiane antiche e moderne, vol. 349, Silvestri Editore, Milano, pag. 6

[57] A. D'ALOIA, op. cit., pag. 20

ley calla y el poder legislativo no se preocupa por compensar el defecto de las leyes, ¿el jurisconsulto puede ver que la arbitrariedad del magistrado al menos no viola las relaciones de razón y equidad natural, si antes no tiene un modelo, es decir, un sistema de principios sólidos y reglas naturales que deben compensar con precisión el silencio o el descuido de la autoridad legislativa civil?"[58] Un debate que todavía es extremadamente moderno y que todavía surge hoy en día sobre el delicado conflicto entre la norma o el poder legislativo y la decisión del juez.

En resumen, todas estas características modernas del pensamiento de Romagnosi, que hoy nos parecen ingeniosas y útiles para comprender la corriente, alguna vez, seguramente, fueron mal entendidas o entendidas por pocos, y la desgracia de la poca popularidad de Romagnosi tuvo un impacto negativo en su destino, retomado después de 100 años de historia. Romagnosi aún no tenía un aparato constitucional maduro ante él, razonó por inducción, partió de sus intuiciones personales para llevarlos a una realidad normativa teórica y no jurídica-normativa. Según Brunialti, "Romagnosi recoge el pensamiento jurídico del siglo que lo precede y le da la condena, con vigor de grandes ideas, restablece las ciencias político-legales y comienza la filosofía civil que lo condujo al conocimiento exacto de las leyes de hecho y leyes de origen de la sociedad civil."[59]; Romagnosi insiste en la Constitución como una ley fundamental que limita los poderes, vinculando el aspecto jurídico al político, a su vez estrechamente relacionado con una cultura científica y de la ilustración como elemento del progreso civil. "Ética, política y derecho", escribe, "pueden distinguirse, pero no separarse. No existe una ética práctica, excepto a través de buenas leyes y buenas administraciones[60]". Consejos que también debemos escuchar hoy.

[58] A. D'Aloia, op. cit., pag. 36

[59] V. A Brunialti, "Il diritto costituzionale e la politica nella scienza e nelle istituzioni", 1896, Torino, pag. 207

[60] G. Sacchi, "Appunti e pensieri inediti di Gian Domenico Romagnosi. Raccolti e pubblicati da un suo antico discepolo, in memoria del grande restauratore della filosofia civile in Italia." 1873, Tipografia Editrice Lombarda, pag. 2-3

PANORAMA DO DIREITO IMOBILIÁRIO NO SÉCULO XXI[1]

GISELDA MARIA FERNANDES NOVAES HIRONAKA*

INTRODUÇÃO

Desde a pré-história humana, a ocupação de espaços e o preenchimento deles com edificações, plantações ou criações é fator de relevância crucial para a humanidade. A capacidade de criar, a partir dos elementos naturais, um *abrigo* foi fundamental para a sobrevivência do homem enquanto espécie. A relação da sociedade com o terreno, com as plantações e com as edificações sempre foi um marco da cultura de um povo e sempre consistiu em algo que evoluiu com o tempo. E, realmente, a arquitetura e as relações entre as pessoas e os imóveis são reveladoras da cultura adjacente, de modo que se pode reconhecer, de forma praticamente instantânea, uma construção como sendo grega, ou egípcia, ou inglesa (inclusive com variação de períodos), e assim por diante.

Sendo faceta tão relevante da cultura humana, não é de se estranhar que haja um ramo do Direito que especificamente regule as relações daí deri-

* Professora Titular da Faculdade de Direito da USP. Livre-docente, Doutora e Mestre em Direito pela USP. Coordenadora e Professora Titular do Programa de Mestrado e Doutorado da FADISP. Coordenadora Titular da área de Direito Civil da Escola Paulista de Direito. Ex-Procuradora Federal. Fundadora e Diretora Nacional do IBDFAM (região sudeste). Diretora Nacional do IBDCivil (região sudeste).

[1] Este artigo nasceu de reflexões sobre Direito Imobiliário, economia e tecnologia, em virtude de evento do qual participei sobre o tema, realizado em Washington (DC), nos Estados Unidos da América, em fevereiro de 2020, e que reúne anualmente diversos juristas e magistrados do Brasil e dos Estados Unidos.

vadas. É nesse sentido que se fala em Direito Imobiliário, isto é, o Direito que regula as interações entre as pessoas e os imóveis. Segundo Vicente Ráo, "se as regras de direito se incorporam em institutos jurídicos, por sua vez e em razão das mesmas causas, os institutos jurídicos, segundo sua natureza, também se agrupam e formam o conteúdo de cada ramo do direito"[2]. Então, especificamente com relação à formação do Direito Imobiliário, verifica-se que se trata de um conjunto de normas jurídicas de diversos ramos do Direito e relacionadas com a aquisição e eficácia das posições registrais e outras situações jurídicas imobiliárias, isto é, relacionadas com direitos e deveres sobre imóveis[3].

É de se ter em mente que o estudo das categorias jurídicas por meio do foco na área de aplicação – e não por meio do foco no ramo do Direito – é de grande valia prática para o uso efetivo dos institutos jurídicos. Nesse sentido, Pietro Perlingieri propõe o estudo do Direito por "problemas", e não por ramo do direito. Ele diz que "o fracionamento da matéria jurídica e do ordenamento em ramos tem um sentido porque divide por competências e por necessidade de exposição uma matéria única em si mesma, mas não deve significar que a realidade do ordenamento é divisível em diversos setores, dos quais um é totalmente autônomo em relação ao outro, de tal modo que possa ser proclamada a sua independência. O estudo do direito não deve ser feito por setores pré-constituídos, mas por problemas, com especial atenção às exigências emergentes como, por exemplo, a habitação, saúde, etc."[4].

Assim, no que toca ao tema em estudo, ensina Luciano Lopes Passarelli que o Direito registral engloba normas de vários ramos do Direito, tais como Direito Constitucional, Direito Tributário, Direito Agrário, Direito Ambiental, Direito Urbanístico, Direito Processual etc., tendo vários importantes diplomas normativos, como a Lei n. 6.015/1973 e a Lei n. 8.935/1994[5]. Nesse sentido, sem querer ficar adstrita especificamente a certos e específicos ramos jurídicos – como o registral, ou o civil, ou o

[2] Ráo, Vicente. *O direito e a vida dos direitos*. 5. ed. por Ovídio Rocha Barros Sandoval. São Paulo: Ed. RT, 1999. p. 228.

[3] Ortiz, Jose Maria Chico Y. *Estudios sobre derecho hipotecario*. Madrid: Marcial Pons, 1989.

[4] Perlingieri, Pietro. *Perfis do direito civil:* introdução ao Direito Civil Constitucional. Tradução de Maria Cristina De Cicco. 2. ed. Rio de Janeiro: Renovar, 2002. p. 55-56.

[5] Passarelli, Luciano Lopes. *Da autonomia do direito registral imobiliário*. Revista de Direito Imobiliário, São Paulo, v. 75, jul./dez. 2013. p. 15.

empresarial, o trabalhista ou o previdenciário –, mas, ainda assim, com enfoque no Direito Privado, passo a apresentar os principais marcos e tendências, do passado, do presente e do futuro, relacionados com o Direito Imobiliário do século XXI.

1. A HERANÇA RECEBIDA PELO DIREITO IMOBILIÁRIO DO SÉCULO XXI NO BRASIL

O Direito Imobiliário tem na segurança jurídica uma importante pedra de toque, sobretudo quando considerados os desdobramentos dela, como a publicidade dos atos e a estabilidade dos registros. A publicidade de certos atos jurídicos dá segurança para as relações jurídicas privadas nascidas tendo como objeto bens imóveis. Aliás, a própria razão de ser do Direito registral imobiliário é justamente a de ser um instrumento de segurança, isto é, uma forma de dar previsibilidade, calculabilidade e publicidade para as situações jurídicas imobiliárias. Conforme ensina Humberto Ávila, sabe-se que a segurança jurídica deve ser entendida:

> Como sendo uma norma-princípio que exige, dos Poderes Legislativo, Executivo e Judiciário, a adoção de comportamentos que contribuam mais para a existência, em benefício dos cidadãos e na sua perspectiva, de um estado de confiabilidade e de calculabilidade jurídica, com base na sua cognoscibilidade, por meio da controlabilidade jurídico-racional das estruturas argumentativas reconstrutivas de normas gerais e individuais, como instrumento garantidor do respeito à sua capacidade de – sem engano, frustração, surpresa e arbitrariedade – plasmar digna e responsavelmente o seu presente e fazer um planejamento estratégico juridicamente informado de seu futuro[6].

Assim sendo, é da essência do Direito Imobiliário perseguir essa segurança, eis que ele nasceu para promover esse *estado de confiabilidade e de calculabilidade jurídica*, sendo que isso justifica toda a existência de um sistema registral de direitos reais. Deveras, tanto isso é verdade que – conforme magistério de Ricardo Dip – o Direito registral imobiliário brasileiro nasce inicialmente com o fito de publicizar e regular os efeitos das hipotecas, haja vista a ocorrência, no início do século XIX, das chamadas "hipotecas ocultas", isto é, hipotecas instituídas por escritura pública, mas não publi-

[6] ÁVILA, Humberto. *Teoria da segurança jurídica*. 3. ed. rev., atual., e ampl. São Paulo: Malheiros, 2014. p. 282.

cizadas em um registro público vinculado ao imóvel afetado, circunstância que gerava problemas graves quando imóveis eram alienados e o adquirente era surpreendido com a alegação, por um terceiro, de que aquele imóvel estava garantindo uma dívida[7].

A solução só viria com a Lei Orçamentária n. 317, de 21 de outubro de 1843[8], que instituiu o Registro Hipotecário. Por essa lei as hipotecas passaram a ser averbadas em um registro do imóvel, o que deu muita segurança jurídica para o instituto. Assim, tendo em vista o sucesso do sistema, esse registro imobiliário passou a ser utilizado também para as aquisições imobiliárias e a inscrição de outros ônus reais, o que ocorreria com a edição da Lei n. 1.237, de 24 de setembro de 1864[9], regulamentada pelo Decreto n. 3.453, de 26 de abril de 1865[10]. Essa Lei foi muito importante, porque substituiu a tradição da coisa pela transcrição do título como forma de aquisição da propriedade.

Ademais, esses diplomas normativos deixam claro que o legislador brasileiro adotou o "Sistema de Registro de Direitos", que é reconhecidamente

[7] DIP, Ricardo. *Registros sobre registros*. Artigo. Brasília/DF (Brasil): Portal da Associação dos Notários e Registradores do Brasil, 12 fev. 2019. Disponível em: http://iregistradores.org.br/registros-sobre-registros-142/. Acesso em: 28 jan. 2020.

[8] "Art. 35. Fica creado um Registro geral de hypothecas, nos lugares e pelo modo que o Governo estabelecer nos seus Regulamentos", cf. BRASIL. *Lei n. 317, de 21 de outubro de 1843.* Fixando a Despeza e orçando a Receita para os exercícios de 1843-1844, e 1844-1845. Rio de Janeiro: Portal da Legislação do Governo Federal (Planalto), 1843 (ano da publicação originária da lei). Disponível em: http://www.planalto.gov.br/ccivil_03/leis/lim/LIM317.htm. Acesso em: 28 jan. 2020.

[9] "Art. 7º O registro geral comprehende: A transcripção dos titulos da transmissão dos immoveis susceptiveis de hypotheca e a instituição dos onus reaes. A inscripção das hypothecas. § 1º A transcripção e inscripção devem ser feitas na Comarca ou Comarcas onde forem os bens situados. § 2º As despezas da transcripção incumbem ao adquirente. As despezas da inscripção competem ao devedor. § 3º Este registro fica encarregado aos Tabelliães creados ou designados pelo Decreto n. 482 de 14 de Novembro de 1846", cf. BRASIL. *Lei n. 1.237, de 24 de setembro de 1864.* Reforma a Legislação Hypothecaria, e estabelece as bases das sociedades de credito real. Portal da Legislação do Governo Federal (Planalto), 1864 (ano da publicação originária da lei). Disponível em: http://www.planalto.gov.br/ccivil_03/leis/lim/ LIM1237.htm. Acesso em: 28 jan. 2020.

[10] BRASIL. *Lei n. 3.453, de 26 de abril de 1865.* Manda observar o Regulamento para execução da Lei n. 1.237, de 24 de setembro de 1864, que reformou a legislação hypothecaria. Portal da Legislação do Governo Federal (Planalto), 1865 (ano da publicação originária da lei). Disponível em: http://www.planalto.gov.br/ccivil_03/decreto/historicos/dim/DIM3453.htm. Acesso em: 28 jan. 2020.

uma forma muito segura de se transmitir, averbar, modificar ou extinguir direitos reais. Sabe-se que existem, basicamente, três modelos de sistemas registrários no mundo, a saber: (a) Registro de documentos; (b) Contratação privada; e (c) Registro de direitos.

Basicamente, pelo sistema do *Registro de documentos,* o registro é realizado por meio da conservação do próprio título que materializa o contrato privado no registro do imóvel, o que se faz com o intuito de disponibilizar provas documentais da titularidade dos bens e que são posteriormente utilizáveis pelas Cortes e interessados. Esse sistema é utilizado atualmente na França e em Estados dos Estados Unidos da América (EUA). Depois, há o sistema da *Contratação privada,* utilizado na Inglaterra até meados do século XX, e por meio do qual o Direito Real é registrado (e provado) com os próprios títulos contratuais por meio dos quais foi constituído. Finalmente, há o *Sistema de Registro de Direitos,* utilizado na Alemanha, Espanha e Brasil, por meio do qual o registro, em vez de se focar em transcrever informações sobre os títulos modificativos de direitos reais, concentra-se em deixar registrada a própria constituição do direito real, o que demanda uma avaliação rigorosa de validade e possibilidade jurídica do registro por meio da aferição de conformidade com princípios como o princípio da anterioridade, o princípio da continuidade registral, o princípio do trato sucessivo, o princípio da rogação etc.[11].

Posteriormente, houve a edição do Decreto n. 3.272, de 5 de outubro de 1885[12]; o Decreto n. 169-A, de 19 de janeiro de 1890[13], e o Decreto n. 370, de 2 de maio de 1890[14], que modificaram a legislação de 1864 e tiveram a

[11] MELO, Marcelo Augusto Santana de. *Breves anotações sobre o Registro de Imóveis.* Artigo. Brasília/DF (Brasil): Portal da Associação dos Notários e Registradores do Brasil, 2001?. Disponível em: https://anoreg.org.br/images/arquivos/parecerrr.pdf. Acesso em: 28 jan. 2020.

[12] BRASIL. *Decreto n. 3.272, de 5 de outubro de 1885.* Altera diversas disposições referentes ás execuções civeis e commerciaes. Portal da Câmara dos Deputados, 1885 (ano da publicação originária da lei). Disponível em: https://www2.camara.leg.br/legin/fed/decret/1824-1899/decreto-3272-5-outubro-1885-543469-publicacaooriginal-53793-pl.html. Acesso em: 29 jan. 2020.

[13] BRASIL. *Decreto n. 169-A, de 19 de janeiro de 1890.* Substitue as Leis n. 1.237, de 24 de setembro de 1864, e n. 3.272, de 5 de outubro de 1885. Portal da Câmara dos Deputados, 1890 (ano da publicação originária da lei). Disponível em: https://www2.camara.leg.br/legin/fed/decret/1824-1899/decreto-169-a-19-janeiro-1890-516767-publicacaooriginal-1-pe.html. Acesso em: 29 jan. 2020.

[14] BRASIL. *Decreto n. 370, de 2 de maio de 1890.* Manda observar o regulamento para execução do decreto n. 169-A, de 19 de janeiro de 1890, sobre operações de crédito móvel. Portal da

importância de estipular que o contrato, enquanto não transcrito, só conferia direitos *pessoais* aos contratantes. Em 1916, o Brasil editou o seu primeiro Código Civil (CC/1916), instituído pela Lei n. 3.071, de 1º de janeiro de 1916[15], e no qual a transcrição do título hábil, no registro imobiliário da situação do imóvel, passou a constituir exigência para a aquisição da propriedade imóvel[16]. O artigo 530 do Código Civil de 1916 determinou que "adquire-se a propriedade imóvel: I – pela transcrição do título de transferência no registro do imóvel"[17]. Adicionalmente, capítulos inteiros foram dedicados a regular os direitos reais e sua eficácia, merecendo destaque o fato de que os direitos reais sobre imóveis negociados por atos intervivos só são adquiridos após a transcrição do respectivo título translativo no registro de imóveis, conforme estabelecem diversas normas presentes entre os artigos 532 e 676 do CC/1916. Também há a criação da presunção segundo a qual o direito real se presume pertencer à pessoa em cujo nome se inscreveu, ou transcreveu (CC/1916, art. 859). Ademais, os atos jurídicos sujeitos à transcrição não transferem domínio, senão na data em que foram transcritos (CC/1916, art. 533).

Vale mencionar, ainda com relação à regulamentação dos ônus reais no Código Civil de 1916, que as hipotecas deveriam ser inscritas no lugar do imóvel, conforme determinou o artigo 831 do CC/1916[18]. O número

Legislação do Governo Federal, 1890 (ano da publicação originária da lei). Disponível em: http://www.planalto.gov.br/ccivil_03/decreto/1851-1899/D370.htm. Acesso em: 29 jan. 2020.

[15] BRASIL. União. *Lei n. 3.071, de 1º de janeiro de 1916. Código Civil dos Estados Unidos do Brasil.* (CC/1916 – Código Civil). Rio de Janeiro/RJ (Brasil): Congresso Nacional, 1916 (ano da publicação originária). Disponível em: http://www.planalto.gov.br/ccivil_03/LEIS/L3071.htm. Acesso em: 22 dez. 2019.

[16] PAIVA, João Pedro Lamana. *Curso em direito imobiliário registral aplicado aos bens públicos.* Porto Alegre/RS (Brasil): Registro de Imóveis 1ª Zona de Porto Alegre, 2014. Disponível em: http://www.planejamento.gov.br/assuntos/patrimonio-da-uniao/programa-de-modernizacao/linha-do-tempo/arquivos-e-publicacoes/historia-do-sistema-registral-brasileiro.pdf. Acesso em: 29 jan. 2020.

[17] BRASIL. União. *Lei n. 3.071, de 1º de janeiro de 1916. Código Civil dos Estados Unidos do Brasil.* (CC/1916 – Código Civil). Rio de Janeiro/RJ (Brasil): Congresso Nacional, 1916 (ano da publicação originária). Disponível em: http://www.planalto.gov.br/ccivil_03/LEIS/L3071.htm. Acesso em: 22 dez. 2019.

[18] Corresponde ao artigo 1.492 do CC/2002, que diz: "Art. 1.492. As hipotecas serão registradas no cartório do lugar do imóvel, ou no de cada um deles, se o título se referir a mais de um. Parágrafo único. Compete aos interessados, exibido o título, requerer o registro da hipoteca", cf. BRASIL. União. *Lei n. 10.406, de 10 de janeiro de 2002.* Institui o Código Civil (CC/02

de ordem estipula a preferência entre as hipotecas (CC/1916, art. 853, parágrafo único). E as hipotecas só geram efeitos perante terceiros após o registro, sendo que antes disso possuem efeitos *inter partes*, conforme determinou o artigo 848 do Código Civil de 1916. Portanto, o Código Civil de 1916 consagrou a máxima de que *a propriedade imóvel só se adquire pelo registro*.

Na sequência, o Decreto-lei n. 1.000, de 21 de novembro de 1969[19], atualizou as normas registrais, tendo havido uma grande preocupação em eliminar procedimentos ineficientes e técnicas registrais obsoletas. Esse decreto vigeu até a edição da Lei n. 6.015, de 31 de dezembro de 1973[20], que consolidou as normas de Direito registral (muitas das quais, portanto, relacionadas com o Direito Imobiliário).

A mais importante alteração do ponto de vista de Direito Imobiliário e Registral foi a adoção do modelo de registro por *matrículas*, no qual um documento – a matrícula – reúne todas as informações juridicamente relevantes do imóvel, incluindo a sua descrição e também todos os atos jurídicos, alterações e informações relevantes relacionados com o bem. Como diz Lamana Paiva, a matrícula consiste em um "autêntico *curriculum vitae* da propriedade imobiliária"[21], contendo tudo o que é juridicamente importante sobre o imóvel reunido em um único documento. O sistema de matrícula só foi implementado a partir de 1º de janeiro de 1976, sem imposição de obrigação para os registradores de converterem todas as transcrições até então existentes para o novo modelo. Assim, muito embora todos os novos registros sejam realizados em matrículas, ainda hoje convivem os dois modelos – modelo *por matrículas* e modelo *por transcrições* –, eis que,

– Código Civil). Brasília/DF (Brasil): Portal da Legislação do Governo Federal, 2002 (ano da publicação originária). Disponível em: http://www.planalto.gov.br/ccivil_03/leis/2002/L10406.htm. Acesso em: 22 dez. 2019.

19 BRASIL. União. *Decreto-lei n. 1.000, de 21 de novembro de 1969*. Brasília/DF (Brasil): Portal de Legislação do Governo Federal, 1969. Disponível em: http://www.planalto.gov.br/ccivil_03/Decreto-Lei/1965-1988/Del1000.htm. Acesso em: 29 jan. 2020.

20 BRASIL. União. *Lei n. 6.015, de 31 de dezembro de 1973*. Dispõe sobre os registros públicos, e dá outras providências. Brasília/DF (Brasil): Portal da Legislação do Governo Federal, 1973 (ano da publicação originária da lei). Disponível em: http://www.planalto.gov.br/ccivil_03/leis/L6015 compilada.htm. Acesso em: 13 jan. 2019.

21 PAIVA, João Pedro Lamana. *Curso em direito imobiliário registral aplicado aos bens públicos*. Porto Alegre/RS (Brasil): Registro de Imóveis 1ª Zona de Porto Alegre, 2014. Disponível em: http://www.planejamento.gov.br/assuntos/patrimonio-da-uniao/programa-de-modernizacao/linha-do-tempo/arquivos-e-publicacoes/historia-do-sistema-registral-brasileiro.pdf. Acesso em: 29 jan. 2020.

nos imóveis antigos e em que não há averbação de novidades, persiste o registro segundo o modelo anterior.

Um caso muito marcante na história do Direito Imobiliário brasileiro foi aquele que ficou conhecido como "Caso Encol". A falência da Incorporadora Encol ocorreu devido a uma prática comum na época entre as construtoras com dificuldades financeiras, na qual recursos financeiros eram utilizados por essas construtoras de uma obra para outra, prática essa que, em longo prazo, levou a empreiteira à falência, deixando mais de 700 compradores com seus imóveis inacabados em 1999[22].

A prática da empresa era financiar suas obras atuais com dinheiro recebido para novas obras. Assim, se a empresa não vendesse, ela não conseguia terminar as obras em andamento e que já tinham sido vendidas antes. Por causa disso, a Encol usava estratégias de vendas extremamente agressivas, incluindo aceitar carros usados como pagamento, telefones (na época valiam muito!) e outros imóveis, além de dar garantias absurdas para os compradores, prometendo a recompra de apartamentos pagando juros e correção. Tudo era para que a empresa não parasse de vender em hipótese alguma, pois a Encol precisava de muita renda no fluxo de caixa para continuar sobrevivendo. Evidentemente, esse modelo de negócios se mostrou insustentável e levou a incorporadora à falência.

Esse processo falimentar foi extremamente complexo e deixou muitas pessoas lesadas. Conta-se que o relatório final da falida Encol foi entregue à Justiça somente em maio de 2013. O processo durou mais de quatorze anos, contendo mais de 153 mil páginas distribuídas em mais de 500 volumes. As dívidas da Encol ultrapassaram um bilhão de reais, deixando 710 obras Brasil afora, milhares de funcionários desempregados e centenas de clientes sem dinheiro e sem os imóveis que haviam comprado. Assim, um divisor de águas a partir desse caso foi a criação do chamado *patrimônio de afetação,* concebido exatamente com o objetivo de assegurar a imediata e plena recomposição dos patrimônios dos adquirentes em caso de quebra do incorporador, bem como evitar pirâmides financeiras e outros malabarismos econômicos que antes eram possíveis[23].

[22] URBE.ME. Patrimônio de afetação: lições do caso Encol. Itajubá/MG (Brasil). *Dinheirama*, 2019. Disponível em: https://dinheirama.com/patrimonio-de-afetacao-licoes-do-caso-encol/. Acesso em: 29 jan. 2020.

[23] GABRIEL, Caio César Lazare; ROCHA, Ana Carla de Paiva; FERNANDES, Graziella; SULINA, Vanessa; PAULA, Jefferson de; CURTI, Kaue Almeida; OLIVEIRA, Nathalia Gomes

O patrimônio de afetação consiste na segregação patrimonial de bens do incorporador para uma atividade específica, assegurando-se assim a continuidade e entrega das unidades em construção aos adquirentes, mesmo que ocorra a falência ou insolvência do incorporador[24]. Então, essa situação ocorrida com a Encol resultou diretamente na criação de um novo instituto no Direito Imobiliário brasileiro (*patrimônio de afetação,* regulamentado pela Lei n. 10.931, de 2 de agosto de 2004). De forma semelhante, ao longo do século XX, a prática trouxe a necessidade por diversas inovações cruciais para o Direito Imobiliário. Além do já citado advento do regime de patrimônio de afetação, viu-se a criação da Lei sobre o Parcelamento do Solo Urbano, em 1979, da Lei do Inquilinato, em 1991, do Estatuto da Terra, em 1964; da Lei da alienação fiduciária, em 1997, e tantas outras normas relevantes. Todo esse cabedal histórico é recebido pelo Direito Imobiliário do novo século, justificando o que hoje existe no Direito Imobiliário do século XXI.

2. ESTADO ATUAL DO DIREITO IMOBILIÁRIO BRASILEIRO DO SÉCULO XXI

O atual sistema de Direito Imobiliário brasileiro envolve a conjugação de diversos institutos, regidos por diplomas normativos de vários ramos do Direito. Luiz Antonio Scavone Junior indica as seguintes instituições como as mais importantes do Direito Imobiliário atual: os Direitos Reais (CC/2002); Direito Registral (LRP/1973); Direito cartorial (Lei n. 8.935/1994[25]), outorga conjugal; desapropriação; posse e as ações possessórias; usucapião; regularização fundiária urbana (Reurb); o parcelamento do solo urbano (Lei n. 6.766, de 19 de dezembro de 1979[26]); as incorporações imobiliárias; os fundos de investimento imobiliário; a aplicabili-

de. Patrimônio de afetação: o caso Encol. *Jus.com.br*, 2016. Disponível em: https://jus.com.br/artigos/47503/patrimonio-de-afetacao-o-caso-encol. Acesso em: 28 jan. 2020.

[24] PAIVA, João Pedro Lamana. Patrimônio de afetação: segurança jurídica na aquisição de imóvel em planta. Porto Alegre/RS (Brasil): *Site Registro de Imóveis 1ª zona de Porto Alegre.* Disponível em: http://registrodeimoveis1zona.com.br/?p=202. Acesso em: 29 jan. 2020.

[25] BRASIL. *Lei n. 8.935, de 18 de novembro de 1994.* Regulamenta o art. 236 da Constituição Federal, dispondo sobre serviços notariais e de registro. Brasília/DF (Brasil): Portal da Legislação do Governo Federal, 1994 (ano da publicação originária da lei). Disponível em: http://www.planalto.gov.br/ ccivil_03/LEIS/L8935.htm. Acesso em: 29 jan. 2020.

[26] BRASIL. *Lei n. 6.766, de 19 de dezembro de 1979.* Dispõe sobre o Parcelamento do Solo Urbano e dá outras Providências. Brasília/DF (Brasil): Portal da Legislação do Governo Federal, 1979

dade do Código de Defesa do Consumidor (CDC/1990); a promessa de compra e venda; os distratos e resoluções de compromissos de compra e venda ("Lei do Distrato"[27]); corretagem; estudo da mora; vícios ocultos; execução hipotecária por agente financeiro (Lei n. 5.741/1971); alienação fiduciária de bem imóvel (Lei do Sistema Financeiro Imobiliário – SFI[28]); fraude contra credores; fraude à execução; condomínio; direitos de vizinhança; locação imobiliária urbana ("lei do inquilinato"[29]); entre outros. Como se percebe, o sistema brasileiro de Direito Imobiliário é intrincado e envolve a conjugação de muitos institutos jurídicos diferentes.

O Código Civil de 2002, a teor do que já acontecera com o Código Civil de 1916, também se manteve em posição de destaque no Direito Imobiliário. Isso se dá, em primeiro lugar, porque ratificou os avanços que haviam sido obtidos com o Código Civil de 1916. Com efeito, o artigo 1.245 do Código Civil de 2002 afirma – em clara continuidade do bem-sucedido sistema que havia sido anteriormente estabelecido – que "transfere-se entre vivos a propriedade mediante o registro do título translativo no Registro de Imóveis"[30]. A mesma lógica serve para os demais direitos reais, pois, nos casos em que o registro não tem efeito constitutivo, ele pelo menos serve como modal de eficácia perante terceiros. É a publicidade do ato que dá a ele oponibilidade *erga omnes*.

(ano da publicação originária da lei). Disponível em: http://www.planalto.gov.br/ccivil_03/LEIS/L6766.htm. Acesso em: 29 jan. 2020.

[27] BRASIL. *Lei n. 13.786, de 27 de dezembro de 2018.* Altera as Leis n. 4.591, de 16 de dezembro de 1964, e 6.766, de 19 de dezembro de 1979, para disciplinar a resolução do contrato por inadimplemento do adquirente de unidade imobiliária em incorporação imobiliária e em parcelamento de solo urbano. Brasília/DF (Brasil): Portal da Legislação do Governo Federal, 2018 (ano da publicação originária da lei). Disponível em: http://www.planalto.gov.br/ccivil_03/_Ato2015-2018/2018/Lei/L13786.htm. Acesso em: 29 jan. 2020.

[28] BRASIL. União. *Lei n. 9.514, de 20 de novembro de 1997.* Dispõe sobre o Sistema de Financiamento Imobiliário, institui a alienação fiduciária de coisa imóvel e dá outras providências. Brasília: Portal da Legislação do Governo Federal, 1997 (data da publicação originária). Disponível em: http://www.planalto.gov.br/ccivil_03/leis/L9514.htm. Acesso em: 1º jul. 2018.

[29] BRASIL. União. *Lei federal n. 8.245, de 18 de outubro de 1991 [Lei do Inquilinato].* Brasília: Congresso Nacional, 1991. Disponível no Portal da Legislação do Governo Federal: http://www.planalto.gov.br/ ccivil_03/leis/L8245.htm. Acesso em: 20 jun. 2017.

[30] BRASIL. União. *Lei n. 10.406, de 10 de janeiro de 2002.* Institui o Código Civil (CC/02 – Código Civil). Brasília/DF (Brasil): Portal da Legislação do Governo Federal, 2002 (ano da publicação originária). Disponível em: http://www.planalto.gov.br/ccivil_03/leis/2002/L10406.htm. Acesso em: 22 dez. 2019.

Além do Código Civil de 2002, como já foi visto, há diversas legislações de grande interesse para o Direito Imobiliário. Adicionalmente, a jurisprudência brasileira também tem prestado importante contribuição para o desenvolvimento desse centro de questões jurídicas. Exemplificando, sobre a recente Lei do Distrato Imobiliário (Lei n. 13.786/2018[31]), o Superior Tribunal de Justiça já se manifestou no sentido de que a legislação em questão não se aplica aos contratos firmados antes da vigência dela[32]. Isso dá segurança jurídica – que é a pedra de toque do Direito Imobiliário –, eis que pessoas que já celebraram seus contratos não serão surpreendidas com a legislação nova. No mesmo julgado (REsp 1.498.484-DF[33]), que foi afetado ao rito dos recursos repetitivos e publicado no Informativo n. 651 da Corte Especial, ficou decidido, ainda, que "a cláusula penal moratória tem a finalidade de indenizar pelo adimplemento tardio da obrigação, e, em regra, estabelecida em valor equivalente ao locativo, afasta-se sua cumulação com lucros cessantes"[34]. O *decisum* é salutar porque afasta a possibilidade de enriquecimento sem causa e equaliza o *quantum* de multa que será pago entre as partes. O valor equivalente à locação já serve como indenização pelo não uso do adquirente. Não há razão para isso ser somado a lucros cessantes, eis que estes seriam, fatalmente, aquilo que a pessoa deixou de ganhar a título de locação, o que é exatamente o que ela está recebendo.

Ainda sobre a Lei de Distrato, vale pontuar que entre as principais alterações está a fixação de percentual de retenção de até 25% para os incorpo-

[31] BRASIL. União. *Lei n. 13.786, de 27 de dezembro de 2018*. Altera as Leis n. 4.591, de 16 de dezembro de 1964, e 6.766, de 19 de dezembro de 1979, para disciplinar a resolução do contrato por inadimplemento do adquirente de unidade imobiliária em incorporação imobiliária e em parcelamento de solo urbano. Brasília: Portal de Legislação do Governo Federal, 2018. Disponível em: http://www.planalto.gov.br/ ccivil_03/_Ato2015-2018/2018/Lei/L13786.htm. Acesso em: 29 jan. 2020.

[32] COMPRA DE IMÓVEIS. Lei do Distrato não vale para contratos firmados antes de sua vigência. São Paulo/SP (Brasil): *Site Consultor Jurídico*, 28 mar. 2019. Disponível em: https://www.conjur.com.br/2019-mar-28/lei-distrato-nao-vale-contratos-anteriores-vigencia. Acesso em: 29 jan. 2020.

[33] BRASIL. Superior Tribunal de Justiça (STJ). REsp n. 1498484/DF (2014/0306634-9), autuado em 25.11.2014. Relator Min. Luis Felipe Salomão – Segunda seção. *DJe* 25 jun. 2019. Disponível em: https://ww2.stj.jus.br/processo/revista/documento/mediado/?componente=ITA&sequencial=1744759&num_registro=201403066349&data=20190625&formato=PDF. Acesso em: 29 jan. 2020.

[34] Destaque do Informativo n. 651 do STJ, disponível em: https://ww2.stj.jus.br/jurisprudencia/ externo/informativo/?acao=pesquisar&processo=1498484&operador=mesmo&b=INFJ&thesaurus=JURIDICO&p=true. Acesso em: 29 de janeiro de 2020.

radores quando a desistência da compra partir do consumidor adquirente (Lei n. 4.591/1964, art. 67-A[35]). Se a obra estiver submetida ao regime do Patrimônio de Afetação, essa retenção passa para 50% (Lei n. 4.591/1964, art. 67-A, § 5º[36]).

A norma também trouxe como novidade a possibilidade de aplicação do direito de arrependimento por parte do adquirente se a aquisição do imóvel ocorrer em estande de venda e fora da sede do incorporador, desde que essa desistência seja manifestada pelo adquirente em até 7 dias corridos da compra. Nesse caso, todos os valores pagos pelo adquirente deverão ser reembolsados, incluindo a comissão de corretagem (Lei n. 4.591/1964, art. 67-A, §§ 10, 11 e 12[37]). Se o imóvel tiver sido adquirido via financiamento que envolveu alienação fiduciária, devem ser respeitados os termos e condições da referida lei, e, na hipótese de leilão da unidade por execução, a devolução dos valores ao adquirente deverá observar as condições estabelecidas pela Lei da Alienação Fiduciária[38]. Isso é importante pois,

[35] BRASIL. União. *Lei n. 4.591, de 16 de dezembro de 1964.* Dispõe sobre o condomínio em edificações e as incorporações imobiliárias. Brasília/DF (Brasil): Portal de Legislação do Governo Federal, 1964. Disponível em: http://www.planalto.gov.br/ccivil_03/leis/l4591.htm. Acesso em: 29 jan. 2020.

[36] "§ 5º Quando a incorporação estiver submetida ao regime do patrimônio de afetação, de que tratam os arts. 31-A a 31-F desta Lei, o incorporador restituirá os valores pagos pelo adquirente, deduzidos os valores descritos neste artigo e atualizados com base no índice contratualmente estabelecido para a correção monetária das parcelas do preço do imóvel, no prazo máximo de 30 (trinta) dias após o habite-se ou documento equivalente expedido pelo órgão público municipal competente, admitindo-se, nessa hipótese, que a pena referida no inciso II do *caput* deste artigo seja estabelecida até o limite de 50% (cinquenta por cento) da quantia paga", cf. BRASIL. União. *Lei n. 4.591, de 16 de dezembro de 1964*, cit.

[37] "§ 10. Os contratos firmados em estandes de vendas e fora da sede do incorporador permitem ao adquirente o exercício do direito de arrependimento, durante o prazo improrrogável de 7 (sete) dias, com a devolução de todos os valores eventualmente antecipados, inclusive a comissão de corretagem. § 11. Caberá ao adquirente demonstrar o exercício tempestivo do direito de arrependimento por meio de carta registrada, com aviso de recebimento, considerada a data da postagem como data inicial da contagem do prazo a que se refere o § 10 deste artigo. § 12. Transcorrido o prazo de 7 (sete) dias a que se refere o § 10 deste artigo sem que tenha sido exercido o direito de arrependimento, será observada a irretratabilidade do contrato de incorporação imobiliária, conforme disposto no § 2º do art. 32 da Lei n. 4.591, de 16 de dezembro de 1964", cf. BRASIL. União. *Lei n. 4.591, de 16 de dezembro de 1964*, cit.

[38] MUDANÇAS PARA CONSUMIDOR. Comissão do Senado aprova projeto de lei sobre distratos em compras de imóveis (Artigo). São Paulo/SP (Brasil): *Site Consultor Jurídico*, 9 nov. 2018. Disponível em: https://www.conjur.com.br/2018-nov-09/comissao-senado-aprova-projeto-lei-distratos-imoveis. Acesso em: 29 jan. 2020.

como se sabe, o procedimento de execução extrajudicial previsto naquela lei permite a venda do imóvel por valor inferior ao do imóvel (art. 27, § 2º, da Lei n. 9.514/97[39]).

Evidentemente, essas questões apenas pincelam esse ramo jurídico tão amplo que é o Direito Imobiliário. O importante é notar que se trata de uma parte muito viva do Direito nacional. O sistema imobiliário sofre mudanças constantemente, e essas mudanças são sentidas de maneira muito direta pela sociedade. Basta lembrar do julgado histórico sobre a ilegalidade da cobrança da Taxa de Assessoria Técnico-Imobiliária (SATI) e da legalidade da cobrança da comissão de corretagem na compra de imóveis na planta. Nessa ocasião, o Ministro relator – Paulo de Tarso Sanseverino – afirmou que "essa assessoria [SATI] prestada ao consumidor por técnicos vinculados ao vendedor constitui mera prestação de serviço inerente à celebração do próprio contrato, inclusive no que tange ao dever de informação, não constituindo serviço autônomo, oferecido ao cliente, como ocorre

[39] "Art. 27. Uma vez consolidada a propriedade em seu nome, o fiduciário, no prazo de trinta dias, contados da data do registro de que trata o § 7º do artigo anterior, promoverá público leilão para a alienação do imóvel. § 1º Se, no primeiro público leilão, o maior lance oferecido for inferior ao valor do imóvel, estipulado na forma do inciso VI do art. 24, será realizado o segundo leilão, nos quinze dias seguintes. § 1º Se no primeiro leilão público o maior lance oferecido for inferior ao valor do imóvel, estipulado na forma do inciso VI e do parágrafo único do art. 24 desta Lei, será realizado o segundo leilão nos quinze dias seguintes. (Redação dada pela Lei n. 13.465, de 2017) § 2º No segundo leilão, será aceito o maior lance oferecido, desde que igual ou superior ao valor da dívida, das despesas, dos prêmios de seguro, dos encargos legais, inclusive tributos, e das contribuições condominiais. § 2º-A. Para os fins do disposto nos §§ 1º e 2º deste artigo, as datas, horários e locais dos leilões serão comunicados ao devedor mediante correspondência dirigida aos endereços constantes do contrato, inclusive ao endereço eletrônico. (Incluído pela Lei n. 13.465, de 2017) § 2º-B. Após a averbação da consolidação da propriedade fiduciária no patrimônio do credor fiduciário e até a data da realização do segundo leilão, é assegurado ao devedor fiduciante o direito de preferência para adquirir o imóvel por preço correspondente ao valor da dívida, somado aos encargos e despesas de que trata o § 2º deste artigo, aos valores correspondentes ao imposto sobre transmissão *inter vivos* e ao laudêmio, se for o caso, pagos para efeito de consolidação da propriedade fiduciária no patrimônio do credor fiduciário, e às despesas inerentes ao procedimento de cobrança e leilão, incumbindo, também, ao devedor fiduciante o pagamento dos encargos tributários e despesas exigíveis para a nova aquisição do imóvel, de que trata este parágrafo, inclusive custas e emolumentos. (Incluído pela Lei n. 13.465, de 2017)", cf. BRASIL. União. *Lei n. 9.514, de 20 de novembro de 1997.* Dispõe sobre o Sistema de Financiamento Imobiliário, institui a alienação fiduciária de coisa imóvel e dá outras providências. Brasília: Portal da Legislação do Governo Federal, 1997 (data da publicação originária). Disponível em: http://www.planalto.gov.br/ccivil_03/leis/L9514.htm. Acesso em: 1º jul. 2018.

com a corretagem. Verifica-se nesse caso flagrante violação dos deveres de lealdade e transparência impostos pela boa-fé objetiva, tendo em vista a cobrança da SATI pelo cumprimento de deveres inerentes ao próprio contrato celebrado"[40]. Como se percebe, a decisão é importantíssima, recente (2016) e impacta diretamente na vida de milhares de cidadãos.

Apenas para ilustrar com outro exemplo, recentemente (26.11.2019) foi afetada para julgamento sob rito dos recursos repetitivos a controvérsia sobre a possibilidade de apreciação da contestação oferecida antes da execução de liminar de busca e apreensão deferida com base no Decreto-Lei n. 911/1969 (ProAfR no REsp 1799367/MG)[41], medida de iniciativa

[40] Trecho do voto do Ministro Relator. O julgado foi ementado da seguinte forma: "RECURSO ESPECIAL REPETITIVO. DIREITO CIVIL E DO CONSUMIDOR. PROCESSUAL CIVIL. INCORPORAÇÃO IMOBILIÁRIA. VENDA DE UNIDADES AUTÔNOMAS EM ESTANDE DE VENDAS. CORRETAGEM. CLÁUSULA DE TRANSFERÊNCIA DA OBRIGAÇÃO AO CONSUMIDOR. ALEGAÇÃO DE ABUSIVIDADE. TEORIA DA ASSERÇÃO. LEGITIMIDADE PASSIVA DA INCORPORADORA. VALIDADE DA CLÁUSULA. SERVIÇO DE ASSESSORIA TÉCNICO-IMOBILIÁRIA (SATI). COBRANÇA. DESCABIMENTO. ABUSIVIDADE. 1. TESE PARA OS FINS DO ART. 1.040 DO CPC/2015: 1.1. Legitimidade passiva 'ad causam' da incorporadora, na condição de promitente-vendedora, para responder pela restituição ao consumidor dos valores pagos a título de comissão de corretagem e de taxa de assessoria técnico-imobiliária, nas demandas em que se alega prática abusiva na transferência desses encargos ao consumidor. 2. CASO CONCRETO: 2.1. Aplicação da tese ao caso concreto, rejeitando-se a preliminar de ilegitimidade. 2.2. 'Validade da cláusula contratual que transfere ao promitente-comprador a obrigação de pagar a comissão de corretagem nos contratos de promessa de compra e venda de unidade autônoma em regime de incorporação imobiliária, desde que previamente informado o preço total da aquisição da unidade autônoma, com o destaque do valor da comissão de corretagem' (tese firmada no julgamento do REsp 1.599.511/SP). 2.3. 'Abusividade da cobrança pelo promitente-vendedor do serviço de assessoria técnico-imobiliária (SATI), ou atividade congênere, vinculado à celebração de promessa de compra e venda de imóvel' (tese firmada no julgamento do REsp 1.599.511/SP). 2.4. Improcedência do pedido de restituição da comissão de corretagem e procedência do pedido de restituição da SATI. 3. RECURSO ESPECIAL PROVIDO, EM PARTE" (REsp 1551951/SP, Rel. Ministro Paulo de Tarso Sanseverino, Segunda Seção, julgado em 24.08.2016, *DJe* 06.09.2016).

[41] "PROPOSTA DE AFETAÇÃO. RITO DOS RECURSOS ESPECIAIS REPETITIVOS. DIREITO CIVIL E PROCESSUAL CIVIL (CPC/2015). RECURSO ESPECIAL INTERPOSTO EM INCIDENTE DE RESOLUÇÃO DE DEMANDAS REPETITIVAS – IRDR. CAUSA-PILOTO DE ALIENAÇÃO FIDUCIÁRIA EM GARANTIA. BUSCA E APREENSÃO. RITO DO DECRETO-LEI 911/1969. CONTESTAÇÃO OFERECIDA ANTES DA EFETIVAÇÃO DA LIMINAR. CONTROVÉRSIA ACERCA DA POSSIBILIDADE DE APRECIAÇÃO DA RESPOSTA. 1. Controvérsia acerca da possibilidade de apreciação da contestação oferecida antes da execução de liminar de busca e apreensão deferida com base no Decreto-Lei 911/1969.

do Relator do caso, o Min. Paulo de Tarso Sanseverino. O que ocorre é que o Decreto-Lei n. 911/1969, em seu artigo 3º, determina que "o proprietário fiduciário ou credor poderá, desde que comprovada a mora, na forma estabelecida pelo § 2º do art. 2º, ou o inadimplemento, requerer contra o devedor ou terceiro a busca e apreensão do bem alienado fiduciariamente, a qual será concedida liminarmente, podendo ser apreciada em plantão judiciário"[42]. Assim sendo, conforme se percebe, há a previsão de que a busca e apreensão é deferida liminarmente, *inaudita altera parte*, e apenas depois o réu será citado e apresentará sua defesa. Entretanto, o que ocorre na hipótese em que, sem aguardar o cumprimento da medida liminar, o réu apresenta sua contestação com matéria de fato e de direito extintiva, modificativa ou obstativa do direito alegado pelo autor? Duas hipóteses de solução surgem a partir daí. Pela primeira, o juiz deve esperar o cumprimento da liminar para somente depois fazer qualquer avaliação da contestação oferecida pelo réu, pois, em tese, o autor teria realmente o direito de ver cumprida sua liminar antes de ser o réu citado. Pela segunda hipótese, o juiz não deve esperar o cumprimento da liminar para somente depois fazer qualquer avaliação da contestação oferecida pelo réu – pelo contrário, deverá ele imediatamente verificar, pelo menos, se é o caso de revogar a medida anteriormente concedida –, pois o fato de a lei prever em favor do credor a liminar significa apenas que ela pretendia não impor ao credor o ônus da demora do processo, mas de modo algum significaria que ela teria

2. Nos termos do art. 3º, § 3º, do Decreto-Lei 911/1969, 'o devedor fiduciante apresentará resposta no prazo de quinze dias da execução da liminar'. 3. Julgamento de IRDR a respeito desse tema no Tribunal de origem, tendo-se firmado tese nos seguintes termos: 'Na ação de busca e apreensão, a análise da contestação somente deve ocorrer após a execução da medida liminar' (IRDR 13/TJMG). 4. Necessidade de formação de precedente qualificado a respeito desse tema no âmbito deste Tribunal Superior, a fim de preservar a missão constitucional deste Tribunal Superior como Corte de vértice em matéria de interpretação da lei federal. 5. Delimitação da controvérsia: 'Possibilidade de apreciação da contestação oferecida antes da execução da liminar de busca e apreensão deferida com base no Decreto-Lei 911/1969'. 6. RECURSO ESPECIAL AFETADO AO RITO DO ART. 1.036 DO CPC/2015" (ProAfR no REsp 1799367/MG, Rel. Ministro Paulo de Tarso Sanseverino, Segunda Seção, julgado em 26.11.2019, *DJe* 10.12.2019).

[42] BRASIL. *Decreto-lei n. 911, de 1º de outubro de 1969.* Altera a redação do art. 66, da Lei n. 4.728, de 14 de julho de 1965, estabelece normas de processo sôbre alienação fiduciária e dá outras providências. Brasília/DF (Brasil): Portal de Legislação do Governo Federal, 1969. Disponível em: http://www.planalto.gov.br/ccivil_03/Decreto-Lei/1965-1988/Del0911.htm. Acesso em: 29 jan. 2020.

concedido ao autor um direito subjetivo de que o juiz só poderá se valer das asserções do autor para aferir a viabilidade da tutela provisória, mesmo quando já há outros elementos nos autos que poderiam infirmar essa conclusão. Como se percebe – e o próprio fato de o caso ter sido afetado para julgamento em sede de recursos repetitivos prova esse ponto –, o Direito Imobiliário possui grande relevância na atualidade; suas mudanças afetam diretamente a vida das pessoas; e essas mudanças são frequentes e constantes. É um ramo jurídico muito vivo e rico em desdobramentos e concreções. Assim sendo, o Direito Imobiliário remanesce sendo área de grande importância jurídica e econômica no cenário socioeconômico brasileiro.

3. TENDÊNCIAS E POSSIBILIDADES PARA O FUTURO DO DIREITO IMOBILIÁRIO

3.1. MULTIPROPRIEDADE E OUTRAS FORMAS DE EXERCÍCIO DE DIREITOS REAIS

Em 21 de dezembro de 2018, foi publicada a Lei n. 13.777, que estabeleceu a chamada *multipropriedade imobiliária* no Direito brasileiro[43]. O instituto já era conhecido dos portugueses (*direito real de habitação periódica*), dos espanhóis (*contrato de aprovechamiento por turno de bienes inmuebles*), dos franceses (*droit de jouissance à temps partagé*; *propriété spatio-temporelle; multijouissance; multiproprietà*), da própria União Europeia como um todo (Diretiva 2008/122/CE, de 14 de janeiro de 2009) e também nos países de *common law* (*time sharing*)[44]. Gustavo Tepedino conceituou o instituto como "relação jurídica de aproveitamento econômico de uma coisa móvel ou imóvel repartida em unidades fixas de tempo, de modo que diversos titulares possam, cada qual a seu turno, utilizar-se da coisa com exclusividade e de maneira perpétua"[45].

[43] BRASIL, União. *Lei n. 13.777, de 20 de dezembro de 2018.* Altera as Leis n. 10.406, de 10 de janeiro de 2002 (Código Civil), e 6.015, de 31 de dezembro de 1973 (Lei dos Registros Públicos), para dispor sobre o regime jurídico da multipropriedade e seu registro. Brasília/DF (Brasil): Portal de Legislação do Governo Federal, 2018. Disponível em: http://www.planalto.gov.br/ccivil_03/_Ato2015-2018/2018/Lei/L13777. htm. Acesso em: 29 jan. 2020.

[44] Cf. Oliveira, Carlos Eduardo Elias. Análise detalhada da multipropriedade no Brasil após a Lei n. 13.777/2018: pontos polêmicos e aspectos de registros públicos. São Paulo/SP (Brasil): *GenJurídico.com.br*, 21 mar. 2019. Disponível em: http://genjuridico.com.br/2019/03/21/analise-detalhada-da-multipropriedade-no-brasil-apos-a-lei-no-13-777-2018-pontos-polemicos-e-aspectos-de-registros-publicos/. Acesso em: 29 jan. 2020.

[45] Tepedino, Gustavo. *Multipropriedade imobiliária.* São Paulo: Saraiva, 1993. p. 1.

Isso significa que um mesmo bem pode ser utilizado por diferentes titulares de forma integral e quase plena, cada um em determinado momento no tempo. O *time sharing* é empregado de forma otimizada, ou utilizado com maior aproveitamento, em casas de praia, de veraneio, ou outros locais de temporada, que se frequenta com finalidade de descanso, lazer e outras atividades recreativas e lúdicas. Quando são submetidos a um regime de propriedade simples (ou propriedade singular), esses bens costumam ficar vazios grande período do ano. Por isso, a multipropriedade potencializa a utilização e fruição deles, pois, quando um titular termina de o utilizar, o outro pode iniciar a sua utilização, dinâmica que cria um verdadeiro revezamento recreativo, uma espécie de rodízio no (bom) ócio[46].

A Lei da Multipropriedade (Lei n. 13.777/2018) incluiu os artigos 1.358-B a 1.358-U no Código Civil de 2002, inserindo, assim, o Capítulo VII-A, "do condomínio em multipropriedade". Diz o artigo 1.358-C do Código Civil de 2002 que a "multipropriedade é o regime de condomínio em que cada um dos proprietários de um mesmo imóvel é titular de uma fração de tempo, à qual corresponde a faculdade de uso e gozo, com exclusividade, da totalidade do imóvel, a ser exercida pelos proprietários de forma alternada"[47].

A multipropriedade representa uma tendência não apenas porque é uma novidade do ponto de vista dos direitos reais, mas porque representa muito bem uma ideia: a busca pela eficiência máxima; pela otimização das possíveis receitas; pela redução de custos. Por um lado, embora haja a percepção de que as pessoas estão cada dia mais consumistas[48], ao mesmo

[46] No mesmo sentido, ver: SCHREIBER, Anderson. Multipropriedade imobiliária e a Lei 13.777/18. *JusBrasil*, 2019. Disponível em: https://flaviotartuce.jusbrasil.com.br/artigos/664096447/multipropriedade -imobiliaria-e-a-lei-13777-18. Acesso em: 29 jan. 2020.

[47] BRASIL. União. *Lei n. 10.406, de 10 de janeiro de 2002.* Institui o Código Civil. (CC/02 – Código Civil). Brasília/DF (Brasil): Portal da Legislação do Governo Federal, 2002 (ano da publicação originária). Disponível em: http://www.planalto.gov.br/ccivil_03/leis/2002/L10406.htm. Acesso em: 22 dez. 2019.

[48] Ver, por exemplo, GONZALEZ, Amelia. Pesquisa mostra que 76% não praticam consumo consciente no Brasil. Rio de Janeiro/RJ (Brasil): *Portal G1*, 25 jul. 2018. Disponível em: https://g1.globo.com/ natureza/blog/amelia-gonzalez/post/2018/07/25/pesquisa-mostra-que-76-nao-praticam-consumo-consciente-no-brasil.ghtml. Acesso em: 29 jan. 2020; NINNI, Karina. Consumo cresce seis vezes em 50 anos. São Paulo/SP (Brasil): *Site do Estadão*, 29 jun. 2010. Disponível em: https://sustentabilidade. estadao.com.br/noticias/geral,consumo-cresce-seis-vezes-em-50-anos,573880. Acesso em: 29 jan. 2020; DEARO, Guilherme. As 10 tendências

tempo há uma curiosa tendência de as pessoas não *terem* mais coisas no sentido que antes essa palavra designava, isto é, nesse sentido clássico-jurídico de *ser proprietário* com todos os *poderes da propriedade.* Hoje, quem *tem* algo frequentemente quer fazer essa coisa render (em vez de usar a coisa diretamente). Os exemplos são muitos: o motorista de aplicativo com relação ao seu carro; a empresa de mobilidade urbana com relação às suas bicicletas e aos seus patinetes, o anunciante de casa em aplicativo com relação ao seu imóvel, e assim por diante. Está cada vez mais difundida a ideia de que *ter* um carro envolve despesas que fazem compensar mais usar táxi ou motoristas privados[49], ou de que uma casa *não é um ativo*[50], e que o melhor é simplesmente não ter a casa própria ou somente a adquirir quando ela representar uma parcela ínfima do patrimônio total da pessoa. A mesma lógica aos poucos se espraia por classes cada vez mais amplas de ativos e em camadas cada vez maiores da sociedade, consistindo em clara tendência moderna que abarca o Direito Imobiliário.

Está havendo uma transformação na forma de *ter coisas,* e é claro que isso se reflete nos direitos reais e, mais precisamente, no Direito Imobiliário. O "sonho da casa própria" não tem mais tanta força quanto outrora tinha. Isso dá azo a um enfraquecimento da categoria da propriedade simples e dá força para institutos que promovam arranjos diferentes, como é o caso da multipropriedade, da locação intermediada por aplicativo, e outras novidades. Assim sendo, essa é uma tendência importante para o futuro: a caminhada para formas alternativas de uso dos bens, de modo a promover a otimização do uso e da fruição dos bens e diminuição de custos para aquele que figura como proprietário direto.

globais de consumo em 2019. São Paulo/SP (Brasil): *Site Exame,* 15 jan. 2019. Disponível em: https://exame.abril.com.br/marketing/as-10-tendencias-globais-de-consumo-em-2019/. Acesso em: 29 jan. 2020.

[49] EMPIRICUS. *Carro:* ter ou não ter? Vídeo postado no YouTube pelo usuário Empiricus em 18 set. 2018. Disponível em: https://www.youtube.com/watch?v=EHdf-MdxXh>. Acesso em: 29 jan. 2020.

[50] Kiyosaki, Robert T. *Pai rico, pai pobre (Rich Dad Poor Dad).* Edição comemorativa. Tradução de Maria José Cyhlar Monteiro. Rio de Janeiro: Alta Books, 2018. Versão digital (Kindle), loc. 1197.

3.2. DESBUROCRATIZAÇÃO DE PROCEDIMENTOS E EXTRAJUDICIALIZAÇÃO DOS ATOS JURÍDICOS

Uma tendência importante para o futuro do Direito Imobiliário é a desburocratização dos procedimentos registrais e de celebração dos atos jurídicos em geral. Nesse sentido, vale como exemplo o Projeto de Lei n. 7.790/2014[51], transformado na Lei Ordinária n. 13.838, de 4 de junho de 2019[52], que alterou o artigo 176 da Lei de Registros Públicos (Lei n. 6.015/1973 – "LRP/1973") para dispensar a anuência dos confrontantes na averbação do georreferenciamento de imóvel rural, bastando, para tanto, a declaração do requerente da averbação do georreferenciamento no sentido de que respeitou os limites e as confrontações do imóvel. Isso só é possível porque, diferentemente dos antigos sistemas de marcação topográfica do terreno, o georreferenciamento permite – através do uso de avançada tecnologia de referenciação em modelos tridimensionais e de equipamentos outrora impensáveis como satélites – que se marque o solo de maneira precisa e com chance mínima de erro, o que torna sem sentido o procedimento, assaz demorado e dispendioso, de obtenção de anuência de todos os confrontantes, que podem ser muitos, podem estar em local incerto e não sabido, ou, pior, podem ser desconhecidos.

Esse georreferenciamento eletrônico das propriedades rurais é realizado, no Brasil, pelo Instituto Nacional de Colonização e Reforma Agrária (INCRA), fundado pelo Decreto n. 1.110, de 9 de julho de 1970, com a missão de manter o cadastro nacional de imóveis rurais, administrar as terras públicas da União e promover a reforma agrária[53]. Para tanto, o

[51] BRASIL. Câmara dos Deputados. *Projeto de Lei n. 7.790/2014*. Acresce o § 9º ao art. 176 da Lei n. 6.015, de 31 de dezembro de 1973, que dispõe sobre os registros públicos e dá outras providências, para dispensar a apresentação de carta de anuência de confrontantes na averbação do georreferenciamento de imóveis rurais. Brasília/DF (Brasil): Portal da Câmara dos Deputados Federais, 2014. Disponível em: https://www.camara.leg.br/proposicoesWeb/fichadetramitacao?idProposicao=619907. Acesso em: 2 jan. 2020.

[52] BRASIL. *Lei n. 13.838, de 4 de junho de 2019*. Altera a Lei n. 6.015, de 31 de dezembro de 1973 (Lei de Registros Públicos), para dispensar a anuência dos confrontantes na averbação do georreferenciamento de imóvel rural. Brasília/DF (Brasil): Portal de Legislação do Governo Federal, 2019. Disponível em: http://www.planalto.gov.br/ccivil_03/_ato2019-2022/2019/lei/L13838.htm. Acesso em: 29 jan. 2020.

[53] BRASIL. *Decreto-lei n. 1.110, de 9 de julho de 1970*. Cria o Instituto Nacional de Colonização e Reforma Agrária (INCRA), extingue o Instituto Brasileiro de Reforma Agrária, o Instituto Nacional de Desenvolvimento Agrário e o Grupo Executivo da Reforma Agrária e dá outras

INCRA se vale do chamado Sistema de Gestão Fundiária (SIGEF), que é acessível pelo público[54] e que está em plena expansão. Com a evolução de técnicas como a do georreferenciamento e a do sistema de posicionamento global (*Global Positioning System – GPS*), a marcação precisa e segura das dimensões e confrontações de imóveis se torna algo muito mais simples e factível. A tendência é, cada vez mais, esses registros começarem a adotar a forma de georreferenciamento, inclusive mediante armazenamento de dados em forma eletrônica, abandonando-se o antigo sistema de marcações topográficas.

De forma correlata, existe também uma tendência a tornar os atos jurídicos tanto mais extrajudiciais quanto seja possível. Há, pois, uma "extrajudicialização" do Direito, o que ocorre, principalmente, em atenção ao nível alarmante de abarrotamento da Justiça brasileira, que em 2018 indicou a existência de 78,7 milhões de processos em tramitação[55]. Para se ter uma ideia comparativa, os Estados Unidos – que são um país continental maior do que o Brasil – têm bem menos processos do que nós. Enquanto a Justiça Federal do Brasil contabilizou, em 2018, 4.203.804 (quatro milhões, duzentos e três mil, oitocentos e quatro) casos novos[56], a Justiça Federal dos Estados Unidos contabilizou 358.563 (trezentos e cinquenta e oito mil, quinhentos e sessenta e três casos)[57]. A diferença é gritante. São representativos dessa tendência de "extrajudicialização" o sistema brasileiro de alienação fiduciária de imóveis (Lei n. 9.514, de 20 de novembro de 1997); o Projeto de Lei que pretende admitir a execução civil extrajudicial (PL

providências. Brasília/DF (Brasil): Portal de Legislação do Governo Federal, 1970. Disponível em: http://www.planalto.gov.br/ ccivil_03/Decreto-Lei/1965-1988/Del1110.htm. Acesso em: 29 jan. 2020.

[54] BRASIL. *Site* do Sistema de Gestão Fundiária (SIGEF): Sistema desenvolvido pelo INCRA/MDA para gestão de informações fundiárias do meio rural brasileiro. Brasília/DF (Brasil): Ministério do Desenvolvimento Agrário. Disponível em: https://sigef.incra.gov.br. Acesso em: 29 jan. 2020.

[55] BRASIL. Conselho Nacional de Justiça (CNJ). *Justiça em Números 2019:* ano-base 2018. Brasília/DF: CNJ, 2019. Disponível em: https://www.cnj.jus.br/pesquisas-judiciarias/justica-em-numeros/. Acesso em: 21 nov. 2019. p. 79.

[56] BRASIL. Conselho Nacional de Justiça (CNJ). *Justiça em Números 2019:* ano-base 2018. Brasília/DF: CNJ, 2019. Disponível em: https://www.cnj.jus.br/pesquisas-judiciarias/justica-em-numeros/. Acesso em: 21 nov. 2019. p. 84.

[57] USA. *Federal Judicial Caseload Statistics 2018.* Washington/DC (USA): Site United States Courts, 2019. Disponível em: https://www.uscourts.gov/statistics-reports/federal-judicial-caseload-statistics-2018. Acesso em: 29 jan. 2020.

6.204/2019) e a possibilidade da usucapião extrajudicial (CPC/2015, art. 1.071; e LRP/1973, art. 216-A).

CONCLUSÕES

Portanto, verifica-se que o Direito Imobiliário do século XXI veio como continuidade de um ramo jurídico cuja pedra de toque são a segurança jurídica e a publicidade. Atualmente, esse importante ramo do Direito se apresenta como um conjunto de normas muito variadas - incluindo disposições de diversas áreas clássicas como Direito Tributário, Direito Trabalhista, Direito Previdenciário, Direito Ambiental, Direito Empresarial, Direito Falimentar, Direito Civil, Direito Consumerista e assim por diante - e inclui disposições que estão esparsas em diversas legislações (como a Lei da Alienação Fiduciária, a Lei da Multipropriedade, a Lei do Distrato Imobiliário, a Lei das Locações Urbanas, o próprio Estatuto da Terra, entre outros diplomas normativos) e julgados relevantes. Tendo em vista a evolução contínua desse ramo do Direito, para o futuro se observa uma tendência ao uso da tecnologia e dos meios de comunicação para criar direitos reais ou direitos pessoais relacionados com imóveis que sejam cada vez mais flexíveis e que propiciem o máximo de otimização do uso e fruição dos ativos. Observa-se também uma clara tendência à digitalização, desburocratização e extrajudicialização dos atos jurídicos, sendo muito clara a existência de um caminho cuja direção aponta para a criação de um registro imobiliário unificado e digital, o uso de tecnologias como o GPS, a solução de controvérsias em cartórios extrajudiciais, entre outras repercussões.

REFERÊNCIAS

ÁVILA, Humberto. *Teoria da segurança jurídica.* 3. ed. rev., atual., e ampl. São Paulo: Malheiros, 2014.

BRASIL, União. *Lei n. 13.777, de 20 de dezembro de 2018.* Altera as Leis n. 10.406, de 10 de janeiro de 2002 (Código Civil), e 6.015, de 31 de dezembro de 1973 (Lei dos Registros Públicos), para dispor sobre o regime jurídico da multipropriedade e seu registro. Brasília/DF (Brasil): Portal de Legislação do Governo Federal, 2018. Disponível em: http://www.planalto.gov.br/ccivil_03/_Ato2015-2018/2018/Lei/L13777.htm. Acesso em: 29 jan. 2020.

BRASIL. Câmara dos Deputados. *Projeto de Lei n. 7.790/2014.* Acresce o § 9º ao art. 176 da Lei n. 6.015, de 31 de dezembro de 1973, que dispõe sobre os registros públicos e dá outras providências, para dispensar a apresentação de carta de anuência de confrontantes na averbação do georreferenciamento de imóveis rurais.

Brasília/DF (Brasil): Portal da Câmara dos Deputados Federais, 2014. Disponível em: https://www.camara.leg.br/proposicoesWeb/fichadetramitacao?idProposicao=619907. Acesso em: 2 jan. 2020.

BRASIL. Conselho Nacional de Justiça (CNJ). *Justiça em Números 2019:* ano-base 2018. Brasília/DF: CNJ, 2019. Disponível em: https://www.cnj.jus.br/pesquisas-judiciarias/justica-em-numeros/. Acesso em: 21 nov. 2019.

BRASIL. *Decreto n. 169-A, de 19 de janeiro de 1890.* Substitue as Leis n. 1.237, de 24 de setembro de 1864, e n. 3.272, de 5 de outubro de 1885. Portal da Câmara dos Deputados, 1890 (ano da publicação originária da lei). Disponível em: https://www2.camara.leg.br/legin/fed/decret/1824-1899/decreto-169-a-19-janeiro-1890-516767-publicacaooriginal-1-pe.html. Acesso em: 29 jan. 2020.

BRASIL. *Decreto n. 3.272, de 5 de outubro de 1885.* Altera diversas disposições referentes ás execuções civeis e commerciaes. Portal da Câmara dos Deputados, 1885 (ano da publicação originária da lei). Disponível em: https://www2.camara.leg.br/legin/fed/decret/1824-1899/decreto-3272-5-outubro-1885-543469-publicacaooriginal-53793-pl.html. Acesso em: 29 jan. 2020.

BRASIL. *Decreto n. 370, de 2 de maio de 1890.* Manda observar o regulamento para execução do decreto n. 169-A, de 19 de janeiro de 1890, sobre operações de crédito móvel. Portal da Legislação do Governo Federal, 1890 (ano da publicação originária da lei). Disponível em: http://www.planalto.gov.br/ccivil_03/decreto/1851-1899/D370.htm. Acesso em: 29 jan. 2020.

BRASIL. *Decreto-lei n. 1.110, de 9 de julho de 1970.* Cria o Instituto Nacional de Colonização e Reforma Agrária (INCRA), extingue o Instituto Brasileiro de Reforma Agrária, o Instituto Nacional de Desenvolvimento Agrário e o Grupo Executivo da Reforma Agrária e dá outras providências. Brasília/DF (Brasil): Portal de Legislação do Governo Federal, 1970. Disponível em: http://www.planalto.gov.br/ccivil_03/Decreto-Lei/1965-1988/Del1110.htm. Acesso em: 29 jan. 2020.

BRASIL. *Decreto-lei n. 911, de 1º de outubro de 1969.* Altera a redação do art. 66, da Lei n. 4.728, de 14 de julho de 1965, estabelece normas de processo sôbre alienação fiduciária e dá outras providências. Brasília/DF (Brasil): Portal de Legislação do Governo Federal, 1969. Disponível em: http://www.planalto.gov.br/ccivil_03/Decreto-Lei/1965-1988/Del0911.htm. Acesso em: 29 jan. 2020.

BRASIL. *Lei n. 1.237, de 24 de setembro de 1864.* Reforma a Legislação Hypothecaria, e estabelece as bases das sociedades de credito real. Portal da Legislação do Governo Federal (Planalto), 1864 (ano da publicação originária da lei). Disponível em: http://www.planalto.gov.br/ccivil_03/leis/lim/LIM1237.htm. Acesso em: 28 jan. 2020.

BRASIL. *Lei n. 13.786, de 27 de dezembro de 2018.* Altera as Leis n. 4.591, de 16 de dezembro de 1964, e 6.766, de 19 de dezembro de 1979, para disciplinar a resolução do contrato por inadimplemento do adquirente de unidade imobiliária em incorporação imobiliária e em parcelamento de solo urbano. Brasília/DF (Brasil): Portal da Legislação do Governo Federal, 2018 (ano da publicação originária da lei). Disponível em: http://www.planalto.gov.br/ccivil_03/_Ato2015-2018/2018/Lei/L13786.htm. Acesso em: 29 jan. 2020.

BRASIL. *Lei n. 13.838, de 4 de junho de 2019.* Altera a Lei n. 6.015, de 31 de dezembro de 1973 (Lei de Registros Públicos), para dispensar a anuência dos confrontantes na averbação do georreferenciamento de imóvel rural. Brasília/DF (Brasil): Portal de Legislação do Governo Federal, 2019. Disponível em: http://www.planalto.gov.br/ccivil_03/_ato2019-2022/2019/lei/L13838.htm. Acesso em: 29 jan. 2020.

BRASIL. *Lei n. 3.453, de 26 de abril de 1865.* Manda observar o Regulamento para execução da Lei n. 1.237, de 24 de setembro de 1864, que reformou a legislação hypothecaria. Portal da Legislação do Governo Federal (Planalto), 1865 (ano da publicação originária da lei). Disponível em: http://www.planalto.gov.br/ccivil_03/decreto/historicos/dim/DIM3453.htm. Acesso em: 28 jan. 2020.

BRASIL. *Lei n. 317, de 21 de outubro de 1843.* Fixando a Despeza e orçando a Receita para os exercícios de 1843-1844, e 1844-1845. Rio de Janeiro: Portal da Legislação do Governo Federal (Planalto), 1843 (ano da publicação originária da lei). Disponível em: http://www.planalto.gov.br/ccivil_03/leis/lim/LIM317.htm. Acesso em: 28 jan. 2020.

BRASIL. *Lei n. 6.766, de 19 de dezembro de 1979.* Dispõe sobre o Parcelamento do Solo Urbano e dá outras Providências. Brasília/DF (Brasil): Portal da Legislação do Governo Federal, 1979 (ano da publicação originária da lei). Disponível em: http://www.planalto.gov.br/ccivil_03/LEIS/L6766.htm. Acesso em: 29 jan. 2020.

BRASIL. *Lei n. 8.935, de 18 de novembro de 1994.* Regulamenta o art. 236 da Constituição Federal, dispondo sobre serviços notariais e de registro. Brasília/DF (Brasil): Portal da Legislação do Governo Federal, 1994 (ano da publicação originária da lei). Disponível em: http://www.planalto.gov.br/ccivil_03/LEIS/L8935.htm. Acesso em: 29 jan. 2020.

BRASIL. *Site* do Sistema de Gestão Fundiária (SIGEF): Sistema desenvolvido pelo INCRA/MDA para gestão de informações fundiárias do meio rural brasileiro. Brasília/DF (Brasil): Ministério do Desenvolvimento Agrário. Disponível em: https://sigef.incra.gov.br. Acesso em: 29 jan. 2020.

BRASIL. Superior Tribunal de Justiça (STJ). *Agravo Interno no Recurso Especial (AgInt em REsp) n. 1.758.854-SP.* Sobre a diferença entre hipoteca e alienação fiduciária. Relator: Paulo de Tarso Sanseverino – Brasília/DF (Brasil): STJ, 13 dez. 2019 (data de publicação). Disponível em: https://ww2.stj.jus.br/processo/julgamento/eletronico/documento/mediado/?documento_tipo=91&documento_sequencial=103446777&registro_numero=201701760987&publicacao_data=20191213&formato=PDF. Acesso em: 28 jan. 2020.

BRASIL. Superior Tribunal de Justiça (STJ). REsp 1498484/DF (2014/0306634-9), autuado em 25.11.2014. Relator Min. Luis Felipe Salomão – Segunda Seção. *DJe* 25 jun. 2019. Disponível em: https://ww2.stj.jus.br/processo/revista/documento/mediado/?componente=ITA&sequencial=1744759&num_registro=201403066349&data=20190625&formato=PDF. Acesso em: 29 jan. 2020.

BRASIL. União. *Decreto-lei n. 1.000, de 21 de novembro de 1969.* Brasília/DF (Brasil): Portal de Legislação do Governo Federal, 1969. Disponível em: http://www.planalto.gov.br/ccivil_03/Decreto-Lei/1965-1988/Del1000.htm. Acesso em: 29 jan. 2020.

BRASIL. União. *Lei federal n. 8.245, de 18 de outubro de 1991 [Lei do Inquilinato].* Brasília: Congresso Nacional, 1991. Disponível no Portal da Legislação do Governo Federal: http://www.planalto.gov.br/ccivil_03/leis/L8245.htm. Acesso em: 20 jun. 2017.

BRASIL. União. *Lei n. 10.406, de 10 de janeiro de 2002.* Institui o Código Civil (CC/02 – Código Civil). Brasília/DF (Brasil): Portal da Legislação do Governo Federal, 2002 (ano da publicação originária). Disponível em: http://www.planalto.gov.br/ccivil_03/leis/2002/L10406.htm. Acesso em: 22 dez. 2019.

BRASIL. União. *Lei n. 3.071, de 1º de janeiro de 1916. Código Civil dos Estados Unidos do Brasil* (CC/1916 – Código Civil). Rio de Janeiro/RJ (Brasil): Congresso Nacional, 1916 (ano da publicação originária). Disponível em: http://www.planalto.gov.br/ccivil_03/LEIS/L3071.htm. Acesso em: 22 dez. 2019.

BRASIL. União. *Lei n. 4.591, de 16 de dezembro de 1964*. Dispõe sobre o condomínio em edificações e as incorporações imobiliárias. Brasília/DF (Brasil): Portal de Legislação do Governo Federal, 1964. Disponível em: http://www.planalto.gov.br/ccivil_03/leis/l4591.htm. Acesso em: 29 jan. 2020.

BRASIL. União. *Lei n. 6.015, de 31 de dezembro de 1973*. Dispõe sobre os registros públicos, e dá outras providências. Brasília: Portal da Legislação do Governo Federal, 1973 (ano da publicação originária da lei). Disponível em: http://www.planalto.gov.br/ccivil_03/leis/L6015compilada.htm. Acesso em: 13 jan. 2019.

BRASIL. União. *Lei n. 9.514, de 20 de novembro de 1997*. Dispõe sobre o Sistema de Financiamento Imobiliário, institui a alienação fiduciária de coisa imóvel e dá outras providências. Brasília: Portal da Legislação do Governo Federal, 1997 (data da publicação originária). Disponível em: http://www.planalto.gov.br/ccivil_03/leis/L9514.htm. Acesso em: 1º jul. 2018.

COMPRA DE IMÓVEIS. Lei do Distrato não vale para contratos firmados antes de sua vigência. São Paulo/SP (Brasil): *Site Consultor Jurídico*, 28 mar. 2019. Disponível em: https://www.conjur.com.br/2019-mar-28/lei-distrato-nao-vale-contratos-anteriores--vigencia. Acesso em: 29 jan. 2020.

Dearo, Guilherme. As 10 tendências globais de consumo em 2019. São Paulo/SP (Brasil): *Site Exame*, 15 jan. 2019. Disponível em: https://exame.abril.com.br/marketing/as-10--tendencias-globais-de-consumo-em-2019/. Acesso em: 29 jan. 2020.

Dip, Ricardo. *Registros sobre registros*. Artigo. Brasília/DF (Brasil): Portal da Associação dos Notários e Registradores do Brasil, 12 fev. 2019. Disponível em: http://iregistradores.org.br/registros-sobre-registros-142/. Acesso em: 28 jan. 2020.

EMPIRICUS. *Carro:* ter ou não ter? Vídeo postado no YouTube pelo usuário Empiricus em 18 set. 2018. Disponível em: https://www.youtube.com/watch?v=EHdf-MdxXh>. Acesso em: 29 jan. 2020.

Gabriel, Caio César Lazare; Rocha, Ana Carla de Paiva; Fernandes, Graziella; Sulina, Vanessa; Paula, Jefferson de; Curti, Kaue Almeida; Oliveira, Nathalia Gomes de. Patrimônio de afetação: o caso Encol. *Jus.com.br*, 2016. Disponível em: https://jus.com.br/artigos/47503/patrimonio-de-afetacao-o-caso-encol. Acesso em: 28 jan. 2020.

Gonzalez, Amelia. Pesquisa mostra que 76% não praticam consumo consciente no Brasil. Rio de Janeiro/RJ (Brasil): *Portal G1*, 25 jul. 2018. Disponível em: https://g1.globo.com/natureza/blog/amelia-gonzalez/post/2018/07/25/pesquisa-mostra-que-76-nao--praticam-consumo-consciente-no-brasil.ghtml. Acesso em: 29 jan. 2020

Kiyosaki, Robert T. *Pai rico, pai pobre (Rich Dad Poor Dad)*. Edição comemorativa. Tradução de Maria José Cyhlar Monteiro. Rio de Janeiro: Alta Books, 2018. Versão digital (Kindle).

MARTINS-COSTA, Judith. *Comentários ao novo Código Civil*. Coord. Sálvio de Figueiredo Teixeira. Rio de Janeiro: Forense, 2003.

MELO, Marcelo Augusto Santana de. *Breves anotações sobre o Registro de Imóveis*. Artigo. Brasília/DF (Brasil): Portal da Associação dos Notários e Registradores do Brasil, 2001?. Disponível em: https://anoreg.org.br/images/arquivos/parecerrr.pdf . Acesso em: 28 jan. 2020.

MUDANÇAS PARA CONSUMIDOR. Comissão do Senado aprova projeto de lei sobre distratos em compras de imóveis (Artigo). São Paulo/SP (Brasil): *Site Consultor Jurídico*, 9 nov. 2018. Disponível em: https://www.conjur.com.br/2018-nov-09/comissao-senado-aprova-projeto-lei-distratos-imoveis. Acesso em: 29 jan. 2020.

NINNI, Karina. Consumo cresce seis vezes em 50 anos. São Paulo/SP (Brasil): *Site do Estadão*, 29 jun. 2010. Disponível em: https://sustentabilidade.estadao.com.br/noticias/geral,consumo-cresce-seis-vezes-em-50-anos,573880. Acesso em: 29 jan. 2020.

OLIVEIRA, Carlos Eduardo Elias. Análise detalhada da multipropriedade no Brasil após a Lei n. 13.777/2018: pontos polêmicos e aspectos de registros públicos. São Paulo/SP (Brasil): *GenJurídico.com.br*, 21 mar. 2019. Disponível em: http://genjuridico.com.br/2019/03/21/analise-detalhada-da-multipropriedade-no-brasil-apos-a-lei-no-13-777-2018-pontos-polemicos-e-aspectos-de-registros-publicos/. Acesso em: 29 jan. 2020.

ORTIZ, Jose Maria Chico Y. *Estudios sobre derecho hipotecario*. Madrid: Marcial Pons, 1989.

PAIVA, João Pedro Lamana. *Curso em direito imobiliário registral aplicado aos bens públicos*. Porto Alegre/RS (Brasil): Registro de Imóveis 1ª Zona de Porto Alegre, 2014. Disponível em: http://www.planejamento.gov.br/assuntos/patrimonio-da-uniao/programa-de-modernizacao/linha-do-tempo/arquivos-e-publicacoes/historia-do-sistema-registral-brasileiro.pdf. Acesso em: 29 jan. 2020.

PAIVA, João Pedro Lamana. Patrimônio de afetação: segurança jurídica na aquisição de imóvel em planta. Porto Alegre/RS (Brasil): *Site Registro de Imóveis 1ª zona de Porto Alegre*. Disponível em: http://registrodeimoveis1zona.com.br/?p=202. Acesso em: 29 jan. 2020.

PASSARELLI, Luciano Lopes. *Da autonomia do direito registral imobiliário*. Revista de Direito Imobiliário, São Paulo, v. 75, jul./dez. 2013.

PERLINGIERI, Pietro. *Perfis do direito civil:* introdução ao Direito Civil Constitucional. Tradução de Maria Cristina De Cicco. 2. ed. Rio de Janeiro: Renovar, 2002.

RÁO, Vicente. *O direito e a vida dos direitos*. 5.ed. por Ovídio Rocha Barros Sandoval. São Paulo: Ed. RT, 1999.

SCHREIBER, Anderson. Multipropriedade imobiliária e a Lei 13.777/18. *JusBrasil*, 2019. Disponível em: https://flaviotartuce.jusbrasil.com.br/artigos/664096447/multipropriedade-imobiliaria-e-a-lei-13777-18. Acesso em: 29 jan. 2020.

TEPEDINO, Gustavo. *Multipropriedade imobiliária*. São Paulo: Saraiva, 1993.

URBE.ME. Patrimônio de afetação*:* lições do caso Encol. Itajubá/MG (Brasil). *Dinheirama*, 2019. Disponível em: https://dinheirama.com/patrimonio-de-afetacao-licoes-do-caso-encol/. Acesso em: 29 jan. 2020.

USA. *Federal Judicial Caseload Statistics 2018*. Washington/DC (USA): Site United States Courts, 2019. Disponível em: https://www.uscourts.gov/statistics-reports/federal-judicial-caseload-statistics-2018. Acesso em: 29 jan. 2020.

CÁLCULO, SOLUÇÃO DE ANTINOMIAS E DERIVAÇÃO DE PRINCÍPIOS[1]

JONATHAN BARROS VITA[*]

INTRODUÇÃO

O tema dos princípios há tempos traz especulações dos estudiosos do direito e permeia um sem fim de tomos jurídicos dedicados a identificação conceitual dos mesmos e sua relação com regras[2], valores (e sua contraparte limites objetivos)[3], garantias[4] e vários outros termos. É dizer, há pouco consenso no plano da definição do conceito de princípio além da aposição de vários denotadores negativos, não existindo concretamente uma definição positiva do termo, que é citado inclusive em textos constitucionais e precedentes judiciais, mas nada se sabe.

[*] Doutor e Mestre em Direito pela PUC-SP. Coordenador e professor do Mestrado e Doutorado em Direito da UNIMAR. Conselheiro do Conselho Municipal de Tributos de São Paulo. Ex-Conselheiro do CARF, Conselho Administrativo de Recursos Fiscais. Ex-Juiz do Tribunal de Impostos e Taxas do Estado de São Paulo. Ex-Secretário da Comissão Especial de Direito Tributário do Conselho Federal da OAB. Contador e Advogado.

[1] Este artigo é a segunda parte de dois artigos sobre estrutura, classificação e cálculo de princípios.

[2] Mais proeminentemente em: ÁVILA, Humberto. **Teoria dos princípios – Da definição à aplicação dos princípios jurídicos.** São Paulo: Malheiros, 2005.

[3] CARVALHO, Paulo de Barros. **Direito Tributário: linguagem e método.** 5ª edição. São Paulo: Noeses, 2013.

[4] TORRES, Heleno Taveira. **Direito Constitucional Tributário e Segurança Jurídica: metódica da segurança jurídica do Sistema Constitucional Tributário.** 3ª ed. São Paulo: Revista dos Tribunais, 2019.

De qualquer forma, essa etapa do centro de especulações já foi superada, estabelecendo os princípios como normas que se coordenam com as normas de competência em sentido amplo no processo de positivação e contém no seu consequente valores que são ponderados e calculados entre si. Esse segundo ponto merece um maior aprofundamento ainda, vez que não foram todas as matizes do cálculo de princípios que foram analisados, deixando-se normalmente de lado os estudos sobre solução de antinomias e como funciona a derivação de princípios.

Ainda, neste ponto, deve ser reforçado que como se tem a premissa de que cada norma de princípio contém no objeto de seu consequente/prescritor apenas um valor, uma série de interações entre essas normas existem para informar, como dito, a norma de competência seu giro semântico. Para atingir os objetivos delimitados neste trabalho, primeiro dos itens deste trabalho lidará com a identificação das formas de cálculo de princípios, inicialmente, uma introdução a solução de antinomias e suas especificidades em relação aos princípios

O segundo item retratará os contornos gerais do cálculo de princípios, entendido como contraposição dos consequentes das normas de princípios em busca de um vetor comum de aplicação. O terceiro e último item traz o conceito de derivação de princípios e seus contornos no direito brasileiro, identificando na pragmática dos princípios as relações hierárquicas que os sustentam, o que será realizado a partir da proposta de classificação contida no primeiro dos artigos dessa série.

Finalmente, para atingir os objetivos traçados nesse artigo, o método aplicável é o empírico-dialético, utilizando-se de técnicas de pesquisa bibliográfica e de levantamento de jurisprudência, e o sistema de referência utilizado[5] é formado da conjugação entre a Teoria dos Sistemas de Niklas Luhmann[6], o Construtivismo Lógico-Semântico de Barros Carvalho[7] e ferramentas específicas do *Law and Economics*[8/9/10].

[5] Para a visão mais atual deste sistema de referência proposto: VITA, Jonathan Barros. **Teoria Geral do Direito: Direito Internacional e Direito Tributário.** São Paulo: Quartier Latin 2011.

[6] LUHMANN, Niklas. **Law as a social system.** Oxford: Oxford University Press, 2004.

[7] CARVALHO, Paulo de Barros. **Direito Tributário: linguagem e método.** 5ª edição. São Paulo: Noeses, 2013.

[8] Como representação do texto clássico sobre o tema: POSNER, Richard A. **Economic Analysis of Law.** 9a ed. New York: Wolters Kluwer, 2014.

1. SOBRE A SOLUÇÃO DE ANTINOMIAS E SUA APLICABILIDADE AOS PRINCÍPIOS

1.1. NOTAS SOBRE A SOLUÇÃO DE ANTINOMIAS

Antinomias são contradições existentes no plano do objeto de estudo, em que há a existência de duas proposições contraditórias sobre um mesmo dado de mundo[11]. No caso jurídico, ou seja, é a regulação excludente/contraditória por meio de duas ou mais regras jurídicas, editadas por autoridades competentes e com sujeitos competentes, sem contar com a materialidade prevista na regra de competência[12]. Logo, a definição do conceito de antinomias passa pelos denotadores negativos da definição (negativa) dos conceitos de validade, revogação e lacuna.

Ou seja, quando se fala de antinomia, portanto, deve se falar que não se trata de revogação, de retirada de validade ou de lacunas no direito, já que, no caso de antinomia, não há expulsão de regra do sistema, de não existência jurídica de uma dada norma ou, mesmo, de situações não reguladas pelo direito. Lembra-se que as antinomias existem no plano abstrato, mas, em alguns casos, são expressas para criar exceções que recortam a regra, a norma jurídica.

Elucidando, vários textos/normas são potencialmente antinômicos entre si, parcialmente, do que a regra mais geral é recortada pelas exclusões dadas pelas regras específicas, como no exemplo de uma norma que proíbe fumar e outra que diz da permissão de fumar em locais abertos. Conforme pôde ser dessumido da primeira frase, as antinomias são conflitos estruturados logicamente segundo a lei da não contradição, que é uma

9 Como exemplos de coletâneas que representam os clássicos autores do tema: ROEMER, Andrés. **Derecho y economía: uma revisión de la literatura.** Cidade do México: ITAM, 2000; ZYLBERSZTAJN, Décio; STAJN, Rachel. **Direito e economia: analise econômica do direito e das organizações.** Rio de Janeiro: Campus juridico, 2005.

10 Como exemplos bem acabados de um sistema de referência baseado nos clássicos autores americanos aplicados ao direito tributário: CALIENDO, Paulo. **Direito tributário e análise econômica do direito: uma visão crítica.** Rio de Janeiro: Elsevier, 2009; e CARVALHO, Cristiano Rosa de. **Teoria do sistema jurídico: direito, economia, tributação.** São Paulo: Ed. Quartier Latin, 2005.

11 Para o clássico inaugural (e, muitas vezes contraditado aqui neste artigo) a respeito do tema: BOBBIO, Norberto. **Teoria do ordenamento jurídico.** 7ª edição. Brasília: UNB, 1996.

12 Como autora que estabelece os clássicos a respeito da solução de antinomias e os ubica dentro do direito brasileiro: DINIZ, Maria Helena. **Compêndio de Introdução à Ciência do Direito.** 21ª ed. São Paulo: Saraiva, 2010.

lei lógica consistente na impossibilidade de que dois eixos de linguagem existam ou inexistam ao mesmo tempo. Lembra-se que na contradição há a impossibilidade de que ambas as normas sejam falsas ou verdadeiras simultaneamente, diversamente da contrariedade em que ambos podem o ser, mas nunca as duas verdadeiras ao mesmo tempo. Tal afirmação pode ser vista no quadro de oposições deôntico[13]:

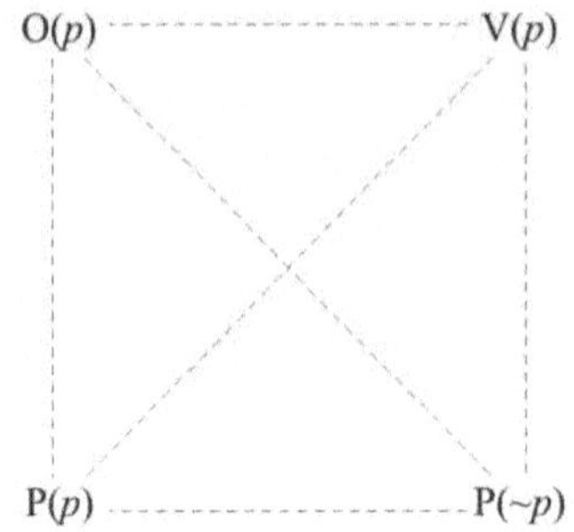

Nas situações O (p) x V(p); além de P (p) e P (~p) há contrariedade, enquanto na V (p) e P (p); e O (p) e P (~p) haveria contradição. Antinomia normativa é, portanto, a identidade entre os critérios do antecedente e consequente com a variação do modal deôntico aplicado ao dever ser contido no consequente jurídico.

Dentro do conceito de ordenamento/sistema jurídico (estática e dinâmica) inserido como forma de aperfeiçoamento das estruturas jurídicas para gerar maior consistência, surge à ideia de que, no S4 de Barros Carvalho[14], ou seja, no plexo da recombinação das normas jurídicas sob a forma de sistema, exista uma impossibilidade de contradição entre normas jurídicas. Tal ideia surge pelo fato que o S4 é o sistema do direito[15] elaborado pelo cientista sem quaisquer contradições, do que as antinomias neste sis-

[13] Esse quadro foi formalizado por, entre outros: ECHAVE, Delia Tereza; URQUIJO, Maria Eugenia; GUIBOURG, Ricardo. **Lógica, proposición y norma.** Buenos Aires: Astrea, 1991.

[14] CARVALHO, Paulo de Barros. **Direito Tributário: linguagem e método.** 5ª edição. São Paulo: Noeses, 2013.

[15] Lembra-se que as ideias de ordenamento e sistema jurídicos adotadas são de que o ordenamento jurídico é o dado bruto e o sistema jurídico o conjunto de proposições/normas jurídicas estruturado sob a forma lógica de sistema com partes estruturadas sintaticamente de forma homogênea com interações entre si, dissimilar ao apresentado em; ROBLES, Gregório. **O direito como texto: quatro estudos de teoria comunicacional do direito.** Barueri – SP: Manole, 2005.

tema seriam impossíveis, já que extrato acabado de uma realidade bruta plena de contradições.

No caso específico, se se analisasse o conjunto S1, S2 ou S3, poder-se-ia encontrar normas jurídicas conflitantes entre si, do que se opta por utilizar o S4 sob a denominação de sistema jurídico e não o S3. Portanto, reelucidando, poder-se-ia encontrar antinomias jurídicas no conjunto de normas jurídicas produzidas a partir dos enunciados prescritivos, em se entendendo antinomias no pré-sistema jurídico, que seja, o ordenamento jurídico.

Cita-se que, com relação à solução de antinomias no sistema jurídico pode existir no S3, em que uma delas é selecionada para o S4, de acordo com os critérios estabelecidos pelo sistema/usuário do sistema como será visto. Em um primeiro momento, opera-se com as antinomias sob uma perspectiva de evitar a aplicação das duas em um mesmo momento, gerando uma ineficácia técnico sintática positiva[16], posteriormente gerando a invalidação desta norma por outro comando normativo. Nesta perspectiva, a sentença de um juiz que aplica uma dada norma em detrimento de outra trata da ineficácia daquela segunda, porém quando há uma declaração de inconstitucionalidade por um órgão competente para o sistema (STF, a exemplo) há a invalidade desta norma, solucionando a antinomia pela expulsão da norma do sistema.

1.2. ANTINOMIAS E PRINCÍPIOS

Elaborando o dito na introdução deste título e, a partir do repertório de premissas estabelecidas, interessante é notar a interação entre as antinomias e os princípios, em especial no que trata da forma de interação entre princípios quando um se sobrepõe aos demais princípios. A preferibilidade aludida normalmente aos valores, tem sua aplicação entre os princípios e opera sob a forma de solução de antinomias, que surge no ato de aplicação e não gera a revogação de uma dada norma.

[16] Essa perspectiva sobre a eficácia foi extrapolada a partir de: CARVALHO, Paulo de Barros. **Direito Tributário: linguagem e método.** 5ª edição. São Paulo: Noeses, 2013.

1.3. INVALIDADE POR DESUSO DE KELSEN – CONTINGENCIA NORMATIVA E VALIDAÇÃO CONSTANTE DO SISTEMA JURÍDICO, A FALIBILIDADE DO SISTEMA JURÍDICO É MANIFESTADA TAMBÉM NO PLANO DOS PRINCÍPIOS

Logo, a não aplicação de um princípio em detrimento de outro (positivados ou não) acaba por ser a demonstração de que a forma de ação de um valor/princípio no ordenamento jurídico é idêntica a o de uma norma jurídica qualquer. Obviamente, esta forma de solução de antinomias a partir da definição de um mesmo conceito por normas diversas acaba por de extrema dificuldade para a sua aplicação, mas, aparentemente, é a solução mais adequada para este problema.

Logo, utilizam-se os critérios de solução de antinomias positivados no direito brasileiro como padrão de comportamento no que diz respeito a determinar o que ocorre quando um princípio entra em conflito com outro conflito. Sinteticamente, uma norma quando entra em conflito com outra norma, no caso as normas de princípios entrando em conflito entre si, ocorre, no momento do ato de aplicação, a incidência de uma em detrimento da outra, ainda que elas pudessem ser aplicadas ao mesmo tempo, conforme será elucidado no ponto seguinte.

Conclui-se, portanto, que a solução de antinomias normativas é a forma de operacionalização das preferibilidades de um sujeito frente à forma de positivação de uma dada outra norma jurídica através do supracitado acoplamento, necessário, entre a norma de princípio e a norma de competência.

2. NOTAS SOBRE O CÁLCULO DE PRINCÍPIOS

Segunda forma de cálculo de princípios existe quando dois princípios são aplicados concomitantemente com relação a uma mesma norma de competência. Neste ponto, duas formas de visualização podem ser produzidas: uma que trata do uso da teoria das classes para permitir a ideia de aplicação e outra que trata, de maneira superficial, sobre o problema material da aplicação concomitante dos princípios a um mesmo dado bruto.

Como primeiro ponto, trata-se do uso da teoria das classes para tratar sobre o assunto, já que o que ocorre é a conhecida relação um vários no que diz respeito à forma de operacionalização da aplicação concomitante de princípios jurídicos. Nota-se, desde já que o processo que ocorre com frequência, no caso da aplicação concomitante de princípios, logicamente, é o produto relativo de relações, em que há: a relação R entre x elemento de A e z (xRz); e a relação R' entre y elemento de B e z (yR'z), simultaneamente – do que o produto relativo desta relação (R/R').

Nesta situação a norma de princípio x diferente de y está em relação com uma dada competência e ambas se aplicam diretamente, produzindo uma nova relação. De outro lado, ocorre é uma relação uni-plurívoca, em que um mesmo fato (potencial uso da competência) implica mais de um consequente. Aqui, dividem-se duas situações, uma é quando os princípios não são contraditórios entre si e permitem que sejam aplicados concomitantemente, caso de simples solução pela mera aplicação possível de mais de uma norma a um mesmo evento do mundo fenomênico. A segunda ocorre quando os princípios são contraditórios, mas o resultado de sua aplicação pode ser percebido concomitantemente ou disjuntamente (como no caso supracitado de solução de antinomias). No caso concreto, apesar de as dificuldades material são muito mais complexas, operacionalmente a forma de compatibilização é idêntica a do exemplo anterior, que seja, a possibilidade de aplicação de mais de uma norma a um mesmo evento, já que a ideia de as normas serem contrárias ou contraditórias está na mente do intérprete e não são dados ontológicos. Nota deve ser feita, já que os valores jurídicos não são bipolares por si mesmos, não existindo, no direito, muitos casos desta bipolaridade de um mesmo valor, mas um cone de penumbra entre dois valores potencialmente contraditórios.

A segunda ideia desta parte é inspirada indiretamente nos textos de Robert Alexy[17] sobre a ideia de balanceamento de princípios e a sua aplicabilidade aos casos concretos. Basicamente, esta ideia trata da materialidade dos princípios, suas derivações e as formas de aplicação de princípios aos casos concretos. Aqui, uma análise material e racional é empreendida para que a solução das antinomias entre princípios ou, mesmo, a aplicação em maior grau ou menor grau de um princípio em relação a outro na determinação da forma de exercício material de uma competência.

Em outro giro, quando dos processos de decisão dos agentes competentes do sistema, deve haver um peso entre a norma a ser produzida e seu impacto por meio de um cálculo entre um maior peso a um dado princípio em detrimento de outro. Estas situações ocorrem frequentemente na

[17] ALEXY, Robert. **Constitutional Rights, Balancing and Rationality.** In: Ratio Juris. Vol. 16 No. 2 June 2003 (131–40).

dosimetria da pena no direito penal ou, mesmo, no *quantum* de indenizações por danos em matérias de direito civil.

3. DERIVAÇÃO DE PRINCÍPIOS

Como primeiro ponto, novamente ressalta-se a ideia de definição e conceito como elementos fundamentais no tratamento do problema da derivação de princípios. Interessante é notar que os conceitos dos de uma série de princípios, intuitivamente, são relacionados, mas a definição deles possui diferenças que fazem com que eles sejam princípios distintos entre si.

Logo, nas derivações comuns, um princípio mais geral dá fundamento de validade a um de mesmo nível classificatório ou mais específico. Estruturalmente, como forma de derivação ocorre a partir do produto relativo de relações ou da inclusão de relações, já que, nesta, há a inclusão de uma classe dentro de outra e, naquela, trata-se da zona de intersecção entre duas classes. Portanto, a derivação de princípios segue a regra de que um princípio mais geral apenas gera um geral ou um mais específico. Consequentemente, a derivação de princípios decorre de aplicação de princípios gerais com um maior reforço ou especificidade, ou do cálculo de:

a) Vários princípios gerais entre si produzindo princípios gerais ou específicos (gerais ou específicos);
b) Princípios gerais e específicos gerais, gerando específicos gerais ou específicos específicos;
c) Princípios gerais e específicos específicos gerando específicos específicos;
d) Princípios específicos gerais com específicos gerais gerando específicos gerais ou específicos;
e) Princípios específicos gerais com específicos específicos gerando específicos específicos;
f) Princípios específicos específicos com princípios específicos específicos gerando específicos específicos
g) Combinações entre as regras apresentadas, como no caso de princípios gerais, específicos gerais e específicos específicos gerando específicos específicos[18].

[18] Estes exemplos citados são os logicamente possíveis a partir da classificação apresentada, já que uma classe é mais específica do que outra, impedindo que o processo contrário ocorra.

Lembra-se que estas são, apenas, estruturações a respeito do assunto, do que, podem existir outras formas de derivação difusas, que são alcançadas através outros processos inferenciais, mas que podem ser, ao menos, teoricamente, reconduzidas a uma das estruturas apresentadas. Como exemplo de reforço dos princípios gerais produzindo um específico, tem-se o princípio geral da legalidade e o princípio geral tributário da legalidade estrita. Exemplo derivação através da inclusão de mais elementos na inclusão da classe, gerando um princípio específico com mais elementos da definição do conceito deste princípio, mas sem entrar, obviamente, em contradição com o que lhe dá fundamento de validade: tem-se o princípio da irretroatividade da lei, do qual se derivam a noventena e a irretroatividade como princípios tributários específicos.

Na segunda modalidade, como exemplos desta derivação a partir do cálculo de princípios, pode ser citado: a derivação, a partir do princípio da certeza (princípio geral) do direito e segurança jurídica (princípio geral) do princípio da irretroatividade das leis (princípio geral). Outro exemplo é o do princípio do mínimo existencial (princípio geral) adicionando-se o princípio da vedação de tributo com efeito de confisco (princípio geral tributário (específico)), cria-se a capacidade contributiva (princípio específico tributário). Lembra-se, ainda, que as derivações estruturadas acima podem se apresentar concomitantemente, como no exemplo da derivação/relação existente entre a segurança jurídica, certeza do direito, previsibilidade irretroatividade, derivando a anterioridade. Por fim, nota-se que esta derivação de princípios existe, também, no plano da classificação apresentada, já que existem princípios que tomam como fundamento de validade outros princípios. Interessante é notar que, apesar das classes apresentadas serem disjuntas, o fato de ser um sistema, com interação entre suas partes homogêneas gera situações inusitadas em que a revogação de um dado princípio acaba por produzir o perecimento de outros que são vinculados mediatamente a este, mas não implica infirmação de suas separações para o fim de classificação.

CONCLUSÕES

No processo de positivação, há um acoplamento/ligação/adição entre a norma de competência com uma norma que possui em seu consequente um determinado valor, a norma de princípio. Neste contexto, os princípios se classificam através de um critério de diferenciação do campo semântico (classe geral, classe específica, disjuntas) de irradiação deste princípio, sendo, classificado, fractalmente (forma dentro da forma) a partir da distinção entre princípios gerais e específicos, os quais se subdividem em gerais e específicos.

Para visualizar tais problemas e mais especificamente, inicia-se o trabalho com as duas formas básicas no trato do cálculo de princípios: uma ocorre quando um princípio é aplicado em detrimento de outro; e quando um princípio é aplicado concomitantemente a outro. Neste contexto, as contradições entre princípios são, apenas, aparentes, já que, em alguns casos há uma solução de antinomia e, em outros, há, tão-somente, a aplicação de mais de uma norma a uma mesma irritação do sistema.

Os princípios se regem mediante processos de derivação para a sua produção e de cálculo para a sua produção. Duas formas de cálculo de princípios existem para a sua aplicação, uma, através do processo de solução de antinomias explicam quando um princípio se aplica em detrimento do outro e este não é revogado; a segunda ocorre quando dois princípios são aplicados concomitantemente, já que são dois fatos criados a partir de um mesmo evento e que expressam realidades distintas. No plano da derivação de princípios, vários são os processos envolvidos, mas a regra geral é de que um princípio geral somente pode gerar um geral ou um mais específico.

REFERÊNCIAS

ALEXY, Robert. *Constitutional Rights, Balancing and Rationality*. In: Ratio Juris. Vol. 16 No. 2 June 2003 (131–40).

ÁVILA, Humberto. *Teoria dos princípios – Da definição à aplicação dos princípios jurídicos*. São Paulo: Malheiros, 2005.

BOBBIO, Norberto. *Teoria do ordenamento jurídico*. 7ª edição. Brasília: UNB, 1996.

CALIENDO, Paulo. *Direito tributário e análise econômica do direito: uma visão crítica*. Rio de Janeiro: Elsevier, 2009.

CARVALHO, Cristiano Rosa de. *Teoria do sistema jurídico: direito, economia, tributação*. São Paulo: Ed. Quartier Latin, 2005.

CARVALHO, Paulo de Barros. *Direito Tributário: linguagem e método*. 5ª edição. São Paulo: Noeses, 2013.

DINIZ, Maria Helena. *Compêndio de Introdução à Ciência do Direito*. 21ª ed. São Paulo: Saraiva, 2010.

ECHAVE, Delia Tereza; URQUIJO, Maria Eugenia; GUIBOURG, Ricardo. *Lógica, proposición y norma*. Buenos Aires: Astrea, 1991.

ENGISCH, Karl. *Introdução ao Pensamento Jurídico*. 7ª Ed. Lisboa: Fundação Calouste Gulbenkian, 1996.

GAMA, Tácio Lacerda. *Competência Tributária – Fundamentos para uma teoria da nulidade.* São Paulo: Noeses, 2011.

KELSEN, Hans. *Teoria pura do direito.* 6ª Ed. São Paulo: Martins Fontes, 2003.

LUHMANN, Niklas. *Law as a social system.* Oxford: Oxford University Press, 2004.

MARMOR, Andrei. *Interpretation and Legal Theory. Revised Second Edition.* Oxford and Portland, Oregon: Hart, 2005.

MOUSSALEM, Tárek Moysés. *Fontes do direito tributário.* São Paulo: Noeses, 2007.

POSNER, Richard A. *Economic Analysis of Law. 9a ed.* New York: Wolters Kluwer, 2014.

REALE, Miguel. *Introdução à Filosofia.* 4ª Ed. São Paulo: Saraiva, 2007.

ROBLES, Gregório. *O direito como texto: quatro estudos de teoria comunicacional do direito.* Barueri – SP: Manole, 2005.

ROEMER, Andrés. *Derecho y economía: uma revisión de la literatura.* Cidade do México: ITAM, 2000.

SANTI, Eurico Marcos Diniz. *Tributo e classificação das espécies no sistema tributário brasileiro.* In: http://www.fiscosoft.com.br/main_artigos_index.php?PID=267444&printpage=_ (acesso em 30/10/2019)

TORRES, Heleno Taveira. *Direito Constitucional Tributário e Segurança Jurídica: metódica da segurança jurídica do Sistema Constitucional Tributário.* 3ª ed. São Paulo: Revista dos Tribunais, 2019.

VILANOVA, Lourival. *Causalidade e relação no direito.* São Paulo: Saraiva, 1989.

VITA, Jonathan Barros. *Teoria Geral do Direito: Direito Internacional e Direito Tributário.* São Paulo: Quartier Latin 2011.

ZYLBERSZTAJN, Décio; STAJN, Rachel. *Direito e economia: analise econômica do direito e das organizações.* Rio de Janeiro: Campus juridico, 2005.

A PANDEMIA DO CORONAVÍRUS COMO ELEMENTO CONSTITUTIVO PARA A APLICAÇÃO DA TEORIA DA IMPREVISÃO E DA ONEROSIDADE EXCESSIVA AOS CONTRATOS BANCÁRIOS E SEUS ACESSÓRIOS

JOSE LUIZ RAGAZZI*

INTRODUÇÃO

Em 26 de fevereiro de 2020 surgia o primeiro caso confirmando a infecção de uma pessoa pelo Coronavírus no Brasil, moléstia que já se alastrava fortemente pela China e Europa, chamando assim a atenção das autoridades brasileiras. Logo na data de 11/03/2020 a Organização Mundial da Saúde decretou a pandemia do coronavírus, denominado SARS-CoV-2, causador da doença denominada Covid-19.

Atualmente, o Brasil é um dos países mais afetados pela pandemia, ultrapassando a expressiva marca de 370.000 mil infecções e mais de 23 mil mortes[1], e uma série de medidas governamentais que visam contar a disseminação do vírus, medidas estas consistentes em leis e decretos expedidos pelos Poderes Executivos de todas as esferas, v .g., Lei

* Doutor em Direito Processual Civil pela PUC-SP. Mestre em Direito pela Faculdade de Direito de Bauru. Professor do mestrado e doutorado da Instituição Toledo de Ensino-ITE. Advogado.

1 https://g1.globo.com/bemestar/coronavirus/noticia/2020/05/25/casos-de-coronavirus-e-numero-de-mortes-no-brasil-em-25-de-maio.ghtml. Acesso em 26/05/2020.

nº 13.979/2020[2], Decreto 64.881/2020 do Governo do Estado de São Paulo[3], Lei nº 17.340/2020[4] do Município de São Paulo, etc.

Tais medidas impactaram no cenário econômico do país, especialmente com relação aos autônomos, micro e pequenos empresários que viram seus negócios estagnarem frente às medidas governamentais, o que vem causando repercussões políticas e jurídicas, já que estes personagens passaram a acionar o Poder Judiciário invocando a aplicação da Teoria da Imprevisão e da Onerosidade Excessiva, para a alteração do cumprimento das obrigações contratuais.

Como se sabe, o Código Civil permite a relativização do *pacta sunt servanda*, autorizando a alteração das condições contratuais quando houver desequilíbrio entre as partes, adotando assim a Teoria de Imprevisão e da Onerosidade Excessiva, decorrentes da cláusula rebus sic stantibus e boa-fé contratual (art. 317[5], 478[6], 479[7] e 480[8]).

E com base nestes postulados passaram a ser aforadas várias demandas judiciais, muitas vezes por pessoas jurídicas insumidoras de crédito bancário, buscando a revisão dos contratos, visando especialmente a prorrogação de parcelas e liberação de garantias atreladas (travas bancárias) a

[2] Dispõe sobre as medidas para enfrentamento da emergência de saúde pública de importância internacional decorrente do coronavírus responsável pelo surto de 2019.

[3] Decreta quarentena no Estado de São Paulo, no contexto da pandemia do COVID-19 (Novo Coronavírus), e dá providências complementares.

[4] Dispõe sobre medidas de proteção da saúde pública e de assistência, bem como relativas a dilação e suspensão de prazos de alvarás e concursos públicos para o enfrentamento da Emergência de Saúde Pública em decorrência da Infecção Humana pelo Coronavírus (COVID-19) no âmbito do Município de São Paulo; cria o Selo Empresa Parceira da Cidade de São Paulo e o Mês do Combate ao Coronavírus e autoriza doação de imóvel da União com o encargo social que especifica.

[5] Art. 317. Quando, por motivos imprevisíveis, sobrevier desproporção manifesta entre o valor da prestação devida e o do momento de sua execução, poderá o juiz corrigi-lo, a pedido da parte, de modo que assegure, quanto possível, o valor real da prestação.

[6] Art. 478. Nos contratos de execução continuada ou diferida, se a prestação de uma das partes se tornar excessivamente onerosa, com extrema vantagem para a outra, em virtude de acontecimentos extraordinários e imprevisíveis, poderá o devedor pedir a resolução do contrato. Os efeitos da sentença que a decretar retroagirão à data da citação.

[7] Art. 479. A resolução poderá ser evitada, oferecendo-se o réu a modificar eqüitativamente as condições do contrato.

[8] Art. 480. Se no contrato as obrigações couberem a apenas uma das partes, poderá ela pleitear que a sua prestação seja reduzida, ou alterado o modo de executá-la, a fim de evitar a onerosidade excessiva.

contratos bancários (mútuos), sob o argumento de que os negócios desenvolvidos teriam sido fortemente afetados pela pandemia, o que culminou na concessão de medidas liminares neste sentido.

Contudo, ante a atual situação, as demandas acompanhadas de pedidos liminares, propostas por empresas insumidoras de crédito, devem ser vistas com reservas, especialmente no que tange à análise do preenchimento pelo interessado dos requisitos para a invocação da aplicação da Teoria da Imprevisão e da Onerosidade Excessiva, sob pena de se impor o desequilíbrio contratual ao demandado, o que provocará reflexos negativos na economia.

1. BREVES CONSIDERAÇÕES ACERCA DA TEORIA DA IMPREVISÃO E DOS REQUISITOS PARA SUA APLICABILIDADE

Como cediço, a Teoria da Imprevisão decorre da cláusula rebus sic stantibus, inserta de forma tácita em todos os contratos, e possibilita a alteração do trato negocial quando verificadas alterações fáticas que impliquem modificação nas bases contratuais. Analisando a origem da cláusula rebus sic stantibus comenta Silvio Salvo Venosa (2017, p. 89):

> Parece que o fenômeno já era conhecido antes do direito romano, o qual, entretanto, não o sistematizou, mas plenamente o conheceu e aplicou. Ganha-altura na Idade Média, passa um tempo esquecido, para ressurgir com força após a Primeira Guerra Mundial. Esta conflagração de 1914-1918 trouxe um desequilíbrio para os contratos a longo prazo. Conhecida é a famosa Lei Failliot, da França, de 21-1-1918, que autorizou a resolução dos contratos concluídos antes da guerra porque sua execução se tornara muito onerosa. Esse diploma demandava a participação obrigatória do juiz.

Neste mesmo sentido é o comentário de Anderson Schreiber (2020, p. 702):

> Não se encontrando sob a sujeição de uma norma tão rígida quanto o art. 1.134 do Código Civil francês, ao afirmar que o contrato faz lei entre as partes, e se beneficiando do fato de que o brocardo latino do pacta sunt servanda era amplamente ignorado pela teoria geral dos contratos administrativos, o Conseil d'État passou a admitir a modificação dos contratos celebrados com entes públicos em razão de uma alteração imprevisível que afetasse o equilíbrio econômico original do ajuste.

No Brasil, tal tema passou a ser enfrentando no início do século XX, não sendo demais lembrar que o Código Civil de 1916 nada dispunha sobre a possibilidade de relativização dos contratos por fatores imprevisíveis, sendo inicialmente uma construção doutrinária e jurisprudencial, vindo o tema a ser enfrentado pelo Supremo Tribunal Federal no ano de 1938, por ocasião do julgamento do Recurso Extraordinário nº 2.675, de relatoria do Ministro Laudo de Camargo. A necessidade de que a legislação disciplinasse a Teoria da Imprevisão era latente, como alerta Maria Helena Diniz ao discorrer sobre a etiologia histórica do Código Civil Brasileiro (2012, p. 65):

> Em verdade, depois de 1916 os acontecimentos alteraram, profundamente, os fatos sociais, requerendo maior ingerência do juiz nos negócios jurídicos, derrogando o princípio pacta sunt servanda. (...) **o direito obrigacional exigia que se alargasse a noção de responsabilidade civil, que se consignassem normas sobre a teoria da imprevisão**, que se disciplinasse o instituto da lesão e o do estado de perigo, que se fixasse a questão do abuso de direito, que se cogitasse da reserva mental, que se tratasse da cessão de débito paralela à do crédito; o direito da personalidade requeria uma construção dogmática; (Grifos e destaques nossos).

Após os entendimentos jurisprudenciais sobre o assunto, no ano de 1990 foi criada a Lei nº 8.078/90 (Código de Defesa do Consumidor), que assegura ao consumidor a possibilidade de "modificação das cláusulas contratuais que estabeleçam prestações desproporcionais ou sua revisão em razão de fatos supervenientes que as tornem excessivamente onerosas" (art. 6º, V, CDC). Encampando esta teoria, o Código Civil de 2002 em seu art. 478 assim dispôs:

> Nos contratos de execução continuada ou diferida, se a prestação de uma das partes se tornar excessivamente onerosa, com extrema vantagem para a outra, em virtude de acontecimentos extraordinários e imprevisíveis, poderá o devedor pedir a resolução do contrato. Os efeitos da sentença que a decretar retroagirão à data da citação.

A propósito, confira-se a lição de Maria Helena Diniz (2007, p. 93/94) comentado a novidade:

> Além disso, urge ressaltar que, pelo art. 317 do Código Civil, o órgão judicante poderá, mediante requerimento da parte interessada, atualizar

> monetariamente o valor da prestação devida em caso de contrato de execução continuada, se motivos imprevisíveis e supervenientes o tornarem desproporcional em relação com o estipulado ao tempo da efetivação negocial. A correção judicial do contrato em razão de desproporção, provocada por motivo imprevisível (motivo de desproporção não previsível ou previsível, mas de resultado imprevisível — Enunciado n. 17, aprovado na Jornada de Direito Civil, promovida, em setembro de 2002, pelo Centro de Estudos Judiciários do Conselho da Justiça Federal), manifesta, ou evidente, entre o valor da prestação devida e o do momento de sua execução só pode dar-se, mediante requerimento da parte interessada, em caso de contrato de execução continuada, sendo inadmissível nos contratos de execução imediata. (...) Aceita está a "teoria" da imprevisão (CC, art. 317 c/c os arts. 478 a 480), por isso melhor seria dizer que se terá, na verdade, revisão por imprevisibilidade.

Deve ser registrada aqui a diferença entre os dispositivos legais: o Código de Defesa do Consumidor não exige que o fato superveniente seja imprevisível, ao passo que o Código Civil assim o exige, sendo assim imperiosa a clara distinção do cenário que se analisa, a propósito, assim ensina Rizzatto Nunes (2018, p. 131):

> A teoria da imprevisão prevista na regra da cláusula rebus sic stantibus tem como pressuposto o fato de que, na oportunidade da assinatura do contrato, as partes não tinham condições de prever aqueles acontecimentos, que acabaram surgindo. Por isso se fala em imprevisão. A alteração do contrato em época futura tem como base certos fatos que no passado, quando do fechamento do negócio, as partes não tinham condições de prever. Na sistemática do CDC não há necessidade desse exercício todo. Para que se faça a revisão do contrato basta que, após ter ele sido firmado, surjam fatos que o tornem excessivamente oneroso. Não se pergunta, nem interessa saber, se, na data de seu fechamento, as partes podiam ou não prever os acontecimentos futuros. Basta ter havido alteração substancial capaz de tornar o contrato excessivo para o consumidor.

Portanto, da fria análise do art. 478, CC, tem-se que são pressupostos para a aplicação da Teoria da Imprevisão: 1) configuração de eventos extraordinários e imprevisíveis; 2) comprovação da onerosidade excessiva que causa a insuportabilidade do cumprimento do acordo para um dos contratantes; 3) extrema vantagem para o outro polo da relação; e, 4) que o contrato seja de execução continuada ou de execução diferida. A propósito, analisando o referido artigo, Cleysson de Moraes Mello (2017, p. 197) assim disserta:

> O contrato será considerado excessivamente oneroso a partir do momento em que causar um desequilíbrio economicamente insuportável para um dos contraentes. É uma espécie de cláusula aberta. Neste caso, o magistrado deverá utilizar a discricionariedade para decidir o caso concreto decidendo. Mais uma vez lembramos que discricionariedade não significa arbitrariedade. No caso concreto decidendo o juiz deverá analisar a possibilidade de ocorrência de um prejuízo patrimonial sofrido por uma das partes contratantes que venha a modificar o equilíbrio econômico da avença. Ao verificarmos a regra do artigo 478, constata-se que o pedido de resolução do contrato ocorre em razão da "imprevisibilidade" e "extraordinariedade" do acontecimento. Assim, de certa forma, o referido artigo se aproxima da teoria da imprevisão stricto sensu, já que o magistrado para acolher a pretensão resolutória, deverá verificar se o acontecimento invocado pela parte era imprevisível ao homem comum. **Portanto, a resolução por onerosidade excessiva apresenta as seguintes exigências: que o acontecimento seja extraordinário, imprevisível e excessivamente oneroso para uma das partes, além de informar que exista extrema vantagem para outra parte contratante.** (Grifos e destaques nossos).

Hodiernamente, o Superior Tribunal de Justiça assim vem se posicionando com relação aplicação da Teoria da Imprevisão:

> A intervenção do Poder Judiciário nos contratos, à luz da teoria da imprevisão ou da teoria da onerosidade excessiva, **exige a demonstração** de mudanças supervenientes das circunstâncias iniciais vigentes à época da realização do negócio, oriundas de evento imprevisível (teoria da imprevisão) e de evento imprevisível e extraordinário (teoria da onerosidade excessiva), **que comprometa o valor da prestação, demandando tutela jurisdicional específica.**" (REsp 1321614/SP, Rel. Ministro PAULO DE TARSO SANSEVERINO, Rel. p/ Acórdão Ministro RICARDO VILLAS BÔAS CUEVA, TERCEIRA TURMA, julgado em 16/12/2014, DJe 03/03/2015). (Grifos e destaques nossos).

Ainda, analisando a jurisprudência do Superior Tribunal de Justiça, observa-se que a Teoria da Imprevisão apenas tem lugar quando o fato imprevisível provoque a onerosidade excessiva do contrato alterando a base do negócio:

> 2. **A teoria da imprevisão – corolário dos princípios da boa-fé e da função social do contrato -, a qual autoriza a revisão das obrigações contratuais, apenas se configura quando há onerosidade excessiva decorrente da superveniência de um evento imprevisível, alterador da base econômica objetiva do contrato, hipótese inocorrente no caso.** (AgInt no REsp 1514093/CE, Rel. Ministro MARCO BUZZI, QUARTA TURMA, julgado em 25/10/2016, DJe 07/11/2016). (Grifos e destaques nossos).

Silvio Rodrigues (2002, p. 134) analisando o assunto assim discorre:

> A resolução por onerosidade excessiva tem por campo apenas o contrato de execução continuada ou diferida no futuro, o que equivale a excluir de seu alcance o contrato de execução imediata. É a idéia da velha cláusula rebus sic standibus, em que se dizia que os contratos que têm duração continuada, ou dependência de futuro, são entendidos como se as coisas permanecessem as mesmas, (...) **A idéia é evitar que nos contratos comutativos em que, por definição, há uma presumível equivalência das prestações, o tempo desequilibre a antiga igualdade, tornando a prestação de uma das partes excessivamente onerosa em relação à da outra. Se isso ocorrer e inspirado no preceito que evita o enriquecimento sem causa [...], permite o legislador que, a pedido do interessado, o juiz determine a rescisão do contrato.** Note-se que o desequilíbrio das prestações deve derivar de acontecimentos extraordinários e imprevisíveis, pois a fonte inspiradora do codificador de 2002 foi a conhecida teoria da imprevisão. (...) Determinada a lei que a resolução do contrato poderá ser evitada se o réu se oferecer para modificar eqüitativamente as suas condições (art. 479). Ora grifei a expressão "eqüitativamente" porque a idéia de eqüitatividade é imprecisa. Quem vai estabelecer se a proposta do réu é eqüitativa ou não é o juiz em sentença final, pois a mera circunstância de haver uma decisão prova que a tentativa de composição, feita na audiência de conciliação, se frustrou. A lei contempla, ainda, a hipótese de no contrato caberem as obrigações apenas a uma das partes, como, por exemplo, no caso de a outra já haver cumprido a prestação a ela incumbente. A solução é a mesma: se aquela obrigação devida se tiver tornado excessivamente onerosa, pode o devedor pleitear que seja ela reduzida, ou alterado o modo de executá-la (art. 480). (Grifos e destaques nossos).

Merece atenção especial o requisito da extrema vantagem, expressamente previsto pelo art. 478, CC, eis que a doutrina diverge acerca da necessidade de seu preenchimento, destacando Anderson Schereiber (2020, p. 710) que alguns autores sugerem seja o requisito ignorado. Interessante observar que no Projeto de Lei nº 6.960/02 (BRASÍLIA, 2002, P. 42), de autoria de Ricardo Fiuza, se propunha uma alteração no referido dispositivo, sob o argumento de que "não se deve configurar a onerosidade excessiva, na dependência do contraponto de um grau de extrema vantagem. Isto significaria atenuar o instituto, sopesado por uma compreensão menor.", destacando ainda que o benefício apenas teria lugar em não havendo mora. Confira-se como ficaria a redação do disposto acaso o projeto houvesse sido aprovado:

> "Art. 472. Nos contratos de execução sucessiva ou diferida, tornando-se desproporcionais ou excessivamente onerosas suas prestações em decorrência de acontecimento extraordinário e estranho aos contratantes à época da celebração contratual, pode a parte prejudicada demandar a revisão contratual, desde que a desproporção ou a onerosidade exceda os riscos normais do contrato.
>
> § 1º. Nada impede que a parte deduza, em juízo, pedidos cumulados, na forma alternativa, possibilitando, assim, o exame judicial do que venha a ser mais justo para o caso concreto;
>
> **§ 2º – Não pode requerer a revisão do contrato quem se encontrar em mora no momento da alteração das circunstâncias;**
>
> § 3º – Os efeitos da revisão contratual não se estendem às prestações satisfeitas, mas somente às ainda devidas, resguardados os direitos adquiridos por terceiros". (NR)" (Grifos e destaques nossos).

Em que pesem as vozes em contrário, o Superior Tribunal de Justiça, no julgamento do Recurso Especial 1.034.702/ES, ocorrido em 15/04/2008, sob relatoria do Min. João Otávio Noronha, assentou que:

> (...) Ao decidir a respeito da matéria, o magistrado deve ter em mente o contrato como um elo da atividade de produção e repartição de riquezas, de prestação de serviços e de consumo, ou seja, a resolução contratual entendida como a solução recomendada para evitar que o credor de uma prestação tornada excessivamente onerosa receba, como empresário, "uma vantagem concorrencialmente injustificada" à custa de outra, que sofreria um dano sem

nenhuma utilidade funcional ou econômica. **Ultima ratio, evitar o enriquecimento sem causa de um dos contratantes em detrimento da ruína do outro sob a ótica da função social do contrato no sentido de garantia de equilíbrio e, ao mesmo tempo, fomento ao crescimento e desenvolvimento econômico.** (...). (Grifos e destaques nossos).

Este posicionamento serviu como fundamento para o recente julgamento do Agravo Interno no Agravo em Recurso Especial nº 1.340.589/SE, ocorrido em 23/04/2019, sob relatoria do Min. Raul Araújo, onde restou assentado que **"a caracterização da onerosidade excessiva pressupõe a existência de vantagem extrema da outra parte".** (Grifos e destaques nossos). Assim, de se concluir que não há como se afastar a necessidade de comprovação da "vantagem extrema" pela outra parte contratante, já que há julgados neste sentido, além do que, já se entendeu que acaso se constate que ambas partes tenham sido afetadas pelo evento imprevisível é inaplicável a revisão das obrigações:

> (...) 14. **Em relação à onerosidade excessiva alegada, verifica-se que a teoria da imprevisão autoriza a revisão das obrigações contratuais apenas quando há onerosidade excessiva decorrente da superveniência de um evento imprevisível, alterador da base econômica objetiva do contrato. No entanto, no presente caso, a alteração afetou ambos os contratantes, razão pela qual inaplicável a teoria na hipótese.** (...) (REsp 1632842/RS, Rel. Ministro PAULO DE TARSO SANSEVERINO, TERCEIRA TURMA, julgado em 12/09/2017, DJe 15/09/2017). (Grifos, destaques e omissos nossos).

Lógica, portanto, a conclusão de que o elemento "vantagem extrema" é imprescindível para a invocação da Teoria da Imprevisão, e deve ser objeto de análise acurada pelo julgador, sob pena de se subverter a inteligência do instituto que não serve para beneficiar uma ou outra parte, mas sim para reestabelecer o equilíbrio do contrato, em atendimento à sua função social.

2. CONDIÇÕES PARA QUE A PANDEMIA POSSA SER UTILIZADA COMO FUNDAMENTO PARA A APLICAÇÃO DA TEORIA DA IMPREVISÃO

Primeiramente deve se destacar que o presente trabalho não aborda as relações de consumo, cuja legislação permite a revisão de contratos independentemente de que o fato superveniente seja imprevisível (arts. 6º, V[9] e 51, IV[10], ambos do CDC), exigindo apenas a ocorrência de fatos supervenientes que torne o contrato oneroso (art. 6º, V) e nulifica cláusulas desproporcionais (art. 51, IV), ao contrário do Código Civil que exige mais requisitos conforme visto no item anterior.

Com efeito, o presente estudo tem por finalidade analisar a crise pandêmica como fundamento para se pleitear a resolução ou revisão de contratos celebrados por pessoas jurídicas insumidoras de crédito bancário, com base na Teoria de Imprevisão, cujos requisitos vão além do que estipula o Código de Defesa do Consumidor.

É inegável que a pandemia do Coronavírus se trata de um evento imprevisível e extraordinário, perfeitamente acobertado pela regra do art. 478, CC, contudo, e malgrado os fatos que acometeram o país, a verdade é em uma demanda judicial o interessado deve apresentar provas indispensáveis para ser agraciado com a aplicação da Teoria da Imprevisão, que exige, dentre outros elementos, a prova de que o contrato se tornou **excessivamente oneroso** para si e **extremamente vantajoso** para a outra parte.

Ocorre que na maioria dos casos que estão sendo postos à apreciação judicial o jurisdicionado se limita a invocar a seu favor a pandemia (evento notório) e os decretos governamentais (que limitam o trabalho/produção) que visam impedir a disseminação do vírus Covid-19, o que, *data venia*, não se revela suficiente para endossar a sua pretensão. Não por outra razão é possível encontrar arestos do Tribunal de Justiça do Estado de São Paulo rechaçando pedidos liminares para alteração na forma de cumprimento do contrato, confira-se exemplos:

> Agravo de instrumento. Ação de suspensão de cobrança. Decisão que indeferiu o pedido de antecipação de tutela para suspender os boletos de cobrança, débitos e contas vincendas dos agravantes. A despeito da crise econômica decorrente do COVID-19 e ressalvada eventual revisão dos contratos, as condições originalmente firmadas devem ser cumpridas pelas partes, diante do

[9] Art. 6º São direitos básicos do consumidor: (...) V – a modificação das cláusulas contratuais que estabeleçam prestações desproporcionais ou sua revisão em razão de fatos supervenientes que as tornem excessivamente onerosas.

[10] Art. 51. São nulas de pleno direito, entre outras, as cláusulas contratuais relativas ao fornecimento de produtos e serviços que:(...) IV – estabeleçam obrigações consideradas iníquas, abusivas, que coloquem o consumidor em desvantagem exagerada, ou sejam incompatíveis com a boa-fé ou a equidade.

princípio da força obrigatória dos contratos. Não preenchimento dos requisitos para concessão da tutela provisória de urgência. Pedido de sigilo dos autos não acolhido que não se enquadra nas hipóteses do art. 189 do CPC. Insurgência contra o indeferimento da gratuidade não conhecida diante da ausência de apreciação da questão pelo despacho agravado. Decisão mantida. Recurso desprovido. (TJSP; Agravo de Instrumento 2067476-26.2020.8.26.0000; Relator (a): Pedro Kodama; Órgão Julgador: 37ª Câmara de Direito Privado; Foro de Bauru – 5ª. Vara Cível; Data do Julgamento: 26/05/2020; Data de Registro: 26/05/2020).

AGRAVO DE INSTRUMENTO. AÇÃO DE REVISÃO CONTRATUAL C/C PEDIDO DE TUTELA DE URGÊNCIA. EMPRESA TÊXTIL QUE ALEGA CRISE FINANCEIRA DADA A DESCONTINUIDADE DE ATIVIDADES NESSE PERÍODO DE PANDEMIA RELATIVA À COVID-19. TUTELA PROVISÓRIA. PEDIDO DE SUSTAÇÃO DO PROTESTO. AUSENTES OS REQUISITOS LEGAIS AUTORIZADORES DA CONCESSÃO DA TUTELA. PROBABILIDADE DO DIREITO ALEGADO NÃO DEMONSTRADA. INEXISTÊNCIA DE DEMONSTRAÇÃO DA IMPOSSIBILIDADE DO CUMPRIMENTO DA OBRIGAÇÃO TENDO COMO CAUSA DIRETA A PANDEMIA OCASIONADA PELO VÍRUS SARS-COV-2. – RECURSO DESPROVIDO. (TJSP; Agravo de Instrumento 2090679-17.2020.8.26.0000; Relator (a): Edgard Rosa; Órgão Julgador: 22ª Câmara de Direito Privado; Foro de Nova Odessa – 2ª Vara Judicial; Data do Julgamento: 13/05/2020; Data de Registro: 13/05/2020).

Os contratos bancários, na maioria das vezes submetidos a discussão judicial, são contratos de mútuo de natureza comutativa, ou seja, os contratantes podem antever as prestações, sendo que em referidos contratos há que haver uma presumível equivalência entre as prestações, o que compõe o conceito da referida espécie contratual. Como já comentado, para que a referida equivalência seja mantida, o legislador, prevendo a possibilidade de ocorrência de fatores externos (como a pandemia), possibilitou a resolução do ajuste por onerosidade excessiva ou ainda a modificação das prestações de modo a manter o equilíbrio do contrato (arts. 478/480 do Código Civil).

Entretanto, como visto alhures, além da demonstração do fator externo – evento imprevisível – deve o interessado demonstrar que as prestações se tornaram excessivamente onerosas, a ponto de impedi-lhe de cumpri-las em conformidade com o ajuste e a extrema vantagem para a parte adversa, sob pena de não poder pleitear a resolução do contrato ou a modificação da forma de seu cumprimento. A propósito, o Tribunal de Justiça do Estado de São Paulo, escudado no aqui citado Agravo Interno no Agravo em Recurso Especial nº 1.340.589/SE, assim já decidiu:

> (...) Não ficou demonstrada pelo réu a ocorrência de fato superveniente que tenha tornado a prestação excessiva, nem a ausência de equivalência entre a prestação e a contraprestação, a qual pudesse implicar extrema vantagem do autor em detrimento do réu. (...) (TJSP; Apelação Cível 1018449-19.2018.8.26.0564; Relator (a): José Marcos Marrone; Órgão Julgador: 23ª Câmara de Direito Privado; Foro de São Bernardo do Campo – 8ª Vara Cível; Data do Julgamento: 28/11/2019; Data de Registro: 28/11/2019).

Assim, para que se tenha sucesso na invocação da Teoria da Imprevisão, com sustentáculo na pandemia (evento imprevisível) o interessado deve instruir sua inicial, provando que a avença se tornou onerosa a ele e vantajosa à outra parte, como reclama a lei e orienta a jurisprudência. A onerosidade excessiva, por exemplo, deve ser comprovada através da juntada de documentos tais como balaços financeiros demonstrando expressiva queda o faturamento após a ocorrência do evento imprevisível (no caso, a pandemia), despesas totais da empresa (salários, energia, limpeza, logística, insumos, etc).

A extrema vantagem para a outra parte deve ser demonstrada com provas de que esta não foi afetada pelo evento imprevisível e que o que está lucrando com a manutenção do contrato é expressivamente mais vantajoso do que quando celebrado o contrato. Neste particular, oportuna a citação da interpretação de Maria Helena Diniz (2010, p. 399) que destaca o dever do magistrado quando da análise de demandas desta natureza:

> O magistrado deverá, para dar ganho de causa ao lesado, apurar rigorosamente a ocorrência dos seguintes requisitos: a) vigência de um contrato comutativo de execução continuada; b) alteração radical das condições econômicas no momento da execução do contrato, em confronto com as do instante de sua formação; c) onerosidade excessiva para um dos contratantes e benefício exagerado para o outro; e d) imprevisibilidade e extraordinariedade daquela modificação, pois é necessário que as partes, quando celebraram o contrato, não possam ter previsto o evento anormal.

Por exemplo: imagine-se que a pandemia houvesse se restringido ao Brasil, e uma determinada empresa brasileira, possuindo um contrato atrelado ao dólar com uma empresa estrangeira (portanto não atingida pelo evento imprevisível), fosse gravemente afetada com as atuais medidas governamentais e principalmente com a alta do dólar. Evidente que no exemplo a empresa estrangeira auferiria uma vantagem excessiva, tendo em vista que a alta do dólar, embora previsível, não ocorre de forma abrupta como nos atuais tempos de pandemia, assim, fazendo com que receba mais dinheiro do que o que se imaginava receber quando da celebração do contrato.

A empresa brasileira, por outro lado, além de estar com suas atividades comprometidas (faturamento baixo, funcionários licenciados, baixa produção), vê as prestações de seus contratos ficarem extremamente mais elevadas em decorrência das sucessivas altas abruptas do dólar, estando em extrema desvantagem. Com efeito, a pandemia afetou o país – e o mundo – em geral, sendo que na maioria das demandas ambas partes litigantes foram atingidas de alguma forma, sendo que por vezes se verifica que o contrato não se tornou excessivamente oneroso para uma parte e extremamente vantajoso para outra, não tendo lugar, portanto a aplicação da Teoria da Imprevisão. Por exemplo: imagine-se uma empresa que atue com a venda de eletroeletrônicos e possua alto faturamento anual, comercializando produtos via internet, inclusive, (setor que não foi atingido por atos governamentais) e possua contrato de mútuo bancário para o fomento de suas atividades.

À referida empresa não será lícito postular a revisão de seu contrato de mútuo com base na pandemia, sem que demonstre que o contrato ficou extremamente oneroso para si e extremamente vantajoso ao Banco, pois o Banco não está recebendo nada além do contratado e, igualmente, sofre os impactos da crise ao conceder moratórias (suspendendo contratos) a outros clientes que realmente necessitem de moratórias. É preciso que o magistrado afira caso a caso o regular preenchimento dos requisitos do art. 478, CC para se impor a resolução ou revisão de um contrato, especialmente quando esta análise for realizada para fins de apreciação de pedidos liminares, sob pena de se provocar desequilíbrio na relação contratual.

3. DA SITUAÇÃO DAS GARANTIAS CONTRATUAIS

Conforme alinhavado, muitas das demandas aforadas visam, além da prorrogação das parcelas do contrato, a liberação das garantias (travas bancárias) atreladas a ele, onde a Casa Financeira acaba sendo compelida a liberar todo o numerário que serve de garantia ao mútuo, cujos valores já foram disponibilizados e consumidos pelo cliente no passado. Neste outro cenário a situação se torna delicada, pois independentemente de que o interessado demonstre a vantagem extrema auferida pela parte contrária, e acabe sendo agraciado com a alteração do modo de cumprimento da avença, a liberação das garantias do contrato imporia o desequilíbrio contratual.

Neste eito, tem-se que o Código de Processo Civil Brasileiro fixou como regra geral que o devedor responde com **todos os seus bens presentes e futuros para o cumprimento de suas obrigações**, salvo as restrições estabelecidas em lei (Código de Processo Civil, art. 789). Em outras palavras, a inobservância das obrigações assumidas contratualmente resulta na responsabilização patrimonial do devedor para que a dívida seja satisfeita, de modo que, uma vez celebrado contrato com cláusula de garantia, seja pessoal ou real, fica o devedor obrigado a saldar a dívida perante o credor, sob pena de responder com o seu patrimônio, especialmente aquele entregue em garantia.

Neste ponto, pertinente citar a lição de Pontes de Miranda (1958, p. 19) que assevera que "o direito real persiste enquanto persiste a dívida e depois, enquanto não se cancela o registro, se o há." Com base nestas ponderações, não se pode concordar, sob o argumento da imprevisibilidade ou de onerosidade excessiva passageira, com a aniquilação das garantias contratuais regularmente constituídas e livremente pactuadas. Inclusive, analisando situação similar, o Superior Tribunal de Justiça assim já assentou:

> Crédito documentário. Importação e exportação. Variação do dólar em decorrência da maxidesvalorização. Código de Defesa do Consumidor. Não-configuração da onerosidade excessiva nem da teoria da imprevisão relativamente ao importador e ao banco emitente da garantia. 1. Embora pertinente o enquadramento da relação entre o importador e o banco emitente da garantia no Código de Defesa do Consumidor, **não é possível enxergar onerosidade excessiva ou a teoria da imprevisão, porquanto o banco é apenas um garantidor da operação comercial entre o exportador e o importador, assegurando o pagamento da obrigação assumida pelo último, nos ter-**

mos e valores contratados, não podendo receber menos do que pagou em razão da garantia decorrente do crédito documentário. 2. Recurso especial não conhecido. (REsp 654.969/PR, Rel. Ministro CARLOS ALBERTO MENEZES DIREITO, TERCEIRA TURMA, julgado em 07/12/2004, DJ 28/03/2005, p. 255). (grifos e destaques nossos).

A tudo isso se alie as novas diretrizes trazidas ao Código Civil pela lei nº 13.874/19, que atribuiu maior faculdade aos particulares quando da celebração dos contratos, limitando a intervenção do estado nas avenças:

> Art. 421. A liberdade contratual será exercida nos limites da função social do contrato. (Redação dada pela Lei nº 13.874, de 2019)
> **Parágrafo único. Nas relações contratuais privadas, prevalecerão o princípio da intervenção mínima e a excepcionalidade da revisão contratual.** (grifos e destaques nossos).

Ainda, o art. 421-A do Código Civil assim dispõe:

> Art. 421-A. Os contratos civis e empresariais presumem-se paritários e simétricos até a presença de elementos concretos que justifiquem o afastamento dessa presunção, ressalvados os regimes jurídicos previstos em leis especiais, garantido também que: (Incluído pela Lei nº 13.874, de 2019)
> I – **as partes negociantes poderão estabelecer parâmetros objetivos para a interpretação das cláusulas negociais e de seus pressupostos de revisão ou de resolução**; (Incluído pela Lei nº 13.874, de 2019)
> II – **a alocação de riscos definida pelas partes deve ser respeitada e observada;** e (Incluído pela Lei nº 13.874, de 2019)
> **III – a revisão contratual somente ocorrerá de maneira excepcional e limitada.**

Assim, aceitar que dificuldades passageiras experimentadas pelo devedor que o impossibilitem de adimplir as prestações do contrato na forma convencionada **implica e autoriza** a liberação de garantias atreladas ao contrato, provocará manifesta insegurança jurídica às partes, pois se desconstituirá uma garantia contratual, sem qualquer prova de que será futuramente substituída, em decorrência única e exclusiva de uma situação passageira, que pode ser sanada com a prorrogação das parcelas do contrato (ou outras condições), sem que altere as garantias prestadas. É imperioso que o Poder Judiciário assegure o reequilíbrio do contrato na hipótese de constatar imprevisibilidade ou onerosidade excessiva, **sem que ao mesmo tempo promova a extinção de uma garantia contratual**, condição que traz ao credor a segurança que dela se espera, sob pena de se transferir ao credor todo o risco pelo evento imprevisível, deixando de privilegiar a cooperação, boa-fé e a manutenção das relações contratuais em momentos e crise.

Em outros termos, acaso em virtude de uma situação transitória se aplique a Teoria da Imprevisão e se promova alterações no trato negocial, suprimindo-se ainda garantias contratuais, evidente que quando a situação transitória for sanada (e o será), é possível que o credor não mais goze das garantias prestadas, ficando exposto ao risco do total inadimplemento da avença. Neste sentido, o Tribunal de Justiça do Estado de São Paulo assim já decidiu:

> EMENTA – Locação de imóvel comercial. **Tutela de urgência destinada a suspender a exigibilidade dos aluguéis em face da quarentena decorrente da pandemia por COVID-19. Descabimento. Moratória que pelo regime legal não pode ser imposta ao credor pelo Juiz, devendo decorrer de ato negocial entre as partes ou por força de especial disposição legal. Evocação do caso fortuito e força maior que tampouco autoriza aquela medida.** Cabimento, porém, da vedação à extração de protesto de título representativo do crédito por aluguéis. Recurso parcialmente provido. (TJSP, Agravo de Instrumento n. 2063701-03.2020.8.26.0000 – 36ª Câmara de Direito Privado Relator Desembargador Arantes Teodoro, j. 06/04/2020) (Grifos e destaques e grifos nossos).

A suspensão/prorrogação das parcelas, em tese, é medida que atende a situação de emergência transitória reclamada pelo interessado, mas, liberar as garantias ao cumprimento do contrato é medida desproporcional e que não encontra qualquer referencial válido à luz dos arts. 314 e 480 do Código Civil. Ademais, nos termos do art. 1.421 do Código Civil tem-se que o "pagamento de uma ou mais prestações da dívida não importa exoneração correspondente da garantia, ainda que esta compreenda vários bens, salvo disposição expressa no título ou na quitação. Ora, se o pagamento das prestações não exonera a correspondente garantia, não há dúvidas de que a garantia contratual não possa ser suprimida da relação contratual com a eventual prorrogação do pagamento das parcelas contratuais em razão de evento imprevisível ou onerosidade excessiva.

CONCLUSÕES

À vista do exposto, conclui-se que a pandemia do Coronavírus, inequivocamente, é um evento imprevisível e extraordinário, que preenche um dos requisitos previstos pelo art. 478, CC, e enseja a postulação judicial pela revisão ou resolução de um contrato. Todavia, no atual cenário, observa-se que várias demandas aforadas por pessoas jurídicas insumidoras de crédito – portanto alheias à aplicação do Código de Defesa do Consumidor – têm como fundamento apenas o evento pandêmico, o que não basta para decretar a revisão ou resolução do contrato, carecendo ainda a comprovação de outros fatores, em especial, a onerosidade excessiva e a extrema vantagem percebida pela outra parte.

Como exemplificado através de julgados emanados do Superior Tribunal de Justiça, apesar de vozes em contrário, a onerosidade excessiva da obrigação e a extrema vantagem para a outra parte são requisitos fundamentais para que o interessado postule a revisão ou resolução de um contrato com fundamento na Teoria da Imprevisão, sob pena de ver sua demanda trilhar o caminho do insucesso.

Além disso, acaso os contratos submetidos à discussão sejam contratos bancários com garantias atreladas, tem-se que estas não poderão ser revistas por meio da aplicação da Teoria da Imprevisão, sob pena de se desequilibrar a relação contratual, deixando com que o credor suporte todos os riscos do negócio, onde muitas vezes já antecipou valores ao devedor.

Desta forma, impõe-se ao jurisdicionado a meticulosa tarefa de bem instruir sua inicial, com as provas cabais para fundamentar seu pedido revisional, e ao Poder Judiciário, impõe-se o dever de bem sopesar os fatos e provas, a fim de se evitar a prolação de decisões que, embora busquem reequilibrar a relação, acabem por desequilibrá-las, como por exemplo, liberando-se em favor do devedor as garantias atreladas ao contrato.

REFERÊNCIAS

BRASIL. Código Civil. Lei 10.406, de 10 de janeiro de 2002. Disponível em: < http://www.planalto.gov.br/ccivil_03/leis/2002/l10406.htm >. Acesso em: 26 de maio de 2020.

BRASIL. Código Civil. Lei 8.078, de 11 de setembro de 1990. Disponível em: <http://www.planalto.gov.br/ccivil_03/leis/l8078.htm>. Acesso em: 26 de maio de 2020.

BRASÍLIA. Câmara dos Deputados. Projeto de Lei 6960/2002. Dá nova redação aos artigos 2º, 11, 12, 43, 66, 151,224, 243, 244,246, 262, 273,281,283, 286, 294,299, 300, 302, 306,309,328, 338,369, 421, 422, 423, 425, 429, 450, 456, 471, 472, 473, 474, 475, 478, 479, 480,482, 496,502, 506, 533, 549, 557, 558, 559, 563, 574,576, 596, 599, 602, 603, 607, 623, 624, 625, 633, 637, 642, 655, 765, 788, 790, 872, 927, 928,931, 944, 947, 949,950, 953, 954,966, 977,999, 1053, 1060, 1086, 1094, 1099, 1158, 1160, 1163, 1165, 1166, 1168, 1196, 1197, 1204, 1210, 1228, 1273, 1274, 1276, 1316, 1341, 1347, 1352, 1354, 1361, 1362, 1365,1369, 1371, 1374, 1378, 1379, 1434, 1436, 1456, 1457,1473, 1479, 1481, 1512, 1515, 1516,1521, 1526, 1561, 1563, 1573, 1574, 1575, 1576, 1581, 1583, 1586, 1589, 1597, 1601, 1605, 1606, 1609, 1614, 1615, 1618, 1623, 1625, 1626, 1628, 1629, 1641, 1642, 1660, 1665, 1668, 1694, 1700, 1701, 1707, 1709, 1717, 1719, 1721, 1722, 1723, 1725, 1726, 1727, 1729, 1731, 1736, 1768, 1788, 1790, 1800, 1801, 1815, 1829, 1831, 1834, 1835, 1848, 1859, 1860, 1864, 1881, 1909, 1963, 1965, 2002, 2038 e 2045 da Lei nº 10.406 de 10 de janeiro de 2002, que "Institui o Código Civil", acrescenta dispositivos e dá outras providências. Disponível em: < https://www.camara.leg.br/proposicoesWeb/fichadetramitacao?idProposicao=56549 >. Acesso em 27/05/2020.

Bittar, Carlos Alberto Filho. Teoria da Imprevisão, dos poderes do juiz. São Paulo: Revista dos Tribunais, 1993.

Diniz, Maria Helena. Curso de Direito Civil Brasileiro: Teoria Geral das Obrigações. Volume 2. 22ª ed. São Paulo: Saraiva, 2007.

Diniz, Maria Helena. Curso de Direito Civil Brasileiro: Teoria Geral do Direito Civil. Volume 1. 29ª ed. São Paulo: Saraiva, 2012.

Diniz. Maria Helena. Código Civil Anotado. 15º ed. São Paulo: Saraiva, 2010.

Miranda, Pontes de. Tratado de direito privado. Parte especial. Tomo XX. Direito das coisas: direitos reais de garantia. Hipoteca, penhor e anticrese. Rio de Janeiro: Editor Borsoi, 1958.

Mello, Cleysson de Moraes. Direito Civil: Contratos. 2ª ed. Rio de Janeiro: Freitas Bastos Editora, 2017.

Nunes, Rizzatto. Curso de Direito do Consumidor. 12ª Ed. São Paulo: Saraiva Educação, 2018.

Rodrigues, Silvio. Direito Civil. Dos contratos e das declarações unilaterais de vontade. Volume 3. 28. ed. São Paulo: Saraiva, 2002.

Schreiber, Anderson. Manual de Direito Civil Contemporâneo. 3º ed. São Paulo: Saraiva, 2020.

SUPERIOR TRIBUNAL DE JUSTIÇA (STJ). Rel. Ministro Paulo De Tarso Sanseverino. REsp 1321614/SP. Julgado em 16/12/2014. Disponível em www.stj.jus.br.

SUPERIOR TRIBUNAL DE JUSTIÇA (STJ). Rel. Ministro Marco Buzzi. AgInt no REsp 1514093/CE. Julgado em 25/10/2016. Disponível em www.stj.jus.br.

SUPERIOR TRIBUNAL DE JUSTIÇA (STJ). Rel. Ministro Paulo De Tarso Sanseverino. REsp 1632842/RS. Julgado em 12/09/2017. Disponível em www.stj.jus.br.

SUPERIOR TRIBUNAL DE JUSTIÇA (STJ). Rel. Ministro Carlos Alberto Menezes Direito. REsp 654.969/PR. Julgado em 07/12/2004. Disponível em www.stj.jus.br.

Tartuce, Flávio. Manual de Direito Civil. 10º ed. São Paulo: GEN, 2019.

TRIBUNAL DE JUSTIÇA DO ESTADO DE SÃO PAULO (TJSP). Rel. Pedro Kodama. Agravo de Instrumento 2067476-26.2020.8.26.0000. Julgado em 26/05/2020. Disponível em www.tjsp.jus.br.

TRIBUNAL DE JUSTIÇA DO ESTADO DE SÃO PAULO (TJSP). Rel. Edgard Rosa. Agravo de Instrumento 2090679-17.2020.8.26.0000. Julgado em 13/05/2020. Disponível em www.tjsp.jus.br.

TRIBUNAL DE JUSTIÇA DO ESTADO DE SÃO PAULO (TJSP). Rel. José Marcos Marrone. Apelação Cível 1018449-19.2018.8.26.0564. Julgado em 28/11/2019. Disponível em www.tjsp.jus.br.

TRIBUNAL DE JUSTIÇA DO ESTADO DE SÃO PAULO (TJSP). Rel. Arantes Teodoro. Agravo de Instrumento n. 2063701-03.2020.8.26.0000. Julgado em 06/04/2019. Disponível em www.tjsp.jus.br.

VENOSA, Silvio de Salvo. Direito Civil. Contratos. 17ª ed. São Paulo: Saraiva, 2017.

OS ALIMENTOS AVOENGOS DIANTE DO RECONHECIMENTO DA SOCIOAFETIVIDADE E DA MULTIPARENTALIDADE[1]

LUCAS ABREU BARROSO[*]
DANIELLA GONÇALVES STEFANELLI[**]

INTRODUÇÃO

A modernidade perdurou de meados do século XVIII até meados do século XX e foi caracterizada pela intensa busca de uma unidade sistêmica e razão totalizadora, orientadas pelo ideal de emancipação universal. Não por outra razão, o paradigma jurídico da modernidade estava pautado por modelos teóricos lineares, rígidos e totalizadores, que se demonstraram insuficientes para compreender toda a dinamicidade, pluralidade e complexidade de uma sociedade que enfrentava o crescente desenvolvimento dos meios de produção, como também do conhecimento científico.[2]

[*] Doutor em Direito pela PUC-SP. Professor na Faculdade de Direito da Universidade Federal do Espírito Santo. Líder do Grupo de Pesquisa "O direito civil na pós-modernidade jurídica". Advogado.

[**] Mestranda e Bacharel em Direito pela Universidade Federal do Espírito Santo. Membro do Grupo de Pesquisa "O direito civil na pós-modernidade jurídica". Advogada.

[1] Este capítulo foi concluído na semana em que a tragédia global provocada pela COVID-19 fez milhares de vítimas, no Brasil e no mundo. Infelizmente, com muito pesar, uma entre elas se destaca. Por isso, o autor Lucas Abreu Barroso dedica sua publicação nesta importante obra ao amigo de uma vida inteira, Wilton Oliveira da Rocha. Um admirador da família, que amava sua família e que tinha nos amigos uma grande família.

[2] AMARAL, Francisco. O direito civil na pós-modernidade. *In*: NAVES, Bruno Torquato de Oliveira; FIUZA, César; SÁ, Maria de Fátima Freire de (coord.). *Direito civil:* atualidades. Belo Horizonte: Del Rey, 2003. p. 63.

Constatou-se um enorme distanciamento entre os modelos jurídicos e a realidade social, sobretudo considerando que o contexto descrito fomentou ou evidenciou a formação de novos arranjos interpessoais e sociais, inclusive no âmbito das relações familiares. Como consequência, tornou-se necessária a revisão e a reestruturação da epistemologia jurídica,[3] para restabelecer uma correlação mínima entre o direito e a sociedade; caso contrário, restariam negadas as funções primordiais do direito na contemporaneidade, de "decidir casos, justificar decisões e produzir normas"[4].

Superado o paradigma da modernidade, o pensamento jurídico passou a ser orientado pelo constitucionalismo principiológico, concretizando uma nova teoria constitucional "preocupada com a consolidação e a garantia dos direitos humano-fundamentais"[5] e que encampou a teoria dos princípios (agora revestidos de forma e força normativa)[6] como discurso a densificar e assegurar os direitos previstos nos textos constitucionais, produzindo efeitos sobre todo o campo jurídico.

O direito civil pós-1988 experimentou a reconfiguração de seus três pilares, "em cujos vértices se assentam a estrutura do sistema privado clássico"[7]: os modos de apropriação, os contratos e as famílias. Entretanto, o anteprojeto do código civil de 2002 em muito antecedeu à redemocratização do País. Por essa razão, observados no contexto cultural e social, muitos direitos relativos às famílias receberam tratamento demasiado tímido ou nem sequer foram disciplinados, a exemplo da socioafetividade e da multiparentalidade.

Observa-se a ausência de regulamentação no que concerne à interferência na esfera jurídica de terceiros, alheios ao processo de formação dos

[3] ARONE, Ricardo. Sistema jurídico e unidade axiológica: contorno metodológico do direito civil constitucional. *Revista de Propriedade Intelectual*, Aracaju, a. 2, n. 3, p. 153-184, jun. 2013. p. 154.

[4] BARROSO, Lucas Abreu. Para além do positivismo jurídico: a metodologia jurisprudencialista de A. Castanheira Neves. *Revista Eletrônica do Mestrado em Direito da UFAL*, Maceió, v. 6, n. 1, p. 61-68, 2015. p. 64.

[5] HOFFMAM, Fernando; CAVALHEIRO, Larissa Nunes; NASCIMENTO, Valéria Ribas do. O constitucionalismo principiológico como condição de possibilidade para a concretização dos direitos humano-fundamentais. *Revista Eletrônica Direito e Política*, Itajaí, v. 6, n. 1, p. 101-119, abr. 2011. p. 110.

[6] FIUZA, César. Diretrizes hermenêuticas do direito de família. *In*: PEREIRA, Rodrigo da Cunha (coord.). *Família e dignidade humana*: V congresso brasileiro de direito de família. São Paulo: IOB Thomson, 2006. p. 235.

[7] FACHIN, Luiz Edson. *Teoria crítica do direito civil*. 3. ed. Rio de Janeiro: Renovar, 2012. p. 13-14.

vínculos parentais dessas naturezas, inclusive para imposição de alguns ônus legais. É justamente nesse ponto que se encontra o problema objeto do presente estudo, especificamente, o ônus alimentar avoengo decorrente da socioafetividade e da multiparentalidade, quando estas assim restarem configuradas, independentemente da preexistência da afetividade entre avós e netos.

A socioafetividade e a multiparentalidade serão abordadas envoltas nos obstáculos encontrados pelos tribunais pátrios e pela doutrina nacional para sua definição, como, também, para a fixação dos seus requisitos configuradores, diante das várias conformações familiares que a nova ordem constitucional permite, com vistas a melhor decotar a prestação alimentar pelos avós, aqui englobados os biológicos e os afetivos. Cumpre esclarecer que as relações parentais pautadas pela adoção não compõem este estudo, porque, além de contar com tutela jurídica específica, a constituição do vínculo entre adotante e adotado enseja o desligamento de toda e qualquer conexão deste para com seus parentes consanguíneos (biológicos), "salvo para efeito de impedimento matrimonial"[8], hipótese que, de regra, exclui a multiparentalidade.

1. A AFETIVIDADE[9] COMO CRITÉRIO JURÍDICO PARA A CONSTITUIÇÃO E PARA O RECONHECIMENTO DE RELAÇÕES FAMILIARES

Oportunizado pelo constitucionalismo democrático pós-1988, o critério jurídico da afetividade trouxe outras possibilidades para a constituição e para o reconhecimento de relações familiares, porquanto representativo do exercício do afeto objetivamente verificável em situações existenciais intersubjetivas,[10] ensejando novas modalidades de parentesco civil. Antes da promulgação da vigente Constituição, a família era matrimonializada,

[8] DINIZ, Maria Helena. *Curso de direito civil brasileiro*. 22. ed. São Paulo: Saraiva, 2007. v. 5. p. 411.

[9] Este estudo, contrariamente à doutrina familiarista majoritária, não trabalha com a noção de afeto, mas de afetividade, haja vista consistir o afeto em "sentimento anímico de aspecto subjetivo (inapreensível de forma direta pelo Direito)", enquanto a afetividade consubstancia "atividade exteriorizadora do afeto; conjunto de atos concretos representativos de um dado sentimento afetivo por outrem (esses atos concretos são captáveis pelo Direito, pelos seus meios usuais de prova)" (CALDERÓN, Ricardo. *Princípio da afetividade no direito de família*. 2. ed. Rio de Janeiro: Forense, 2017. p. 152. *Versão digital*.).

[10] CALDERÓN, Ricardo. *Princípio da afetividade no direito de família*. 2. ed. Rio de Janeiro: Forense, 2017. p. 152. *Versão digital*.

patrimonializada e hierarquizada. O rompimento com esses arquétipos viabilizou a compreensão da família como uma "verdadeira comunidade de afeto, para que o indivíduo venha a obter plena realização da sua dignidade enquanto ser humano, porque o elo entre os integrantes da família deixa de ter conotação patrimonial para envolver, sobretudo, o afeto, o carinho, o amor e a ajuda mútua"[11].

Os vínculos e as estruturas familiares são as melhores amostras do dinamismo social que qualifica a contemporaneidade, visto que a família, "organização social essencial à base do sistema"[12], fica exposta e suscetível às mutabilidades das relações interpessoais. Tal afirmação é corroborada pelo caráter histórico e relativo do seu próprio conceito, que, por sua vez, não comporta definições peremptórias e absolutas.[13]

Com efeito, o art. 1.593 do Código Civil recepcionou noção mais abrangente de parentesco civil, proveniente de qualquer origem, não apenas da consanguinidade, como a união estável, o matrimônio, a adoção e outras, pressupondo a afetividade.[14] Nessa conjuntura, a relação de parentesco pode estar firmada biologicamente ou afetivamente; esses fatores não são excludentes entre si, embora não guardem dependência, o que importa dizer que os critérios sanguíneo e afetivo podem coexistir em um mesmo vínculo de parentesco e que a ausência de qualquer deles não impede a conservação do laço familiar pelo outro.

Idêntico raciocínio aplica-se para questões referentes à parentalidade, considerando que a filiação biológica não encerra, automática e necessariamente, sentimentos entre filhos e pais, como a filiação socioafetiva não reclama identidade do tronco ancestral entre ambos.[15] A partir dessa ideia, o Enunciado n. 256 do Conselho da Justiça Federal propõe: "a posse do estado de filho (parentalidade socioafetiva) constitui modalidade [autônoma] de parentesco civil".

[11] ALVES, Leonardo Barreto Moreira. *Direito de família mínimo*: a possibilidade de aplicação e o campo de incidência da autonomia privada no direito de família. Rio de Janeiro: Lumen Juris, 2010. p. 119.

[12] FACHIN, Luiz Edson. *Teoria crítica do direito civil*. 3. ed. Rio de Janeiro: Renovar, 2012. p. 14.

[13] AMARAL, Francisco. *Direito civil:* introdução. 8. ed. Rio de Janeiro: Renovar, 2014. p. 176.

[14] DINIZ, Maria Helena. *Curso de direito civil brasileiro*. 22. ed. São Paulo: Saraiva, 2007. v. 5. p. 411.

[15] DINIZ, Maria Helena. *Curso de direito civil brasileiro*. 22. ed. São Paulo: Saraiva, 2007. v. 5. p. 409-411.

O tema aparenta simplicidade, mormente quando se sabe que a parentalidade biológica advém das semelhanças gênicas entre os ascendentes e os descendentes, imprescindível à manutenção da vida humana, porquanto a parentalidade socioafetiva resulta de atos de vontade,[16] cujo critério estrutural é a afetividade.[17] Porém, a afetividade, por si só, não é suficiente para que o laço parental reste configurado, sendo a legislação omissa acerca dos requisitos para tanto.

Diante disso, a doutrina e a jurisprudência, objetivando aproximar os ditames normativos e as demandas sociais, como, também, buscando conferir novas dimensões para o direito das famílias, a fim de amenizar os efeitos negativos da inércia legislativa, debruçaram-se sobre o problema, o que resultou na fixação dos pressupostos para a filiação afetiva.

Antônio Cezar Quevedo Goulart Filho, ao defender que a investigação jurídica do afeto somente é possível na esfera objetiva,[18] mediante a exteriorização de comportamentos capazes de expressar sentimentos relativos a outrem, consubstanciando, assim, a afetividade,[19] assevera de maneira categórica que:

> Em todas as relações de família, conjugalidade e parentesco, se faz presente a afetividade enquanto princípio jurídico deontológico [criador de deveres jurídicos]. Aqui importa dizer que não deve a afetividade ser confundida com amor [...] Não há um dever de amor, pois a amar não se pode ser compelido pelo direito, mas há um dever de cuidado, que significa 'garantir às crianças e aos adolescentes [como aos demais membros] condições de desenvolvimento físico e emocional adequado, que lhes permita, inclusive, o sentimento de fazer parte de uma família'.[20]

[16] NERY, Rosa Maria de Andrade; NERY JUNIOR, Nelson. *Instituições de direito civil:* família e sucessões. 2. ed. São Paulo: Thomson Reuters Brasil, 2019. v. 4. p. 405.

[17] CASSETTARI, Christiano. *Multiparentalidade e parentalidade socioafetiva*: efeitos jurídicos. 3. ed. São Paulo: Atlas, 2017. Capítulo 1. Item 1.3. p. 25. *Versão digital.*

[18] GOULART FILHO, Antônio Cezar Quevedo. *Relação avoenga*: apreensão jurídica e expressão eficacial na senda das vulnerabilidades. 2016. 195 f. Dissertação (Mestrado em Direito) – Programa de Pós-Graduação em Direito, Setor de Ciências Jurídicas, Universidade Federal do Paraná, Curitiba, 2016. p. 22-23.

[19] CALDERÓN, Ricardo. *Princípio da afetividade no direito de família.* 2. ed. Rio de Janeiro: Forense, 2017. p. 152. *Versão digital.*

[20] GOULART FILHO, Antônio Cezar Quevedo. *Relação avoenga*: apreensão jurídica e expressão eficacial na senda das vulnerabilidades. 2016. 195 f. Dissertação (Mestrado em Direito) –

Esse entendimento já havia sido exposto pela Ministra Nancy Andrighi na relatoria do Recurso Especial n. 1.159.242/SP, oportunidade em que aduziu que "o amor diz respeito à motivação, questão que refoge os lindes legais, situando-se, pela sua subjetividade e impossibilidade de precisa materialização, no universo meta-jurídico da filosofia, da psicologia ou da religião"[21]. Por essa razão, coloca o cuidado, percebido como um valor jurídico, cujo cumprimento pode ser verificado e comprovado objetivamente, como cerne da análise e da discussão de questões concernentes à parentalidade e à afetividade, pois, segundo ela, "amar é faculdade, cuidar é dever"[22].

Nesse diapasão, para o reconhecimento do vínculo parental socioafetivo é necessário, para além do elo afetivo propriamente dito, o comportamento social típico de pais e de filhos, assim como a convivência familiar duradoura, consoante Paulo Lôbo.[23] O laço de afetividade e o tempo de convivência também são considerados por Christiano Cassettari[24], que considera, ainda, a solidez do vínculo afetivo em cada caso concreto.

Por sua vez, quando da análise da Repercussão Geral n. 622, decorrente do julgamento do Recurso Extraordinário n. 898.060/SC,[25] o Supremo Tribunal Federal confirmou que já vinha sendo reconhecida a posse do estado de filho; portanto, vínculo parental socioafetivo "em favor daquele [que] utilizasse o nome da família (*nominatio*), fosse tratado como filho pelo pai (*tractatio*) e gozasse de reconhecimento da sua condição de descendente

Programa de Pós-Graduação em Direito, Setor de Ciências Jurídicas, Universidade Federal do Paraná, Curitiba, 2016. p. 22-23 e 96.

[21] BRASIL. Superior Tribunal de Justiça. Recurso Especial nº 1.159.242/SP. 3. T. Relatora: Min. Nancy Andrighi, j. 24/04/2012. *Diário da Justiça Eletrônico*, Brasília-DF, 10 maio 2012. Disponível em: https://ww2.stj.jus.br/processo/revista/documento/ mediado/?componente=ITA&sequencial=1067604&num_registro=200901937019&data=20120510&formato=PDF. Acesso em: 24 maio 2020.

[22] BRASIL. Superior Tribunal de Justiça. Recurso Especial nº 1.159.242/SP. 3. T. Relatora: Min. Nancy Andrighi, j. 24/04/2012. *Diário da Justiça Eletrônico*, Brasília-DF, 10 maio 2012. Disponível em: https://ww2.stj.jus.br/processo/revista/documento/ mediado/?componente=ITA&sequencial=1067604&num_registro=200901937019&data=20120510&formato=PDF. Acesso em: 24 maio 2020.

[23] Lôbo, Paulo. *Direito civil:* direito de família. 9. ed. São Paulo: Saraiva, 2019. v. 5. p. 231-233.

[24] Cassettari, Christiano. *Multiparentalidade e parentalidade socioafetiva*: efeitos jurídicos. 3. ed. São Paulo: Atlas, 2017. Capítulo 1. Item 1.4. *passim*. *Versão digital.*

[25] Ver a ementa completa no Anexo A.

pela comunidade (*reputatio*)"[26], evidenciando, assim, certa semelhança e homogeneidade no trato do tema pela doutrina e pela jurisprudência, a despeito de sutis distinções terminológicas, como ora observado.[27] Tomando por empréstimo a nomenclatura utilizada por Paulo Lôbo, o comportamento social típico de pais e de filhos pode ser sintetizado como percepção social do caráter filial da relação entre as partes que figuram em um vínculo afetivo, a partir de condutas objetivas e subjetivas comuns a todo elo parental.[28] O mencionado jurista indica a *nominatio*, a *tractatio* e a *reputatio*, adotadas pela Suprema Corte, como possíveis desdobramentos daquele requisito.

Aqui, mister destacar o cuidado,[29] valor jurídico que atua para "informar a melhor interpretação de quais direitos ou deveres jurídicos decorrem"[30] do critério jurídico da afetividade, norteando as condutas a serem segui-

[26] BRASIL. Supremo Tribunal Federal. Recurso Extraordinário nº 898.060/SC. Relator: Min. Luiz Fux j. 29/09/2016. *Diário da Justiça Eletrônico*, Brasília-DF, 30 set. 2016. Disponível em: http://stf.jus.br/portal/diarioJustica/verDiarioProcesso.asp?numDj=209 &dataPublicacaoDj=30/09/2016&incidente=4803092&codCapitulo=2&numMateria=29&codMateria=4. Acesso em: 20 maio 2020.

[27] Embora muito se tenha falado a respeito do laço afetivo, todos os requisitos têm igual relevância, posto que cumulativos.

[28] LÔBO, Paulo. *Direito civil:* direito de família. 9. ed. São Paulo: Saraiva, 2019. v. 5. p. 231-232.

[29] Consiste em uma das formas de manifestação da afetividade, senão a principal delas. O cuidado atua tanto na configuração, quanto na definição dos deveres jurídicos de cada sujeito nas relações familiares. Para a doutrina, "cuidado é, acima de tudo, uma postura ética diversa. Um modo-de-ser-no-mundo diferente do padrão de comportamento que a humanidade vem adotando nos últimos séculos. Diferente do modo-de-ser-trabalho, que objetifica e subjuga tudo ao nosso redor, para colocar aos interesses pessoais e coletivos, o modo-de-ser-cuidado adota uma noção de con-vivência, de inter-ação e de comunhão, que valoriza a natureza, o outro ser humano e a si mesmo não pelo que podem ter de utilidade, mas pelo valor intrínseco que têm. É a compreensão de que só se pode ser humano enquanto não se desoreza [*sic*] a dimensão da *pathos*, do sentimento, em prol do *logos*, da razão, e o cuidado se insere nesta lógica própria do coração que é a emoção humana. [...] Quando se trata de afetividade nas relações de família, busca-se o reconhecimento do caráter normativo de deveres pautados em condutas que, se esperaria, a família mantivesse espontaneamente. A dimensão deontológica jurídica, então, tem lugar, a partir do substrato afetivo que se imprimiu ao modelo jurídico do ser em família" (GOULART FILHO, Antônio Cezar Quevedo. *Relação avoenga*: apreensão jurídica e expressão eficacial na senda das vulnerabilidades. 2016. 195 f. Dissertação (Mestrado em Direito) – Programa de Pós-Graduação em Direito, Setor de Ciências Jurídicas, Universidade Federal do Paraná, Curitiba, 2016. p. 69-70).

[30] GOULART FILHO, Antônio Cezar Quevedo. *Relação avoenga*: apreensão jurídica e expressão eficacial na senda das vulnerabilidades. 2016. 195 f. Dissertação (Mestrado em Direito) –

das no bojo das relações familiares. Noutro giro, a convivência familiar duradoura nada mais é que a consolidação de um comportamento social de pais e de filhos, a propiciar a formação de uma entidade familiar juridicamente reconhecida. Não há lapso temporal previsto na legislação para a convivência, basta que permita identificar "laços familiares efetivos e não apenas relações afetivas"[31].

Uma vez preenchidos os pressupostos, estará configurada a posse do estado de filho, com o reconhecimento da parentalidade socioafetiva, ante o art. 1.605, II, do código civil, que ao tratar a existência de presunções veementes "resultantes de fatos já certos", como prova da filiação em caso de falta ou de defeito do termo de nascimento, abarca esse estado como um fato gerador da parentalidade em estudo, apesar de inexistir previsão legal nesse sentido. A doutrina e a jurisprudência denotam, ainda que implicitamente, a dispensabilidade da *nominatio* para a constatação do fenômeno em tela, sobremodo ante a paternidade socioafetiva, independentemente da sua declaração em registro público, conforme a tese fixada na Repercussão Geral n. 622, posição que parece ser a mais acertada. Caso contrário, todo vínculo parental socioafetivo se convolaria em adoção formal, o que obstaria e negaria tutela jurídica às relações parentais afetivas não registrais.

Com substrato nesse arcabouço teórico, constata-se que, apesar de a lei ser tímida quanto ao tema, aparentando até certa exclusão dos filhos socioafetivos pela dicção do art. 1.596 do código civil, por mencionar apenas os filhos biológicos, havidos ou não na relação matrimonial, bem como os adotivos, frutos do estabelecimento de um vínculo civil, o fato é que a parentalidade socioafetiva tornou-se uma realidade amplamente admitida pelo direito brasileiro.

2. A REDE DE PARENTESCO DECORRENTE DOS VÍNCULOS BIOLÓGICOS E AFETIVOS

O quanto posto até o momento permite asseverar que o art. 1.593 do código civil abrange, entre outras modalidades, os parentescos consanguíneo e socioafetivo, este como uma espécie de parentesco civil,[32] com todos os

Programa de Pós-Graduação em Direito, Setor de Ciências Jurídicas, Universidade Federal do Paraná, Curitiba, 2016. p. 70.

[31] Lôbo, Paulo. *Direito civil:* direito de família. 9. ed. São Paulo: Saraiva, 2019. v. 5. p. 232.

[32] Calderón, Ricardo. *Princípio da afetividade no direito de família*. 2. ed. Rio de Janeiro: Forense, 2017. p. 58. *Versão digital.*

efeitos que são próprios das relações de filiação. Somado a isso, observa-se a diferença de fatores fundantes dos laços de parentalidade, os quais, como abordado, não necessariamente se concentram numa mesma pessoa; aliás, a dissociação dos vínculos sanguíneo e afetivo é tema bastante comum na jurisprudência dos tribunais superiores.

Isso porque a formação do laço parental socioafetivo com pessoa diversa do genitor biológico, com exceção das hipóteses de adoção regularizada, tem, por consequência, a dupla parentalidade, isto é, a coexistência entre a filiação biológica e a filiação afetiva. Desse modo, uma mesma pessoa passa a ter dois pais, duas mães, duas famílias.[33] Esse cenário levantou dúvidas a respeito da concomitância ou da prevalência entre os vínculos, tendo a doutrina se posicionado a favor da primeira, com respaldo no princípio da igualdade entre as filiações, a teor do art. 227, § 6º, da Constituição.[34]

Tal corrente encontra assento na teoria tridimensional do direito de família, para a qual a condição humana cumula as dimensões genética, afetiva e ontológica, impondo a outorga dos efeitos jurídicos das paternidades biológica e afetiva à pessoa. Para Belmiro Pedro Welter, "a compreensão do ser humano não é efetivada somente pelo comportamento com o mundo das coisas (mundo genético), mas, também, pelo modo de ser-em-família e sociedade (mundo desafetivo) e pelo próprio modo de relacionar consigo mesmo (mundo ontológico)"[35]. Destarte, todas as dimensões precisam ser satisfeitas, pois diretamente relacionadas a uma contínua formação da existencialidade humana. As paternidades genética e afetiva, ainda que não representadas na mesma pessoa, não são excludentes entre si, devendo ser conciliadas.

Ocorre que a falta de disciplinamento jurídico dessas realidades acarreta diversos problemas práticos, o que provocou a manifestação do Supremo Tribunal Federal por meio da Repercussão Geral n. 622, proveniente do Recurso Extraordinário n. 898.060/SC: "A paternidade socioafetiva, declarada ou não em registro público, não impede o reconhecimento do vín-

[33] CALDERÓN, Ricardo. *Princípio da afetividade no direito de família*. 2. ed. Rio de Janeiro: Forense, 2017. p. 212. *Versão digital*.

[34] CASSETTARI, Christiano. *Multiparentalidade e parentalidade socioafetiva*: efeitos jurídicos. 3. ed. São Paulo: Atlas, 2017. Capítulo 3. Item 3.4. *passim*. *Versão digital*.

[35] WELTER, Belmiro Pedro. Teoria tridimensional no direito de família: reconhecimento de todos os direitos das filiações genética e socioafetiva. *Revista do Ministério Público do RS*, Porto Alegre, n. 62, p. 9-25, nov. 2008/abr. 2009. p. 19.

culo de filiação concomitante baseado na origem biológica, com efeitos jurídicos próprios".

O julgamento visava decidir se os deveres legais, impostos para a parentalidade biológica, foram supridos/afastados pela filiação socioafetiva que se desenvolveu de forma paralela com terceira pessoa, o que foi negado. Nesta oportunidade, a Suprema Corte, amparada na dignidade da pessoa humana, na busca da felicidade, na igualdade entre as filiações e na paternidade responsável, posicionou-se a favor da concomitância dos vínculos consanguíneo e afetivo, dando ensejo à multiparentalidade. Entre os vários argumentos debatidos, vale trazer à colação a impossibilidade da redução das realidades familiares aos modelos previamente estabelecidos. O texto constitucional vigente preza pela atipicidade do conceito e da conformação das entidades familiares, porquanto instrumentos de realização plena da personalidade.[36]

Com efeito, o acolhimento dos vínculos biológico e afetivo é medida que se impõe, "quando o melhor interesse do descendente for o reconhecimento jurídico de ambos"[37], a ser aferido *in concreto* pelo julgador,[38] por não haver, até o momento, normativa jurídica regulamentando no seu todo a multiparentalidade. Assim concluiu a Suprema Corte:

> Os arranjos familiares alheios à regulação estatal, por omissão, não podem restar ao desabrigo da proteção a situações de pluriparentalidade, por isso que merecem tutela jurídica concomitante, para todos os fins de direito, os vínculos parentais de origem afetiva e biológica, a fim de prover a mais completa e adequada tutela aos sujeitos envolvidos, ante os princípios constitucionais da dignidade da pessoa humana (art. 1º, III) e da paternidade responsável (art. 226, § 7º).[39]

[36] ALVES, Leonardo Barreto Moreira. *Direito de família mínimo*: a possibilidade de aplicação e o campo de incidência da autonomia privada no direito de família. Rio de Janeiro: Lumen Juris, 2010. p. 119.

[37] BRASIL. Supremo Tribunal Federal. Recurso Extraordinário nº 898.060/SC. Relator: Min. Luiz Fux j. 29/09/2016. *Diário da Justiça Eletrônico*, Brasília-DF, 30 set. 2016. Disponível em: http://stf.jus.br/portal/diarioJustica/verDiarioProcesso.asp?numDj=209 &dataPublicacaoDj=30/09/2016&incidente=4803092&codCapitulo=2&numMateria=29&codMateria=4. Acesso em: 20 maio 2020.

[38] LÔBO, Paulo. *Direito civil:* direito de família. 9. ed. São Paulo: Saraiva, 2019. v. 5. p. 232.

[39] BRASIL. Supremo Tribunal Federal. Recurso Extraordinário nº 898.060/SC. Relator: Min. Luiz Fux j. 29/09/2016. *Diário da Justiça Eletrônico*, Brasília-DF, 30 set. 2016. Disponível em: http://stf.jus.br/portal/diarioJustica/verDiarioProcesso.asp?numDj=209 &dataPublicac

A decisão, acima parcialmente ementada, deu significação jurídica para a afetividade e para a multiparentalidade, mesmo diante da ausência de um regramento legal que lhes ofereça contornos próprios.[40] À vista disto, os efeitos e as regras gerais, relativos ao direito das famílias, devem incidir sobre os casos em que configuradas a socioafetividade e a multiparentalidade. O entendimento consolidado no Supremo Tribunal Federal e no Superior Tribunal de Justiça prenuncia conclusões alinhadas com o tema central deste estudo, a saber: a viabilidade da concomitância dos laços parentais biológicos e afetivos; logo, é admitida a multiparentalidade no direito pátrio. Entretanto, seu reconhecimento deve ser orientado pela análise casuística[41] do melhor interesse da criança (ou do descendente), razão pela qual a prevalência de um vínculo sobre o outro pode ser, apenas excepcionalmente, autorizada mediante processo judicial.

Não há, tanto na doutrina quanto na jurisprudência, justificativas prévias para que um vínculo parental se sobreponha ao outro, impedindo, dessa maneira, a indicação de um padrão para essas circunstâncias. A manutenção dos efeitos jurídicos de apenas um desses vínculos é sustentada em julgados mais antigos, que prezavam pela prevalência das relações de filiação explicitadas nos registros de nascimento, tendo sido prolatados anteriormente à manifestação do Supremo Tribunal Federal sobre o tema na Repercussão Geral n. 622.

3. O ÔNUS ALIMENTAR AVOENGO NO CONTEXTO DA SOCIOAFETIVIDADE E DA MULTIPARENTALIDADE

Em poucas palavras, a prestação alimentar é composta por "tudo aquilo de que alguém necessita para sobreviver"[42], cuja finalidade é garantir o sustento àquele que não possui meios ou condições para prover sua pró-

aoDj=30/09/2016&incidente=4803092&codCapitulo=2&numMateria=29&codMateria=4. Acesso em: 20 maio 2020.

[40] Calderón, Ricardo. *Princípio da afetividade no direito de família*. 2. ed. Rio de Janeiro: Forense, 2017. p. 212. p. 223. *Versão digital.*

[41] BRASIL. Superior Tribunal de Justiça. Recurso Especial nº 1.674.849/RS. 3. T. Relator: Min. Marco Aurélio Bellizze, j. 17/04/2018. *Diário da Justiça Eletrônico*, Brasília-DF, 23 abr. 2018. Disponível em: https://ww2.stj.jus.br/processo/revista/documento/mediad o/?componente=ITA&sequencial=1698834&num_registro=201602213860&data=20180423&formato=PDF. Acesso em: 20 maio 2020.

[42] Nery, Rosa Maria de Andrade; Nery Junior, Nelson. *Instituições de direito civil*: família e sucessões. 2. ed. São Paulo: Revista dos Tribunais, 2019. v. 4. p. 501.

pria mantença. O instituto encontra respaldo nos princípios constitucionais da dignidade da pessoa humana e da solidariedade familiar,[43] com tratamento infraconstitucional ancorado no disposto pelo art. 1.694 e ss. do código civil. Por determinação do art. 1.694 e do art. 1.696, ambos do código civil, a obrigação alimentar contempla os parentes, os cônjuges e os companheiros. Contudo, nas relações parentais, guarda a peculiaridade da reciprocidade entre pais e filhos, sendo "extensivo a todos os ascendentes, recaindo a obrigação nos mais próximos em grau, uns em falta dos outros".

Desse modo, quando os genitores não dispuserem de recursos suficientes para oferecer o mínimo existencial para sua prole, esta tem a faculdade de expandir o ônus alimentar em desfavor dos avós, tanto paternos quanto maternos, por se tratar de descendentes e ascendentes, nesta ordem, atraindo a incidência do previsto no art. 1.696 do Código Civil. Assim, não restam dúvidas acerca da obrigação alimentar dos avós com relação aos netos, ainda que de forma subsidiária, complementar e sucessiva,[44] porque a ordem de preferência trazida pela legislação civil não faculta a exclusão da obrigação alimentar dos parentes mais remotos, somente fixando a sequência a ser seguida quando de sua imposição, segundo a proximidade entre alimentante e alimentando. Isso "não impede que sejam chamados dois ou mais parentes para prestarem alimentos, desde que obedecidos os graus da ordem"[45].

A situação jurídica dos avós é tranquilamente captada na parentalidade consanguínea, porém parece demasiado abstrata no contexto da socioafetividade e da multiparentalidade, muito em razão do papel exercido pela autonomia privada na constituição e no reconhecimento do vínculo parental afetivo. Na lição de Rosa Maria de Andrade Nery e Nelson Nery Junior, a manifestação da vontade livre torna possível a formação do parentesco civil nos moldes da filiação socioafetiva. Para esses autores, a posse do estado de filho, *in casu*, pressupõe uma reciprocidade entre as partes envolvidas: é preciso que o pai e/ou a mãe reconheça(m) a existência de um laço substanciado na afetividade, com aptidão para deflagrar uma filiação não imposta por lei ou por origem biológica; igualmente, o filho deve

[43] Lôbo, Paulo. *Direito civil:* direito de família. 9. ed. São Paulo: Saraiva, 2019. v. 5. p. 384.

[44] Campos, Gustavo de Castro. *Alimentos avoengos*. 2015. 63 f. TCC (Graduação em Direito) – Universidade Federal do Paraná, Curitiba, 2015. p. 12.

[45] Campos, Gustavo de Castro. *Alimentos avoengos*. 2015. 63 f. TCC (Graduação em Direito) – Universidade Federal do Paraná, Curitiba, 2015. p. 22.

identificar-se como tal, independentemente da existência de registros formais de parentalidade.[46]

Uma vez constituída a relação filial afetiva, terá esta aptidão para produzir todos os efeitos jurídicos próprios da filiação, extensíveis a terceiros, até mesmo com a imposição de obrigações para aqueles que não participaram da formação do vínculo familiar. Isso ocorre em razão da idoneidade da afetividade para estabelecer uma rede de parentesco, tal qual o vínculo biológico, permeada por direitos e deveres que se prolongam para os demais parentes, indiferentemente, por não haver hierarquia ou diferença de qualidade jurídica entre a filiação consanguínea e a afetiva,[47] como restou sedimentado na Repercussão Geral n. 622.

Cumpre ressaltar que a autonomia privada deve ser examinada tão somente para averiguar a conformação do vínculo parental socioafetivo, isto é, entre os pais e os filhos, não subsistindo fundamentos para ser perscrutada em relações com os demais parentes. Isso porque aos terceiros não incumbe a negativa do vínculo socioafetivo ou da relação multiparental[48], visando exonerar-se das obrigações e dos deveres familiares legalmente impostos. Posicionamento em sentido diverso desafiaria a isonomia e a lealdade que devem respaldar e orientar todas as relações interpessoais, sem exceção, principalmente as de caráter familiar.

Cabe apontar que se o vínculo socioafetivo não pode servir de escusa para os parentes biológicos omitirem-se de suas responsabilidades familiares, igualmente o vínculo biológico não pode servir de justificativa para os parentes socioafetivos relegarem suas responsabilidades familiares, considerando o princípio da solidariedade familiar. Não é demais dizer que os avós socioafetivos até podem escolher os netos que serão contemplados com o seu amor e afeto, mas não têm liberdade para definir as circunstâncias em que os efeitos jurídicos próprios das relações familiares os atin-

[46] NERY, Rosa Maria de Andrade; NERY JUNIOR, Nelson. *Instituições de direito civil*: família e sucessões. 2. ed. São Paulo: Revista dos Tribunais, 2019. v. 4. p. 405.

[47] BRASIL. Supremo Tribunal Federal. Recurso Extraordinário nº 898.060/SC. Relator: Min. Luiz Fux j. 29/09/2016. *Diário da Justiça Eletrônico*, Brasília-DF, 30 set. 2016. Disponível em: http://stf.jus.br/portal/diarioJustica/verDiarioProcesso.asp?numDj=209 &dataPublicacaoDj=30/09/2016&incidente=4803092&codCapitulo=2&numMateria=29&codMateria=4. Acesso em: 20 maio 2020.

[48] NERY, Rosa Maria de Andrade; NERY JUNIOR, Nelson. *Instituições de direito civil*: família e sucessões. 2. ed. São Paulo: Revista dos Tribunais, 2019. v. 4. p. 409-410.

girão, visto que as obrigações inerentes ao direito das famílias aplicam-se extensivamente nas hipóteses de parentesco socioafetivo.

Com Maurício Requião é possível concluir que a questão conduz à hipótese de limitação relacional da autonomia privada dos avós socioafetivos, embora específica, estabelecida a partir da principiologia constitucional, com o objetivo único de proteger os interesses pessoais de terceiro que poderia ser atingido por eventual negativa da afetividade, o neto, a despeito da inexistência de relação prévia entre ambos.[49] Assim, parece correto afirmar que a prestação alimentar também é devida no contexto de reconhecimento da socioafetividade e da multiparentalidade, por qualquer das pessoas listadas no art. 1.694 e no art. 1.696, ambos do código civil, dentre elas, os avós.

Em sentido oposto, além de afrontar diretrizes constitucionais e legais, qualquer entendimento poderá privar o neto da fruição integral da dimensão existencial material dos alimentos, assim como poderá recair no equívoco de sugerir certa hierarquia entre a parentalidade biológica e a afetiva. Os vínculos consanguíneos, decorrentes de causa biológica, prescindem da vontade de parentes outros que não os genitores. Dessa forma, os avós biológicos, assim o são como resultado da escolha de seus descendentes, que desencadeou na prole. Ainda que a contragosto, os avós biológicos estão submetidos a todo um regramento legal que tutela a família, o qual abarca o dever de prestar alimentos aos netos, entre outras responsabilidades que lhes são postas, extensíveis ao contexto da afetividade.

Não é demais lembrar que o constitucionalismo principiológico promoveu a releitura da família que, desde então, tornou-se um "centro de promoção da dignidade humana; da dignidade dos filhos, cujo tratamento partirá dos princípios da igualdade, do melhor interesse do menor e do filiocentrismo"[50], entre outros. Em assim sendo, o ônus alimentar avoengo deve ser interpretado à luz da hermenêutica constitucional, com vistas a mitigar o princípio da autonomia privada e o minimalismo no direito das famílias, em proveito da promoção dos direitos e das garantias fundamentais da pessoa do neto, como viver com dignidade, dispondo de um mínimo

[49] REQUIÃO, Maurício. Autonomias e suas limitações. *Revista de Direito Privado*, São Paulo, v. 60, p. 85-96, dez. 2014. p. 90.

[50] FIÚZA, César. Diretrizes hermenêuticas do direito de família. *In*: PEREIRA, Rodrigo da Cunha (coord.). *Família e dignidade humana*: V congresso brasileiro de direito de família. São Paulo: IOB Thomson, 2006. p. 235.

existencial, sobretudo quando não conseguir provê-lo por si próprio. Ademais, o sustento material e imaterial é imposto pela solidariedade familiar, que "assume um caráter de dever ser, gerando deveres jurídicos"[51]. Tratando o tema a partir da solidariedade intergeracional e do dever de cuidado, Antônio Cezar Quevedo Goulart Filho coloca a obrigação alimentar entre as inúmeras regras e os diversos institutos que decorrem da solidariedade, obrigando os ascendentes e os descendentes a cuidarem uns dos outros, reciprocamente.[52]

Para o citado autor, o valor jurídico do cuidado impõe um *modo-de-ser--cuidado em família* que compreende "uma série de obrigações entre avós, pais e netos no tocante à relação avoenga"[53], a qual deve ser orientada por comportamentos objetivos, ainda que praticados por observância de determinação legal, quando ausente qualquer sentimento ou espontaneidade, ante a incidência da afetividade em seu caráter deontológico, com aptidão para impor, por si só, "determinados deveres jurídicos, como a prestação alimentar"[54], inclusive dos avós em favor dos netos.

Devidos os alimentos, de início, legítimos e côngruos,[55] pelos avós, diante do reconhecimento da socioafetividade e da multiparentalidade, concretizando, assim, a solidariedade familiar como dever jurídico decor-

[51] GOULART FILHO, Antônio Cezar Quevedo. *Relação avoenga*: apreensão jurídica e expressão eficacial na senda das vulnerabilidades. 2016. 195 f. Dissertação (Mestrado em Direito) – Programa de Pós-Graduação em Direito, Setor de Ciências Jurídicas, Universidade Federal do Paraná, Curitiba, 2016. p. 66.

[52] GOULART FILHO, Antônio Cezar Quevedo. *Relação avoenga*: apreensão jurídica e expressão eficacial na senda das vulnerabilidades. 2016. 195 f. Dissertação (Mestrado em Direito) – Programa de Pós-Graduação em Direito, Setor de Ciências Jurídicas, Universidade Federal do Paraná, Curitiba, 2016. p. 67-68 e 96.

[53] GOULART FILHO, Antônio Cezar Quevedo. *Relação avoenga*: apreensão jurídica e expressão eficacial na senda das vulnerabilidades. 2016. 195 f. Dissertação (Mestrado em Direito) – Programa de Pós-Graduação em Direito, Setor de Ciências Jurídicas, Universidade Federal do Paraná, Curitiba, 2016. p. 67.

[54] GOULART FILHO, Antônio Cezar Quevedo. *Relação avoenga*: apreensão jurídica e expressão eficacial na senda das vulnerabilidades. 2016. 195 f. Dissertação (Mestrado em Direito) – Programa de Pós-Graduação em Direito, Setor de Ciências Jurídicas, Universidade Federal do Paraná, Curitiba, 2016. p. 68.

[55] GOULART FILHO, Antônio Cezar Quevedo. *Relação avoenga*: apreensão jurídica e expressão eficacial na senda das vulnerabilidades. 2016. 195 f. Dissertação (Mestrado em Direito) – Programa de Pós-Graduação em Direito, Setor de Ciências Jurídicas, Universidade Federal do Paraná, Curitiba, 2016. p. 152.

rente da solidariedade social, que subsiste em face de parentes, como os ascendentes,[56] a prestação alimentar, nos termos delineados pelo art. 1.694 e ss. do código civil, será orientada pelo trinômio: necessidade, possibilidade e razoabilidade.[57] Isso não significa dizer que as disposições do diploma civil sejam suficientes ou adequadas para efetivar a prestação alimentar no cenário da multiparentalidade. Mesmo porque, diante do número de avós de quem figura, simultaneamente, em relações consanguínea e afetiva, a causa de alimentos tende a atingir níveis mais complexos, o que pode dificultar a tutela jurisdicional. Os obstáculos eventualmente gerados pelas peculiaridades do caso *sub judice* deverão ser contornados pelo julgador, com o uso de instrumentos processuais que promovam a adequação do procedimento aos pedidos.

Por fim, os alimentos são devidos pelos avós, paternos e/ou maternos, biológicos e/ou socioafetivos, ainda que no contexto da multiparentalidade, dada a divisibilidade do ônus[58] que coobriga "todos os ascendentes de mesmo grau"[59], conforme as possibilidades demonstradas por cada um – em razão da incidência de princípios constitucionais como o melhor interesse da criança, a dignidade da pessoa humana, a igualdade entre os filhos e a solidariedade familiar –, a prevalecer sobre o primado civilístico da autonomia privada, dada a sua indispensabilidade para a formação do vínculo familiar socioafetivo.

CONCLUSÕES

Este estudo dedicou-se à análise constitucional da família, com foco no ônus alimentar avoengo no contexto da socioafetividade e da multiparentalidade. Foram investigados os elos familiares socioafetivos e as estruturas familiares multiparentais, seguidos das análises geral e específica da prestação alimentar no direito brasileiro, o que permitiu concluir que os

[56] CAMPOS, Gustavo de Castro. *Alimentos avoengos*. 2015. 63 f. TCC (Graduação em Direito) – Universidade Federal do Paraná, Curitiba, 2015. p. 11.

[57] LÔBO, Paulo. *Direito civil:* direito de família. 9. ed. São Paulo: Saraiva, 2019. v. 5. p. 388-390.

[58] CAMPOS, Gustavo de Castro. *Alimentos avoengos*. 2015. 63 f. TCC (Graduação em Direito) – Universidade Federal do Paraná, Curitiba, 2015. p. 17.

[59] GOULART FILHO, Antônio Cezar Quevedo. *Relação avoenga*: apreensão jurídica e expressão eficacial na senda das vulnerabilidades. 2016. 195 f. Dissertação (Mestrado em Direito) – Programa de Pós-Graduação em Direito, Setor de Ciências Jurídicas, Universidade Federal do Paraná, Curitiba, 2016. p. 158.

avós, sejam biológicos ou afetivos, têm obrigação alimentar para com os netos, com alicerce, entre outros, nos princípios da dignidade da pessoa humana, da igualdade entre os filhos, do melhor interesse da criança, da solidariedade familiar.

Embora a vigente legislação seja omissa quanto aos novos arranjos familiares oriundos da dinâmica dos relacionamentos pessoais, a doutrina e a jurisprudência debruçaram-se sobre os efeitos jurídicos e as implicações práticas das famílias socioafetivas e multiparentais para apreender a complexidade dessas relações amplamente verificadas no cotidiano social. A insuficiência legislativa foi suprida pela fixação de requisitos que permitem o adequado reconhecimento do parentesco socioafetivo, como o vínculo filial afetivo, o comportamento social típico de pais e filhos e a convivência familiar duradoura. Estes, quando verificados cumulativamente, *in concreto*, permitem a configuração da posse do estado de filho, manifestando socialmente e fundamentando juridicamente a filiação decorrente da afetividade.

De igual modo ocorre com a multiparentalidade. Apesar da inexistência de previsão legal, o Supremo Tribunal Federal, orientado pelas diretrizes do constitucionalismo principiológico e pelo processo hermenêutico constitucional, próprios do paradigma jurídico contemporâneo, posicionou-se favoravelmente à concomitância dos elos biológico e afetivo, ambos com aptidão para a produção dos efeitos jurídicos próprios das relações parentais, afastando qualquer hierarquização entre os vínculos.

Com efeito, tanto os efeitos jurídicos quanto os enunciados normativos que incidem sobre as relações parentais consanguíneas, amplamente reguladas pelo código civil, estendem-se à filiação socioafetiva e, por consequência, à multiparentalidade, inclusive o ônus alimentar avoengo, com fulcro no art. 1.694 e no art. 1.696 do código civil, a impor a obrigação aos avós biológicos, ainda que de forma subsidiária, complementar e sucessiva.

Concluir em sentido diverso importaria em violação aos princípios constitucionais que norteiam a matéria, sobretudo a dignidade da pessoa humana e o melhor interesse da criança. Por tratar-se de questão existencial, relacionada com a subsistência dos descendentes, tais princípios devem prevalecer sobre a autonomia privada, tendo em vista que esta tem maior amplitude quando da constituição do vínculo filial afetivo, não possuindo o condão de ilidir a rede de parentescos por ele formada, nem os direitos e os deveres dele decorrentes. Sem adentrar as particularidades da socioafetividade e da multiparentalidade, a imposição do ônus alimentar aos avós afetivos assemelha-se ao ônus alimentar dos avós biológicos, porquanto esses assumirão as obrigações titularizadas por seus descendentes.

REFERÊNCIAS

ALVES, Leonardo Barreto Moreira. *Direito de família mínimo*: a possibilidade de aplicação e o campo de incidência da autonomia privada no direito de família. Rio de Janeiro: Lumen Juris, 2010.

AMARAL, Francisco. *Direito civil:* introdução. 8. ed. Rio de Janeiro: Renovar, 2014.

AMARAL, Francisco. O direito civil na pós-modernidade. *In*: NAVES, Bruno Torquato de Oliveira; FIUZA, César; SÁ, Maria de Fátima Freire de (coord.). *Direito civil:* atualidades. Belo Horizonte: Del Rey, 2003. p. 61-77.

ARONE, Ricardo. Sistema jurídico e unidade axiológica: contorno metodológico do direito civil constitucional. *Revista de Propriedade Intelectual*, Aracaju, a. 2, n. 3, p. 153-184, jun. 2013.

BARROSO, Lucas Abreu. Para além do positivismo jurídico: a metodologia jurisprudencialista de A. Castanheira Neves. *Revista Eletrônica do Mestrado em Direito da UFAL*, Maceió, v. 6, n. 1, p. 61-68, 2015.

BRASIL. Superior Tribunal de Justiça. Recurso Especial nº 1.159.242/SP. 3. T. Relatora: Min. Nancy Andrighi, j. 24/04/2012. *Diário da Justiça Eletrônico*, Brasília-DF, 10 maio 2012. Disponível em: https://ww2.stj.jus.br/processo/revista/documento/ mediado/?componente=ITA&sequencial=1067604&num_registro=200901937019&data=20120510&formato=PDF. Acesso em: 24 maio 2020.

BRASIL. Superior Tribunal de Justiça. Recurso Especial nº 1.674.849/RS. 3. T. Relator: Min. Marco Aurélio Bellizze, j. 17/04/2018. *Diário da Justiça Eletrônico*, Brasília-DF, 23 abr. 2018. Disponível em: https://ww2.stj.jus.br/processo/revista/documento/mediado/?componente=ITA&sequencial=1698834&num_registro=201602213860&data=20180423&formato=PDF. Acesso em: 20 maio 2020.

BRASIL. Supremo Tribunal Federal. Recurso Extraordinário nº 898.060/SC. Relator: Min. Luiz Fux j. 29/09/2016. *Diário da Justiça Eletrônico*, Brasília-DF, 30 set. 2016. Disponível em: http://stf.jus.br/portal/diarioJustica/verDiarioProcesso.asp?numDj=209 &dataPublicacaoDj=30/09/2016&incidente=4803092&codCapitulo=2&numMateria=29&codMateria=4. Acesso em: 20 maio 2020.

CALDERÓN, Ricardo. *Princípio da afetividade no direito de família*. 2. ed. Rio de Janeiro: Forense, 2017. *Versão digital.*

CAMPOS, Gustavo de Castro. *Alimentos avoengos*. 2015. 63 f. TCC (Graduação em Direito) – Universidade Federal do Paraná, Curitiba, 2015.

CASSETTARI, Christiano. *Multiparentalidade e parentalidade socioafetiva*: efeitos jurídicos. 3. ed. São Paulo: Atlas, 2017. *Versão digital.*

DINIZ, Maria Helena. *Curso de direito civil brasileiro*. 22. ed. São Paulo: Saraiva, 2007. v. 5.

FACHIN, Luiz Edson. *Teoria crítica do direito civil*. 3. ed. Rio de Janeiro: Renovar, 2012.

FIÚZA, César. Diretrizes hermenêuticas do direito de família. *In*: PEREIRA, Rodrigo da Cunha (coord.). *Família e dignidade humana*: V congresso brasileiro de direito de família. São Paulo: IOB Thomson, 2006. p. 223-239.

GOULART FILHO, Antônio Cezar Quevedo. *Relação avoenga*: apreensão jurídica e expressão eficacial na senda das vulnerabilidades. 2016. 195 f. Dissertação (Mestrado em Direito) – Programa de Pós-Graduação em Direito, Setor de Ciências Jurídicas, Universidade Federal do Paraná, Curitiba, 2016.

HOFFMAM, Fernando; CAVALHEIRO, Larissa Nunes; NASCIMENTO, Valéria Ribas do. O constitucionalismo principiológico como condição de possibilidade para a concretização dos direitos humano-fundamentais. *Revista Eletrônica Direito e Política*, Itajaí, v. 6, n. 1, p. 101-119, abr. 2011.

LÔBO, Paulo. *Direito civil:* direito de família. 9. ed. São Paulo: Saraiva, 2019. v. 5.

NERY, Rosa Maria de Andrade; NERY JUNIOR, Nelson. *Instituições de direito civil*: família e sucessões. 2. ed. São Paulo: Revista dos Tribunais, 2019. v. 4.

REQUIÃO, Maurício. Autonomias e suas limitações. *Revista de Direito Privado*, São Paulo, v. 60, p. 85-96, dez. 2014.

WELTER, Belmiro Pedro. Teoria tridimensional no direito de família: reconhecimento de todos os direitos das filiações genética e socioafetiva. *Revista do Ministério Público do RS*, Porto Alegre, n. 62, p. 9-25, nov. 2008/abr. 2009.

ANEXO A – Ementa do Recurso Extraordinário n. 898.060/SC

Recurso Extraordinário. Repercussão Geral reconhecida. Direito Civil e Constitucional. Conflito entre paternidades socioafetiva e biológica. Paradigma do casamento. Superação pela Constituição de 1988. Eixo central do Direito de Família: deslocamento para o plano constitucional. Sobreprincípio da dignidade humana (art. 1º, III, da CRFB). Superação de óbices legais ao pleno desenvolvimento das famílias. Direito à busca da felicidade. Princípio constitucional implícito. Indivíduo como centro do ordenamento jurídico--político. Impossibilidade de redução das realidades familiares a modelos pré-concebidos. Atipicidade constitucional do conceito de entidades familiares. União estável (art. 226, § 3º, CRFB) e família monoparental (art. 226, § 4º, CRFB). Vedação à discriminação e hierarquização entre espécies de filiação (art. 227, § 6º, CRFB). Parentalidade presuntiva, biológica ou afetiva. Necessidade de tutela jurídica ampla. Multiplicidade de vínculos parentais. Reconhecimento concomitante. Possibilidade. Pluriparentalidade. Princípio da paternidade responsável (art. 226, § 7º, CRFB). Recurso a que se nega provimento. Fixação de tese para aplicação a casos semelhantes. 1. O prequestionamento revela-se autorizado quando as instâncias inferiores abordam a matéria jurídica invocada no Recurso Extraordinário na fundamentação do julgado recorrido, tanto mais que a Súmula n. 279 desta Egrégia Corte indica que o apelo extremo deve ser apreciado à luz das assertivas fáticas estabelecidas na origem. 2. A família, à luz dos preceitos constitucionais introduzidos pela Carta de 1988, apartou-se definitivamente da vetusta distinção entre filhos legítimos, legitimados e ilegítimos que informava o sistema do Código Civil de 1916, cujo paradigma em matéria de filiação, por adotar presunção baseada na centralidade do casamento, desconsiderava tanto o critério biológico quanto o afetivo. 3. A família, objeto do deslocamento do eixo central de seu regramento normativo para o plano constitucional, reclama a reformulação do tratamento jurídico dos vínculos parentais à luz do sobreprincípio da dignidade humana (art. 1º, III, da CRFB) e da busca da felicidade. 4. A dignidade humana compreende o ser humano como um ser intelectual e moral, capaz de determinar-se e desenvolver-se em liberdade, de modo que a eleição individual dos próprios objetivos de vida tem preferência absoluta em relação a eventuais formulações legais definidoras de modelos preconcebidos, destinados a resultados eleitos a priori pelo legislador. Jurisprudência do Tribunal Constitucional alemão (BVerfGE 45, 187). 5. A superação de óbices legais ao pleno desenvolvimento das famílias construídas pelas relações afetivas interpessoais dos próprios indivíduos é corolário do sobreprincípio da dignidade humana. 6. O direito à busca da felicidade, implícito ao art. 1º, III, da Constituição, ao tempo que eleva o indivíduo à centralidade do ordenamento jurídico-político, reconhece as suas capacidades de autodeterminação, autossuficiência e liberdade de escolha dos próprios objetivos, proibindo que o governo se imiscua nos meios eleitos pelos cidadãos para a persecução das vontades particulares. Precedentes da Suprema Corte dos Estados Unidos da América e deste Egrégio Supremo Tribunal Federal: RE 477.554-AgR, Rel. Min. Celso de Mello, DJe de 26/08/2011; ADPF 132, Rel. Min. Ayres Britto, DJe de 14/10/2011. 7. O indivíduo jamais pode ser reduzido a mero instrumento de consecução das vontades dos governantes, por isso que o direito à busca da felicidade protege o ser humano em face de tentativas do Estado de enquadrar a sua realidade familiar em modelos pré-concebidos pela lei. 8. A Constituição de 1988, em caráter meramente exemplificativo, reconhece como legítimos modelos de família independentes do casamento, como a união estável (art. 226, § 3º) e a comunidade formada por qualquer dos pais e seus descendentes, cognominada "família monoparental" (art. 226, § 4º), além de enfatizar que espécies de filiação dissociadas do matrimônio entre os pais merecem equivalente tutela diante da lei, sendo vedada discriminação e, portanto, qualquer tipo de hierarquia entre elas (art. 227, § 6º). 9. As uniões estáveis homoafetivas, consideradas pela jurisprudência desta Corte como entidade familiar, conduziram à imperiosidade da interpretação não-reducionista do conceito de família como instituição que também se forma por vias distintas do casamento civil (ADI nº. 4277, Relator(a): Min. AYRES BRITTO, Tribunal Pleno, julgado em 05/05/2011). 10. A compreensão jurídica cosmopolita das famílias exige a ampliação da tutela normativa a todas as formas pelas quais a parentalidade pode se manifestar, a saber: (i) pela presunção decorrente do casamento ou outras hipóteses legais, (ii) pela descendência biológica ou (iii) pela afetividade. 11. A evolução científica responsável pela popularização do exame de DNA conduziu ao reforço de importância do critério biológico, tanto para fins de filiação quanto para concretizar o direito fundamental à busca da identidade genética, como natural emanação do direito de personalidade de um ser. 12. A afetividade enquanto critério, por sua vez, gozava de aplicação por doutrina e jurisprudência desde o Código Civil de 1916 para evitar situações de extrema injustiça, reconhecendo-se a posse do estado de filho, e consequentemente o vínculo parental, em favor daquele utilizasse o nome da família (nominatio), fosse tratado como filho pelo pai (tractatio) e gozasse do reconhecimento da sua condição de descendente pela comunidade (reputatio). 13. A paternidade responsável, enunciada expressamente no art. 226, § 7º, da Constituição, na perspectiva da dignidade humana e da busca pela felicidade, impõe o acolhimento, no espectro legal, tanto dos vínculos de filiação construídos pela relação afetiva entre os envolvidos, quanto daqueles originados da ascendência biológica, sem que seja necessário decidir entre um ou outro vínculo quando o melhor interesse do descendente for o reconhecimento jurídico de ambos. 14. A pluriparentalidade, no Direito Comparado, pode ser exemplificada pelo conceito de "dupla paternidade" (dual paternity), construído pela Suprema Corte do Estado da Louisiana, EUA, desde a década de 1980 para atender, ao mesmo tempo, ao melhor interesse da criança e ao direito do genitor à declaração da paternidade. Doutrina. 15. Os arranjos familiares alheios à regulação estatal, por omissão, não podem restar ao desabrigo da proteção a situações de pluriparentalidade, por isso que merecem tutela jurídica concomitante, para todos os fins de direito, os vínculos parentais de origem afetiva e biológica, a fim de prover a mais completa e adequada tutela aos sujeitos envolvidos, ante os princípios constitucionais da dignidade da pessoa humana (art. 1º, III) e da paternidade responsável (art. 226, § 7º). 16. Recurso Extraordinário a que se nega provimento, fixando-se a seguinte tese jurídica para aplicação a casos semelhantes: "A paternidade socioafetiva, declarada ou não em registro público, não impede o reconhecimento do vínculo de filiação concomitante baseado na origem biológica, com os efeitos jurídicos próprios".

DO INSTITUTO DA LESÃO: APLICABILIDADE E PRINCÍPIOS NORTEADORES

LUIZ ALFREDO ANGELICO SOARES CABRAL*

INTRODUÇÃO

O instituto da lesão sempre esteve presente nas sociedades, independentemente das épocas e países. Apesar de sua difícil aplicação o instituto da lesão é um instrumento poderoso e atualíssimo no sistema jurídico pátrio e se contada a infinidade de contratos e negócios que são firmados todos os dias na nossa sociedade moderna e o risco de ocorrência de vícios de consentimento o Código Civil traz os institutos e as ferramentas de correção. O objetivo do presente trabalho é identificar e conceituar os princípios mais relevantes que norteiam o instituto da lesão.

É a base principiológica do instituto da lesão que permitirá a intérpretes e aplicadores do Direito a sua utilização cada vez mais frequente e efetiva no ordenamento jurídico pátrio. Afinal, difícil é sua aplicabilidade, mas o instituto da lesão se mostrou um essencial instrumento para atingirmos a equidade e a justiça.

1. DA APLICABILIDADE DA LESÃO NO ORDENAMENTO JURÍDICO

Caso ocorra nas relações entre particulares a lesão, cabe ao magistrado, quando acionado, restabelecer a igualdade ou corrigir a injustiça, pois a justiça é regra universal. Não devemos esquecer a afirmativa de Aristóte-

* Mestre em Direito pela PUC-SP. Advogado.

les: "O magistrado é um guardião da justiça e, portanto, também guardião da igualdade".[1] A aplicação da lesão está intrinsecamente ligada à aplicação da justiça. Não podemos aplicá-la conforme a conveniência, variável no desenrolar histórico do homem, pelas mais variadas "justificativas"[2]: "estabilidade econômica", "sustentação dos valores econômicos", "estabilidade das relações jurídicas", "favorecimento da classe dominante em detrimento do mais fraco" ou melhor, o mais atual "favorecimento do desenvolvimento econômico", etc., os quais tem lugar em detrimento da justiça finalidade do direito.

Necessário se faz lembrar as lições de Aristóteles: "As coisas que são justas apenas em virtude da convenção e da conveniência assemelham-se a medidas, pois as medidas para o vinho e para o trigo não são iguais em toda parte, mas maiores nos mercados atacadistas e menores nos retalhistas. Da mesma maneira, as coisas que são justas não por natureza, mas por decisão humana, não são as mesmas em todos os lugares, uma vez que as próprias constituições não são as mesmas, embora haja apenas uma que é, por natureza, a melhor em todos os lugares. Cada uma das regras de justiça se relaciona com as coisas justas e legítimas como o universal se relaciona com os seus casos particulares, pois as coisas praticadas são muitas, ao passo que cada regra é universal."[3]

Desde o surgimento do homem e da sociedade a desigualdade e a injustiça sempre existiram em detrimento dos mais fracos, independentemente da classe dominante da época: seja religiosa, econômica, política etc. A verdade universal é que a maior parte dos homens, quando está em posição de domínio, luta para não perdê-lo. Cabe aos homens que têm esta percepção de consciência reverter essas injustiças, não se deixando enganar por falsas doutrinas, normalmente convenientes aos "poderosos" da vez.

Lembrando ensinamento de San Tiago Dantas, em sua teoria dos contratos, mencionado por Edvaldo Brito: "a proteção a hipossuficientes independe dos particularismos de cada época e sociedade por encarnar a universalidade e a racionalidade que lhe têm permitido adaptar-se a novas exigências econômicas, sobretudo – citando Josserand – na 'proteção social

[1] Aristóteles, *Ética a Nicômaco*, São Paulo, Martin Claret, 2002, p.116.

[2] As "justificativas" as quais nos referirmos acima são baseadas em premissas "relativamente" verdadeiras, para justificarem alguma finalidade interessante a algum "grupo dominante", ou seja, para não aplicarem ou desvirtuarem a aplicação da finalidade do direito, que é a justiça.

[3] Aristóteles, *Ética a Nicômaco*, cit., p.118.

dos mais fracos, destinada que é a corrigir as consequências desumanas do liberalismo jurídico – favorecendo o empregado em relação ao empregador; o devedor em relação ao credor; o inquilino em relação ao senhorio; a vítima em relação ao autor do dano ou ao seu responsável indireto; o consumidor em relação ao fornecedor.' ".[4] Mas não devemos esquecer que esta proteção é concedida somente às "vítimas" deste liberalismo jurídico, e não a todas as pessoas que se enquadrarem em determinada categoria, acima mencionada, pois a aplicação cega do direito gera injustiças. Favorecer em todas as demandas o devedor, o consumidor, o empregado e etc., também seria injusto, pois a desigualdade não deve ser presumida, mas verificada.

Concordamos com a afirmativa de Caio Mario da Silva Pereira, quanto à timidez da aplicação do instituto da lesão nos tribunais: "Não me faltou a ilustração jurisprudencial que bem revela a timidez (e até mesmo a repulsa) de nossos tribunais na aceitação do instituto (ao contrário do que se passa na França, segundo o testemunho de Weill e Terré (*Droit Civil*, vol.3, *Obligations*, nº204). Neste caso, não é mal advertir que o instituto da LESÃO nasceu sob o signo da equidade, e que há de sobreviver no propósito de reprimir a exploração de um contratante pelo outro, incutindo na vida negocial o respeito pela eternidade filosófica da regra moral, em um mundo cada vez mais egoísta."[5]

2. DO INSTITUTO DA LESÃO NO CÓDIGO CIVIL

2.1. CONCEITO, FUNDAMENTOS E NATUREZA JURÍDICA

O conceito da lesão é descrito com certa unifomidade, por inúmeros doutrinadores, a maioria da enfase ao elemento objetivo da lesão, dando mais importância para desproporção das prestações, do que ao elemento subjetivo, inexperiência, necessidade, etc.. Para Renan Lotufo[6]: "A lesão é caracterizada com uma situação de desequilíbrio entre a prestação e a contraprestação, grave, que autoriza o prejudicado a anular o negócio, pela simples existência de *lesão*.". Silvio Rodrigues[7] entende: "A lesão, na forma como a define Demontès, é o prejuízo que um contratante experi-

[4] Orlando Gomes, *Raízes históricas e sociológicas do código civil brasileiro*, São Paulo, Martins Fontes, 2003, p. XIV.

[5] Caio Mario da Silva Pereira, *Lesão nos contratos*, 6ª edição, Rio de Janeiro, Forense, 2001, p.VIII.

[6] Renan Lotufo, *Código Civil Comentado*, São Paulo, Saraiva, 2003, vol.1, p.439.

[7] Silvio Rodrigues, *Dos vícios de consentimento*, São Paulo, Saraiva, 1989, p.209.

menta quando, em contrato comutativo, não recebe, da outra parte, valor igual ao da prestação que forneceu.". Para Darcy Berssone[8]: "A lesão é o prejuízo que, nos contratos comutativos, resulta da desproporção das prestações reciprocamente prometidas pelos contratantes.". Outros também incluem na definição elementos subjetivos.

Segundo Maria Helena Diniz[9]: "O instituto da *lesão* visa proteger o contratante, que se encontra em posição de inferioridade, ante o prejuízo por ele sofrido na conclusão do contrato comutativo, devido à considerável desproporção existente, no momento da efetivação do contrato, entre as prestações das duas partes.". Hélio Borghi[10] ensina: "(...) a lesão é vista atualmente pelas legislações mais modernas que a acolhe em sua forma que conjuga os elementos objetivos e subjetivos, pode-se, num primeiro ensaio, definí-la como sendo uma proteção posta à disposição por essas legislações, no sentido de ser considerado nulo, ou de ser anulado, um ato ou negócio jurídico, de caráter comutativo, em que as prestações devidas pelas partes, no momento da celebração da avença, não sejam proporcionais em relação ao quanto que tais legislações fixem, ou ao arbitrado por juiz, e que tal desproporção seja originada da inexperiência, leviandade ou estado de necessidade da parte lesada na avença, podendo tal anulação ser evitada com a complementação do preço ao valor real, ou, se o lesado for o comprador que pagou mais pelo que valia menos (observando-se os mesmos pressupostos), a devolução, pela parte a que aproveitou a desproporção, do equivalente ao excesso do justo preço, podendo tal complementação ou devolução ser diminuída ou acrescida de um décimo do valor.".

Observamos que a existência do instituto da lesão na evolução do tempo está ligado a inconformidade do ser humano em ser lesado, estando intrinsecamente ligado a justiça e a equidade, pois a injustiça não deixa de ser imoral e a boa-fé nas relações contratuais e genericamente nas relações humanas é condição *sine qua non* para o convívio social. O liberalismo individualista e a prevalência da autonomia da vontade, levado ao extremismo racionalista, demonstrou-se um excelente instrumento para o cometimento de injustiças, pois o "racionalismo cego" ausente de humanidade e espiritualidade demonstra a limitação existencial da nossa espécie.

[8] Darcy Bessone, *Do contrato teoria geral*, 4ª edição, São Paulo, Saraiva, 1997, p.205.

[9] Maria Helena Diniz, *Curso de direito civil brasileiro,* São Paulo, Saraiva, 2005, v.1, p.451.

[10] Hélio Borghi, *A lesão no direito civil,* São Paulo, Leud, 1998, p.22.

O Código Civil de 10 de janeiro de 2002, refere-se a **lesão especial** ou lesão-vício, admitindo a aplicação da mesma fundada no artigo 157, e §§ 1º e 2º:

> *"Art. 157. Ocorre lesão quando uma pessoa, sob premente necessidade, ou por inexperiência, se obriga a prestação manifestamente desproporcional ao valor da prestação oposta.*
>
> *§1º Aprecia-se a desproporção das prestações segundo os valores vigentes ao tempo em que foi celebrado o negócio jurídico.*
>
> *§2º Não se decretará a anulação do negócio, se for oferecido suplemento suficiente, ou se a parte favorecida concordar com a redução do proveito."*

Desprendemos pela redação do dispositivo legal acima transcrito, que ocorrerá a lesão quando uma pessoa, sob premente necessidade e por leviandade ou inexperiência, face uma situação de desigualdade (elemento subjetivo), obriga-se a prestações nitidamente desproporcionais (elemento objetivo). Segundo Maria Helena Diniz[11]: "É um vício de consentimento decorrente do abuso praticado em situação de desigualdade de um dos contratantes, por estar sob premente necessidade, ou por inexperiência, visando protegê-lo, ante o prejuízo sofrido na conclusão do contrato, devido à desproporção existente entre as prestações das duas partes, dipensando-se a verificação do dolo, ou má-fé, da parte que se aproveitou.".

Para Humberto Theodoro Júnior[12]: "A lesão que o novo Código admite como vício de consentimento para gerar a anulabilidade consiste na hipótese em que a pactuação do negócio tenha sido fruto de premente necessidade ou de inexperiência de uma das partes, circunstâncias que foram determinantes das prestações avençadas de maneira manifestamente desproporcional."[13]

A natureza jurídica da lesão, conforme verificado, constitui vício do negócio jurídico, para que ocorra a realização do negócio jurídico é essen-

[11] Maria Helena Diniz, *Código civil anotado,* São Paulo, Saraiva, 2002, p.148.

[12] Humberto Theodoro Júnior, *Comentários ao novo código cívil*, Rio de Janeiro, Forense, 2003, vol.III, tomo I, p.225.

[13] Maria Helena Diniz, *Curso de direito civil brasileiro,* cit., v.1, p.398 à 403; Maria Helena Diniz, *Código civil,* cit., p.148/149; Renan Lotufo, *Código Civil Comentado,* cit., p.434 à 443; Marcelo Guerra Martins, *Lesão contratual no direito brasileiro,* São Paulo, Renovar, 2001, p.95 à 109; Humberto Theodoro Júnior, *Comentários ao novo código ,cit.*, p.225.

cial a manifestação de vontade. Ensina Maria Helena Diniz[14]: "Toda doutrina é unânime em salientar que a declaração da vontade é elemento essencial do negócio jurídico. Para que este validamente exista, é indispensável a presença da vontade e que esta haja funcionado normalmente. Só então o negócio produz os efeitos jurídicos colimados pelas partes. Tanto isso é verdade que se a vontade for inexistente o negócio jurídico existe apenas de fato na aparência, mas não no mundo jurídico, pois será nulo". Mas não é pacífica esta ideia, pois observa Darcy Bessone que quando a vontade existe, mas não reflete com aquela que o agente exteriorizar, o negócio jurídico será viciado, ocorrendo assim, os vícios de consentimento, como o erro, o dolo, a coação, o estado de perigo e a lesão, que estão fundados no desequilíbrio da atuação volitiva relativamente a sua declaração, ou seja, a vontade real não corresponde a vontade declarada. Para Washington de Barros Monteiro[15] o "negócio jurídico é manifestação da vontade tendente a criar, modificar ou extinguir um direito. A vontade é, pois, base e fundamento do ato, sua razão de ser, a alma do negócio jurídico.".

A maioria dos autores considera a lesão um vício de consentimento, conforme acima mencionado, mas destacamos algumas opiniões diversas. Para Renan Lotufo[16]: "É muito discutido o enquadramento da lesão como defeito do negócio, pois, estabelecido o acordo de vontades, aparentemente o negócio está perfeito e acabado, sendo anulável tão-só por uma *correção social* ao desequilíbrio do contrato.". Roberto Senise Lisboa[17] afirma, por sua vez, que "muitos colocam indevidamente a lesão como vício de consentimento, ao lado do erro, dolo ou coação, salientando haver nela declaração de vontade viciada. Não se confunde, todavia, com quaisquer dos vícios aludidos. Enquanto nestes se verifica uma desconformidade entre a vontade real e sua declaração exteriorizada, na lesão ocorre a desproporção da prestação.", pois qualifica a lesão como sendo um instituto próximo dos atos ilícitos.

Já Darcy Bersone[18] invoca "razões de humanidade ou considerações de equidade. Parece que é a melhor explicação. A teoria dos vícios de consen-

14 Maria Helena Diniz, *Curso de direito civil brasileiro,* cit., v.1, p.430.

15 Washington de Barros Monteiro, *Curso de direito civil – parte geral,* v.1, São Paulo, Saraiva, 2003, p.219.

16 Renan Lotufo, *Código Civil Comentado,* cit., p.440.

17 Roberto Senise Lisboa, *Contornos atuais da teoria dos contratos* – A lesão nos contratos, *in Revista dos Tribunais, s/d,* São Paulo, p.64.

18 Darcy Bessone, *Do contrato,* cit., p.210/211.

timento, a da causa, a do enriquecimento ilícito, a do abuso de direito só podem ter aplicação quando se apresentem os elementos que as caracterizam. Entretanto, em muitas oportunidades, sem que, a rigor, concorram esses elementos, configuram-se situações de injustiça manifesta, para as quais a equidade reclama uma solução, que, precisamente por não concorrerem as características que as singularizam, não pode ser por elas fornecida.".

Apesar das interessantes posições opostas consideramos a lesão como um dos vícios de consentimento, pois todo negócio jurídico está alicerçado na manifestação de vontade, sendo esta, o principal suporte para a validade do negócio jurídico, estando a vontade viciada também estará o negócio. O Código Civil brasileiro prevê a lesão (artigo 157) como um dos vícios de consentimento, estando previstos também o erro (artigo 138 e seguintes), o dolo (artigo 145 e seguintes), a coação (artigo 151 e seguintes) e o estado de perigo (artigo 156), temos ainda, os vícios sociais, como a simulação (artigo 167, *caput*) e a fraude contra credores (artigo 171,II, *in fine* e artigo 178,II), que ocorre quando a vontade funciona normalmente, ou seja, a vontade interna corresponde com sua manifestação, mas ela desvia da lei e da boa-fé, infringindo direito e prejudicando terceiros, comprometendo a ordem jurídica pela afronta à lisura, à honestidade e à regularidade do comércio jurídico, nas palavras de Washington de Barros Monteiro[19] a "simulação e fraude contra credores, rigorosamente falando, não são vícios da vontade. Com mais precisão, diríamos que são vícios sociais, comprometedores da ordem jurídica, pela deliberada afronta à lisura, à honestidade e à regularidade do comércio jurídico.".

Lembramos, ainda, que os vícios sociais não se confundem com a lesão especial, elencada nos vícios de consentimento, pois se dá nos casos em que a vontade do contratante atua de modo essencial e absoluto para a formação do ato ou negócio jurídico. A seguir faremos uma breve comparação e a distinção da lesão especial e os demais vícios de consentimento, como também sua diferenciação dos vícios sociais:

a) **erro ou ingnorância e lesão** – no erro necessariamente não importa a vantagem excessiva da parte, mas a falsa percepção dos fatos ou seu desconhecimento, por fator externo, que interfere na vontade

[19] Washington de Barros Monteiro, *Curso de direito civil*, cit.,v.1, p.220.

do indivíduo. Maria Helena Diniz[20] ensina: "Num sentido geral erro é uma noção inexata, não verdadeira sobre alguma coisa, objeto ou pessoa, que influencia a formação da vontade" e a ingorância é "a ausência completa de conhecimento sobre algo (...) o legislador os equiparou nos seus efeitos jurídicos". Segundo Washington de Barros Monteiro[21]: "Ignorância é o completo deconhecimento acerca de um objeto. Erro é a noção falsa a respeito desse mesmo objeto ou de determinada pessoa. Por outras palavras, na primeira, a mente está *in albis*; na segunda, o que nela está registrado é falso.". Somente o erro substancial (artigo 138), que qualquer pessoa capaz e inteligente poderia cometer, levará a anulabilidade do negócio jurídico, pois o erro acidental, relativo a quantidade e qualidade, não gera anulabilidade. Já na lesão independentemente do elemento subjetivo, que é essencial no erro (devido a falsa noção de uma realidade negocial), verifica-se a desproporção das prestações, podendo inclusive conter elementos subjetivos de necessidade e inexperiência;

b) **dolo e lesão** – o dolo ocorre por qualquer ato positivo ou negativo do agente, através do emprego de artifício ou expediente astucioso, buscando prejudicar ou auferir vantagem ilícita para si ou terceiro. Segundo Clóvis Bevilaqua[22]: "Dolo é o artifício ou expediente astucioso, empregado para induzir alguém à prática de um ato, que o prejudica, e aproveita o autor do dolo ou terceiro.". O dolo pode ser **principal** (artigo 145), quando atingir causa determinante para realização do ato ou negócio jurídico, sem o qual não teria ocorrido, acarretando sua anulabilidade, ou **acidental** (artigo 146), quando leva a vítima a realizar o ato ou negócio jurídico, porém em condições menos vantajosas, não afetando sua declaração de vontade, embora provoque desvios, não acarreta anulação do contrato, mas acarreta em perdas e danos ou em uma redução da prestação acordada. Quanto a sua gravidade, pode ser dolo *bonus* ou *malus*, podendo o primeiro ser tolerado e o segundo pode causar a anulabilidade do negócio jurídico. No dolo, face ao ardil de uma das partes, a outra não está plenamente consciente do negócio que realiza,

[20] Maria Helena Diniz, *Curso de direito civil brasileiro,* cit., v.1, p.431/432.
[21] Washington de Barros Monteiro, *Curso de direito civil,* cit.,v.1, p.220.
[22] Clóvis Bevilaqua, *Comentários ao Código Civil,* Rio de Janeiro, 1927, p.363.

conforme acima exposto, na lesão deverá ocorrer a desproporção entre as prestações, podendo estar aliada à premente necessidade e a inexperiência.;

c) **coação e lesão** – a "coação seria qualquer pressão física ou moral exercida sobre a pessoa, os bens ou a honra de um contratante para obrigá-lo ou induzi-lo a efetivar negócio jurídico[23]". Ocorre a coação física ou *vis absoluta*, quando o constrangimento corporal retira toda a capacidade da pessoa, implicando ausência total de consentimento, o que acarreta a nulidade do ato, não se tratando de vício de vontade. Já a coação moral ou *vis compulsiva* (artigos 171,II e 178, I), atua sobre a vontade da vítima sem aniquilar o consentimento, pois conserva uma liberdade relativa, embora maculada a vontade, podendo acarretar a anulabilidade do negócio jurídico ou optar pela realização do mesmo, sendo indenizado por perdas e danos. Na coação a vontade está inibida, podendo ser considerada como inexistente, o que não ocorre na lesão, pois a vontade está presente.;

d) **estado de perigo e lesão**- no estado de perigo (artigo 156) "haverá temor de iminente e grave dano moral (direto ou indireto) ou material, ou seja, patrimonial indireto à pessoa ou a algum parente seu que compele o declarante a concluir contrato, mediante prestação exorbitante[24]", ou seja, no estado de perigo, o contratante que se aproveita desta situação deverá estar ciente que está se aproveitando desta situação, enquanto na lesão, haverá a desproporção da prestações, podendo ser causada pela premente necessidade, em virtude de **risco patrimonial** relativo a algum dano material (falência, ruína negocial, etc.) ou até mesmo em virtude de um **risco pessoal** (perigo de vida; lesão a saúde, à integridade física ou psíquica, etc) que diminui a capacidade de disposição livre e consciente, na lesão não há necessidade do conhecimento do contratante, que vem a se aproveitar do negócio. Lembramos que ambos os atos podem ser praticados em estado de necessidade. Quanto aos vícios sociais:

   a) **simulação e lesão** – na simulação ocorre a falsa manifestação da vontade, declarando o que não é verdadeiro, pretendendo preju-

[23] Maria Helena Diniz, *Curso de direito civil brasileiro,* cit., v.1, p.447.

[24] Maria Helena Diniz, *Curso de direito civil brasileiro,* cit., v.1, p.455.

dicar terceiros, na lesão não se busca esconder ou alcançar interesses diversos, para prejudicar terceiros, não há esta intenção.;

b) **fraude contra credores e lesão** – "Diz-se haver fraude contra credores, quando o devedor insolvente, ou na iminência de tornar-se tal, pratica atos suscetíveis de diminuir seu patrimônio, reduzindo, desse modo, a garantia que este representa, para resgate de suas dívidas.[25]". Notamos que a lesão difere da fraude contra credores, pois não tem a intenção de prejudicar terceiro.

Conforme observamos, a lesão é um vício de consentimento, que gera defeito no negócio jurídico, diverso dos demais vícios de consentimento (erro, dolo, coação e estado de perigo) e dos vícios sociais (simulação e fraude contra credores). Concordamos com Humberto Theodoro Júnior[26] quando afirma "todas as figuras do vício de consentimento passam pelo terreno da boa-fé e da probidade negocial (artigo 177)".[27]

2.2. ELEMENTOS E CARACTERES DA LESÃO

Conforme conceituado pelo artigo 157 acima referido, existem dois elementos que configuram a lesão, o elemento objetivo (desproporção das prestações) e os elementos subjetivos (premente necessidade, inexperiência ou leviandade).

O elemento objetivo da lesão se refere ao princípio da equivalência das prestações, pois o contrato deve ser justo e moral, não devendo haver desproporções exageradas. Segundo Maria Helena Diniz[28]: "O Código Civil, por referir-se à *lesão especial* ou lesão-vício, dispensa, por sua vez, como vimos, a verificação e a prova do dolo da parte que tirou proveito com a lesão, ordenando a anulabilidade ou a possibilidade de complementação contratual, bastando, para tanto, que haja prejuízo (desproporção das prestações – requisito objetivo), prova da ocorrência do ato em caso de premência de necessidade, leviandade ou por inexperiência (requisito

[25] Silvio Rodrigues, *Direito civil- parte geral,* São Paulo, Saraiva, 2003, v.1, p.228.

[26] Humberto Theodoro Júnior, *Comentários ao novo código ,cit.* , p.241.

[27] Marcelo Guerra Martins, *Lesão,* cit., p.95 à 109; Hélio Borghi, *A lesão,* cit., p.30 à 35; Arnaldo Rizzardo,*Da ineficácia dos atos jurídicos e da lesão no direito,* Rio de Janeiro, Forense, 1983, p.108 à 112; Roberto Senise Lisboa, *Contornos,* cit., p.64 à 66; Maria Helena Diniz, *Curso de direito civil brasileiro,* cit., v.1, p.428 à 472.

[28] Maria Helena Diniz, *Curso de direito civil brasileiro,* cit., v.1, p.454.

subjetivo). Daí ser a lesão objetiva, pois, juridicamente, pouco importará o fato de o outro contratante ter, ou não, conhecimento das condições de necessidade ou inexperiência da vítima. Não será preciso comprovação que houve dolo de aproveitamento (intuito de obter vantagem excessiva da situação do lesado) por parte de quem tirou proveito".

Esta desproporção das prestações, ocorrendo lesão deverá ser apreciada segundo os valores vigentes ao tempo da celebração do negócio jurídico pela técnica pericial e avaliada pelo magistrado. Humberto Theodoro Júnior[29] explica o critério a ser adotado pelo juiz, para averiguar a desproporção entre as prestações: "adota-se um conceito vago, cujo conteúdo haverá de ser completado, caso a caso, pelo juiz, segundo prudente arbítrio, à luz da boa-fé, da equidade e dos usos e costumes". Se a desproporcionaldade for superveniente à formação do negócio, será juridicamente irrelevante.

A avaliação da desproporção estre as prestações, exige o Código, deve ser feita "segundo os valores vigentes ao tempo em que foi celebrado o negócio jurídico" (artigo 157,§ 2º). Entendemos que o legislador foi feliz ao excluir o tarifamento da lesão, mencionando apenas no texto legal a expressão "prestação manifestamente desproporcional ao valor da prestação oposta"(artigo 157, *caput*), deixando ao arbítrio do juiz no caso concreto avaliar a ocorrência ou não da lesão. Concordamos com as palavras de Caio Mário da Silva Pereira[30] quando afirma: "Mas é evidente que o recurso ao tarifamento não satisfaz, por não comportar a variedade enorme das convenções humanas.

Não há dúvida que certos tipos de contrato comportam perfeitamente o tabelamento das prestações. É muito simples dizer que na compra e venda o desfazimento do ato está sujeito à verificação, se o vendedor deu por menos de metade a coisa sua. Aqui a dificuldade estará apenas na prova do valor exato, ou à sua falta na aferição do valor corrente do bem no momento da venda. Mas, na sociedade moderna este não é propriamente um problema. A multiplicidade dos negócios é tão grande, e sua publicidade tão frequente (registro imobiliário, registro de documentos, cotação da bolsa, lançamento tributário, registro em livros comerciais etc.) que a estimativa não se apresenta revestida de dificuldade absoluta.". Mas há inúmeras convenções nas quais o tarifamento torna-se impossível, face ao

[29] Humberto Theodoro Júnior, *Comentários ao novo código ,cit.* , p.227.

[30] Caio Mario da Silva Pereira, *Lesão,* cit., p.111.

objeto da prestação, em relação às partes contratantes, ou edições de leis econômicas que podem alterar determinada contratação, realidades estas que o universo jurídico não pode ignorar[31].

Quanto aos elementos subjetivos dizem respeito ao estado psicológico das partes, ante ao estado de "premente necessidade", "inexperiência" ou "leviandade". A "premente necessidade" pode "advir da iminência de um dano patrimonial, como urgência de evitar processo falimentar, mas nem sempre está ligada a condições econômico-financeiras, pois poderá dizer respeito à impossibilidade, em razão da situação em que a pessoa se encontra, de evitar a efetivação de um dado contrato" ou seja, o lesado encontra-se precionado e debilitado para agir. Nas palavras de Humberto Theodoro Júnior[32] "*necessidade premente* deve-se entender a que provém de imperativos tanto de ordem material como de ordem espiritual".

A "inexperiência" não se "refere a falta de cultura ou mesmo erudição mas a familiaridade do mundo negocial[33]". Segundo Caio Mário[34]: "inexperiência não quer dizer incultura, pois que um homem erudito, letrado, inteligente, muitas vezes se acha, em contraposição com o co-contratante arguto, na situação de não perceber bem o alcance do contrato que faz, por escapar aquilo à sua atividade comum". A inexperiência contratual deverá ser auferida face a natureza da transação e a pessoa da outra parte. Humberto Theodoro Júnior[35], ensina que "quando a lesão tenha sido motivada por *inexperiência* da parte, há um *déficit* na formação da vontade. (...) O dado é concreto e deve ser analisado como falta de prática no terreno em que o contrato se consumou. Pode, assim, uma pessoa do comércio apresentar-se como inexperiente quando se dispõe a aferir as condições do contrato estranho ao seu *métier*".

A "leviandade" ocorre quando não houve uma necessária reflexão em torno das consequências da avença. Segundo Caio Mario[36]: "será a incúria, a indiferença, o descaso pelas consequências que possam advir do ato".[37]

[31] Caio Mario da Silva Pereira, *Lesão*, cit., p.112.

[32] Humberto Theodoro Júnior, *Comentários ao novo código ,cit.* , p.228.

[33] Marcelo Guerra Martins, *Lesão*, cit., p.89-90.

[34] Caio Mario da Silva Pereira, *Lesão*, cit., p.167.

[35] Humberto Theodoro Júnior, *Comentários ao novo código ,cit.* , p.228.

[36] Caio Mario da Silva Pereira, *Lesão*, cit., p.167.

[37] Marcelo Guerra Martins, *Lesão*, cit., p.80 à 95; Maria Helena Diniz, *Curso de direito civil brasileiro*, cit., v.1, p.453-454; Maria Helena Diniz, *Código civil*, cit., p.148/149; Humberto

2.3. PRINCÍPIOS INSPIRADORES PARA CONFIGURAÇÃO DO INSTITUTO DA LESÃO NO BRASIL

A lesão atualmente está inspirada pelos institutos e princípios abordados abaixo, que se trata de institutos eminentemente protetivos, na medida em que buscam um equilíbrio contratual. O rol abaixo não é taxativo e estudaremos os principais, princípios, quais sejam, da boa-fé objetiva, da probidade, da comutatividade ou equivalência das prestações, da autonomia da vontade, das limitações da disponibilidade contratual em face da edição de normas de ordem pública e dos bons costumes e o da função social do contrato como diretriz fundamental.

Lembramos as palavras de Maria Helena Diniz[38] quando afirma que: "Todos os princípios contratuais estão ligados ao do respeito e proteção à dignidade da pessoa humana (CF, art.1º, III), dando tutela jurídica aos contratantes, para que se efetivem a função social da propriedade (CC, art.1.118, §1º), a do contrato (CC, art.421) e a justiça social (CF, art.170)".

2.3.1. PRINCÍPIOS DA BOA-FÉ OBJETIVA E DA PROBIDADE

O princípio da **boa-fé objetiva**[39] tem como característica uma atuação positiva, pois visa o interesse social de segurança nas relações jurídicas, devendo as partes agirem com lealdade, honestidade, honradez, coragem e confiança recíproca, e com transparência, procurando o equilíbrio das prestações e impedindo o enriquecimento indevido, e, na interpretação do contrato deverá prevalecer a intenção da declaração de vontade das partes, e não seu sentido literal, pois é pedra basilar das relações contratuais.

Theodoro Júnior, *Comentários ao novo código ,cit.* , p.226 à 231; Renan Lotufo, *Código Civil Comentado,* cit., p.440 à 443.

[38] Maria Helena Diniz, *Curso de direito civil brasileiro,* São Paulo, Saraiva, vol 3., 21ªedição, p.44.

[39] Apesar de não haver unanimidade quanto à diferenciação ontológica de boa-fé objetiva e boa-fé subjetiva, Laerte Marrone de Castro Sampaio (*A boa-fé objetiva na relação contratual,* São Paulo, Manole, 2004, p.26) informa sobre a diferenciação proposta por António Manuel da Rocha Menezes de Cordeiro (*Direito das obrigações,* v.1, Lisboa, Associação Acadêmica da Faculdade de Direito de Lisboa, 1986, p.126/132.) a seguir expressa: "A boa-fé, enquanto norma de conduta, pode ser acatada ou não, pelos particulares. Quando se verifique o seu acatamento, a situação jurídica do sujeito em causa é caracterizada pela conformidade com a boa fé objectiva, podendo, assim, considerar-se, ela própria como sendo uma situação jurídica de boa fé e estando o sujeito considerado de boa-fé. É a boa fé do sujeito ou boa fé subjectiva. Pelo contrário, quando os sujeito não acate o Direito objectivo em sede de boa fé, isto é, a boa fé objectiva, a sua situação jurídica caracterizar-se-á, nesse ponto, pela não boa-fé, ou, na linguagem consagrada, pela má fé. Esta, obviamente, não pode ser senão subjectiva.".

Segundo Karl Larenz[40], a boa fé objetiva consiste num elemento ético-social, fundada na ideia da confiança entre as pessoas, para uma convivência em sociedade próspera e pacífica. Já Fernando Noronha[41] entende que o conteúdo da boa-fé objetiva está pautado nas noções de lealdade e confiança, ou seja, em outras palavras, no "dever de lealdade de uma parte, expectativa de confiança da contraparte".

Este princípio deverá ser instrínseco em todas as relações jurídicas, constituindo, segundo Français Gorphe[42], o "dever moral de não enganar outrem", no campo dos contratos, "baseados essencialmente sobre a justa equivalência dos direitos e a reciprocidade das obrigações". Caio Mário da Silva Pereira lembra que, em Roma, estava em toda parte, respondendo com a pureza do seu direito, associando-se à força criadora do *aequitas,* trazendo sentido de humanidade ao *ius romanum,* inspirando-o, na grandeza de sua floração, a boa-fé nos contratos, que, na época clássica, era denominada: *Bona fides quae in contractibus exigitur aequitatem summam desiderat.*

Nosso Código Comercial de 1850 expressa o princípio da boa-fé como regra de interpretação das cláusulas contratuais, estabelecendo o seguinte: "artigo 131, nº1 – Sendo necessário interpretar as cláusulas do contrato, a interpretação, além das regras sobreditas, será regulada sobre as seguintes bases: 1. a inteligência simples e adequada, que for mais conforme à boa-fé e ao verdadeiro espírito e natureza do contrato, deverá sempre prevalecer à rigorosa e restrita significação das palavras.".

O Código Civil de 1916 não fez menção expressa à boa-fé como o Código Suíço das Obrigações, apenas se refere à intenção volitiva, ao sentido literal da linguagem (artigo 85), mas, nesta busca subjetiva, é imprescindível a existência da boa-fé, pois a deslealdade no contrato, a malícia e o desacordo moral encontram repulsa no direito aplicado e dinâmico.

O Código de Defesa do Consumidor (Lei nº 8078/90) elegeu a boa-fé como um dos princípios basilares da relação de consumo, pois, em caso de relação de consumo haverá nulidade, de pleno direito, das cláusulas abusivas, desleais, ou leoninas (artigo 51, incs. I a XVI), conforme elencou Maria

[40] Karl Larenz (*Derecho civil – parte general,* Madri, Edersa, 1978, p.58/59) *apud* Laerte Marrone de Castro Sampaio (*A boa-fé objetiva,* cit., p.28).

[41] Fernando Noronha, *O direito dos contratos e seus princípios fundamentais,* São Paulo, Saraiva, 1994, p.138.

[42] François Gorphe, *Le principe de la bonne foi,* Dallaz Paris, 1928, p.45 *apud* Caio Mario da Silva Pereira, *Lesão,* cit., p.104/105.

Helena Diniz a que ora trascrevemos: "a) exonerarem ou atenuarem a responsabilidade do fornecedor por vício dos produtos ou serviços, ou transferirem sua responsabilidade a terceiro; b) quando prescreverem inversão do ônus da prova em prejuízo do consumidor; c) deixarem ao fornecedor a opção de concluir ou não o contrato, embora obrigando o consumidor; d) autorizarem o fornecedor a cancelar, modificar o contrato ou a variar o preço unilateralmente; e) possibilitarem a renúncia do direito de indenização por benfeitorias necessárias".

Entretanto, a cláusula que contiver conteúdo desleal não invalidará o contrato, nas relações de consumo, salvo quando sua ausência implicar em ônus excessivo a qualquer das partes (artigo 51,§ 2º). A interpretação do contrato deverá, ainda, respeitar o interesse social de segurança das relações jurídicas, uma vez que as partes deverão agir com lealdade e confiança recíprocas, e, a esse respeito o Código Civil, promulgado em 10 de janeiro de 2002, em seu artigo 422 estatui: "Os contratantes são obrigados a guardar, assim na conclusão do contrato, como em sua execução, os princípios de probidade e boa-fé".

Segundo Maria Helena Diniz[43], "O princípio da probidade e da boa-fé está ligado não só à interpretação do contrato, pois, segundo ele, o sentido literal da linguagem não deverá prevalecer sobre a intenção inferida da declaração de vontade das partes, mas também ao interesse social de segurança das relações jurídicas, uma vez que as partes têm o dever de agir com lealdade e confiança recíprocas, isto é, proceder com boa-fé tanto na conclusão do contrato como em sua execução, impedindo que uma dificulte a ação da outra."A boa-fé objetiva está ligada à violação positiva da obrigação contratual. O contratante que não cumprir seu dever estará transgredindo a boa-fé objetiva, independentemente de culpa.[44]

[43] Maria Helena Diniz, *Código civil*,cit., p.306.

[44] Informamos ainda a redação dos enunciados aprovados na I Jornada de Direito Civil do Conselho de Justiça Federal, realizado em 2002, relativos ao princípio da boa-fé objetiva: "24 – Art.422: em virtude do princípio da boa-fé, positivado no art.422 do novo Código Civil, a violação dos deveres anexos constitui espécie de inadimplemento, independentemente de culpa; 25- Art.422: o art.422 do Código Civil não inviabiliza a aplicação pelo julgador do princípio da boa-fé nas fases pré-contratual e pós- contratual; 26- Art.422: a cláusula geral contida no art.422 do novo Código Civil impõe ao juiz interpretar e, quando necessário, suprir e corrigir o contrato segundo a boa-fé objetiva, entendida como a exigência de comportamento leal dos contratantes; 27-Art.422: na interpretação da cláusula geral da boa-fé, deve-se levar em

O Projeto de Lei nº 6.960/02, em face das conclusões da I Jornada de Direito Civil do Conselho de Justiça Federal, procurou alterar as disposições do artigo 422, que dispõe que: "os contratantes são obrigados a guardar, tanto nas negociações preliminares e na conclusão do contrato, como na sua execução e fase pós-contratual, os princípios de probidade e boa fé e tudo mais que resultar da natureza do contrato, da lei, dos usos e das exigências da razão e da equidade, salientando, assim, a necessidade da boa-fé objetiva tanto na fase pré- contratual como na pós-contratual". Maria Helena Diniz, em relação a esse último dispositivo, menciona o parecer de Vicente Arruda, que é o seguinte: "Pela manutenção do texto, que fala em 'conclusão do contrato', que compreende a fase de negociação, elaboração, assinatura, e da sua 'execução', que compreende o cumprimento ou descuprimento das obrigações contratuais, bem como a solução dos conflitos entre as partes. Não devemos ceder à tentação de deixar tudo explícito, até mesmo o óbvio".

A boa-fé objetiva deverá ser verificada no caso concreto, após cautelosa análise dos aspectos fáticos que envolvam determinado negócio jurídico, para poder aferir a quebra da boa-fé objetiva. De acordo com Judith Martins Costa:[45] "Não é possível, efetivamente, tabular, *a priori,* o significado da valoração a ser procedida mediante a boa-fé objetiva, porque se trata de uma norma cujo conteúdo não pode ser rigidamente fixado, dependendo sempre das concretas circunstâncias do caso. Mas é, incontroversamente, regra de caráter marcadamente técnico-jurídico, porque enseja a solução dos casos particulares no quadro dos demais modelos jurídicos postos em cada ordenamento, à vista das suas particulares circunstâncias.

A solução jurídica, repito, e não de cunho moral, advindo a sua juricidade do fato de remeter e submeter a solução do caso concreto à estrutura, às normas e aos modelos do sistema, considerado este de modo aberto.". Já o artigo 187 do Código Civil, concebe a boa-fé como norma de conduta, impondo limites aos contraentes, exigindo que as partes, ao fazer valerem seus direitos, atuem com moderação. Conforme despreendemos da redação do artigo supra, e que é a seguir transcrito: "Também comete ato ilícito o titular de um direito que, ao exercê-lo, excede manifestamente os

conta o sistema do Código Civil e as conexões sistemáticas com outros estatutos normativos e fatores metajurídicos.".

[45] Judith Martins- Costa, *A boa-fé no direito privado,* São Paulo, Revista dos Tribunais, 1999, p.412/413.

limites impostos pelo seu fim econômico ou social, pela boa-fé ou pelos bons costumes". Mário Julio de Almeida Costa[46] entende abusivo o exercício do direito "sempre que a conduta do respectivo titular se revele, no caso concreto, gravemente chocante e reprovável para o sentimento ético-jurídico prevalecente na colectividade", pois não admite que o exercício de um direito contraste com o "sentimento de justiça dominante na comunidade social.".

Para Karl Larenz[47], a boa-fé é o mais importante limite para o gozo de um direito, e não é possível delimitar exaustivamente quando o exercício de um direito infringe a boa-fé. Mas descreveremos a seguir algumas categorias encontradas na doutrina[48]:

a) *venire contra factum proprium*- que expressa a ideia de que à parte não é permitido agir em contradição a um comportamento assumido anteriormente, pois sua conduta anterior gerou uma expectativa na outra parte, para que atuasse em um determinado sentido, e essa incoerência no exercício de um direito, rompe a lealdade e a confiança;
b) *supressio* – que ocorre quando o não exercício de um direito for claramente excessivo, gerando uma legítima expectativa em outra parte, constituindo uma limitação ao exercício de direito subjetivo, em razão da boa-fé objetiva. A respeito da *supressio* Judith Martins – Costa informa que, para sua configuração, se faz necessário que: "(I) o decurso de prazo sem exercício do direito com indícios objetivos de que o direito não mais seria exercido, e (II) desequilíbrio, pela ação do tempo, entre o benefício do credor e o prejuízo do devedor.";
c) *surrectio*- que utiliza o raciocínio inverso da *suppressio*, ou seja, diz respeito ao exercício de um direito, à prática reiterada de certos atos, gerando a convicção de que a outra parte possui tal direito;

[46] Mario Júlio de Almeida Costa (*Direito das obrigações*, Coimbra, Almedina, 1999, p.68/69) *apud* Laerte Marrone de Castro Sampaio (*A boa-fé objetiva*, cit., p.77).

[47] Karl Larenz (*Derecho civil*, cit., p.299/300) *apud* Laerte Marrone de Castro Sampaio (*A boa-fé objetiva*, cit., p.77/78).

[48] A classificação abaixo utilizada está descrita nas seguintes obras: Laerte Marrone de Castro Sampaio, *A boa-fé objetiva*, cit., p.78 à 84, Judith Martins- Costa, *A boa-fé*, cit., p.462 e Judith Martins- Costa e outro, *Diretrizes Teóricas do Novo Código Civil Brasileiro*, São Paulo, Saraiva, 2002, p.214 à 221; Fernando Noronha, *O direito dos contratos*, cit., p.186.

d) *tu quoque*- que veda à pessoa que viole uma norma jurídica a posterior invocação da mesma em seu favor – a *tu quoque* corresponde ao juízo mencionado no famoso brocardo romano *nemo creditur turpitudinem suam allegans*, que significa: "ninguém alcança acolhida alegando a própria torpeza";
e) abuso de nulidades por motivos formais – que ocorre nas situações em que agir com lealdade e retidão implicaria a impossibilidade da alegação de vícios quanto à forma do negócio realizado, ou seja, quando uma das partes, conhecendo o defeito de forma, cumpre negócio jurídico nulo ou aceita o cumprimento realizado pela outra parte, não podendo posteriormente questionar a validade do contrato;
f) adimplemento substancial – que significa que a boa-fé protege o contraente que cumpriu, quase integralmente, a obrigação a que estava submetido, e que o exercício do direito do credor em resolver o contrato, nessas condições, demonstra deslealdade, ficando assim, excluído o direito de resolução, podendo pedir o credor o adimplemento da obrigação e perdas e danos;
g) exercício desequilibrado de direitos – ofende a boa-fé objetiva a vantagem desproporcionalmente obtida, com o exercício do direito pelo seu titular, em sacrifício de outrem. O princípio da boa-fé objetiva encontra-se intrínsicamente ligado aos assuntos relativos à justiça contratual, servindo-lhe de instrumento, pois garante a relação de equilíbrio entre prestação e contraprestação nos contratos comutativos, sendo a manutenção da equivalência econômica, entre prestação e contraprestação também uma das funções deste princípio.

Segundo Karl Larenz[49], duas são as formas de se garantir a justiça contratual: a primeira pela equivalência objetiva das prestações, e a segunda, pela contraprestação e distribuição justa de ônus e risco. Judith Martins-Costa comenta os pontos importantes para a construção deste princípio: 1-) "o princípio da boa- fé objetiva é via para a concretização, no domínio das relações obrigacionais, notadamente as contratuais, dos deveres que defluem da diretriz constitucional da solidariedade social."; 2-) assinala à

[49] Karl Larenz (*Derecho civil*, cit., p.61/65) *apud* Laerte Marrone de Castro Sampaio (*A boa-fé objetiva*, cit., p.87).

"responsabilidade da doutrina ao apontar os modelos hermenêuticos que auxiliarão o juiz, e mesmo o legislador, na elaboração dos modelos jurídicos. Vivemos em um tempo que se tem pressa, mas a atividade doutrinária não pode prescindir da reflexão, do tempo de maturação das ideias e das novas concepções, equilibrando-se na tensão entre o apontar de novos caminhos, constitutivos da sua missão antecipante de novas soluções, e a necessidade de ponderação, a cada dia mais dificultosa e necessária porque, como disse Hannah Arendt[50], a irreflexão, 'a imprudência temerária ou irremediável confusão ou repetição complacente de 'verdades', que se tornam triviais e vazias, parece ser uma das principais características do nosso tempo.'."; 3-) menciona a missão da jurisprudência, ao afirmar que o "o Direito não é 'dado' ao jurista recebe, 'é uma tarefa que o concita a um ingente esforço e a uma profunda responsabilidade', devemos considerar que o princípio da boa-fé objetiva, justamente por configurar norma vaga, semanticamente aberta, carreia, para o juiz, um extraordinário acréscimo de sua responsabilidade. Não pode nem recair no crasso decisionismo, nem no voluntarismo, tanto primário quanto perigoso aos valores da Democracia.".

A boa-fé objetiva tem como função otimizar o comportamento contratual pela imposição de deveres de cooperação e de proteção dos interesses recíprocos, pois visa à satisfação dos interesses globais envolvidos, auxiliando a realização positiva da finalidade contratual e a proteção das pessoas e de seus bens, devendo o princípio da boa-fé objetiva ser utilizado na interpretação e integração do contrato, em consonância com a função econômico-social que concretamente deverá realizar[51].

[50] Hannah Arendt (*A condição humana*, 5.ed., Rio de Janeiro, Forense, 1991, p.13) *apud* Judith Martins- Costa e outro (*Diretrizes Teóricas*, cit., p.220).

[51] Maria Helena Diniz, *Curso de direito civil*, vol 3.,cit., p.41 à 44; Caio Mario da Silva Pereira, *Lesão*, cit., p.104/105; Marcelo Guerra Martins, *Lesão*, cit., p.156 à 161; Laerte Marrone de Castro Sampaio, *A boa-fé objetiva*, cit., p.25 à 32 e 76 à 88; Judith Martins- Costa e outro, *Diretrizes Teóricas*, cit., p.199/200 e 214 à 221; Fernando Noronha, *O direito dos contratos*, cit., p.186. Informamos ainda a redação dos enunciados aprovados na III Jornada de Direito Civil do Conselho de Justiça Federal, realizado em 2004, relativos ao princípio da boa-fé objetiva: "167 – Art.421 a 424: Com o advento do Código Civil de 2002, houve forte aproximação principiológica entre esse Código e o Código de Defesa do Consumidor, no que respeita à regulação contratual, uma vez que ambos são incorporadores de uma nova teoria geral dos contratos; 168 – Art. 422: O princípio da boa-fé objetiva importa no reconhecimento de um direito a cumprir em favor do titular passivo da obrigação; 169- Art. 422: O princípio da boa-

2.3.2. PRINCÍPIO DA EQUIVALÊNCIA DAS PRESTAÇÕES

O conceito de equidade, que buscamos ao analisar o instituto da lesão, visando uma proteção contratual, é o da justiça no caso concreto. Caio Mario, ao mencionar a Teoria da Equidade de Edmundo Lins, esclarece que o vocábulo jurídico possui vários conceitos e está subdividido em três sentidos: "A primeira, 'sinônima de direito natural ou ideal', é a 'prática da justiça nos casos obscuros ou duvidosos', nas omissões da lei naqueles "deixados ao prudente arbítrio do juiz'. A segunda é a 'aplicação da lei de modo a satisfazer às novas necessidades sociais'. E a terceira será um 'temperamento ou abrandamento ao rigor do direito positivo, fazendo o juiz, como *bom judge*, a justiça de cada caso particular'.

Depois de mostrar os diversos casos em que, na prática da *aequitas*, o pretor romano se mostrou verdadeiro legislador e construiu e decretou normas de cunho legislativo, quando estuda o direito moderno evidencia que a equidade já não pode ter toda aquela extensão, porém reduz-se ao primeiro desses sentidos, por não ser facultado ao juiz introduzir modificações na lei, a fim de adaptá-las às convivências, nem lhe ser mais lícito amputar na lei sob pretexto de abrandar os seu rigor, porque a atribuição legiferante é conferida a outro poder".

Marcelo Martins Guerra informa, nas palavras de Limongi França que, "Enquanto os preceitos de justiça são de natureza geral (*commune praeceptum*), os da equidade são particulares, isto é, atendem às particularidades de cada espécie, imprevisíveis de antemão. É a *epieikeia* dos gregos, e, segundo São Tomás de Aquino, é mais alta e mais extensa que a justiça.". Segundo Arnaldo Rizzardo: "A equidade, no ensinamento de Pothier, o grand inspirador do Código Francês, impõe a igualdade de proteção e a equivalência de pretações. Revela-se a iniquidade quando notável uma desproporção injusta, o que significa a negação do direito em si.".

Conforme menciona Silvio Rodrigues, após mencionar a Lei Segunda de Deocleciano e Maximiliano, "Trata-se de instituição fundada na equidade, como bem diz a lei citada, ao empregar a expressão *humanum est*; e, decerto, se inspira na ideia de equivalência das prestações, que deve existir nos contratos comutativos.". O princípio da equidade foi positivado no

-fé objetiva deve levar o credor a evitar o agravamento do próprio prejuízo; 170 – Art.422: A boa-fé objetiva deve ser observada pelas partes na fase de negociações preliminares e após a execução do contrato, quando tal exigência decorrer na natureza do contrato.".

Direito Brasileiro, através do artigo 51, inciso IV, do Código de Defesa do Consumidor, que considera nula as cláusulas contratuais incompatíveis com a boa-fé e a equidade, nas palavras de Cláudia Lima Marques: "é o *Princípio da Equidade Contratual,* do equilíbrio de direitos e deveres nos contratos, para alcançar a justiça contratual. (...) O princípio da equidade, do equilíbrio contratual é cogente; a lei brasileira, como veremos, não exige que a cláusula abusiva tenha sido incluída no contrato por 'abuso do poderio econômico' do fornecedor, como exige a lei francesa; ao contrário, o CDC sanciona e afasta apenas o resultado, o desequilíbrio, não exige um ato reprovável do fornecedor; a cláusula pode ter sido aceita conscientemente pelo consumidor, mas se traz vantagem excessiva para o fornecedor, se é abusiva, o resultado é contrário à ordem pública, contrária às novas normas de ordem pública de proteção do CDC, e a autonomia de vontade não prevalecerá.".[52]

Confome observamos na evolução deste trabalho, o instituto da lesão visa proteger a equivelência das prestações nos contratos comutativos. E, segundo Maria Helena Diniz, "Será comutativo o contrato a título oneroso e bilateral em que a extensão das prestações de ambas as partes, conhecida desde o momento da formação do vínculo contratual, é certa, determinada e definitiva, apresentando uma relativa equivalência de valores, que, por sua vez, são insuscetíveis de variação durante o implemento do contrato, embora, algumas vezes, corram riscos relativos à coisa ou à oscilação do seu valor, o que, contudo, são circunstâncias independentes do contrato.".

Na afirmação de Orlando Gomes, "Nos *contratos comutativos,* a relação entre *vantagem* e *sacrifício* é subjetivamente equivalente, havendo certeza quanto às prestações (...) pode não haver *equivalência objetiva* das prestações exigível, tão-só, nos que podem ser rescindidos por *lesão.*". É muito difícil que, nos contratos comutativos, as prestações entre as partes seja idêntica, mas o lucro excessivo é condenável, pois afronta as regras éticas e morais.

Concordamos com Arnaldo Rizzardo quando afirma que, "Quanto à desproporção, a obrigação de pagar o preço é a causa da obrigação de entregar a coisa. Dentro dos princípios da seriedade que regem os negócios, não se admite uma desigualdade exagerada. Esclarecem, com muita proprie-

[52] Caio Mario da Silva Pereira, *Lesão,* cit.,p. 151 a 154; Marcelo Guerra Martins, *Lesão,* cit., p.151 a 161; Arnaldo Rizzardo,*Da ineficácia*, cit., p.111; Silvio Rodrigues, *Dos vícios de consentimento,* São Paulo, Saraiva, p.210; Cláudia Lima Marques, *Contratos no código de defesa*, cit., p.390/391.

dade, Planiol e Ripert, em tradução para o espanhol: '...ha de existir cierta equivalencia entre el precio y el valor de la cosa; de hecho, esto es así por regla general y es evidente que el valor de una cosa queda determinado por su precio de venta. Sin embargo, a veces ocurre que existe desproporción entre el precio prometido por el comprador y el valor normal de la cosa.' (...) Clóvis Bevilaqua, com a sua autoridade, acrescenta: 'O preço deve ser justo, isto é, equivalente ao valor aproximado da coisa vendida... Havendo diferença, para mais ou para menos, as partes só poderão exigir a retificação do preço ou resilir o contrato, havendo vício de consentimento.'. ". Os contratos têm por essência a realização de negócios jurídicos, baseados nas vontades das partes, mas serão limitados quando injustamente prejudicarem um dos contratantes.[53]

2.3.3. PRINCÍPIO DA AUTONOMIA DA VONTADE E AS LIMITAÇÕES DE NORMA DE ORDEM PÚBLICA E DOS BONS COSTUMES

O princípio da autonomia da vontade funda-se na liberdade de cada indivíduo de poder estipular livremente, mediante acordo de vontades, seus interesses, que geram efeitos tutelados pela ordem jurídica. Esta liberdade contratual, conforme ensina Maria Helena Diniz[54], abrange: "a) a liberdade de contratar ou não contratar, isto é, o poder de decidir, segundo seus interesses, se e quando estabelecerá com outrem uma relação jurídica contratual. Todavia, o princípio de que a pessoa pode abster-se de contratar sofre exceções, como, p. ex., quando o indivíduo tem obrigação de contratar imposta pela lei, como é o caso das companhias seguradoras relativamente aos seguros obrigatórios; b) a liberdade de escolher o outro contraente, embora às vezes a pessoa do outro contratante seja insuscetível de opção, como, p.ex., nas hipóteses de serviço público concedido sob regime de monopólio, ou seja, das empresas concessionárias de serviço público; c) a liberdade de fixar o conteúdo do contrato, escolhendo qualquer uma das modalidades contratuais reguladas por lei (contratos nominados), introduzindo alterações ou cláusulas (*RT*,481: 120) que melhor se coadunem com seus interesses e com as peculiaridades do negócio,

[53] Maria Helena Diniz, *Curso de direito civil,* vol.3, cit., p.84; Orlando Gomes, *Contratos,* Rio de Janeiro, Forense, 1998, p.74/75; Arnaldo Rizzardo, *Da ineficácia,* cit., p.114/146; Marcelo Guerra Martins, *Lesão,* cit., p.151 a 161.

[54] Maria Helena Diniz, *Curso de direito civil,* vol.3, cit., p.33.

ampliando ou restringindo os efeitos do vínculo contratual, ou adotando novos tipos contratuais, distintos dos modelos previstos pela ordem jurídica, conforme as necessidades do negócio jurídico, dando origem, assim, aos contratos inominados. O conteúdo pertence à livre determinação das partes contratantes, embora, como logo mais veremos, alguns contratos se formem pela adesão de uma das partes às cláusulas impostas pela outra.".

Já José Puig Brutau[55] define o princípio da autonomia da vontade como "A possibilidade de duas ou mais pessoas se obrigarem por sua própria iniciativa significa o reconhecimento do poder criador da autonomia da vontade. Essa autonomia significa que, em princípio, todo particular pode contratar quando queira, como queira e com quem queira.".

Lembramos que o princípio da liberdade contratual não é ilimitado ou absoluto, pois está limitado ao princípio da supremacia da ordem pública, que veda convenções contrárias aos bons costumes, de forma que a vontade dos contratantes está subordianada ao interesse coletivo. Não prevalecerão as convenções que contrariarem preceitos de ordem pública, tais como a função social da propriedade, estabelecida no artigo 2.035 do Código vigente.

Segundo Orlando Gomes[56], "O conceito de *liberdade de contratar* abrange os poderes de auto-regência de interesses, de livre discussão das condições contratuais e, por fim, de escolha do tipo de contrato conveniente à atuação da vontade. Manifesta-se, por conseguinte, sob tríplice aspecto: a)*liberdade de contratar propriamente dita;* b) *liberdade de estipular o contrato;* c)*liberdade de determinar o conteúdo do contrato.* (...) O *princípio da liberdade de contratar* torna-se mais intelegível à luz da distinção entre *leis coativas* e *supletivas.* As primeiras ordenam ou proíbem algum ato, determinado o que se deve e o que não se deve fazer. Quando ordenam, dizem-se *imperativas.* Quando proíbem, *proibitivas.* Destinam-se as *leis supletivas* a suprir ou completar a vontade do indivíduo, aplicando-se quando ele não a declara. Ora, O Direito Contratual constitui-se, predominantemente, de *normas supletivas,* deixando, por tanto, larga margem à vontade dos que agem em sua esfera. Nesse território, a *liberdade de contratar* domina amplamente.".

[55] José Puig Bruteu (*Fundamentos de derecho civil,* 3ed., Barcelona, Bosh, s.d, p.5) *apud* Marcelo Guerra Martins, *Lesão,* cit., p.167.

[56] Orlando Gomes, *Contratos,* Rio de Janeiro, Forense, 1998, p.22/23.

Henri de Page[57] afirma que lei de ordem pública seria "aquela que entende com os interesses essenciais do Estado ou da coletividade, ou que fixa, no Direito Privado, as bases jurídicas fundamentais sobre as quais repousa a ordem econômica ou moral de determinada sociedade". Em seguida, tenta classificá-los exemplificativamente: "1º) as leis que consagram ou salvaguardam o princípio da liberdade e da igualdade dos cidadãos, e, particularmente, as que estabelecem o princípio da liberdade de trabalho, de comércio e de indústria; 2º) as leis relativas a certos princípios de responsabilidade civil ou a certas responsabilidades determinadas; 3º) as leis que asseguram ao operário proteção especial; 4º) as leis sobre o estado e a capacidade das pessoas; 5º) as leis sobre o estado civil; 6º) certos princípios básicos do direito hereditário como os relativos à legítima e o que proíbe os pactos sobre sucessão futura; 7º) as leis relativas à composição do domínio público; 8º) os princípios fundamentais do direito de propriedade; 9º) as leis monetárias; e 10º) a proibição do anatocismo.".

O princípio da autonomia da vontade, que é o poder conferido aos contratantes para estabelecer vínculo obrigacional, está submetido às normas jurídicas e aos bons costumes. Esta restrição trazida pelo "dirigismo contratual", que é a intervenção estatal na economia do negócio contratual, busca aplicar medidas restritivas estatais, invocando a supremacia dos interesses coletivos sobre os individuais dos contratantes, pois o Estado tem por escopo executar sua política de coordenar os vários setores da vida econômica e proteger os economicamente mais fracos, sacrificando às vezes alguns benefícios particulares em prol da coletividade, mas sempre buscando conciliar os interesses das partes e da sociedade.

Nas palavras de Maria Helena Diniz[58], "A expressão *dirigismo contratual* é aplicável às medidas restritivas estatais que invocam a supremacia dos interesses coletivos sobre os meros interesses individuais dos contraentes, com o escopo de dar execução à política do Estado de coordenar os vários setores da vida econômica e de proteger os economicamente mais fracos, sacrificando benefícios particulares em prol da coletividade, mas sempre conciliando os interesses das partes e os da sociedade.".

O Estado poderá intervir de várias formas, mediante a aplicação de normas de ordem pública e também através do judiciário, revisado os con-

[57] Henri de Page (*Traité élémentaire de droit civil belge*,t.I., p.100/103) *apud* Orlando Gomes, *Contratos*, cit., p.24/25.
[58] Maria Helena Diniz, *Curso de direito civil*, vol.3, cit., p.36.

tratos, estabelecendo condições de execução e, até mesmo, exonerando a parte lesada, confome o caso, mas sempre fundados no princípio da boa-fé e do interesse coletivo, no amparo do fraco contra o forte. Exemplo disto é a cláusula penal prevista no artigo 413 do Código Civil, que autoriza o juiz a reduzir proporcionalmente a pena estipulada, quando o valor da pena exceder ao do contrato principal, e quando ocorrer o cumprimento parcial da obrigação, independentemente deste dispositivo, pois o Poder Judiciário tem o dever e o direito de intervir, observando o alcance da finalidade do negócio e a harmonia social, conforme disposto no artigo 5º da Lei de Introdução às Normas do Direito Brasileiro. Maria Helena Diniz[59] ensina que os contratantes deverão sujeitar sua vontade: "a) às *normas de ordem pública*, que fixam, atendendo aos interesses da coletividade, as bases jurídicas fundamentais em que repousam a ordem econômica e moral da sociedade, uma vez que são atinentes ao estado e à capacidade das pessoas; à organização da família; aos princípios básicos da ordem de vocação hereditária, da sucessão testamentária, do direito de propriedade, da responsabilidade civil, da liberdade e da igualdade dos cidadãos, da liberdade de trabalho, de comércio e de indústria; e à organização política, administrativa e econômica do Estado; e b) aos *bons costumes*, relativos à moralidade social, de forma que sejam proibidos, p.ex., contratos que versem sobre exploração de casas de tolerância, corretagem matrimonial, usura, por contrariarem os bons costumes.".

Laerte Marrone de Castro Sampaio[60] informa: "Menezes de Cordeiro afirma que os bons costumes surgem sempre como algo exterior que limita o âmbito da autonomia privada, sem, todavia, determinar o teor do comportamento a exigir, como o faz a boa-fé.(...)" mais adiante acrescenta, "na linha de Massimo Bianca, pode-se afirmar que os preceitos relativos aos bons costumes assumem caráter negativo – impõem ao sujeito uma abstenção, um não agir contra o senso comum de honestidade, enquanto os de boa-fé guardam natureza positiva, reclamando um comportamento em favor do outro.".[61]

[59] Maria Helena Diniz, *Curso de direito civil*, vol.3, cit., p.34/35.

[60] António Manuel da Rocha Menezes de Cordeiro (*Direito das obrigações*, cit., p.1213.) e Massimo Bianca (*Diritto civili*,v.3, Milão, Giuffrè, 2000, p.15) *apud* Laerte Marrone de Castro Sampaio, *A boa-fé objetiva*, cit., p.31/32.

[61] Maria Helena Diniz, *Curso de direito civil*, vol.3, cit., p.33/34; Marcelo Guerra Martins, *Lesão*, cit., p.166 a 177; Caio Mario da Silva Pereira, *Lesão*, cit., p.186/187; Laerte Marrone de Castro Sampaio, *A boa-fé objetiva*, cit., p.31/32; Orlando Gomes, *Contratos*, cit., p.22 à 25.

2.3.4. PRINCÍPIO DA FUNÇÃO SOCIAL DO CONTRATO COMO DIRETRIZ FUNDAMENTAL

Os contratos deverão ter por finalidade e limite sua **função**[62] social, pois o individualismo foi repelido em face da positivação infraconstitucional explícita, no artigo 421 do novo Código Civil[63]: "A liberdade de contratar será exercida em razão e nos limites da função social do contrato", e este artigo seguiu as diretrizes postas pela Constituição de 1988, em seus artigos 1º, IV, 5º, XXIII, e 170,III, que postulam que, o contrato deverá ter utilidade social, pois limitado está a autonomia da vontade em face da intervenção estatal, e ante à função econômico-social do ato negocial. Como ensina Maria Helena Diniz[64], "A liberdade contratual é reconhecida, mas seu exercício está condicionado à função social do contrato e implica valores de boa fé e probidade (CC, art. 422). Logo, a função social do contrato, dirigida à satisfação de interesses sociais, não elimina o princípio da autonomia contratual, mas atenua ou reduz seu alcance, quando estiverem presentes interesses meta – individuais ou interesse individual coletivo relativo à dignidade da pessoa humana (Enunciado do STJ n.23, aprovado na Jornada de Direito Civil, promovida, em setembro de 2002, pelo Centro de Estudos Judiciários do Conselho da Justiça Federal).

A autonomia privada como autorregulamentação de interesses só se justificaria se o contrato corresponder a uma função considerada socialmente útil pelo ordenamento.". Lembramos que o princípio da função

[62] Antônio Jeová Santos (*Função social lesão e onerosidade excessiva nos contratos,* São Paulo, Método, 2002, p.103) infoma o singnificado de "função", apesar da definição abaixo ter critérios biológicos, fazendo analogia ao significado "função protetora-repressiva" do direito, para Norberto Bobbio, que "é a prestação continuada que um determinado órgão dá para a conservação e desenvolvimento, segundo um ritmo de nascimento, crescimento e morte, de todo o organismo, é dizer, do organismo considerado como um todo.".

[63] Informamos ainda a redação dos enunciados aprovados na I Jornada de Direito Civil do Conselho de Justiça Federal, realizado em 2002, relativos ao princípio geral da função social dos contratos: "21- Art.421: a função social do contrato, prevista no art.421 do novo Código Civil, constitui cláusula geral a impor a revisão do princípio da relatividade dos efeitos do contrato em relação a terceiros, implicando a tutela externa do crédito; 22- Art.421: a função social do contrato, prevista no art.421 do novo Código Civil, constitui cláusula geral que reforça o princípio de conservação do contrato, assegurando trocas úteis e justas; Art. 421: a função social do contrato, prevista no art.421 do novo Código Civil não elimina o princípio da autonomia contratual, mas atenua ou reduz o alcance desse princípio quando presentes interesses metaindividuais ou interesse individual relativo a dignidade da pessoa humana.".

[64] Maria Helena Diniz, *Curso de direito civil,* vol.3, cit., p.35.

social do contrato decorre do princípio constitucional da função social da propriedade e da justiça que norteiam a ordem econômica, sempre visando, a boa-fé entre contratantes, a transparência nas negociações e a efetivação da justiça contratual.

Para Antonio Jeová Santos[65]: "A função social do contrato obriga a todos do mundo jurídico a harmonizar o direito com a vontade de lucrar muito e mais, como é próprio do sistema capitalista. Além de enxergar o contrato como instrumento jurídico, terá de observar que ele tem forte conteúdo de justiça e de utilidade.(...) Na vida econômica e social, o contrato não afeta somente interesses dos que nele intervêm, mas se transforma numa instituição social.".

O artigo 421 declara a limitação à vontade de contratar pela função social do contrato, o princípio da autonomia da vontade deverá estar atrelado também ao da **sociabilidade**[66], devendo atender aos fins sociais, limitando o arbítrio dos contratantes, criando condições para um equilíbrio econômico-contratual, facilitando o reajuste das prestações e, até mesmo, sua resolução. Para Miguel Reali[67] "o reconhecimento da função social do contrato é mero corolário dos imperativos constitucionais relativos à 'função social de propriedade' e à justiça que deve presidir a ordem econômica.". Já Teresa Negreiros[68] entende que o "princípio da função social encontra fundamento constitucional no princípio da solidariedade, a exigir

[65] Antônio Jeová Santos, *Função social lesão*, cit., p.126.

[66] Judith Martins- Costa e outro (*Diretrizes Teóricas*, cit., p.144) ensinam: "Se a eticidade está no fundamento das regras civis, dúvidas não há de que o Direito Civil em nossos dias é também marcado pela socialidade, pela situação de suas regras no plano da vida comunitária. A relação entre a dimensão individual e a comunitária do ser humano constitui tema de debate que tem atravessado os séculos, desde, pelo menos, Aristóteles, constituindo, mais propriamente, um problema de filosofia política, por isso devendo ser apanhado pelo Direito posto conforme os valores de nossa – atual – experiência jurídica. O quadro que hoje se apresenta ao Direito Civil é o da reação ao excessivo individualismo característico da Era codificatória oitocentista que tantos e tão fundos reflexos ainda nos lega. Se às Constituições cabe proclamar o princípio da função social – o que vem sendo regra desde Weimer –, é ao Direito Civil que incumbe transformá-lo em concreto instrumento de ação. Mediante o recurso à função social e também à boa-fé – que tem uma face marcadamente ética e outra solidarista – instrumentaliza o Código agora aprovado a diretriz constitucional da *solidariedade social*, posta como um dos 'objetivos fundamentais da Repúblia'.".

[67] Miguel Reali, *O projeto do novo código civil*, Saraiva, São Paulo, 1999, p.32.

[68] Teresa Negreiros, *Teoria do contrato novos paradigmas*, Rio de Janeiro, Renovar, 2002, p. 207/208.

que os contratantes e os terceiros colaborem entre si, respeitando as situações jurídicas anteriormente constituídas, ainda que as mesmas não sejam providas de eficácia real, mas desde que a sua prévia existência seja conhecida pelas pessoas implicadas.(...) Vale dizer: a função social, muito além de ser mais um princípio, com finalidades delimitativas, é elemento de qualificação que varia conforme a concreta correlação de interesses em causa.".

Antonio Jeová Santos[69] afirma que "o contrato atinge sua função social quando o dever de não lesar outrem é incorporado ao direito subjetivo, dever que condiciona o exercício e que se aproxima da busca de um satisfatório resultado social. Simulaneamente a esse resultado social a ser atingido, o âmbito de poder do titular haverá de ser preservado, desde que não vulnere o fim social a que se destina o contrato.".

Para Laerte Marrone de Castro Sampaio, o contrato há que atender o valor da justiça e da utilidade, para ajustar-se à função social, pois a liberdade contratual somente é admissível para atingí-la. O contrato reveste de juridicidade, as operações econômicas, instrumentalizando a circulação de riquezas, transferindo a riqueza de um para outro, o patrimônio de um para o outro. Nas palavras de Judith Martins Costa[70], "A constituição econômica de uma sociedade, todos o sabemos, não é matéria de interesse individual, ou particular, mas atinge – e interessa – a todos. O contrato, veste jurídica das operações de circulação de riqueza, tem, inegavelmente, função social, assim como a disciplina das Obrigações, pois não devemos esquecer, no exame das projeções da diretriz da sociabilidade, a estrutura sistemática do Código.".[71]

2.4. EFEITOS DA LESÃO

A lesão inclui-se entre os vícios de consentimento e acarretará a anulabilidade do negócio (artigo 171, II). Havendo uma ressalva que impede a decretação da anulação, permitindo-se, assim, para evita-la, a oferta de suplemento suficiente ou se o favorecido concordar com a redução da vantagem, aproveitando, assim, o negócio, por restabelecer o reequilíbrio con-

[69] Antônio Jeová Santos, *Função social lesão*, cit., p.127.

[70] Judith Martins- Costa e outro, *Diretrizes Teóricas*, cit., p.158.

[71] Maria Helena Diniz, *Curso de direito civil*, vol.3, cit., p.33 à 43; Judith Martins- Costa e outro, *Diretrizes Teóricas*, cit., p.156 à 160; Antônio Jeová Santos, *Função social lesão*, cit., p.116 à 127; Laerte Marrone de Castro Sampaio, *A boa-fé objetiva*, cit., p.22, Teresa Negreiros, *Teoria do contrato*, cit., p. 205 à 210.

tratual (artigo 157, §2º). O prejudicado terá duas vias de ação em juízo, a de anulação de contrato e a de revisão do contrato, optando pela anulação, caberá ao outro contratante ilidir a pretensão de ruptura contratual (artigo 157, §2º).

O Código Civil ao incluir a lesão entre os vícios de consentimento, atribuiu seu reconhecimento em juízo a uma ação de anulação (artigos 171, II, 177 e 157, §2º), podendo negar seu cabimento por meio de exceção (contestação). As causas de anulabilidade são manejáveis tanto por ação como por exceção, em qualquer caso prevalecerá o prazo decadencial de 4 (quatro) anos estatuído pelo artigo 178, II, cuja aplicação aplicação poderá ser feita pelo juiz *ex ofício* (artigo 210), ou seja, a ação constitutiva (artigo 177) deve ser proposta dentro de 4 (quatro) anos contados do dia em que se realizou o negócio jurídico (artigo 178, II), a exceção, quando manejada, também deverá observa-lo. Não se sujeitando as suspenções e interrupções relativas a prescrição (artigos 207 e 208). Humberto Theodoro Júnior[72] lembra para levarmos em conta "o prestígio que o Código dispensa ao princípio da conservação do negócio, mesmo quando afetado por nulidade (artigos 170, 176, 178, etc.), não será injurídico pretender que quem pode o mais pode o menos. Se à parte prejudicada cabe o direito de desconstituir todo o negócio, não é desarrazoado admitir que possa pleitear apenas a redução do preço, para eliminar a lesão nele contida".[73]

CONCLUSÕES

É no contexto desta base de principios que a lesão tem de ser aplicada no ordenamento jurídico pátrio. Todos os princípios contratuais estão ligados ao do respeito e proteção à dignidade da pessoa humana, dando tutela jurídica aos contratantes, para que se efetivem a função social da propriedade, a do contrato e a justiça social.

A lesão é um vício de consentimento do negócio jurídico e se a vontade estiver viciada também estará o negócio jurídico, pois todo negócio jurídico está alicerçado na manifestação de vontade, mas não devemos olvidar que todas as figuras do vício de consentimento passam pelo terreno da boa-fé e da probidade negocial.

[72] Humberto Theodoro Júnior, *Comentários ao novo código ,cit.*, p.237.

[73] Humberto Theodoro Júnior, *Comentários ao novo código ,cit.*, p.242-243;Maria Helena Diniz, *Curso de direito civil brasileiro,* cit., v.1, p.511; Maria Helena Diniz, *Código civil,* cit., p.148/149; Caio Mario da Silva Pereira, *Lesão,* cit.,p. 190.

REFERÊNCIAS

ARISTÓTELES – *Ética a Nicômaco,* São Paulo, Martin Claret, 2002.

_____ *Os pensadores Aristóteles: Poética, Organon, Política e Constituição de Atenas,* São Paulo, Nova Cultural, 1999.

BECKER, Anelise – *Teoria geral da lesão nos contratos,* São Paulo, Saraiva, 2000.

BESSONE, Darcy – *Do contrato teoria geral,* 4º edição, São Paulo, Saraiva, 1997.

BEVILAQUA, Clóvis – *Comentários ao Código Civil,* Rio de Janeiro, 1927.

BORGHI, Hélio – *A lesão no direito civil,*São Paulo, Leud, 1988.

DINIZ, Maria Helena – *Compêndio de introdução à ciência do direito,* 11ª edição, São Paulo, Saraiva, 1999.

_____ *A ciência jurídica,* 4ª edição, São Paulo, Saraiva, 1996.

_____ *Curso de direito civil brasileiro,* São Paulo, Saraiva, 2005, v.3 (*Teoria das obrigações contratuais e extracontratuais*), 21ª edição.

_____ *Curso de direito civil brasileiro,* São Paulo, Saraiva, 2005, v.1 (*Teoria geral do direito civil*), 22ª edição.

_____ *Código civil anotado,* São Paulo, Saraiva, 2002.

_____ *Dicionário jurídico,* São Paulo, Saraiva, 2005, obra em 4 volumes, 2ª edição.

GOMES, Orlando – *A crise do direito,* São Paulo, Max Limonad, 1955.

_____ *Raízes históricas e sociológicas do código civil brasileiro,* São Paulo, Martins Fontes, 2003.

_____ *Contratos,* Rio de Janeiro, Forense, 1998.

LARENZ, Karl – *Derecho civil – parte general,* Madri, Edersa, 1978.

LIMA MARQUES, Cláudia – *Contratos no código de defesa do consumidor,* São Paulo, RT, 1999.

LOTUFO, Renan – *Código civil comentado,* São Paulo, Saraiva, 2003, vol.1.

MARTINS, Marcelo Guerra – *Lesão contratual no direito brasileiro,* São Paulo, Renovar, 2001.

MARTINS-COSTA, Judith – *A boa-fé no direito privado,* São Paulo, Revista dos Tribunais, 1999.

MARTINS-COSTA, Judith e BRANCO, Gerson Luiz Carlos – *Diretrizes Teóricas do Novo Código Civil Brasileiro,* São Paulo, Saraiva, 2002.

MONTEIRO, Washington de Barros – *Curso de direito civil – parte geral,* v.1, São Paulo, Saraiva, 2003.

NEGREIROS, Teresa – *Teoria do contrato novos paradigmas,* Rio de Janeiro, Renovar, 2002.

NORONHA, Fernando – *O direito dos contratos e seus princípios fundamentais,* São Paulo, Saraiva, 1994.

PEREIRA, Caio Mario da Silva – *Lesão nos contratos,* 6ª edição, Rio de Janeiro, Forense, 2001.

REALE, Miguel – *O projeto do novo código civil,* Saraiva, São Paulo, 1999.

RIZZARDO, Arnaldo – *Da ineficácia dos atos jurídicos e da lesão no direito,* Rio de Janeiro, Forense, 1983.

RODRIGUES, Silvio – *Dos vícios de consentimento,* São Paulo, Saraiva, 1989.

_____ *Direito civil- parte geral,* São Paulo, Saraiva, 2003, v.1.

SAMPAIO, Laerte Marrone de Castro – *A boa-fé objetiva na relação contratual,* São Paulo, Manole, 2004.

SANTOS, Antônio Jeová – *Função social lesão e onerosidade excessiva no contratos,* São Paulo, Método,2002.

THEODORO JÚNIOR, Humberto – *Comentários ao novo código civil,* Rio de Janeiro, Forense, 2003, vol.III, tomo I.

LISBOA, Roberto Senise – Contornos atuais da teoria dos contratos – A lesão nos contratos, in *Revista dos Tribunais,* s/d., São Paulo.

PROTEÇÃO DA FAUNA: GARANTIA DA SUSTENTABILIDADE AMBIENTAL[1]

Maria Helena Diniz*

1. IMPORTÂNCIA DA FAUNA SILVESTRE E SUA FUNÇÃO ECOLÓGICA

A fauna silvestre ou nativa é uma locução que abrange os que pertencem as espécies nativas, migratórias, aquáticas ou terrestres, que tenham, total ou parcialmente, seu ciclo de vida nos limites do território brasileiro ou nas águas jurisdicionais do Brasil. A fauna nativa tem uma função ecológica e grande é a sua importância para manter o equilíbrio ambiental, ou seja, os ecossistemas, pois há uma teia infinita de relações, por existir uma interdependência entre os fatores antrópicos, bióticos e abióticos. Erica Bechara[2] observa que

* Professora Titular de direito civil da PUC-SP. Livre-docente, Doutora e Mestre em Teoria Geral do Direito e Filosofia do Direito pela PUC-SP. Professora de Direito Civil no curso de graduação da PUCSP. Professora de Filosofia do Direito, de Teoria Geral do Direito e de Direito Civil Comparado nos cursos de pós-graduação (mestrado e doutorado) em Direito da PUC-SP. Coordenadora do Núcleo de Pesquisa em Direito Civil Comparado nos Cursos de pós-graduação em Direito da PUCSP. Membro da Academia Paulista de Direito (cadeira 62-patrono Oswaldo Aranha Bandeira de Mello), da Academia Notarial Brasileira (cadeira 16-patrono Francisco Cavalcanti Pontes de Miranda), do Instituto dos Advogados de São Paulo e do Instituto de Direito Comparado Luso-brasileiro. Presidente do Instituto Internacional de Direito.

[1] Artigo publicado na Revista Brasileira de Direito Animal, ISSN 2317-4552, Vol. 12, Num. 1, Jan.-Abr./2017, p.15-52.

[2] Bechara, E. *A proteção da fauna sob a ótica constitucional.* SPaulo: Juarez de Oliveira, 2003. p. 54.

> a harmonia de um ecossistema repousa na interação de todas as espécies, cada qual cumprindo uma função ecológica própria, e se nenhuma espécie pode ser considerada inútil, é natural que a ausência de um elemento só que seja nesse ciclo natural deixará um vazio irreparável, pois que dificilmente esse vácuo será preenchido pela espécie vizinha por mais que semelhante.

O ecossistema abrange animais e vegetais que sempre estão interagindo entre si e com outros elementos do meio ambiente, dando sustentação à diversidade biológica. Por isso, a fauna e a flora, que estão em interação mútua, devem ser preservadas. Urge tutelar a fauna, impondo penalidades não só ao caçador não portador de autorização do órgão competente, como também ao que, indiscriminadamente, destrói a flora provocando morte de animais silvestres que vivem nas florestas[3]. Imprescindível será evitar a extinção das espécies e respeitar o meio ambiente, pois cada ecossistema desempenha verdadeira função na natureza, sob pena de acarretar o desequilíbrio ambiental, que constitui grave ameaça à rica biodiversidade do planeta Terra e à humanidade, que, então, perderia o que tem de mais precioso: seu direito à vida, ou melhor, à sadia qualidade de vida.

Uma vida sensível implica o direito a um ambiente ecologicamente equilibrado, que deverá ser garantido tendo em vista as presentes e futuras gerações[4]. O desenvolvimento econômico e a sobrevivência do ser humano, da fauna e da flora requerem o saneamento da terra e uma boa administração dos recursos naturais[5]. Com muita propriedade, o Santo Papa João Paulo II[6] alerta que o homem contemporâneo está ameaçado pelo resultado da obra de sua inteligência e vontade e, por tal razão, será necessário acompanhar o progresso moderno, pois "existe já um real e perceptível perigo de que, enquanto progride enormemente o domínio do homem sobre o mundo das coisas, ele perca os fios essenciais deste seu domínio e, de diversas maneiras, submeta a elas a sua humanidade, e ele próprio

[3] Sirvinskas, Luis Paulo. *Manual de direito ambiental.* SPaulo: Saraiva, 2015. pp. 621 e 622.

[4] Purvin de Figueiredo, Guilherme Jose e SILVA, Solange Teles da. Elementos balizadores da ação estatal na defesa dos bens ambientais para as presentes e futuras gerações. IN: *Temas de direito ambiental e urbanístico.* Guilherme Jose Purvin de Figueiredo (org.). SPaulo: Max Limonad, n.3, 1998. p. 137.

[5] Milaré, E. Tutela jurisdicional do ambiente. *Revista do Advogado,* 37:5.

[6] Sartori, Frei Luís Mª, A. (org) Enciclicas do Papa João Paulo II (Encíclica *Redemptor Hominis,* 4. 3. 19 – 9) SP:LTR, 1999. p.31 – 34.

se torne objeto de multiforme manipulação, se bem que muitas vezes não diretamente perceptível". Diante do avanço tecnológico as futuras gerações dependem muito da atual.

Jose Eduardo Faria[7] observa que se a globalização mudou o perfil e a escala dos conflitos e exige novos padrões de responsabilidade, controle, segurança, deve a ética avançar ou ceder mais espaço nesse contexto. Mas parece que o ser humano, a sociedade e o Poder público não se conscientizaram da importância da preservação da natureza. Ramón Martín Mateo[8] pondera: *"El hombre de hoy usa y abusa de la naturaleza como si hubiera de ser el ultimo inquilino de este desgraciado planeta, como si detrás de él no se anunciara un futuro. La naturaleza se convierte aí en el chivo expiatorio del progreso"*. Em nome do progresso econômico e social, desenvolveram-se técnicas que, por explorar inadequadamente a natureza, causam poluição de toda sorte e degradação do meio ambiente, colocando em risco a vida do homem e das demais espécies que povoam a terra, dando origem à crise ambiental[9].

As agressões ecológicas ou assaltos ao meio ambiente atingem os animais, surgindo as questões: Quanto vale um metro cúbico de biodiversidade? Como compatibilizar as tendências do progresso socioeconômico com a preservação do equilíbrio ecológico? Como o desenvolvimento industrial poderia ser compatível com a restauração do meio ambiente? A riqueza gerada com a poluição compensaria os danos causados à fauna e à flora? Como explorar adequadamente os recursos naturais e recuperar a qualidade ambiental? Como progredir e manter a diversidade biológica? Qual o risco da ausência ou do declínio populacional de uma espécie animal no meio ambiente? Como pôr um fim à cultura predatória e à defaunação?[10] Urge uma conscientização de todos quanto aos grandes riscos decorrentes dessa desordem ecológica dando preponderância ao ecodesenvolvimento, ou melhor, ao desenvolvimento sustentável, na busca de uma conciliação entre o desenvolvimento, a preservação ecológica, como nos ensina Édis Milare[11].

[7] FARIA, J.E. *O direito na economia globalizada*. SPaulo: Malheiros, 1999. p.8.

[8] MATEO, Ramón M. *Derecho ambiental*. Madrid: s/e, 1977. p. 21.

[9] TOURINHO NETO, Fernando do C. Dano ambiental. *Consulex*, 2 : 19 – 20; SANTOS, Antonio Silveira R. Dos. Vida selvagem: importância e proteção. *Revista* APMP, 31 : 71 – 3.

[10] DINIZ, M.Helena. *O estado atual do biodireito*. SPaulo: Saraiva, 2014. pp. 844 a 849.

[11] MILARE, Edis. Tutela jurisdicional do ambiente. *Revista do advogado* 37 : 7 – 8.

2. DEFAUNAÇÃO DIRETA E INDIRETA

Os animais, pelo importante papel que exercem para o equilíbrio do meio ambiente, merecem tutela jurídica. A proteção à fauna, por sua vez, conduz à tutela da vida do ser humano, por tal razão alguns países se preocuparam em resguardar os animais. A Suíça, em 1992, reconheceu, no art. 26 da sua Constituição o respeito à dignidade da criatura, que deve ser respeitada no âmbito das leis que regem à engenharia genética. A Alemanha, em 2002, alterou o art. 20 da Lei Fundamental substituindo a locução "vida humana" por "bases naturais da vida", incluindo a proteção aos animais, não humanos, e a França também fez o mesmo.

Pelo Código Civil brasileiro de 2002 (art. 82), os animais são bens semoventes, por isso o direito os protege indiretamente ao tutelar o patrimônio do homem. Pela Constituição Federal de nosso País, embora os animais não tenham o *status* jurídico de pessoa, têm um *status* moral relevante, que requer proteção jurídica, ante o principio da solidariedade humana[12]. A fauna é abordada na nossa Carta Magna nos arts. 23, VII, 24 VI, 225, § 1º, VII. A norma constitucional protege, expressamente, a fauna e proíbe maus tratos a animais, apresentando uma visão do ecocentrismo, apesar da predominação do antropocentrismo[13], que está centrada no animal, ao auxiliar o entendimento de como o sistema biótico sobrevive e se modifica, ante a interligação de todos os elementos da biota (as espécies e seus meios ambientes)[14]. E a Declaração Universal dos Direitos dos Animais, por sua vez, prescreve:

> Art. 2º. 2 – " O homem como espécie animal, não pode exterminar os outros animais ou explorá-los violando esse direito, tem o dever de pôr os seus conhecimentos ao serviço dos animais".
>
> Art. 3º. 1- "Nenhum animal será submetido nem a maus tratos nem a atos cruéis".

[12] ELER, Kalline C. G. A tutela dos animais pela personalidade: melhor caminho? *Animais – Bioética e Direito.* Tereza R. Vieira e Camilo H. Silva (coord.). Brasília, Portal Juridico, 2016, p. 18.

[13] Pela ótica antropocêntrica, o ser humano é o centro do Universo, as demais formas de vida somente terão importância na medida em que proporcionam o seu bem-estar. Consulte: KORTENKAM, K.V. e MOORE, CF. Ecocentrism and anthropocentrism: moral reasoning about ecological commons dilemmas. *Journal* of *Environmental Psychology*, 21: 261 – 276, 2001.

[14] MOTA, Jose A. e BURSZTYN, Marcel. O valor da natureza como apoio à decisão pública. *Revista Paranaense de Desenvolvimento,* Curitiba. V. 34, n. 125, pp. 39 – 56, 2013.

> Art. 4º. 1 – "Todo animal pertencente a uma espécie selvagem tem o direito de viver livre no seu próprio ambiente natural, terrestre, aéreo ou aquático e tem o direito de se reproduzir".
>
> Art. 4º. 2 – "Toda privação de liberdade, mesmo que tenha fins educativos, é contraria a esse direito."
>
> Art. 8º. 1 – "A experimentação animal que implique sofrimento físico ou psicológico é incompatível com os direitos do animal, quer se trate de uma experiência médica, científica, comercial ou qualquer que seja a forma de experimentação."
>
> Art. 12. 1 – "Todo ato que implique na morte de grande numero de animais selvagens é um genocídio, isto é, um crime contra a espécie."
>
> Art.12. 2 – "A poluição e a destruição do ambiente natural conduzem ao genocídio."

O Brasil é subscritor da Declaração Universal dos Direitos dos Animais (1978), que no art. 12 prevê o genocídio animal pela poluição e destruição do ambiente natural, ou seja, pela prática de exterminação indireta, contra o meio em que ele habita, e, com isso, veda, terminantemente, a defaunação. A defaunação é a extinção ou a diminuição populacional de espécies animais em seu *habitat*. Problema tão grave quanto o desmatamento, porque o desaparecimento das espécies influencia na função dos ecossistemas naturais[15].

Tal defaunação será: a) *direta* quando o objetivo da atividade é o próprio animal ou seus subprodutos, como a caça de subsistência ou desportiva, o trafico ou captura de animais silvestres, b) *indireta* se houver um distúrbio ambiental, que, apesar de não visar a espécie animal, provoca a sua remoção ou sua morte, como perda e degradação de *habitats*, advindas de catástrofes naturais (mudanças climáticas etc., por ex. os dinossauros tiveram sua extinção provocada por fator externo: o período glacial) aglomerações urbanas, empreendimentos agropecuários, rodovias, usinas hidroelétricas, mineração etc.[16]. Os animais são bens semoventes (CC, arts. 82, 445, 936, 1442, V) mas são seres sencientes, pois, na visão do *ecocentrismo*, podem sofrer, por terem capacidade de sentir[17].

[15] DIRZO. R. e outros. Defaunation in the antropocene science, 2014, v. 345, pp. 401–406.

[16] ROCHA VILELA, Daniel A. da e outros. Principais ameaças e medidas de salvaguarda aos animais silvestres. *MPMG jurídico – Revista MPEMG* – Edição Defesa da Fauna, 201, pp. 18–23.

[17] MCINTYRE, s. *Animals are now legally recognised as sentient beigns in New Zealand*, 2015.

Se o ser humano exerce domínio sobre animais, sendo o senhor de seu destino, é preciso uma tomada de consciência sobre suas atividades em relação à fauna, cabendo-lhe estabelecer seus objetivos, evitando defaunação. É preciso controlar as ameaças que levam a extinção de fauna. Constituem, como veremos, ameaças ao desaparecimento de animais silvestre, dentre outras: caça e tráfico para subsistência, que provoca morte de animais silvestres, em busca de carnes, peles de catetos, queixadas, capivaras e jacarés para serem vendidas no mercado nacional e internacional; perda de *habitat*; impacto de rodovias; introdução de espécies exóticas, advindas de outros países[18].

A proteção dos animais contra sua extinção e maus tratos por seres humanos se justifica numa visão kantiana pois não se pode admitir o abandono moral daquele que os maltrata. Com isso estar-se-ia, como diz Seher, protegendo não o animal, mas a pessoa humana, para que não fique abandonada moralmente. É preciso que haja uma conscientização social voltada ao respeito dos animais[19].

3. PRINCIPAIS FATORES DE EXTINÇÃO DA FAUNA NATIVA

A fauna silvestre é o conjunto de animais que vive em certa região e é um bem ambiental, que integra o meio ambiente ecologicamente equilibrado. A esgotabilidade e o escasseamento da fauna repercutem, por esse motivo, negativamente, na manutenção e no equilíbrio ecológico, tão essencial à sadia qualidade de vida do povo. A extinção da fauna liga-se a alguns fatores, dentre eles podemos citar[20]:

A) *a fragmentação e destruição do "habitat"* ou do local (abrigos, ninhos, criadouros naturais, matas, rios e marés etc.) onde naturalmente vive, fora do cativeiro, uma espécie animal, mediante condutas humanas como expansão urbana e pecuária, queimadas, poluição de rios, dizimação de

[18] ROCHA VILELA E OUTROS. Principais ameaças e medidas de salvaguarda aos animais silvestres. *MPMG jurídico – Revista MPEMG* – Edição Defesa da Fauna, 201, pp. 19 e 20.

[19] SEHER, Gerhard. La legitimación de normas penales basada en principios y el concepto de bien jurídico. in. HEFENDHEL, Roland. *La teoría del bien jurídico.* Fundamento de legitimación del derecho penal o juego de abalorios dogmático? Madrid: Marcial Pons, 2007, p. 87.

[20] BECHARA, Erika. *A proteção da fauna sob a ótica constitucional.* SPaulo: Juarez de Oliveira, 2003. pp. 123 – 4, 126 – 7, 130, 134 e 261; DINIZ, M. Helena. O *estado..* , cit .,p. 882 a 885; PRINGLE. *Ecologia: ciencia* da *sobrevivência.* Rio de Janeiro, 1977. p. 14; LINDAHLN- CURRY. *Ecologia* – conservar para *sobreviver.* p. 284 e s; FIORILLO e RODRIGUES, *Manual...* , cit, pp. 318 – 43; CAUGHLEY. Directions in conservation biology. *Journal of Animas Ecology*, 63 : 215 – 44.

florestas para exploração madeireira ou formação de área de cultivo, uso de herbicidas e agrotóxicos, que envenenam a terra. Todos esses atos atingem ecossistemas, matando animais pela degradação ou perda de *habitat.*

Realmente, diante da poluição aquática provocada pela atividade humana (vazamento de óleo, uso de fertilizantes ou de produtos químicos, dejetos industriais, tubulações de esgoto doméstico, lançamento de lixo plástico, que provoca extinção de milhares de albatrozes), os rios e mares estão perdendo a sua capacidade de autorregeneração. Há queda acentuada de cardumes de peixes e de mamíferos marinhos (focas, leões-marinhos), crescimento de algas tóxicas, que matam seres marinhos, águas vivas, proliferação de bactérias, aumento de morte de peixes pelas marés vermelhas.

Portanto, são poluentes altamente danosos à vida aquática: pesca predatória, mediante aplicação intensa de novas tecnologias de captura, que aumentaram, aceleradamente, a produção pesqueira nas ultimas décadas; plásticos e restos de redes de pesca; petróleo, introduzido no mar por afluentes terrestres, pela exploração *off shore* e pelo tráfego marítimo, gerando catastróficos acidentes, como, por ex, o do navio *Torrey Canyon,* nas costas da Cornualha; metais pesados, esgotos industriais e domésticos, agrotóxicos, fertilizantes ou lixo tóxico, alijados no mar ou nos rios[21].

Isto é assim, porque o mar, apesar de ser tido como a grande "lixeira" do mundo, não consegue reciclar, em curto ou médio prazo, as inúmeras substâncias químicas, latas, borrachas, enfim, tudo que nele é lançado, e isso sem falar do lixo atômico dos submarinos russos afundados no mar de Barentz. Consequentemente, certos ecossistemas marinhos, degradam-se, às vezes de modo irreversível, diante não só da falta de técnicas eficientes ou de recursos para a introdução de tecnologias para limpar o meio ambiente já devastado, mas também uma tomada de consciência para o uso sustentável e a conservação dos recursos vivos marinhos e fluviais. Urge proporcionar uma *window of opportunity* (janela de oportunidade) para a adoção de medidas legais à proteção e à gestão desses recursos[22].

[21] GUSMÃO CÂMARA, Ibsen de. O ambiente marinho e as consequências da poluição. *Questões importantes referentes ao mar.* Georgette Nacarato Nazo (coord.). SPaulo: Soamar, 1996. pp. 48 – 9; DINIZ, M. Helena. *O estado...*, cit., pp. 1008 e 1009.

[22] BALSA, Elizabeth S. Ambiente marinho e a poluição. *Questões importantes referente ao mar.* Georgette Nacarato Nazo (coord.), cit. p. 54; MESQUITA PEREIRA, Rodrigo de. A proteção dos recursos hídricos – aspectos legais e práticos. *Manual prático da Promotoria de Justiça do Meio Ambiente* (vários autores). SPaulo: Imesp, 1999. pp. 247–260; DINIZ, M. Helena, *O estado...*, cit., p. 1010.

Muitas aves migratórias que proveriam nos EUA utilizam-se, no inverno, de florestas tropicais da America Latina, e, assim, sendo, havendo desmatamento, com a destruição de seu *habitat*, perdidas estarão essas espécies de aves. Sem duvida, o desmatamento provoca desequilíbrio ambiental, em virtude, por ex. da função ecológica desempenhada pelas florestas no meio ambiente, na manutenção de elementos básicos para a preservação dos *habitats* para animais silvestres.

Realmente, degradação do *habitat* pelo desmatamento para dar espaço, por ex. à pecuária, à agricultura, a empreendimentos de grande porte como hidrelétricas e minerações, afeta muito a fauna silvestre, podendo ameaçá-las de extinção, ou deslocá-las de seu *habitat*, causando forte impacto sócio ambiental.

A construção de estradas e o fluxo de veículos, também, podem causar perda de *habitat*, pois, em razão de atropelamentos da fauna silvestre provocados pela colisão de veiculo com animais, Forman, Seiler, Helldin, Glista e outros apontam as seguintes soluções preventivas para reduzir o impacto das estradas, ferrovias e rodovias sobre a fauna nativa, que devem ser implantadas pelo poder público ou pelas concessionárias[23]: a) construção de passagens (viadutos, pontes, túneis) para a fauna; b) uso de muros, cercas e telas para bloquear locais de risco e conduzir animais para um lugar de travessia mais adequado; c) adoção de medidas para reduzir velocidade com lombadas, radares, redutores eletrônicos etc.; d) manejo da vegetação na borda da estrada; e e) educação ambiental no trânsito e campanhas informativas.

Como se vê, sempre será possível uma solução, sem ameaçar a vida silvestre e sem que se trave o progresso. Outra causa é o aquecimento global (efeito estufa), provocado pela ação humana (queima de combustíveis fósseis), que vem afetando ecossistemas terrestres e marinhos, causando fortes impactos sobre a fauna e a flora, em diferentes regiões, por exemplo: forçando a migração de aves e fuga de espécies animais para regiões mais frias, alterando a reprodução do atum – de – barbatana-azul; provocando, branqueamento de corais, diminuindo o estoque de *Krill* no oce-

23 FORMAN, R.T e outros. *Road ecology*. Science and Solutions, Island Press: Washington, D.C. 2003, p. 481; SEILER e HELLDIN. Mortality in wildlife due to transportation in Davenport. The *Ecology of Transportation: managing Mobility for the Environment*, Kluwer, 2006, p. 392; GLISTA e outros. A review of mitigation measures for reducing wildlife mortality on roadways. *Landscape and urban Planning*, v. 91', n -1 pp. 1 – 7, 2009.

ano Austral. O ritmo de desaparecimento das espécies é de 100 extinções por milhão de espécies por ano[24].

Observa Luis Paulo Sirvinskas[25], "que os seres vivos da Terra não estão enfrentando uma extinção tão catastrófica quanto a que deu cabo dos dinossauros, mas estão caminhando a passos largos para esta hecatombe". Perda e fragmentação de *habitat* é uma grande ameaça à biodiversidade, visto que provoca remoção imediata da fauna nativa e desaparecimento ou redução da espécie[26].

B) *A caça e a pesca excessivas*, que se dão quando uma população for explorada acima de seu limite de reposição. Foi o que ocorreu, por ex. em 1907, no planalto de Kaiab (Arizona), quando os caçadores, para manter 4000 veados, mataram a maior parte de lobos, coiotes e leões-de-montanha, que deles se alimentavam. Com isso, em 1924, os veados, que já eram 100.000, destruíram a vegetação, e, em dois invernos consecutivos, mais da metade da manada morreu de fome. A caça predatória, por ter finalidade comercial (caça profissional, se visar lucro com a venda do produto ou subproduto extraído do animal silvestre) ou de mero deleite (caça desportiva, ou caça sanguinária), visto que deixa o animal morto no local sem qualquer utilidade[27]. A caça não predatória é a que tem um objetivo especifico. Pode ser: **a)** caça de controle, destinada a proteção de saúde pública, e da agricultura. Sendo permitida se os animais silvestres estiverem lesando plantações ou destruindo rebanhos, ou colocando em risco a saúde humana; **b)** caça amadorista ou desportiva é praticada por caçador que integra uma associação ou clube de caça ou tiro ao vôo, desde que munido de licença especial para transitarem com arma de esporte. Tal licença será concedida se ocorrer superpopulação de animais silvestres; **c)** caça de subsistência é a realizada por índios, caboclos, caiçaras, que, por viverem em local distante do centro urbano, caçam para manter sua subsistência, e esse fato não é crime ambiental (Lei n. 9.605/98, art. 37,I); e **d)** caça cientifica (lei n. 5.197/67, art. 14) é a feita, com permissão, a cientistas para coleta de material, a ser usado para a descoberta de remédios.

24 Garcia, Rafael. Homem acelerou ritmo de extinção em mil vezes. *Folha de SPaulo* – ciencia + Saúde, 30.5.2014, p. 11.

25 Sirvinskas, L. Paulo. *Manual de direito ambiental*. SPaulo: Saraiva, 2015. p. 661.

26 Dirzo, R. e Raven P.H. Global state of biodiversity and loss. *Annual Review of Environment and Resources*, v. 28, pp. 137–167, julho 2003.

27 Sirvinskas, Luis Paulo. *Manual...*, cit., pp. 415 – 416.

A Lei n. 11.794/2008, regulamentada pelo Dec. 6.899/2009, disciplina o uso de animais em experimentos científicos e criou o CONCEA (Conselho Nacional de Controle de Experimentação Animal) e a CEUA (Comissão de Ética no Uso de Animais). É preciso não olvidar que a pesquisa científica pode ter propósitos diferentes, alguns revestem-se de certa importância outros causam muita dor aos animais (por ex. existem experimentos feitos em animais para produção de cosméticos, testando-os nos olhos de coelhos, por ex., causando-lhes malefícios) e outros não lhes infligem nenhum mal (por ex. observação de animais).

A experimentação animal para fins didáticos ou de pesquisa, abrange a vivissecção, procedimento cirúrgico em animal vivo (ratos, coelhos, macacos, pombos, peixes etc.). Experimento cruel, praticado mundialmente, fazendo com que diariamente um incontável numero de animais perca a vida, em razão de testes comportamentais, neurológicos, cirúrgicos, toxicológicos, cutâneos é punido no art. 32 § 1º da Lei n. 9.605/98 e só pode ser realizado na ausência de métodos alternativos (necrópsia, biópsia, sistema biológico *"in vitro"*, cultura de bactérias etc.)[28].

Sobre vivissecção, experimentação e pesquisas com animais vivos, que são sacrificados em prol da humanidade, há registro de que mais de 100 milhões perdem a vida, anualmente, no mundo inteiro, "em laboratórios de vivissecção, a pretexto de servirem à ciencia médica e às indústrias de alimentos ou de cosméticos"[29]. As técnicas de pesquisas de vivissecção vêm sendo feitas em animais para testes militares, espaciais, cosmetológicos, farmacêuticos etc. Para tanto há afogamento de animais, amputação de membros, esmagamento de órgãos, provocação de ataques cardíacos, convulsões, paralisia, inalação de fumaça, ingestão de drogas ou álcool etc. Além de levar esses animais à morte, tais técnicas causam sofrimento, exposição à radiação. Singer observa que essa pesquisa na indústria alimentícia, para conservantes, aditivos e corantes, (LD 50), que tem por escopo descobrir a dose letal, pode levar à morte de 50% de cem amostras de animais[30].

[28] LEVAI, Laerte F. A experimentação animal e a proteção da fauna. *Manual prático da Promotoria de Justiça do Meio Ambiente*, vol. 1, SPaulo, Imprensa Oficial, 2005, pp. 502 a 514.

[29] LEVAI, Laerte F. *Direito dos animais*. Campos de Jordão: Mantiqueira, 1998. p. 76.

[30] SINGER, P. *Libertação animal*. SPaulo: M. Fontes, 2010; REGAN, *Jaulas vazias*: encarando desafio dos direito animais. Porto Alegre: Lugano, 2006. p. 214.

A Lei Federal n. 9605/1998, art. 32,§§ 1º e 2º, define como crime de maus-tratos a animais experiência cruel ou dolorosa em animal vivo, ainda que para fins didáticos ou científicos, se existirem recursos alternativos[31]. Pesquisas em animais vivos estão sendo substituídas por métodos alternativos como: biópsias, cultura de bactérias, uso de placenta ou de cordão umbilical; farmacologia, cromatografia, sistemas biológicos *in vitro* etc.

Atualmente a engenharia genética tem provocado uma verdadeira revolução científica, pois a tecnologia do DNA recombinante e o mapeamento sequencial do genomas, como um passe de mágica, vem resolvendo certos problemas mediante a alteração da composição genética da flora e da fauna. Não será difícil que, dentro de alguns anos, haja uma recodificação genética, provocando criações inusitadas como por ex. animais quiméricos, como os da mitologia grega ou clones de animais, novas raças, animais transgênicos (ANGM'S). Não se pode negar o forte impacto da engenharia genética ou da biotecnologia no meio ambiente ao criar, mediante a manipulação de moléculas ADN/ARN recombinantes ou de fusão celular, organismos geneticamente modificados (OGMS)[32].

Chegou-se até mesmo a misturar vegetal e animal, por ex, como se deu, com a transferência do gene que provoca a bioluminescência do vagalume para a célula da planta de fumo, que passou a brilhar, ou de gene do *hamster* chinês no genoma do tabaco, para aumentar a produção do esterol ou de gene de rato na alface para aumentar sua produção de vitamina C[33].

A produção de organismos transgênicos produz impacto no meio ambiente e pode ameaçar a extinção de espécies existentes, p. ex. bactérias modificadas podem despoluir rios e mares, decompor hidrocarbonetos do petróleo, limpar lençóis freáticos contaminados, tornar certos solventes tóxicos inofensivos, mas poderá trazer riscos ao meio ambiente e provocar morte de animais aquáticos.

Indaga-se: Quais as reais consequências, a longo prazo, das transformações biotecnológicas? Quais os efeitos que, no futuro, poderão advir das mutações genéticas artificiais, praticadas em laboratórios, em animais e plantas? Quais os riscos que meio ambiente poderá sofrer com a introdu-

31 ALVIM, Mariana Spacek. Experimentação animal na nova Lei n. 11.798/2008 à luz da interpretação conforme a Constituição. *Revista Brasileira de Direito Animal*, 2014.

32 DINIZ, Maria Helena. *O estado*..., cit., pp. 886-887.

33 SZKLAROWSKY, Léon F. Transgênicos. *Consulex*, 34 : 19; DINIZ, Maria Helena. *O estado*..., cit., p. 892.

ção dessa civilização transgênica ou com a criação de organismos geneticamente modificados? Será que o ser humano teria direito de alterar geneticamente um animal, criando espécie diferente da existente? Seria possível admitir o transporte de genes de uma espécie a outra? A formação de novas espécies mais resistentes não seria um modo de fazer uma seleção natural artificial?[34]

Como não se pode prever, com certeza, quais os efeitos da engenharia genética no meio ambiente, a CF/88, no art. 225, § 1º II, incumbe o Poder Público de preservar a diversidade e a integridade do patrimônio genético do País e de fiscalizar as entidades dedicadas à pesquisa e manipulação de material genético. A norma constitucional ordena a preservação da diversidade biológica já existente e do patrimônio genético de todos os seres vivos, inclusive dos organismos geneticamente modificados, desde que haja não só um controle do Poder Público da sua produção e comercialização, bem como do emprego das técnicas, métodos e substâncias que comportem risco para vida, a qualidade de vida e o meio ambiente (CF, art. 225, V), mas também um resguardo da função ecológica dos OGMs derivados da associação de genes da mesma espécie (CF, art. 2255, VII). Com isso, proibidas estão as práticas que coloquem em risco a função ecológica dos organismos que provoquem a extinção das espécies ou que submetam os animais à crueldade, mediante o emprego de métodos inadequados e impróprios à pesquisa ou de procedimentos que não sejam indolores[35].

Na caça está proibida a utilização de instrumentos que possam maltratar os animais como veneno, armadilhas, atiradeiras, e armas a bala com calibre 22 para animais de porte superior ao tapiti (35 cms). Em certos locais a caça não é permitida: zonas urbanas, suburbanas, povoadas, estâncias hidrominerais e climáticas, açudes etc.[36]. Está vedada a pesca: **a)** de espécies que devam ser preservadas ou com tamanhos inferiores aos permitidos; **b)** de quantidades superiores as permitidas ou mediante uso de petrechos ou métodos proibidos; **c)** por meio de explosivos ou de substâncias tóxicas.

A Lei n. 11.959/2009 disciplina o exercício da pesca contendo normas sobre sua permissão, autorização ou licença pelo órgão competente, sem

[34] DINIZ, Maria Helena. *O estado...*, cit., p. 930.

[35] FIORILLO e RODRIGUES. *Manual...*, cit., pp. 475-8; DINIZ, Maria Helena. *O estado...*, cit., p. 935.

[36] SIRVINSKAS, Luis Paulo. *Manual...*, cit., pp. 630 a 635.

prejuízo das analises de impacto ambiental, observando-se os períodos, tamanhos de espécies e locais proibidos previamente estabelecidos pelo Poder Público. Imprescindível será o controle da pesca para evitar diminuição ou extinção de espécies aquáticas em risco de desaparecimento. Daí a importância de se fixar normativamente os períodos de proibição de pesca ou os locais interditados, levando-se em conta as peculiaridades de cada região para proteção da fauna e da flora aquáticas, e principalmente das espécies ameaçadas de extinção.

A Lei n. 9605/98, arts. 34 a 36, por sua vez, trata dos crimes da pesca, não permitindo: **a)** pesca em período no qual a pesca é proibida (piracema - 1º/11 a 28/2), porque os peixes buscam locais adequados para desova e alimentação. Nesse período só é permitida, no Estado de Minas Gerais (Portaria/MG – IEF/2015), pesca com limite de quantidade para espécies exóticas (de outros países), alóctones (de outras bacias brasileiras), híbridas (produzidas em laboratórios, além de pouca espécies autóctones[37]; **b)** pescar peixes ameaçados de extinção ou de tamanhos inferiores aos permitidos; **c)** usar aparelhos, apetrechos, técnicas, métodos/vedados (lambada, arrasto, batida etc.).

A preservação da fauna deve ser um dos principais objetivos da lei que visa proteger o meio ambiente, coibindo ação maléfica de caçadores e de pescadores.

C) O comercio ilegal de animais silvestres, por incentivo a sua caça, captura ou procura por toda sorte de pessoas ávidas por seu trafico, tendo-se em vista a venda de peles de diferentes animais e, ainda, o fato de que em alguns restaurantes vem-se tornando moda o ato de servir animais silvestres, como javali, tartarugas, capivaras, jacarés, fazendo com que sejam capturados, para ser criados para abate, mas só poderão sê-lo em criadouros credenciados, para que haja controle dessa atividade. Além disso, aves, animais silvestres ou exóticos (p. ex. iguanas, salamandras, hamster, chinchila, jiboias, leões, tigres etc.) têm despertado atenção de algumas pessoas que os adquirem por meio de internet, anuncio em *site*, leilão eletrônico, sala de bate papo e os mantém em casa, retirando-os do seu *habitat*.

A caça e captura por traficantes de aves (tucanos, aracaris, arapongas) tem provocado alteração no tamanho dos frutos de palmito – juçara, pois

[37] CARRILHO, Luciana Mª C. Pontos controvertidos do crime de pesca. *MPMG Jurídico. Revista do Ministerio Publico de MG*. Ed. Defesa da Fauna, 2016, p. 62.

as aves menores não conseguem se alimentar dos frutos grandes. Com isso, a defaunação vem dando origem à produção de sementes menores, influindo na flora.

A captura e o comércio (interno ou internacional) clandestino de animais silvestres e de seus subprodutos causam, portanto, lesão à biodiversidade por retirá-los de seu ambiente natural, levando à sua extinção, como ocorreu, p. ex. com a ararinha azul (*cyanopsitta spixii*), ou ameaça de extinção, como o bicudo (*sporophila maximiliani*) e o curió (*sporophila angolensis*). Grande é a responsabilidade do trafico ilegal de milhares de animais silvestres, na extinção da fauna, visto que cerca de 12 milhões de animais são retirados de seu *habitats* e a *Environment Investigation Agency* relata que muitos animais transportados por via aérea ou fluvial, no comércio ilegal, chegam mortos a seu destino.

É importante que haja uma maior fiscalização para evitar a retirada dos animais do seu ambiente e implantação de um maior numero de CETAS para receber, cuidar e recuperar animais silvestres apreendidos, recolhidos para preservação da fauna nativa. As aves apreendidas ilegalmente, em gaiolas devem ser levadas aos centros de readaptação (viveiros), para sua ulterior soltura em seu *habitat*.

Para evitar isso, vários países assinaram, em 1973, a Convenção sobre o Comércio Internacional das Espécies da Fauna e Flora Selvagens em Perigo de Extinção. A Convenção sobre o Comercio Internacional das Espécies da Fauna e Flora Selvagens em perigo de extinção – CITES – reconhece a fauna e a flora como portadoras de valores biológicos, científicos, culturais que devem ser protegidas no interesse da atual e futura geração. Os Estados por tal razão devem combater práticas como tráfico de animais silvestres[38].

Urge, como ensina MARTINS,[39] entender que o tráfico de animais influi na teia de interrelações ecossistêmicas, de modo que um ecossistema não pode ser entendido isoladamente. Assim se um papagaio for retirado de seu *habitat* para ser mantido em cativeiro, traz séria consequência danosa à biodiversidade, pois os papagaios que ficaram no ninho não serão alimentados e perecerão, as sementes dos frutos que o alimentavam não são

[38] BENJAMIN, A.H. Constitucionalização do Ambiente e ecologização da Constituição brasileira. CANOTILHO e LEITE (org.). *Direito constitucional ambiental brasileiro*. SPaulo: Saraiva, 2007, pp. 57–130.

[39] MARTINS, G.S. *Norma Ambiental: complexidade e concretização*. Dissertação de mestrado apresentada na UFSC, 2013. pp. 22 e 23.

dispersadas, comprometendo a manutenção da floresta. Além disso, aves traficadas para guarda doméstica ilegal morrem pelo caminho e deixam de reproduzir. Deveras, um papagaio pode gerar 4 filhotes por ano, ao fim de 35 anos, com a retirada de um exemplar da espécie, 3500 papagaios deixarão de nascer.

O tráfico de animais silvestres constitui um dos maiores desafios do direito ambiental no século XXI. Mas não é um fenômeno novo, visto que desde a época colonial houve tráfico ilegal no Brasil, pois por ex., em 1532, portugueses ao capturarem a nau francesa Peregrina nela encontraram três mil peles de onça, 15 mil toras de pau-brasil, 600 papagaios e 1,8 toneladas de algodão, óleos medicinais, pimenta, sementes de algodão e amostras de minerais apreendidos pela tripulação durante sua estada de 4 meses no Brasil, e isso provocou o rompimento das relações entre Portugal e França[40]. É tido como ilícito qualquer comportamento que venda, exponha à venda, exporte ou adquira, guarde ou tenha em cativeiro espécies da fauna silvestre, sem a permissão, autorização ou licença da autoridade competente. (Lei 9605/98, art. 29 e §§ 1º e 3º).

O tráfico de animais requer por parte do Poder Público uma prevenção e repressão maior, para salvaguardar o patrimônio faunístico brasileiro, porque: **a)** sob o prisma penal tem sido entendido como crime de menor potencial ofensivo conducente à transação penal ou aplicação de pena restritiva de direitos, com a mesma duração da que restringe a liberdade, como prestação de serviço à comunidade, interdição temporária de direitos e recolhimento domiciliar[41]; **b)** sob o aspecto administrativo ambiental não tem havido execução da maior parte das multas aplicadas ao traficante de animais; **c)** sob o enfoque civil, a responsabilidade civil por dano à fauna, não tem sido eficaz.

Para Luciano J. Alvarenga[42] o tráfico de animais silvestres apresenta cinco caracteres de crime organizado: a) articulação por grandes redes de rotas para o traslado dos animais, quer no interior, quer para o exterior do país; b) recurso ao apoio de atores-chave no *métier* político, para proteção discreta e efetiva das atividades criminosas; c) corrupção de atores gover-

[40] BUENO. *Capitães do Brasil*: a saga dos primeiros colonizadores. Rio de Janeiro: Objetiva, 1999. pp. 7 e 8.

[41] RAPHAELLI, R. *Noções sobre o trafico de animais no Brasil*. 2012.

[42] ALVARENGA, L. J . Trafico de animais silvestres: historiografia e lógicas de continuidade. *MPMG Jurídico*, Rev. MPEMG, 2016, Ed. Defesa da Fauna, p. 37.

namentais, nomeadamente dos afetos às atividades fiscalizatórias, como fato, e, em alguns casos, como estratégia, que dá sustentação à prática; 4) conectividade dinâmica e sincronismo com outras atividades ilícitas como o tráfico de drogas e de armas. Hernandez[43] esclarece que a *United Nations Interregional Crime and Justice Institut*, apurou uma conexão entre as atividades do tráfico de drogas e o de animais, e às vezes se observa o que causa perplexidade, um ou mais espécimes serem usadas como instrumentos de crime; 5) estruturação hierárquica interna entre os agentes do tráfico similar à das organizações criminosas profissionais, marcada por uma divisão clara de funções e benefícios entre os participantes (pessoas hipossuficientes economicamente, em condições de vulnerabilidade sociopolítica, subordinando-se a membros com maior poderio).

A Lei n.5197/67, art.3º, veda comércio de espécies de fauna silvestre que implique caça, perseguição, destruição ou apanha como o dos produtos e objetos dela provenientes, mas admite caça de espécies silvestres e o comércio dos produtos manufaturados provenientes de criadouros artificiais, desde que haja autorização do poder público competente.

D) a extinção em cadeia, que ocorre quando a perda de uma espécie conduz à de outra, como, por ex, se dá com a espécie predadora, quando a espécie que serve de presa é extinta, fazendo, então, com que aquela não mais possa prover sua subsistência, por não conseguir substituir sua alimentação por outro produto existente no *habitat*.

E) a introdução de espécies exóticas em ecossistema estranho a elas, com o escopo de melhorar os animais existentes no local ou para que cacem outros, que, na verdade, trazem consequências nefastas, tornando-se uma praga destruidora do ambiente. Foi o que ocorreu, por ex: na Austrália em 1858, que introduziu em sua fauna o gambá-de-rabo-peludo para aproveitamento de sua pele, causando enormes prejuízos a pastagens e florestas e, em 1859, com a introdução de coelhos, que três anos depois tornaram-se uma praga e catástrofe nacional. Na Nova Zelândia, ao se introduzir fauna exótica, doméstica e selvagem, na nativa, com o objetivo de aumentar a população de caça, dizimaram-se florestas, cereais, répteis, anfíbios e outros animais nativos.

Destruição de *habitats* e invasão de espécies invasoras ameaçam a biodiversidade provocada pela mudança climática global, pois aves, desorien-

[43] HERNANDES, E.F.T. Das redes e do tráfico de animais. *Geografia*, n. 11, 2002, p. 277.

tadas pelo clima, acabam mudando rotas de migração, correndo risco de extinção. Pinguins ante o aquecimento global, migram do sul para o litoral brasileiro em busca de comida, porque o derretimento do gelo afasta o *Krill* que é sua principal fonte de alimentação e acabam morrendo nas praias do sudeste e nordeste brasileiro[44].

É preciso evitar introdução deliberada ou acidental nos *habitats* de espécies não nativas que pode trazer deslocamento da fauna nativa, causando dano ao funcionamento do ecossistema e graves consequências econômicas. Foi o que ocorreu com a introdução do javali (*Sus Scrofa*) no Brasil, que, por ser animal de grande porte, competiu por *habitat* com espécies nativas de porcos do mato ou de catetos (*Pecari Tajacu*), depredando plantas e animais.

4. CRITÉRIOS ÉTICO-JURÍDICOS EM RELAÇÃO À DEFAUNAÇÃO: UMA CONTRIBUIÇÃO PARA A SUSTENTABILIDADE AMBIENTAL

Não há como negar os serviços prestados à humanidade pelos ecossistemas, mas, ao lado desses benefícios, a crescente urbanização, a caça e a pesca predatória, as agressões às florestas com o desmatamento para afins agrícolas, pecuários ou industriais, o uso de energia nuclear, o desenvolvimento da tecnologia do DNA recombinante, a introdução no meio ambiente de organismos engenheirados, a criação de animais transgênicos, depauperação da camada de ozônio, escassez de água, intoxicação de uso desmedido de agrotóxicos, poluição, ressecamento do solo, destruição de *habitats*, iminência de esgotamento de recursos naturais não renováveis etc., alteraram a ordem natural da Terra, trazendo fatos danosos ao ser humano, à fauna e à flora.

Tudo isso traz, em seu bojo: a iminência da crescente falta de recursos naturais não renováveis[45]; o perigoso desfaunamento, ou seja, a extinção de animais inclusive nas áreas preservadas; o devastador impacto da ação da humanidade na natureza, reduzindo a biodiversidade; o empobrecimento e destruição de *habitats* naturais; a competição com espécies invasores; o

[44] GERAQUE, Eduardo. Aquecimento faz pinguim morrer nas praias do Brasil. *Folha de SPaulo*, 19.10.2008, p. c-13.

[45] HOKKANEN e LYNCH. *Biological control:benefits and risks*. Cambridge, 1995; PAVIANI, Aldo. Impactos ambientais da população. *Bioética*, 4: 195–20.

aquecimento global que provoca alterações climáticas; a poluição; a super exploração das espécies, flagelos que atingem a biodiversidade.

E, com isso, prejudicada está a função ecológica da fauna tão preconizada constitucionalmente. Urge uma efetiva proteção jurídica dos animais, alterando as normas, garantindo-lhes uma existência digna[46]. As leis ambientais devem priorizar a proteção da fauna silvestre, por estar inserida no contexto dos ecossistemas e da biodiversidade. É preciso deter o avanço da caça de animais em risco de extinção (mico-leão-dourado, veado campeiro, jacaré-do-papo-amarelo, a lontra, o cervo-do-pantanal, lobo-guará, ararinha azul, flamingo), e da pesca, desde que, clandestinas ou impulsionadas pela oferta e procura e o mercado conduzindo o tráfico ilegal[47].

Deveras, sem um controle legal às condutas humanas, a flora e a fauna correm o risco de extinção e, até mesmo, de perder sua função ecológica (CF, art.225, § 1º, VII), ou seja, sua participação na manutenção e equilíbrio do ecossistema, acarretando desequilíbrio do meio ambiente[48]. O poder público tem dever imposto pela CF, art, 225 e VII, de defender e preservar o meio ambiente, para tanto deverá proteger a fauna e vedar, por meio de lei, práticas que coloquem em risco sua função ecológica, provoquem a extinção de espécies ou submetam os animais a crueldade.

Berque[49] observa que o direito deve: reconhecer que a biosfera tem capacidade de autorregulação limitada; respeitar os ecossistemas locais e reinstaurar os destruídos; salvaguardar estabilidade ecológica e recarga hídrica; manter a diversidade fitofisionômica e florística e o fluxo de espécies faunísticas. Isto porque, o direito ao meio ambiente ecologicamente equilibrado, adquire hoje o *status* de direito fundamental[50]. Consequentemente, nenhum agente público ou privado, poderá tratá-lo como algo de

[46] SARLET, I.W e FENSTERSEIFER. T. Algumas notas sobre a dimensão ecológica da dignidade da pessoa humana e sobre a dignidade da vida em geral, in MOLINARO, C. A. e outros (org). *A dignidade e os direitos fundamentais para além dos humanos: uma discussão necessária.* Belo Horizonte. Fórum, 2008. pp. 175-205.

[47] LEVAI, Laerte F. Proteção Juridica da fauna. *Manual prático da Promotoria da Justiça do Meio Ambiente.* Spaulo: Imprensa Oficial, vol. 1, pp. 565–89.

[48] FIORILLO, Celso A. P. e RODRIGUES, Marcelo Abelha. *Manual de direito ambiental* e *legislação aplicável.* SPaulo: Max Limonad, 1999. p. 357: DINIZ, Maria Helena. *O estado* ..., cit., p. 880.

[49] BERQUE A. A. Ecúmena: medida terrestre ao homem, medida humana da terra. In: Serrão, A.V.S (org). *Filosofia da paisagem uma antologia.* Lisboa, 2011. p. 196.

[50] CANOTILHO, Jose J.G. e MOREIRA, Vital. *Constituição da Republica Portuguesa anotada.* Coimbra, 1993. p. 37.

valor menor. É preciso retirar o poder público da atmosfera de *laissez-faire* ambiental para que venha a atuar, positivamente, em prol do ambiente e contra a sua degradação, recompondo-se, impondo sanções ao degradador, prevenindo atentados. Deve haver uma preocupação cívica da degradação ambiental, voltada: à proibição de captura de animais; ao treinamento de funcionários para proteção de animais; à implantação de sistema de fiscalização de estabelecimentos que comercializem animais etc.

Na seara jurídica os animais, embora dotados de sensibilidade e de movimento próprio, são apenas considerados em função de interesse humano, daí serem bens semoventes (CC, arts. 82, 445, 936 e 1442). Embora submetidos ao extermínio sistemático (caça, pesca), à ponta dos arpões, às gaiolas, às prisões perpétuas dos zoos, têm direito a uma proteção jurídica.

A fauna representa um componente imprescindível ao equilíbrio da natureza, urge impedir, por meio de leis rigorosas e de efetiva atuação do poder público e da sociedade, práticas que coloquem em risco a sua função ecológica e que provoquem extinção de espécies. Para tanto, bastaria uma política ambiental direcionada a gestão racional e planejada dos recursos da natureza, evitando seu uso predatório, preservando as biodiversidades. É preciso dentro dos limites da capacidade de suporte dos ecossistemas, adotar medidas, sem rejeitar os avanços tecnológicos, que tragam benefício para a fauna, a flora e a humanidade. Não há por que parar com a extração da madeira, com a pesca, com a caça, com a indústria etc., pois tudo isso poderá continuar, mas de forma racional, sem o uso de instrumentos devastadores e sem a brutal agressão ao meio ambiente[51].

Para que haja equilíbrio e higidez do meio ambiente, sem alteração dos ecossistemas, o ser humano, a sociedade e o Estado deverão enfrentar no século XXI, o desafio ecológico, impondo padrões de comportamento que sejam cogentes para que haja maior preservação da natureza por ocasião da exploração de seus recursos. Seria imprescindível o reforço da função socioambiental da propriedade urbana e rural, garantindo a perpetuação das riquezas ambientais, mediante aproveitamento adequado dos recursos naturais disponíveis; o controle das atividades predatórias; a preser-

[51] Fiorillo, Celso A.P. e Diaféria, Adriana. *Biodiversidade e patrimônio genético no direito ambiental brasileiro*. SPaulo: Max Limonad, 1999. pp. 31-32; Tourinho Neto, Fernando da Costa. Dano ambiental. *Consulex*, cit., pp. 20 -21; Diniz, Maria Helena. *O estado...*, cit., pp. 850 -851.

vação do meio ambiente; a proteção das espécies ameaçadas de extinção (por ex., o mico-leão dourado); o estabelecimento de Reservas Particulares do Patrimônio Natural (RPPN); a restauração das reservas legais e das áreas de proteção permanente nas propriedades; o fomento de educação ambiental; a efetivação não, de programas de monitoramento ambiental relativos à instalação de hidrelétricas e minerações e aos efeitos da operação desses empreendimentos sobre as espécies, mas também de programas de controle de poluição; o ataque às causas e aos fatores conducentes à prática de crimes ambientais etc.[52]

A Constituição Federal de 1988 (art. 225 *caput*, art 1º III) requer um meio ambiente ecologicamente equilibrado que possibilite a concretização do respeito à dignidade humana, por ser oriundo do direito a vida, salvaguardando a fauna e flora. No artigo 225, § 1º, I a VII, visa: a) preservar e restaurar processos ecológicos essenciais, como manejo ecológico de espécies e ecossistemas; b) preservar a diversidade e a integridade do patrimônio genético do país; c) instituir, em todos os Estados da Federação, Espaços Territoriais Especialmente Protegidos (ETEP); d) exigir estudo prévio de impacto ambiental para instalação de obra ou atividade potencialmente causadora de degradação do meio ambiente; e) controlar a produção, comercialização e emprego de técnicas e substâncias que coloquem em risco a vida, a qualidade de vida e o meio ambiente; f) promover educação ambiental em todos os níveis de ensino e a conscientização pública para a preservação do meio ambiente; g) proteger a fauna e a flora vedando legalmente, práticas que coloquem em risco sua função ecológica e provoquem a extinção de espécies ou submetam animais à crueldade.

O direito ao meio ambiente sadio e ecologicamente equilibrado é o direito à vida e à preservação de tudo que for imprescindível para sua boa qualidade, e somente poderá ser conquistado pela conformação das atividades socioeconômicas no sentido de que se deve respeitar a biodiversidade para evitar a degradação ambiental[53].

[52] Diniz, Maria Helena. *O estado...*, cit., pp. 851-852; Piovesan, Flavia. O direito ao meio ambiente e a Constituição de 1988: diagnósticos e perspectivas. *Caderno de Direito Constitucional e Ciência Política*, 4 : 80-81, 85, 95 e 96.

[53] Diniz, Maria Helena. *O estado...*, cit., pp. 853-854; Purvin de Figueiredo, Guilherme J e Silva, Solangee Teles de. Elementos balizadores..., cit., pp. 143-144.

CONCLUSÕES

A humanidade não está preparada para o impacto ambiental provocado pela biotecnologia, que pode trazer extinção de espécies animais e riscos sem limites para a saúde do ser humano e para o meio ambiente, por isso, imprescindível será uma tomada de consciência pelos órgãos políticos e legislativos quanto a esse grave e sério problema[54].

Não seria necessária a implantação de políticas compreensivas de desenvolvimento urbano e rural que controlassem as atividades econômicas predatórias? Como reduzir os impactos ambientais se o direito ficar inerte à devastação ecológica provocada pela defaunação? Se sem proteção ambiental não há direito à saúde, nem a uma vida digna como assegurar a efetividade do direito ao meio ambiente sadio e ecologicamente equilibrado sem que a norma jurídica apresente não só as fontes de recursos que, de fato, viabilizassem o implemento de políticas públicas voltadas à tutela do meio ambiente, mas também os mecanismos hábeis de responsabilização do Poder Publico pela sua omissão ante os impactos ambientais? Será que se teria o esgotamento do modelo liberal do Estado diante do aumento de bens tutelados que exigem a eficiência de um Estado de bem-estar social ou intervencionista?

Fácil é perceber que o bem ambiental não é *res nullius*, por ser, diante do comando constitucional, uma *res communi omnium*. A sua titularidade é do povo. O meio ambiente sadio e ecologicamente equilibrado é um bem de uso comum do povo, não integrando o patrimônio particular de qualquer pessoa física ou jurídica. O bem ambiental possui a natureza jurídica de direito difuso, assumindo a feição de direito transindividual, tendo como titulares pessoas ligadas apenas por circunstâncias fáticas, podendo ser desfrutado por qualquer pessoa dentro das restrições impostas legal e constitucionalmente[55].

A preservação da biodiversidade dos ecossistemas somente será possível pelo uso sustentável, ou melhor, pela utilização de componentes da diversidade biológica de modo e em ritmo tais que não levem, a longo prazo, à diminuição da diversidade biológica, mantendo assim seu potencial para atender às necessidades e aspirações das gerações presentes e futuras[56].

[54] DINIZ, Maria Helena. *O estado...*, cit., pp. 942-943.

[55] FIORILLO e DIAFERIA. *Biodiversidade...*, cit., p.27; SILVA, Jose Afonso da. *Direito ambiental Constitucional*. São Paulo: Malheiros, 1994. p. 15; DINIZ, Maria Helena. *O estado...*, cit., p. 885.

[56] art. 4º, da Lei estadual do Acre n. 1235/97.

Quando o artigo 225 de CF/88 estabeleceu que "todos têm direitos ao meio ambiente ecologicamente equilibrado, bem de uso comum do povo e essencial à sadia qualidade de vida, impondo-se ao Poder Publico e à coletividade o dever de defendê-lo e preservá-lo para as presentes e futuras gerações" consagrou o direito ambiental, que tem por bases fundamentais: o direito de todos ao equilíbrio ecológico do meio ambiente; o meio ambiente considerado como bem de uso comum do povo e essencial à sadia qualidade de vida e a defesa e preservação do bem ambiental para as presentes e futuras gerações como dever do Poder Publico e de toda a coletividade ou das ONGS[57].

A proteção da fauna é uma garantia da biodversidade, por tal razão sua tutela, encontra-se, como vimos, no Brasil prevista na CF, pois apesar do fundamento antropocêntrico que a norteia, apresenta uma base ecocêntrica, contendo limitações ao ser humano em suas atividades em relação ao animal, em busca de seu bem estar. Não há dúvida que o declínio e a extinção da fauna nativa é uma crise atual da biodiversidade. Por isso, urge evitar a perda de *habitats*, que ameaça a manutenção de biomas. É preciso conservar a fauna *in situ*, criando áreas protegidas que permitam o manejo sustentável da biodiversidade, possibilitando recuperar espécies e reintroduzi-las no ambiente natural.

Tanto o poder público como a iniciativa particular podem e devem tomar medidas para controlar na degradação ambiental e a defaunação, por ex: observando a legislação ambiental, adotando tecnologias agropecuárias, ambientalmente, corretas, criando reservas particulares. Todo país tem soberania no que concerne aos seus próprios recursos biológicos, tendo responsabilidade pela preservação de biodiversidade, pelo uso sustentável de sua fauna, flora e riquezas minerais. Pelo princípio de participação. Estado e sociedade civil deverão atuar conjuntamente, na escolha dos meios preventivos para preservação ambiental, e dos reparatórios, para recomposição e proteção do meio ambiente[58].

É lamentável que não haja uma conscientização de que ambiente saudável e equilibrado requer a manutenção e integridade de todas as espécies da fauna silvestre. Finalizando esse breve estudo poder-se-á dizer, como

[57] Diniz, Maria Helena. *O estado...*, cit., p. 885.

[58] Fiorillo e Diaféria. *Biodiversidade...*, cit., pp. 35 – 6; Diniz, Maria Helena. *O estado...*, cit., p. 953.

São Francisco de Assis, que "todos os animais da criação são filhos do Pai e irmãos do homem. Deus quer que auxiliemos os animais, se necessitarem de ajuda, e toda criatura em desamparo tem o mesmo direito de proteção".

REFERÊNCIAS

ALVARENGA, L. J. Tráfico de animais silvestres: historiografia e lógicas de continuidade. *MPMG Jurídico.* Rev. MPEMG. Ed. Defesa da Fauna, 2016.

ALVIM, Mariana Spacek. Experimentação animal na nova Lei n. 11.798/2008 à luz da interpretação conforme a Constituição. *Revista Brasileira de Direito Animal*, 2014.

BALSA, Elizabeth S. Ambiente marinho e a poluição. *Questões importantes referentes ao mar.* Georgete N. Nazo (coord.). São Paulo: Soamar, 1996.

BECHARA, E. *A proteção da fauna sob a ótica constitucional.* SPaulo: Juarez de Oliveira, 2003.

BENJAMIN, A.H. Constitucionalização do Ambiente e ecologização da Constituição brasileira. In: CANOTILHO e LEITE (orgs.). *Direito constitucional ambiental brasileiro.* São Paulo: Saraiva, 2007.

BERQUE A. A. Ecúmena: medida terrestre ao homem, medida humana da terra. In: Serrão, A.V.S (org). *Filosofia da paisagem uma antologia.* Lisboa, 2011.

BUENO. *Capitães do Brasil: a saga dos primeiros colonizadores.* S/l: s/e, 1999.

CANOTILHO, Jose G. e MOREIRA, Vital. *Constituição da Republica Portuguesa anotada.* Coimbra: Coimbra, 1993.

CARRILHO, Luciana Mª C. Pontos controvertidos do crime de pesca. *MPMG Jurídico. Revista* do MPMG. Ed. Defesa da Fauna, 2016.

CAUGHLEY. Directions in conservation biology. *Journal of Animas Ecology*, 63: 215–44.

DINIZ, Maria Helena. *O estado atual do biodireito.* SPaulo: Saraiva, 2014.

DIRZO. R. e outros. Antropocene. *Science*, 2014, v. 345.

DIRZO, R. e RAVEN P.H. Global state of biodiversity and loss. *Annual Review of Environment and Resources*, v. 28, 2003.

ELER, Kalline C. G. A tutela dos animais pela personalidade: melhor caminho? *Animais – Bioética e Direito.* Tereza R. Vieira e Camilo H. Silva (coords.). Brasília, Portal Jurídico, 2016.

HOKKANEN e LYNCH. *Biological control:benefits and risks.* Cambridge, 1995.

FARIA, Jose Eduardo. *O direito na economia globalizada.* SPaulo: Malheiros, 1999.

FIORILLO, Celso A.P. e DIAFÉRIA, Adriana. *Biodiversidade e patrimônio genético no direito ambiental brasileiro.* SPaulo: Max Limonad, 1999.

FIORILLO e RODRIGUES. *Manual de direito ambiental e legislação aplicável.* SPaulo: Max Limonad, 1999.

FORMAN, R.T e outros. *Road ecology.* Science and Solutions. Washington: Island Press, 2003.

GARCIA, Rafael. Homem acelerou ritmo de extinção em mil vezes. *Folha de SPaulo* – ciencia + Saúde, 30.5.2014, p. c-11.

GERAQUE, Eduardo. Aquecimento faz pinguim morrer nas praias do Brasil. *Folha de SPaulo.* 19.10.2008, p. c-13.

GLISTA e outros. A review of mitigation measures for reducing wildlife mortality on roadways. *Landscape and urban Planning*, v. 91, n. 1, 2009.

GUSMÃO CÂMARA, Ibsen de. O ambiente marinho e as consequências da poluição. *Questões importantes referentes ao mar.* Georgette Nacarato Nazo (coord.). SPaulo: Soamar, 1996.

KORTENKAM, K.V. e MOORE, CF. Ecocentrism and anthropocentrism: moral reasoning about ecological commons dilemmas. *Journal of Environmental Psychology*, 21: 261 – 276, 2001.

LEVAI, Laerte F. *Direito dos animais.* Campos do Jordão: Mantiqueira, 1998.

LEVAI, Laerte F. Proteção Jurídica da fauna. *Manual prático da Promotoria da Justiça do Meio Ambiente.* SPaulo: Imprensa Oficial, vol. 1, pp. 56 – 89.

LINDAHL-CURRY, Kai. *Ecologia: conservar para sobreviver.* São Paulo: Cultrix, 1972.

MARTINS, G.S. *Norma Ambiental: complexidade e concretização.* Dissertação (mestrado), Universidade Federal de Santa Catarina, Centro Ciências Jurídicas, Programa de Pós-Graduação em Direito, Florianópolis, 2013.

MATEO, Ramón M. *Derecho ambiental.* Madrid: s/e, 1977.

MILARÉ, Edis. Tutela jurisdicional do ambiente. *Revista do Advogado*, 37:5 e ss.

MOTA, Jose A e BURSZTYN, Marcel. O valor da natureza como apoio à decisão publica. *Revista Paranaense de Desenvolvimento*, Curitiba, v. 34, n. 125, pp. 39-56, 2015.

PAVIANI, Aldo. Impactos ambientais da população. *Bioética*, 4: 195–220.

PIOVESAN, Flavia. O direito ao meio ambiente e a Constituição de 1988: diagnósticos e perspectivas. *Cadernos de Direito Constitucional e Ciência Política*, 4 : 80-96.

PURVIN DE FIGUEIREDO, Guilherme Jose e SILVA, Solange Teles da. Elementos balizadores da ação estatal na defesa dos bens ambientais para as presentes e futuras gerações. *Temas de direito ambiental e urbanístico.* Guilherme Jose Purvin de Figueiredo (org.). SPaulo: Max Limonad, n.3, 1998.

PRINGLE. *Ecologia: ciência da sobrevivência.* Rio de Janeiro: s/e, 1977.

RAPHAELLI, R. *Noções sobre o tráfico de animais no Brasil.* 2012.

REGAN, *Jaulas vazias.* Encarando o desafio dos direitos animais. Porto Alegre: Lugano, 2006.

ROCHA VILELA, Daniel A. e outros. Principais ameaças e medidas de salvaguarda aos animais silvestres. MPMG jurídico. Rev. MPEMG. Ed. Defesa da Fauna, 2016, pp. 18-23.

SANTOS, Antonio Silveira R. dos. Vida Selvagem: importância e proteção. *Revista APMP, 31* : 71–73.

SARLET, I.W e FENSTERSEIFER. T. Algumas notas sobre a dimensão ecológica da dignidade da pessoa humana e sobre a dignidade da vida em geral. In: MOLINARO, C. A. e outros (orgs). *A dignidade e os direitos fundamentais para além dos humanos: uma discussão necessária.* Belo Horizonte: Fórum, 2008.

SARTORI, Frei Luís Mª, A. (org). Encíclicas do Papa João Paulo II (*Encíclica Redemptor Hominis*, 4. 3. 1979). SPaulo: LTR, 1999.

SEHER, Gerhard. La legitimación de normas penales basada en principios y el concepto de bien jurídico. In: HEFENDHEL, Roland. *La teoría del bien jurídico. Fundamento de legitimación del derecho penal o juego de abalorios dogmático?* Madrid: Marcial Pons, 2007.

SEILER e HELLDIN. Mortality in wildlife due to transportation. In: Davenport (ed.) *The Ecology of Transportation: managing mobility for the Environment.* Kluwer, 2006.

SILVA, Jose Afonso da. *Direito ambiental Constitucional.* São Paulo: Malheiros, 1994.

SINGER, P. *Libertação animal.* SPaulo: M. Fontes, 2010.

SIRVINSKAS, Luis Paulo. *Manual de direito ambiental.* SPaulo: Saraiva, 2015.

TOURINHO NETO, Fernando do C. Dano ambiental. *Consulex*, 2 : 19–20.

TEORIA DO ADIMPLEMENTO SUBSTANCIAL E ATIVISMO JUDICIAL

MILTON FLÁVIO DE A. C. LAUTENSCHLÄGER*
ODETE NOVAIS CARNEIRO QUEIROZ**

INTRODUÇÃO

Os contratos, como de resto todos os negócios jurídicos, têm um ciclo vital: nascem do acordo de vontades, produzem os efeitos que lhes são próprios e se extinguem com o adimplemento das prestações avençadas[1]. Em regra, a extinção do contrato se dá mediante a sua *execução*, seja ela *instantânea*, *diferida* ou *continuada*. Portanto, o *meio normal de extinção* do contrato é o *cumprimento da prestação pelo devedor*, de modo a *satisfazer o credor* (v. artigos 304 a 388 do Código Civil brasileiro). Às vezes, contudo, o contrato se extingue sem que as obrigações tenham sido adequadamente cumpridas. Várias são as *causas* que acarretam a *extinção anormal do contrato*. Algumas são *anteriores* ou *contemporâneas* à formação do contrato, outras são causas *supervenientes* à sua formação.

* Doutor, Mestre e Bacharel em Direito pela PUC-SP. Diretor Administrativo do Instituto dos Advogados de São Paulo – IASP (2016-2018). Advogado.

** Doutora e Mestre em Direito pela PUC/SP. Professora da Faculdade de Direito da PUC-SP. Advogada.

[1] GONÇALVES, Carlos Roberto. Direito Civil Brasileiro. 3º Volume. São Paulo: Editora Saraiva, 2004, p. 154.

São causas anteriores ou contemporâneas à formação do contrato:

a) as *invalidades gerais* (arts. 166, 167 e 171 do Código Civil brasileiro); e
b) as *invalidades específicas* (v.g.: arts. 489, 496, 548 e 550 do Código Civil brasileiro).

Por outro lado, são hipóteses de dissolução do contrato em função de causas posteriores à sua celebração:

a) a *dissolução reflexa* (*resolução*): (i) *culposa* (art. 475 do Código Civil brasileiro), nos casos de *mora* (art. 394 do Código Civil brasileiro), *inadimplemento absoluto* (art. 395 do Código Civil brasileiro), *cláusula resolutiva expressa* ou *tácita* (art. 474 do Código Civil brasileiro) e de *exceção do contrato não cumprido* (art. 476 e 477 do Código Civil brasileiro); ou (ii) *não culposa*, nos casos de *fortuito* ou *força maior* (art. 393 do Código Civil brasileiro) e de *onerosidade excessiva* (art. 478 a 480 do Código Civil brasileiro); e
b) a *dissolução deliberada* (*resilição*): (i) *bilateral* (*distrato*) (art. 472 do Código Civil brasileiro); ou (ii) *unilateral* (art. 473 do Código Civil brasileiro), nos casos de *denúncia*, *revogação*, *resgate* e *exercício do direito de arrependimento convencionado.*

A resolução contratual culposa produz efeitos *ex tunc*, extinguindo aquilo que foi executado, obrigando as partes a promoverem restituições recíprocas, sujeitando o inadimplente ao pagamento de eventuais perdas e danos e, ainda, ao pagamento da cláusula penal convencionada, seja para a hipótese de total inadimplemento da prestação (*cláusula penal compensatória*), seja para a garantia de alguma cláusula especial, ou mesmo para evitar o retardamento no cumprimento das obrigações (*cláusula penal moratória*), nos termos dos artigos 409, 410, 411 e 475, todos do Código Civil brasileiro. Ela só não produz efeitos pretéritos (não obrigando a restituição das prestações cumpridas) nas hipóteses de contratos de *trato sucessivo* (v.g.: contratos de prestação de serviços de transporte, locação, seguro etc.). Nestes casos, o seu efeito é *ex nunc.*

É preciso registrar, contudo, que nem toda falta confere à parte prejudicada o direito de resolver o contrato. Neste artigo, examinaremos melhor esta hipótese (do inadimplemento sem a resolução contratual) e as suas eventuais consequências para a regular atividade jurisdicional.

1. A TEORIA DO ADIMPLEMENTO SUSBTANCIAL

Ao longo dos anos, doutrina e jurisprudência nacionais passaram a questionar se toda ou qualquer falta deveria conferir à parte prejudicada o direito de resolver o contrato. E foi assim que, sob a inspiração do instituto inglês do "substantial performance", nasce no Brasil a chamada *teoria do adimplemento substancial*.

O surgimento do "substantial performance" remonta ao século XVIII, fruto de evidências recolhidas pelas Cortes de *Equity*, acerca da "desproporcionalidade" de algumas resoluções contratuais, aplicadas incondicionalmente em determinadas situações nas quais a "obrigação principal" havia sido cumprida pelo devedor, restando inadimplida, apenas, a "obrigação secundária"[2].

Essa doutrina espraiou-se também para países de tradição romano-germânica, com especial destaque para o Direito italiano, cujo artigo 1.455 de seu Código Civil trata da "*importanza dell'inadempimento*". Na mesma esteira, o Direito português impede a resolução do negócio jurídico "se o não cumprimento parcial, atendendo ao seu interesse [do credor], tiver escassa importância" (art. 802, 2, do Código Civil). A "Convenção das Nações Unidas sobre os Contratos de Compra e Venda Internacional de Mercadorias" (Viena, 1980), por seu turno, autoriza que o comprador declare resolvido o contrato, mas apenas se "a inexecução pelo vendedor (...) constituir uma infração essencial (...)" (art. 49, 1, "a").

No Brasil, a introdução deste tema é atribuída à doutrina de Clóvis Veríssimo do Couto e Silva – estudioso de diversos institutos do direito comparado -, bem como à atuação na magistratura de um de seus alunos, o Ministro do Superior Tribunal de Justiça Ruy Rosado de Aguiar. O pri-

[2] No Direito inglês é frequente a citação ao caso Boone *vs.* Eyre, relatado por Lord Mansfield, em 1777, e que teve por objeto um contrato no qual o autor, Boone, pretendia traditar uma fazenda e seus escravos ao réu, Eyre, mediante o pagamento de 500 libras, acrescido de prestações anuais de 160 libras, em caráter perpétuo. Boone alienou a propriedade, mas não tinha direito de transferir os escravos. Eyre sobrestou o pagamento das prestações anuais, alegando a *exceptio non adimpleti contractus*. Ao decidir o caso, Lord Mansfield entendeu que o comprador não poderia deixar de pagar as prestações avençadas, pois a obrigação de dar a coisa (os escravos) não seria condição precedente à obrigação de pagar as prestações anuais perpétuas. Mansfield qualificou a entrega dos escravos como "obrigação secundária" e, como tal, insuficiente para ensejar a resolução do contrato. Ao autor coube, então e apenas, reivindicar eventual reparação por perdas e danos (V. Min. Antônio Carlos Ferreira, em voto lançados nos autos do Resp nº 1.581.505)

meiro acórdão do Superior Tribunal de Justiça que registra abordagem sobre o tema é o Resp n. 76.362/MT, julgado em 11 de dezembro de 1995 pela Quarta Turma (DJ de 01/04/1996). No caso, dois segurados promoveram ação de cobrança para receber a cobertura securitária devida em razão de acidente de veículo. Logo na inicial, os autores confessaram que deixaram de pagar a última parcela do prêmio. Noticiaram, ainda, que a purgação da prestação inadimplida foi rejeitada pela empresa ré. Apreciada a ação pelo Tribunal de Justiça do Mato Grosso, entendeu aquela Corte que os segurados tinham "obrigação primordial" de pagar o "prêmio do seguro". Sem isso, nada poderiam exigir da seguradora, na hipótese de se acharem em estado de inadimplência. No entanto, o recurso dos segurados foi provido, sob o amparo da doutrina do adimplemento substancial, por meio de acórdão cuja ementa é a seguinte:

> "SEGURO. INADIMPLEMENTO DA SEGURADA. FALTA DE PAGAMENTO DA ÚLTIMA PRESTAÇÃO. ADIMPLEMENTO SUBSTANCIAL. RESOLUÇÃO. A COMPANHIA SEGURADORA NÃO PODE DAR POR EXTINTO O CONTRATO DE SEGURO, POR FALTA DE PAGAMENTO DA ÚLTIMA PRESTAÇÃO DO PRÊMIO, POR TRÊS RAZÕES: A) SEMPRE RECEBEU AS PRESTAÇÕES COM ATRASO, O QUE ESTAVA, ALIÁS, PREVISTO NO CONTRATO, SENDO INADMISSÍVEL QUE APENAS REJEITE A PRESTAÇÃO QUANDO OCORRA O SINISTRO; B) A SEGURADA CUMPRIU SUBSTANCIALMENTE COM A SUA OBRIGAÇÃO, NÃO SENDO A SUA FALTA SUFICIENTE PARA EXTINGUIR O CONTRATO; C) A RESOLUÇÃO DO CONTRATO DEVE SER REQUERIDA EM JUÍZO, QUANDO SERÁ POSSÍVEL AVALIAR A IMPORTÂNCIA DO INADIMPLEMENTO, SUFICIENTE PARA A EXTINÇÃO DO NEGÓCIO. RECURSO CONHECIDO E PROVIDO." (REsp 76.362/MT, Rel. Ministro RUY ROSADO DE AGUIAR, QUARTA TURMA, julgado em 11/12/1995, DJ 01/04/1996, p. 9917)

De lá para cá, as decisões sobre este tema, proferidas no âmbito do Superior Tribunal de Justiça, concentram esforços no sentido de clarificar o que poderia configurar o "*descumprimento mínimo*" suficiente para justificar a invocação da teoria do adimplemento substancial e afastar os efeitos da mora. São exemplos: a) atraso na última parcela: REsp. 76.362/MT; b) inadimplemento de 2 (duas) parcelas: REsp. 912.697/GO; c) inadimplemento de valores correspondentes a 20% (vinte por cento) do valor total do bem: REsp. 469.577/SC; d) inadimplemento de 10% (dez por cento) do valor total do bem: AgRg no AgREsp 155.885/MS; e) inadimplemento de 5 (cinco) parcelas de um total de 36 (trinta e seis), correspondendo a 14% (quatorze por cento) do total devido: Resp. 1.051.270/RS.

Como se pode notar, a jurisprudência do Superior Tribunal de Justiça vem oscilando no exame do requisito objetivo do adimplemento substancial, principalmente porque "em cada caso aqui [STJ] julgado há peculiaridades muito próprias a serem consideradas para efeito de avaliar a importância do inadimplemento frente ao contexto de todo o contrato e os demais elementos que envolvem a controvérsia"[3].

Essa vinculação aos elementos do caso concreto é um dado objetivo que a doutrina internacional e a nacional reconhecem. Eduardo Luiz Bussata, a esse propósito, leciona:

> "A indagação quanto à extensão, à intensidade e às demais características do inadimplemento é que conduz à sua adjetivação como sendo ou não de 'escassa importância'. É o que se buscará neste momento. Contudo, antes disso, é necessário fazer uma advertência: a verificação da importância ou não importância do inadimplemento há de ser feita diante do caso concreto, ou seja, diante da situação de fato ocorrida, ponderando os interesses em jogo, a conduta das partes e de todas as demais circunstâncias que no caso se mostrarem relevantes."[4]

Com efeito, ressalvada a hipótese de evidente relevância, "o julgamento sobre a substancialidade do descumprimento contratual não se deve prender ao exclusivo exame do critério quantitativo". Há outros tantos *elementos qualitativos* que também envolvem a contratação e devem ser considerados para efeito de se avaliar a extensão do adimplemento.

No julgado pioneiro do Superior Tribunal de Justiça, antes referido (REsp 76.362/MT), foram delineados alguns requisitos que devem ser examinados pelo juiz para aplicação da teoria do adimplemento substancial, sem prejuízo da avaliação de circunstâncias específicas do caso sob julgamento. São eles: a) a existência de *expectativas legítimas* geradas pelo

[3] Trecho destacado do voto do Ministro Antonio Carlos Ferreira, lançado nos autos do Resp nº 1.581.505.

[4] Bussata, Eduardo Luiz. Resolução dos contratos e teoria do adimplemento substancial. 2ª ed. São Paulo: Saraiva, 2008, p. 106.

comportamento das partes (exemplo disso está no recebimento reiterado de parcelas em atraso no contrato de seguro e a posterior mudança de atitude quando do último pagamento, o que quebraria essas expectativas legítimas e levaria a um comportamento contraditório); b) o pagamento faltante há de ser *ínfimo*, se considerado o total do negócio (correlação que permite formular um juízo sobre o caráter substancial do adimplemento realizado); e c) deve ser possível a *conservação da eficácia do negócio*, sem prejuízo ao direito do credor de pleitear a quantia devida pelos meios ordinários.

Atualmente, os autores ingleses, tomando como fundamento a gravidade objetiva do prejuízo causado ao credor pelo não cumprimento da prestação, formulam três requisitos para admitir a *substancial performance*: a) *insignificância* do inadimplemento; b) satisfação do *interesse* do credor; e c) *diligência* por parte do devedor no desempenho de sua prestação, ainda que a mesma se tenha operado imperfeitamente[5].

O uso do instituto da *substantial performance* não pode ser estimulado a ponto de inverter a ordem lógico-jurídica que assenta o integral e regular cumprimento do contrato como meio esperado de extinção das obrigações. A sua incidência é excepcional, reservada para os casos nos quais a rescisão contratual traduz, *icto oculi*, solução evidentemente desproporcional. Mais do que isso. A sua má utilização pode caracterizar o chamado *ativismo judicial*.

2. A ESTRUTURA DO ATIVISMO JUDICIAL[6]

A doutrina nacional avalia as *condutas ativistas*, ora de forma *positiva*, ora de forma *negativa*. De todo modo, tanto um como o outro lado afirmam a existência de *limites*, fronteira além da qual a jurisdição não pode, nem deve ir. Aqueles que enxergam o ativismo judicial como algo negativo, em geral associam o mesmo à ultrapassagem desses limites, ou seja, a uma atuação além das fronteiras conferidas à jurisdição pelo ordenamento jurídico (atuação supostamente ilícita, portanto). De modo oposto, aqueles que avaliam o ativismo como algo positivo enxergam o magistrado atuando,

[5] Cf. Rodrigues Junior, Otavio Luiz. Revisão Judicial dos Contratos – Autonomia da vontade e teoria da imprevisão. 2ª edição revista, ampliada e atualizada. São Paulo: Editora Atlas, 2006, p.72.

[6] Ver: "Contornos teóricos do ativismo judicial em matéria contratual" (Lautenschläger, Milton Flávio de Almeida Camargo. 449 folhas. Tese de Doutorado em Direito. Faculdade de Direito, Pontifícia Universidade Católica de São Paulo – PUC/SP, 2015).

mesmo nestas específicas circunstâncias, dentro dos limites conferidos pelo ordenamento à jurisdição (atuação supostamente lícita).

Tal divergência de opiniões acerca do correto posicionamento do ativismo judicial frente aos limites do ordenamento jurídico – ora colocando o ativista dentro dos limites do ordenamento, ora colocando o ativista fora destes limites – merece detida análise. Em primeiro lugar, é preciso compreender o que é o "*limite da jurisdição*". "Limite" é a "linha real ou imaginária que separa dois terrenos ou territórios contíguos"[7]. Por outro lado, "jurisdição" é o poderio que o magistrado tem para submeter um caso particular e concreto ao império de uma norma jurídica. De onde se retira, portanto, que "limite da jurisdição" é a fronteira que delimita a seara onde o magistrado está autorizado, pelo ordenamento jurídico, a decidir um caso concreto. Fora desse específico território, jurisdição não há.

O exercício da jurisdição se dá por intermédio do "processo", que cumpre função instrumental, não do direito material, mas da própria jurisdição, como forma tradicional de solução de conflitos. E na qualidade de instrumento da jurisdição, é evidente que "o processo" também deve encontrar limites, os quais são efetivamente impostos pelo ordenamento jurídico pátrio. São exemplos desses limites os informados pelos princípios da inércia (art. 2º do Código de Processo civil: "O processo começa por iniciativa da parte e se desenvolve por impulso oficial, salvo as exceções previstas em lei."), da investidura (somente os magistrados poderão exercer a Jurisdição), da territorialidade (a função jurisdicional é limitada ao território nacional), da indelegabilidade (o Judiciário não pode delegar o poder jurisdicional a outrem), do juiz natural (a demanda deve ser apreciada pelo órgão e juiz competentes), dentre muitos outros.

No entanto, não só de limites formais está cercado o magistrado no desempenho de seu mister. É certo que existem também *limites materiais*, que dizem respeito ao próprio direito a ser atribuído aos interessados. Os limites materiais da atividade jurisdicional, tal qual ocorre com os limites formais, são extraídos do próprio ordenamento jurídico, e variam segundo a *natureza da demanda* ou *da controvérsia* apresentada pelas partes.

Para os fins deste artigo, interessa analisar apenas os limites materiais da jurisdição, e não aqueles formais. Pois bem. É sabido que, na maioria

[7] FERREIRA, Aurélio Buarque de Holanda. Dicionário Aurélio básico da língua portuguesa. Rio de Janeiro: Editora Nova Fronteira, p. 395.

das situações cotidianas, as divergências são de *fácil solução*, resolvidas com base no raciocínio dedutivo de uma norma válida, aceita pela comunidade. Os *casos difíceis*, que constituem exceção à regra, são aqueles em que se detectam *dificuldades* no *elemento normativo*, no *fático* ou na própria *dedução* de uma norma válida, aceita pela comunidade[8].

Em um caso fácil, o magistrado deve delimitar os fatos, identificar a norma ou o conjunto de premissas jurídicas válidas que permitam formular um enunciado normativo geral e determinar o sentido dessas premissas jurídicas. Feito isso, deve o juiz solucionar o caso pela via da dedução. No entanto, se o magistrado ignorar os fatos provados, se não invocar as normas, ou se invocar normas derrogadas ou não aplicáveis, configurada estará uma *decisão infundada, arbitrária*[9]. E, por contrariarem o ordenamento jurídico vigente, tanto os casos de *arbitrariedade normativa* quanto os casos de *arbitrariedade fática* constituem exemplos de *atuação judicial ilícita*.
Por outro lado, nos casos *complexos* ou *difíceis* (aqueles que não permitem deduzir da lei a solução de modo simples, seja em função de dificuldades relacionadas à norma aplicável, seja em virtude de sua interpretação), o juiz é guiado por princípios, decidindo mediante um *juízo de ponderação*[10]. Nestas particulares circunstâncias, é bastante comum que o magistrado, ser humano que é, julgue de forma equivocada (*error in judicando*), isto é, produza uma sentença injusta[11]. Por isso, nada mais natural e compreensível os ordenamentos jurídicos de todos os povos, com o propósito de assegurar justiça o quanto possível perfeita, propiciarem a possibilidade de reexame ou de reforma das decisões por outros juízes, ou mesmo pelos próprios juízes que as proferirem.

[8] LORENZETTI, Ricardo Luis. Teoria da Decisão Judicial – Fundamentos de Direito. Tradução de Bruno Miragem, Notas da tradução de Cláudia Lima Marques. 2ª edição revista. São Paulo: Editora Revista dos Tribunais, 2011, p. 158-159.

[9] Teoria da Decisão Judicial – Fundamentos de Direito, cit., p. 160.

[10] Teoria da Decisão Judicial – Fundamentos de Direito, cit., p. 163.

[11] A palavra "justiça" é polissêmica. Assim, para os estreitos fins deste artigo, tomaremos a expressão "decisão justa" no sentido de "a melhor decisão para o caso concreto". *A contrario sensu*, sempre que mencionarmos "decisão injusta", estaremos usando a expressão no sentido de que a mesma não se constitui "na melhor decisão para o caso concreto". Não há um critério objetivo de justiça. Assegurar algo como justo ou injusto é um julgamento de valor, efetivado segundo um determinado escopo. E valorar é ato, predominantemente, de natureza subjetiva; é um ato de preferência; de escolha daquilo que alguém imagina ser "a melhor" alternativa.

Note-se que, ao errar, o magistrado não imagina atuar em desconformidade com o ordenamento jurídico. Muito ao contrário. Em sua visão (ainda que equivocada), ele fez cumprir aquilo que a ordem jurídica determinava. Neste caso, portanto, há uma decisão lícita, porque idealmente proferida em conformidade com o ordenamento jurídico; porém, equivocada, injusta. Muito diferente é a situação do juiz que, diante de um caso simples, inexplicavelmente atua contra a norma imperativa vigente; ou o magistrado que, em sua decisão, ofende deliberadamente a ordem pública, a boa-fé ou os bons costumes. Nestas hipóteses, a decisão é ilícita, ou porque *ilegal* (quando ofender norma imperativa vigente), ou porque *proibida* (quando ofender a ordem pública), ou porque *imoral* (quando ofender a boa-fé e os bons costumes).

Ultrapassar ou exceder os limites materiais da jurisdição significa atuar em desconformidade com o ordenamento jurídico, ou seja, ilicitamente. Todavia, repise-se, o ativismo judicial não está propriamente relacionado a uma atuação fora dos limites materiais da jurisdição, mas ao seu *exercício equivocado*. Este é o motivo por que se reputa a *decisão judicial equivocada* como *elemento do ativismo judicial*. Em outras palavras: inexistindo uma decisão judicial equivocada[12], não há que se falar em ativismo judicial.

Vale ressalvar, contudo, que a ocorrência de uma decisão judicial equivocada ou injusta, por si só, não é suficiente à caracterização do ativismo judicial. O que autoriza qualificar uma determinada postura judicial como ativista são, na realidade, algumas *características especiais* de uma decisão judicial equivocada. Mas quais seriam estas características especiais? Originalmente, a expressão "ativismo judicial" (*judicial activism*) nasceu para designar a ação do magistrado capaz de desempenhar um *papel afirmativo, proativo*, em contraposição à *postura judicial autocomedida, passiva* (*self-restraint*). Desde então, em quaisquer das acepções conferidas à expressão, o ativismo judicial está sempre relacionado à *ampliação* dos poderes jurisdicionais, ao passo que o chamado passivismo está vinculado à sua *compressão*.

Traçando, pois, um paralelo, é possível dizer que a postura ativista corrobora para inflar, avultar, elastecer os limites da jurisdição, enquanto a postura autocomedida causa o seu esvaziamento, afrouxamento, a sua

12 O equívoco judicial (*error in judicando*) é fruto da complexidade do caso a ser julgado. Logo, se o equívoco é elemento do ativismo judicial, então só se pode cogitar em ativismo judicial nas decisões proferidas em casos complexos.

depressão. Mas não é só. Ao conferir limites à atuação jurisdicional, o ordenamento jurídico o faz, em tese, de *forma simétrica*, isto é, guardando uma proporção ideal entre o território reservado à atuação jurisdicional e aquele destinado aos *agentes limitadores* desta atividade, tais como, a *lei*, os *atos administrativos* e a própria *vontade das partes* (no caso dos negócios jurídicos).

Se o ativismo judicial é caracterizado pela ampliação equivocada dos limites da jurisdição, ele implica, obrigatoriamente, na restrição do campo de atuação daqueles outros agentes, rompendo com a simetria original e idealmente prevista pelo ordenamento jurídico. Por esta razão é que os limites da jurisdição, quando vitimados por uma decisão ativista, sofrem de uma *distensão assimétrica*, isto é, de uma distorção, em grandeza, inflando o território idealmente reservado à atuação jurisdicional, e esvaziando aquele determinado, concretamente, por um dos citados agentes limitadores da sua atividade.

Vale ressaltar, outrossim, que a aferição do alargamento das fronteiras conferidas pelo ordenamento à jurisdição só pode ser feita caso a caso. Apenas diante de uma situação concreta é possível identificar qual providência judicial será adequada à solução da controvérsia, bem como a exata medida da intervenção a ser realizada. E para concluir: além de uma decisão judicial equivocada, que tenha por resultado o alargamento assimétrico dos limites conferidos pelo ordenamento jurídico à jurisdição, aquilo que de fato estimula e induz a doutrina a usar a expressão "ativismo judicial" (ainda que, por vezes, de forma nada técnica) são determinadas *posturas jurisdicionais* ou *sociais* que, por si sós, sugerem um *protagonismo* do Poder Judiciário, frente aos papéis ordinariamente reservados aos demais atores sociais que, com ele (Judiciário), dividem a incumbência de criar, interpretar e aplicar o direito de forma legítima.

O que se percebe é que, independentemente do desrespeito ou não aos limites impostos pelo ordenamento à jurisdição (o que denotará uma atuação lícita ou ilícita), se o ato de decidir não estiver aliado a uma postura que evidencie um determinado protagonismo do Poder Judiciário, a tendência é que tal atuação não seja reconhecida e qualificada, pela comunidade jurídica e pela sociedade, como uma atuação ativista. Vale dizer, um juiz que, embora decida para além das fronteiras da jurisdição (de forma ilícita, portanto), o faça para reforçar o poderio do Poder Legislativo, seguramente não será identificado como um "ativista judicial" (embora deva ser configurado como um magistrado arbitrário). Da mesma forma, o magistrado que, não obstante aja excedendo os limites jurisdicionais, o faça para reforçar a vontade das partes manifestadas em contrato, muito provavelmente não será tido, pela comunidade jurídica ou pela sociedade, como um "ativista".

Por tudo isso, a postura jurisdicional que denote um protagonismo do Poder Judiciário, nos moldes aqui delimitados, é outro *requisito* essencial à configuração do ativismo judicial. Em síntese: ao menos no âmbito deste artigo, o "ativismo judicial" deve ser entendido como uma disfunção especial da atividade jurisdicional, consistente em uma *decisão judicial equivocada*, que tenha por resultado o *alargamento assimétrico dos limites conferidos pelo ordenamento jurídico à jurisdição*, e que denote um *protagonismo do Poder Judiciário* frente aos papéis ordinariamente reservados aos demais atores sociais que, com ele, dividem a incumbência legítima de criar, interpretar e aplicar o direito.

3. ADIMPLEMENTO SUBSTANCIAL E ATIVISMO JUDICIAL[13]

Vista a estrutura básica do adimplemento substancial e do ativismo judicial, resta a derradeira pergunta: uma decisão judicial que deixa de resolver um contrato com fundamento na teoria do adimplemento substancial pode configurar ativismo judicial? A resposta correta é: em determinadas circunstâncias, sim. Explica-se. O conceito geral de ativismo judicial, tal como antes referido, não é suficiente para revelar todas as minúcias teóricas do *ativismo judicial em matéria contratual*. Existem características próprias desta seara jurídica que precisam ser descritas e analisadas, para somente então serem cotejadas com a estrutura geral do ativismo.

A primeira dessas particularidades refere-se aos limites do território disponível para o exercício da jurisdição. Mais especificamente, é importante compreender a maneira pela qual a atividade jurisdicional e as *fontes do regulamento contratual* se relacionam.

3.1. AS "FONTES" DO REGULAMENTO CONTRATUAL E A ATIVIDADE JURISDICIONAL

Sabe-se que as partes determinam o regulamento ou o conteúdo contratual, com o fito de definir o arranjo recíproco que envolverá os seus

[13] Ver: "Contornos teóricos do ativismo judicial em matéria contratual" (LAUTENSCHLÄGER, Milton Flávio de Almeida Camargo, Tese de Doutorado em Direito, cit.).

interesses através do vínculo jurídico contratualmente estabelecido. O regulamento ou conteúdo contratual, portanto, fixa e determina a operação econômica e os compromissos jurídicos assumidos pelos contratantes. Em um sistema capitalista, fundado no princípio da *liberdade da iniciativa privada*, é natural e lógico que, sob o ponto de vista do conteúdo negocial, vigore o *princípio da liberdade privada de determinação do regulamento contratual*. De uma forma geral, os particulares têm *autonomia*[14], isto é, são livres para se obrigar, segundo as suas próprias conveniências. Logo, a *livre iniciativa das partes*, manifestada através de uma declaração de vontade, constitui o mais autêntico e amplo território dos contratos.

Sucede que a liberdade contratual não é ilimitada. São muitas as *restrições* ao livre poder de determinar o conteúdo do regulamento contratual. Aliás, a própria liberdade de escolher a celebração ou não de um determinado contrato possui limites que se concretizam na presença de verdadeiras "obrigações de contratar", impostas por lei a sujeitos que se encontrem em determinadas circunstâncias (de monopólio, por exemplo).

Esses limites e restrições à autonomia contratual dos particulares não derivam apenas da lei, isto é, das normas que operam diretamente sobre o regulamento contratual. Muitas vezes, os limites e restrições decorrem de *decisões judiciais* ou de *atos das autoridades administrativas*. Se uma cláusula contratual contraditória ou ambígua é declarada inválida por decisão judicial, por exemplo, resta evidente a importante atuação do magistrado como agente inibidor da liberdade contratual, ainda que tal atuação tenha sempre por fundamento o arcabouço legal vigente.

Portanto, as normas legais, as decisões judiciais e os atos das autoridades administrativas, juntamente com a vontade das partes, que exprime o poder de autonomia, são "os agentes típicos das limitações impostas à liberdade contratual dos particulares"[15], isto é, são as *fontes do regulamento contratual*, para cuja concreta determinação podem, segundo as circuns-

[14] "Autonomia significa, etimologicamente, poder de modelar por si – e não por imposição externa – as regras da sua própria conduta; e autonomia privada, ou autonomia contratual, significa liberdade dos sujeitos de determinar com a sua vontade, eventualmente aliada à vontade de uma contraparte no 'consenso' contratual, o conteúdo das obrigações que se pretende assumir, das modificações que se pretende introduzir no seu património" (Roppo, Enzo. O contrato. Tradução de Ana Coimbra e M. Januário C. Gomes. Coimbra: Almedina, 2009, p. 128).

[15] Roppo, Enzo, O contrato, cit., p. 140.

tâncias e em diferentes medidas, concorrer. E como se dá tal concurso das fontes do regulamento contratual?

Embora a declaração de vontade das partes deva ser considerada como a principal das fontes de determinação do regulamento contratual[16], entre o dogma da vontade e a tutela da autonomia privada não há coincidência necessária. Muitas vezes, ao contrário, a lógica do negócio levado a cabo pelas partes só poderá ser protegida através da limitação da vontade declarada.

A *operatividade* de todas as fontes de determinação (limitação) do conteúdo do contrato, diversas da declaração de vontade das partes (*fontes heterônomas*, portanto), pressupõe a *intervenção combinada* da *lei* e do *juiz*. Significa dizer que, de um lado, estão as hipóteses em que a *norma* intervém pontual e precisamente na determinação do regulamento contratual (embora necessariamente *ativada* pelo magistrado), com o fito de exprimir a escolha do legislador e, portanto, reduzir ao mínimo a discricionariedade do órgão julgador; do outro lado, estão as hipóteses nas quais a determinação do regulamento se dá através da aplicação de regras formuladas de modo genérico, recheadas de conceitos indeterminados, conferindo ao *juiz* (ou à autoridade administrativa, em alguns casos) o exercício de um poder amplo de valoração autônoma[17].

Ainda a respeito das fontes de determinação do regulamento contratual, é fundamental notar que, se as *determinações voluntárias* do regulamento contratual exprimem sempre os poderes e interesses da autonomia privada (ressalvados os casos de vício da vontade), as fontes "*heterônomas*" do regulamento contratual (as leis, as decisões judiciais e os atos da autoridade administrativa) podem, diferentemente, operar de acordo com as seguintes variantes: a) *valorações legais contrastantes* com a autonomia privada; b) *valorações legais homogêneas* e *instrumentais* da autonomia privada; c) *valorações judiciais contrastantes* com a autonomia privada; e d) *valorações judiciais homogêneas* e *instrumentais* da autonomia privada[18]. Consoante será demonstrado mais adiante, tais variantes são importantes à caracterização de eventual ativismo judicial em matéria contratual.

[16] "O princípio da autonomia privada (embora acolhido no nosso ordenamento, como se viu, em termos não absolutos e ilimitados) implica que a vontade das partes deve considerar-se como a principal das fontes de determinação do regulamento contratual" (ROPPO, Enzo, O contrato, cit., p. 142).

[17] Ver: ROPPO, Enzo, O contrato, cit., p. 166-167.

[18] ROPPO, Enzo, O contrato, cit., p. 168.

3.2. A INTERVENÇÃO JUDICIAL EM MATÉRIA CONTRATUAL

Além de uma boa compreensão acerca da relação existente entre a atividade jurisdicional e as fontes do regulamento contratual, é preciso lembrar que a eventual ocorrência de ativismo judicial decorre, necessariamente, de uma prévia *intervenção judicial*. A depender da sua natureza, a atuação judicial em matéria contratual pode ser classificada como um *simples instrumento de intervenção legal* (intervenção judicial "lato sensu") ou, diversamente, como uma *verdadeira intervenção judicial* (intervenção judicial "stricto sensu").

Nas hipóteses em que *a norma* intervém pontual e precisamente na determinação do regulamento contratual (embora necessariamente ativada pelo magistrado), com o fito de exprimir a escolha do legislador e, portanto, reduzir ao mínimo a discricionariedade do órgão julgador (são circunstâncias em que o desfecho da controvérsia se dá através de simples raciocínio dedutivo de uma norma válida, aceita pela comunidade), tem-se uma *atuação judicial instrumental da intervenção legal* ou, em outros termos, uma *intervenção judicial "lato sensu"*. De outra banda, nas hipóteses nas quais a determinação do regulamento contratual se dá através da aplicação de regras formuladas de modo genérico, com conceitos indeterminados, sugerindo ou mesmo impondo ao juiz o exercício de um *poder amplo de valoração autônoma*, a fonte de determinação do regulamento contratual é a *atividade valorativa do magistrado* e não a lei. Neste caso, tem-se uma *verdadeira intervenção judicial* (intervenção judicial "stricto sensu").

Embora não seja a regra, o Código Civil brasileiro prescreve alguns artigos que tratam especificamente da intervenção judicial nos contratos. São eles: o artigo 413, que prevê a possibilidade de redução equitativa da multa em caso de cumprimento parcial da obrigação; o artigo 473, que prevê a possibilidade de o juiz intervir para manter o contrato em caso de resilição unilateral, havida quando uma das partes tenha efetuado substanciais investimentos em decorrência da respectiva celebração; o artigo 572, que trata da possibilidade do juiz reduzir o valor da indenização em casos de locação; e o artigo 581, que cuida da possibilidade de o juiz reduzir o prazo do comodato, na hipótese de necessidade imprevista e urgente.

Por se tratar de intervenções judiciais expressamente previstas em lei, são as chamadas *intervenções judiciais típicas*. Ao lado delas, encontram-se as *intervenções judiciais atípicas*, isto é, aquelas que, embora fundadas na lei, em princípios ou no próprio regulamento contratual, neles não se encontram expressamente previstas.

Diferenciar as simples *atuações judiciais* das *intervenções judiciais*, e classificá-las como de baixa ou alta complexidade, justas ou injustas, contratuais ou não contratuais, intervenções judiciais *lato sensu* ou *stricto sensu*, típicas ou atípicas etc. tem clara utilidade didática. Mas além do caráter pedagógico, tais diferenças e classificações são fundamentais para compreender os contornos teóricos do ativismo judicial em matéria contratual.

3.3. AS CIRCUNSTÂNCIAS QUE AUTORIZAM A INTERVENÇÃO JUDICIAL NOS CONTRATOS

Como se viu, a verdadeira intervenção judicial sucede apenas em casos cuja solução impõe ao magistrado um amplo poder de valoração autônoma (*casos difíceis*). E isso ocorre nas situações em que o regulamento contratual é constituído ou limitado por regras formuladas de modo genérico, com conceitos jurídicos indeterminados. Diferentemente, nos casos em que o desfecho da controvérsia se dá através de simples raciocínio dedutivo de uma norma válida (*casos fáceis*), é vedado ao magistrado impor a sua vontade ou intervir no contrato, sob pena de configurar uma atuação arbitrária[19].

E se não se vislumbra intervenção judicial *stricto sensu* nos casos fáceis, é possível concluir que *a chamada intervenção judicial no âmbito dos contratos está limitada aos casos de alta complexidade* (ou difíceis), isto é, àqueles que não permitem deduzir da lei a solução de modo simples, seja em função de dificuldades relacionadas à norma aplicável (contratual ou legal), seja em virtude de sua interpretação, impondo ao juiz orientar-se através de princípios, mediante um juízo de ponderação.

Sob tal perspectiva, pode se inferir ao menos três circunstâncias que, combinadas, autorizam uma intervenção judicial nos contratos:

a) o surgimento de um conflito de interesses relacionado a um contrato ou às partes por ele afetadas – inclusive terceiros;
b) o pedido da tutela jurídica do Estado pelo interessado através de uma ação judicial, desde que preenchidos os pressupostos processuais e as condições para tanto; e
c) a alta complexidade do caso a ser solucionado.

[19] Nos casos de baixa complexidade, a atuação do juiz deve limitar-se a exprimir a escolha dos próprios contratantes ou do legislador (esta última hipótese, no caso da vontade dos contratantes ofenderem preceito legal ou princípio vigente em nosso ordenamento jurídico).

3.4. A AMPLITUDE E INTENSIDADE DAS INTERFERÊNCIAS JUDICIAIS NO ÂMBITO DOS CONTRATOS[20]

É preciso lembrar, ainda, que os limites impostos à jurisdição não orientam apenas a *licitude*, mas, também, a *medida* da atuação judicial. Significa que, ao decidir, o juiz deve agir ou interferir nos contratos na *proporção necessária* à solução da controvérsia – nem mais, nem menos. Por isso, é importante compreender quais são os fatores que fazem variar a *amplitude* (extensão) e a *intensidade* (força) da atuação ou intervenção judicial nos contratos.

A *amplitude* da atuação ou da intervenção judicial nos contratos guarda estreita relação com a *autonomia* que o magistrado tem para solucionar um determinado caso. Veja. Os casos fáceis, como vimos, são geralmente solucionados através de um simples raciocínio dedutivo, com pouca ou nenhuma margem à criatividade ou à discricionariedade judicial. Já os casos difíceis, por sua vez, permitem soluções mais amplas, fundadas em cláusulas gerais, conceitos jurídicos indeterminados ou, até mesmo, em princípios sobre os quais se formula um juízo de ponderação. Nesse sentido, é possível afirmar que quanto *mais complexa* for a solução da controvérsia contratual, maior será a discricionariedade judicial no desempenho dessa tarefa e, por consequência, *mais amplo* será o *poder de intervenção* do magistrado nos contratos.

Mas além da complexidade da controvérsia, outros fatores fazem variar a amplitude da intervenção judicial no âmbito contratual. O *modo da negociação* estabelecida entre as partes, a *natureza do objeto da prestação contratual* e a *finalidade da contratação* são outros fatores determinantes para uma atuação judicial mais ou menos extensa. No que se refere ao modo da negociação entre as partes e o tempo da sua execução, os contratos podem ser classificados em: (i) *contratos isolados* (descontínuos ou singulares) e (ii) *contratos relacionais.*

Os contratos isolados ou instantâneos são aqueles cuja manifestação de vontade e execução ocorrem de uma só vez, em função das circunstâncias presentes no momento da celebração[21]. Já os contratos relacionais são aqueles nos quais a determinação do conteúdo ou de alguns de seus ele-

[20] Aqui englobadas as intervenções judiciais *lato sensu* e as intervenções judiciais *stricto sensu.*

[21] Aguiar Júnior, Ruy Rosado de. Contratos relacionais, existenciais e de lucro. Revista Trimestral de Direito Civil – RTDC. Volume 45. Rio de Janeiro: Editora Padma, p. 91-110, jan./mar., 2011, p. 97.

mentos essenciais se realiza mediante a remissão a elementos estranhos ao mesmo (*relatio*)[22].

O contrato relacional se caracteriza por ser um *contrato de duração* e que exige forte colaboração entre as partes interessadas. Antonio Junqueira de Azevedo, a propósito, leciona: "São relacionais todos os contratos que, sendo de duração, têm por objeto colaboração (sociedade, parcerias etc.) e, ainda, os que, mesmo não tendo por objeto a colaboração, exigem-na intensa para poder atingir os seus fins, como os de distribuição e da franquia, já referidos"[23]. Em função dessas características, o contrato relacional é aquele que melhor se adapta à negociação entre empresas, e no qual a *gestão do risco da superveniência* é uma questão a ser superada, seja através da renegociação, seja através da revisão das cláusulas pelo juiz ou pelo árbitro.

Por outro lado, o relacionamento continuado requer das partes um "comportamento adequado a cada nova situação, e com isso abre a oportunidade para que tais condutas sejam analisadas à luz da boa-fé, do fim social e da equidade"[24]. Logo, a própria natureza dos contratos relacionais exige uma amplitude maior da intervenção heterônoma, do que aquela ordinariamente necessária nos contratos isolados ou instantâneos. Relativamente à natureza do objeto da prestação contratada e à sua finalidade, os contratos podem ser classificados em: (i) *contratos existenciais* e (ii) *contratos de lucro*[25].

Segundo Antonio Junqueira de Azevedo, os contratos existenciais são aqueles que têm como uma das partes, ou ambas, as pessoas naturais[26], as

[22] Aguiar Júnior, Ruy Rosado de, Contratos relacionais, existenciais e de lucro, Revista Trimestral de Direito Civil – RTDC, Volume 45, cit., p. 98.

[23] Parecer jurídico: Natureza jurídica do contrato de consórcio. Classificação dos atos jurídicos quanto ao número de partes e quanto aos efeitos. Os contratos relacionais. A boa-fé nos contratos relacionais. Contratos de duração. Alteração das circunstâncias e onerosidade excessiva. Sinalagma e resolução contratual. Resolução parcial do contrato. Função social do contrato. Revista dos Tribunais. Ano 94. Volume 832, fevereiro de 2005, p. 115-137, p. 123.

[24] Aguiar Júnior, Ruy Rosado de, Contratos relacionais, existenciais e de lucro, Revista Trimestral de Direito Civil – RTDC, Volume 45, cit., p. 99.

[25] Ruy Rosado de Aguiar Júnior distingue os contratos de lucro dos empresariais, "porque nem sempre os empresariais têm por propósito a obtenção de uma vantagem patrimonial (v. Contratos relacionais, existenciais e de lucro, Revista Trimestral de Direito Civil – RTDC, Volume 45, cit., p. 105-106).

[26] Junqueira também admite, nesta categoria, as pessoas jurídicas sem fins lucrativos.

quais *negociam visando à sua subsistência* ou *necessidades fundamentais* (direito à vida, à integridade física, à saúde, à habitação etc.)[27].

Dentre os chamados contratos existenciais estariam parte dos contratos de consumo, os contratos de trabalho, os de locação residencial, compra e venda de casa própria e, de uma maneira geral, os que dizem respeito à *subsistência humana*. Trata-se de contratos que exigem um regime jurídico que privilegie a sua função social, seja interna (equivalência), seja externa (realização dos fins sociais para os quais existe o contrato), com o intuito último de assegurar os valores inerentes à dignidade da pessoa humana[28]. Por conta disso, são contratos que admitem uma maior participação do magistrado na apreciação do seu conteúdo e nos casos de eventual revisão, com o propósito de respeitar a sua função social.

De outra parte, os contratos de lucro são aqueles celebrados entre empresas ou entre profissionais, com o propósito de atingir os *fins* que lhes são próprios (ordinariamente, o lucro). Aqui, leva-se em consideração não o objeto da prestação contratada, mas a sua própria função econômica[29], isto é, de transferir patrimônio com vantagem para o contratante.

No caso desses contratos de lucro, afirma Antonio Junqueira de Azevedo, "a interferência dos juízes perturba o funcionamento do mercado ou o exercício das profissões; o princípio *pacta sunt servanda* tem que ter aí maior força (...) especialmente nas situações limítrofes como as de pessoas naturais, que mesmo fora do exercício profissional, visam lucro, ou as de empresas muito pequenas etc.".[30] Portanto, nos contratos empresariais e nos de lucro, a intervenção judicial deve se dar, como regra[31], em menor medida.

27 Diálogos com a doutrina: entrevista com Antonio Junqueira de Azevedo, Revista Trimestral de Direito Civil, v. 9, nº 34, cit., p. 304-305.

28 Alpa, Guido. Manuale di diritto privato. 4ª edição. Padova: CEDAM, 2005, p. 543, *apud* Aguiar Júnior, Ruy Rosado de. Contratos relacionais, existenciais e de lucro, Revista Trimestral de Direito Civil – RTDC. Volume 45, cit., p. 106.

29 Aguiar Júnior, Ruy Rosado de, Contratos relacionais, existenciais e de lucro, Revista Trimestral de Direito Civil – RTDC, volume 45, cit., p. 103.

30 Diálogos com a doutrina: entrevista com Antonio Junqueira de Azevedo. Revista Trimestral de Direito Civil, v. 9, nº 34. Rio de Janeiro, abr./jun., 2008, p. 304-305.

31 Para Ruy Rosado de Aguiar Júnior, "a tese da menor intervenção estatal (judicial) sobre o conteúdo dos contratos de lucro está hoje em parte derrogada pela crise de 2008 no mercado financeiro, que está exigindo dos Estados regulamentação rigorosa desses negócios" Contratos relacionais, existenciais e de lucro, Revista Trimestral de Direito Civil – RTDC, volume 45, cit., p. 110).

Pois bem. Se a amplitude da intervenção judicial varia de acordo com a complexidade da controvérsia, o modo da negociação e a natureza das relações jurídicas firmadas, a intensidade da interferência judicial está relacionada, por seu turno, à *relevância* e *potencial impacto social* da divergência contratual suscitada, bem como à *natureza da intervenção judicial* a ser realizada. Evidentemente, a não observância ou o desrespeito a um preceito constitucional, legal ou infralegal (norma geral) é mais grave do que a não observância ou o desrespeito a uma determinada cláusula contratual (norma particular). Afinal, se a infração a uma norma geral tem potencial ofensivo suficiente para atingir toda a sociedade, o desrespeito a uma cláusula contratual pode alcançar apenas as partes contratantes (e, excepcionalmente, terceiros ao contrato vinculados). Por esta mesma razão, uma controvérsia contratual decorrente da não observância ou do desrespeito a uma norma de ordem pública merece maior reprimenda do Estado do que a inobservância ou a infração a uma norma de ordem privada. No que toca à natureza da intervenção judicial a ser executada, o Judiciário pode ser chamado a interpretar, integrar ou modificar um contrato ou uma determinada cláusula contratual. Nestes casos, avaliamos que há maior intervenção judicial quando se modifica um contrato ou uma cláusula contratual, do que quando se integra ou se interpreta um ou a outra. Isso porque, ao se modificar um contrato ou uma cláusula contratual, há verdadeira *substituição da vontade originalmente declarada* pelos contratantes por outra fonte de conteúdo contratual, isto é, a lei ou a decisão judicial. Na interpretação ou integração, por seu turno, há apenas uma *complementação* desta vontade original pelas fontes heterônomas do regulamento contratual. Em síntese:

a) Quanto à amplitude das interferências judiciais no âmbito dos contratos:
   (i) Quanto mais complexa for a solução da controvérsia contratual, mais amplo será o poder de intervenção do magistrado nos contratos.
   (ii) Os contratos relacionais propiciam uma intervenção judicial mais ampla do que os contratos isolados ou instantâneos.
   (iii) Os contratos existenciais carecem, em regra, de uma maior atenção do magistrado na apreciação do seu conteúdo do que os contratos empresariais ou de lucro.

b) Quanto à intensidade das interferências judiciais no âmbito dos contratos:
   (i) Uma controvérsia contratual decorrente da não observância ou do desrespeito a uma norma de ordem pública merece maior reprimenda do Estado do que a inobservância ou a infração a uma norma de ordem privada.
   (ii) Há maior intervenção judicial quando se modifica um contrato ou uma cláusula contratual, do que quando se integra ou se interpreta um ou a outra.

3.5. OS NÍVEIS E GRAUS DA INTERFERÊNCIA JUDICIAL NO ÂMBITO DOS CONTRATOS

Há diferentes providências judiciais possíveis por ocasião da solução de uma controvérsia contratual. A depender da natureza, do impacto e relevância social da divergência, a atuação judicial pode variar de um simples esclarecimento da melhor forma de interpretar um contrato até a sua modificação, a sua resolução, o reconhecimento da prática de um ato ilícito, a nulidade do quanto avençado, a condenação em multas contratuais, a eventual reparação de danos materiais e morais etc.

Ao menos em tese, portanto, a interferência judicial nos contratos varia de *alta a baixa*, no que tange à *amplitude*; e de *máxima a mínima*, no que se refere à *intensidade*. Ademais, por traduzirem diferentes critérios, ambas as classificações podem ser *combinadas*, de modo a que se tenha casos de interferência alta, média ou baixa, de grau máximo, médio ou mínimo.

Seguindo este raciocínio:

1.a) *Interferência alta de grau máximo*: casos difíceis, solucionados através de um juízo de ponderação fundado em normas-princípio, que resultem na nulidade de uma cláusula contratual ou do contrato como um todo; ou na resolução do mesmo, acrescida das penalidades contratuais e eventuais reparações cabíveis.

1.b) *Interferência alta de grau médio*: casos difíceis, solucionados através de um juízo de ponderação fundado em normas-princípio, que resultem na modificação de uma cláusula ou do próprio contrato.

1.c) *Interferência alta de grau mínimo*: casos difíceis, solucionados através de um juízo de ponderação fundado em normas-princípio, que tenham por fim preencher uma lacuna contratual, ou o esclarecimento do sentido e alcance de uma cláusula ou do próprio contrato.

2.a) *Interferência média de grau máximo*: casos difíceis, solucionados através da aplicação de imposições legais ou infralegais abertas e flexíveis (cláusulas gerais ou conceitos jurídicos indeterminados), que resultem na nulidade de uma cláusula contratual ou do contrato como um todo, ou na resolução do mesmo, acrescida das penalidades contratuais e eventuais reparações cabíveis.

2.b) *Interferência média de grau médio*: casos difíceis, solucionados através da aplicação de imposições legais ou infralegais abertas e flexíveis (cláusulas gerais ou conceitos jurídicos indeterminados), que resultem na modificação de uma cláusula ou do próprio contrato.

2.c) *Interferência média de grau mínimo*: casos difíceis, solucionados através da aplicação de imposições legais ou infralegais abertas e flexíveis (cláusulas gerais ou conceitos jurídicos indeterminados), que tenham por fim preencher uma lacuna contratual, ou o esclarecimento do sentido e alcance de uma cláusula ou do próprio contrato.

3.a) *Interferência baixa de grau máximo*: casos fáceis, solucionados através de um simples raciocínio dedutivo, que resultem no reconhecimento da inexistência de um determinado negócio jurídico, na nulidade de uma cláusula contratual ou do contrato como um todo, na resolução do mesmo, acrescida das penalidades contratuais e eventuais reparações cabíveis; ou no reconhecimento da decadência de um determinado direito, acrescido das penalidades contratuais e eventuais reparações cabíveis.

3.b) *Interferência baixa de grau médio*: casos fáceis, solucionados através de um simples raciocínio dedutivo, que resultem na modificação de uma cláusula ou do próprio contrato; na anulabilidade ou ineficácia de uma cláusula contratual ou do contrato como um todo, acrescida das penalidades contratuais e eventuais reparações cabíveis; ou no reconhecimento da prescrição do exercício de um determinado direito, acrescido das penalidades contratuais e eventuais reparações cabíveis.

3.c) *Interferência baixa de grau mínimo*: casos fáceis, solucionados através de um simples raciocínio dedutivo, que tenham por fim preencher uma lacuna contratual, ou o esclarecimento do sentido e alcance de uma cláusula ou do próprio contrato.

3.6. A INTERVENÇÃO JUDICIAL EQUIVOCADA COMO ELEMENTO DO ATIVISMO JUDICIAL EM MATÉRIA CONTRATUAL

Uma intervenção judicial *desmedida*, seja em sua amplitude, seja em sua intensidade, pode configurar erro judicial (*error in judicando*), a merecer o imediato reexame e eventual correção em sede recursal. Entretanto, caso tal desproporção se faça de modo a *ampliar* os limites impostos pelo ordenamento à jurisdição, evidenciando um suposto *protagonismo* do Poder Judiciário, nos moldes já delineados nesta obra, então estar-se-á diante de um caso típico de ativismo judicial.

A caracterização do equívoco da decisão judicial na seara contratual só pode ser aferida caso a caso. Apenas diante de uma situação concreta é possível identificar a providência judicial adequada à solução da controvérsia, bem como a exata medida da intervenção a ser realizada no contrato ou na respectiva cláusula contratual. Assim sendo, é importante compreender a amplitude, a intensidade, os níveis e graus das intervenções judiciais nos contratos, de modo que se obtenham critérios úteis à identificação dos eventuais excessos, a serem revistos e corrigidos pelos meios processuais aplicáveis na espécie.

Para ilustrar o quanto referido, vale rememorar o célebre caso do Resp n. 76.362/MT, neste trabalho já ventilado, no qual dois segurados promovem ação de cobrança para receber a cobertura securitária devida em razão de acidente de veículo. Imagine agora, apenas por hipótese, que os autores confessem dever não só a última, mas 20% (vinte por cento) das parcelas do contrato. Apreciada a ação pelo respectivo Tribunal de Justiça, entende aquela Corte que o segurado tinha como principal obrigação pagar o "prêmio do seguro", dando por resolvido o contrato, e condenando os inadimplentes ao pagamento da cláusula penal convencionada, além das verbas sucumbenciais[32]. Inconformados, os segurados interpõem recurso especial e, para surpresa geral, obtêm o seu provimento, com fundamento na doutrina do adimplemento substancial, para declarar subsistente o contrato e condenar os segurados, apenas, no pagamento das parcelas inadimplidas, devidamente corrigidas e acrescidas de juros de mora, além da cláusula penal convencionada.

Note-se que o caso é indiscutivelmente difícil, uma vez que requer solução através de um juízo de ponderação fundado em normas-princí-

[32] Conforme prescreve o ordenamento positivo brasileiro, a teor dos artigos 757 e 763 do Código Civil.

pio (princípio da força obrigatória dos contratos, da conservação dos contratos, da boa-fé objetiva, da função social, da equivalência material dos contratos, dentre outros). Por outro lado, são duas as possíveis providências judiciais a serem tomadas na hipótese: uma delas de grau máximo (a resolução do contrato) e outra de grau médio (a modificação da cláusula contratual que previa a resolução do contrato na hipótese de inadimplemento dos segurados).

Evidentemente, dentre as opções possíveis, existe aquela que se afigura a melhor (idealmente), a mais adequada para o caso concreto. A despeito disso, pode não ser ela a opção do magistrado. Em outras palavras, é possível que o juiz *erre* e opte pela solução que lhe pareceu a mais justa, mas que se mostre, na avaliação de uma das partes e, até mesmo, de outros magistrados, como injusta. Neste caso, estar-se-á diante de uma decisão lícita, porém *equivocada*.

Vale ressalvar, contudo, que a ocorrência de uma decisão judicial equivocada ou injusta, por si só, não é suficiente à caracterização do ativismo judicial. O que autoriza qualificar uma determinada postura judicial como ativista são algumas *características especiais* da decisão judicial equivocada, a seguir delineadas.

3.7. O ALARGAMENTO ASSIMÉTRICO DAS FRONTEIRAS DA JURISDIÇÃO COMO REQUISITO DO ATIVISMO JUDICIAL EM MATÉRIA CONTRATUAL

Como anteriormente exposto, ao conferir limites à atuação jurisdicional, o ordenamento jurídico o faz, em tese, de forma simétrica, isto é, guardando uma proporção ideal entre o território reservado à atuação jurisdicional e aquele destinado aos demais agentes limitadores da liberdade contratual.

Se o ativismo judicial é caracterizado pela ampliação dos limites ideais da jurisdição, isto significa, de algum modo, restringir o campo de atuação dos outros agentes, rompendo com uma simetria originalmente prevista pelo ordenamento jurídico. Por esta razão, afirma-se que os limites da jurisdição, quando vitimados por uma decisão ativista, sofrem de uma distensão assimétrica, isto é, de uma distorção, em grandeza, envolvendo o território idealmente reservado à atuação jurisdicional e aquele determinado, concretamente, por um dos citados agentes de limitação da liberdade contratual.

Volte-se, então, ao caso hipotético mencionado no compartimento anterior, consistente no inadimplemento de 20% (vinte por cento) das parcelas do contrato de seguro. Imagine, agora, que a decisão mais justa para o caso, diante de todas as circunstâncias concretas, fosse a resolução do contrato, e que, não obstante isso, o magistrado tenha decidido, com fundamento no princípio do adimplemento substancial do contrato, manter íntegro o negócio, condenando os devedores, apenas, no pagamento das parcelas inadimplidas, devidamente corrigidas e acrescidas de juros de mora, além da cláusula penal convencionada. Ora, não há dúvida que a citada decisão judicial limitou aquilo que havia sido ajustado sob o império da liberdade contratual dos particulares. Vale dizer, o que as partes contrataram (a resolução do contrato, na hipótese de inadimplemento), o Poder Judiciário houve por bem "descontratar". O caso, portanto, é um exemplo clássico de distorção, em grandeza, envolvendo o território idealmente reservado à atuação jurisdicional (nesta hipótese, o regulamento contratual) e aquele determinado, concretamente, por um dos citados agentes de limitação da liberdade contratual (nesta hipótese, a decisão judicial).

Ainda assim, o equívoco da decisão judicial e o alargamento assimétrico das fronteiras da jurisdição não são motivos suficientes para decretar a configuração do ativismo judicial. Resta, para tanto, apurar se a intervenção judicial, tal qual realizada, denotaria ou não um *protagonismo* do Poder Judiciário.

3.8. O "PROTAGONISMO DO JUDICIÁRIO" COMO REQUISITO DO ATIVISMO JUDICIAL EM MATÉRIA CONTRATUAL

A comunidade jurídica e a sociedade só reconhecem e qualificam uma atuação judicial como ativista, se a mesma denotar um *protagonismo do Poder Judiciário* frente aos papéis ordinariamente reservados aos demais atores sociais que, com ele, dividem a incumbência legítima de criar, interpretar e aplicar o direito. Ademais, se as determinações voluntárias do regulamento contratual traduzem sempre os poderes e interesses da autonomia privada, as fontes "heterônomas" do regulamento contratual (as leis e as decisões judiciais) podem, diferentemente, operar de acordo com as seguintes variantes: a) valorações legais contrastantes com a autonomia privada; b) valorações legais homogêneas e instrumentais da autonomia privada; c) valorações judiciais contrastantes com a autonomia privada; e d) valorações judiciais homogêneas e instrumentais da autonomia privada.

As valorações legais do regulamento contratual, por não demandarem uma participação extraordinária do magistrado (responsável apenas pela ativação da norma), não são atuações capazes de evidenciar a importância do Poder Judiciário, mas, sim, do próprio legislador. Afinal, nestes casos, a lei é a verdadeira fonte de determinação do regulamento contratual.

Seguindo o mesmo raciocínio, no que tange às valorações judiciais, apenas aquelas que *contrastam* com a *autonomia privada* podem ser configuradas como ativistas. Vale dizer, as valorações judiciais homogêneas e instrumentais da autonomia privada, ao ratificarem a vontade natural expressada pelas partes na avença, também não são capazes de destacar a atuação excepcional do Poder Judiciário. Na realidade, elas denotam um protagonismo da autonomia privada.

Em resumo: se o regulamento contratual pode ser concebido pelos próprios contratantes, e retocado pela lei, pelas autoridades administrativas ou pelo Judiciário, toda vez que o magistrado, ao intervir em um determinado contrato, o fizer segundo a *sua valoração* (judicial), em *detrimento* da *valoração voluntária* (a fonte autêntica do regulamento contratual), estar-se-á diante de uma circunstância capaz de sugerir um predomínio (protagonismo) do Poder Judiciário em relação à autonomia privada (ou mesmo ao legislador) e, consequentemente, de um potencial exemplo de ativismo judicial em matéria contratual.

Vale registrar, ainda, que entre todos os atos ou eventos capazes de originar uma controvérsia contratual, destacam-se apenas três que comportam as sobreditas intervenções judiciais suscetíveis de serem reconhecidas como "ativistas". São eles: a) a suposta não observância ou o desrespeito a normas-princípio no âmbito de uma relação contratual; b) a suposta não observância ou o desrespeito, no âmbito de uma relação contratual, a imposições legais ou infralegais abertas e flexíveis (cláusulas gerais ou conceitos jurídicos indeterminados); e c) a suposta necessidade de interpretar, integrar ou modificar um determinado contrato ou cláusula contratual.

Note-se que nessas três hipóteses, a determinação do regulamento contratual se dá através da aplicação de regras formuladas de modo genérico, recheadas de conceitos indeterminados, sugerindo ou mesmo impondo ao juiz o exercício de um poder amplo de valoração autônoma (decisão difícil). Apenas para exemplificar o quanto teoricamente exposto, volta-se, pela derradeira vez, ao caso ilustrativo trazido nos dois últimos compartimentos, no qual dois segurados, muito embora inadimplentes com

20% (vinte por cento) das parcelas do seu contrato de seguro, promovem ação de cobrança para receber a cobertura securitária devida em razão de acidente de veículo.

Para efeito didático, considere-se, uma vez mais, que a decisão mais justa para o caso seria a resolução contratual, mas que, a despeito disso, o magistrado tenha decidido, por equívoco, manter o contrato, com fundamento na teoria do adimplemento substancial. A hipótese, pois, é um exemplo clássico de distorção, em grandeza, envolvendo o território idealmente reservado à atuação jurisdicional (o regulamento contratual) e aquele determinado, concretamente, por um dos citados agentes de limitação da liberdade contratual (o juiz). Sucede que, como visto, para a caracterização do ativismo judicial não basta a comprovação de uma decisão judicial equivocada, que resulte no alargamento assimétrico das fronteiras da jurisdição. É preciso, ainda, apurar se a intervenção judicial, tal qual realizada, denota ou não um protagonismo do Poder Judiciário.

Pois bem. Ao julgar através de um juízo de ponderação baseado em normas-princípio (as cláusulas gerais da boa-fé, da função social do contrato etc.), o magistrado ressaltou a importância da sua valoração pessoal para a construção da norma de decisão, ou seja, conferiu protagonismo ao Poder Judiciário (do qual é membro) e não à vontade das partes (expressão da autonomia privada). Ademais, a solução encontrada pelo juiz imaginário mostrou-se absolutamente contrária àquela propugnada pelas partes, no momento em que celebraram o negócio (a resolução contratual, na hipótese de inadimplemento das parcelas devidas). Repise-se: o que as partes contrataram, o Poder Judiciário desconsiderou. O caso, portanto, é de uma providência judicial operada através de uma valoração judicial (baseada em cláusulas gerais) contrastante com a autonomia privada.

Toda vez que o magistrado, ao intervir em um determinado contrato, o fizer segundo a sua valoração (judicial), em detrimento da valoração voluntária (a fonte autêntica do regulamento contratual), estar-se-á diante de uma circunstância capaz de sugerir um predomínio do Poder Judiciário em relação à autonomia privada e, consequentemente, de um potencial exemplo de ativismo judicial. Por isso, a hipótese aqui trazida como ilustração é reprodução fiel de uma ocorrência de ativismo judicial em matéria contratual, fruto da equivocada aplicação da teoria do adimplemento substancial.

CONCLUSÕES

Com base em todos os argumentos trazidos neste artigo, pode-se afirmar que a caracterização do ativismo judicial em matéria contratual pressupõe:

a) um conflito de interesses relacionado a um contrato ou às partes por ele afetadas – inclusive terceiros;
b) o pedido da tutela jurídica do Estado pelo interessado através de uma ação judicial, desde que preenchidos os pressupostos processuais e as condições para tanto;
c) a alta complexidade do caso a ser solucionado;
d) uma controvérsia contratual fundada: (i) na inobservância ou no desrespeito a normas-princípio; (ii) na inobservância ou no desrespeito a imposições legais ou infralegais abertas e flexíveis; ou (iii) na necessidade de interpretar, integrar ou modificar um determinado contrato ou cláusula contratual; e
e) uma intervenção judicial equivocada, concretizada através da formulação de uma norma de decisão inadequada ou desmedida (decisão injusta), além de contrária à vontade originalmente declarada pelos contratantes.

Em outras palavras: haverá ativismo judicial em matéria contratual toda vez que, diante de uma controvérsia contratual complexa, fundada na inobservância ou no desrespeito a normas-princípio, na inobservância ou no desrespeito a imposições legais ou infralegais abertas e flexíveis, ou na necessidade de interpretar, integrar ou modificar um determinado contrato ou cláusula contratual, o magistrado intervenha de modo equivocado, formulando uma norma de decisão inadequada ou desmedida, além de contrária à vontade originalmente declarada pelos contratantes. Nestes termos, reafirma-se: em determinadas circunstâncias, uma decisão judicial que deixa de resolver um contrato com fundamento na teoria do adimplemento substancial pode configurar ativismo judicial.

REFERÊNCIAS

AGUIAR JÚNIOR, Ruy Rosado de. *Contratos relacionais, existenciais e de lucro*. Revista Trimestral de Direito Civil – RTDC. Volume 45. Rio de Janeiro: Editora Padma, p. 91-110, jan./mar., 2011.

BUSSATA, Eduardo Luiz. *Resolução dos contratos e teoria do adimplemento substancial*. 2ª ed. São Paulo: Saraiva, 2008.

Ferreira, Aurélio Buarque de Holanda. *Dicionário Aurélio básico da língua portuguesa*. Rio de Janeiro: Editora Nova Fronteira.

Gonçalves, Carlos Roberto. *Direito Civil Brasileiro*. 3º Volume. São Paulo: Editora Saraiva, 2004.

Junqueira de Azevedo, Antonio. *Parecer jurídico:* Natureza jurídica do contrato de consórcio. Classificação dos atos jurídicos quanto ao número de partes e quanto aos efeitos. Os contratos relacionais. A boa-fé nos contratos relacionais. Contratos de duração. Alteração das circunstâncias e onerosidade excessiva. Sinalagma e resolução contratual. Resolução parcial do contrato. Função social do contrato. Revista dos Tribunais. Ano 94. Volume 832, fevereiro de 2005, p. 115-137.

____. *Diálogos com a doutrina: entrevista com Antonio Junqueira de Azevedo*, Revista Trimestral de Direito Civil, v. 9, nº 34, cit., p. 304-305.

Lautenschläger, Milton Flávio de Almeida Camargo. *Ativismo judicial disfuncional nos contratos*. São Paulo: Editora IASP, 2018.

Lorenzetti, Ricardo Luis. *Teoria da Decisão Judicial* – Fundamentos de Direito. Tradução de Bruno Miragem, Notas da tradução de Cláudia Lima Marques. 2ª edição revista. São Paulo: Editora Revista dos Tribunais, 2011.

Rodrigues Junior, Otavio Luiz. *Revisão Judicial dos Contratos* – Autonomia da vontade e teoria da imprevisão. 2ª edição revista, ampliada e atualizada. São Paulo: Editora Atlas, 2006.

Roppo, Enzo. *O contrato*. Tradução de Ana Coimbra e M. Januário C. Gomes. Coimbra: Almedina, 2009.

A LEGITIMIDADE DE POSTULADOS DA JUSTIÇA RESTAURATIVA NA ESFERA CÍVEL COMO UMA QUESTÃO DE ALTERIDADE

Mônica Aguiar*
Sara Bomfim Santa Rosa**

INTRODUÇÃO

O presente artigo se propõe a estudar a flexibilização do procedimento voluntário nas ações de direito de família, ao refletir sobre a utilização do negócio jurídico processual atípico pelas partes, num conflito familiar. Assim, analisa-se as influências que a flexibilização voluntária do procedimento trazida pela legislação processual civil pode exercer sobre as ações de família, a exemplo dos casos de alienação parental.

Sustenta-se que isto permite a aplicação das ideias do processo restaurativo de justiça na esfera cível, na medida em que viabiliza a alteração procedimental de acordo com as necessidades do caso concreto, sem afastar a fiscalização do Poder Estatal quanto ao respeito atribuído às garantias fundamentais e condições gerais do negócio jurídico. Assim como, entende-se que tal possibilidade é um reflexo da inclusão do pressuposto da alteridade no ordenamento jurídico brasileiro.

A relevância sócio-jurídica desta pesquisa consiste na demonstração de que o art. 190 do Código de Processo Civil ampliou o leque para que

* Doutora em Direito pela PUC-SP. Professora da Universidade Católica do Salvador e da Universidade Federal da Bahia.Coordenadora do Mestrado em Direito da Universidade Católica do Salvador.
** Mestranda em Direito pela Universidade Católica do Salvador. Advogada.

os conflitos possam ser solucionados pelas próprias partes tendo o Estado, apenas, o papel fiscalizador. Deste modo, o presente artigo possibilita o diálogo com a concepção de alteridade em duas frentes: a primeira reside no fato de o Estado enxergar os litigantes como sujeitos como protagonistas mais atuantes na solução do próprio litígio, afinal eles são os maiores interessados na resolução eficaz do conflito; e a segunda consiste na alteridade entre as partes, na medida em que uma consegue visualizar as necessidades da outra, as quais podem ser diferentes das suas. Neste diapasão, percebe-se que ambas as hipóteses são verificadas no modelo restaurativo de justiça. Tem-se como objetivo, ainda, demonstrar que a perspectiva de privatização do direito processual civil quando feita nos limites legais e constitucionais permite a efetivação do princípio da alteridade, único capaz de reconhecer idêntico valor às diferentes partes do processo.

A metodologia escolhida é a pesquisa bibliográfica com natureza qualitativa, pois artigos e livros foram consultados como fonte de pesquisa, por meio do método dedutivo.Inicialmente, é realizado um estudo conceitual a respeito dos negócios jurídicos processuais dentro do Código de Processo Civil brasileiro com o recorte de aprofundamento do estudo nos negócios jurídicos processuais atípicos versando sobre suas características e base legal. Posteriormente, são estudados os modelos de flexibilização procedimental existentes, priorizando aquele escolhido pelo ordenamento positivo brasileiro.

Por fim, é analisada a aplicação dos postulados da Justiça Restaurativa como uma forma de negócio jurídico processual atípico, isto é, carreando-a do direito penal para a esfera cível. De forma exemplificativa, fala-se nos círculos familiares discutidos por Howard Zehr, o qual trata essa temática nas ações de família. Vale ressaltar que o conceito e o significado do princípio da alteridade fundamenta essa perspectiva.

1. O NEGÓCIO JURÍDICO PROCESSUAL E O CPC

O Código de Processo Civil de 1973 afirmava em seu art. 125, que a forma como o processo seria administrado era determinada pelo juiz, na medida em que ele era o seu personagem principal. Por outro lado, o atual CPC (Código de Processo Civil) assevera que as escolhas das partes durante o processo devem ser fruto da autonomia delas para que o procedimento se desenrole em conformidade com seu objetivo de efetividade diante da situação jurídica concreta. (PONTE; ROMÃO, 2015, p.312; 318). Nessa perspectiva, o negócio jurídico processual é o fato proposto, voluntariamente, por algum sujeito processual que repercute no universo jurídico tendo como escopo atribuir às partes a capacidade de, mediante o respeito ao ordenamento jurídico, atribuir legitimidade a algumas maleabilidades dentro do processo, inclusive, à mudança do procedimento. (Didier, 2012, p. 59-60). Paula Sarno Braga dialoga com Fredie Didier ao afirmar que um processo que requeira a atuação do Poder Judiciário e se estabeleça numa democracia necessita da "participação das partes, que serão atingidas pelos efeitos do ato decisório (normativo) ali produzido". (Braga, *et al,* 2017, p. 435).

O entendimento da autora se fundamenta no fato de o objetivo primordial da sistemática processual brasileira ser o de regozijar os sujeitos processuais pela resolução do seu problema, o que permite a pacificação social, por intermédio do apoio de todas as partes para a resolução do caso concreto da ação judicial. Essa compreensão se torna real, por meio da inclusão do órgão julgador nas tratativas, com o intuito de fiscalizá-las e dialogá-las, sendo um *plus* ao princípio do contraditório já conhecido ao permitir a melhor escuta de todos os sujeitos do processo. (Matta, 2015, p. 134; 146). Nessa toada, a negociação de procedimentos jurídicos pelas partes se torna fundamento da norma jurídica, o que proporciona a vinculação do juízo às regras e aos princípios jurídicos, os quais devem ser respeitados numa democracia. (Cabral, 2015, p. 240). Paula Sarno Braga assevera que processo é, em sua essência, um ato, que objetiva a criação de normas e tem como valor permitir a participação democrática. (Braga, *et al,* 2017, p. 434).

Posto isto, o que se tem como escopo é que haja um diálogo entre o procedimento e as singularidades da causa de pedir para que a resolução seja dotada de efetividade para as partes envolvidas. Nessa perspectiva, "as partes, ao convencionarem sobre aspectos procedimentais, assumem parcela do protagonismo do juiz, adaptando o procedimento de maneira que tenha melhor adequação aos seus interesses". (Matta, 2015, p. 152). Sob essa ótica, destaca-se que o CPC brasileiro aborda alguns tipos de negócios jurídicos. Este artigo se restringirá aos atípicos, ou seja, àqueles que não estão previstos expressamente em lei. Este tipo de negócio ganha validade, por causa da cláusula geral do art. 190 do CPC combinado com o princípio do autorregramento da vontade do processo, o qual efetiva o direito fundamental à liberdade na esfera pública do direito, podendo, por exemplo, mudar a ordem dos atos processuais ou sua configuração.

(Didier, 2018, p. 443). Isso implica em convencionar que a resposta do Poder Judiciário à resolução do processo será baseada no senso de justiça ou no direito costumeiro. (Cadiet, 2014, p. 21-22). É importante frisar que o negócio jurídico processual atípico, como qualquer negocio jurídico, deve se submeter ao disposto no art. 200 do CPC. Além disso, pode ser realizado com a participação do órgão julgador quando este estará exercendo a função de fiscalização imediata da conformidade desse negócio à lei. Ademais, eles podem ocorrer antes ou depois da discussão ensejadora do litígio. (DIDIER, 2018, p. 447).

Por fim, para que tenha validade jurídica, deve ter objeto lícito e ser feito conforme a legislação determinar ou não proibir, sendo que caso não cumpra os requisitos tecidos no parágrafo supracitado, ocasionará dano à relação jurídica; o que provocará a sua nulidade. (Almeida, 2014, p. 124). No que se refere à forma e à revogabilidade do negócio jurídico processual atípico, aquela é desprendida de rigidez, podendo ser feita pela oralidade ou pela documentação, de forma evidente ou oculta; e nela a irrevogabilidade dos atos processuais praticados prospera. (Didier, 2018, p. 456-459).

Ademais, caso o cumprimento de uma decisão judicial esteja pesado demais para uma das partes, poderá haver a extinção ou modificação dela, e, se uma das partes estiver inadimplente numa obrigação prolongada no tempo, então a outra deverá informar isso em juízo sob pena de perder a possibilidade de efetivar o ato processual de cobrança. (Didier, 2018, p. 456-459). Ressalte-se que esses negócios estão incluídos nas regras e nos princípios gerais dos negócios jurídicos dispostos no Código Civil brasileiro, tais como: a boa-fé processual e a intenção das partes nas suas falas. (Didier, 2018, p. 456-459).

Assim sendo, ante o exposto no art. 190 do CPC, verifica-se que o Poder Legislativo ampliou as possibilidades de as partes gerirem o procedimento processual demonstrando uma abolição da ideia de que o processo é regido, unicamente, pelo juiz em detrimento de que ele seja mais democrático e participativo. (Ponte, Romão, 2015, p.317-318). Sustenta-se que a democracia e a participação pode ser evidenciada na possibilidade de uma parte numa ação de família optar por ideias oriundas do modelo restaurativo de justiça para solucionar seus litígios mudando, totalmente ou em parte, o procedimento processual positivado, desde que o Estado, por meio do Poder Judiciário, fiscalize as modificações para que elas não venham a mitigar direitos fundamentais dos envolvidos.

2. A FLEXIBILIZAÇÃO PROCEDIMENTAL VOLUNTÁRIA NO CPC

No que tange à teoria da flexibilização procedimental, é importante frisar que, de acordo com Gajardoni, ela pode ser estabelecida sob dupla ótica. A primeira consiste no sistema da legalidade das formas procedimentais, segundo a qual para se ter segurança jurídica é preciso que haja burocracia processual e que se ocorrer algum erro, deve existir a invalidade do procedimento ou do ato resultante.(Gajardoni, 2011, p. 1-2). Enquanto que a segunda conclama que para que haja a flexibilidade da ordem processual, se faz necessário a existência de uma maior liberdade procedimental. Esta é a preponderante na legislação ordinária (Gajardoni, 2011, p. 1-2). Vale salientar, inclusive, que já existia o embrião da flexibilização procedimental no CPC de 73, o qual tratava do princípio da instrumentalidade das formas. Dessa forma:

Alinhando a esse entendimento, o CPC/1973, nos arts. 154, 24411 e 25012, criou mecanismos para afastar o excesso de formalismo. A literalidade de tais regras aponta para a possibilidade de convalidação de atos processuais executados de maneira diversa a da lei, quando estes conseguirem atingir sua finalidade essencial, ainda que provenientes de uma violação formal que o próprio sistema puna com pena de nulidade. Nesse caso, o princípio da instrumentalidade se manifesta no sentido de tornar a atividade jurisdicional mais compatível com as noções de economia processual, celeridade e tutela eficiente do direito. Além do mais, vale ressaltar que o princípio da instrumentalidade das formas também cumpre com os princípios da convalidação, da causalidade e do interesse processual, todos pretendendo salvaguardar o processo das consequências do ato nulo, relativizando assim o desatendimento à forma em sentido estrito. (Ono, 2015, p. 5)

Neste ponto, Paula Sarno Braga defende que o contraditório não é um condicionante da existência de um processo, todavia um requisito de validade; na medida em que "de tudo devem estar as partes cientes, de tudo devem participar, sempre com oportunidade de se manifestar, com poder de influência e cooperativamente". (Braga, *et al*, 2017, p. 438-439).

Deste modo, já existe no processo civil brasileiro, uma proliferação da concepção de que o direito precisa ser efetivo e, para tanto, o processo, deve ser cooperativo. Esse novo olhar sob o processo revela que a possibilidade de negociar o procedimento a ser utilizado para sanar o direito material não surgiu do acaso, mas é resultado de uma ampliação paulatina da privatização do processo. (Migliavacca; Fortes, 2014, p. 4).

Assim, com o atual CPC há uma maior mitigação do modelo da legalidade das formas procedimentais viabilizando que tanto o juiz como as partes, diante da insuficiência do procedimento, possa adaptá-lo às singularidades objetivas e subjetivas do caso concreto. (Gajardoni, 2011, p. 3-4). Entende-se que o objetivo do legislador com a flexibilização voluntária do procedimento no art. 190 do CPC brasileiro é demonstrar que um processo não deve servir para reafirmar o poder do Estado, mas para garantir que, através do contraditório, as partes alcancem a melhor solução para o litígio que protagonizam.

Hodiernamente, há uma simplificação formal e ritual no CPC, por meio de uma supressão de obstáculos, sem renúncia aos direitos e garantias processuais, isto é, de uma processuais convencionais sem efetividade. Isso em virtude duma recriação do processo com o aperfeiçoamento das formalidades provenientes da demanda objetivando garantir um processo civil seguro e cadenciado. (Gajardoni, 2011, p. 4). De forma ilustrativa, existe uma substituição dos procedimentos cognitivos ordinário e sumário pelo procedimento comum melhorado, por intermédio da extinção da fase de arrolamento das testemunhas, da ampliação da improcedência liminar do pedido, do julgamento antecipado do mérito da audiência de conciliação, da análise sobre a competência do juízo como preliminar da contestação, da possibilidade de emenda a inicial após a contestação por motivo de ilegitimidade passiva, da diminuição do prazo da fazenda pública do quádruplo para o dobro. Ademais, tem-se o fim dos procedimentos comuns cautelares e a instituição de apenas dois requisitos para a tutela de urgência ou de evidência: o *fumus boni iuris* e o *periculum in mora*. (Gajardoni, 2011, p. 4 e ss).

Assim sendo, mediante o alargamento da flexibilização do procedimento, o processo civil consegue acompanhar a melhor rota a ser seguida para a resolução do conflito oriundo do direito material. Nessa linha de raciocínio, destaca-se que o medo de condutas arbitrárias do Poder Judiciário diminui, na medida em que as partes atuam no processo de maneira mais ostensiva e cooperativa. Contudo, para que o art. 190 do CPC brasileiro torne-se costumeiro nas relações jurídicas processuais precisa-se que não só a legislação se modernize, mas também a forma que a sociedade enxerga o Direito. (Migliavacca; Fortes, 2014, p. 17).

Nesse diapasão, aborda-se que o CPC brasileiro traz, em seu bojo, o princípio da adequação formal, o qual marginaliza a concepção de que o procedimento deve ser rígido, isto é, de que a inflexibilidade é uma regra de ordem pública. Isto porque, o rito processual não é criado para a atuação da função soberana do Estado, mas para as partes dirimirem o seu conflito. Assim, não há mais a ideia de que um procedimento rígido deve existir para se garantir a previsibilidade e a disciplina, tendo em vista que o que se visa é uma maior eficiência processual quando o Poder Judiciário tiver de sanar um litígio. (GAJARDONI, 2011, p. 11 *apud* GAJARDONI, 2007, p. 85).

Sob essa ótica, a flexibilização do procedimento é condição *sine qua non* da aplicação do princípio da adaptabilidade. Este, por sua vez, consiste em tornar o processo mais pessoal para as partes ao analisar o objeto dele, por meio da ampliação de procedimentos conforme as carências do caso concreto, ou seja, ajustar o processo à melhor forma para que ele possa auxiliar na resolução do litígio advindo do direito material. (GAJARDONI; SOUZA, 2016, p. 2).

É necessário desproteger a ideia de que os atos do processo devem estar adstritos a certa forma anteriormente dita, sem que o órgão julgador possa torná-la maleável diante do caso fático que se apresente. Afinal, "o formalismo exagerado é incompatível com a visão social do processo". Nessa linha de raciocínio, não se pode esquecer que o Poder Estatal está enredado na resolução dos litígios não com a colocação dele numa caixa processual incapaz de garantir a eficácia da solução alcançada, mas com um posicionamento democrático e efetivo para o acesso à justiça. (PONTE; ROMÃO, 2015, p. 315). Nesse ponto, destaca-se que existem duas vertentes e o legislador optou pelo encontro entre elas: a flexibilização legal genérica, a qual permite que o juiz exerça com maior liberdade o controle temporal do processo; e a flexibilização legal alternativa, segundo a qual o Poder Judiciário pode se imiscuir nos prazos processuais, porém essa possibilidade está restrita às opções dispostas em lei e a adequação à situação jurídica concreta. (GAJARDONI; SOUZA, 2016, p. 11, 13).

Vale ressaltar que "no anteprojeto elaborado pela Comissão de Juristas responsável pelo CPC/2015, pretendia-se substituir tal modelo rígido do CPC/73 (flexibilização legal alternativa) pelo sistema da flexibilização legal genérico", todavia temeu-se que esse comportamento atribuísse muita liberdade ao Poder Judiciário e que ele poderia não saber administrar essa autonomia. (GAJARDONI; SOUZA, 2016, p. 11, 13). Dentro desse prisma de dialeticidade, percebe-se que o CPC brasileiro foi mais além quando trouxe para si a valorização da vontade das partes, por meio da clausula geral da flexibilização voluntária do procedimento. (PONTE; ROMÃO, 2015, p. 313).

A flexibilização voluntária do procedimento é verificada no art.190 do CPC brasileiro, sendo ele responsável por permitir às partes capazes de fato e de direito negociarem ajustes procedimentais para a viabilidade de um julgamento melhor do direito material. Assim como, acordem a respeito dos "ônus, poderes, faculdades e deveres processuais, antes ou durante o processo", desde que sejam relações jurídicas permissionárias de autocomposição, isto é, de criação de um método de resolução dos problemas *inter partes*. (BRASIL, 2015). A flexibilização pode ser realizada desde que sejam respeitadas algumas condições: finalidade, motivação e contraditório útil. A primeira visa resguardar o esquema formal desenhado pelo legislador por uma questão da manutenção da confiança e da expectativa adstrita à lei. A segunda objetiva demonstrar que o Poder Judiciário deve interpretar o arcabouço probatório de forma holística para proferir as suas decisões. (GAJARDONI; SOUZA, 2016, p. 16-20).

A terceira intenciona permitir que as partes possam ser ouvidas, sob a égide da cooperação, a respeito das medidas tomadas pelo juiz, ou seja, para saber se há imparcialidade, correição e justiça nelas. Sob essa ótica, verifica-se a necessidade das condições supracitadas e descritas para garantir o espírito dialético do processo e a capacidade de assegurar vantagem à parte com a flexibilização do procedimento processual. (GAJARDONI; SOUZA, 2016, p. 16-20). Assim sendo, pelo modelo da flexibilidade procedimental voluntária, é dever dos sujeitos do processo escolher o "procedimento processual adequado, ou ao menos parte dos atos processuais da série". Nesse tipo de modelo, a participação do Poder Judiciário é minorada ante a vontade das partes. (PONTE; ROMÃO, 2015, p. 317). Diante deste pano de fundo processual, o CPC se inclina a um "modelo mais cooperativo", no qual os sujeitos processuais junto com seus advogados e os órgãos julgadores "unam forças para resolução do conflito, deixando para trás atos e argumentos meramente protelatórios". (MATTA, 2015, p. 134).

Compreende-se que as ideias nascidas através dos estudos sobre justiça restaurativa fomentam a cooperação processual, bem como a sua eficácia no que concerne à obtenção de justiça, principalmente nas ações de família. Por isso, a adequação do modelo restaurativo de justiça como uma possibilidade diante da flexibilização voluntária do procedimento para dinamizar as ações da família permite que as partes resolvam o conflito familiar da forma que entendam ser mais efetiva sem ferir garantias fundamentais como a proteção integral do infantojuvenil. Daí porque, por exemplo, mitiga os julgamentos feitos por um agente público sem qualquer formação em psicologia a respeito da confirmação ou não de alienação parental. (Zehr, 2018, p. 35-38).

3. O MODELO COOPERATIVO DA FLEXIBILIZAÇÃO VOLUNTÁRIA DO PROCEDIMENTO E OS POSTULADOS DA JUSTIÇA RESTAURATIVA: DO DIREITO PENAL PARA A ESFERA CÍVEL

A Justiça Restaurativa, como modelo alternativo de solução de conflitos, trazido ao Poder Judiciário possibilita a apropriação do problema pelas partes envolvidas justamente para não deixar o litígio, unicamente, sob os ditames do Estado em administrar inteiramente situações que a vítima ou uma comissão representadora pode resolver, pois não há advogado, promotor ou juiz que saiba mais sobre a dor de ser lesado do que aquele que efetivamente o foi. (Achutti, 2012, p. 6). Nessa linha de raciocínio, a justiça restaurativa consiste num modelo de justiça que prioriza os interesses daqueles que estão vivenciando o litígio permitindo, com isso, uma melhor percepção e solução do conflito. (Achutti, 2012, p. 6). Perceber os atores jurídicos é um desafio inquietante, pois é através do olhar mais aprofundando para o problema apresentado pelas partes que se torna possível enxergá-las mais e flexibilizar formas de resolver os seus conflitos dando a elas a permissão para pensar o melhor caminho. Esse entendimento é ilustrado na obra "Nenhuma verdade se escreve no singular" de Cláudia Cruz Santos quando o narrador expõe o que se passava na mente da personagem Amália, a qual exerce o papel de juíza na trama:

Amália não desconhece, claro está, que a vítima pode participar no processo e que há momentos em que tem a oportunidade de dar a sua versão, contar a sua história, tornar conhecido o seu sofrimento, manifestar as suas necessidades. Mas não é para isso que sobretudo serve o processo penal. E indaga-se, com frequência, sobre se não haveria algo que se pudesse mudar para evitar que, como tantas vezes sente que sucede, a passagem pelo seu tribunal signifique para as vítimas sobretudo um novo padecimento, uma outra decepção, uma diferente forma de exclusão. (Santos, 2017, p. 144 e 145)

Percebe-se que o procedimento restaurativo de justiça não se condiciona a focar na culpa, mas se posiciona para permitir que todos os envolvidos possam ter direito de fala, de explicações e esclarecimentos, ou seja, se permite o diálogo de forma equitativa e atribuindo valor ao diferente, ao estranho, pois, dessa forma, se estabelece uma relação ética e de cuidado com o Outro. Por isso, a justiça restaurativa possibilita soluções mais efetivas a casos concretos, pois mitiga o olhar no fato isolado e entende as conexões que a situação tem com outras questões tão importantes quanto a que originou o litígio. Nessa perspectiva, sabe-se que atribuir valor ao diferente, isto é, ao estranho vai depender de como a pessoa o reconhece, ou seja, de "como se coloca a ele a questão da alteridade". Assim, o outro é o esquisito que incomoda nas relações e o seu reconhecimento é condição fundamental para que a relação seja saudável. (Thones; Pereira, 2013, p. 10).

Sabe-se que as ideias basilares do modelo restaurativo de justiça fomentam a necessidade de se desburocratizar o acesso das partes ao Poder Estatal quando elas almejam "a reconstrução dos laços que se viram desfeitos pelo rompimento produzido pela relação conflituosa". Essa mudança de perspectiva permite a afirmação da alteridade, ou seja, da valorização das ideias de soluções diferentes da sua, porém suficientes para o outro. (Salm; Leal, 2012, p.196). Nesse diapasão, entende-se que para que haja a transformação da visão clássica do direito pela inserção do conceito de alteridade a ela, se faz necessário desproteger "os modelos construídos". Essa ação permite que se perceba a fluidez do direito, bem como a sua capacidade de acumular direitos inerentes ao ser humano. (Aguiar, 2006, p. 13).

Cumpre ressaltar que a palavra alteridade tem sua origem na língua latina significando a pluralidade diversa entre o eu e o outro, sendo que esse outro não está restrito ao homem, mas aberto à vida na sua completude. O conceito da palavra foi sendo construído, paulatinamente, na história. Inicialmente, o outro era visto como menor do que o eu numa percepção hierárquica de importância; depois o outro passou a existir em função do eu, até que o outro começou a ter vida, valor independente do eu, tendo um rosto. (Neves, 2017, p.71-72). Nessa toada, afirma-se que a Justiça Restaurativa se coloca como um meio jurídico para alcançar a justiça incluindo os envolvidos no processo como protagonistas e não figurantes, ou seja, libertando-os de uma perspectiva utilitária. Sob essa ótica, por intermédio das técnicas do modelo restaurativo de justiça o objetivo do Estado deixa de ser o de atribuir culpa a alguém por uma determinada conduta, mas as consequências do ato ilegal. (Aguinsky; Capitão, 2008, p.262-263).

Nessa linha de raciocínio, percebe-se que é necessário fazer uma análise crítica sobre a história que chega aos ouvidos de cada ser humano, o qual, muitas vezes, tem dificuldade de aceitar o novo, com isso, prefere rejeitá-lo. De forma ilustrativa, muitos preferem venerar o modelo tradicional de justiça existente, porque acreditam que ele já é suficiente para a solução dos problemas. (SANTOS, 2014, p. 125). Esse mesmo raciocínio pode ser compreendido no âmbito do Poder Estatal, na medida em que ele precisa alcançar a compreensão de que não deve ser protagonista da busca dos cidadãos pela obtenção de justiça nos casos concretos. Logo, que ser o personagem principal dessa empreitada, durante séculos, o afastou da efetivação da justiça, por sua vez, da alteridade. (THONES; PEREIRA, 2013, p. 5-8).

Assim como, que se o Poder Estatal tiver a compreensão de que o processo e o interesse maior pela obtenção da justiça são das partes, então ele entenderá que a sua função é, apenas, fiscalizar o procedimento escolhido e adotado. Essa mudança de paradigma levará o Estado a vivenciar a angústia pelo novo que desmistifica tudo o que ele defende. (THONES; PEREIRA, 2013, p. 5-8). Daí porque, a ideia da alteridade consiste na ciência de que o outro é digno de respeito da maneira como é, o que garante o seu direito à liberdade de escolhas. Assim sendo, o objetivo do princípio da alteridade é efetivar ações de cuidado entre estranhos. (MEIRELES; AGUIAR, 2018, p. 125). Nesse ponto, a Justiça Restaurativa surge como uma possibilidade de efetivação da alteridade seja porque o estudo do modelo restaurativo de justiça está permeado por diversas compreensões psicológicas, sociológicas, filosóficas, ou seja, pela pluralidade de ciências, que juntas solucionam melhor os problemas jurídicos seja porque é capaz de promover valores iguais a polos distintos. A justiça restaurativa é uma justiça que serve como modelo de resposta a qualquer conflito, e não apenas ao criminal, pois as técnicas de mediação não são exclusividade do direito penal, mas podem ser úteis para resolver diversos litígios, tais como os familiares.

Afinal, conforme dispõe Raquel Tiveron, o objetivo do modelo restaurativo de justiça só se efetiva mediante a ação de "colocar-se no lugar do outro" focando nas possíveis resultantes para o futuro, ao invés de nas ações ensejadoras do problema no passado. Esse comportamento deve ser apoiado para que não haja uma exacerbação da culpa, mas a propagação de "um justiça que olha, escuta, compreende bem diferente da deusa tradicional, surda, muda, cega, empunhando a espada". (TIVERON, 2014).

Assim, constata-se que a Justiça Restaurativa tem por escopo permitir a ampliação do diálogo das partes no processo para que elas, que sofreram as consequências do litígio, participem mais do trâmite processual possibilitando, assim, que as suas necessidades sejam o centro da discussão. (ZEHR, 2018, p.35-38).

De forma exemplificativa, seria relevante poder opinar, por exemplo, a respeito do momento em que uma criança será ouvida em processos de alienação parental, o qual pode ser no início de todo o deslinde processual para resguardar ao máximo a veracidade das memórias desse infantojuvenil diante do tempo. (ZEHR, 2018, p.35-38). Esse pensamento permite a aplicação do princípio da alteridade paradigma essencial nas relações familiares; o que possibilita uma mitigação das práticas de alienação dos lares ou a sua solução mais eficaz, isto é, menos lesiva ao contexto familiar. (AGUIAR, 2014, p. 242)

É importante esclarecer que a alienação parental consiste numa patologia no convívio familiar entre, por exemplo, pais e filhos, que oprime as relações entre eles. (AGUIAR, 2014, p.243). Vale lembrar que a legislação brasileira compreende como prática de alienação parental qualquer ação dos pais ou outra autoridade familiar que macule o psicológico do infantojuvenil provocando o distanciamento, por exemplo, da criança do seu genitor. (BRASIL, 2010). Ilustra-se a possibilidade de a mãe ou a avó contratarem um profissional para que seja realizada uma pericia psicológica na criança ou no adolescente e transpor essa perícia ao processo como prova pré-constituída. Ao invés de aceitar sem questionamentos a ordem processual da oitiva correndo-se o risco de que as lembranças da criança se percam ou sejam distorcidas pelo genitor alienante. (ZEHR, 2018, p. 35-38). O caminho restaurativo se inicia com as desavenças, isto é, os pré-conflitos ou conflitos menos gravosos; evoluindo para o diálogo, ou seja, para a comunidade circundante culminando com a restauração de laços. Essa, por sua vez, ocorre através de um debate com assunção de responsabilidades pelos envolvidos no litígio num circulo de resolução de conflitos. (ZEHR, 2018).

Nessa linha de raciocínio, entende-se que conflitos familiares como os que envolvem a prática de alienação parental podem se resolvidos, através do diálogo sugerido, haja vista que a principal vítima é o infantojuvenil e a melhor solução para ele não é vislumbrar seus pais proferindo farpas judicialmente ou tendo de vivenciar as etapas de um procedimento comum, mas ter a possibilidade de vivenciar o processo de forma menos gravosa para o seu desenvolvimento enquanto pessoa. Dessa forma, se trata de uma questão casuística, afinal as famílias e os conflitos produzidos por elas são distintos.

Por isso, defende-se que o entendimento do Estado sobre o significado de gozo, alegria, paz, pode não ser o mesmo das partes. Assim sendo, caso o Poder Estatal se recuse a enxerga-las como diferentes dele, logo com necessidades e realidades próprias, então ele continuará a afirmar que os sujeitos processuais são uma extensão de sua vontade e não pessoas além dele e do que ele entende como justiça. Tal ação não permitiria a manifestação do princípio da alteridade, e, portanto, mitigará a possibilidade de se efetivar a justiça nos casos concretos. (NEVES, 2017, p.81-82).

4. AS CONFERÊNCIAS DE GRUPOS FAMILIARES COMO UMA POSSIBILIDADE DE FLEXIBILIZAÇÃO PROCEDIMENTAL VOLUNTÁRIA DO PROCEDIMENTO COMUM EM AÇÕES DE FAMÍLIA

Percebe-se que a relação conflituosa existe quando se colocam vontades em situação de confrontação quando o que se quer é que uma se curve à outra pela imposição de uma solução, o que promove a criação de inimizades., verifica-se que o litígio judicial está inserido no conjunto de formas jurídicas de resolver os conflitos; o qual pode ser impulsionado ou marginalizado a depender da cultura da sociedade analisada. (GIMENEZ; SPENGLER, 2018, p. 247). Assim sendo, caso a justiça seja culturalmente "especializada, autônoma, burocrática e sistematizada, orientada para atividades rigidamente definidas e hierarquizadas" num dado ambiente social; então tanto a forma como o problema será resolvido de maneira impessoal, padronizada, demorada e ineficaz, ou seja, despreocupada com o crédito que os atos jurídicos precisam transmitir. (GIMENEZ; SPENGLER, 2018, p. 247).

Dentro desse prisma, destaca-se que as Conferências de Grupos Familiares têm como condão oferecer um ambiente para que se discuta os fatos, a exemplo das possibilidades de mediação, na qual não só as vítimas e os ofensores são ouvidos, mas também os seus familiares próximos e remotos. Assim como, pessoas que por algum motivo sejam quase parte da família e o representante do Ministério Público devem comparecer para velar pelos direitos da criança e do adolescente. (ZEHR, 2018, p. 174-175). Aliás, "o direito é um fenômeno de relação entre um e outro, daí a necessidade de reafirmarmos que ele é o reino da alteridade. A presença de um outro é condição para a existência jurídica". (Aguiar, 2006, p. 15).

Nesse ponto, nota-se o princípio da alteridade como pressuposto às Conferências de Grupos Familiares, na medida em que ele permite a mitigação do excesso de regras e hierarquizações como forma de escora do Estado no ordenamento jurídico processual civilista. Assim como, "muitas vezes causada pela concorrência frequente entre os cônjuges, razão mais próxima do desencadeamento da alienação parental". Desse modo, apenas, a alteridade pode viabilizar relacionamentos saudáveis dentro das famílias. (Aguiar, 2014, p. 246). Entende-se que uma forma de se ter a manifestação da alteridade nas soluções ofertadas aos litígios familiares é a possibilidade positivada no art. 190 do CPC brasileiro de flexibilizar o procedimento processual carreando ao processo ideias provenientes do modelo restaurativo de justiça.

Deste modo, a relação ética e justa se estabelece, isto é, se promove a aplicação do princípio da alteridade, o que ocorre quando o eu (Poder Estatal) passa a enxergar o outro (partes, novidade jurídica) nas suas particularidades e não como uma projeção espelhada de si. Daí porque, "só a ética é capaz de libertar o outro do jugo do eu". (Neves, 2017, p. 76-79).

Assim, o arquétipo da alteridade traz a capacidade de confronto, elaboração e integração dos opostos que deve permear as vivências parentais, de tal modo que à criança seja permitida a elaboração simbólica das características de ambos os pais, sem a intervenção nociva de qualquer deles, em nenhuma esfera. Permitir ao filho a possibilidade de enxergar o Outro (pai ou mãe) da forma como lhe convier e elaborar simbolicamente estas percepções é tarefa que deve ser desenvolvida sob a ótica da alteridade. (Aguiar, 2014, p.246)

Nessa perspectiva, possibilitar a negociação do procedimento a ser adotado processualmente, quando for possível a autocomposição, é forma de uma parte se forjar e se compreender melhor consigo mesmo, com o Estado e com a outra parte. (Neves, 2017, p.76-79). A Justiça Restaurativa intenta devolver aos reais interessados na solução do problema o principal papel como resolvedores. Esse entendimento permite a reflexão a respeito da perspectiva de culpabilidade, lamentavelmente inserida no conceito de alienação parental pelo legislador brasileiro. Com efeito, o legislador intenciona encontrar um culpado das práticas e apená-lo de alguma forma quando, na realidade, não há como estabelecer onde um conflito familiar começa ou de quem parte as primeiras desavenças. O mais importante é garantir que sejam mitigadas as consequências do conflito para a criança e o adolescente. Assim, faz-se necessário olhar os fatos ocorridos na família por prismas novos e diferentes focados nas carências e emoções dos envolvidos. (Gimenez; Spengler, 2018, p. 249-250).

A mudança de perspectiva ocorre mediante a ressignificação do estigma vergonhoso de ser o ofensor ou alienante para o de vergonha que reintegra ao seio familiar, demonstrando para os envolvidos um caminho de volta, uma possibilidade de perdão, principalmente para os principais sacrificados no âmbito da alienação, isto é, os infantojuvenis. (Zehr, 2018, p. 176). As Conferências de Grupos Familiares possibilitam que a vítima possa expor as suas dores demonstrando uma maneira de resolução do problema, que, de fato, concerte o prejuízo que lhe foi causado e evite que a situação fática se repita; e, assim, mediante o desagravo o acusado não tenha mais que carregar esse estigma, na medida em que as emoções dos envolvidos foram equilibradas. (Gimenez; Spengler, 2018, p. 249-250). Esse raciocínio pode ser aplicado em ações de divórcio, alimentos, investigação de paternidade, definição de guarda ou em qualquer temática que envolva o direito de família, pois ele é um ramo do ordenamento jurídico que comporta bem o raciocínio *alter* proposto.

É tremendo o potencial de denúncia do erro dentro do circulo familiar. Já é ruim passar vergonha diante da vítima, imagine diante de seu avô e sua avó! Mas como o ofensor é parte da família, as CGF também oferecem incentivo para a afirmação do valor do ofensor. Segundo relatos, os membros da família manifestam seu desapontamento e raiva em relação ao comportamento, mas também afirmam o valor essencial e dons do jovem que cometeu a ofensa. Trabalhando juntos como uma família, eles chegam a estratégias de colaboração através da discussão que permite ao ofensor assumir a responsabilidade de corrigir as coisas e se sentir apoiado ao longo do processo. (Zehr, 2018, p. 176)

Posto isto, a participação de todos no processo restaurativo de justiça permite que haja o aprimoramento do êxito, o que estimula os familiares a vistoriarem a concretização do acordado. (Zehr, 2018, p. 176). Assim, se o ofensor lograr êxito em entender as nuances da situação e a vítima em se desvincular dessa condição para a de sobrevivente; chega-se ao objetivo final do procedimento. Isso só pode ocorrer quando se cria um local com capacidade de ouvir as histórias e as dores, por intermédio da qual se estabelece o diálogo na comunidade familiar, diferente do que ocorre na sistemática judiciária hodierna. (Gimenez; Spengler, 2018, p. 254-256).

CONCLUSÕES

Este artigo traz uma construção histórica e teórica da flexibilização do procedimento processual no direito pátrio até alcançar-se o procedimento voluntário, o qual dar vida ao negócio jurídico processual atípico. Sob essa ótica, nota-se que a vertente de flexibilização procedimental escolhida pelo legislador pátrio foi a flexibilização legal alternativa de forma mitigada o que deu azo à chamada flexibilização procedimental voluntária e com ela ao negócio jurídico processual atípico. Isto, desde que o ato que enseje a modificação ou alteração do procedimento tenha finalidade, motivação e contraditório útil.

Sustenta-se que as ideias da justiça restaurativa podem ser trazidas para o processo civil, por meio do negócio jurídico atípico disposto no art. 190 do CPC, bem como que ele expressa a apropriação da zetética pela dogmática, na medida em que o ordenamento positivo incorpora a filosofia ética proposta pela alteridade permitindo que os conflitos sejam resolvidos conforme as peculiaridades de cada grupo familiar. Nessa linha de raciocínio, verifica-se que é possível adequar premissas da justiça restaurativa na seara civilista, tendo em vista que o paradigma de justiça alternativa em comento permite a modificação do procedimento conforme as necessidades das partes, bem como a supervisão do Estado no que se refere à acuidade perante as garantias constitucionais e condições comuns a todos os negócios jurídicos.

Esse entendimento procura solidificar a alteridade, na medida em que tanto o Estado como as partes se permitem ao diálogo, a flexibilizações para que o direito material seja de fato alcançado mesmo que para isso o processo tenha de ser mais maleável. Nessa linha de raciocínio, demonstrou-se que o fato de a justiça restaurativa ter como berço o direito penal e processual penal, seus pressupostos, seus ideais, sua base de pensamento também podem ser estudados na esfera civil. Nessa seara, inclusive, destacou-se um dos procedimentos de justiça restaurativa conceituados por Howard Zehr – Círculos Familiares -, os quais podem ser aplicados nas ações de família, a exemplo dos casos de alienação parental, por meio do fenômeno da ampliação da privatização do direito publicista processual cível com a alteração procedimental; resguardando-se as garantias constitucionais e os preceitos básicos dos negócios jurídicos.

Enfim, o objetivo do processo é diligenciar o diálogo entre as partes e garantir que o Estado supervisione os trâmites dessa operação para que o caminho a ser percorrido até o alcance da solução do direito material seja espelhado na alteridade. Desta forma, a partir do momento em que a lei processual possui um dispositivo legal que flexibiliza ainda mais o procedimento pode-se afirmar que ele está fomentando a alteridade ao permitir que os conflitos familiares sejam ainda mais protagonizados pelas partes e, portanto, solucionados de forma a resgatar o afeto dentro da família e não, apenas, extinguir um processo com resolução do mérito.

REFERÊNCIAS

ACHUTTI, D. Justiça Restaurativa e Sistema Penal:contribuições abolicionistas para uma política criminal do encontro. Tese de Doutorado – Pontifícia Universidade Católica do Rio Grande do Sul, Porto Alegre, 2012. Disponível em: http://tede2.pucrs.br/tede2/handle/tede/4901. [Acesso em: 05 jul. 2019].

AGUIAR, M. O arquétipo da alteridade como paradigma necessário ao afastamento da alienação parental. Direito de Família I. 1ed. Florianópolis: CONPEDI, 2014, v. XXIII, p. 241-256. Disponível em: http://publicadireito.com.br/publicacao/ufpb/livro.php?gt=245. [Acesso em: 10 ago. 2019].

AGUIAR, R. Alteridade e Rede no Direito. Revista Veredas do Direito, Belo Horizonte, v.3 n.6, Julho-Dezembro de 2006, p.11-43. Disponível em: http://repositorio.unb.br/bitstream/10482/7564/1/ARTIGO_AlteridadeRedeDireito.PDF. [Acesso em: 07 ago. 2019].

AGUINSKY, B; CAPITÃO, L. Violência e socioeducação: uma interpelação ética a partir de contribuições da Justiça Restaurativa. Rev. Katál. Florianópolis, v. 11, n. 2, jul./dez, 2008, p. 257-264. Disponível em: http://www.scielo.br/scielo.php?pid=S1414-49802008000200011&script=sci_abstract&tlng=pt. [Acesso em: 05 jul. 2019].

ALMEIDA, D. Das Convenções Processuais no Processo Civil. Tese (Doutorado em Direito Processual). Faculdade de Direito, Universidade do Estado do Rio de Janeiro, Rio de Janeiro, 2014. Disponível em: http://bdtd.ibict.br/vufind/Record/UERJ_1a46d725f58dd6f586384fe24e1903da. [Acesso em: 05 jul. 2019].

BRAGA, Paula. *et al.* Competência legislativa dos estados-membros em torno dos negócios processuais. Coletânea Mulheres no Processo Civil Brasileiro – Negócios Processuais. 1ed. Salvador: Jus Podivm, 2017, v. 1, p. 431-460.

BRASIL. Lei nº 12.318, de 26 de agosto de 2010. Alienação Parental. Acesso em: 07/09/2019; Disponível em: http://www.planalto.gov.br/ccivil_03/decreto-lei/Del2848compilado.htm.

BRASIL Lei – n. 13.105 de 16 de março de 2015. Código de Processo Civil. Acesso em: 07/09/2019; Disponível em: http://www.planalto.gov.br/ccivil_03/_ato2015-2018/2015/lei/l13105.htm.

CABRAL, Antônio. Convenções processuais: entre publicismo e privatismo. Tese de livre-docência. São Paulo. Universidade de São Paulo, Faculdade de Direito, 2015.

CADIET, L. Los acuerdos procesales em derecho francés: situación de actual de La contractualización Del processo y de la justicia em Francia. Civil procedure Review, v.3, n.3, 2014, p. 3-35. Disponível em: http://www.civilprocedurereview.com/busca/baixa_arquivo.php?id=59&embedded=true. [Acesso em: 07 set. 2019].

DIDIER, F; NOGUEIRA, P. Teoria dos fatos jurídicos processuais. 2ª ed. Salvador: Editora JusPodivm, 2012.

DIDER, F. Curso de Direito Processual Civil: Introdução ao Direito Processual Civil, parte geral e processo do conhecimento. 20ª ed. Salvador. Editora JusPodivm, 2018.

GAJARDONI, F; Procedimentos, déficit procedimental e flexibilização procedimental no novo CPC. Revista de informação legislativa, v. 48, n. 190 t.1, Brasília, abr./jun. 2011, p. 163-177. Disponível em: https://www2.senado.leg.br/bdsf/bitstream/handle/id/242889/000923104.pdf?sequence=1. [Acesso em: 13 out. 2019].

GAJARDONI, F; SOUZA, M. Os princípios da adequação, da adaptabilidade e da flexibilização procedimental pelo juiz no novo CPC. Revista do Tribunal Superior do Trabalho: Vol. 82, n. 3 (jul./set. 2016), 2016, p. 165-187. Disponível em: https://juslaboris.tst.jus.br/bitstream/handle/20.500.12178/96971/2016_gajardoni_fernando_principios_adequacao.pdf?sequence=1. [Acesso em: 13 out. 2019].

GIMENEZ, C; SPENGLER, F. A justiça restaurativa como instrumento de fortalecimento da cultura de paz: uma nova perspectiva para a execução das medidas socioeducativas no Brasil. Revista. Bras. Políticas Públicas, Brasília, v. 8, nº 1, 2018, p. 243-259. Disponível em: https://www.publicacoesacademicas.uniceub.br/RBPP/article/view/5100. [Acesso em: 15 out. 2019].

MATTA, D. O processo colaborativo para a busca da efetiva tutela jurisdicional. Revista Eletrônica de Direito Processual, v. 16, nº16, Rio de Janeiro, 2015. Disponível em: https://www.e-publicacoes.uerj.br/index.php/redp/article/view/17978. [Acesso em: 20 ago. 2019].

MEIRELES, A.T; AGUIAR, M. Autonomia e alteridade como fundamentos da construção do sentido de dignidade existencial diante do direito à vida. Revista Brasileira de Direito Animal, V.13, N. 01, Salvador, 2018, p. 123-147. Disponível em: https://portalseer.ufba.br/index.php/RBDA/article/view/26220. [Acesso em: 10 ago. 2019].

MIGLIAVACCA, L; FORTES, V. Flexibilização do procedimento e cooperação: Um novo olhar sobre o processo. CONPEDI, 2014, v. XXIII, p. 237-255. Disponível em: http://publicadireito.com.br/publicacao/ufsc/livro.php?gt=198. [Acesso em: 15 out. 2019].

MIRANDA, F. Comentários ao Código de Processo Civil. Atualização legislativa de Sérgio Bermudes. 4ª ed. Rio de Janeiro. Forense, 1997.

NEVES, M.C. Alteridade e Deveres Fundamentais: Uma abordagem ética. Revista Direitos Fundamentais e Alteridade, Salvador, v. I nº 01, jul-dez, 2017, p. 69-86. Disponível em: file:///C:/Users/sarii/AppData/Local/Temp/429-1066-1-SM.pdf. [Acesso em: 07 ago. 2019].

ONO, T. A flexibilização do procedimento e sua abordagem na tramitação legislativa do novo código de processo civil. Revista Eletrônica de Direito Processual, v. 16, n 16, 2015, p. 664-683. Disponível em: https://www.e-publicacoes.uerj.br/index.php/redp/article/view/18733. [Acesso em: 17 ago. 2019].

PONTES, M; ROMÃO, P. Negócio Jurídico Processual e a flexibilização do procedimento: As influências da autonomia privada no paradigma publicista do Direito Processual

Civil. Revista Eletrônica de Direito Processual, Rio de Janeiro, v. 16, nº 16, 2015, p. 305-334. Disponível em: https://www.e-publicacoes.uerj.br/index.php/redp/article/view/19968. [Acesso em: 08/10/2019].

SALM, J; LEAL, J. A Justiça Restaurativa: multidimensionalidade humana e seu convidado de honra. Revista Sequência,v. 33, n. 64, jul, 2012, p. 195-226. Disponível em: https://periodicos.ufsc.br/index.php/sequencia/article/view/2177-7055.2012v33n64p195. [Acesso em: 13/05/2019].

SANTOS, C. A Justiça Restaurativa. Um modelo de reação ao crime diferente da justiça penal. Porquê, para quê e como?; 1ª ed; Ed. Coimbra, 2014.

SANTOS, C. Nenhuma verdade se escreve no singular. 1ª ed, Editora Bertrand, Lisboa, 2017.

THONES, A.P; PEREIRA, M. Um entre o Outro e Eu: do estranho e da alteridade na educação. Porto Alegre. Revista Educação e Realidade, v. 38, n.2, abr./jun. 2013, p. 501-520. Disponível em: https://www.scielo.br/scielo.php?pid=S2175-62362013000200009&script=sci_abstract&tlng=pt [Acesso em: 15 out. 2019].

TIVERON, R. Justiça Restaurativa e emergência da cidadania na dicção dos direitos: A construção de um novo paradigma de Justiça Criminal. Editora Thesaurus Jurídica, Brasília, 2014.

ZEHR, H. Trocando as lentes: Justiça Restaurativa para o nosso tempo. Ed 3º, Editora Palas Athena, São Paulo, 2018.

A EVOLUÇÃO RECENTE DO REGIME JURÍDICO DO TETO DOS GASTOS DE CAMPANHA

OLIVIA RAPOSO DA SILVA TELLES*

A primeira missão que incumbe ao regime jurídico do financiamento eleitoral, em todas as democracias, é fixar um limite máximo para os gastos de campanha. Isso porque a ausência de um limite assim atenta contra o princípio da igualdade de oportunidades entre todos os candidatos. No entanto, o que se verificava, no que diz respeito ao conjunto das regras que se aplicava ao financiamento eleitoral, tal como estava posto no texto original da Lei das Eleições (Lei nº 9.504/1997), é que ao invés de coibir, ele favorecia sobremaneira a influência do poder econômico nas eleições.

Assim, não surpreende que a disciplina do teto de gastos, no texto original dessa lei, fosse de fato das mais insatisfatórias. Não havia um limite fixo, igual para todos os candidatos ao mesmo cargo, na mesma circunscrição. O que havia era a previsão de que os partidos deviam, juntamente com o pedido de registro de seus candidatos, comunicar à Justiça Eleitoral os valores máximos de gastos que fariam por cada tipo de candidatura, em cada eleição em que concorressem.

Esse sistema, por demais iníquo, perdurou intocado até 2006. No ano anterior, 2005, eclodiu o escândalo do "Mensalão", que pôs em relevo algumas das falhas do regime jurídico do financiamento eleitoral. Por exem-

* Doutora pela Universidade de Paris 1 (Panthéon-Sorbonne). Bacharel em Direito pela USP. Colaboradora em matéria de direito eleitoral do Movimento de Combate à Corrupção Eleitoral. Advogada.

plo, o insuficiente sancionamento do caixa dois. A forte reação da opinião pública mobilizou o Congresso Nacional a editar a minirreforma eleitoral de 2006 (Lei nº 11.300), introduzindo mudanças com vistas sobretudo a tornar mais efetivas as regras então vigentes.

No que concerne ao teto dos gastos, ficou estabelecido, na ocasião, que em todo ano eleitoral um limite de gastos de campanha deveria ser fixado *por lei* para os cargos em disputa. Entretanto, o paradoxo que marca o direito eleitoral – ser feito pelos políticos para disciplinar a forma como eles próprios chegam ao poder – se fez sentir então fortemente. Como não interessava aos partidos perder a liberdade para fixar seu próprio limite de gastos em cada eleição, como ocorreria se houvesse um limite fixo igual para todos previsto em lei, essa mudança foi enfraquecida. Assim, ficou estabelecido que caso a lei não fosse editada até a data prevista, tudo ficaria como antes – caberia a cada partido fixar o limite de gastos e comunicá-lo à Justiça Eleitoral.

Desse modo, para as eleições de 2008, de 2010, de 2012 e de 2014, o Congresso Nacional deixou de editar a referida lei, tendo sido mantida nesses anos eleitorais a regra da fixação do próprio limite de gastos por cada partido político. Esse sistema favorecia a corrupção, além de ser iníquo – porque os partidos tinham acesso desigual às fontes privadas de financiamento, na época oriundo sobretudo de doações de empresas. Nada impedia que os que recebiam doações maiores fixassem tetos de gastos mais altos para si.

Dois fatores contribuíram para uma certa mudança de mentalidade nessa matéria. Um foi a propositura, pela OAB, da ADI que questionou a constitucionalidade da permissão legal para doações de pessoas jurídicas para partidos e candidatos. A ação foi proposta a pedido do MCCE, que atuou como Amicus Curiae. Ela culminou com o banimento, em decisão proferida pelo STF em 2015, dessa modalidade de financiamento eleitoral. Outro foi a eclosão do escândalo do "Petrolão", objeto da Operação Lava Jato da Polícia Federal, que teve início em 2014. Como se sabe, esse escândalo revelou que doações de empresas para campanhas eleitorais, ainda que declaradas à Justiça Eleitoral, vulgo caixa um, podiam constituir na verdade contrapartida de favorecimentos em licitações públicas.

Tudo isso contribuiu para uma certa tomada de consciência, por parte da sociedade brasileira, do fato de que o próprio regime jurídico do financiamento eleitoral, tal como previsto em lei, tendia no sentido de favorecer a influência do poder econômico nas eleições. Pressionado, em 2015 o Congresso Nacional mudou a disciplina do teto dos gastos, dando nova redação ao art. 18 da Lei das Eleições. Essa minirreforma (Lei nº 13.165/2015) estabeleceu parâmetros gerais para fixação do teto. Esses parâmetros consistiam em porcentagens do maior gasto informado na eleição anterior. Pela primeira vez, tínhamos limites iguais para todos os candidatos ao mesmo cargo, na mesma circunscrição. E essa minirreforma conferiu à Justiça Eleitoral a atribuição de fazer os cálculos, com base nessas regras, e dar publicidade aos números.

Porém, fixar os limites com base nas prestações de contas da eleição anterior talvez não tenha sido a medida mais acertada. Como é sabido, nas prestações de contas alguns candidatos declaram o movimento real da campanha e outros omitem gastos. Por essa razão, foram observadas na campanha de 2016 acentuadas discrepâncias, de um município para o outro, entre o número de eleitores e o teto de gastos. Assim, municípios com número maior de eleitores tiveram teto de gastos fixado em valor inferior ao de municípios com eleitorado menor.

Quanto à sanção, como sói acontecer, quando a regra é mais estrita, de mais difícil observância, ela costuma ser mais branda, e é o que se verifica no presente caso: antes, em caso de extrapolação do teto, aplicava-se multa no valor de 5 a 10 vezes a quantia em excesso. Desde a reforma de 2015, ano em que o financiamento por empresas foi banido, a sanção passou a ser o pagamento de multa em valor equivalente a 100% da quantia que ultrapassar o limite estabelecido (ou seja, uma vez a quantia em excesso, e não mais de 5 a 10 vezes) (art. 18-B da Lei das Eleições, incluído pela Lei nº 13.165/2015).

Ao que parece, a campanha eleitoral de 2016 se ressentiu da escassez de recursos, em razão do banimento das doações de pessoas jurídicas, que eram responsáveis por grande parte do financiamento eleitoral. Por essa razão, em 2017, a disciplina do financiamento eleitoral foi modificada novamente. O Congresso Nacional criou o Fundo Especial de Financiamento de Campanha (FEFC), ampliando o financiamento público das campanhas (Lei nº 13.487/2017).

Na ocasião, o tratamento do teto dos gastos eleitorais foi também alterado. Por força da redação dada pela Lei nº 13.488/2017 ao caput do art. 18 da Lei das Eleições, os parâmetros fixados em 2015 foram revogados. Ficou estabelecido que "os limites de gastos de campanha serão definidos em lei e divulgados pelo Tribunal Superior Eleitoral". Essa mesma lei de 2017 estabeleceu os limites aplicáveis às eleições gerais de 2018. O teto de gastos para a campanha para o cargo de presidente da República foi fixado em 70 milhões de reais, com acréscimo de 35 milhões para o segundo turno.

Para se ter uma ideia, na eleição presidencial de 2014, ainda no sistema anterior, do limite auto declarado e com financiamento por pessoas jurídicas, a campanha de Dilma Rousseff informou à Justiça Eleitoral gastos de mais de 350 milhões de reais, e a de Aécio Neves, de mais de 223 milhões de reais. Uma vez implantado o FEFC, em 2018 o MDB foi a sigla que recebeu a maior fatia, um montante aproximado de 230 milhões de reais, de um total de 1,7 bilhão de reais, distribuído entre 35 partidos.

Exceção feita ao dever de destinar no mínimo 30% para campanhas de candidatas mulheres, objeto de Consulta respondida pelo TSE, não há regras disciplinando a distribuição do FEFC entre os candidatos de um mesmo partido. Sendo assim, no regime de financiamento majoritariamente público, o teto de gastos mantém sua importância, por ser o único limite legal que impede que um dado partido concentre grande parte dos recursos do FEFC por ele recebidos em apenas uma ou em poucas candidaturas.

Como é óbvio, essa minireforma de 2017 instalou o risco de que em anos eleitorais vindouros os gastos de campanha fiquem ilimitados, caso o Congresso deixe de editar a referida lei, como ocorreu tantas vezes no passado. Para atenuar essa incerteza, pelo menos quanto às eleições municipais, em 2019 foi editada a Lei nº 13.878, que incluiu o art. 18-C na Lei das Eleições. Esse artigo fixou o teto de gastos nas eleições municipais de forma geral. Supostamente, aplica-se a todas as eleições municipais vindouras, e não apenas às eleições municipais de 2020: "O limite de gastos nas campanhas dos candidatos às eleições para prefeito e vereador, na respectiva circunscrição, será equivalente ao limite para os respectivos cargos nas eleições de 2016, atualizado pelo Índice Nacional de Preços ao Consumidor Amplo (IPCA), aferido pela Fundação Instituto Brasileiro de Geografia e Estatística (IBGE), ou por índice que o substituir. Parágrafo único. Nas campanhas para segundo turno das eleições para prefeito, onde houver, o limite de gastos de cada candidato será de 40% (quarenta por cento) do limite previsto no *caput* deste artigo."

Como dito, o teto de gastos fixado para a campanha de 2016 esteve na origem de acentuadas discrepâncias, razão pela qual não parece sensata essa repetição na eleição de 2020. A esta altura, em razão da pandemia, ainda não é possível saber se as eleições municipais de 2020 se realizarão de fato este ano, ou se serão adiadas. Além disso, discute-se se o FEFC de 2 bilhões de reais deverá ou não ser destinado ao combate ao coronavirus. Há óbices jurídicos, mas é o que pretendem ações em juízo e projetos de lei. Quanto às eleições gerais, os limites seguem indefinidos.

Seja como for, é de notar que deve observar o teto de gastos a soma de (quase) todas as despesas realizadas pelo candidato durante a campanha, bem como de (quase) todas as despesas realizadas pelo partido que tenham sido feitas em favor da campanha do candidato em questão. Não importa se a fonte dos recursos despendidos é pública (Fundo Partidário e FEFC) ou privada (doações de pessoas físicas e autofinanciamento). Por que dissemos *quase*? É que a reforma de 2019 (Lei nº 13.877) introduziu uma exceção: os gastos com honorários de advogados e contadores, relacionados à prestação de serviços em campanhas eleitorais, bem como para defesa em juízo de interesses de candidatos e partidos, doravante não precisam mais ser contabilizados para os fins da observância do teto.

Com ou sem razão, os políticos provavelmente consideraram que os elevados gastos com honorários de advogados e contadores, embora necessários, restringiriam os gastos com propaganda eleitoral, que é a principal prioridade das campanhas, se fossem mantidos no conjunto de gastos que, somados, estão submetidos ao teto. Mas, como não há um teto específico para esses gastos com honorários de advogados e contadores, houve quem estimasse que essa regra constitui uma brecha para contornar os limites fixos – até o momento estabelecidos ao menos para as campanhas municipais.

Por esse e por outros motivos, a fiscalização é importante. Esse sempre foi um grande desafio para a Justiça Eleitoral, que sempre tendeu a fazer um exame perfunctório das prestações de contas de candidatos e partidos. Se as contas estivessem formalmente bem prestadas, tendiam a ser aprovadas, embora não refletissem, nem de longe, a realidade das campanhas.

A fiscalização, pela Justiça Eleitoral, da realidade da arrecadação e dos gastos de campanha, durante todo processo eleitoral, não se limitando simplesmente à análise das prestações de contas, está prevista pelo menos desde 2014. Desde então, as resoluções do TSE que disciplinam a arrecadação e os gastos de campanha contêm a previsão de que, durante todo o processso eleitoral, a Justiça Eleitoral pode fiscalizar a arrecadação e aplicação de recursos, visando subsidiar a análise das prestações de contas. O passo mais importante foi dado a partir da minirreforma de 2015, que estabeleceu o dever de divulgação, durante a campanha, dos recursos recebidos, que devem ser publicados na internet em até 72 horas do seu recebimento ; e de de todos os recursos recebidos e todas as despesas realizadas em prestação de contas parcial, no dia 15 de setembro (Lei das Eleições, art. 28, § 4º).

Nas eleições de 2016, a Justiça Eleitoral criou um Núcleo de Inteligência, formado por representantes do TSE, dos TREs, do Ministério Público Federal, da Polícia Federal, do Tribunal de Contas da União, da Receita Federal e do Coaf. Nas eleições de 2018, o capítulo sobre fiscalização contido na resolução sobre arrecadação e gastos de campanha foi intitulado "Controle e Fiscalização Concomitante", e trouxe normas detalhadas sobre a fiscalização pela Justiça Eleitoral, o encaminhamento ao MP dos indícios de irregularidade, indícios esses obtidos mediante cruzamento de informações, a apuração pelo MP e a comunicação à autoridade judiciária.

A matéria teve o mesmo tratamento na Resolução TSE nº 23.607/2019, que disciplinou a arrecadação e os gastos de campanha nas eleições de 2020 (art. 89). Em suma, o Brasil partiu de um sistema insatisfatório, de limites auto declarados. O sistema aos poucos evoluiu, e nas campanhas eleitorais de 2016 e de 2018 houve tetos fixos e iguais para todos, previstos em lei e estabelecidos em patamares menores do que se praticava anteriormente. Uma vez implantado o financiamento majoritariamente público, o teto de gastos segue relevante. O Brasil tem no presente momento um limite para campanhas municipais, mas nas eleições gerais os limites estão indefinidos. O limite para campanhas municipais baseia-se em critério que dá ensejo a discrepâncias. Uma brecha permite que parte dos gastos não se submeta ao teto. É importante agora que uma lei estabeleça limites para as eleições gerais. A fiscalização, ponto tradicionalmente fraco do sistema, evoluiu com a divulgação da movimentação financeira das campanhas antes da eleição. Cumpre à Justiça Eleitoral exercer um controle concomitante e eficaz.

REFERÊNCIAS

BORGES, Iara Farias. Senadores querem destinar recursos do Fundo Eleitoral ao combate à covid-19. Senado Notícias, 2 de abril de 2020. Disponível em : <https://www12.senado.leg.br/noticias/audios/2020/04/senadores-querem-destinar-recursos-do-fundo-eleitoral-ao-combate-a-covid-19>. Acesso em: 6 maio 2020.

EM, BB/JP. TSE aprova com ressalvas contas de Dilma e de Comitê Financeiro para presidente da República. *Tribunal Superior Eleitoral*, 10 de dezembro de 2014. Disponível em : <http://www.tse.jus.br/imprensa/noticias-tse/2014/Dezembro/tse-aprova-com-ressalvas-contas-de-dilma-e-de-comite-financeiro-para-presidente-da-republica>. Acesso em: 5 maio 2020.

FP/TC. Eleições 2016: Justiça Eleitoral institui Núcleo de Inteligência para atuar na fiscalização das contas de camapnha. *Tribunal Superior Eleitoral*, 12 de agosto de 2016. Disponível em: <http://www.tse.jus.br/imprensa/noticias-tse/2016/Agosto/eleicoes-2016-justica-eleitoral-institui-nucleo-de-inteligencia-para-atuar-na-fiscalizacao-das-contas-de-campanha>. Acesso em: 6 maio 2020.

MARTINS, Helena. Campanhas de Aécio e Dilma juntas gastaram mais de 570 milhões. *Agência Brasil*, 25 de novembro de 2014. Disponível em: <https://agenciabrasil.ebc.com.br/geral/noticia/2014-11/campanhas-de-aecio-e-dilma-juntos-gastaram-mais-de-r-570-milhoes>. Acesso em: 5 maio 2020.

PEREIRA, Sandra. Embu terá campanha para prefeito e vereador mais cara que Taboão e Itapecerica. *Jornal na Net*, 21 de julho de 2016. Disponível em: <https://www.jornalnanet.com.br/noticias/14073/> . Acesso em: 5 maio 2020.

X. JF/DF bloqueia fundos eleitoral e partidário e autoriza uso para combate ao coronavirus. *Migalhas*, 7 de abril de 2020. Disponível em: <https://www.migalhas.com.br/quentes/324027/jf-df-bloqueia-fundos-eleitoral-e-partidario-e-autoriza-uso-para-combate-ao-coronavirus>. Acesso em: 6 maio 2020.

A RESPEITO DA LIBERDADE

Paulo de Barros Carvalho[*]

O homem é o único animal que não coincide com o mundo; seu destino é dilatá-lo, expandi-lo até o ponto em que puder chegar sua fantasia, até o céu..., como diria Teixeira de Pascoaes. E suas ações se coordenam na esfera daquele conceito tão grandioso e discutido que chamamos de *liberdade*, ponto de encontro das consciências e fundamento último das concepções filosóficas. Aliás, para Sartre, *o homem é liberdade* ou, dito de outro modo, *está condenado a ser livre.*

O tema da *liberdade*, que atormenta o espírito irrequieto dos grandes pensadores da história desde a antemanhã de sua existência, está ligado a uma série de questões da mais alta indagação e, dentre elas, a de ser a criatura humana um *ser pleno* ou um *ser carente.* Com efeito, muitos entendem que o atributo da razão de que é dotado o homem, proporcionando-lhe a possibilidade de raciocinar e, portanto, de locomover-se no espaço social com a lucidez de sua mente, dominando a natureza circunstante para fazer prevalecer seus desígnios, seria motivo suficiente para dar-lhe acesso às verdades absolutas, onde estão depositadas as razões últimas do existir. Outros, porém, tomam-no como um ser carente, prisioneiro de incontáveis limitações de ordem física, biológica, psicológica e moral, atrelado mui-

[*] Livre Docente, Doutor, Mestre e Bacharel em Direito pela PUC-SP. Professor Titular da Faculdade de Direito da PUC-SP. Professor Titular da Faculdade de Direito da USP. Presidente do IBET – Instituto Brasileiro de Estudos Tributários. Advogado.

tas vezes de maneira desfavorável aos laços da contingência, condenado a lutar incessantemente para sobreviver no intermundo de suas necessidades básicas. Nos domínios da aquisição do conhecimento, como anotou Kant, seu saber há de contentar-se com aquilo que simplesmente aparece (fenômeno), não tendo como atingir as essências (noumeno), apoderar-se da verdade incisiva e definitiva que viesse a pôr termo às suas inquietações. Essas ideias valem para o plano do conhecimento científico (episteme), sobrando ao homem o amplo território da crença (doxa). Afinal de contas, houve uma hora em que o mundo foi dado aos poetas..., a quem se confia a produção da linguagem, constituidora e propagadora da realidade em que vivemos.

Creio poder admitir-se uma analogia entre o *ser pleno* e os ontólogos; entre o *ser carente* e os retóricos. Acontece que o campo de irradiação semântica da palavra *liberdade* é muito amplo, havendo multiplicidade de sentidos para o termo. A escolha de opções requer o procedimento que consiste em promover incisões radicais e enérgicas, cortando e recortando o material significativo dessa noção grandiosa. Lembremo-nos de Pontes de Miranda (O problema fundamental do conhecimento), para repetir: *o cindir é desde o início.* A apologia do corte, aliás, impõe-nos a função indispensável para o aperfeiçoamento das comunicações, em todos os setores da interação social.

Nicola Abbagnano acentua três conteúdos de significação que julga ser os mais relevantes para fazer menção à palavra: *(i) a liberdade como autodeterminação*, em que o indivíduo aparece como causa de si próprio, isto é, sua vontade, fortalecida por desejáveis níveis de desenvolvimento, faria convergir para a pessoa mesma o centro de irradiação do conceito libertário, exibindo, com jactância essa prerrogativa sobranceira; seus efeitos, naturalmente, são nefastos, caminhando de mãos dadas com as posturas autoritárias inerentes à verdade absoluta; *(ii) a liberdade do indivíduo que se esteia numa ordem superior*, imposta pelo Estado que se auto-atribui a liberdade absoluta. Suas conseqüências, da mesma forma, são desastrosas, como bem o demonstram as experiências históricas conhecidas. A prepotência do Estado acaba por transmitir-se imediatamente para o indivíduo que tende a reproduzir o autoritarismo da ordem superior. Nessas duas acepções, Abbagnano identifica a presença da chamada *verdade absoluta*. Mas é na terceira dimensão de sentido *(iii) em que surge a liberdade como possibilidade de escolha que se faz diante de limitações.* Nesse nível de significação, a ordem superior, digamos, o Estado, definindo o campo de suas preferências, estabelece fronteiras demarcadoras, dentro das quais a escolha do indivíduo poderá movimentar-se. Trata-se da *liberdade relativa*, mantida entre marcos que delimitam a extensão das prerrogativas outorgadas, sendo certo que ele mesmo, o Estado, se autolimita, restringindo também sua conduta dentro de setor adredemente conhecido. Eis o encontro de faixas de opções valorativas, que facilita o aparecimento da chamada *liberdade de escolha*. Neste tópico, aliás, cabe uma consideração de superior importância: vista a liberdade como opção de conduta entre os marcos estabelecidos como balizas, torna-se possível uma definição objetiva de *responsabilidade: é a consciência que o indivíduo tem dos limites que determinam o espaço de sua liberdade.*

A *liberdade*, contudo, experimenta outras manifestações de ordem semântica. Quer em termos antropológicos ou sociológicos, a ideia expressa pelo termo comparece, invariavelmente, como relação, como vínculo, vale dizer, o conceito de liberdade pressupõe sempre o outro, é *aliorelativo*, não fazendo sentido admiti-lo simplesmente como atributo ou predicado de um ser. Ninguém é livre como privilégio pessoal, perante si mesmo. O conceito há de submeter-se, desse modo, a tudo que diz respeito à teoria das relações, ou lógica dos predicados poliádicos. Esta é a feição sintática ou lógica da *liberdade*.

Para o direito, da mesma forma, a noção de *liberdade* cumpre papel relevantíssimo. Não é exagero anunciar que reveste o caráter de pressuposto ontológico do direito, pois não caberia imaginar disciplina das condutas intersubjetivas no contexto social, sem que os destinatários das normas tivessem a possibilidade de optar entre duas ou mais condutas. Seria até um absurdo deôntico obrigar, proibir ou permitir, sem que os sujeitos receptores pudessem escolher entre cumprir a conduta ou omiti-la. Por exemplo, trancar alguém na sala de aula e, em seguida, enunciar a ordem de que está obrigado a sair ou a ficar, proibido de sair ou de ficar, permitido de sair ou de permanecer naquele lugar. Sem a liberdade de escolha o sentido deôntico ficará, desde logo, comprometido. Ao mesmo tempo, todas as ordens jurídicas consagram a tutela de situações em que o sujeito de direito, obrigado a um comportamento, vê-se obstado de praticá-lo. Na ordem jurídica brasileira, para assegurar o direito de cumprir as próprias obrigações, quando pecuniárias, há a ação de consignação em pagamento: (Op -> Pp), isto é, se alguém está obrigado a cumprir a conduta p, então tem que ter a permissão de cumpri-la. Da mesma forma, se alguém estiver proibido de exercitar certo comportamento p, tem que ter a permissão de omiti-lo. Dito em linguagem formalizada, (Vp -> P-p).

Outro dado curioso do universo jurídico é *a impossibilidade da escravidão absoluta*. De fato, se retirarmos todos os direitos de um cidadão, impondo-lhe somente obrigações e proibições, ao menos um haverá de ser inexoravelmente preservado: o direito de cumprir os deveres estipulados, bem como o de omitir as condutas proibidas. Em lógica deôntico-jurídica, a fórmula que expressa o direito de liberdade é representada assim (Pp v P-p), que pode ser interpretada: uma conduta p ou está permitido cumpri-la ou sua omissão –p está permitida. Não há outra possibilidade. No território dos teoremas deônticos, como homenagem ao princípio da liberdade, essa fórmula molecular é tomada como axioma.

Sobre o tema que faz aqui nossos cuidados, vale a pena transcrever trecho do Prof. Lourival Vilanova ("Fundamentos do Estado de Direito" – in Escritos Jurídicos e Filosóficos, volume I. pág. 413 – Noeses – 2004): *Na ordem do conhecimento científico, que sejamos relativistas. Na ordem da ação humana, porém, é indispensável manter o postulado da dignidade ética do homem – suporte dos direitos humanos e núcleo antropocêntrico do direito positivo. Mas, com a liberdade não se pode ir ao ponto de ser livre para dispor da própria liberdade, renunciando-a. Por isso, também, com a democracia, que é forma política de constitucionalizar a liberdade jurídica, não é legítimo usá-la com o fim de implantar a antidemocracia. (O grifo é meu).* O direito de liberdade vem referido, com tintas fortes e de maneira eloqüente no expressivo preâmbulo da Constituição da República.

Nós, representantes do povo brasileiro, reunidos em Assembleia Nacional Constituinte para instituir um Estado Democrático, destinado a assegurar o exercício dos direitos sociais e individuais, a liberdade, a segurança, o bem estar, o desenvolvimento, a igualdade e a justiça como valores supremos de uma sociedade fraterna, pluralista e sem preconceitos, fundada na harmonia social e comprometida, na ordem interna e internacional com a solução pacífica das controvérsias, promulgamos, sob a proteção de Deus, a seguinte Constituição da República Federativa do Brasil (O grifo é meu).

Vê-se, desde logo, que ao anunciar o rol dos direitos fundamentais, a *liberdade* aparece em primeiro lugar, confirmando o aspecto de pressuposto ontológico a que me referi linhas acima. Nenhuma regulação de comportamentos interpessoais torna-se possível sem atinência a esse primado estruturante que está na raiz das demais prerrogativas indicadas no

Texto Supremo. Eis aí a *liberdade* alçada à condição de princípio dos princípios, de sobreprincípio, consagrada como valor fundamental da ordem jurídica brasileira, de tal modo que qualquer dos direitos mencionados na redação magnífica desse preâmbulo, com toda a energia e determinação de sua força prescritiva, repousará, certamente, na extensão do conceito de *liberdade*.

Deixei por último a caracterização da *liberdade* como entidade axiológica, como valor, dada a importância extraordinária que ela representa. O direito inscreve-se na região ôntica dos objetos culturais, assim considerados todos aqueles que, produzidos pelo ser humano no curso de sua trajetória existencial, transformam a natureza circunstante para atingir e implantar um fim. Agora, se nos lembrarmos das lições de Miguel Reale, segundo as quais o fim, o objetivo, a finalidade nada mais é do que um valor, tomado como razão de ser da conduta, torna-se intuitivo concluir que o objeto cultural, na sua entidade constitutiva, na sua intimidade estrutural requer a presença insofismável do dado axiológico, do valor ou da estimativa, como quisermos. O universo da cultura é o mundo dos valores! Ora, valores, para Tércio Sampaio Ferraz Jr. são preferências por núcleos de significação, ou melhor, são centros significativos que expressam preferibilidade por certos conteúdos de expectativa. Em outras palavras, posso dizer que é a não indiferença de alguma coisa relativamente a um sujeito ou a uma consciência motivada, ou uma relação entre o sujeito dotado de uma necessidade qualquer e um objeto ou algo que possua qualidade ou possibilidade real de satisfazê-lo. Valor é o vínculo que se institui entre o agente do conhecimento e o objeto, tal que o sujeito, movido por uma necessidade, não se comporta com indiferença, atribuindo-lhe qualidades positivas ou negativas. Nesse ângulo, é possível falar em valor como ato de valorar. Uma atitude do sujeito perante o objeto, já que as estimativas não têm existência concreta, não têm expressão ôntica: elas não são, não consistem em algo, mas valem e só se pode predicar sua existência como algo aderente ao ser e não como alguma coisa que tenha um ser. Haveria uma dependência ontológica dos valores com relação ao ser, daí o definir-se o objeto cultural como a conjunção de um suporte físico mais o ato de valoração que sobre ele o homem faz incidir.

Miguel Reale (Introdução à Filosofia, Saraiva, 3ª edição, 1994, p. 141), desvinculando os valores dos objetos ideais, logrou dar *status* autônomo à Axiologia ou Teoria dos Valores. Consoante as ponderações do jusfilósofo, seguindo a trilha de Hessen, há traços que assinalam a presença de valores, permitindo identificá-los em contraste com entidades próximas. São autênticos elementos lógicos que estão em todos os valores. Acrescentei aos nove itens indicados por Hessen, três outros que vejo integrarem a compostura dos entes axiológicos. Vejamos quais são eles e como se manifestam no valor *liberdade.*

A *bipolaridade,* apenas possível nos objetos metafísicos e culturais, é marca obrigatória dos valores. Onde houver valor, haverá, como contraponto, o desvalor, de tal modo que os valores positivos e negativos implicam-se mutuamente, daí (2) a *implicação recíproca:* a liberdade é o valor e a escravidão o desvalor. A terceira nota (3) é a necessidade de sentido ou *referibilidade,* querendo significar que o valor importa sempre uma tomada de posição do ser humano perante alguma coisa a que está referido, e este algo, no caso da liberdade é a possibilidade de escolha entre duas ou mais condutas possíveis. Além disso as estimativas são (4) entidades vetoriais, apontando para uma direção determinada, para um fim e denunciando, com isso, *preferibilidade.* Por outro lado, não sendo susceptíveis de medição, os valores são (5) *incomensuráveis.* A liberdade, por exemplo não pode ser medida, avaliada em termos quantitativos. Mas os valores apresentam forte tendência à (6) *graduação_hierárquica.* Encontrando-se em relações mútuas e tendo em vista o mesmo sujeito axiológico, tendem a se acomodar em ordem escalonada, como fiz, aliás, para dar preeminência à liberdade em face de outras diretrizes previstas no preâmbulo da Constituição. Mais um item que comparece na configuração de cada valor que analisamos é a (7) *objetividade,* importa dizer: requerem eles objetos da experiência para neles se agregar. Não se revelam sem algo que lhes sirva de suporte e sem uma ou mais consciências às quais se refiram. A objetividade é conseqüência da particular condição ontológica dos valores. Se eles se configuram como qualidades aderentes, que os seres humanos predicam dos objetos (reais e ideais), hão de requerer, invariavelmente, a presença desses mesmos objetos. Chamo aqui de objetividade a esse atributo intrínseco aos valores, a despeito de sua verificação cognoscitiva processar-se mais emocional do que racionalmente. No caso da liberdade, é claro que se exige uma situação tal que a escolha das condutas seja possível.

QUALIDADES FEMININAS E MASCULINAS NAS IMAGENS DA JUSTIÇA*

RAFAEL CHAGAS MANCEBO**

1. JUSTIFICATIVA DO TEMA: PERCEPÇÃO E PLURALIDADE DA JUSTIÇA

A Justiça é um valor humano básico que trespassa a realidade científica e ideal. Assim como os valores-conceitos mais básicos, a Justiça tem realidade metafísica, ideática, cultural e natural, nos diversos quadrantes de realidade (Husserl 1985). Natural, porque a Justiça é um Interpretante pragmático básico (Peirce 1983) da expressão humana, assim como o Amor, Vida, a Fé. Símbolo básico, o valor Justiça vai além de uma definição estrita, completa, cabíveis apenas em temas matemáticos, como o triângulo, reta, planeta, asteroide, bissetriz, baricentro. Além de verbo, o valor Justiça é um sentido básico da experiência humana. Por tal razão, comunica-se na religião, filosofia, política, direito, ciências. Por tal razão, este valor tem ênfase fundamental no ambiente cultural e é interpretante básico de fenômenos sociais mais amplos e um tanto indefiníveis, como é o caso de outros conceitos básicos: Cultura, Psique Social, Bem Social.

Em razão desta generalidade, amplitude, polissemia da Justiça, seu tema pode se tornar um lugar comum e aí possível razão de uma falta de estudos mais aprofundados sobre o seu conceito e realização, pois o discurso de

* Artigo originalmente publicado na Cartografia Sociali, – Rivista de Sociologia e Scienze Umane –, ano III, n. 5, maio de 2018.

** Doutor, Mestre e Bacharel em Direito pela PUC-SP.

Justiça pode ser facilmente simplificado em "clichês". Apesar desta limitação pragmática, toda relação humana ganha mais plenos sentidos quando trazidos para os argumentos bem ponderados de Justiça. E este é um artigo em que se propõe discutir a Justiça é tornada em culturas antigas na forma de imagens e deidades na fluência de suas dinâmicas sociopolíticas.

Visto que é um valor interpretante básico do fenômeno humano, a Justiça interpreta e conecta todas as humanidades (filosofia – ética, estética, metafísica-, Psicologia, Antropologia, Linguística, Música, Pedagogia, Política, História, Sociologia, Economia, Culturalidade) e mediatamente, o critério ponderação e decisão (balança e espada) dá contexto às matemáticas e biológicas. O valor Justiça é tão básico à nossa condição existencial que toca os conceitos mais profundos e altos – o Infinito, o Nada, a Lógica, o Irracional – e também os conceitos mais cotidianos e da experiência prática de vida são interpretáveis pelo valor Justiça. Natural então que a Justiça escapa às palavras, à escrita.

Tal valor-conceito ocorre e mistura-se ao próprio contexto cultural em que é fluente, por tal razão sua conceituação seja necessariamente aberta, polissêmica, dependente do Tempo (*Zeitgeist*), do Ambiente Social (*Volksgeist*) e da Concepção (*Weltanschauung*), para referenciar os conceitos elaborados no "*Erklärung*" alemão, em especial de Herder e Hamman. Diante desta magnitude linguística, filosófica e existencial do conceito de Justiça, muitos juristas se mantêm no discurso mais seguro dos argumentos da "Lei e da Ordem", na perda patente de propostas políticas mais significativas para além das banalidades que dominam a vida política. O tema exige uma maleabilidade e policontextualidade mais encontrável nas artes plásticas e na música do que na escrita. Aí o porquê da utilidade de imagens e notas mitológicas do senso de Justiça, por meio das qualidades femininas e masculinas nas imagens da Justiça, que dão notas de outras experiências sociais, além dum discurso estritamente filosófico e de organização escrita.

2. QUIRALIDADE

Quiralidade é um atributo geométrico pelo qual um objeto é "espelhado" por sua contraparte, assim como a mão esquerda se relaciona diametralmente à mão direita. *Kíron* é sufixo de mão (χείρ) e cirurgia (χειρουργική *cheirourgikē*), que significa "trabalho de mão". Quíron é o Centauro que ensina Asclépio a arte da medicina, ao mesmo tempo em que é vitimado pelas flechas envenenadas na Guerra dos Centauros, arma que ele mesmo inventou.

Asclépio (Ἀσκληπιός, Asklēpiós), filho de Apolo, funda a medicina grega com o manuseio e sínteses das ervas e plantas, no aprendizado de Quíron[1]. Isto porque a QUIRALIDADE acontece frequentemente nas (1) microrrealidades, na química, física e astrobiologia (2) na realidade biológica, na fauna e flora (a própria estrutura corporal humana é quiral, pelo lado esquerdo e direito) e na (3) – realidade cultural, como no caso Feminino-Masculino, Pessoa-Grupo, Lei-Justiça, Purgação da Condição Social. Basta o conceito do "spin" na co-criação e relação entre moléculas a girarem inversamente, uma gira para a direita (dextrógira) enquanto outra molécula gira para a esquerda (levógira).

Não faço uma extensão indutiva para forçar uma conclusão generalizante de que tudo é formado por estrutura dual do micro ao macro, apenas indico a nossa tendência costumeira em pensar a partir desta estrutura dualística na percepção da realidade cultural. Nossa intelecção carrega traços duais e a percepção da Política e Cultura se conduz por seu ambiente, a Natureza.

Esta estrutura dual básica impele pensamentos clássicos (no exemplo do Maniqueísmo filosófico, a distinção entre sujeito e objeto, no próprio taoísmo – com imagético no Yin e Yang – ou as imagens implícita da lógica formal: Princípio da Identidade (P Λ NP), Princípio da Não-contradição (P≠NP) e Princípio do Terceiro Excluído (P V NP) ou na relação dual "causa e consequência") e contemporâneos (vide no estruturalismo fundado na distinção entre língua e fala – Wölflin, 1996, Saussure 2001).

A quiralidade imprime o modelo da contraposição (*Coincidentia Oppositorum*) na vida jurídica e cotidiana porque é simples e muito e direta. Por tal razão se extende a modelos de pensamento, como a teoria das cores, a

[1] Ainda que haja absorção e reelaborações semânticas, a palavra "cirurgião" tem raiz indiana, advém do médico "Sushrutha", (circa VI A.C.), reputado o primeiro cirurgião praticante e autor do livro "Suśruta-samhitā", fundamental para o Ayurveda e para a técnica da cirurgia. Há uma circulação cultural do Oriente para o Ocidente, mas deixamos considerar outros fundadores míticos da Medicina, como foi Imhotep (Egito, 27 A.C.), o Livro do Imperador Amarelo, fundante da Medicina Chinesa (entre V e II A.C., coevo à Era dos Reinos Combatentes ou Dinastia Han) e outro fundador mítico, "Obaluayê/Xapanã/Omulu", o Orixá (=Ancestral, Energia, Princípio) das doenças e das curas no Candomblé e no sincretismo da Umbanda, intepolado da África Yoruba, Fon e Jejê/Ewe para as Américas. O argumento mitológico grego funciona apenas paraenfatizar a dualidade presente na percepção da vida cultural.

contraposição de notas musicais no pentagrama ou o modelo geométrico implícito nas formas básicas de nosso pensamento. Por nossa estrutura mental, a quiralidade é verificável nas microrrealidades e nas macrorrealidades, porém pode se tornar uma limitação cognitiva humana. O senso da dualidade é arraigado na estrutura fisiológica e cultural da experiência humana e se praticarmos os limites desta forma de pensamento, podemos alcançar novas sínteses sobre o Feminino e o Masculino no senso de Justiça.

3. QUIRALIDADE FÍSICA E QUIRALIDADE INTELECTUAL

Há experiências que depuram o bom senso em regras lógicas (Hume 2009, Leibniz 1988). Há uma correspondência sincrônica entre pensamento e a Terra (*anima telluris*), na opinião de Leibniz, na "... *harmonia preestabelecida*, isto é, de um sincronismo absoluto dos acontecimentos psíquicos e físicos" (Jung 2004, pag. 64). Pensamos a partir de imagem (Aristóteles 2006). O modelo existencial influencia o modelo de pensamento. Isto pode ser reduzido a simplificações classificatórias, binarismo, estruturalismo basal, basismo de gênero sexual, truísmos, preconceitos etc. Percebemos os diversos argumentos dualísticos que se perdem e se esvaziam de sentidos, refletem a linguagem indiciária do discurso científico e humanístico contemporâneo. Numa guerra dos sexos, a assunção de papéis masculinos por mulheres varia de momento a momento.

Até para fugir ao erro da simplificação dual, são pertinentes fundamentos menos analíticos e mais sutis. O Taoísmo – na leitura mais acessível do Tao Te King- propõe a contraposição entre o Yin (feminino) e Yang (masculino), que pode ser tomado metaforicamente como feminino, masculino, frio, quente, noite, dia. Assim, a diferença entre energia feminina e energia masculina (Chi) é percebida além das diferenças entre a máscara feminina e a máscara masculina, plastificam a transcendência desta relação feminina-masculina que coabitam tanto no homem quanto a mulher (Jung 1992), numa geometria de tendências infindas. É recorrente esta união entre o feminino e o masculino em várias culturas. Por vezes, nesta permeabilidade energética, na androginia, bissexualismo (Zeus e a sedução de Ganimedes) ou no travestismo (como no trabalho de Thor em resgatar Freya, refém dos Gigantes de Jottunheim), em mitos dados em variadas civilizações, como é o caso do valor Justiça.

No âmbito filosófico, esta discussão permeia o fluxo da Vida, o HILOZOÍSMO e o HILOMORFISMO, que se dá em correntes por vezes incompreensíveis, mas conduzem as formas sociais – cidades, rituais e papéis-, ainda que as horas do cotidiano tenda a esmaecer este pulso vital. Tudo para concluir que as relações latentes entre energia do ambiente e energia cultural, entre causalidades e irrazões mediadas pelo imagético político, embebidas em recorrências de imemórias de sangue ou espiritual.

4. GÊNERO E ENERGIA SEXUAL

Num primeiro momento, a Justiça é uma entidade feminina e eis então que seja muito comum a energia masculina para reinterpretá-la, dizê-la, ritualizá-la. No exemplo das primeiras divindades femininas a representar a Justiça, a egípcia deusa Maát serve também de balança pela qual o masculino Deus Osiris faça o julgamento das almas de sua cultura. As qualidades femininas e masculinas comunicadas pelas imagens de Justiça são intercambiantes. Isto gera sínteses comportamentais menos radicais nos opostos. Por tal razão trabalhamos na lógica empírica da "ambivalência" (Touraine, 2010) ao invés de decisões duras por lógicas do "*a priori*", tendentes a um "silogismo" desconectado dos fatos da vida. Aí uma lógica compreensiva que aceita a incerteza (Prigogine), para citarmos discussões de racionalidade nas humanidades que ainda não foram absorvidas, pois a lógica das humanidades se pauta em imagens e racionalidades típicas das exatas, entretanto insuficientes para entender relações de causalidade nas humanidades, que se operam mais por probabilística, em manchas de possibilidades antes que pontos de verdade.[2]

O "senso" de Justiça interpreta o direito e também outras humanidades, brota de dentro, da experiência própria e ao mesmo tempo, vem de fora, pela lei. Esta percepção não foge ao neopositivismo do jurista Hans Kelsen, que percebe a inconsistência do argumento "da lei pela autoridade e a autoridade pela lei" (Kelsen) e o próprio conceito de "mínimo eficacial da norma jurídica", o "umbigo sociopolítico" que sustenta o sistema "puro" de direito, negando o caráter de "pureza" do direito.

"A verdade está no fundo" (Heráclito 2002). Esta conexão ajusta o indivíduo como também o contato emocional, o "*Pathos*" político que impele as

[2] Por tal razão, a tendência da lógica contemporânea torna-se interessantes para as ciências humanas: "*paralogia*", "*fuzzy logics*", "lógica probabilística", todas estas lógicas que desenham menos a regra dura da lei, mas realçam a "plasticidade" de símbolos sociais básicos como é o da Justiça, ainda que esta ambivalência e suspensão da certeza não tenha amplo lastro nos costumes da realidade jurídica.

leis, toca argumentos pré-verbais de Justiçam, em âmbito de sensibilidade e exortação. Tais aspectos foram atribuídos à uma *psique social*, por meio do *inconsciente coletivo*, que guarda forte influência do *Volksgeist* do *Erklärung* e articula o conceito aberto de Soberania e as crises de populismo que é a "*sombra*" (Jung) permanente da Democracia, numa relação de Medida, Desmedida e Nêmesis, tensionadas numa relação de "*exaltação-banalização*" (Diel 2004). Jung (1992) propõe argumentos nesta ambivalência entre indivíduo-grupo/feminino-masculino de nosso "*Zeitgeist*" através dos símbolos *antropomorfizados*, como é o caso da Justiça. São os conceitos "*anima*" e "*animus*", em que "*anima*" é o aspecto inconsciente no homem e "*animus*", o aspecto inconsciente na mulher. Este jogo é patentemente inspirado na interdependência do símbolo YinYang tendente à infindade. A imagem do Yin e do Yang contém um pingo do outro ao contrário de cortar expressõoes do indivíduo, fragmentando-lhe o *Self* (Jung, 1991, p. 119).

5. SOBREPOSIÇÃO SIMBÓLICA E ATUALIZAÇÃO MITOPOIÉTICA

Santidades, divindades e heróis representam e narram estórias que se repetem arquetipicamente nas experiências pessoais e de grupo (Brandão, 1989ª, Campbell s/d). O Mito é um Método, etimologicamente sígnica "seguir um caminho", uma "narrativa" e portanto a tensão existencial em "vivenciar" um caminho pessoal ou social, que "replica" uma experiência religiosa, fora do tempo (daí o "Mito = modelo exemplar", Eliade, 2001, p. 84), ainda que em particularidades e soluções poéticas próprias (Jung, 1991, p. 85), cumprem uma função pedagógica existencial particulares.

Em ambiente coletivo e difuso, as imagens da Justiça dispõem de imagens próprias, mas também intercambiáveis, justaponíveis, em sobreposição de figuras, numa "fantasmagoria" (Cassirer, 2003, p. 21) de imagens. Há a perda de corte definitório, mas ganho de modulação e difusão social, na manutenção do discurso vivo. Esta abertura conceitual possibilita uma utopia poética (Vico, 1974) na atualização permanente do que seja a Justiça, intérprete das questões "práticas" do cotidiano das Leis, adequando-se a temas profundos: Igualdade, Liberdade, Bem Comum, Democracia etc.

A "fantasmagoria" entre imagens e narrativas míticas da Justiça é a condição comum em diversas expressões culturais. Ocorre nas religiões afro-americanas ou mesmo no paganismo europeu, no exemplo em que as titânicas Gaia (Geia), Réa e finalmente, Athena e Apolo, intérpretes da Ordem Olímpica, todos mútuos interpretantes para expressar energias e princípios. Tais holografias são patentes na cultura indiana (Zimmer, 2005), em que o fundamento da transmigração da alma (*metempsicose*) facilita a aceitação desta dinâmica de imagens e no fim, o discurso escrito sobre as propostas. O sistema jurídico se dá nestas afasias comunicacionais, em meio a um "inferno linguístico" (Bittar, 2006 apud Foucault) comum em ordens nacionais e internacionais, visto que refletem as inconsistências conceituais humanas (Jung, 2006, pag. 3; Freud, s/d).

Percebe-se a inabilidade do discurso jurídico moderno/científico em trabalhar argumentos metajurídicos –filosofia, cultura, psicologia– de modo mais compreensivo, na absorção da capacidade midiática de ampla difusão, tecnologia social ainda por se formatar. Tais "ondas de longuíssima geração" (Braudel, 1992, Bloch, 2002) sintonizam expressões culturais de "curta duração" do século XX, como nos movimentos de contracultura "hippie", "beatinik", "new age", bem exemplificado pela propagação de Sri Paramahansa Yogananda nos anos 60 na Califórnia.

A Igreja Católica Romana articula tais fatos com Revelação, Milagre, Visão, Sonhos, Graça e pelo negativo no Domínio do Exorcismo, enquanto muitos movimentos neoevangélicos correntes no Brasil absorvem vários atos e discursos do espiritualismo, inclusive com sessões de "incorporações", "exorcismo", "descarrego" televisionados. Esta sutileza de percepção do fluxo interpretativo simbólico é refinada na memória indígena e africana brasileira, ainda que a matriz europeia também seja maleável, visto que advinda de uma Europa Proto-Moderna, mística, agrária ou marinha, dotada de uma percepção direta da natureza, "fisiocrática", chamadas as três raízes de "realismo ingênuo" (Cassirer, 2003) pela Sociedade "Industrial-Carbonífera", até que esta Sociedade Carbonífera se depare com o vazio de seu protagonismo retórico, entre o suicídio e a "idiotia", em desconsideração à Mãe-Terra e à "sabedoria agrária" (άγροιχοζ σοφία) (Cassirer, p. 16).

Talvez até por estas superposições de imagens religiosas de diferentes fontes no Brasil Colonial e Agrário, incluindo a matriz ibérica com diferentes imagens místicas– católicas, sefaraditas e muçulmanas, espelhando a matriz mediterrânea – explique a extrema facilidade da cultura brasileira na lida com diferentes imagens de diversas matrizes culturais, o que torna fácil penetração da voga moderna do espiritismo já nos XIX, no Rio de Janeiro. O "Séance" do século XIX e XX, muito em voga na França, Inglaterra e Estados Unidos, encontra ressonância no imágetico embebido em fontes indígenas assentadas em lugares como México e Cuba e Brasil. A proposta de comunicação com o Além toma diferentes colorações culturais: Espiritualismo, Séance, Espiritismo ou Xamanismo.

Natural esta retomada da "paranormalidade" e "reencarnação" no século XIX e XX como um ponto de inflexões de culturas antigas, como o "bramanismo" e o "budismo" (Zimmer, 2005), que trabalha temas vitalistas e telúricos, a "reencarnação" e *"karma"* e "energias primais", como as culturas não escritas brasílicas. Este é o ambiente multicultural que projetam sentidos metafísicos e culturais nas de imagens da Justiça. Vamos a algumas delas.

6. SINCRETISMO DE CULTURAS, IMAGENS E NARRATIVAS

O Novo Mundo é uma convergência do *ius sanguinis* e de *ius soli*. Num sentido telúrico e vitalista, justiça da terra e justiça biofisiológica conectam instintos e razões que impelem a ética pessoal e social. A aceitação da alteridade cultural – apesar de críticas atuais sobre a "democracia racial" como algo postiço – sempre teve forte impulso no Brasil, até porque a aceitação e absorção da recém-chegada cultura europeia pelos índios tupys foi condição para o sucesso da colonização brasileira desde os 1500. Sem esta absorção cultural proto-brasílica, "de dentro para fora" (Braudel, 1992) seria impossível a expansão civilizatória indígena-lusitana – "de fora para dentro" – e a formação do Estado brasileiro. Esta expansão, que se confirma ao próprio território do Brasil atual, foi lastreada no conhecimento de rotas (os chamados *Peabirus*), alimentos, modos, remédios negociados pela logística indígena. Vale a provocação, as primeiras indústrias brasileiras, nas Capitanias de São Vicente, Pernambuco e Bahia foram a de "*know-how*" cultural, agrofloresta, mineração e logística, na mistura cultural e racial, contra a opinão de Furtado (2005), que toma a cana-de-açúcar como a primeira indústria brasileira. O chão cultural brasileiro é indígena e daí podemos pensar o europeu e o africano.

Há uma contiguidade entre o Mar Mediterrâneo e o Mar Atlântico (os Deuses Poseidon e Okeanos, respectivamente) que comunica as Américas à Fenícia, à África, à Europa, Ás Arábias, à China e à Índia, o que é marcante mesmo numa expressão brasileira, mandinda – tomada como feitiço ou truque – enraizada em certos tipos de escravos islâmicos, que tinham uma miniatura de livro trazido no colar, o Corão. O Brasil recepciona a cultura escrita e não-escrita de diversos povos da Europa, África e

Oriente, tanto por sangue quanto por linguagem. Este intróito vale para realçar algo da tecnologia social e talento em lidar com a pluralidade tanto por miscigenação (*Eros*) quanto por guerra (*Polemos*), nas expressões de Empédocles, nas sombras da luta do Bem (*Ahúra Mazda*) e do Mal (*Arumã*) do Zoroastrismo.

Ao contrário da proposta pós-modernista, a complexidade social brasílica já é corrente desde a chegada dos europeus no Brasil, que se depararam com guerras indígenas de heterogêneas tribos, algumas vindo do Norte, outras vindo do Pacífico, possivelmente algumas mais antigas vindas da África e Mediterrâneo, o que recua a complexidade social desde a "invenção" do Brasil. A cultura brasileira recebe o influxo da energia da terra e de populações. Apesar da memória escrita recente, carrega um potencial de memória cultural, por vezes dormentes nos próprios países de origem, o que dá a interessante percepção de cultura nova, mas com dizeres, modos e percepções de sabedorias antigas, culturas depuradas em lógica (Leibniz; Hume).

7. ÁFRICA-BRASIL

O *Candomblé* e a *Umbanda* são as mais eminentes religiões de cunho afro-brasileiro e suas narrativas da Justiça são polifacetadas, podem se ater a ordens mais antigas, como no Criador *Olorun*, divindade representada pela Abóbada Celeste, esposo de *Aye*, a Terra. Olorun se fez realizar na Terra por seu filho-represente, *Oxalá* e neste mito houve a separação entre o Céu e a Terra (Verger, 2000). De outra parte, *Olokun*, Deus andrógino do Oceano, do Mar Profundo, com rabo de peixe, como Okeanos e Poseidon. Olokun é pai de *Iemanjá*, Mãe dos Orixás, dos Homens e dos Peixes. *Oxumaré*, Deus do Arco-Íris, semelhante ao *Ourobouros*, também é andrógino, 6 meses homem, 6 meses mulher, o que se repete em outras narrativas, a de passar por baixo do Arco-Íris e trocar de sexo e tem rabo de cobra.

Esta sutileza da androginia ou sexualidade indistinta no *Candomblé* e na *Umbanda* acontece também no antigo Egito, que gera a "proliferação mítica" (Bastide, 2005, tomando a Bergson). Brandão (1989b) comenta a Androginia ou Hierogamia Primordial como algo comum em diversas civilizações do Mediterrâneo. Há notas de outras energias sexuais completas, de *Hierogamia/ Androginia* (Brandão, 1989b) ou dinâmica feminino-masculinho no Candomblé e na Umbanda. O próprio filho de Olorun, Oxalá tem designações no masculino e eventualmente no feminino

(Bastide, pag. 241), sendo certo que de suas outras identidade ou holografias – Oxalufã, Obatalá, Ossaguian- uma – Oduduá – é patentemente de narrativa confusa, ora entendido como esposa de Obatalá, ora como competidor, ora como continuador na função de fazer o mundo e até, muito interessante, um irmão gêmeo de Obatalá contactado com o Islã, sendo Obatalá ligado à Cristandade (Verger, *idem*). As divindades do Candomblé, de matrizes africanas (nações Nagô, Ketu e Bantu e a denominação Jeje, os povos "estrangeiros", como os Daomé, Mahi, Axânti, Abomey) e presentes também na religião brasileira da Umbanda, sincrética a diversas inspirações (ameríndias, kardecistas, celta, ciganas, africanas e brasílicas) tomam o entendimento dos *Orixás* como as divindades orientadoras (guias) da pessoa, casa espiritual, tempo[3]. Há outras manifestações religiosas de cunho mais regional, como o perseguido e quase extinto "*Xangô*" em Pernambuco, mas tomaremos o Candomblé e a Umbanda por seu maior acesso ao imagético nacional.

O "*Orixá*" pode ainda ser tomado por um Ancestral Mítico ou Energia Predominante na Pessoa, arquétipo que alude tanto ao *jus sanguinis* quanto ao *jus soli*, visto que tem caráter imanentista. Há uma certa semelhança no conceito de Orixá e outros em diferentes culturas: "Deuses e Deusas", "Avataras", "Kuannon", "Djinn", "Divindade", "Ancestral Mítico", "Herói/Heroína", "Padroeira/Padroeiro", "Santos". O Candomblé e Umbanda religiões de incorporação dos mediums, isto é a pessoa entre em transe/êxtase e segue um ritual próprio de cada Orixá no Terreiro, o local religioso. Há uma gradação de dignidade e contato destes Orixás, sendo que Olorun e Olokun não se manifestam em mediums, assim como a Titânica Thêmis-Justiça divina não pisa o chão da Terra. Tais divindades mais próximas ao Mundo dos Homens são: Exú, Ogum, Oxóssi, Ossaim, Oxumaré, Xaponan, Nanan, Oxum, Iansan, Ossaim, Iemanjá, Xangô e Oxalá. Alguns destes circundam o valor Justiça, pelo quê falaremos de suas imagens. O *Orixá Ogum* (Gu) representa a Lei, o Ferro, a Instrumentação Religiosa, da

[3] A Umbanda é sincretizada no século XX, na cidade do Rio de Janeiro por Zelio Fernandino de Morais, entre 1907/8, após divergência com o espiritismo kardecista, visto que os orientadores espirituais de Zelio não se apresentavam como "espíritos evoluídos". Apresentavam-se como espírito de "prêto velho" – no Brasil identificado como um velho escravo negro e guia de sua comunidade – e também o espírito de um índio, o "Caboclo das Sete Encruzilhadas". O "Caboclo das Sete Encruzilhadas" seria a reencarnação do Missionário Jesuíta Gabriel Malagrida, cuja Ordem encontrava-se em confronto direto com o absolutismo pombalino.

Guerra, dos Caminhos, Tecnologia e Avanços. É sincretizado na Umbanda com São Jorge, no Sul e Sudeste, e com Santo Antônio no Nordeste Brasileiro. Guarda relação com a realização da lei romana, o *FAS*. O *Orixá* da Justiça, do Fogo, dos Raios e do Trovão é Xangô (Şango).

Xangô guarda relação direta com o JUS romano, o valor Justiça. Ambos têm suas afinidades e diferenças, "*coincidentia oppositorum*", assim como na contemporaneidade, há convergências e contradições entre a lei e a justiça. Xangô tem sincretismo com São Sebastião no Rio de Janeiro e em São Paulo, enquanto guarda aproximação com São Bento na Bahia. Ambos Ogum e Xangô têm traços de existência histórica. Xangô teria sido um rei mítico histórico fundador da cidade de Oyo da Cultura Iorubá (circa sec. XIV) e Ogum, fundador mítico da Cidade de Ifé, da cultura do tronco linguístico do Volta-Niger, recuando a pelo menos VII a.C.

Numa dinâmica mais sutil, as Orixás femininas se alternam como pares complementares destes dois Orixás masculinos. *Oxum*, ligada à energia de vida (*Axé*), beleza, sensibilidade, magia e trabalho tem sua contraparte em *Iansã* – muitos tomam por Oya-. De caráter mais guerreiro, Iansã é a divindade que controla os Ventos, ação da justiça, traz a Verdade. *Iansã* era a divindade e antigo nome do atual rio Niger. Ambas foram alternadamente mulheres de Ogum e de Xangô e completam a relação lei-justiça patentes em Ogum e Xangô. Oxum pelo arquétipo materno e mágico, das riquezas terrenas, da percepção do jogo social. Iansã pela mobilidade dos ventos e a força da Verdade. A díade feminina tem o mesmo respeito e apelo popular dos seus correspondentes masculinos, o que recebe maior impulso no fato de que a interpolação cultural da África para o Brasil contou com o denodado esforço e liderança das mulheres (Mães de Santo famosas, como Mãe Senhora, Mãe Menininha do Gantois, Mãe Stella de Oxóssi[4]). Note-se que há uma semelhança e possível troca cultural entre as civilizações do centro-leste africano e mediterrâneas, visto que as Divindades guardam semelhantes funções e mesmo semelhantes sonoridades. Os deuses "Oxalá" e Hitita "Sharumma", que decorre do Assírio/Sumério/Babilônico "Samas", o Deus-Sol. O próprio Deus Sol latino. O jogo divinatório de Ifá (Búzios) é dito ter sido trazido do Egito ou Mesopotâmia. Neste curto espaço que temos, vamos tomar um atalho da África-Brasil para o Egito.

[4] Para maior percepção, Mãe Stella de Oxóssi, com mais de 90 anos, dispõoe de um canal de videos no Youtube.

8. EGITO

Podemos dizer que o mais antigo símbolo da Justiça como ponderação e balança é a egípcia. Esta ponderação do justo ocorre na ponderação entre o "coração" da pessoa e o o peso da Pena de Maát, para se chegar a uma sentença favorável ou desfavorável (Budge, 2010). A ritualística egípcia revelada nos hieróglifos – isto é o autor quem nos afirma – mais se aproxima de "Capítulos de Sair à Luz" para uma vida Além da Morte. A escatologia egípcia tem esta passagem pelo julgamento da vida após a morte com o aniquilamento ou a continuidade da Vida ao Além Morte, em novos "Capítulos de Sair à Luz" (Budge, 2010). Em alguns hieróglifos, depreende-se que este julgamento é presidido por Osiris e lavrado por Toth, juiz da Justiça e da Verdade, Escriba dos Deuses, segundo correntes inscrições e em outras tantas imagens, por Anúbis, ainda em outros, é presidido pela própria Deusa Maát, cuja pena serve de contrapeso da balança. A qualidade Justiça é portanto, simbolizada tanto por Anúbis, por Toth ou por Maat. «esposa de TOT e filha de Râ; assistiu à obra da criação. É a deusa da regularidade e da ordem absolutas, da retidão moral, da justiça e da verdade. Seu emblema é a pena» (Budge, 2010, pag. 524). A troca e sinonímia da Justiça-qualidade divina e Justiça-ação entre Osíris, Tot, Maat, Anúbis, Pena de Maat e mesmo outras divindades, argumenta o egiptólogo Budge, era prática bastante comum da liberdade artística do desenhista, escultor ou gravurista sobre a Justiça da Vida, o que é reforçado no longo arco de tempo desde o Império Antigo até o Novo em que este julgamento final foi amplamente e livremente representado.

Esta rica variância das imagens indica qualidades tanto femininas quanto masculinas no valor Justiça na cultura do Egito Antigo contorna a atribuição deste valor somente à Deusa Maat, que compartilha o ritual e julgamento da Justiça com Osiris e Tot além de um séquito de divindades. Há uma "diacronia linguística" (Saussure, 2001) tendente à fusões e ressignificações de sentidos religiosos e mesmo políticos, conducentes ao amálgama de divindades oriundas de diversas tribos que se fundem e se facetam na mesma divindade no correr dos tempos, para lembrar a "fantasmagoria" de Cassirer.

Vê-se a força da sutileza na célebre revolução da Ordem Religiosa dada no Egito, quando o Faraó Aquenaton e da Farani Nefertiti propugnam a passagem da adoração do Deus do Vento, *Amon*, ("O Oculto", "O Escondido"), para o Deus-Sol, Aton, ambos em semelhantes tendências monoteísticas tanto na Ordem Antiga de Amon quanto na Ordem Nova de Aton. Isto ocorre também na Índia, com a prevalência dos três Deuses, Brahman (Criação) Vishnu (Manutenção) e Shiva (Destruição), configurando o "Trimurti", o "Hendriati" (três por um), filhos de Durga, Deusa Mãe que concentra as armas e poderes de seus três filhos.

É notável a ciência embebida na referência do "Hendriate" como expressão da condição de conhecimento humano dado pela experiência da tridimensionalidade e o Tempo, como quarta dimensão implícita, visto queo "Trimurti" representa o próprio fluxo da vida, a roda da vida (Chacra). Tais ressignificações talvez se simplificariam com as Imagens de Justiça. Num tom mais sintético, vamos argumentar como é o talento grego para conectar o muito novo e o muito antigo.

9. GRÉCIA

A mitologia grega é irresistível por diversos motivos. Um deles é que seus enredos, morais e imagens são de mais fácil compreensão do que de outras matrizes, mais próximas à realidade brasileira. Outro ponto é que as imagens de Justiça são refletidas em vários mitos gregos, visto que a "*Justitia*" romana foi uma adequação da Deusa Themis para a cultura dominante, trazida por Augusto, circa I A.C. *Themis* é a Deusa grega da Justiça Maior, da Lei Divina, do Sábio Conselho, da Previdência, do Conhecimento Popular. Filha de Uranos e Gaia, da Abóbada Celeste e da Terra, assim como o Iorubá *Obatalá*.

Themis, apesar de titânide, permanece como força vital na nova ordem olímpica que se sucede à Titanomaquia entre os Olímpicos e os Titãs. Permanece até porque representa a conexão entre ordem Cósmica transurânica, Ordem Olímpica e Ordem Social. Por uma Ordem Olímpica, mais nova e solar, surge a personificação da Justiça pela Deusa *Diké*, a Justiça Vingativa, com a espada em mãos, significante desta nova reorganização. Ela é irmã de *Eunomia* , "Boa Ordem", imagem da lei e da condução da boa vida das leis e finalmente, de *Eirene* a Paz. Juntas, elas são as Horas e formam um "*Hendriati*" (*Hen dia treis*" um por três), como o *Trimurti* (*Bramahn, Vishnu* e *Shiva*) indiano e carregam o caráter cíclico da vida social e de um retorno a um "*mundo edêmico*" (Eliade, pag. 63 e ss.).

Nota-se que a diferença entre Themis e Diké é a mesma diferença entre a ponderação da justiça e a ação da justiça, valor que permanece mais à Moral, ou à Ética, e que não tem o caráter sancionador da lei. Esta imagem foi latinizada para *Iustitia*, divindade que é trazida para Roma no período greco-romano pelo Imperador Augusto (I a.C.) e fundado seu templo por Tibério (13 a.C.) em imagem que já carrega tanto a espada quanto a balança, já uma imagem cooptada pelo estamento político antes que fruto duma síntese cultural mais fluida.

Esta relação mãe e filha -Justiça Ideal e Justiça no fato- é o ponto de contato entre as realidades metafísicas e ideias às realidades factuais e culturais, mediada pela linguagem, visto que mitos, cultos e imagens religiosas são mensageadas por linguagem e apontamos que o a estrutura de pensamento mítica, mágica do homem religioso ("homus religiosus" de Mircea Eliade) permanece no discurso contemporâneo, ainda que o discurso se diga laico, descrente e totalmente científico. Esta mesma paixão exaltada, descomedida, bem representada pela Deusa da Vingança é permanente no trato da vida social.

Isto nos faz repensar o Iluminismo um tanto ideático de Cesare de Beccaria, sobre a função predominantemente educativa da pena, frente ao caldo romântico e basal que é o senso comum e da adstrição, congruência, legitimidade e eficácia do sistema jurídico na realidade comum, mais atraído pela espada da vingança que pela ponderação da balança, revelando que o problema de qualquer sistema jurídico tem como infraestrutura a Cultura e uma Cultura de Paz.

A Paz é representado pela Divina *Eirene*, valor que na modernidade influencia o movimento irenista no âmbito internacional -pré-Estado Moderno- que seria um fiel da balança da Justiça internacional, a influenciar e fundamentar o pensamento religioso, filosófico e político de Erasmo de Roterdam, Leibniz Hugo Grotius, Samuel Pufendorf, Immanuel Kant, entre tantos outros. De volta às considerações ideais, ainda na Grécia, outra imagem e mito independente da Justiça é *Astraea*, "Noite Estrelada", referenciada por Virgílio, personifica tanto a castidade, pureza, qualidades intérpretes da Justiça e também o retorno da antiga Themis, da época de Ouro, de Cronos, titânica ou "saturnina".

Contraposta às irmãs *Horas*, a imagem da Deusa *Atena* também interpreta o senso de Justiça. Segundo um antigo oráculo das *Velhas*, responsáveis pelo Destino, o rebento da Oceanide Methis iria sobrepujar Zeus. A divindade podia se transformar em qualquer coisa, pelo quê Zeus pergunta se ela seria capaz de se transformar numa gota d´água. Assim que se transforma, Zeus Methis, que já está grávida. Por tal razão o feto de Methis, Atena, sobrevive e é gestada na cabeça de Zeus.

Algum tempo se passa sem que ninguém saiba desta gestação. Zeus, sofrendo de terríveis dores, pede a Hefesto que lhe martele a têmpora e após o golpe, Atena salta da cabeça do Deus-Rei. Nasce a Deusa de "partenogênese", assim como acontece com Dionisio, gestado na coxa de Zeus, e veremos porque Dionisio representa um aspecto mais terreno do discurso de Justiça. *Atena* é a Deusa da Sabedoria, da Civilização, da Justiça, da Habilidade, das Artes, do Artifício, da Força, da Guerra, de caráter racional, distante, frio, calculista, abstêmia, estrategista, qualidades um tanto masculinas. A imagem de Atena acaba por aglutinar a Ordem Social e a Justiça e intercambiante com as três irmãs *Horas*. Por sua psiqué e representações, Atena é uma imagem de Justiça comumente conectada ao patriarcado apolíneo grego antes que do matriarcado titânico (Brandão, 1989c) e ressalta a energia feminina-masculina (Jung, 1992) ínsita na realidade humana.

Além destas imagens patentes da Justiça, vale a atenção da passagem da Ordem Titânica para a a Ordem Olímpica, que implicam no rearranjo político da Justiça, e na passagem da imagem de Methis, o oráculo das três Velhas (Geias), que fiam, medem e cortam o fio da vida, invertido pelo ato de Zeus, organizador da Ordem Olímpica, com as repaginadas imagens de Diké, Atenas e Astraea, a seguir o complemento trino proposto por Junito de Souza Brandão em seus estudos sobre a Mitologia.

Figuras masculinas também implicam em atos de julgamento de Justiça. O próprio Zeus concentra o poder julgador, juntamente com seu irmão, Hades, senhor do mundo inferior, cuja palavra não volta atrás (sentença final). Esta troca de ordens religiosas e políticas pelas metáforas das divindades pode se sobrepor a transição do Período Micênico (Séc. XIV-XI a.C.) ao Período Geométrico ou Homérico (sec. XI-IX a.C.), assim como a divindade Themis é rearranjada a novas expressões da justiça, notadamente Diké e possivelmente Astraea, se esta é realmente anterior aos escritos de Virgílio.

Mito fundamental que aglutina imagem, rito (processo) e sentença em polaridades feminino-masculino e pessoal/social é a transição do Oráculo Pítico para o Oráculo Délfico. Há uma transição de ordens (Brandão, 1989b, pag. 95) que implicam novas formas e modos religiosos, em que a Ordem Solar de Apolo toma a Ordem Telúrica, pontificada pela Píton, uma Dragão Fêmea ou Grande Serpente, símbolo da conexão entre o eu-terreno e o eu-solar. Píton era filha da própria Terra, Geia, energias mais fundamentais que são representadas (ou civilizadas) na Ordem Olímpica pela

Deusa Hera, Deusa Mãe, esposa de Zeus, deusa do matrimônio. Esta envia a entidade Píton para matar Leto e seus filhos naturais de Zeus, Ártemis e Apolo. Há variantes da narrativa, em que Píton era já a substituta de mais pristína Dragão-Fêmea, *Delfine*. Fato é que Píton foi morta por Apolo este devia, por um senso divino, purgar o assassinato de uma Entidade basal com uma oferenda. E aí nasceu o Templo de Delfos.

Estas trocas de ordem religiosa e cosmológica representam a troca social, em "valências cosmológicas" (Brandão, 1989b, pag. 95), e significam a transição 1. de um Matriarcado (ou Androginia) para um Patriarcado 2. De uma Ordem Terrena para uma Ordem Solar e uma mudança ritual, com ênfase na "inspiracão", mais ao céu, que pela "incubação" mais ligada ao aspecto físico, da Terra, ainda que a imagem de Dioniso, pois é o responsável tanto pelo Êxtase, Inspiração, "Mania" quanto pela incubação, visto que ele próprio foi "gestado" na coxa de Zeus. Dionísio, com suas qualidades terreais, complementa o ritual solar apolíneo, facilita este contato na relação Terra e Céu, através do Templo de Delfo, cujo centro é o OMPHALÓS, o umbigo do mundo (Brandão, 1989ª, 95; Eliade, pag.38). Esta transição civilizatória da Ordem Pítica à Ordem Délfica implica em mudanças no pensamento político que se irradiam até a contemporaneidade, num contributo essencial do direito grego, no exemplo da passagem da Justiça pessoal, para a Justiça dos Tribunais (Brandão, 1989ª, pag. 91), a Justiça Pública.

Num argumento final e que parece contactar os problemas bem contemporâneos de falta de contato e humanidade na realidade industrial, tenho a impressão de que o rito por "incubação", mais físico, mais ao umbigo, "ventral" seja mais imediato aos "instintos" enquanto a "inspiração", mediada pelo ar, imediatize-se ao lampejo, à "intuição". Por uma manifestação interna ou externa, há um contato com o divino, a "*hierofania*" (brilho, manifesto do sagrado) ou a "*epifania*" (manifestação, aparição súbita, *insight*, "ter uma luz") conducentes ao "*conhecer-se a si mesmo*" délfico.

O "sexto sentido", que podemos tomar empiricamente como a pré-cognição apurada e harmônica tanto do "instinto" quanto da "intuição". Pode-se distribuir esta combinação no sistema indiano dos chacras. Interessante, a Ordem Apolínea enfatiza a "inspiração, mais aérea, luz, porém permanecem valores píticos-telúricos, fogo, na ritualística grega, até pelo fato do próprio Apolo passar período de purgação, o que pode ser tomado como um ritual de "incubação" pelo fato de ter matado a Píton, Entidade

Viva. Esta passagem de uma Mântica Telúrica, dada pela Dragão Delfine para uma subsequente Ordem telúrica, a do Dragão Píton, possibilita a impressão da energia feminina E masculina num mesmo corpo, ou seja à "*androginia*" ou "*hierogamia*" primordial (Bachofen, Brandão, 1989c, pag. 337), numa completude de energias masculina feminina o que é associado a mitos de serpentes, peixes e dragões -animais totêmicos pristínos/primais e por tal razão ligados à origem do mundo mágico e memo biológico, cosmogônicos- como vimos nos Orixás *Olokun*, dos Mares Profundos e *Oxumaré*, do Arco-Íris.

REFERÊNCIAS

Aristóteles, 2006, De Anima III, Editora 34, Brasil.

Bachofen, J. J., 1992, Myth, Religion, and Mother Right: Selected Writings of (Bollingen Series).

Bastide, R., 2005, O Candomblé na Bahia – o rito nagô-, Editora Companhia das Letras, Brasil.

Bittar, E. C. Bianca, 2006, Linguagem Jurídica, Saraiva, São Paulo.

Bloch, M., 2002, Apologia da História ou o Ofício do Historiador, Zahar Editores, Brasil.

Brandão, J. S., 1989a, Mitologia Grega, Volume I.

—, 1989b, Mitologia Grega, Volume II.

—, 1989c, Mitologia Grega, Volume III.

Braudel, F., 1992, Escritos sobre a História, Editora Perspectiva, São Paulo.

Budge, E. A. Wallis, 2010, O Livro Egípicio dos Mortos, Editora Pensamento, São Paulo.

Cassirer, E., 2003, Linguagem e Mito, Editora Perspectiva, São Paulo.

Campbell, J., s/d, Cambpell, Entrevista "A Jornada do Herói", Documentário Coleção "O Poder do Mito", Logon Editora Multimídia.

Diel, P., 2004, O simbolismo na mitologia grega, Editora Attar, Brasil.

Eliade, M., 2001, O sagrado e o profano, Editora Martins Fontes, São Paulo.

Freud, S., s/d, artigo Qualidades psíquicas, Obras Psicológicas Completas, Imago Editora, Rio de Janeiro, volume IV, versão digital.

Furtado, C., 2005, Formação Econômica do Brasil, Companhia Editora Nacional, Brasil.

Heráclito, 2002, Fragmentos contextualizados, Editora Difel, Brasil.

Hume, D., 2009, Tratado da Natureza Humana, São Paulo, Editora Unesp.

Husserl, E., 1985, Investigações Lógicas, Editor Victor Civita.

Jung, C. G., 1991, O espírito na arte e na ciência, Editora Vozes, Petrópolis. —, 1992, O Homem e seus Símbolos, Nova Fronteira, São Paulo.

—, 2006, O Eu o Inconsciente, Editora Vozes, 19ª Edição, Petrópolis, 2006.

Kelsen, H., 1998, Teoria Pura do Direito, Editora Martins Fontes, São Paulo.

Leibniz, G. W., 1988, Novos Ensaios sobre o Entendimento Humano, Nova Cultural Editora, São Paulo.

Peirce, C. S., 1983, Ensaios Coligidos, Editora Victor Civita.

—, 1999, Semiótica, Editora Perspectiva, São Paulo.

PRIGOGINE, Y., 2002, As leis do caos, Editora Unesp, São Paulo.

TOURAINE, A., 2010, O mundo das mulheres, Editora Vozes, Rio de Janeiro, 2ª Edição.

SAUSSURE, F. de, 2001, Curso de Linguística Geral, Editora Cultrix, São Paulo.

VERGER, P., 2000, Notas sobre o Culto aos Orixás e Voduns, Editora Edusp, São Paulo.

VICO, G., 1974, Princípios de (uma) ciência Nova (acerca da natureza comum das nações, Editora Abril Cultural.

WÖLFLIN, Heirich, 1996, Conceitos Fundamentais da História da Arte, Editora Martins Fontes.

ZIMMER, H., 2005, Filosofias da Índia, Editora Palas Athena, Brasil.

PRINCÍPIOS INFORMADORES DA TEORIA GERAL DO DIREITO DE DANOS

ROMUALDO BAPTISTA DOS SANTOS*

INTRODUÇÃO

Não resta dúvida que o direito é regido por princípios gerais que orientam desde a elaboração das normas até sua interpretação e aplicação aos fatos concretos. Os princípios contêm forte carga axiológica, de sorte que seu conteúdo é flexível e varia de acordo com o tempo e lugar. Observada a tridimensionalidade jurídica de que fala Miguel Reale, os princípios incidiriam sobre o aspecto valorativo da normatividade. São alguns princípios gerais que regem o direito contemporâneo a dignidade humana, a igualdade e a solidariedade.

Todavia, o direito se organiza em vários ramos que se orientam por princípios próprios e específicos, como é o caso da autonomia privada, da boa-fé objetiva e da função social que regem o direito contratual; os princípios da legalidade estrita, da presunção de inocência e da tipicidade no direito penal; os princípios a do contraditório e da ampla defesa no direito processual etc. É possível afirmar que a existência de uma principiologia própria delimita os campos e marca a autonomia dos institutos jurídicos. Assim também a responsabilidade civil, que agora se organiza como direito

* Doutor e Mestre em Direito Civil pela USP. Especialista em Direito Contratual e Direito de Danos (Contratos y Daños) pela Universidade de Salamanca. Professor convidado em cursos de pós-graduação. Membro do Instituto Brasileiro de Estudos da Responsabilidade Civil – IBERC. Advogado.

de danos, emerge como instituto jurídico autônomo na medida em que se orienta por uma principiologia que lhe confere identidade própria.

Neste trabalho buscaremos fixar os contornos gerais do direito de danos na atualidade e identificar quais seriam os princípios que regem essa disciplina jurídica, de sorte a conferir-lhe autonomia em relação aos institutos jurídicos correlatos e a delimitar seu campo de aplicação.

1. DESDOBRAMENTOS DA RESPONSABILIDADE CIVIL AO LONGO DA MODERNIDADE

A responsabilidade civil é um instituto jurídico moderno, não porque tenha sido inventado pelos modernos, mas porque adquiriu autonomia dogmática a bordo das transformações sociais, políticas e econômicas que culminaram com a promulgação do *Code Napoleon*, nos primórdios da modernidade.

Ademais, a teoria da responsabilidade civil encontra-se em permanente processo de evolução que acompanha aproximadamente os desdobramentos da própria modernidade. Assim, a teoria da culpa era adequada e suficiente para resolver os problemas que surgiam entre sujeitos de direito, num ambiente individualista de numa sociedade eminentemente agrária. A teoria do risco veio a lume para suprir a insuficiência da teoria da culpa a respeito dos danos decorrentes das atividades voltadas para a produção de bens em larga escala, em que não era possível individualizar a culpa. Presentemente, a teoria da responsabilidade civil se depara com danos de causalidade múltipla e indeterminada, decorrentes de atividades indispensáveis ao modo de vida nas sociedades contemporâneas.[1] Ainda em linha com os desdobramentos da Era Moderna, é possível identificar ao menos três fases na teoria e na prática da responsabilidade civil.[2]

[1] Sobre os desdobramentos da teoria da responsabilidade civil, confira-se no Brasil HIRONAKA, Giselda Maria Fernandes Novaes. *Responsabilidade pressuposta*. Belo Horizonte: Del Rey, 2005, p. 71-102. Na doutrina espanhola, DÍEZ-PICAZO, Luis e GULLÓN, Antonio. *Instituciones de derecho civil*, vol. I. Madrid: Tecnos, 1995, p. 820-824. Entre os autores argentinos, MESA, Marcelo J. López. *Presupuestos de la responsabilidad civil*. Buenos Aires: Astrea, 2013, p. 25 e 37.

[2] Sobre as características da modernidade, confira-se: BAUMAN, Zygmunt. *Modernidade líquida*. Tradução de Plínio Dentzien. Rio de Janeiro: Jorge Zahar Editor, 2001, passim; BITTAR, Eduardo Carlos Bianca. *O direito na pós-modernidade*. 2. ed. Rio de Janeiro: Forense Universitária, 2009, p. 33-183.

1.1. PRIMEIRA FASE

Em seu primeiro momento, a responsabilidade civil se pauta na culpa civil e na autonomia individual, nos moldes da cláusula geral inscrita no art. 1.382 do *Code Napoleon* e seus correlatos nas demais codificações ocidentais. É corrente na doutrina a afirmação de que a responsabilidade civil individual, fundada na culpa, era adequada e suficiente para dar conta das relações intersubjetivas, típicas de uma sociedade predominantemente agrária.[3]

Três fatores marcam essa fase da teoria geral da responsabilidade civil: a) em princípio, o indivíduo deveria suportar os danos que se abatessem sobre seus bens, segundo a máxima *res perit domino,* só podendo transferir a responsabilidade a terceiro, excepcionalmente, mediante comprovação de culpa; b) por via de consequência, o indivíduo causador só estava obrigado a indenizar os danos decorrentes de sua conduta culposa; c) o indivíduo que causasse dano a outro teria o dever de indenizar e de tomar o prejuízo para si.[4]

Estes aspectos marcam o caráter excludente e excepcional da responsabilidade civil por culpa, pois em princípio a vítima deveria absorver os prejuízos que se abatessem sobre seus bens. A responsabilidade só poderia ser atribuída a terceiro mediante comprovação da culpa, a essa altura erigida à categoria de erro de conduta. Então, a responsabilidade civil estava umbilicalmente atrelada à ideia de ilicitude jurídica ou antijuridicidade da conduta. A reparação do dano valia como reprovação à conduta culposa, considerada ilícita.[5]

1.2. SEGUNDA FASE

A cláusula geral de responsabilidade civil por culpa logo se mostrou insuficiente para dar conta dos danos causados pelas atividades indus-

[3] MESA, Marcelo J. López. *Presupuestos de la responsabilidad civil,* p. 25 e 37.

[4] MESA, Marcelo J. López. *Presupuestos de la responsabilidad civil,* p. 26.

[5] DÍEZ-PICAZO Y GULLÓN sustentam que: "El sistema subjetivo de responsabilidad se estructura en torno a la idea de que no basta que una persona sufra un daño para que el autor de la acción u omisión que sea su causa esté obligado a repararlo; es menester que su acto u omisión se daba a que por lo menos ha sido negligente, descuidado, no ha previsto sus consecuencias dañosas para evitarlas, en suma, a un reproche que se hace a su proceder" (DÍEZ-PICAZO, Luis e GULLÓN, Antonio. *Instituciones de derecho civil,* vol. I, p. 821). No Brasil, Caio Mário assinala, com base nas lições de De Page, o caráter excludente da responsabilidade civil subjetiva: "A irresponsabilidade é a regra; a responsabilidade a exceção" (PEREIRA, Caio Mário da Silva. *Responsabilidade civil.* Rio de Janeiro: Forense, 1989, p. 35).

triais e até mesmo pelas atividades agrícolas executadas com emprego de tecnologia e mecanização. A essa altura, podia-se relacionar o dano a determinada pessoa ou empresa responsável pela atividade industrial ou agrícola, mas não era possível individualizar o agente causador direto nem demonstrar a negligência, imprudência ou imperícia na execução da atividade.[6]

Não por acaso, o caso pioneiro de reconhecimento de responsabilidade civil sem culpa se deu no âmbito das relações de trabalho, no direito francês, a partir do Parecer Cames, proferido pelo Comissário Romieu em 1895, em que o Conselho de Estado reconheceu a responsabilidade do Estado por acidente sofrido por um trabalhador na construção de uma estrada de ferro. Este teria sido o ponto de partida para a teoria da responsabilidade civil objetiva, em sua primeira formulação, que dispensa a vítima de individualizar o agente causador do dano e de comprovar a negligência, a imprudência ou a imperícia.[7]

Observa-se, porém, que a teoria da responsabilidade civil objetiva, nessa primeira formulação, assume a mesma estrutura da teoria subjetiva, apenas dispensando a vítima de comprovar a culpa do agente. Trata-se ainda de uma responsabilidade civil retrospectiva, que se destina à reparação dos danos causados e que impõe ao causador do dano a obrigação de assumir e absorver o prejuízo decorrente da reparação.[8]

1.3. TERCEIRA FASE

A possibilidade de imposição de responsabilidade sem verificação da culpa conduz logicamente a dois fenômenos que marcam a terceira fase da teoria da responsabilidade civil: o gerenciamento dos riscos e a socialização dos

[6] Lopez Mesa observa que, para tanto, seria necessário que a vítima conhecesse o processo de produção para identificar em que consistiu eventual falha de conduta ou de procedimento (MESA, Marcelo J. López. *Presupuestos de la responsabilidad civil*, p. 25).

[7] VARELLA, Marcelo Dias (Coord.). *Responsabilidade e sociedade do risco/Relatório público considerações gerais*. Conselho de Estado da França. Tradução de Michel Abes. Brasília: UniCEUB, 2006, p. 23.

[8] DÍEZ-PICAZO Y GULLÓN anotam que, diante da insuficiência do sistema da culpa em face dos novos danos, a jurisprudência passou a recorrer à presunção de responsabilidade, com dispensa da vítima de comprovar a culpa do agente e com flexibilização do nexo de causalidade, em um movimento de objetivação da responsabilidade civil (DÍEZ-PICAZO, Luis e GULLÓN, Antonio. *Instituciones de derecho civil*, vol. I. Madrid: Tecnos, 1995, p. 821; ____________, *Sistema de derecho de daños, vol. II*. 11ª ed. Madrid: Tecnos: 2015, p. 317).

danos.[9] De outro lado, observa-se o incremento exponencial das atividades de produção, com o emprego de elevados índices de automação para produção de alimentos e comodidades em alta escala, assim como a fluidez e despersonificação do capital e o desaparecimento da figura do responsável pelas atividades econômicas. As atividades são desempenhadas por entidades que, embora fisicamente existentes, são altamente virtualizadas, no sentido de que seus donos são acionistas ou investidores que podem retirar ou transferir seus recursos a qualquer momento para outras empresas ou atividades.[10] Há algum tempo, verifica-se o surgimento e o crescimento das empresas de tecnologia, cujas atividades impactam a vida das pessoas e podem causar danos de diversas ordens. Nos dias atuais, surgem as denominadas plataformas digitais, que sequer existem fisicamente, mas desempenham atividades, contratam empregados ou colaboradores.

De todo modo, as atividades são desempenhadas pelas empresas e pelo poder público para atender às necessidades e comodidades da vida contemporânea. Por outro lado, os danos decorrentes dessas atividades são incorporados aos balanços financeiros das empresas, aos orçamentos dos entes públicos ou ao cálculo atuarial das seguradoras, conduzindo a uma espécie de solidarização ou socialização dos deveres de responsabilidade, baseada nos princípios da solidariedade social e da igualdade frente aos encargos públicos.[11]

[9] Encontramos em Díez-Picazo e Gullón a descrição desse desdobramento da teoria do risco: *"Nacida la teoría del riesgo para explicar fundamentalmente la obligación de indemnizar del patrono por el accidente de trabajo sufrido por el obrero, ha alcanzado una extraordinaria fortuna en los tiempos actuales merced a la aparición de instrumentos creadores de riesgos muy cualificados (utilización de energía nuclear, vehículos de motor, aviación, etc.), y pugna por abrirse paso en todos los campos"* (Díez-Picazo, Luis e Gullón, Antonio. *Instituciones de derecho civil*, vol. I. p. 821-822; ______________. *Sistema de derecho civil*, vol. II, p. 317-318). No mesmo sentido, confira-se: Delmas-Marty, Mireille. *Por um direito comum*, p. 16-17); Mesa, Marcelo J. López. *Presupuestos de la responsabilidad civil*, p. 24-30.

[10] "Proprietários ausentes" é a expressão utilizada por Bauman para se referir à despersonificação do capital (Bauman, Zygmunt. *Globalização*. Tradução de Marcus Penchel. Rio de Janeiro: Zahar, 1999, p. 16-17). Em outra obra, Bauman afirma que *"Tendo se livrado do entulho do maquinário volumoso e das enormes equipes de fabrica, o capital viaja leve, apenas com a bagagem de mão – pasta, computador portátil e telefone celular" (...) "A habilidade de desaparecer como Houdini, 'artista da fuga', a estratégia do desvio e da evitação e a prontidão e capacidade de fugir se necessário, esse núcleo da nova política de desengajamento e descomprometimento, são hoje sinais de saber e sucesso gerenciais"* (Bauman, Zygmunt. *Modernidade líquida*, p. 173).

[11] Varella, Marcelo Dias (Coord.). *Responsabilidade e sociedade do risco/Relatório público considerações gerais*, p. 7. No mesmo sentido, confira-se: Roger-Lacan, Cyril. *Specialité, gravité et*

A terceira fase da teoria da responsabilidade civil é marcada também pela magnitude dos danos decorrentes das atividades, que são desempenhadas em escala cada vez maior e com grandes intervenções na vida social e no ambiente natural.[12] Esse aspecto é determinante para que os danos sejam tratados *a priori*, pelo prisma da prevenção e da precaução dos danos potenciais, além da reparação dos danos efetivos.[13]

Portanto, é possível afirmar que a teoria geral da responsabilidade civil ingressa em sua terceira fase, em linha com os desdobramentos da modernidade, cujo ponto de partida é a identificação e delimitação de uma modalidade específica de dano, o dano-atividade ou dano-acidente, relacionado com as atividades desenvolvidas pelas empresas e pelo poder público em benefício da coletividade.

2. DELINEAMENTO DA TEORIA GERAL DO DIREITO DE DANOS

Nessa terceira fase de seu desenvolvimento, a teoria geral da responsabilidade civil se organiza sob a rubrica do direito de danos, cujo enfoque é a prevenção/precaução e a reparação dos danos e menor ênfase sobre a punição/dissuasão do agente. Nesse cenário, há um deslocamento do centro de gravidade da responsabilidade civil, de sorte que a vítima ocupa posição de

anormalité das la responsabilité sans faute: conclusions sur Conseil d'État, 1er février 2012, M. Bizouerne et outre, nº 347205 et 347446, in: Revue Française de Droit Administratif, nº 2, mars-avril/2000, p. 335: «En effet, en matière de ruipture d'egalité devent les charges publiques, quand sont en cause des préjudices économiques, le seuil de gravité excédant l'aléa normal d'une intreprise ou d'une explotation doit être à la fois celui qui caractérise le catactère anormal du préjudice et celui borne le montant de l'indemnisation possible».

12 O dano enorme pode ser definido como o dano de proporções catastróficas, decorrentes de atividades típicas do modo de vida nas sociedades contemporâneas, de causalidade múltipla ou indeterminada e de consequências difusas (SANTOS, Romualdo Baptista dos. *Responsabilidade civil por dano enorme.* Curitiba: Juruá Editora; Porto: Juruá Editorial, 2018, p. 201-204). Sobre danos de causalidade múltipla, veja-se também: DÍEZ-PICAZO, Luis e GULLÓN, Antonio. *Instituciones de derecho civil*, vol. I, p. 821-822; LLAMAS POMBO, Eugenio. *Reflexiones sobre Derecho de Daños: casos y opiniones*, p. 104-105.

13 Segundo Comandé, o grau de gravidade e irreversibilidade determina o modo de tratamento do dano: em grau mínimo, reparação a posteriori; em grau médio, assunção do risco; em grau máximo, prevenção/precaução (COMANDÉ, Giovanni. *L'assicurazione e la responsabilità civile come strumenti e veicoli del principio di precauzione.* In: COMANDÉ, Giovani. *Gli strumenti della precauzione:* nuovi rischi, assicurazione e responsabilità. Milano: Giuffrè, 2006, p. 42 e 46).

destaque e o dano se apresenta como elemento desencadeador dos deveres de responsabilidade (prevenção/precaução e reparação).[14]

Disso resulta que, em princípio, todo dano deve ser reparado, de modo que a base do sistema é a reparação e não a responsabilidade. Verifica-se uma mudança de perspectiva, da punição da conduta do agente para o direito da vítima, uma vez que não mais se busca tanto a atribuição de responsabilidade a um culpado, mas sim a promoção do ressarcimento dos danos sofridos pela vítima.[15]

Nesta terceira fase, há três modalidades de danos que fundamentam a atuação das três teorias da responsabilidade civil: a) o dano-culposo, de caráter individual e intersubjetivo, que exige atuação da teoria da culpa sobre o dano causado e impõe ao culpado o dever de assumir e absorver o encargo da reparação; b) o dano sem culpa, que exige atuação da teoria da responsabilidade civil objetiva em sua primeira formulação, com a mesma estrutura da teoria da culpa, apenas dispensando a vítima de comprovar a culpa do agente causador (risco individual); c) o dano-atividade ou dano--acidente, inerente às atividades de risco desempenhadas pelas empresas e pelo poder público em benefício da sociedade, que exige atuação dos deveres de prevenção/precaução e de reparação cujos encargos são diluídos reflexivamente na própria sociedade (risco coletivo ou risco solidário).[16]

[14] Ricardo Lorenzetti ressalta a preponderância do direito da vítima e a centralidade do dano para o sistema do direito de danos (LORENZETTI, Ricardo Luis. *Reflexiones acerca de la responsabilidad civil en el siglo XX*, p. 7). Também López Mesa explica que a teoria da responsabilidade civil na atualidade pretende cumprir antes de tudo sua função ressarcitória, sem maiores indagações sobre a atitude subjetiva daquele que deu causa ao dano. (MESA, Marcelo J. López. *Presupuestos de la responsabilidad civil*, p. 27). Por fim, Calvo Costa explica que a razão de ser da responsabilidade civil já não é o ato ilícito praticado pelo causador do prejuízo, mas o dano sofrido pela vítima (CALVO COSTA, Carlos Alberto. *Daño resarcible*. Buenos Aires: Hamurabi, 2005, p. 51).

[15] GHERBI, Carlos Alberto. *Teoría general de la reparación de daños*. 3. ed. Buenos Aires: Astrea, 2003, passim, particularmente a introdução, p. 1-13; CALVO COSTA, Carlos Alberto. *Daño resarcible*, p. 171; DELMAS-MARTY, Mireille. *Por um direito comum*, p. 15-16; DESIDERI, Jean-Pierre. *La précaution en droit privé*. Revue Française de Droit Administratif, Paris: Dalloz, p. 238-242, mar./abr. 2012. p. 241.

[16] Giovanni Comandé identifica três cenários no desenvolvimento da teoria da responsabilidade civil ao longo do século XX: a) o da responsabilidade civil subjetiva, associada à culpa e previdência; b) o do risco profissional ou de empresa, em que se rompe o nexo causal entre o indivíduo e o incidente, tendo como objetivo a distribuição dos custos em uma lógica de eficiência e solidariedade; c) o da superação da responsabilidade em uma plena socialização

Com isso, a teoria da responsabilidade civil se encaminha a formulação de um direito de danos, cujas principais características são: [1] a centralidade do dano como elemento desencadeador dos deveres de responsabilidade; [2] o protagonismo da vítima e seu direito à precaução e à reparação; [3] a atuação do princípio da prevenção/precaução quanto aos danos potenciais ao lado da reparação dos danos efetivos.

São pressupostos dessa terceira fase da responsabilidade civil que: [1] as atividades públicas e empresariais são desenvolvidas e desempenhadas em benefício da coletividade, justificando-se que seus efeitos negativos sejam diluídos na própria sociedade pelos mecanismos de socialização; [2] as atividades devem ser desempenhadas de maneira sustentável, sustentabilidade socioambiental, de maneira a produzir a menor quantidade de danos possível; [3] a pessoa não está obrigada a suportar os danos decorrentes das atividades públicas e privadas, fazendo jus à prevenção/precaução dos danos potenciais e à reparação dos danos efetivos.

Considerando a correlação entre os desdobramentos da modernidade e o desenvolvimento da teoria geral da responsabilidade civil, é fácil intuir que os princípios que informaram o instituto nos primórdios da modernidade perderam a força, haja vista as transformações sociais, políticas e econômicas verificadas nos últimos tempos. Basta dizer que o individualismo que é marca da primeira modernidade cedeu lugar a alguma forma de solidarismo na contemporaneidade. Assim também o patrimonialismo abriu espaço para a despatrimonialização ou repersonalização do direito, particularmente do direito privado que não mais se destina à proteção do patrimônio individual, mas à tutela da pessoa em toda sua complexidade e circunstancialidade.[17]

dos custos (COMANDÉ, Giovanni. *L'assicurazione e la responsabilità civile come strumenti e veicoli del principio di precauzione*, p. 62-63).

[17] Sobre a passagem do individualismo para o solidarismo, confira-se: DELMAS-MARTY, Meirelle. *Por um direito comum*, p. 15-16; MESA, Marcelo J. López. *Presupuestos de la responsabilidad civil*, p. 24-25. Sobre a despatrimonialização ou repersonalização do direito, confira-se: PERLINGIERI, Pietro. *Perfis do direito civil:* introdução do direito civil constitucional. Tradução de Maria Cristina de Cicco. 2. ed. Rio de Janeiro: Renovar, 2002, p. 33-34; FACHIN, Luiz Edson. *Teoria crítica do direito civil: à luz do novo Código Civil brasileiro.* 2. ed. rev. e atual. Rio de Janeiro: Renovar, 2003, p. 78; BARROSO, Luís Roberto. *O neoconstitucionalismo e constitucionalização do direito*: o triunfo tardio do direito constitucional no Brasil. Disponível em: <http://www.luisrobertobarroso.com.br/wp-content/themes/LRB/pdf/neoconstitucionalismo_e_constitucionalizacao_do_direito_pt.pdf>. Acesso em: 12 mar. 2019.

Com força nisso, é possível perquirir sobre quais princípios regem a teoria geral da responsabilidade civil, nessa sua terceira fase de desenvolvimento, em que se organiza sob a rubrica de um direito de danos.

3. PRINCÍPIOS QUE ORIENTAM A TEORIA GERAL DO DIREITO DE DANOS

A teoria geral do direito de danos que se delineia na contemporaneidade tem como fundamentos a centralidade do dano como elemento desencadeador dos deveres de responsabilidade e o protagonismo da vítima e seu direito à precaução e à reparação. No que se refere aos danos decorrentes das atividades de risco, o direito de danos pressupõe que [1] as atividades devem ser desempenhadas de modo sustentável, que [2] a vítima não tem obrigação de suportar os danos decorrentes das atividades alheias e que [3] os encargos da precaução e da reparação dos danos devem ser diluídos na sociedade.

Alguns princípios informam a teoria geral do direito de danos, podendo-se destacar os seguintes: princípio de responsabilidade, princípio de solidariedade social e da igualdade frente aos encargos públicos, princípio *favor victimae* ou *pro damnato,* princípio da prevenção/precaução e princípio da justa reparação.

3.1. PRINCÍPIO DE RESPONSABILIDADE

O princípio de responsabilidade tem fundamentação ética, de contornos filosóficos, visto que se refere ao modo de ser e de agir das pessoas, das comunidades e da sociedade. Há diversas abordagens acerca da questão ética, mas uma das mais relevantes é aquela em que o *ethus* significa o modo de ser e de agir da pessoa ou da coletividade. Por conseguinte, a ética possui dupla funcionalidade: impõe ao sujeito a observância de deveres em relação ao outro e determina o modo de ser das pessoas e da sociedade.[18]

[18] Segundo Eduardo Bittar, o termo "ética" tem raízes etimológicas no *éthos* grego, que no singular significa hábito ou comportamento decorrente da natureza, das convenções sociais ou da educação. O plural, *éthe,* significa o conjunto dos hábitos e comportamentos dos grupos ou coletividades, podendo corresponder aos costumes. Disso resulta que o *éthos* não diz respeito à ação isolada do indivíduo, mas ao seu comportamento habitual, enquanto o *éthe* envolve o comportamento habitual da comunidade, que pode ser traduzido por costume. O *éthos* e o *éthe,* então, são o modo constante de ser, que ordinariamente se apresenta como adequado para o sujeito e para o Outro (BITTAR, Eduardo Carlos Bianca. *Curso de ética jurídica:* ética

A responsabilidade está presente em todo o direito, dado que este constitui uma das dimensões do agir humano e, portanto, um dos campos da ética.[19] De fato, o direito objetivo se constitui de uma bilateralidade atributiva, no sentido de que atribui direitos subjetivos a uns ao tempo em que atribui deveres e obrigações a outros. Desse modo, ao direito subjetivo de alguém corresponde o dever ou a obrigação de outrem. A responsabilidade reside nessa parte da bilateralidade atributiva que corresponde aos deveres e obrigações atribuídas a alguém de satisfazer o direito subjetivo de outrem.[20]

Em reforço a esse argumento, merece ser lembrada a teoria dualista da *obligatio,* desenvolvida por Aloys Ritter von Brinz (1820-1887) e Ernst Immanuel Bekker (1827-1916), que decompõe o vínculo obrigacional em dois elementos: a dívida (Schuld) e a responsabilidade (Haftung). De acordo com essa teoria, a responsabilidade estaria contida no vínculo que submete o ofensor, ou um terceiro em seu lugar, à vingança privada do ofendido.[21]

Não bastasse, o direito contemporâneo, particularmente o direito civil, é informado pelo princípio da eticidade, que consiste na observância de valores éticos caros à vida em sociedade. Vale dizer que a responsabilidade não se resume à satisfação do direito subjetivo da outra parte na relação

geral e profissional. 6. ed. São Paulo: Saraiva, 2009, p. 6-7). Esse entendimento se harmoniza com o pensamento de Aristóteles, para quem a virtude é uma prática que se adquire pelo hábito (ARISTÓTELES. *Ética a Nicômaco.* Tradução de Pietro Nassetti. São Paulo: Martin Claret, 2003. Livro II, 1, 1103a-15 a 1103b-25).

19 Miguel Reale explica que há cinco modalidades de conduta ética: religiosa, afetiva, moral, costumeira e jurídica, além das condutas econômica e política que dizem respeito às relações com a riqueza e com o poder (REALE, Miguel. *Filosofia do direito.* 19. ed. São Paulo: Saraiva, 2002, p. 394-406).

20 REALE, Miguel. *Filosofia do direito,* p. 384-386; REALE, Miguel. *Lições preliminares de direito.* 8. ed. rev. São Paulo: Saraiva, 1981, p. 27-29. Também Inocêncio Galvão explica que o termo "obrigação" pode ser empregado para designar a posição jurídica daquele que ocupa a face passiva da relação jurídica, bem como para designar a relação jurídica como um todo (GALVÃO, Inocêncio Telles. *Direito das obrigações.* 7. ed. Coimbra: Ed. Coimbra, 2014. p. 11). Em igual sentido, confira-se DÍEZ-PICAZO, Luis e GULLÓN, Antonio. *Instituciones de derecho civil,* vol. I, p. 469-470.

21 A esse respeito, confira-se: DÍEZ-PICAZO, Luis e GULLÓN, Antonio. *Instituciones de derecho civil,* vol. I, p. 469-470. No Brasil, confira-se: ALVES, José Carlos Moreira. *Direito romano,* v. II. 3. ed. Rio de Janeiro: Forense, 1980, p. 5-7; SIMÃO, José Fernando, *A teoria dualista do vínculo obrigacional e sua aplicação ao direito civil brasileiro.* Revista Jurídica ESMP-SP, v. 3, p. 165-181, 2013.

jurídica, mas deve ter em conta a denominada ecologia da ação, ou seja, as repercussões que a conduta produz sobre as demais pessoas, a sociedade, o meio ambiente etc.[22]

Portanto, a responsabilidade corresponde à dimensão ética do direito que diz respeito à observância das normas de conduta que se dirigem necessariamente ao outro. Diante de danos efetivos ou potenciais, a vítima tem direito subjetivo às medidas de prevenção/precaução e à reparação, ao qual correspondem deveres e obrigações atribuíveis a um responsável. Por essa razão, a responsabilidade constitui um dos fundamentos do direito de danos que, em última análise, cuida da imposição de deveres e obrigações relacionados com a ocorrência de danos efetivos ou potenciais.

Todavia, a questão da responsabilidade perpassa o fenômeno da modernização do mundo, com a passagem do individualismo para o solidarismo. O direito moderno, em linha com o pensamento dominante na primeira modernidade, volta-se à proteção do indivíduo e seu patrimônio (individualismo e patrimonialismo), de sorte que a responsabilidade civil se estabelece nas relações jurídicas intersubjetivas, entre o causador e a vítima. Nesse contexto, o direito se orienta pela ética do dever, de matiz kantiano, baseada na autonomia individual e na capacidade de autodeterminação dos indivíduos.[23]

Sob a égide da ética do dever, a responsabilidade é uma questão de escolha racional pautada no conceito kantiano de *boa vontade*, que é transcendental e é boa em si mesma, *a priori*.[24] Ademais, a responsabilidade assume um viés antropocêntrico, pois se estabelece sempre e necessariamente entre dois indivíduos humanos, com exclusão de qualquer outro. Nesse contexto, a responsabilidade civil se mostra excludente, vez que em

[22] Sobre a diretriz principiológica que rege o direito privado, confira-se REALE, Miguel. *Visão geral do projeto de Código Civil.* Disponível em: <www.miguelreale.com.br>. Acesso em: 12 mar. 2019. Sobre a ecologia da ação, confira-se: MORIN, Edgar. *Os sete saberes necessários à educação do futuro*, p. 79.

[23] A ética do dever é antropocêntrica, pois se baseia na supremacia do ser humano sobre todas as coisas e sobre todas as espécies. A dignidade humana tem fundamento na capacidade racional do homem. Por ser racional, o homem é superior a todas as coisas e não pode jamais ser tomado como meio, mas sempre como um fim em si mesmo (KANT, Immanuel. *Fundamentação da metafísica dos costumes.* Tradução de Leopoldo Holzbach. São Paulo: Martin Claret, 2005. p. 29 e 59).

[24] KANT, Immanuel. *Crítica da razão pura.* Tradução de Valério Rohden e Udo Bardur Moosburger. São Paulo: Nova Cultural, 1999. p. 23.

princípio o indivíduo deve suportar eventuais danos que se abaterem sobre seus bens, segundo a máxima *res perit domino,* salvo se conseguir demonstrar que os danos advieram de negligência, imprudência ou imperícia de outro indivíduo. Em contrapartida, o causador só responde estritamente pelos decorrentes de sua conduta culposa.[25]

Na contemporaneidade, observa-se uma ampliação do senso de responsabilidade, que não mais se estabelece exclusivamente entre indivíduos autônomos, mas envolve grandezas não humanas, como a natureza, os animais, o meio ambiente, o planeta; e coletivas, como a comunidade, a coletividade, a sociedade.[26] Ademais, a responsabilidade não tem sua origem na *boa vontade* transcendental nem no senso de dever individual, mas sim na vulnerabilidade do Outro.[27] Sob o prisma da ética da outridade, a responsabilidade do sujeito é despertada em razão da vulnerabilidade do Outro. E aqui há dois conceitos que merecem esclarecimento: o Outro, que não é alguém determinado, mas dimensão de outridade que corresponde a tudo que não é o próprio sujeito; a vulnerabilidade, que é inerente ao Outro e, portanto, existe como possibilidade de que o Outro venha a sofrer um dano. Vale dizer que a simples presença do Outro torna o sujeito responsável por algo que lhe possa acontecer. E mais: a responsabilidade do sujeito é indeclinável e inalienável, visto que tem que dar uma

[25] Mesa, Marcelo J. López. *Presupuestos de la responsabilidad civil,* p. 24-30; Díez-Picazo, Luis e Gullón, Antonio. *Instituciones de derecho civil,* vol. I, p. 821; Pereira, Caio Mário da Silva. *Responsabilidade civil,* p. 35.

[26] Na ética da outridade, de Emmanuel Levinas, o Outro é dimensão de outridade, que não pode ser reduzida a um Mesmo, formulação essa que possibilita a ampliação da noção de Outro também no campo da responsabilidade civil, de modo a envolver não somente as outras pessoas, mas também dimensões não humanas e coletivas, como a natureza, os animais, o meio ambiente e a coletividade (Bernardes, Cláudio Teles de Toledo. *A ética da alteridade em Emmanuel Levinas – uma contribuição atual ao discurso da moral cristã. Revista de Cultura Teológica,* v. 20, n. 78, p. 83-101, abr./jun. 2012, p. 86-87; Levinas, Emmanuel. *Totalité et infini:* essai sur l'extériorité. Livre de Poche, 4120, Paris: Livrairie Générale Française, 2014. p. 24-27 e 211-212).

[27] Emmanuel Levinas escreve que "Não matarás" é a primeira palavra do rosto. Confira-se: «Le 'Tu ne tueras point' est la première parole du visage. Or c'est un ordre. Il y a dans l'apparition du visage un commandement, comme se un maître me parlait. Pourtant, en même temps, le visage d'autrui est dénué; c'est le pauvre pour lequel je peux tout et à qui je dois tout. Et moi, qui que je sois, mais en tant que 'première personne', je suis celui qui se trouve des ressources pour répondre à l'apple » (Levinas, Emmanuel. *Éthique et infini,* p. 83).

resposta diante da vulnerabilidade do Outro, mesmo porque sua omissão também conta como resposta.[28]

Sem muito esforço pode-se compreender que a responsabilidade é constitutiva da personalidade, pois só os entes personalizados são capazes de responder; e da identidade, visto que a qualidade da resposta molda a personalidade e identifica o sujeito. Com base nessa formulação, é possível dizer que a maneira como tratamos o outro determina o que somos, enquanto pessoas e enquanto sociedade.[29]

Essas considerações repercutem sobre a teoria da responsabilidade civil e conferem justificação ética a uma teoria geral do direito de danos. Em primeiro lugar, a inversão lógica do princípio de responsabilidade, de modo a conceber que a responsabilidade tem sua origem na vulnerabilidade do Outro, justifica a proeminência da posição da vítima no plano da responsabilidade civil. Ademais, a noção de que a responsabilidade existe desde logo, ante a possibilidade do Outro vir a sofrer um dano, justifica a incidência dos deveres de prevenção e de precaução no âmbito da responsabilidade civil. Por fim, a compreensão de que o Outro é dimensão de outridade amplia o alcance da responsabilidade civil, que se estende sobre grandezas não humanas como os animais, a natureza, o meio ambiente; e coletivas, como a coletividade e a sociedade como um todo.[30]

[28] A questão do Outro e sua vulnerabilidade intrínseca constitui o núcleo do pensamento de Emmanuel Levinas e, em razão de sua complexidade, não pode ser aprofundada nos limites do presente estudo. Um resumo mais amplo sobre o pensamento de Emmanuel Levinas pode ser encontrado em BERNARDES, Cláudio Teles de Toledo. *A ética da alteridade em Emmanuel Levinas – uma contribuição atual ao discurso da moral cristã.* Revista de Cultura Teológica, v. 20, n. 78, p. 83-101, abr./jun. 2012. Ver também: SANTOS, Romualdo Baptista dos. *Responsabilidade civil por dano enorme.* Curitiba: Juruá Editora; Porto: Juruá Editorial, 2018, p. 52-55.

[29] Frase forjada com base na ética da outridade, de Emmanuel Levinas (BERNARDES, Cláudio Teles de Toledo. A ética da alteridade em Emmanuel Levinas – uma contribuição atual ao discurso da moral cristã, p. 86-87; RIPANTI, Graziano. *Introdução: Emmanuel Levinas e o infinito diálogo.* In: LEVINAS, Emmanuel. *Violência do rosto.* Tradução de Fernando Soares Moreira. São Paulo: Loyola, 2014. p. 9; LEVINAS, Emmanuel. *Totalité et infini:* essai sur l'extériorité, p. 24-27 e 211-212.

[30] Tese apresentada no Congresso Internacional de Direito Civil – Oitavo Centenário da Universidade de Salamanca, em outubro/2018 e publicada no respectivo livro de ponências: SANTOS, Romualdo Baptista dos. *A dimensão do Outro na configuração da responsabilidade civil.* In: LLAMAS POMBO, Eugenio. *Congreso internacional de derecho civil octavo centenário de la Universidad de Salamanca: libro de ponencias.* Valência: Tirant lo Blanch, Salamanca: Universidad de Salamanca, 2018, p. 435-448.

Como visto, o princípio de responsabilidade constitui um dos fundamentos da teoria geral do direito de danos, mas seu conteúdo evoluiu ao longo da modernidade, com a passagem do individualismo moderno para o solidarismo contemporâneo. O direito de danos se funda na noção de que alguém deve responder pelos danos que se abatem sobre a pessoa e os bens da vítima, mas o alcance e os contornos da responsabilidade sofreram modificação com a passagem da ética do dever para a ética da outridade.

3.2. PRINCÍPIO *PRO DAMNATO* OU *FAVOR VICTIMAE*

O princípio *pro damnato* ou *favor victimae* reflete a influencia da ética da outridade sobre a teoria geral do direito de danos. Trata-se de uma mudança de perspectiva no âmbito da teoria geral da responsabilidade civil, que consiste em olhar para o fenômeno do dano pelo prisma da vítima e não do agente causador. Constitui o ponto de inflexão que indica a passagem da responsabilidade civil individualista e mais voltada à punição da conduta culposa; para o direito de danos, de caráter solidarista e mais voltado para os direitos da vítima.

Um olhar apressado sobre o tema poderia levar o observador a pensar que responsabilidade civil e direito de danos são apenas nomenclaturas distintas para o mesmo objeto. Não se pode perder de vista, porém, que o direito é marcado por um elemento valorativo que atribui sentido à normatividade.[31] Por isso, faz muita diferença o sentido que se atribui aos institutos jurídicos, principalmente em seu momento de interpretação e de aplicação.[32] Ademais, esses aspectos axiológicos são fortemente influenciados por fatores sociais e pelo pensamento filosófico, os quais se modificam incessantemente no curso do tempo.

Por essa razão, afirma-se que a responsabilidade civil baseada na culpa atendia mais ao individualismo que marcou a primeira modernidade, sob a égide de uma ética do dever, individualista, em que cada indivíduo res-

[31] REALE, Miguel. *Filosofia do direito*, p. 497-507. REALE, Miguel. *Teoria tridimensional do direito*, 5ª. ed. São Paulo: Saraiva, 1994, p. 57.

[32] Arturo Solarte explica que o princípio *favor victimae* é um princípio tendencial que constitui forte pauta hermenêutica para juízes e tribunais, no sentido de favorecer a situação da vítima e assegurar a obtenção de uma indenização (RODRIGUEZ, Arturo Solarte. *El principio favor victimae*. In: LLAMAS POMBO, Eugenio (coord.). *Congreso internacional de derecho civil octavo centenário de la Universidad de Salamanca: libro de ponencias*. Valência: Tirant lo Blanch, Salamanca: Universidad de Salamanca, 2018, p. 722-725).

ponderia pelos danos decorrentes de sua conduta culposa, com exclusão de qualquer outro. Nos dias atuais, a responsabilidade é informada por uma ética da outridade, levinassiana, marcada muito mais pela solidariedade do que pela individualidade. Observado o evento danoso pelo prisma da vítima, temos uma mudança de perspectiva: se antes dizíamos que o indivíduo está obrigado a reparar os danos decorrentes de sua conduta, hoje dizemos que a vítima não se encontra obrigada a suportar o dano decorrente da conduta nem da atividade alheia.[33]

Não sem razão, Llamas Pombo observa uma nova mudança no sistema de responsabilidade civil a partir da segunda metade do século XX, pela qual o protagonista deixa de ser o causador do dano e passa a ser a vítima do dano. Pouco importa quem ou porque se causou o dano, mas sim o direito da vítima de ser indenizada.[34] O princípio *pro damnato* ou *favor victimae* consiste no deslocamento do centro de gravidade do sistema de responsabilidade civil: do dever do causador para o direito da vítima à reparação. Com isso, o direito de danos traduz a ideia de que por princípio a vítima tem direito aos deveres de responsabilidade: prevenção/precaução dos danos potenciais e reparação dos danos efetivos; restando em segundo plano o

[33] Segundo Andrés Mariño Lopez, "Las personas tienen derecho a no ser dañadas y el sistema jurídico debe proteger las personas de padecer daños antes que sancionar a un culpable" (MARIÑO LOPEZ, Andrés. *La función preventiva del Derecho de Daños, el princípio de precaución y la protección de la salud humana.* In: LLAMAS POMBO, Eugênio (coord.). *Congreso internacional de derecho civil octavo centenário de la Universidad de Salamanca: libro de ponencias.* Valência: Tirant lo Blanch, Salamanca: Universidad de Salamanca, 2018, p. 643-657).

[34] "En efecto, suelo afirmar, plásticamente, que en la segunda mitad del siglo XX hemos asistido a un cambio de protagonista dentro del teatro de la responsabilidad civil: el «primer actor» ya no es (como en el art. 1.902 del Código Civil) «el que causa daño a otro», ni tampoco (como en el art. 1.101) «los que incurrieran en dolo, negligencia o morosidad...», sino precisamente ese «otro» que es víctima de un daño extracontractual o contractual, de manera que importa poco por quién o por qué motivo se va a afrontar la indemnización de ese daño, con tal de que dicha reparación se produzca" (LLAMAS POMBO, Eugenio. *Reflexiones sobre Derecho de Danos: casos y opiniones*, p. 44). Também Ricardo Lorenzetti sentencia que: "El derecho mira a la víctima, y ya no le interesa castigar, sino reparar; y es preciso atender a la reparación del daño "injustamente sufrido", antes que al 'injustamente causado'. ¿Que ha cambiado con respecto al enfoque anterior? (...) En este enfoque hay un principio 'favor victimae' que tiende a aliviar su carga. La sola existencia de daño dispara una flecha contra una categoria de sujetos y cada uno de ellos debe decir 'yo no fui' para eximirse; ha cambiado el efecto inercial (...) Ahora importa la reparación antes que la sanción de autores que se conocen poco o bien son anónimos o tienen una culpa disminuida (LORENZETTI, Ricardo Luis. *Reflexiones acerca de la responsabilidad civil en el siglo XXI*, p. 7).

problema de quem deve suportar o encargo: o próprio causador, alguém em seu lugar ou a coletividade.[35]

Por força do princípio *pro damnato* ou *favor vitimae*, a ilicitude da conduta ou da atividade que figura como causa do dano fica em segundo plano, mesmo porque o dano muitas vezes decorre de atividade ou de conduta absolutamente lícita.[36] Em sua compreensão mais atual, o dano possui uma ilicitude intrínseca, ou seja, é ilícito em si mesmo, uma vez que a vítima não está obrigada a suportá-lo, seja por força de lei ou em virtude de contrato.[37] Eis a razão pela qual o dano constitui o centro de gravidade sobre o qual se assenta a teoria geral do direito de danos. Por princípio, a vítima tem direito à prevenção/precaução e à reparação porque não está obrigada a suportar o dano, restando em segundo plano a questão de a quem cabe os deveres de responsabilidade.[38]

Em atenção ao princípio *pro damnato* ou *favor victimae*, a cláusula geral de responsabilidade civil constante de todas as codificações ocidentais deveria ser atualizada. Onde consta *"Todo aquele que causa um dano fica obrigado a indenizar"* deveria constar que *"Todo aquele que sofre um dano tem direito à reparação"*. Um passo além, poderíamos acrescentar que *"Todo aquele que se encontra na iminência de sofrer um dano tem direito de exigir que o responsável adote medidas de prevenção e precaução"*.[39] O princípio *pro damnato* ou *favor*

[35] Segundo López Mesa, o problema central da responsabilidade civil na atualidade é a distribuição dos custos e dos riscos dos comportamentos das pessoas na vida em sociedade, a saber se a vítima deve se resignar diante dos danos sofridos ou se tem a opção de transferi-los para terceiros (Mesa, Marcelo J. López. *Presupuestos de la responsabilidad civil*, p. 22-27). Também Guido Alpa analisa o mesmo fenômeno sob o prisma da análise econômica do direito (Alpa, Guido. *Trattato di diritto civile*, v. IV: La responsabilità civile, Milano: Giuffrè, 1999, p. 145-163). No plano da ciência econômica, Ronald Coase enfrenta o problema do custo social das atividades (Coase, Ronald. *O problema do custo social*. Tradução por Francisco Kümmel F. Alves e Renato Vieira Caovilla. In: The Latin American and Caribbean Journal of Legal Studies. Volume 3, Issue 1 2008 Article 9. Disponível em: https://services.bepress.com/lacjls/vol3/iss1/art9/. Visualizado em: 22/12/2019).

[36] Llamas Pombo, Eugenio. *Reflexiones sobre Derecho de Danos: casos y opiniones*, p. 45.

[37] Sobre a ilicitude intrínseca do dano, confira: Santos, Romualdo Baptista dos. *Responsabilidade civil por dano enorme*, p. 150-152.

[38] Segundo Díez-Picazo, *"Además, el principio social es hoy el otro: reparar todos aquellos perjuicios en que no se vea razón clara para que la víctima los suporte por sí sola"* (Díez-Picazo, Luis e Gullón, Antonio. *Instituciones de derecho civil*, vol. I, p. 823).

[39] É o que defende Llamas Pombo: *"El protagonista es ahora la víctima, de manera que la formulación de los preceptos nucleares de nuestro sistema de responsabilidad civil podría ser muy distinta, para*

victimae está em linha com o princípio *favor debilis*, de caráter mais amplo e de observância obrigatória nas relações trabalhistas e consumeiristas, que tem em conta a presunção de vulnerabilidade de uma das partes na relação jurídica.[40] Esses dois princípios, *pro damnato* ou *favor victimae* e *favor debilis*, contrapõem-se ao princípio *favor debitoris*, que visa proteger a posição do devedor no processo de execução da dívida (CPC/1973, art. 620; CPC/2015, art. 805, 829, § 2º, e 847). A aplicação do princípio *favor debitoris* ao direito de danos levaria à ideia de exclusão de responsabilidade, sempre que possível, para proteger a posição do causador do dano. Ao revés, o princípio *favor victimae* ou *pro damnato* visa reforçar o direito da vítima à reparação do dano.[41]

Por fim, cumpre anotar a advertência de Arturo Solarte de que a aplicação desmesurada do princípio *favor victimae* ou *pro damnato* poderia levar ao desprezo dos pressupostos substanciais da responsabilidade civil: o dano, a imputação causal e a atribuição subjetiva ou objetiva. A advertência é válida porque o sentido atribuído por esse princípio de privilegiar a posição da vítima, se levado ao extremo, poderia conduzir a grandes distorções e até mesmo ao esvaziamento do sistema do direito de danos.[42]

señalar que "todo aquel que sufre un daño antijurídico tiene derecho a ser indemnizado", o algo parecido" (LLAMAS POMBO, Eugenio. *Prevención y reparación, las dos caras del derecho de daños*. In: MORENO MARTÍNEZ, Juan Antonio (coord.). La responsabilidad civil y su problemática actual. Madrid: Dykinson, 2007, p. 4).

[40] Não será demasiado esclarecer que nesse caso se trata de vulnerabilidade específica, que não se confunde com a vulnerabilidade genérica presente na teoria da responsabilidade. A vulnerabilidade específica diz respeito à posição de fragilidade da pessoa ou de determinados grupos sociais em relação à outra parte nas relações jurídicas (BARBOZA, Heloísa Helena. *Vulnerabilidade e cuidado: aspectos jurídicos*. In: PEREIRA, Tânia da Silva; OLIVEIRA, Guilherme de (coords.). *Cuidado e vulnerabilidade*. São Paulo: Atlas, 2009. p. 106-118; MARQUES, Claudia Lima. *Introdução ao direito do consumidor*. In: BENJAMIN, Antônio Herman; MARQUES, Claudia Lima; BESSA, Leonardo Roscoe (Coord.). *Manual de direito do consumidor*. 6. ed. São Paulo: RT, 2013. p. 49-50; TARTUCE, Fernanda. *Igualdade e vulnerabilidade no processo civil*. Rio de Janeiro: Forense, 2012. p. 189-210). A vulnerabilidade genérica, presente na responsabilidade civil, significa a possibilidade genérica de o Outro vir a sofrer um dano (LEVINAS, Emmanuel. *Totalité et infini*, p. 24-27 e 211-215; LEVINAS, Emmanuel. *Violência do rosto*, p. 28-29; BERNARDES, Cláudio Teles de Toledo. A ética da alteridade em Emmanuel Levinas, p. 86-87).

[41] LLAMAS POMBO, Eugenio. *Reflexiones sobre Derecho de Danos: casos y opiniones*, p. 45.

[42] RODRIGUEZ, Arturo Solarte. *El princípio favor victimae*, p. 735.

3.3. PRINCÍPIO DE SOLIDARIEDADE SOCIAL E IGUALDADE FRENTE AOS ENCARGOS PÚBLICOS

A solidariedade social significa que, enquanto membro de uma comunidade, toda pessoa deve colaborar para o bem comum, mas também faz jus a um mínimo de proteção necessária à sua sobrevivência e manutenção em face das adversidades.[43] Na contemporaneidade, a solidariedade social desponta como um princípio jurídico, seja porque se encontra inscrito em inúmeras normas jurídicas, seja porque é pressuposto da convivência em sociedade e do Estado Democrático de Direito.[44] Ademais, a solidariedade social se manifesta sob a forma de solidarismo, em diversos institutos jurídicos, como é o caso do sistema previdenciário (CF, art. 40) e dos mecanismos de proteção de vulnerabilidades específicas, como é o caso das crianças e adolescentes, das pessoas com deficiência, dos idosos etc. No plano do direito privado, o princípio de solidariedade implica transigir quanto à autonomia privada em benefício do bem-estar coletivo.[45]

A incidência do princípio da solidariedade social sobre o direito de danos surge da conjugação do princípio de responsabilidade com o princípio *favor victimae*. É dizer que, por princípio, a vítima tem direito aos deve-

[43] Vem da obra de Durkheim a ideia de que o sentimento de solidariedade fundamenta a vida em sociedade, dada a natureza gregária dos seres humanos (https://conceitos.com/solidariedade-social/, visualizado em 12/03/2019). Ver também DURKHEIM, Émile. *Da divisão do trabalho social.* Tradução: Eduardo Brandão. 2. Ed. São Paulo: Martins Fontes, 1999, p. 20/37. Em sentido semelhante, FACHIN, Luiz Edson. *Estatuto jurídico do patrimônio mínimo.* 2ª ed. Rio de Janeiro: Renovar, 2006, p. 47.

[44] A Constituição Federal brasileira de 1988 dispõe em seu preâmbulo sobre o Estado Democrático de Direito fundado, entre outros, nos "valores supremos de uma sociedade fraterna, pluralista e sem preconceitos, fundada na harmonia social". Em seguida, no art. 3º, o constituinte diz que são objetivos da República, entre outros, "construir uma sociedade livre, justa e solidária".

[45] "Adicionalmente, también hay que someter la clásica identificación entre Derecho civil y Derecho Privado al principio de solidaridad, del que habló RODOTÀ, y que obliga a ceder autonomía privada para obtener bienestar colectivo". (...) El civilista moderno no pierde de vista el peso que adquieren los fenómenos colectivos, y la idea social que sustituye unas veces, y se superpone otras, a la idea individual. Frente a un ordenamiento de actividades netamente individuales, el Derecho civil actual es el ordenamiento de las "formas asociativas", de la "cooperación humana", que caracterizan a toda la actividad económica moderna. Las ideas de solidaridad social y protección de los intereses generales y colectivos ya no son ajenas al Derecho civil, y presiden, por imperativo del Estado social y democrático de Derecho, las viejas y las nuevas instituciones que lo Integran". (LLAMAS POMBO, Eugenio. *Prevención y reparación, las dos caras del derecho de daños*, p. 6/7).

res de responsabilidade: prevenção/reparação e reparação, os quais nem sempre são suportados diretamente por outro indivíduo, o causador direto do dano, mas distribuídos pela sociedade mediante mecanismos de socialização.[46] A igualdade frente aos encargos públicos é corolário da solidariedade social, pois considera a pessoa em sua circunstancialidade, isto é, em suas relações com as demais pessoas e com o mundo, bem como que as atividades públicas e privadas são necessárias ao modo de vida na sociedade contemporânea. Se todos são beneficiários das atividades desempenhadas pelo poder público e pelas empresas, todos devem suportar igualmente as consequências negativas decorrentes dessas atividades, mediante algum dos mecanismos de socialização dos danos: estatização, mutualização ou securitização.[47]

Simultaneamente, observa-se uma mudança na compreensão da natureza e do significado dos danos. Se, à luz da teoria subjetiva, os danos eram considerados como maldades praticadas por um indivíduo contra outro, mediante negligência, imprudência ou imperícia, a teoria objetiva os compreende como acidentes que decorrem das atividades desempenhadas pelas empresas e pelo poder público.[48] O surgimento das formas de socialização dos danos é manifestação do princípio da solidariedade social e da igualdade frente aos encargos públicos, que coincide com a passagem do individualismo que marcou a primeira fase da modernidade para o solidarismo que caracteriza a fase atual. Vale dizer que o dano, principalmente o denominado dano-acidente ou dano-atividade, é um fenômeno social relacionado com o modo de vida nas sociedades contemporâneas, de modo que os encargos relacionados com a prevenção/precaução e reparação devem ser suportados pela sociedade e não exclusivamente pela vítima.[49]

[46] Llamas Pombo adverte que estes mecanismos de solidariedade e socialização não se harmonizam com a ideia de indemnização que é própria da responsabilidade civil (LLAMAS POMBO, Eugenio. *Reflexiones sobre Derecho de Daños: casos y opiniones*, p. 114-115).

[47] Marcelo Dias Varella (coord.), *Responsabilidade e sociedade do risco/Relatório público considerações gerais*, p. 7 e 58.

[48] Mireille Delmas-Marty sintetiza que o dano cede lugar ao acidente (Mireille Delmas-Marty, *Por um direito comum*, p. 15-16).

[49] DELMAS-MARTY, Mireille. *Por um direito comum*, p. 15-16; ROGER-LACAN, Cyril. *Specialité, gravité et anormalité das la responsabilité sans faute : conclusions sur Conseil d'État*, p. 333/338.

3.4. PRINCÍPIO DA PREVENÇÃO/PRECAUÇÃO

A prevenção e a precaução estão relacionadas à capacidade de prever a ocorrência de fatos e se antecipar para interferir no resultado, alterando-o ou eliminando-o. Esta capacidade é presente em todos os seres vivos, em razão do instinto de sobrevivência, mas é mais elaborada nos seres humanos, em virtude da complexidade de seu organismo.[50] Trata-se de uma capacidade de perceber o perigo, de realizar causalidades abstratas e adotar medidas para evitar os resultados indesejáveis.

A prevenção e a precaução são indissociáveis da ideia de risco, pois de nada adiantaria perceber o perigo de dano se não fosse para adotar medidas para evitar sua ocorrência. No entanto, prevenção e precaução são conceitos análogos, mas não são sinônimos. A prevenção pressupõe a existência de perigo concreto de dano, ao passo que a precaução tem lugar em caso de incerteza sobre a probabilidade de dano (incerteza probabilizada).[51] A precaução alcançou *statu* de princípio no âmbito do direito ambiental, a partir da Conferência Internacional sobre o Meio-Ambiente, realizada no Rio de janeiro em 1992, a ECO-92, na qual foi editada Declaração do Rio de Janeiro, cujo Princípio 15 dispõe que: com o fim de proteger o meio ambiente, o princípio da precaução deverá ser amplamente observado pelos Estados, de acordo com suas capacidades. Quando houver ameaça de danos graves ou irreversíveis, a ausência de certeza científica absoluta não será utilizada como razão para o adiamento de medidas economicamente viáveis para prevenir a degradação ambiental.

Portanto, a incerteza probabilizada impõe a adoção de medidas de precaução para evitar a ocorrência do dano, bem como para assegurar sua reparação, ainda que não haja certeza cientifica sobre sua ocorrência. Toda-

[50] TELLES JÚNIOR, Goffredo. Direito quântico: ensaio sobre o fundamento da ordem jurídica. 8. ed. rev. São Paulo: Juarez de Oliveira, 2006, p. 272 e 286.

[51] Giovanni Comandé explica que o princípio da precaução se aplica mesmo que os dados científicos não sejam concludentes sobre a probabilidade de concretização dos danos: "Il principio si applica unicamente in un ipotesi di rischio potenziale, anche se questo rischio non può essere interamente dimostrato, o la sua portata quantificata o i suoi effetti determinati per l'insuficienza o il carattere non concludente dei dati scientifici" (COMANDÉ, Giovanni. *L'assicurazione e la responsabilità civile come strumenti e veicoli del principio di precauzione*, p. 31). Confira-se, no mesmo sentido: BESTANI, Adriana. *Principio de precaución*. Buenos Aires: Astrea, 2012, p. 19-20; LOPEZ, Teresa Ancona. *Princípio da precaução e evolução da responsabilidade civil*. São Paulo: Quartier Latin, 2010, p. 101; VARELLA, Marcelo Dias (Coord.). *Responsabilidade e sociedade do risco/Relatório público considerações gerais*, p. 134.

via, a atuação do princípio da precaução não deve restar adstrita aos danos ambientais, mas se estende aos danos sociais de grandes proporções, relacionados com as atividades inerentes ao modo de vida nas sociedades contemporâneas, o dano enorme.[52]

O princípio da precaução é uma novidade na teoria geral da responsabilidade civil, cuja função tradicional é a de reparar os danos causados. A responsabilidade civil subjetiva é retrospectiva ou *post factum*, visto que incide exclusivamente sobre danos ocorridos no passado. Também a responsabilidade civil objetiva, em sua primeira formulação, assumiu a mesma estrutura retrospectiva da teoria da culpa, apenas dispensando a vítima do dever de comprovar a negligência, imprudência ou imperícia do agente causador. A responsabilidade civil por risco da atividade, presente nos dias atuais, tem como substrato fático tanto os danos efetivos, já ocorridos no passado, quanto os danos potenciais, que se desenham como possibilidade de ocorrerem no futuro. Neste caso, a responsabilidade existe desde o momento em que a atividade é colocada em curso e contempla dois tipos de deveres: de prevenção e de precaução quanto aos danos potenciais; de reparação quanto aos danos efetivos.

Llamas Pombo ressalta que a função primordial da responsabilidade civil é a reparação dos danos causados. Todavia, a função inibitória seria a "nova face" do moderno direito de danos. Um dos problemas suscitados é que os sistemas jurídicos ocidentais não contemplam uma cláusula geral (formulação genérica, substantiva, não tipificada) de tutela inibitória dos

[52] Jean-Pierre Desideri entende que a gravidade e a irreversibilidade do dano justificam a atuação do princípio da precaução: "Elle [la précaution] a été d'abord regardée comme un mode d'action opératoire plutôt que comme une règle de droit, pour inspirer l'adoption de mesures effectives et proportionnées visant à prévenir un risque de dommages graves et irrefersibles en l'absence de certitudes" (DESIDERI, Jean-Pierre. *La précaution en droit privé.* Revue Française de Droit Administratif, Paris: Dalloz, p. 238-242, mar./abr. 2012, p. 238). Também Adriana Bressani defende que a precaução é um princípio que se espraia para quase todos os campos do direito: "Este es lo momento del principio de precaución. Un momento que ha llegado para instalarse. Hoy, entiendo, es el tiempo de la cautela, del reforzamiento de las funciones preventivas en casi todas las áreas del derecho" (BESTANI, Adriana. *Principio de precaución,* prefácio). Em sentido semelhante, confira-se: COMANDÉ, Giovanni. *L'assicurazione e la responsabilità civile come strumenti e veicoli del principio di precauzione,* p. 42 e 46. Ver também MARIÑO LOPEZ, Andrés. *La función preventiva del Derecho de Daños, el princípio de precaución y la protección de la salud humana.* In: LLAMAS POMBO, Eugênio (coord.). *Congreso internacional de derecho civil octavo centenário de la Universidad de Salamanca: libro de ponencias.* Valência: Tirant lo Blanch, Salamanca: Universidad de Salamanca, 2018, p. 643-657.

danos ameaçantes. Em geral, esse tipo de tutela é previsto na lei processual, a exemplo do art. 250.1 da Ley de Enjuiciamiento Civil espanhola e do art. 300 a 311 e art. 497 do Código de Processo Civil brasileiro de 2015. Como instituto de natureza processual, a tutela de urgência atende a outros pressupostos – *fumus boni juris* e *periculum in mora* – que visam antes assegurar o resultado útil de um processo judicial. A formulação de uma cláusula geral de tutela inibitória substancial, relacionada aos danos potenciais, deslocaria o instituto para o âmbito do direito de danos, convertendo-se em uma função adicional da responsabilidade civil.[53]

A tutela inibitória substantiva consiste no direito subjetivo da vítima em potencial de requerer ao juiz medidas de precaução a serem adotadas pelo responsável por atividade de risco, com base na noção de causalidade abstrata ou probabilística.[54] Ou seja, a reparação do dano potencial deve se dar *a priori*, antes que se concretize, especialmente em face de danos decorrentes de atividades de risco, em que a responsabilidade existe desde o momento em que a atividade é posta em curso.[55]

É importante ressaltar a natureza movediça, fugidia, do direito de danos, cuja casuística parece estar sempre um passo adiante das formulações teóricas. Ademais, a ciência e a tecnologia modernas, a par de serem fontes de novos danos, são também instrumentos que possibilitam o conhecimento dos danos por antecipação, com elevado grau de certeza. Isso nos põe diante de uma nova realidade, de um novo modo de conhecer e de

[53] Llamas Pombo, Eugenio. *Reflexiones sobre Derecho de Danos: casos y opiniones*, p. 39-40.

[54] Eugenio Facchini Neto se refere a diversas formulações da teoria da causalidade probabilística, as quais procuram evitar que a obscuridade probatória resulte em julgamento desfavorável ao autor (Facchini Neto, Eugenio. *Aumentando a proteção das vítimas de danos: a causalidade probabilística.* In: Llamas Pombo, Eugenio. *Congreso internacional de derecho civil octavo centenário de la Universidad de Salamanca: libro de ponencias.* Valência: Tirant lo Blanch, Salamanca: Universidad de Salamanca, 2018, p. 541-545).

[55] São as palavras de Llamas Pombo: "Admitida la necesidad de un instrumento preventivo de los daños dentro del ordenamiento jurídico privado, y rechazada la bondad del (indirecto y amenzante) mecanismo indemnizatorio para conseguirlo, es preciso establecer un camino que, de manera directa, permita impedir las conductas dañosas y promover los comportamientos minoradores de los efectos del daño. Y esa vía no puede ser otra que la llamada tutela civil inhibitoria aplicada al daño" (Llamas Pombo, Eugenio. *Prevención y reparación, las dos caras del derecho de daños*, p. 23). Ver também: Rosenvald, Nelson. *A responsabilidade civil pelo lucro ilícito: o disgorgment e a indenização restitutória.* Salvador: Juspoduim, 2019. p. 225-233; Venturi, Thaís Goveia Pascoaloto. *Responsabilidade civil preventiva: a proteção contra a violação dos direitos e a tutela inibitória material.* São Paulo: Malheiros, 2014. p. 269-285.

lidar com o mundo, isto é, de uma nova racionalidade, em que os danos são conhecidos por antecipação.[56]

A ideia de risco, inerente às atividades desempenhadas e necessárias à vida moderna, significa que as relações de causa e efeito podem ser percebidas *a priori*, antes mesmo que os danos aconteçam. Não se trata de exercício de futurologia nem de abstração, mas de percepção *a priori* de que determinadas atividades podem causar danos. Diante disso, a racionalidade jurídica não pode se contentar com a reparação de danos causados, devendo atuar também quanto àqueles que, conquanto não causados, se desenham com algum grau de probabilidade, em razão do desempenho de determinadas atividades.[57]

Trata-se, como dito, de um movimento de expansão da responsabilidade civil e do direito de danos, que tem como objeto o tratamento dos danos. Em outros tempos, diante do grau de conhecimento científico e tecnológico disponível, a responsabilidade civil poderia se ocupar satisfatoriamente dos danos causados, em termos de reparação. Hoje, uma vez conhecida a probabilidade de danos relacionados a determinadas atividades, o direito de danos deve ampliar seu espectro de proteção para tratar também dos danos potenciais, em termos de prevenção e de precaução. Essas questões estão entrelaçadas porque a responsabilidade civil é um instituto jurídico moderno, em permanente processo de expansão. A incorporação da função precautória, ao lado da pré-existente função reparatória, parece atender a essa característica dinâmica que é própria da modernidade, que é inerente ao direito de danos.[58]

Como visto, o princípio da precaução se insere no contexto da evolução da teoria geral da responsabilidade civil, nesse momento em que alcança sua terceira fase e se organiza sob a rubrica do direito de danos. Os danos

[56] Não sem razão, Llamas Pombo afirma que se trata de matéria especialmente cambiante e contingente, em constante desenvolvimento, que dificulta alcançar conclusões estáveis e definitivas (LLAMAS POMBO, Eugenio. *Reflexiones sobre Derecho de Danos: casos y opiniones*. Madrid: La Ley, 2010, p. 30).

[57] Llamas Pombo defende a aplicação da teoria da causalidade adequada, devendo o demandante comprovar a vinculação razoável entre a atividade e o dano potencial (LLAMAS POMBO, Eugenio. *Prevención y reparación, las dos caras del derecho de daños*, p. 41).

[58] Tanto isso é fato que Llamas Pombo, inicialmente resistente à incorporação de outras funções à responsabilidade civil, passou a defender a formulação de uma tutela inibitória explícita como parte do Direito de Danos (LLAMAS POMBO, Eugenio. *Reflexiones sobre Derecho de Danos: casos y opiniones*, p. 41).

decorrentes das atividades de risco relacionadas com o modo de vida nas sociedades contemporâneas não podem ser tratados somente pelo prisma da reparação *post factum,* mas demandam um novo tipo de racionalidade jurídica que possa se antecipar à sua ocorrência, seja para evita-los, seja para minimizar seus efeitos. A precaução consiste na adoção de medidas prévias quanto aos danos potenciais, ainda que não haja certeza sobre sua ocorrência (incerteza probabilizada), a fim de evita-los ou de minimizar seus efeitos.

3.5. PRINCÍPIO DA JUSTA REPARAÇÃO

O princípio da justa reparação é a evolução do princípio da reparação integral, presente nas fases anteriores da teoria geral da responsabilidade civil. É frequente na doutrina e na jurisprudência a referência a um suposto princípio da reparação integral, que consistiria no direito subjetivo da vítima de obter reparação completa do dano, com restituição ao *statu quo ante.*[59] Essa ideia tem origem na noção da *restitutio in integrum,* do direito processual romano, decorrente da anulação do processo ou dos atos processuais, com restituição das partes à posição em que se encontravam anteriormente.[60]

Ocorre que o dano é fenômeno que se passa no mundo dos fatos e que sempre deixa um arrasto na esfera de interesses da vítima, que não pode ser totalmente reparado. Enquanto fenômeno que se passa na relação tempo-espaço, o dano é uma experiência que pode ser reparada, mas não pode ser removida da vida da vítima nem do agente causador, visto não ser possível "desacontecer" o acontecido.[61]

[59] SANSEVERINO, Paulo de Tarso Vieira. *Princípio da reparação integral.* São Paulo: Saraiva, 2011, p. 302; CAVALIERI FILHO, Sergio. *Programa de responsabilidade civil.* 11. ed. São Paulo: Atlas, 2014, p. 26; CAVALIERI FILHO, Sergio. *O princípio da reparação integral ("restitutio in integrum") e o seguro de responsabilidade civil.* Disponível em: <http://www.sergiocavalierifilho.com.br/administrativo/artigos/imagens>. Acesso em: 20 jul. 2016.

[60] TUCCI, José Rogério Cruz e. *Breves anotações sobre a "restitutio in integrum" e o processo acusatório romano. Revista Justitia,* São Paulo, 45(122), jul-set. 1983, p. 52/57. Disponível em: <http://www.revistajustitia.com.br/revistas/92c9x5.pdf>. Acesso em: 13 mar. 2019. Confira-se também ALVES, José Carlos Moreira. *Direito romano.* 5. ed. Rio de Janeiro: Forense, 1983. v. I, p. 274-275 e 293-294.

[61] Neste sentido, confiram-se: CALVO COSTA, Carlos Alberto. *Daño resarcible,* p. 51-52; RODRIGUES, Silvio. *Direito civil,* v. 4: responsabilidade civil. 4. ed. São Paulo: Saraiva, 1979, p. 192; FARIAS, Cristiano Chaves de; ROSENVALD, Nelson; BRAGA NETTO, Felipe Peixoto. *Curso de direito civil,* v. 3: responsabilidade civil. 2. ed. São Paulo: Atlas, 2015, p. 22-24; CASILLO, João. *Dano à pessoa e sua indenização.* São Paulo: Revista dos Tribunais, 1987, p. 54.

Portanto, a ideia de reparação comporta temperamentos, uma vez que raramente o dano pode ser integralmente reparado, no sentido de restituir a vítima ao *status quo ante*. O que se consegue na maioria dos casos é a restituição da coisa subtraída, o conserto da coisa danificada ou a reposição de seu equivalente em dinheiro ou ainda o pagamento de uma compensação quando se trate de bens imateriais.[62]

A ideia de reparação integral pode ser relacionada ao problema da monetarização da responsabilidade civil, de cunho liberalista, que reduz o dano à sua dimensão exclusivamente patrimonial.[63] É necessário considerar, porém, que a reparação dos danos pode se dar por diversos modos e não necessariamente pela reposição patrimonial. Ademais, em se tratando de danos extrapatrimoniais, a compensação patrimonial é sempre paliativa, não se prestando à satisfação integral do prejuízo sofrido pela vítima. Não bastasse, registre-se a tendência do direito contemporâneo a permitir a redução equitativa da reparação, conforme consta do art. 10.401 dos Princípios Europeus de Responsabilidade Civil – PETL, do art. VI:6:202 do Projeto de Marco Comum de Referência – DCFR, de vários dispositivos da legislação civil europeia e do art. 944, parágrafo único, do Código Civil brasileiro.[64]

[62] Segundo Zannoni, a reparação do dano pode ser *in natura*, mediante reposição ou conserto da própria coisa destruída ou danificada; ou indenização, mediante pagamento de uma quantia equivalente (Zannoni, Eduardo A. *El daño en la responsabilidad civil*. Buenos Aires: Astrea, 1982, p. 181-182). Llamas Pombo sustenta que há várias formas de reparação, a depender do tipo de dano: a) reparação específica, mediante obrigação de fazer ou não fazer, reposição ou substituição do objeto e reembolso de gastos; b) indenização pecuniária, mediante ressarcimento do valor patrimonial ou compensação do prejuízo corporal ou moral (Llamas Pombo, Eugenio. *Formas de reparación del daño*, Revista de Responsabilidad Civil y Seguros, n. 9 (2010), p. 26).

[63] Giovanni Comandé sustenta que a reversibilidade ou reparabilidade do dano é uma ficção do liberalismo, que reduz o dano a seu aspecto econômico, assim como o princípio da precaução também se assenta sobre a ficção da eliminação dos riscos. Nos dois casos, tanto a reparação integral dos danos quanto a eliminação dos riscos só podem ser concebidas como ideais a serem perseguidos. Confira-se: "La nozione di irreparabilità è relativa, però, perche la riparazione è una fictio sviluppata dalla logica liberalista, e sintetizzata nell'equivalente economico della perdita subita" (Comandé, Giovanni. *L'assicurazione e la responsabilità civile come strumenti e veicoli del principio di precauzione*, p. 46).

[64] Jiménez Triana, Juan Carlos. *La reducción de la indemnización por razones de equidad*. In: Llamas Pombo, Eugenio. *Congreso internacional de derecho civil octavo centenário de la Universidad de Salamanca: libro de ponencias*. Valência: Tirant lo Blanch, Salamanca: Universidad de Salamanca, 2018, p. 627-642.

Por isso, a reparação integral só pode ser admitida como um postulado ético, isto é, como um ideal a ser perseguido, mas que nem sempre pode ser concretizado, particularmente no que tange aos danos morais e aos deveres de precaução. Com isso, o proclamado princípio da reparação integral deve ser interpretado como princípio da justa reparação, no sentido de que a vítima faz jus à reparação mais completa possível.[65]

CONCLUSÕES

Do que se viu até aqui se extrai que:

1. A responsabilidade civil é um instituto jurídico moderno, que adquiriu autonomia dogmática no bojo das transformações sociais e políticas que culminaram com a promulgação do *Code Napoleon.*
2. A evolução da teoria geral da responsabilidade civil acompanha aproximadamente os desdobramentos da modernidade. Em sua primeira fase, baseada na culpa, possuía um caráter individualista e patrimonialista. Na segunda fase, a teoria do risco visa atender os danos que não podiam ser atribuídos à conduta culposa individual. Na fase atual, marcada pelo gerenciamento dos riscos e pela socialização dos danos, a responsabilidade civil se organiza sob a rubrica do direito de danos, com maior ênfase sobre o direito da vítima à prevenção/precaução e à reparação.
3. Em sua terceira fase de desenvolvimento, a teoria da responsabilidade civil se organiza sob a rubrica do direito de danos, que se caracteriza pela centralidade do dano como elemento desencadeador dos deveres de responsabilidade e pelo protagonismo da vítima e seu direito à precaução e à reparação.

[65] Llamas Pombo sustenta que: "La reparación integral del daño constituye, en efecto, un principio, un valor jurídico que ha de inspirar el ordenamiento jurídico, tanto en su construcción como en su interpretación y aplicación. A dicha consideración de principio general del Derecho no obsta la circunstancia, cierta por otra parte, de que la Constitución no contenga ninguna regla o principio alguno que imponga la reparación total de los daños y perjuicios, pues en la suprema norma no son (principios) todos los que están ni están todos los (principios) que son (Llamas Pombo, Eugenio. *Formas de reparación del daño,* Revista de Responsabilidad Civil y Seguros, n. 9 (2010), p. 27). Alonso Perez se refere ao "mito da reparação integral" como uma pretensão inexequível dos juristas romanos que requer um juízo de equidade, muito mais para reduzir do que para alcançar a plenitude indenizatória (Alonso Perez, Mariano. *Prologo.* In: Llamas Pombo, Eugenio. *Reflexiones sobre Derecho de Danos: casos y opiniones.* Madrid: La Ley, 2010, p. 24).

4. São seus pressupostos que as atividades devem ser desenvolvidas de maneira sustentável, que a pessoa não está obrigada a suportar os danos decorrentes das atividades alheias e que os danos devem ser diluídos reflexivamente na sociedade por mecanismos de socialização.
5. Enquanto instituto que busca autonomia no quadro geral das disciplinas jurídicas, o direito de danos se orienta pelos seguintes princípios: da responsabilidade, do *pro damnato* ou *favor victimae*, da solidariedade social e igualdade frente aos encargos públicos, da precaução/prevenção e da justa reparação.

REFERÊNCIAS

ALONSO PEREZ, Mariano. *Prologo.* In: LLAMAS POMBO, Eugenio. *Reflexiones sobre Derecho de Danos: casos y opiniones.* Madrid: La Ley, 2010.

ALPA, Guido. *Trattato di diritto civile*, v. IV: La responsabilità civile, Milano: Giuffrè, 1999.

ALVES, José Carlos Moreira. *Direito romano*, v. I. 5. ed. Rio de Janeiro: Forense, 1983.

ALVES, José Carlos Moreira. *Direito romano*, v. II. 3. ed. Rio de Janeiro: Forense, 1980.

ARISTÓTELES. *Ética a Nicômaco.* Tradução de Pietro Nassetti. São Paulo: Martin Claret, 2003.

BARBOZA, Heloísa Helena. *Vulnerabilidade e cuidado: aspectos jurídicos.* In: PEREIRA, Tânia da Silva; OLIVEIRA, Guilherme de (coords.). *Cuidado e vulnerabilidade.* São Paulo: Atlas, 2009. p. 106-118;

BARROSO, Luís Roberto. *O neoconstitucionalismo e constitucionalização do direito*: o triunfo tardio do direito constitucional no Brasil. Disponível em: <http://www.luisrobertobarroso.com.br/wp-content/themes/LRB/pdf/neoconstitucionalismo_e_constitucionalizacao_do_direito_pt.pdf>. Acesso em: 12 mar. 2019.

BAUMAN, Zygmunt. *Modernidade líquida.* Tradução de Plínio Dentzien. Rio de Janeiro: Jorge Zahar Editor, 2001.

BAUMAN, Zygmunt. Globalização. Tradução de Marcus Penchel. Rio de Janeiro: Zahar, 1999.

BERNARDES, Cláudio Teles de Toledo. *A ética da alteridade em Emmanuel Levinas – uma contribuição atual ao discurso da moral cristã.* Revista de Cultura Teológica, v. 20, n. 78, p. 83-101, abr./jun. 2012.

BESTANI, Adriana. *Principio de precaución.* Buenos Aires: Astrea, 2012.

BITTAR, Eduardo Carlos Bianca. *Curso de ética jurídica:* ética geral e profissional. 6. ed. São Paulo: Saraiva, 2009.

BITTAR, Eduardo Carlos Bianca. *O direito na pós-modernidade.* 2. ed. Rio de Janeiro: Forense Universitária, 2009.

CALVO COSTA, Carlos Alberto. *Daño resarcible.* Buenos Aires: Hamurabi, 2005.

CASILLO, João. *Dano à pessoa e sua indenização.* São Paulo: Revista dos Tribunais, 1987.

CAVALIERI FILHO, Sergio. *Programa de responsabilidade civil.* 11. ed. São Paulo: Atlas, 2014.

CAVALIERI FILHO, Sergio. *O princípio da reparação integral ("restitutio in integrum") e o seguro de responsabilidade civil.* Disponível em: <http://www.sergiocavalierifilho.com.br/administrativo/artigos/imagens>. Acesso em: 20 mar. 2019.

COASE, Ronald. *O problema do custo social.* Tradução por Francisco Kümmel F. Alves e Renato Vieira Caovilla. In: The Latin American and Caribbean Journal of Legal Studies. Volume 3, Issue 1 2008 Article 9. Disponível em: https://services.bepress.com/lacjls/vol3/iss1/art9/. Visualizado em: 22/12/2019.

COMANDÉ, Giovanni. *L'assicurazione e la responsabilità civile come strumenti e veicoli del principio di precauzione.* In: COMANDÉ, Giovani. *Gli strumenti della precauzione:* nuovi rischi, assicurazione e responsabilità. Milano: Giuffrè, 2006.

DELMAS-MARTY, Mireille. *Por um direito comum.* Tradução de Maria Ermantina de Almeida Prado Galvão. São Paulo: Martins Fontes, 2004.

DESIDERI, Jean-Pierre. *La précaution en droit privé.* Revue Française de Droit Administratif, Paris: Dalloz, p. 238-242, mar./abr. 2012.

DÍEZ-PICAZO, Luis y GULLÓN, Antonio. *Instituciones de Derecho civil,* vol. I. Madrid: Tecnos, 1995.

DÍEZ-PICAZO, Luis y GULLÓN, Antonio. *Sistema de Derecho de daños,* vol. II. 11ª ed. Madrid: Tecnos: 2015.

DURKHEIM, Émile. *Da divisão do trabalho social.* Tradução: Eduardo Brandão. 2. Ed. São Paulo: Martins Fontes, 1999.

FACHIN, Luiz Edson. *Estatuto jurídico do patrimônio mínimo.* 2ª ed. Rio de Janeiro: Renovar, 2006.

FACHIN, Luiz Edson. *Teoria crítica do direito civil: à luz do novo Código Civil brasileiro.* 2. ed. rev. e atual. Rio de Janeiro: Renovar, 2003.

FACCHINI NETO, Eugenio. *Aumentando a proteção das vítimas de danos: a causalidade probabilística.* In: LLAMAS POMBO, Eugenio. *Congreso internacional de derecho civil octavo centenário de la Universidad de Salamanca: libro de ponencias.* Valência: Tirant lo Blanch, Salamanca: Universidad de Salamanca, 2018, p. 541-545.

FARIAS, Cristiano Chaves de; ROSENVALD, Nelson; BRAGA NETTO, Felipe Peixoto. *Curso de direito civil,* v. 3: responsabilidade civil. 2. ed. São Paulo: Atlas, 2015.

GALVÃO, Inocêncio Telles. *Direito das obrigações.* 7. ed. Coimbra: Ed. Coimbra, 2014.

GHERBI, Carlos Alberto. *Teoría general de la reparación de daños.* 3. ed. actualizada y ampliada. Buenos Aires: Astrea, 2003.

HIRONAKA, Giselda Maria Fernandes Novaes. *Responsabilidade pressuposta.* Belo Horizonte: Del Rey, 2005.

JIMÉNEZ TRIANA, Juan Carlos. *La reducción de la indemnización por razones de equidad.* In: LLAMAS POMBO, Eugenio. *Congreso internacional de derecho civil octavo centenário de la Universidad de Salamanca: libro de ponencias.* Valência: Tirant lo Blanch, Salamanca: Universidad de Salamanca, 2018, p. 627-642.

LLAMAS POMBO, Eugenio. *Formas de reparación del daño,* Revista de Responsabilidad Civil y Seguros, n. 9 (2010).

LLAMAS POMBO, Eugenio. *Prevención y reparación, las dos caras del derecho de daños.* In: MORENO MARTÍNEZ, Juan Antonio (coord.). La responsabilidad civil y su problemática actual. Madrid: Dykinson, 2007.

LLAMAS POMBO, Eugenio. *Reflexiones sobre Derecho de Danos: casos y opiniones*. Madrid: La Ley, 2010.

LEVINAS, Emmanuel. *Totalité et infini:* essai sur l'extériorité. Livre de Poche, 4120, Paris: Livrairie Générale Française, 2014.

LEVINAS, Emmanuel. *Violência do rosto*. Tradução de Fernando Soares Moreira. São Paulo: Loyola, 2014.

LOPEZ, Teresa Ancona. *Princípio da precaução e evolução da responsabilidade civil*. São Paulo: Quartier Latin, 2010.

LORENZETTI, Ricardo Luis. *Reflexiones acerca de la responsabilidad civil en el siglo XXI*. In: FABIÁN CAPARRÓS, Eduardo A. (coord.): Responsa Iurisperitorum Digesta (volumen 4), Salamanca: Universidad de Salamanca, 2000.

MARIÑO LOPEZ, Andrés. *La función preventiva del Derecho de Daños, el princípio de precaución y la protección de la salud humana*. In: LLAMAS POMBO, Eugênio (coord.). *Congreso internacional de derecho civil octavo centenário de la Universidad de Salamanca: libro de ponencias*. Valência: Tirant lo Blanch, Salamanca: Universidad de Salamanca, 2018, p. 643-657.

MARQUES, Claudia Lima. Introdução ao direito do consumidor. In: BENJAMIN, Antônio Herman; MARQUES, Claudia Lima; BESSA, Leonardo Roscoe (Coord.). Manual de direito do consumidor. 6. ed. São Paulo: RT, 2013.

MESA, Marcelo J. López. *Presupuestos de la responsabilidad civil*. Buenos Aires: Astrea, 2013.

MORIN, Edgar. *Os sete saberes necessários à educação do futuro*. Tradução de Catarina Eleonora F. da Silva e Jeanne Sawaya. Revisão técnica de Edgar de Assis Carvalho. 10. ed. São Paulo: Cortez; Brasília, DF: Unesco, 2005.

PEREIRA, Caio Mário da Silva. *Responsabilidade civil*. Rio de Janeiro: Forense, 1989.

PERLINGIERI, Pietro. *Perfis do direito civil:* introdução ao direito civil constitucional. Tradução de Maria Cristina de Cicco. 2. ed. Rio de Janeiro: Renovar, 2002.

REALE, Miguel. *Lições preliminares de direito*. 8. ed. rev. São Paulo: Saraiva, 1981.

REALE, Miguel. *Filosofia do direito*. 19. ed. São Paulo: Saraiva, 2002.

REALE, Miguel. *Teoria tridimensional do direito*, 5ª. ed. São Paulo: Saraiva, 1994.

REALE, Miguel. *Visão geral do projeto de Código Civil*. Disponível em: <www.miguelreale.com.br>. Acesso em: 24 jun. 2017.

RIPANTI, Graziano. *Introdução: Emmanuel Levinas e o infinito diálogo*. In: LEVINAS, Emmanuel. *Violência do rosto*. Tradução de Fernando Soares Moreira. São Paulo: Loyola, 2014.

RODRIGUES, Silvio. *Direito civil*, v. 4: responsabilidade civil. 4. ed. São Paulo: Saraiva, 1979.

RODRIGUEZ, Arturo Solarte. *El princípio favor victimae*. In: LLAMAS POMBO, Eugenio (coord.). *Congreso internacional de derecho civil octavo centenário de la Universidad de Salamanca: libro de ponencias*. Valência: Tirant lo Blanch, Salamanca: Universidad de Salamanca, 2018, p. 719-736.

ROGER-LACAN, Cyril. *Specialité, gravité et anormalité das la responsabilité sans faute : conclusions sur Conseil d'État, 1er février 2012, M. Bizouerne et outre, nº 347205 et 347446*, in : Revue Française de Droit Administratif, nº 2, mars-avril/2000, p. 333/338.

ROSENVALD, Nelson. *A responsabilidade civil pelo lucro ilícito: o disgorgment e a indenização restitutória*. Salvador: Juspoduim, 2019.

SANTOS, Romualdo Baptista dos. *A dimensão do Outro na configuração da responsabilidade civil*. In: LLAMAS POMBO, Eugenio. *Congreso internacional de derecho civil octavo centenário de la Universidad de Salamanca: libro de ponencias.* Valência: Tirant lo Blanch, Salamanca: Universidad de Salamanca, 2018, p. 435-448.

SANTOS, Romualdo Baptista dos. *Responsabilidade civil por dano enorme.* Curitiba: Juruá Editora; Porto: Juruá Editorial, 2018.

SANSEVERINO, Paulo de Tarso Vieira. *Princípio da reparação integral.* São Paulo: Saraiva, 2011.

SIMÃO, José Fernando, *A teoria dualista do vínculo obrigacional e sua aplicação ao direito civil brasileiro.* Revista Jurídica ESMP-SP, v. 3, p. 165-181, 2013.

TARTUCE, Fernanda. *Igualdade e vulnerabilidade no processo civil.* Rio de Janeiro: Forense, 2012.

TELLES JÚNIOR, Goffredo. *Direito quântico*: ensaio sobre o fundamento da ordem jurídica. 8. ed. rev. São Paulo: Juarez de Oliveira, 2006.

TUCCI, José Rogério Cruz e. *Breves anotações sobre a "restitutio in integrum" e o processo acusatório romano. Revista Justitia,* São Paulo, 45(122), jul-set. 1983, p. 52/57. Disponível em: <http://www.revistajustitia.com. br/revistas/92c9x5.pdf>. Acesso em: 13 mar. 2019.

VARELLA, Marcelo Dias (Coord.). *Responsabilidade e sociedade do risco/Relatório público considerações gerais.* Conselho de Estado da França. Tradução de Michel Abes. Brasília: UniCEUB, 2006.

VENTURI, Thaís Goveia Pascoaloto. *Responsabilidade civil preventiva: a proteção contra a violação dos direitos e a tutela inibitória material.* São Paulo: Malheiros, 2014.

ZANNONI, Eduardo A. *El daño en la responsabilidad civil.* Buenos Aires: Astrea, 1982.

REFLEXÕES DO CORONAVÍRUS (SARS-COV-2) E SEUS EFEITOS NAS RELAÇÕES CONTRATUAIS

SERGIO IGLESIAS NUNES DE SOUZA*

INTRODUÇÃO

O mundo praticamente parou na era contemporânea. A proliferação do vírus SARS-CoV-2 (coronavírus) causador da doença do COVID-19, com origem de seu epicentro na China, na cidade de Wuhan, em outubro de 2019 repercutiu pelo mundo, inclusive, na cidade de Nova York (EUA) atingindo o maior número de casos do planeta em junho de 2020 com 115.590 mil mortos[1] e no Brasil 41.058 mortos em que, como medida de combate à pandemia foi necessário adotar a prevenção comportamental do distanciamento e isolamento social, ante a rápida contaminação e comprometimento da saúde que, em poucos dias, leva à morte, principalmente, os mais idosos ou pessoas com comorbidades que impulsionam o agravamento do quadro de saúde.

Diante da adoção da quarentena com distanciamento social em que muitos países adotaram como controle imediato a fim de reduzir o elevado índice de mortes, bem como pela visível possibilidade de sobrecarregar os leitos de saúde e CTIs de hospitais públicos e privados, as pessoas encontram-se numa situação de total excepcionalidade nunca vista na era moderna no século XXI, em que foram obrigadas a permanecerem em

* Doutor e Mestre em Direito pela PUC-SP. Professor Concursado Titular de Direito Civil na Faculdade de Direito de São Bernardo do Campo. Advogado.

[1] Dados atualizados até 12/06/2020.

suas residências, sem possibilidade de trabalhar, executar as mais simples tarefas diárias, seja produtiva ou de entretenimento e, até mesmo, do lazer e encontro com seus próprios familiares, suspendendo reuniões e outras dezenas de atividades.

A sociedade mundial deparou-se, mesmo com resistência de alguns, com uma nova conjuntura e realidade de combate à pandemia, ante a ausência de medicações seguras e imediatas que evitem o agravamento da saúde de modo a levar a óbito de, talvez, milhões de pessoas, caso nenhuma medida fosse adotada.

Apesar da possibilidade de experimentos científicos trazidos com algum resultado primário, embora sem convalidação pela comunidade científica médica no início da pandemia com o uso de medicações ou formas de tratamento médico alternativos, respectivamente, o uso do sulfato de hidroxicloroquina conjugada com o uso do antibiótico azitromicina no Brasil [2] e em alguns outros países, como Portugal, ou, com o uso de plasma

[2] Em abril de 2020 houve um manifesto redigido pelo médico Dr. Marcos Eberlim, professor da Universidade Presbiteriana Mackenzie, com um texto ressaltando as novidades recentes a respeito do medicamento pelo francês Didier Raoult, carta esta assinada pelos seguintes cientistas: Marcelo Hermes Lima (Universidade de Brasília); Aguimon Alves da Costa (Universidade Cândido Mendes); Alexandre Barbosa Andrade (Universidade Federal de Ouro Preto); Amilcar Baiardi (Universidade Católica de Salvador); Bruno Lima Pessoa (Universidade Federal Fluminense); Carlos Adriano Ferraz (Universidade Federal de Pelotas); Carlos Prudêncio (Instituto Adolfo Lutz); Cláudio Antônio Sorodo Días (Universidade Federal da Grande Dourados); Elvis Böes (Instituto Federal de Brasília); José Carlos Campos Torres (Universidade Estadual de Campinas); Laércio Fidelis Dias (Universidade Estadual Paulista); Leonardo Vizeu Figueiredo (Escola da Advocacia-Geral da União); Milton Gustavo Vasconcelos Barbosa (Universidade Estadual do Piauí); Ney Rômulo de Oliveira Paula (Universidade Federal do Piauí); Pablo Christiano Barboza Lollo (Universidade Federal da Grande Dourados); Pedro Jorge Zany P. M. Caldeira (Universidade Federal do Triângulo Mineiro); Rodrigo Caiado de Lamare (PUC-RJ e University of York); Ronaldo Angelini (Universidade Federal do Rio Grande do Norte); Rosevaldo de Oliveira (Universidade Federal de Rondonópolis); Rui Seabra Ferreira Junior (Universidade Estadual Paulista); Luís Fabiano Farias Borges (Capes); Jane Adriana Ramos Ottoni de Castro (Universidade de Brasília); Martinho Dinoá Medeiros Júnior (Universidade Federal de Pernambuco); Marcos N. Eberlin (Universidade Presbiteriana Mackenzie); Marcus Vinicius Carvalho Guelpeli (Universidade Federal dos Vales do Jequitinhonha e Mucuri); e José Roberto Gomes Rodrigues (Universidade do Estado da Bahia)." Leia mais em: https://www.gazetadopovo.com.br/vida-e-cidadania/carta-aberta-cientistas-coronavirus-cloroquina-efeitos-colaterais/Copyright © 2020, Fonte: Jornal Gazeta do Povo. Acesso em 13/04/2020: https://eur05.safelinks.protection.outlook.com/?url=https%3A%2F%2Fwww.gazetadopovo.com.br%2Fvida-e-cidadania%2Fcarta-aberta-cientistas-coronavirus-cloroquina-efeitos-

sanguíneo com anticorpos de pessoas que já foram contaminadas com o vírus, o distanciamento ou isolamento social como prevenção foi o efetivamente adotado e, com isso, houve um comprometimento econômico ante a suspensão das atividades de trabalho em geral, de produção e serviços que ensejaram na suspensão da execução de inúmeros contratos firmados.

Neste despretensioso artigo, buscaremos categorizar a causa do coronavírus (SARS-CoV-2) nas relações contratuais de prestação continuada ou diferida, se é hipótese de aplicação da teoria da imprevisão ou onerosidade excessiva, fato do príncipe, caso fortuito ou força maior e, se há, em nosso ordenamento jurídico atual, fundamentos principiológicos que autorizem a revisão ou resolução do contrato diante da pandemia que gerou a determinação de uma quarentena social no Brasil e com inúmeras determinações por diversos Estados e Municípios.[3]

1. BREVES CONSIDERAÇÕES DO CONTRATO À LUZ DA SEGURANÇA JURÍDICA

A relação contratual é baseada na vontade entre as partes. MARIA HELENA DINIZ pontifica que o princípio do *pacta sunt servanda* é aquele que:

> "pelo qual as estipulações feitas no contrato deverão ser fielmente cumpridas (*pacta sunt servanda*), sob pena de execução patrimonial contra o inadimplente. Isto é assim porque o contrato, uma vez concluído livremente, incorpora-se ao ordenamento jurídico, constituindo uma verdadeira norma de direito, autorizando, portanto, o contratante a pedir a intervenção estatal para assegurar a execução da obrigação porventura não cumprida segundo a vontade que a constituiu. À ideia da auto-regulamentação dos interesses dos contratantes, baseada no princípio da autonomia da vontade, sucede a da necessidade social de proteger a confiança de cada um deles na observância da avença estipulada, ou melhor, na subordinação à *lex contractus*. O contrato

colaterais%2F&data=02%7C01%7C%7Cff708a38b6e44111d32308d7dfb40bcd%7C84df9e7fe9f640afb435aaaaaaaaaaaa%7C1%7C0%7C637223836706163234&sdata=KOfMtWiT9y0j2M7k5tgFhO9NizLbgUHxTvgFK8%2BgbUs%3D&reserved=0

[3] Arguição de Descumprimento de Preceito Fundamental 672 no STF, Rel. Min. Alexandre de Moraes e na ADI n. 6341, em que referendou a liminar do Min. Marco Aurélio de Mello no entendimento de que as medidas adotadas pelo Governo Federal na Medida Provisória (MP) n. 926/2020 para o enfrentamento do novo coronavírus não afastam a competência concorrente nem a tomada de providências normativas e administrativas pelos Estados, pelo Distrito Federal e pelos Municípios, em sessão realizada por videoconferência, j. 15/04/2020.

é intangível, a menos que ambas as partes o rescindam voluntariamente ou haja escusa por caso fortuito ou força maior. Fora dessas hipóteses ter-se-á a intangibilidade ou a imutabilidade contratual. Esse princípio da força obrigatória funda-se na regra de que o contrato é lei entre as partes, desde que estipulado livremente (RT, 534:243, 478:93), com observância dos requisitos legais. Se os contratantes ajustaram os termos do negócio jurídico contratual, não se poderá alterar o seu conteúdo, nem mesmo judicialmente, qualquer que seja o motivo alegado por uma das partes, e o inadimplemento do avençado autoriza o credor a executar o patrimônio do devedor por meio do Poder Judiciário, desde que não tenha havido força maior ou caso fortuito".[4]

A liberdade de contratar era baseada na soberania da vontade dos contratantes lastreada na vertente individual e liberal dos séculos XVIII e XIX, já que existia o pensamento de que se os contratantes alienavam livremente sua liberdade, deveriam cumprir o acordado, ainda que surgisse para uma das partes um dano considerável.[5] Atualmente, não mais vigora o absolutismo da liberdade contratual e do princípio *pacta sunt servanda*, já que há inúmeras interferências nessa vontade pela lei, no entendimento da doutrina civil e pela própria jurisprudência, daí porque, com acerto a referida autora mencionar as hipóteses de excepcionalidade, tal como a força maior e o caso fortuito.

O conceito de contrato que se desenvolveu com a Revolução Francesa retrata com fidelidade o liberalismo econômico gerado pela Revolução Industrial e pela queda do regime aristocrático que até então dominava a França, com seu epicentro na cidade luz. Por derradeiro, com a liberdade plena tinha, por consequência, a responsabilidade dos contratantes pelos compromissos assumidos, independentemente de fatores exógenos ou posteriores que interferissem nas relações contratuais. Daí porque se fala que firmado o contrato, diz-se que ele tem força de lei entre as partes (*pacta sunt servanda*).

Enzo Roppo afirmou sobre o princípio do *pacta sunt servanda*:

> "... um princípio que, além de indiscutível substância ética, apresentava também um relevante significado econômico: o respeito rigoroso pelos com-

[4] Diniz, Maria Helena Diniz. *Curso de direito civil brasileiro: teoria das obrigações contratuais e extracontratuais*, 10ª Ed., São Paulo: Saraiva, 1995, v. 03, p. 30.

[5] Rodrigues, Silvio. *Direito Civil, dos contratos e das declarações unilaterais de vontade*, 9ª ed., São Paulo: Saraiva, 1980, v. 03, p. 18.

promissos assumidos é, de fato, condição para que as trocas e as outras operações de circulação da riqueza se desenvolvam de modo correto e eficiente segundo a lógica que lhes é própria, para que se não frustrem as previsões e os cálculos dos operadores". [6]

Houve uma evolução social e a substituição do Estado Liberal pelo Estado Social do século XX, pois, há, deveras, uma maior preocupação em se garantir direitos sociais e econômicos dos cidadãos. A CRFB/88 buscou proteger os direitos individuais e sociais, primando pela dignidade da pessoa humana, bem como estabeleceu a possibilidade de intervenção econômica pelo Estado nas relações contratuais, sempre com o objetivo de manter a estabilidade das relações jurídicas, art. 170 do texto constitucional que prescreve que a ordem econômica, fundada na valorização do trabalho humano e na livre iniciativa, tem por fim assegurar a todos existência digna, conforme os ditames da justiça social, observados os princípios da soberania nacional, propriedade privada, função social da propriedade, livre concorrência e a defesa do consumidor, do meio ambiente, redução das desigualdades regionais e sociais, a busca do pleno emprego e o tratamento favorecido para as empresas de pequeno porte.

Por essa razão, numa interpretação lógica e sistemática, há que se observar as disposições do art. 1º, 5º e incisos e 6º da CRFB/88 à luz de uma intervenção Estatal justa, equilibrada, limitada e coerente, de modo que se preserve a vontade das partes contratantes, garanta-se uma economia saudável da sociedade, em prol de um bem comum, preservando-se interesses individuais, mas garantindo-se a sobreposição de interesses coletivos, quando necessário, especialmente, os interesses e bens extrapatrimoniais.

Dá-se a ideia de um capitalismo humanista, já que o torvelinho interpretativo do patrimônio é baseado na dignidade da pessoa humana e nos direitos sociais e extrapatrimoniais. Um exemplo típico dessa posição Estatal deu-se com a contemplação do direito à moradia como direito social no art. 6º da CRFB/88, através da EC 26/2000. Não há intepretação jurídica insustentável, quando esta busca efetivar, com todo o ordenamento, o princípio constitucional da dignidade da pessoa humana, dando a esta o respeito e o direito que tenha de ter.

Por essa razão, institutos jurídicos de ontem e de hoje ganham relevância fundamental para a aplicação de uma reanálise interpretativa e solu-

[6] ROPPO, Enzo. *O contrato*. Coimbra: Almedina, 1988, p. 24-35.

cionadora dos conflitos para a revisão ou resolução dos contratos, tal como ocorrem com o caso fortuito, força maior, teoria da imprevisão, a lesão nos contratos, a par dos demais vícios dos negócios jurídicos, dentre outros. Para a revisão dos contratos deve-se buscar a segurança jurídica tão necessária para que a legislação possa estabelecer os requisitos autorizativos que determinem a possibilidade de reanálise do contrato pelo Poder Judiciário. Daí porque, pontifica DALMO DE ABREU DALLARI que:

> "Entre as principais necessidades e aspirações das sociedades humanas encontra-se a segurança jurídica. Não há pessoa, grupo social, entidade pública ou privada, que não tenha necessidade de segurança jurídica, para atingir seus objetivos e até mesmo para sobreviver".[7]

A segurança jurídica necessita de uma adequada categorização [8] do instituto jurídico que se busque fundamentar a revisão ou resolução do contrato. Sem essa devida categorização tem-se a arbitrariedade do próprio julgador de modo que não poderá legitimar a sua interferência Estatal.

O Direito visa a atender finalidades. Os institutos jurídicos revisionais, igualmente. RUDOLF VON IHERING,[9] renomado jurista alemão do século XIX, falecido em 1892, teve em todas as suas construções teoréticas a busca da finalidade do Direito à luz das finalidades econômicas, por exemplo, na medida em que evoluiu a crítica teórica do dogmatismo da Escola da Jurisprudência dos conceitos, já que, para ele, o Direito é uma consecução de fins, ante a sua pertinente, a nosso ver, visão finalista também da ciência do Direito, quando, por exemplo, tratou do conceito de posse.

Nesse sentido, deve-se compreender que a finalidade dos institutos jurídicos revisionais dos contratos busca o reequilíbrio das partes contratantes em situações excepcionais e específicas, mas, de igual modo, não é de interesse público que dessa tentativa de reequilíbrio possa acarretar um comprometimento econômico coletivo de uma sociedade. Para tanto,

[7] DALLARI, Dalmo de Abreu. Segurança e Direito, in *Renascer do Direito*, 2ª ed., São Paulo: Saraiva, 1980, p. 26.

[8] CRETELLA JÚNIOR, José. As cláusulas de privilégio nos contratos administrativos, *Revista de Informação Legislativa*, Brasília, n. 89, jan./mar., 1986, p. 306: "Categoria jurídica é a formulação genérica, *in abstracto*, com índices essenciais, mas gerais, não comprometida ainda com nenhum dos ramos do direito. Trata-se de figura *iuris* tomada em sua generalidade máxima, caracterizada por conotações típicas do gênero, mas não identificadora da *espécie*".

[9] IHERING, Rudolf von. *Der Zweck im Recht (A finalidade do Direito)*, v. 02, *passim*, 1877-1883.

é necessária a adequada categorização do instituto jurídico da interferência do COVID-19 nas relações contratuais no caso *sub judice*.

Buscar essa categorização é enaltecer a segurança jurídica que não se alcançará com medidas normativas emergenciais em sua essência, estas, por sua vez, nada mais atenuarão determinadas situações em que o Poder legislativo não poderá permanecer inerte e fleumático, por exemplo, quando se está presente uma pandemia pelo Coronavírus, SARS-CoV-2, que, sem dúvida, interferiu em diversas relações contratuais. A figura do Estado Social deverá estar presente nos limites do possível (teoria da reserva do possível).

Sem pontuar a base da segurança jurídica na contratação dos negócios jurídicos, anular-se-á o princípio da legalidade nos contratos, causando uma literal contaminação, não só da saúde de todos, ante o SARS-CoV-2, mas um *vírus jurídico* na base negocial das relações contratuais com efeitos deletérios econômicos, causando amarguras sociais, desequilíbrio monetário e aumento das desigualdades, provocada pela peste uma guerra judicial entre os contratantes, gerando fome e aumento das desigualdades sociais e, por fim, a morte também das relações contratuais. É um efeito inevitável ante a insegurança, quebra da confiança, desequilíbrio e, possível abusividade de ambas as partes, credores ou devedores. Não só a categorização abstrata deve ser adequada, como também a aplicação no caso concreto deve ser aplicada e não há fórmula mágica geral para a solução dos conflitos, quando muito, lenitivos com a intervenção legal emergencial em situações específicas que se fizerem necessárias.

A pandemia gerou a denominada primeira onda devastadora da saúde pública. A segunda, consequente daquela, são os efeitos econômicos e, logicamente, na sua interferência em todas as relações negociais e, por derradeiro, criar-se-á a terceira onda arrebatadora no Poder Judiciário diante do excesso de demandas.

Não se duvida que outras ondas surgirão de modo a causar um verdadeiro tsunami quanto aos efeitos consequentes de uma pandemia desta magnitude, tais como a fome e a miséria, majoração do desemprego e a desestabilização da economia não de apenas um País, mas do mundo, em que sobreviverão aqueles que já estavam em melhores condições de reservas de capital, numa ojeriza seleção dos mais fortes.

A pandemia não coloca todos no mesmo barco, mas na mesma tempestade. Alguns navegam em imensos navios transatlânticos, outros, em médias embarcações e, há, também, aqueles que estão em pequenos botes ou canoas. Há uma simbiose de troca de produtos e serviços entre as embarcações e, nesse percurso, muitos naufragarão. Para estes últimos, urge a necessidade de uma intervenção do Estado Social nas relações contratuais de modo a, ao menos, evitar a extinção de toda e qualquer relação contratual, sempre que possível, posto que o efeito posterior será o grave comprometimento daquela simbiose da cadeia produtiva.

Nas relações contratuais como consequência da pandemia e quarentena, ter-se-á o mesmo efeito já dito por NEYTON FANTONI JÚNIOR[10]:

> "... E com o comprometimento da tranquilidade espiritual, vivencia-se a eliminação da garantia de planejamento à luz de razoável conjuntura de previsibilidade, ensejando crescente desconfiança, desencadeadora de estado permanente de desânimo e decepção, sobrevindo, então, o descaso quanto ao esclarecimento dos direitos e obrigações e quanto à demonstração concreta de seu respeito e do engajamento para a sua efetiva realização."

Desse modo, na tentativa de se evitar o caos social e a intranquilidade jurídica, faz-se necessário analisar os institutos revisionais do contrato a par de seus princípios coligados, tais como a função social, o dever de cooperação, a boa-fé contratual de credor e devedor.

A função social do contrato insculpido no art. 421 do Código Civil de 2002 estabelecida a partir dos princípios da boa-fé objetiva, do dever de cooperação e de lealdade entre as partes contratantes deve ser compreendida como algo compatível com a segurança jurídica. Mesmo os institutos revisionais merecem uma análise pormenorizada de modo que se ajuste devidamente o ocorrido com o COVID-19 que implicou na quarentena social e interferiu, sobremaneira, em todas as relações contratuais. E, a partir disso, buscar-se uma segurança jurídica de modo a estabilizar as relações contratuais.

2. CLÁUSULA *REBUS SIC STANTIBUS* E A TEORIA DA IMPREVISÃO

É necessária uma breve análise histórica de ambas que, a nosso ver, na era moderna não se confundem, já que há uma única diferenciação, isto é, na *cláusula rebus sic stantibus* dispensa-se que o fato seja imprevisível de modo a autorizar a revisão contratual.

[10] FANTONI JÚNIOR, Neyton. "Segurança Jurídica e Interpretação Constitucional". *Revista Jurídica*, v. 238, 1997, p. 14.

Othon Sidou pesquisou e localizou a presença da *rebus sic stantibus* desde o Código de Hamurabi, rei da Babilônia, mais de mil anos antes de Roma, em que se comprovou a seguinte disposição:

> "Se alguém tem um débito a juros, e uma tempestade devasta o campo ou destrói a colheita, ou opor falta de água não cresce o trigo no campo, ele não deverá nesse ano dar trigo ao credor, deverá modificar sua tábua de contrato e não pagar juros por esse ano." [11]

Na Idade Média, século XIII, entre os glosadores medievais, sob a denominação completa *contractus qui habent tractum sucessivum et dependentiam de futuro, rebus sic stantibus intelliguntur,* tem-se a ideia de que os contratos ou pactos de execução continuada e dependentes do futuro entende-se permanecendo as coisas como estão, vale dizer, só se deve cumprir e executar os contratos se não houver alteração essencial das coisas ou nos acontecimentos posteriores, sendo este um entendimento visando a equidade e o maior comprometimento baseado na ética de equilíbrio que deve haver entre credor e devedor.

A referida cláusula *rebus sic stantibus* também foi estabelecida no direito canônico do século XII e XIII, porém, a par do liberalismo ocorrido posteriormente, em que já delineava a implementação dos primeiros Códigos Civis no século XIX no seu quase esquecimento.

Durante a Idade Média a referida cláusula foi totalmente superada, porém, no século XX ressurge diante do comprometimento da economia europeia diante dos efeitos devastadores da Primeira Grande Guerra Mundial que, entretanto, ganhava uma nova roupagem com a inclusão do requisito do fato imprevisível, daí a denominação de "teoria da imprevisão". Cite-se, a lanço de exemplo, nas relações econômicas que envolviam o carvão, já que os fornecedores atrelados a contratos de longo prazo seriam levados à total ruína financeira se aplicassem as regras contratuais e legislação em vigor.

Foi, então, que surgiu a Lei Faillot (1918),[12] na França, que alterou o Código Civil francês, assim como na Inglaterra criou-se a *frustation of the*

[11] Sidou, Othon. *A revisão judicial dos contratos,* 2ª ed., Rio de Janeiro: Forense, 1983, p. 03.

[12] O artigo 1º assim dispunha, tradução livre: "Art. 1º. Enquanto perdurar a guerra e até 03 meses após o fim da cessação das hostilidades, as disposições excepcionais seguintes são aplicadas aos mercados e contratos comerciais para as partes ou apenas uma delas, que foram concluídos

adventure. Por sua vez, a Alemanha buscou a solução desse desequilíbrio financeiro no princípio geral da boa-fé e atrelado esta já na ideia da boa-fé objetiva. No direito italiano, com simplicidade, mas eficácia, apenas aplicou a vetusta e arcaica cláusula do direito medieval: *rebus sic stantibus*.

A cláusula *rebus sic stantibus* está na ideia do sensato que, hoje, com maior tecnicidade, deve se ter na concepção da razoabilidade e proporcionalidade, até mesmo, à luz do direito brasileiro na CRFB/88, numa visão da interpretação do direito civil constitucional. Embora antiga, os princípios da cláusula *rebus sic stantibus* identificam-se com ideais de justiça, de equilíbrio, bem como de cooperação e solidariedade entre credor e devedor, mesmo tendo interesses antagônicos, já que um deve pagar e o outro receber, sob o prisma econômico, mas que, sob o prisma jurídico, são direitos e deveres que se conjugam harmonicamente de modo a executar o contrato (*contractus*). Tal cláusula é tão antiga, que já afirmara ANISIO JOSÉ DE OLIVEIRA que "os princípios de tal cláusula *rebus sic stantibus*, antes de serem carreados para as páginas dos escritos dos Digestos, já se podia ler no próprio coração dos homens". [13]

A cláusula *rebus sic stantibus* tem tamanha força moral que é dispensável, até mesmo a sua disposição expressa no nosso ordenamento jurídico. Com razão, é a lição de CARNEIRO MAIA de que é irrelevante a circunstância de um determinado Código Civil, no caso, o brasileiro, referindo-se ao de 1916, assim como qualquer outro no direito comparado, não contemplar de forma expressa a referida cláusula, pois, o fundamento jurídico da teoria da imprevisão está na "lesão subjetiva", a que "o direito não pode ficar alheio, desde que deva compor o conflito de interesses segundo critério equitativo".[14]

antes de 1º de agosto de 1914, e que cuidem de entrega de mercadorias ou de produtos, sejam outras prestações sucessivas ou apenas diferidas. Art. 2º. Independentemente de a causa da resolução resultar do direito comum ou da convenção, os mercados e contratos atingidos por esta lei, de acordo com o artigo anterior, podem ser resolvidos a pedido de qualquer uma das partes, se restar comprovado que, por virtude do estado de guerra, a execução das obrigações de um dos contratantes acarretará encargos ou causar-lhe-á algum prejuízo, cuja importância ultrapassará e muito as previsões que poderiam ter sido razoavelmente feitas na época da convenção". A referida lei francesa somente foi aplicável aos contratos anteriores à 1ª Guerra Mundial iniciada em 28 de julho de 1914.

[13] OLIVEIRA, Anisio José de. *A cláusula rebus sic stantibus através dos tempos*, Belo Horizonte: Ibérica, 1968, p. 10.

[14] MAIA, Carneiro. *Da cláusula rebus sic stantibus*, n. 47, São Paulo: Saraiva, 1959, p. 246 a 248 e na verbete *Cláusula rebus sic stantibus, in Enciclopédia Saraiva de Direito*, v. 15, p. 155.

Na realidade, a teoria da imprevisão ganhou o requisito para a sua aplicabilidade no sentido de que o fato superveniente seja também imprevisível no momento em que as partes celebraram o negócio. TRABUCCHI pontuou os requisitos de aplicação da teoria da imprevisão: i) que o contrato deva ser de execução continuada, diferida ou periódica, isto é, de execução futura; ii) após a celebração do contrato, deve ter havido a superveniência de eventos extraordinários e imprevisíveis; iii) a prestação para uma das partes deve ter se tornado excessivamente onerosa, ante a nova situação não prevista; iv) a relação entre as prestações, no momento da execução, deve ter se tornado desproporcional relativamente àquilo que se estabelecera no momento da conclusão do contrato.[15]

Para a aplicação da teoria da imprevisão entende-se que o contrato de execução continuada ou diferida deva ter sido celebrado estipulando-se uma execução futura. Entretanto, após a sua celebração, deverá haver três elementos, cumulativos, pertinentes ao fato: superveniência, extraordinário e imprevisível, de modo que se afaste a culpabilidade do devedor da obrigação pelo inadimplemento (art. 396 do Código Civil de 2002).

Apresenta-se o requisito da superveniência, naturalmente, na hipótese em que surge o referido fato que gera o desequilíbrio contratual após o momento da celebração deste. O fato extraordinário é o fora do comum, do habitual, do corriqueiro, isto é, surge um novo fator exógeno e incomum entre as partes contratantes que altera o equilíbrio presumido existente. Nada mais que isso. Não se confunde com a imprevisibilidade.

Diz-se o fato imprevisível, à luz da teoria da imprevisão, aquele que, a par da superveniência e extraordinariedade, também não foi antevisto pelas partes contratantes no momento da celebração do negócio. Se restar comprovado que as partes não poderiam antever aquele fato que resultasse na alteração substancial da relação contratual de modo que comprometesse a vontade contratual, isto é, ao ponto de que as partes (ou uma delas) não desejasse assiná-lo, tem-se o fato imprevisível ensejador da aplicação da teoria da imprevisão.

É importante considerar que a imprevisibilidade do fato deve ser um critério sob análise das partes contratantes e não do especialista em determinada área do conhecimento. O critério norteador do juiz ao aplicá-lo deverá ser do ser humano mediano, tal como comumente se menciona na

[15] TRABUCCHI, *Istituzioni di Diritto Civille*, 17ª ed., Padova: CEDAM, 1968, p. 727-8.

ciência do direito, a do conhecimento do "homem médio". Este deve ser o parâmetro de análise da possibilidade de antever ou não um determinado fato para que se categorize como imprevisível. É o padrão do conhecimento do homem mediano dentro de determinado contexto social de espaço e tempo.

Não pode ser utilizado como parâmetro para a análise do fato imprevisível o conhecimento de uma pessoa com *expertise* em determinada área do conhecimento relacionado ao fato. Cite-se a lanço de exemplo, se uma pessoa (credor) celebra o contrato de venda e compra de um financiamento de um veículo, mas que detém conhecimento ou informação e, até mesmo, formação econômica com conhecimento de dados baseados em diversos estudos técnicos e financeiros, de modo que ela conclua que possivelmente naqueles contratos baseados na variação cambial haverá desajustes com a moeda de seu País.

Se, no momento da celebração, há, *v.g.*, equiparação da moeda do dólar com a moeda nacional de um para um, sabedora ela, de antemão, que essa igualdade em um futuro próximo provavelmente seria quebrada, para mais ou para menos, a seu favor ou não. Nestas condições, poderia ela invocar a teoria da imprevisão? Pensamos que não. Não é este o critério que deve nortear a aplicação do conhecimento do fato antevisto quando se aplicar a teoria da imprevisão. Deve ser baseada na possibilidade do homem mediano que não tem, em situação de normalidade, condições de antever o advento de fato que quebre o equilíbrio econômico do contrato. É uma análise em abstrato apenas.

Logo, se uma das partes, no momento da celebração do contrato, enquadra-se numa situação de homem mediano em que não tinha condições de prever mudanças no estado das coisas, justifica-se a aplicação da teoria da imprevisão, posto que há o requisito do fato ser imprevisível. Imagine-se, hipoteticamente, que uma pessoa, com experiência na área de saúde antevisse a possibilidade de uma pandemia mundial ainda no início da contaminação na cidade de Wuhan, na China, em outubro de 2019. E, assim, celebra um negócio jurídico de prestação diferida. Não se deve perquirir se há o efetivo conhecimento ou não do fato (pandemia), mas, apenas a análise da imprevisibilidade do fato pelo homem mediano. Entretanto, veremos adiante, que a hipótese do vírus SARS-CoV-2, gerador da pandemia e suspensão de atividades na cadeia produtiva, não é hipótese da teoria da imprevisão que autorize a revisão dos contratos.

O outro requisito é o da onerosidade excessiva que está atrelada a duas ideias fundamentais: a cobrança sob o espeque do credor, isto é, a cobrança excessiva diante da nova situação em que se enquadram as partes ante o fato novo e, de outro, a onerosidade, isto é, o dever extremamente gravoso para o devedor se tiver que cumprir a referida obrigação ante o mesmo fato que alterou o equilíbrio antes existente (é uma presunção *juris tantum*).

Quando ocorre a agravação da responsabilidade econômica, ainda ao ponto de trazer para o contratante maior onerosidade, mas que poderia ser razoavelmente prevista, não há que pretender a resolução do contrato ou a alteração de seu conteúdo. Nesses casos, o princípio da força obrigatória dos contratos conserva-se intacto. Para ser afastado, necessário que o acontecimento seja extraordinário e imprevisível. [16] Com efeito, ensina Orlando Gomes:

> "Necessário ainda que a alteração imprevisível do estado de fato determine a dificuldade de o contratante cumprir a obrigação, por se ter tornado excessivamente onerosa a prestação. A modificação quantitativa da prestação há que ser tão vultosa que, para satisfazê-la, o devedor se sacrificaria economicamente. Chega-se a falar em impossibilidade. Pretende-se, até, criar a categoria da impossibilidade econômica, ao lado da física e da jurídica, para justificar a resolução do contrato, mas, se a equiparação procedesse, estar-se-ia nos domínios da força maior, não cabendo, em consequência, outra construção teórica. A onerosidade excessiva não implica, com efeito, impossibilidade superveniente de cumprir a obrigação, mas apenas dificulta, embora extremamente, o adimplemento. Porque se trata de dificuldade, e não de impossibilidade, decorre importante consequência, qual seja a da necessidade de verificação prévia, que se dispensa nos casos de força maior." [17]

A alteração do estado dos fatos ditos imprevisíveis deve ser considerável de modo a interferir na declaração de vontade, isto é, a parte teria deixado de firmar o contrato se conhecesse determinado fato. Mais uma vez, o jurista baiano pontifica:

> "Na fundamentação da retratabilidade, por força da chamada imprevisão, dissentem os escritores. Explicam-na alguns, esclarecendo que a alteração do

[16] Gomes, Orlando. *Contratos*, 24ª Ed., Rio de Janeiro: Forense, 2001, p. 39.
[17] Gomes, Orlando. *ob. cit.*, p. 39.

estado de fato faz desaparecer a vontade contratual, por isso que emitida em atenção às circunstâncias existentes no momento da formação do contrato e às que poderiam ser previstas. Se pudessem as partes prever os acontecimentos que provocaram a alteração fundamental da circunstância, outra seria a declaração de vontade." [18]

Bem verdade que, para outros prosélitos, seria a falta parcial de causa do contrato, no seu aspecto funcional e, para outros, na teoria do abuso do direito. Porém, comungamos do entendimento, seguindo Orlando Gomes, com respaldo em Oertmann, [19] de que as teorias que explicam a necessidade de revisão de certos contratos devem ser pela apreciação da vontade contratual, se persistiria ou não com o fato ocorrido posterior à celebração e imprevisível, já que a ausência da vontade de contratar oferece uma explicação mais satisfatória. Até porque, seja pela falta parcial de causa, abuso do direito, equidade, boa-fé e outras ideias periféricas a esse pensamento estão atreladas, na essência, por mera opção técnica legislativa, do que propriamente uma razão técnico-jurídica.

Na esteira dessas reflexões, o período de quarentena decorrente da pandemia, concebido como o fato imprevisível, deverá ser analisado de modo que justifique a implementação da teoria da imprevisão nos contratos com a seguinte indagação: deixaria o contratante de celebrar o contrato se antevisse a suspensão das atividades durante alguns meses?

A resposta segura dependerá da análise do caso concreto. Entretanto, não é difícil de se imaginar que a imensa maioria dos negócios jurídicos não deixariam de existir em virtude da quarentena provocada pela pandemia. O locatário residencial deixaria de firmar o contrato de aluguel por 30 meses? O empresário não implantaria o seu ponto comercial em um contrato locatício por 03 anos ou mais, por exemplo, a fim de ali fazer de seu sustento? O contrato escolar não seria celebrado naquele ano, porém, com sério comprometimento do ano letivo do discente? São estas, apenas a título de exemplo, algumas das indagações que deverão ser desvendadas pelo juiz de direito ao analisar o caso concreto a fim de se poder afirmar,

[18] Gomes, Orlando, *cit.* p. 39.

[19] Gomes, Orlando, *cit.*, p. 40. Menciona o autor: Nesse sentido, a teoria das bases do negócio jurídico. Cons. Oertmann, *Introducción al Derecho Civil*; Larenz, *Las Bases del Negócio Jurídico*, p. 40.

com serenidade, que houve o comprometimento da vontade se a parte antevisse os efeitos da pandemia do coronavírus.

Concluir, por si só, que se trata da aplicação da teoria da imprevisão de forma abstrata e genérica, parece-nos inadequado e configura atecnia. Seja porque deve ser analisada a ausência da vontade da parte contratante se antevisse o fato, seja, também, porque deve ser comprovada a onerosidade excessiva à luz do credor, que, inegavelmente, também foi afetado diante da simbiose da cadeia produtiva.

Descabe ao legislador, ainda, atribuir aos fatos e dar qualificação jurídica, seja com o intuito de aplicar ou afastar. O anterior Projeto de Lei do Senador Antonio Anastasia, n. 1179/2020, aprovado no dia 03/04/2020, no art. 7º, assim estabelecia: "Não se consideram fatos imprevisíveis, para os fins exclusivos dos art. 478, 479 e 480 do Código Civil, o aumento da inflação, a variação cambial, a desvalorização ou substituição do padrão monetário". Descabe ao Congresso Nacional qualificar ou querer dar uma suposta interpretação dos fatos, já que a interpretação autêntica somente é dada pelo juiz de direito. De mais disso, como veremos adiante, não andaria bem o legislador ao qualificar os fatos como fatos imprevisíveis, já que não é hipótese de aplicação da teoria da imprevisão ou da onerosidade excessiva. De qualquer modo, daquele Projeto de Lei resultou a Lei 14.010 de 10 de junho de 2020 que dispõe sobre o Regime Jurídico Emergencial e Transitório das relações jurídicas de Direito Privado (RJET) no período da pandemia do coronavírus (Covid-19) em que a lei se absteve de tratar do tema como constava no projeto anterior. Nota-se que a Lei 14.010/20 optou pelo princípio da intervenção mínima do Estado nas relações privadas.

Caberia, à luz daquela teoria, o devedor comprovar que o prosseguimento da cobrança pelo credor caracteriza abuso do direito. Considerando-se que os efeitos da pandemia têm potencial de atingir a todos, credor e devedor, de um modo geral, não nos parece que se afigura presente o requisito da abusividade ainda que objetiva do credor da obrigação anteriormente firmada diante do COVID-19. Vale comparar com a Lei Faillot, da França, em 1918, provisória que foi, já que a guerra devastou colheitas e, de forma vertical comprometeu o adimplemento da obrigação dos agricultores e produtores. Na pandemia do COVID-19, parece-nos, que o efeito devastador não só incidiu sobre o devedor, como ocorreu com o efeito da guerra, mas, neste caso, comprometeu também o credor, sob o prisma de circulação das riquezas e da cadeia de produção e econômica, comumente mencionada entre os economistas diante do efeito cascata, sendo imprescindível uma análise interdisciplinar do direito e da economia.[20]

Ainda que os requisitos da teoria da imprevisão incidissem, à luz do art. 478 do Código Civil de 2002, denominada na *Seção IV: Da resolução por onerosidade excessiva*, neste dispositivo, em específico, a solução legal é a resolução do contrato. Aplicar a resolução do contrato a todos os negócios decorrentes da pandemia do COVID-19 seria devastador sob o prisma econômico e não condiz com o texto constitucional da liberdade econômica, pois se extinguiria milhares de contratos em vigor ou, ainda, com a redução indiscriminada da prestação.

O art. 317 do Código Civil de 2002, entretanto, admite que, se por motivos imprevisíveis sobrevier desproporção manifesta entre o valor da prestação devida e o do momento de sua execução, poderá o juiz corrigi-lo, a pedido da parte, de modo que assegure, quando possível, o valor real da prestação. Aqui, há uma permissão legal que, ao invés de resolver o contrato, reduziria a prestação. Igualmente, assim dispõe o art. 480 do Código Civil de 2002, se no contrato couberem a apenas uma das partes a prestação, poderá esta ser reduzida ou alterá-la o modo de sua execução, a fim de evitar a onerosidade excessiva.

O art. 317 menciona a desproporção manifesta que não se confunde com o conceito de onerosidade excessiva, citado no art. 478 e 480, ambos do Código Civil de 2002. Isso porque, a desproporção é mero elemento objetivo que não se analisa a cobrança por abuso do credor. Esse mesmo fenômeno ocorre se comparado o estado de perigo (art. 156 do CC/02)

[20] Ensina ROSSETTI: "O confronto das observações realizadas pelos diversos ramos das Ciências Sociais não só enriquece o contexto analítico empreendido pelas diversas áreas, como também confere maior exatidão aos princípios estabelecidos. Em termos práticos, recorrendo novamente a KOENIG (referindo-se a Samuel Koenig, *Elementos de sociologia*, Rio de Janeiro: Zahar, 1967) pode-se afirmar que: no processo de construção da sociedade futura é essencial que as críticas da ordem atual reconheçam que a estrutura econômica é apenas uma parte, ainda que importante, de um todo integrado, ao qual está inextricavelmente emaranhada. Não nos devemos esquecer de que, além da organização de tarefas de produção e distribuição de bens, o sistema econômico também funciona como uma cadeia que se liga a valores extra econômicos, de grande importância para os homens", p. 38, e, ainda, cita aquele autor: "Daí porque, G. RIPERT, em *Les Aspects Juridiques du Capitalisme Moderne*, observou que as questões da Economia resultariam estéreis se cultivadas em completo isolamento em relação a outros importantes ramos do conhecimento humano", ROSSETTI, José Paschoal, *Introdução à Economia*, 15ª ed., São Paulo: Atlas, 1991, p. 36.

que se refere a uma obrigação excessivamente onerosa com a lesão (art. 157 do CC/02) que estabelece a prestação manifestamente desproporcional. Para a lesão dispensa-se a cobrança abusiva como requisito, basta que seja desproporcional, elemento meramente objetivo.

Neste ponto, o art. 317 do referido *codex* é favorável à sua aplicação em virtude do COVID-19, já que dispensa a prova da abusividade do credor e insere no parâmetro jurídico imprescindível que sobrevenha desproporção manifesta entre o valor da prestação devida e no momento da execução. Por outro lado, o mencionado dispositivo legal permite um novo valor real da prestação. Em princípio, haveria possível interferência para que o juiz reduzisse provisoriamente a prestação continuada no período em que houve, por exemplo, os efeitos da pandemia e da quarentena.

A redução da prestação está condicionada, porém, na comprovação da desproporcionalidade da prestação com a contraprestação futura. O COVID-19 e a suspensão das atividades não criam, por si, só, desproporcionalidade da prestação e da contraprestação, mas um comprometimento no pagamento pelo devedor. Não haverá no período de suspensão de atividades produtivas, a rigor, desproporcionalidade, mas impossibilidade econômica no cumprimento do que antes foi avençado. A proporcionalidade da prestação com o benefício obtido com o contrato é uma relação que, de regra, é mantida após a pandemia. Isto é, prossegue um valor real da prestação diante do benefício ou proveito econômico obtido com o pacto.

O entrave na disposição do art. 317 do CC/02 na questão do COVID-19 é justamente a comprovação de que a prestação se tornou desproporcional em uma determinada relação jurídica, numa análise *inter partes*. A exemplo, o locatário, seja residencial ou comercial, continua com o uso do imóvel e, por sua vez, espera o locador receber o valor convencionado ante o uso de sua propriedade. Ou seja, o COVID-19 e período de quarentena não só compromete o devedor, mas também o credor. Haveria necessidade, à luz de seus requisitos, de que o motivo imprevisível comprometesse apenas o devedor da obrigação em que sobreviesse a desproporcionalidade da obrigação. Tal como ocorre com o fato do príncipe que é espécie de força maior.

Deve haver uma preocupação não só do devedor, mas também do credor, na intepretação legislativa. A esse propósito, o TJDF – Tribunal de Justiça do Distrito Federal, na lição lapidar da atual Min. Nancy Andrighi do STJ – Superior Tribunal de Justiça, externou o seguinte entendimento: "Preocupar-se com apenas uma das partes, ignorando por completo os efeitos que a decisão judicial poderá ter em relação à *ex adversa*, por certo não coaduna com a noção de jurisdição responsável e com o sagrado princípio da igualdade de tratamento". (TJDF, Cons. Da Mag., Ag. 1999.00.2.000303-7, Rel. Des. Nancy Andrighi, ac. 26/02/99, Revista de Direito Bancário e do Mercado De Capitais, v. 05, p. 181).

A função da teoria da imprevisão é restabelecer o equilíbrio contratual, pois não há azo para a revisão das bases do negócio se o ônus que se queixa uma das partes, ainda que decorrentes de uma pandemia, não corresponder a um injustificável acréscimo de vantagens para a outra, visível, pois, quando a lei menciona desproporcionalidade das prestações, ainda que sob uma ótica objetiva da prestação e da contraprestação. E, neste prisma, no geral, inexiste vantagem extrema em favor do credor em razão dos efeitos deletérios da pandemia do COVID-19 a todos, salvo casos específicos.

A depender do ramo do negócio durante a pandemia muitos lucraram de forma demasiada, inclusive, ilegalmente. Aproveitando-se do estado de calamidade pública, sobrelevaram os preços de itens importantes de prevenção da saúde, tais como os álcool em gel ou máscaras de proteção do modelo KN-95 ou de outras com finalidades cirúrgicas ou destinadas à área da saúde, havendo a possibilidade de incidência dos artigos 39, X; art. 51, IV e X do Código de Defesa do Consumidor e, ainda, infração contra a ordem econômica, art. 36, inciso III da Lei 12.529/2011.

A par dessas questões ilegais, outros, no âmbito estreito da legalidade, aumentaram as vendas, tais como os serviços de *delivery* em determinados ramos de produtos alimentícios. Noticiou-se, na Itália, em Bergamo, comuna italiana da região da Lombardia, que comerciantes dobraram as vendas de caixões ante o triste aumento dos mortos decorrentes da contaminação por coronavírus (SARS-CoV-2). No Brasil, *v.g.*, comerciantes de equipamentos de condicionamento físico aumentaram suas vendas ante o interesse por consumidores na prática de exercícios físicos na própria residência por força do isolamento social e, ainda, psicólogos prosseguiram substancialmente com as suas atividades via *on-line.*

Outros, ainda, em que pese o comprometimento comercial, adequaram-se em muitos serviços alternativos, com as referidas vendas por *delivery* e, ainda, pela prestação de serviços por sistema digital *on-line*, em que a *internet* funcionou sobremaneira para uma nova realidade virtual nunca antes experimentada, tais como a prestação de serviços educacionais do ensino básico e universitário.

Daí, porque, a teoria da onerosidade excessiva ou da imprevisão, como a conhecemos, não poderia adequar-se abstratamente à hipótese do COVID-19, pois haveria que se comprovar a cobrança excessiva do credor ou a desproporcionalidade de modo que, se antevisto o fato, o negócio não teria sido celebrado. Este requisito é imprescindível para a sua aplicabilidade, a par, é claro, que a aplicação da teoria da imprevisão a todos os contratos indiscriminadamente, como argumento metajurídico, seria devastador para a economia. Não foi esta a *ratio legis* tanto da *rebus sic stantibus* quanto da referida teoria. A pandemia e a quarentena diante do COVID-19 é um fato de força maior, de maior envergadura de valor jurídico do que a ser considerado como mero fato imprevisível. Não se nega que os efeitos deletérios da pandemia eram imprevisíveis a qualquer contratante, contudo, mais que isso, podem ensejar elemento de força maior que melhor se adequa para solucionar-se o conflito entre os contratantes, justamente, porque, para aplicar a teoria da imprevisão não basta a imprevisibilidade do fato, mas também a onerosidade excessiva em relação a uma das partes. A pandemia atingiu credor e devedor e dependerá do caso concreto, não se justifica traças uma metodologia padrão em favor do devedor diante da pandemia do COVID-19, situação bem diversa, a nosso ver, da que ocorreu com a lei francesa que afetou apenas o devedor em relação a agricultores e produtores rurais.

Entendemos, ainda, que a diferenciação entre a teoria da imprevisão com a cláusula *rebus sic stantibus* consiste na ausência apenas do fato imprevisível. Os demais requisitos são necessários a ambas: contrato de execução diferida ou continuada, fato extraordinário e superveniente que gere desequilíbrio contratual. Em nosso ordenamento jurídico, pode-se afirmar que a cláusula *rebus sic stantibus* está propriamente caracterizada no art. 6º, inciso V do Código de Defesa do Consumidor que determina, na segunda parte do inciso, o direito básico do consumidor à revisão em razão de fatos supervenientes que as tornem excessivamente onerosas.

Denota-se que o CDC não incluiu a necessidade de que fato seja imprevisível, mas apenas superveniente que tornem as prestações excessivamente onerosas para o consumidor. Daí, porque, parte da jurisprudência, inclusive, no STJ, decidiu que a revisão dos contratos *leasing* de veículos importados com base na variação cambial baseada no dólar permitia a revisão ante a brusca elevação do dólar após o ano de 1999, que, antes, estava equiparada de um real para um dólar. Alguns sustentaram certa previsibilidade do fato, que, cedo ou tarde, o dólar iria desequilibrar com a moeda nacional. Outros, entenderam que era imprevisível, inclusive, porque o então Presidente da República do Brasil, antes de sua reeleição, havia garantido a estabilidade da moeda nacional com o dólar. E, apesar disso, não foi o que ocorreu. Daí adveio, dentre tantas, a par da doutrina,[21] a decisão do STJ no REsp 437.660, da lavra do Min. Sálvio de Figueiredo Teixeira, de que:

> "contratos de *leasing* atrelados à variação cambial, os arrendatários, pela própria conveniência e a despeito do risco inerente, escolheram a forma contratual que no momento da realização do negócio lhes garantia prestações mais baixas, posto que o custo financeiro dos empréstimos em dólar era bem menor do que os custos em reais. A súbita alteração na política cambial, condensada na maxidesvalorização do real, ocorrida em janeiro de 1999, entretanto, criou a circunstância da onerosidade excessiva, a justificar a revisão judicial da cláusula que a instituiu".

Entrementes, a jurisprudência hodiernamente é no seguinte sentido:

> "... Com relação à tese da teoria da imprevisão, melhor sorte não espera a demanda, visto que não se fazem presentes os pressupostos para sua aplicação. De fato, nunca se poderia dizer e esperar, em sã consciência, neste país, que já passou por tantos percalços em sua vida econômica e política, que a variação da cotação da moeda norte americana seria um fator estável. Assim, não há que se falar em fato extraordinário e imprevisível, que é um dos requisitos para a aplicação da mencionada teoria (art. 478 do Código Civil de 2002). Como bem nos ensina Carlos Roberto Gonçalves, em sua obra Direito das Obrigações: "Na realidade, a cláusula "rebus sic stantibus" e a teoria da imprevisão têm sido aplicadas entre nós somente em casos excepcionais e com cautela, desde que demonstrados os seguintes requisitos: a) vigência de um contrato comutativo de execução diferida ou de trato sucessivo; b) ocorrência de fato extraordinário e imprevisível; c) considerável alteração da situação de fato existente no momento da execução, em confronto com a que existia por ocasião da celebração; d) onerosidade excessiva para um dos contratantes e vantagem exagerada para o outro". Em se tratando a variação do dólar de fator

[21] Calças, Manoel de Queiroz Pereira. "O Contrato de Arredamento Mercantil [*Leasing*]", *in Atualidades de Direito Civil*, v. I, coord. de Angélica Arruda Alvim e outros, Curitiba: Juruá, 2006, p. 69-83.

incerto e sujeito às mudanças de diretrizes da economia brasileira, afasta-se, sem sombra de dúvida, a possibilidade de invocação da teoria supra mencionada." (Recurso Especial nº 1.374.007 – MG (2013/0072168-3), Relatora: Min. Maria Isabel Gallotti, DJU 03/03/2020)

"... Ademais, a venda antecipada da soja garante a aferição de lucros razoáveis, previamente identificáveis, tornando o contrato infenso a quedas abruptas no preço do produto. Em realidade, não se pode falar em onerosidade excessiva, tampouco em prejuízo para o vendedor, mas tão-somente em percepção de um lucro aquém daquele que teria, caso a venda se aperfeiçoasse em momento futuro". (STJ, REsp 849.228/GO, Rel. Ministro Luis Felipe Salomão, Quarta Turma, j. 03/08/2010, DJe 12/08/2010).

O STJ – Superior Tribunal de Justiça já enfrentou, desde logo, a alegação da cláusula *rebus sic stantibus* em razão da pandemia do COVID-19 sob alegação de impossibilidade de cumprimento da execução da sentença, em que foi denegado o Mandado de Segurança por falta de requisitos legais e, por isso, o mérito não foi apreciado. (STJ, MS n. 025892, DJE 01/04/2020, Rel. Min. Regina Helena Costa). Logo, é correto afirmar-se que o argumento da cláusula *rebus sic stantibus* será invocado corriqueiramente nos Tribunais. [22] A cláusula *rebus sic stantibus* já foi invocada, inclusive, para a alteração das soluções dadas pelo Poder Judiciário conforme o estado das coisas, tal como ocorreu no REsp 1.561.982 – PB (2015/0267120-3), Rel. Min. Og Fernandes, DJe 06/08/2019:

"... Compulsando os autos, entretanto, resta evidenciada a existência de um *distinguishing* entre o precedente invocado e a hipótese em análise, já que a parte agravante defende que a natureza do benefício de aposentadoria por

[22] Nas primeiras decisões enfrentadas pelo Tribunal Bandeirante houve também entendimento que descabe a alteração do valor do aluguel nos contratos de locação, haja vista a possibilidade de emenda da mora em eventual e futura ação de despejo, suspendendo-se apenas a constrição nominal nos órgãos de proteção e crédito: "EMENTA – Locação de imóvel comercial. Tutela de urgência destinada a suspender a exigibilidade dos aluguéis em face da quarentena decorrente da pandemia por COVID-19. Descabimento. Moratória que pelo regime legal não pode ser imposta ao credor pelo Juiz, devendo decorrer de ato negocial entre as partes ou por força de especial disposição legal. Evocação do caso fortuito e força maior que tampouco autoriza aquela medida. Cabimento, porém, da vedação à extração de protesto de título representativo do crédito por aluguéis. Recurso parcialmente provido." (TJSP, Ag. 2063701-03.2020.8.26.0000, 36ª Câmara de Direito Privado, Des. Arantes Theodoro, j. 06/04/2020)

> invalidez é, por si, transitória, restando-lhe ínsita a cláusula *rebus sic stantibus*, isso em função da permanente possibilidade de evolução da medicina e do quadro de saúde do beneficiário, restando, pois, patente a inviabilidade de se cristalizar os efeitos da decadência no presente caso.
>
> (...) A questão deve ser assim entendida porque, em que pese ser requisito para a continuidade à percepção do benefício a sujeição do beneficiário a perícias médicas para fins de comprovação de permanência da condição de incapaz para o trabalho, a lei não trouxe exceção à regra e, entender de modo diverso, viola o Princípio da Segurança Jurídica. Ademais, o exercício da autotutela por parte da Administração não é absoluto, atentando-se para o direito adquirido, uma vez que a apelante percebia o valor referente ao benefício por mais de 12 anos.
>
> Na espécie, a segurada é portadora do Vírus HIV, doença incluída na lei previdenciária no rol de doenças incapacitantes, suscetível de aposentadoria por invalidez ou auxílio-doença (art. 151, da Lei n. 8213/91), estigmatizante e que abala o sistema imunológico humano, tornando-se suscetível de ser acometido por inúmeras outras doenças oportunistas.
>
> Deve-se ressaltar ainda que, tendo sido a ora apelante enfermeira durante sua vida profissional ativa, não se mostra razoável a sua reinserção no mercado de trabalho, porto que inconciliáveis a profissão e a moléstia que detém, pois o retorno ao trabalho colocaria em risco ela própria e os pacientes que viessem a ter contato consigo, face ao caráter infecto-contagioso da referida enfermidade."

E, ainda, na seara do direito penal, igualmente, utilizada a cláusula *rebus sic stantibus*:

> "... Caracterizados concretamente, assim, o *fumus commissi delicti* e o *periculum libertatis*, as custódias devem ser decretadas.
>
> Trata-se de decisão *rebus sic stantibus* (segundo o estado da causa) e, por isso mesmo, poderá ser revogada, se os motivos que a determinaram desaparecerem, bem como de novo ser decretada, se sobrevierem razões que a justifiquem, nos termos do art. 316 do CPP." (STJ, recurso em *Habeas Corpus* nº 73.353 – RS (2016/0185122-3), Rel. Min. Nefi Cordeiro, DJe 01/08/2016)

Por essas razões, parece-nos ser precipitado invocar a teoria da imprevisão ou onerosidade excessiva nas relações contratuais, já que os seus requisitos, ainda que no plano abstrato, não estão presentes, isto é, a onerosidade excessiva, cobrança pelo credor que lhe tenha causado extrema vantagem, já que também acometido de interferência econômica pela pandemia do COVID-19. E, ainda, porque não se trata de mero fato imprevisível a pandemia, mas, força maior que autoriza, se comprovado, a suspensão dos efeitos da mora contratual. E, igualmente, incabível a alegação da cláusula *rebus sic stantibus* nas relações de consumo, já que o requisito da onerosidade excessiva, em tese, inexiste. Assim como, inexiste, numa análise relacional objetiva *inter partes*, a desproporcionalidade entre as prestações, pois é o comprometimento financeiro decorrente da pandemia e o necessário período de quarentena que poderia, em tese, gerar a impossibilidade do adimplemento contratual, em que se afigura outro instituto jurídico aplicável.

3. FATO DO PRÍNCIPE (*FACTUM PRINCIPIS*)

Há que se cogitar se há aplicação da teoria do fato do príncipe diante do vírus SARS-CoV-2 na medida em que muitos estabelecimentos comerciais e empresas foram obrigados a suspender as suas atividades em virtude de determinação de governadores dos Estados no País, inclusive, com afetação das inúmeras relações trabalhistas. Ou, ainda, em virtude da orientação da Organização Mundial da Saúde – OMS com o estabelecimento do *stay home* ou "fique em casa" (no Brasil) por recomendação do Ministério da Saúde. A teoria do fato do príncipe está expressamente estabelecida em nosso ordenamento jurídico nas relações trabalhistas e é contemplada no art. 486 da Consolidação das Leis do Trabalho – CLT, que assim dispõe:

> "No caso de paralisação temporária ou definitiva do trabalho, motivada por ato de autoridade municipal, estadual ou federal, ou pela promulgação de lei ou resolução que impossibilite a continuação da atividade, prevalecerá o pagamento da indenização, que ficará a cargo do governo responsável". (redação dada pela Lei 1.530, de 26.12.1951)

E a pessoa de direito público poderia ser chamada à autoria para alegar o que entende devido em sua defesa, conforme o par. 1º do referido dispositivo celetista, cabendo, se improcedente as suas alegações, na condenação das verbas de natureza trabalhista e indenizatória. A teoria do fato do príncipe é o ato da Administração Pública de natureza administrativa ou legislativa que implica na completa impossibilidade de execução do contrato de trabalho, considerado comumente por como uma espécie do gênero da força maior. Exige-se para a ocorrência do fato do príncipe que o evento seja inevitável; que haja nexo de causalidade entre o ato administrativo do legislativo e a paralisação completa do trabalho e, assim, que haja uma impossibilidade absoluta da continuação do negócio; e, por fim, que o empregador não provoque ou concorra para a sua ocorrência.

A paralisação deve ser completa, pois, não há *factum principis* se o ato da autoridade não impedir absolutamente a continuidade do trabalho, apenas tornando-a mais difícil ou onerosa. Entretanto, muitas empresas tiveram que efetivamente suspender totalmente as atividades em virtude de ato governamental estadual. Por sua vez, o Estado assume a responsabilidade civil quando o fato do príncipe é ato fundado em conveniência e oportunidade ou quando o ato é vinculado. O fundamento da "teoria do fato do príncipe" assenta-se na ideia de que a Administração, se causar danos ou prejuízos aos administrados, ainda que em benefício da coletividade, deverá indenizá-los. A lanço de exemplos, é a hipótese da lei que proíbe a exploração de determinada atividade, antes permitida, suprime empresa pública ou determina a extinção de um cartório. Ou, ainda, na hipótese de encerramento de atividade em virtude de desapropriação do local em que funcionava uma determinada empresa. Nesses casos, é comum a doutrina e jurisprudência admitirem a ocorrência do fato do príncipe.

Entretanto, é importante que se atente que a aplicação do *factum principis* existe somente quando o ato governamental recaia somente sobre uma determinada empresa ou, até mesmo, a um grupo de empresas de determinada atividade econômica. Não foi esse o fenômeno ocorrido com a pandemia e o período de quarentena, até porque, inicialmente, tratou-se de uma orientação da Organização Mundial da Saúde, acolhida por muitos países, tais como na Itália, Alemanha, Reino Unido, Portugal, França e EUA – Estados Unidos da América e, muitos, inclusive, por meio de suas autoridades governamentais arrependeram-se da determinação tardia do distanciamento ou do isolamento social, como ocorreu entre os italianos.

O fato do príncipe supõe três condições para que se verifique: i) um contrato em que a Administração seja parte; ii) medida de Poder Público (lei, regulamento, decisão executória especial), cujo efeito rompe o equilíbrio do contrato; iii) elemento de imprevisão, entendido no sentido seguinte: se a medida de Poder Público intercorrente estivesse nas previsões das partes, no ato de contratar, não há possibilidades de indenização, no momento em que se realiza. A diferença clássica entre o fato do príncipe e a teoria da imprevisão reside que nesta o direito de indenizar surge apenas quando a situação do particular contratante sofreu verdadeiro transtorno, tomando--se insustentável, e pela teoria do fato do príncipe o direito à indenização comumente incide. Por outro lado, ao passo que o fato do príncipe gera direito a uma reparação integral, a imprevisão dá origem apenas a uma participação nos novos encargos. [23] Ao passo que a teoria da imprevisão está subordinada a fatos independentes da vontade da Administração e do concessionário e que originam álea econômica, o fato do príncipe pressupõe um ato voluntário da Administração e que nos coloca em face da álea administrativa. Não foi o que ocorreu no caso da COVID-19. O ato governamental recaiu sobre todas as atividades empresariais de forma indiscriminada a fim de coibir o contágio e pertence a uma álea independente da vontade da Administração, tanto que o isolamento se deu também entre as pessoas naturais. Por essa razão, não há que se falar na aplicação da teoria.

De outra banda, inexiste responsabilidade civil do Estado, já que, em que pese esta ser objetiva, à luz do art. 37, par. 6º da CRFB/88, admite excludentes da responsabilidade e, não se configura, a nosso ver, o ato ilícito diante da tentativa de preservar a segurança física e a saúde da coletividade com o distanciamento social, em prol do bem comum. E, simplesmente, pela inexistência de dano indenizável, ao contrário, buscou-se a preservação da integridade física coletiva e em prol do interesse público. Responsabilizar o Estado pela determinação de suspensão das atividades empresariais em qualquer ramo de atividade, ainda que fosse concebido como ato ilícito, *ad argumendantum tantum*, seria, ao mesmo tempo, agravar os efeitos deletérios da pandemia sobre a sociedade, na medida em que o valor indenizatório, uma vez reconhecido, advém dos cofres públicos em que a conta seria paga pela própria sociedade. Neste cenário, a par de não se caracterizar a ilicitude da atividade Estatal de suspensão das atividades, ao menos aquelas tidas como não essenciais, para se cumprir o isolamento social, tem-se, igualmente, uma solução indenizatória que não atenderia o interesse público.

É de interesse público que se atenda e se garanta certas garantias individuais constitucionais. Entretanto, o interesse público faz-se presente ante a valorização da integridade física, não só sob as vertentes do prisma constitucional, mas também à luz do direito civil, ante a afetação, em primeira análise, da vida e da saúde individual de cada um. A República Federativa

[23] LAUBADERE, Andre de, *Traité elementaire de droit administratif*, Paris: LGDJ, 1953, p. 451.

do Brasil de 1988 tem como fundamento a dignidade da pessoa humana (art. 1º, inciso III da CRFB/88), bem como deve ser garantido aos brasileiros e aos estrangeiros residentes no País a inviolabilidade do direito à vida, expressamente alocados no art. 5º, *caput* e inciso X da Carta Maior. Nesta ordem de pensamento, resta insustentável em situação de excepcionalidade ventilar-se possibilidade de responsabilização da atividade Estatal diante da atitude em se seguir recomendações científicas mundiais praticadas em diversos países, já que, a padronização da conduta diante da pandemia do COVID-19 foi justamente a adoção do distanciamento e isolamento social.

Desse modo, entendemos que não se aplica a teoria do fato do príncipe seja nas relações contratuais trabalhistas ou civis diante da adoção de quarentena pela pandemia do COVID-19, na medida em que as determinações governamentais visavam, assim como ocorreu em inúmeros outros Países, a preservação da saúde da população no mundo. A aplicabilidade da teoria, dentre os demais requisitos, justifica-se por ato governamental em relação a uma determinação de suspensão da atividade total somente a uma pessoa jurídica ou um grupo delas e não a todas, tal como ocorreu em razão da pandemia.

4. ANÁLISE DA APLICAÇÃO DA FORÇA MAIOR E CASO FORTUITO DIANTE DO SARS-COV-2

O caso fortuito e a força maior nas relações contratuais estão estabelecidas expressamente no parágrafo único do art. 393 do Código Civil brasileiro de 2002: "O devedor não responde pelos prejuízos resultantes de caso fortuito ou força maior, se expressamente não se houver por eles responsabilizado. Parágrafo único: O caso fortuito ou de força maior verifica-se no fato necessário, cujos efeitos não era possível evitar ou impedir".[24]

[24] Enunciado 443 da V Jornada de Direito Civil, Superior Tribunal de Justiça: *O caso fortuito e a força maior somente serão considerados como excludentes da responsabilidade civil quando o fato gerador do dano não for conexo à atividade desenvolvida*. No Código Civil Português há similares disposições sobre o caso fortuito: *art. 616, item 02: O adquirente de má fé é responsável pelo valor dos bens que tenha alienado, bem como dos que tenham perecido ou se hajam deteriorado por caso fortuito, salvo se provar que a perda ou deterioração se teriam igualmente verificado no caso de os bens se encontrarem no poder do devedor; Art. 1.462, item 2: Se os animais se perderem, na totalidade ou em parte, por caso fortuito, sem produzirem outros que os substituam, o usufrutuário é tão somente obrigado a entregar as cabeças restantes.* E quanto à força maior no direito lusitano: *Art. 321, item 1: A prescrição suspende-se durante o tempo em que o titular estiver impedido de fazer valer o seu direito, por motivo de força maior, no decurso dos últimos três meses do prazo. Art. 505: Sem prejuízo do disposto no artigo 570º, a responsabilidade fixada*

É de se observar que raramente se entabula no contrato que o devedor se responsabilizará pela obrigação civil diante dos prejuízos resultantes do caso fortuito ou força maior. Desse modo, a regra geral, é a isenção da responsabilidade do devedor por estes prejuízos, livrando-se dos efeitos da mora,[25] tais como juros e multas contratuais estipulados em cláusula penal ou, ainda, decorrentes de lei. O parágrafo único determina o elemento comum do fato nos casos fortuito e força maior, isto é, que o fato seja necessário, *cujos efeitos não era possível evitar ou impedir.*

Neste particular, é crucial, a nosso ver, a noção diferenciadora entre o fato necessário e o fato imprevisível, de modo a não se imiscuir entre a hipótese de caso fortuito ou força maior e a teoria da imprevisão ou onerosidade excessiva. É possível que um fato determinado seja previsível, porém, inevitável. Eis a inevitabilidade do fato, embora previsível. De início, denota-se, por lógica, a diferenciação de conceitos. E, por outro lado, é possível que o fato seja imprevisível, porém, em tese, seria possível evitar de modo que se pudesse cumprir a obrigação, se dele se tivesse, excepcionalmente, o conhecimento prévio. Neste caso, predomina a imprevisibilidade que, por isso, não se pôde evitar o inadimplemento, daí a ausência de culpabilidade do devedor da obrigação. A imprevisibilidade do fato contida na teoria da imprevisão implica numa análise subjetiva das partes, já a inevitabilidade é objetiva.

A inevitabilidade tem uma atuação na relação jurídica de maior amplitude que a imprevisibilidade do fato. Caberá a análise da hipótese para se identificar se o fato é meramente imprevisível e, por isso, não poderia ser evitável ou, se é hipótese de inevitabilidade do fato, independentemente

pelo nº 1 do artigo 503º só é excluída quando o acidente for imputável ao próprio lesado ou a terceiro, ou quando resulte de causa de força maior estranha ao funcionamento do veículo. Art. 509, item 02: Não obrigam a reparação os danos devidos a causa de força maior; considera-se de força maior toda a causa exterior independente do funcionamento e utilização da coisa.

25 Inadimplemento absoluto e relativo. Costumeira flexibilização do *dies ad quem.* A mora e o inadimplemento são, ambos, formas de injúria contratual. No simples caso de mora, porém essa injúria não é irreparável. A mora se distingue do inadimplemento em que este define, à última, a posição do devedor perante o credor, acarretando para aquele as consequências extremas do descumprimento, enquanto a mora se caracteriza por não tirar ao devedor a possibilidade de, mais tarde, cumprir a obrigação. O credor que, habitualmente, não exige pagamento de prestações em tempo certo, como sucede no caso de apólices sorteáveis, arma, como esse teor de proceder, atmosfera de confiança para o devedor, relaxando-se a vigilância quanto ao termo do pagamento (STF, Revista Forense 111/410).

da previsibilidade ou não desse mesmo fato. Na primeira situação, poderia ensejar a aplicação da teoria da onerosidade excessiva ou imprevisão, na segunda, o caso fortuito ou força maior. A lanço de exemplo, imagine-se que uma determinada agência espacial identifica a vinda de um meteoro de proporções tais em direção ao planeta que não se possa impedir a colisão. Haverá a probabilidade e previsibilidade do fato uma vez dada a publicidade mundial deste e, ainda assim, a parte decide por assinar um determinado contrato, mas há a sua inevitabilidade, daí porque os efeitos não é (ou era) possível evitar ou impedir, em que gerou, *a posteriori*, a impossibilidade no cumprimento da obrigação pelo devedor. Sendo, a par dessas considerações, a queda do meteoro decorrente de forças da natureza, tem-se a força maior, logo, é fato necessário e não se qualifica como fato imprevisível.

A pandemia provocada pelo vírus SARS-CoV-2, ainda que, em tese, tivesse sido prevista pelas autoridades governamentais com medidas de contenção de sua propagação imediata e cientificada previamente à sociedade, embora os seus efeitos deletérios pudessem ser minimizados, caracteriza o fato necessário impossível de se evitar ou impedir, pois, consiste justamente na prática de isolamento social mundial com suspensão da cadeia de produção e da atividade econômica em grande escala. Neste sentir, é infértil a pretensão de responsabilização de um país "A" ou "B" pela pandemia diante da natural ausência do controle ante a ágil velocidade do contágio causada pelo coronavírus.

A pandemia do COVID-19 e todos os seus desdobramentos deletérios com o isolamento social consistem em um fato necessário impossível de evitar ou impedir caracterizador exclusivamente da força maior, inclusive, nas relações de consumo. Por esta razão, entendemos que o conceito e extensão de força maior é mais amplo do que o fato imprevisível, já que a força maior poderia até mesmo ser previsível e nem por isso se desnaturaria de sua característica no plano ontológico.

Vislumbra-se a hipótese do parágrafo único do art. 393 do Código Civil de 2002 no caso de pandemia do COVID-19 que decorreu a suspensão das atividades produtivas em geral, pois, o fato é, primordialmente, inevitável, o que afasta, por si, a hipótese da teoria da imprevisão ou da onerosidade excessiva. Não se admite, em nosso ordenamento jurídico, a aplicabilidade de dois institutos revisores ou de autorização da suspensão do cumprimento da obrigação diversos para um mesmo fato. Daí porque o CC/02 abraçou a teoria da onerosidade excessiva no art. 478 e 480 do referido diploma, independentemente das disposições do art. 317 e 393.

O efeito decorrente do caso fortuito[26] ou força maior é o mesmo, isto é, a ausência de culpabilidade do devedor pela obrigação anteriormente assumida, tese já pacífica na doutrina e na jurisprudência. É comum e com acerto a doutrina mencionar que há pouca importância prática na distinção entre força maior e caso fortuito, ante o fato de ambos possuírem idêntica força liberatória, exonerando o devedor de responsabilidade.[27] Distingue a doutrina um e outro, embora muitos autores entendam ser muito difícil a sua conceituação e, já de longa data, para alguns, incluía-se a requisito da imprevisibilidade do fato, tal como ensinava LACERDA DE ALMEIDA: "Força maior diz-se mais propriamente de acontecimento insólito, de impossível ou dificílima previsão, tal uma extraordinária seca, uma inundação, um incêndio, um tufão, etc." [28] Desde a promulgação do Código Civil francês, a maior parte da doutrina francesa limitava-se a afirmar sobre o alcance do caso fortuito e da força maior sem, contudo, distingui-los, já que ambos tratam de acontecimento invencível ou de causa estranha que não é imputável ao devedor e, portanto, isenta-o de responsabilidade pela inexecução da obrigação. Porém, para DEMOLOMBE a força maior trata de um fato decorrente da natureza (*v.g*, inundação, terremoto, etc.) e o caso fortuito (*v.g.*, guerra, violência por terceiro, etc.) decorre de um fato da conduta humana, acolhido majoritariamente pela doutrina nacional. [29]

WASHINGTON DE BARROS MONTEIRO afirmou que teoricamente distinguem-se os dois conceitos de caso fortuito e força maior, diante de várias teorias que tentam delinear as distinções: i) teoria da extraordinariedade; ii) teoria da previsibilidade e da irresistibilidade; iii) teoria da diferenciação quantitativa; iv) teoria do conhecimento; v) teoria do reflexo sobre a vontade humana, vi) teoria das forças naturais e do fato de ter-

[26] No direito norte-americano é definido o caso fortuito como *Act of God* – atos de Deus. No direito brasileiro, em pese essa ideia, não foi acolhida a expressão, na medida em que, historicamente, não contemplaria elemento fático que justifique a revisão.

[27] DINIZ, Maria Helena. *Curso de Direito Civil brasileiro: teoria geral das obrigações*, 30ª Ed., v. 02, São Paulo: Saraiva, 2015, p. 403, assim como sustentou Washington de Barros Monteiro, *Curso de Direito Civil, São Paulo: Saraiva*, 1982, v. 03, p. 331, Clóvis Beviláqua, *Código Civil Comentado*, v. 04, p. 216, dentre outros, conforme noticiado por aquela autora.

[28] ALMEIDA, Lacerda de. *Obrigações*, São Paulo: Livraria Cruz Coutinho, 1897, p. 169.

[29] DINIZ, Maria Helena, *ob. cit.*, p. 402, assim como Orlando Gomes, Washington de Barros Monteiro, Silvio Rodrigues, Serpa Lopes, dentre outros.

ceiro, sendo esta última adotada por aquele autor, [30] seguindo o mesmo entendimento de Clóvis Beviláqua. Pontes de Miranda pontuou importante consideração:

> "A distinção entre força maior e caso fortuito só teria de ser feita, só seria importante, se as regras jurídicas a respeito daquela e desse fossem diferentes, então, ter-se-ia de definir força maior e caso fortuito, conforme a comodidade da exposição. Não ocorrendo tal necessidade, é escusado estarem os juristas a atribuir significados que não têm base histórica, nem segurança em doutrina." [31]

Convém frisar que, modernamente, parece-nos que a legislação atribuiu algumas hipóteses distintas em que, talvez, mereceria reflexos na jurisprudência. Diante do novel Código Civil de 2002, por vezes, este fez menção diferenciada, a saber, menciona o caso fortuito ou a força maior como requisitos para o efeito desejado pela lei como excludente de responsabilidade civil contratual ou extracontratual, são eles, os arts. 246, 393, 399 e 583 e, em outras, somente menciona a hipótese da força maior como excludentes, conforme os arts. 607, 625, 636, 642, 696, 702, 719, 734, 737, 753 e 936. Para tais casos, poder-se-ia afirmar que o caso fortuito não estaria incluso como hipótese de excludente da responsabilidade, mas, tão somente a força maior, havendo, em termos práticos, uma diferença de aplicabilidade nas hipóteses de casos específicos entre o caso fortuito e a força maior.

O Código Civil ao estabelecer situações que não menciona o caso fortuito, igualmente, não o inclui como fator de isenção de responsabilidade e, neste caso, é importante não tratar caso fortuito e força maior como sinônimos, embora muitos dos autores no pretérito assim o tivessem feito. Destarte, a nosso ver, o legislador atual trouxe algum critério diferenciador entre uma hipótese ou outra não quanto aos seus conceitos, mas quanto às hipóteses de sua aplicação no caso concreto.

Na lição lapidar de Maria Helena Diniz tem-se o conceito de ambos distintos:

[30] Monteiro, Washington de Barros. *Curso de Direito Civil: direito das obrigações 1ª parte*, v. 04, 9ª ed., 1970, p. 339-40.

[31] Miranda, Pontes de. *Tratado de direito privado*. t. XXII. São Paulo: Revista dos Tribunais, 2012, p. 158-9.

"Na força maior conhece-se o motivo ou a causa que dá origem ao acontecimento, pois se trata de um fato da natureza, como, p. ex., um raio que provoca um incêndio, inundação, que danifica os produtos ou intercepta as vias de comunicação, impedindo a entrega da mercadoria prometida, ou um terremoto que ocasiona grandes prejuízos, etc. Implica, portanto, uma ideia de relatividade, já que a força do acontecimento é maior do que a suposta, devendo-se fazer uma consideração prévia do estado do sujeito e das circunstâncias espaciotemporais para que se caracterize como eficácia liberatória de responsabilidade civil. No caso fortuito o acidente que acarreta o dano advém de causa desconhecida, como o cabo elétrico aéreo que se rompe e cai sobre fios telefônicos, causando incêndio, explosão de caldeira de usina e provocando a morte. Pode ser ocasionado por fato de terceiro, como greve, que provoca a paralisação da fábrica e impede a entrega de certo produto prometido pelo industrial, motim, mudança de governo, colocação do bem fora do comércio, de modo a causar graves acidentes ou prejuízos, devido à impossibilidade do cumprimento de certas obrigações".[32]

Nota-se que a diferenciação reside, substancialmente, que o caso fortuito é provocado por fato de terceiro ou coisa, já a força maior, decorre da natureza, incluído, por derradeiro, a doença que impede o cumprimento da obrigação pelo devedor. Na hipótese abordada neste estudo, o que determinou a quarentena e a suspensão das atividades produtivas gerais foi um vírus letal (SARS-CoV-2) com possibilidade de contaminação em massa, com maior número de mortes não só no País, como no mundo. A determinação ou orientação geral da OMS – Organização Mundial da Saúde do *stay home* é ato provocado por terceiro, longe de ser ilícito, mas protetivo que, isoladamente, enquadrar-se-ia no caso fortuito (evento provocado por terceiro). Entretanto, é uma determinação derivada, logo, causa próxima, em que a causa remota criadora daquela é, sobremaneira, o referido vírus e a doença provocada por este cujo efeito principal é a velocidade da morte.

Por isso, deve-se tratar como hipótese de força maior todos os efeitos e desdobramentos decorrentes da contaminação do coronavírus, isto é, a quarentena e a suspensão das atividades diversas e isolamento social em todas as relações civis, empresariais ou de consumo. Caberá ao devedor

[32] DINIZ, Maria Helena, *Curso, cit.*, p. 402.

comprovar, cumulativamente, a inimputabilidade do cumprimento da obrigação.

É necessário a prova do fato preciso e determinado que, por ser inevitável, e não culposo, possa exonerar o devedor. Cabe a este comprovar que o seu procedimento está dentro de um padrão de normalidade, isto é, foi prudente e cuidadoso, embora fosse público e notório a causa do seu inadimplemento, isto é, a suspensão das atividades com comprometimento na cadeia produtiva. Insta observar que a ausência de culpa é um gênero, em que o caso fortuito e a força maior é a espécie, diante da inevitabilidade do evento.

Mesmo para as hipóteses de força maior do COVID-19, caberá ao devedor demonstrar a ausência de sua culpa que gere a inimputabilidade civil. Há que se comprovar o nexo de causalidade efetivo da suspensão das atividades produtivas que gere o inadimplemento não culposo e, que, efetivamente, foi o evento que o impediu de executar a obrigação (suspensão das atividades decorrentes do coronavírus) e era, deveras, inevitável adimplir na data aprazada. A existência de recursos financeiros com o isolamento social, por si, só, não justifica o inadimplemento, na medida em que nos dias de hoje os pagamentos poderão dar-se pelos meios alternativos, como os digitais, que não impedem o pagamento das obrigações. Esse entendimento se coaduna com a finalidade de se evitar abusos por parte do devedor da obrigação, pois, descabe a alegação genérica da pandemia de modo a justificar o inadimplemento contratual ou mesmo um acordo judicial lavrado anteriormente.

Há o ônus da prova, como não poderia deixar de ser, de quem alegar a impossibilidade no cumprimento da obrigação decorrente da pandemia, provar, à luz, inclusive, dos preceitos elementares das regras do processo civil, art. 373, inciso I do Código de Processo Civil brasileiro, pois a prova é instituto de caráter misto do direito civil e do processo civil. Cabendo, inclusive, ao magistrado atribuir o ônus diverso, desde que o faça por decisão fundamentada, caso em que deverá dar à parte, oportunidade de se desincumbir do ônus que lhe foi atribuído, nos termos do par. 1º do citado dispositivo.

A comprovação da inimputabilidade do devedor diante do COVID-19 deverá dar-se por todos os meios de prova em direito admitidas, tais como a real ausência de recursos financeiros para o adimplemento do contrato, *v. g.*, pela apresentação de livros contábeis, tratando-se de pessoa jurídica ou, ainda, tratando-se de pessoa natural, a ausência de reservas financeiras em contas bancárias que demonstrem a ausência de liquidez, atrelado, ainda, à análise de sua condição patrimonial ou o período total da execução do contrato diferida no tempo, dentre outros fatores que denotem, cabalmente, a insuficiência de recursos para adimplir na data aprazada. A mera ausência de lucro como anteriormente esperado diante do COVID-19 não dá azo à alegação de força maior que autorize o inadimplemento contratual.

Observa-se que uma vez reconhecido no caso concreto a aplicabilidade da força maior cumulada com a impossibilidade do pagamento por um determinado devedor, tem-se a necessidade do passo seguinte atribuído às contendas judiciais de qual solução cabível deverá ser dada pelo aplicador do direito.

5. NECESSIDADE DE INTERVENÇÃO ESTATAL DIANTE DO SARS-COV-2

Uma vez comprovada a ausência efetiva de possibilidade de adimplemento da obrigação diante da suspensão das atividades por força do COVID-19, exonerar-se-á o devedor dos efeitos da mora, tais como multa e juros. Caberá, porém, o devedor adimplir com a sua obrigação principal, devendo-se ser fixada pelo magistrado o período de seu cumprimento. O grande desafio do Poder Judiciário será fixar esse período determinado e sob quais critérios equitativos na relação contratual.

Entendemos que poderá o magistrado determinar que no mesmo período em que se manteve a quarentena, caberá o devedor cumprir a obrigação faltante cumulada com a obrigação do período respectivo, em ato conjunto, conforme a periodicidade suspensiva. Entretanto, não é difícil de se imaginar que o devedor alegue genericamente a impossibilidade, na medida em que acumulará a obrigação principal atrasada, embora sem juros ou multa, com a obrigação atual do período a ser pago nos contratos de execução continuada. [33] Neste sentido, percebe-se, claramente, que embora incida na hipótese a força maior, ela é insuficiente para solucionar o conflito no sentido de se atribuir uma solução objetiva. Caberá ao juiz

[33] No Agravo de Instrumento n. 2065856-76.2020.8.26.0000, do Tribunal de Justiça de São Paulo, da 1ª Câmara Reservada de Direito Empresarial, Rel. Cesar Ciampolini, foi deferida liminar por tutela recursal de parcelamento de dívida anteriormente acordada decorrente da pandemia. Decisão proferida em 10/04/2020, sob os fundamentos, ao mesmo tempo, da força maior e da teoria da imprevisão.

dispor de nova legislação que venha a definir hipóteses específicas e, não havendo esta, definir, sob seu livre convencimento motivado, a fixação do cumprimento da obrigação postergada no tempo, com equilíbrio, razoabilidade e proporcionalidade.

Trata-se, pois, de uma hipótese excepcional de revisão contratual decorrente de força maior, já que, normalmente, tem-se o inadimplemento relativo das obrigações. E, neste particular, cabível a aplicação do art. 421, par. único do Código Civil de 2002 e art. 421-A, inciso III, ambos conforme a Lei 13.874, de 2019, que deve ser norteada pelo princípio da intervenção mínima. Isso porque, a pandemia causada pelo vírus SARS-CoV-2 é elemento concreto que afasta a presunção do contrato ser paritário e simétrico e, ao mesmo tempo, deve haver alocação de riscos definidos por ambas as partes (credor e devedor) no momento de sua celebração, devendo o negócio ser respeitado.

Os desdobramentos da pandemia, a rigor, não podem ser considerados, em si, inevitáveis ou imprevisíveis a partir do momento da fixação da quarentena. O grave problema reside nos contratos celebrados anteriormente à pandemia. Neste sentido, há que se observar que é necessário a intervenção Estatal (Legislativa e Judiciária) de forma a regular essas relações jurídicas, mas de modo que a legislação aplicável determine, dentro do possível, uma intervenção mínima diante dos reflexos na economia e na cadeia produtiva de forma equilibrada, minimizando os prejuízos não só do devedor, mas também do credor.

Inicialmente, é importante consignar que a melhor solução para as inúmeras divergências nas relações contratuais decorrentes do COVID-19 é a busca das partes por uma conciliação amigável. Restando esta infrutífera, não há dúvidas que a solução final caberá ao Poder Judiciário. Não é possível exigir-se que o devedor comprove uma tentativa de solução amigável antes da propositura de uma ação judicial buscando a revisão do contrato e, mesmo que nada o faça extrajudicialmente e proponha diretamente a ação, não caberá a alegação de falta de interesse de agir, já que nem mesmo poderá a lei condicionar procedimento administrativo prévio de conciliação como requisito de procedibilidade da ação, uma vez que lei não excluirá da apreciação do Poder Judiciário lesão ou ameaça de direito (inciso XXXV, art. 5º da CRFB/88). Inclusive, este é o entendimento pacificado de nossos Tribunais, salvo quando se tratar da existência e eleição da convenção de arbitragem (no *leading case* no STF – Supremo Tribunal

Federal, SE 5.206 que entendeu pela constitucionalidade da Lei de Arbitragem – Lei 9.407/96 – e, ainda, no Superior Tribunal de Justiça, nos REsp 1.550.260; REsp 1.598.220; REsp 1.331.100; REsp 1.753.041; REsp 1.602.076 e REsp 1.082.498 reconhecendo-se a nulidade de algumas cláusulas patológicas e no Conflito de Competência 157.099), em que neste último entendeu-se que as jurisdições estatal e arbitral não se excluem mutuamente, sendo absolutamente possível sua convivência harmônica, exigindo-se, para tanto, que sejam respeitadas suas esferas de competência, que ostentam natureza absoluta.

Caberá ao magistrado analisar diante do COVID-19, mesmo evento que suspendeu a atividade de todos que permitiu a um devedor o cumprimento da obrigação, porém, para outro transpareça com as características que impediram de cumprir a prestação. Não vislumbramos, seguindo raciocínio de Caio Mário da Silva Pereira[34] aí a instituição de um novo requisito na etiologia da força maior, senão a determinação de que os seus elementos sejam apurados sem subordinação a um critério inflexível. Ao contrário, deve ser elástico. Se a inevitabilidade do fato fosse absoluta, então a força maior que incidiu sobre a inexecução da obrigação para aquele devedor não precisaria de apuração. Por ser justamente relativa e por admitir que um devedor teria a força para vencer, o outro, porém, não teve, sendo justo essa aferição conforme as circunstâncias especiais de cada caso.

Se não comprovado pelo devedor a impossibilidade financeira diante do COVID-19 sob a alegação da força maior tem-se a quebra positiva do contrato. Diz-se positiva a quebra porque não se realiza um ato que cumpria fosse praticado, modalidade que vem suscitada no direito modernamente e, no Brasil, desenvolvida por Ruy Rosado de Aguiar Júnior, Clóvis do Couto e Silva e pelo juiz gaúcho Ubirajara Mach de Oliveira.[35]

Poderá o juiz intervir diante da força maior e da impossibilidade comprovada para que determine condição razoável de cumprimento do devedor, livre, total ou parcialmente, dos encargos da mora, consoante o nível de comprometimento da obrigação, sem que isso caracterize ativismo judicial, na medida em que caberá ao juiz decidir, na hipótese de omissão

[34] Pereira, Caio Mário da Silva. *Instituições de direito civil*, v. 02, Rio de Janeiro: Forense, 1976, p. 299.

[35] Rizzardo, Arnaldo. *Contratos*, 2ª ed., Rio de Janeiro: Forense, 2002, p. 133.

da lei, art. 4º e 5º da Lei de Introdução às Normas do Direito Brasileiro. Deve-se evitar, diante do COVID-19, a resolução do contrato, sempre que possível, com fundamento no princípio da conservação dos contratos, da boa-fé objetiva e aos deveres de cooperação e solidariedade entre as partes contratantes. Entretanto, descabe a redução da prestação, quando muito, cabível apenas a moratória proporcional à periodicidade da quarentena.

Nessa intervenção mínima, mas excepcional, há que se ater à ideia fundamental do Estado Social que poderá e, deverá, intervir diante da pandemia provocada pelo SARS-CoV-2 (coronavírus), mas, fundamentalmente, caberá ao devedor efetivamente comprovar a impossibilidade financeira decorrente da suspensão de suas atividades. Há que se ter a lucidez no sentido de identificar a afetação do comprometimento da atividade, por exemplo, se o devedor foi efetivamente acometido pela doença ou, diante da suspensão das atividades, comprove que não tem qualquer reserva financeira para cumprir o que antes se obrigou dada a suspensão das atividades.

A mera alegação teórica e abstrata da força maior sem qualquer vinculação comprobatória da incidência da força maior no caso concreto caracteriza o abuso do direito e, portanto, ato emulativo. A mera alegação de redução de lucros ou daquilo que se esperava ou dificuldade maior no cumprimento da obrigação não dá azo à aplicação da força maior, ao contrário, caracteriza abuso do direito por parte do devedor que tentar afastar ou mitigar os prejuízos diante da pandemia. E cabe não só ao credor, mas também ao devedor, agir consoante os ditames da boa-fé objetiva, atentando-se para os deveres de cooperação e solidariedade. Haverá abuso do direito de revisar o contrato por motivo de força maior ou, equivocadamente, sustente a teoria da imprevisão ou a cláusula *rebus sic stantibus* quando o devedor pleiteia a pretensão sem a efetiva comprovação da ausência de recursos financeiros para adimplir com o contrato anterior. Como dito alhures, inaplicável a teoria da imprevisão ou onerosidade excessiva diante da ausência de comprovação genérica de abuso do credor em prosseguir a cobrança tal como antes firmada, na medida em que, indubitavelmente, foi também afetado pela suspensão de atividades decorrente da pandemia.

Enquadra-se a pandemia na hipótese de força maior sob a perspectiva do devedor da prestação e caberá a sua redução, mas desde que comprove cabalmente os efeitos da pandemia que gere real impossibilidade de pagamento. Entender de forma diversa seria admitir que todos os contratos no País fossem revisados, esta seria a regra, quando deve ser a exceção, comprometendo, substancialmente, a economia e a circulação de riquezas. O efeito deletério não é somente a sobrecarga de demandas judiciais, mas o comprometimento da economia que, por si, só, já foi afetada. Não é a revisão de todos os contratos sob o fundamento da pandemia, de forma genérica e abstrata, que irá se solucionar ou mitigar os problemas decorrentes daquela. Os prejuízos econômicos devem ser suportados solidariamente por ambas as partes contratantes no negócio, tanto o credor como o devedor, afastando-se oportunismos de ambas as partes.

CONCLUSÕES

Diante de todo o exposto, conclui-se que a pandemia do SARS-CoV-2 (coronavírus) e o período de quarentena não configura hipótese de aplicação da teoria da imprevisão ou da onerosidade excessiva ou, ainda, da cláusula *rebus sic stantibus* ou do *factum principis*. Trata-se, deveras, de situação abstrata e geral de força maior, de modo que possa se enquadrar o devedor nas disposições do art. 393, par. único do Código Civil brasileiro de 2002.

Inexiste a aplicabilidade da teoria do fato do príncipe e, incabível, por derradeiro, qualquer responsabilidade Estatal quanto à suspensão das atividades produtivas de comerciantes, já que decorre as medidas de isolamento social de uma orientação de proteção da saúde da população mundial e que, por si, não configura ilicitude, ao contrário, procedimento de segurança da saúde pública coletiva não só no País, como no mundo adotado por diversos países democráticos, tais como EUA, Itália, Espanha, Reino Unido, Portugal e França. Sem pontuar a base da segurança jurídica na contratação dos negócios jurídicos, anular-se-á o princípio da legalidade nos contratos, causando uma literal contaminação, não só da saúde de todos, ante o COVID-19, mas um vírus jurídico na base negocial das relações contratuais com efeitos deletérios econômicos, causando amarguras sociais, desequilíbrio monetário e aumento das desigualdades, provocada pela peste uma guerra judicial entre os contratantes, gerando fome e extrema pobreza e, por fim, a morte também das relações contratuais. É um efeito inevitável ante a insegurança, quebra da confiança, desequilíbrio e, possível abusividade de ambas as partes, credores ou devedores.

Não só a categorização abstrata deve ser adequada como força maior, como também a aplicação no caso concreto deve ser aplicada e não há fórmula mágica geral para a solução dos conflitos ou mitigar estes, quando muito, lenitivos com a intervenção legal emergencial em situações específicas que se fizerem necessárias, evitando-se uma sobrecarga de ações judiciais no Poder Judiciário. A pandemia é a força maior que criou desdobramentos por ato de terceiros que, em si, isoladamente, qualificam-se como caso fortuito. Logo, atos governamentais ou orientação de isolamento social são consequências necessárias e inevitáveis da pandemia. No contexto, incide tão somente a força maior do COVID-19, porém, sem qualquer repercussão prática na qualificação de caso fortuito ou de força maior, já que o efeito será o mesmo: a exoneração do devedor dos encargos moratórios, tais como juros e multa. Não obstante, prosseguirá o devedor obrigado a adimplir com a prestação principal.

Caberá ao devedor, sobretudo, comprovar a impossibilidade financeira diante do período de quarentena decorrente da pandemia sob a alegação da força maior. Não basta a mera alegação para estar livre de quaisquer ônus probatórios. Há que se demonstrar o comprometimento financeiro com ausência de recursos de modo que se autorize a exoneração dos encargos moratórios. A força maior pode ser aplicada, desde que, cumulativamente, comprove-se a impossibilidade financeira pela suspensão das atividades na cadeia produtiva ou, ainda, a lanço de exemplo, pela incidência do acometimento da doença em questão.

A intervenção Estatal sob novas luzes de um Estado Social justifica a intervenção econômica, sem que com isso ofenda os princípios basilares constitucionais da livre economia. Deve haver uma intervenção humanista nestas relações jurídicas de modo a se aplicar uma readequação ou revisão parcial do contrato no período suspensivo de atividades diante do COVID-19, coibindo-se possíveis oportunismos ou abusos, seja do credor ou do devedor.

Decorre uma maior relevância diante do COVID-19 que afetou tanto credor e devedor e interessa não só o sistema jurídico vigente, como, igualmente, os seus efeitos econômicos, na medida que a Ciência do Direito deve também servir a Economia, de modo a não gerar maiores danos e desemprego, dentre outros malefícios. Os efeitos consequentes de uma pandemia desta magnitude será o aumento da fome e a miséria, majoração do desemprego e a desestabilização da economia não de apenas um País, mas do mundo.

O juiz de direito terá a difícil missão em que deverá analisar com prudência as relações contratuais na medida em que as inúmeras ações judiciais contribuirão com o desenlace econômico e o efeito cascata nas relações jurídicas. Há que se evitar a simples resolução do negócio, na medida em que, por vezes, mesmo na ausência de culpa do devedor, com a reverberação dos efeitos da resolução em cadeia não se atingirá o bem comum. Para tanto, os mecanismos legais que poderá e deverá se valer o Poder Judiciário é a aplicabilidade do art. 421, parágrafo único e o 421-A do Código Civil de 2002, trazidos pela recente Lei 13.874/2019, diante da força maior.

A revisão por força maior parcial do negócio jurídico deve limitar-se ao período suspensivo decorrente da pandemia do COVID-19 e deverá estar fundamentada no princípio da intervenção mínima e na excepcionalidade diante dos efeitos ou prejuízos causados por aquela. Só se pode invocar, portanto, a alteração da base do negócio quando a segurança do tráfego não se oponha a tal. E isto só acontecerá quando a alteração da circunstância atingir não um dos contratantes isoladamente, mas afetar a base de valoração "comum a ambas as partes".[36] Por esta razão, imprescindível que se pontue os princípios da boa-fé contratual e da cooperação e solidariedade entre as partes na decisão do caso *sub judice.*

Poderá o juiz intervir diante da força maior e da impossibilidade comprovada para que determine condição razoável de cumprimento do devedor, livre, total ou parcialmente, dos encargos da mora, consoante o nível de comprometimento da obrigação, sem que isso caracterize ativismo judicial, na medida em que caberá ao juiz decidir, na hipótese de omissão da lei, com base no art. 4º e 5º da Lei de Introdução às Normas do Direito Brasileiro (Decreto-Lei 4.657, de 04 de setembro de 1942, com redação da Lei 12.376, de 2010).

Deve-se evitar, diante do COVID-19, a resolução do contrato, sempre que possível, com fundamento no princípio da conservação dos contratos. O princípio da função social dos contratos, mais do que nunca, deve ser analisado diante da funcionalidade social e sua razão de modo a atender o bem comum, este é um *standard* jurídico que deve ser colmatado no caso concreto com prudência e discricionariedade. Há que se buscar a manutenção do contrato, conversando-se o negócio jurídico à luz de uma interpretação do princípio do capitalismo humanista da Constituição da República Federativa do Brasil de 1988, sob o princípio da intervenção mínima e excepcional da revisão dos contratos, tal como é, diante da pandemia do vírus SARS-CoV-2 que gerou a quarentena e o isolamento social

[36] CORDEIRO, Menezes. *Da boa-fé no Direito Civil,* Coimbra: Almedina, 1997, p. 1.065.

coletivo, fato necessário impossível de se evitar ou impedir que gere, comprovadamente, a impossibilidade do adimplemento contratual caracterizador, exclusivamente, da força maior.

REFERÊNCIAS

ALMEIDA, Lacerda de. *Obrigações*, São Paulo: Livraria Cruz Coutinho, 1897.

CALÇAS, Manoel de Queiroz Pereira. "O Contrato de Arredamento Mercantil [*Leasing*]", *in Atualidades de Direito Civil*, v. I, coord. de Angélica Arruda Alvim e outros, Curitiba: Juruá, 2006.

CRETELLA JÚNIOR, José. As cláusulas de privilégio nos contratos administrativos, *Revista de Informação Legislativa*, Brasília, n. 89, jan./mar., 1986.

DALLARI, Dalmo de Abreu. "Segurança e Direito", *Renascer do Direito*, 2ª ed., São Paulo: Saraiva, 1980.

DINIZ, Maria Helena Diniz. *Curso de direito civil brasileiro: teoria das obrigações contratuais e extracontratuais*, 10ª Ed., São Paulo: Saraiva, v. 03, 1995.

FANTONI JÚNIOR, Neyton. "Segurança Jurídica e Interpretação Constitucional". *Revista Jurídica*, v. 238, 1997.

GOMES, Orlando. *Contratos*, 24ª Ed., Rio de Janeiro: Forense, 2001.

IHERING, Rudolf von. *Der Zweck im Recht (A finalidade do Direito)*, v. 02, 1877-1883.

LAUBADERE, Andre de. *Traité elementaire de droit administratif*, Paris: LGDJ, 1953.

MAIA, Carneiro. *Da cláusula rebus sic stantibus*, n. 47, São Paulo: Saraiva, 1959.

MIRANDA, Pontes de. *Tratado de direito privado*. Tomo XXII. São Paulo: Revista dos Tribunais, 2012, p. 158-9.

CORDEIRO, Menezes. *Da boa-fé no Direito* Civil, Coimbra: Almedina, 1997.

OLIVEIRA, Anisio José de. *A cláusula rebus sic stantibus através dos tempos*. Belo Horizonte: Ibérica, 1968.

PEREIRA, Caio Mário da Silva. *Instituições de direito civil*, v. 02, Rio de Janeiro: Forense, 1976.

RIZZARDO, Arnaldo. *Contratos*, 2ª ed., Rio de Janeiro: Forense, 2002.

RODRIGUES, Silvio. *Direito Civil, dos contratos e das declarações unilaterais de vontade*, 9ª ed., São Paulo: Saraiva, v. 03, 1980.

ROPPO, Enzo. *O contrato*. Coimbra: Almedina, 1988.

ROSSETTI, José Paschoal. *Introdução à Economia*, 15ª ed., São Paulo: Atlas, 1991.

SIDOU, Othon. *A revisão judicial dos contratos*, 2ª ed., Rio de Janeiro: Forense, 1983.

TRABUCCHI, *Istituzioni di Diritto Civille*, 17ª ed., Padova: CEDAM, 1968.